A Note from the Publisher

Press Time offers a complete course in journalism. It begins with a consideration of the mass media and their influence on modern life. It then offers extensive coverage of the various skills students need in order to write basic news stories and a number of more specialized stories and articles. The last chapters of the book are devoted to various aspects of producing and financing a school newspaper, as well as to practical advice on preparing for a career in journalism. These are followed by the Editor's Handbook, a detailed guide to the publication of a school newspaper. Features that enhance the student text are listed below with references to pages that give an example of each.

- Each chapter begins with a list of objectives to guide the students' study of the chapter (page 14).
- Important terms are printed in boldface type (page 96), listed at the end of each chapter (page 108), and defined and cross-referenced in the Glossary (page 502).
- Detailed processes are divided into steps to help students master the processes quickly and confidently (page 148).
- Examples from student newspapers are found throughout the text, giving students numerous models to follow (page 188).
- Three or more activities are found within each chapter, allowing students to practice and extend their skills as they progress through each chapter (page 216).
- A checklist in each chapter provides students with an opportunity to check their work or understanding (page 282).
- Each chapter ends with a summary that covers the chapter section by section (page 326).

- Sets of review and discussion questions are also found at the end of each chapter (page 379).
- Each chapter concludes with a chapter project that gives students a chance to apply the skills they have developed in the chapter (page 379).
- The Career Close-Ups in Chapter 20 offer students insights into various careers they may be considering as well as helpful advice (page 431).
- The Editor's Handbook gives students and advisers detailed information about all the stages in the production of a school newspaper (page 449).
- The Glossary at the end of the book covers the important terms in the text as well as other special terms that may be useful in producing a school newspaper (page 502).
- The comprehensive Index that follows the Glossary makes it particularly easy to find any other information needed (page 513).

To assure a highly readable book, the content for this text was selected, organized, and written at a level appropriate for the intended audience. The Dale–Chall and Fry readability formulas were used to control readability level. These scores are available on request from the Educational Book Division, Prentice-Hall, Inc., Englewood Cliffs, New Jersey 07632, or from your local Prentice-Hall representative.

Press Time

Julian Adams

Former Teacher of English and Journalism
Richmond Public Schools
Richmond, California

Kenneth Stratton

Coauthor of the first three editions
Former Chairman and Teacher of English and Journalism
East High School
Des Moines, Iowa

Prentice-Hall, Inc., Englewood Cliffs, New Jersey

Press Time

Acknowledgments

A list of contributing schools and text and photo acknowledgments not included in the text itself are found on pages 525–528.

Supplementary Materials

Teacher's Guide
Practice Book
Annotated Teacher's Edition of the Practice Book

Press Time

Fourth Edition

ISBN 0-13-699116-5

11

PRENTICE-HALL INTERNATIONAL, INC., London
PRENTICE-HALL OF AUSTRALIA, PTY. LTD., Sydney
PRENTICE-HALL CANADA INC., Toronto
PRENTICE-HALL OF INDIA PRIVATE LTD., New Delhi
PRENTICE-HALL OF JAPAN, INC., Tokyo
PRENTICE-HALL OF SOUTHEAST ASIA PTE. LTD., Singapore
WHITEHALL BOOKS LIMITED, Wellington, New Zealand
EDITORA PRENTICE-HALL DO BRASIL LTDA., Rio de Janeiro

Contents

5

UNIT THREE Specialized Writing 210

Editor's Handbook

TO THE STUDENT

Writing for publication is one of the most fascinating activities in which you will ever take part. This book will help you learn the skills you will need for this adventure. It will help you gain a greater understanding of the whole communication process and show you how writers use words to convey ideas and impressions, as well as facts.

In Unit One, you will acquire new insights into the phenomenon of mass communication and its effects on human beings. Unit Two will give you a chance to develop the basic skills needed to gather news and write news stories that people will want to read. In Unit Three, you will learn how to write more specialized kinds of stories and articles. Unit Four focuses on the many other skills needed to produce and finance school newspapers. In Unit Five, you will have a chance to explore careers in journalism and learn how to prepare for such a career. In the Editor's Handbook, which follows Unit Five, you will find a complete and detailed description of the entire newspaper publishing process.

A number of special features have been built into the text to make your study of journalism more rewarding.

Objectives. At the beginning of each chapter, you will find a list of objectives to guide you in your study.

Important Terms. Within each chapter, important new terms are presented in boldface type. These terms are also listed at the end of each chapter and included in the Glossary at the end of the book.

Steps. In the chapters that cover detailed processes—whether for writing an editorial or for taking a photograph—you will find series of steps to follow so that you can proceed with confidence.

Models. Throughout the text, you will find numerous excerpts from school newspapers, showing how other student writers have approached the tasks at hand.

Activities. Each chapter includes a number of activities that will give you a chance to try out or explore further what you are learning.

Checklists. Each chapter also includes a checklist that you can use to check your work or your understanding of an important concept.

Summaries. At the end of each chapter, you will find a concise summary that will prove helpful in previewing or reviewing the material in the chapter.

Review and Discussion Questions. Following the summary and vocabulary list in each chapter, there are review questions that you can use to test your understanding of the chapter and discussion questions that will give you an opportunity to look at a number of broader issues.

Chapter Projects. Each chapter concludes with a major project that allows you to work on your own, applying what you have learned.

Career Close-Ups. In Unit Five, you will read about the careers of real people working in journalism and find out what advice they have for young journalists.

Editor's Handbook. At the end of the book, the Editor's Handbook gives detailed information about the production of a school newspaper, organized into 13 sections for convenient use.

Glossary and Index. The Glossary that follows the Editor's Handbook lists not only the important terms found throughout the text but also a number of other terms that you may find useful in your work in journalism. The Index, found right after the Glossary, will make it easy for you to find anything else you need.

UNIT ONE

The Mass Media and the Student Press

THE
MASS MEDIA
TODAY

When you have completed this chapter you should be able to

Recognize how ideas are communicated from sender to receiver and understand why mass communication is so important to modern living.

Recognize how news is presented through the mass media, especially by means of newscasts, news magazines, and newspapers.

Recognize the place of school newspapers within the news media.

Scene from an old-time movie:

The large smoke-filled news room is noisy and cluttered. Desks are piled high with papers, overflowing ashtrays, and coffee cups. A number of men, their ties loosened and collars unbuttoned, pound frantically at the keys of battered typewriters or shout into telephones. Some gather in corners of the room and argue loudly. Copy boys scurry back and forth carrying piles of paper. Telephones ring constantly. Above the din you can clearly hear the rasping voice of the city editor: "Jones, I want 20 inches on that fire! ... Where's the city council story? ... Tear out the whole front page. We'll feature the election scandal!"

At least in one's imagination, this was the excitement and frenzy of a newspaper city room at deadline time. Not many newspaper offices look that way today. Telephones still ring, but clattering typewriters have been replaced by computer screens and keyboards. Reporters, now just as likely to be women, silently compose and rearrange their stories or read reports coming by wire from other cities. When they are finished, the tap of a key transfers the article to an editor's screen. Another key will send it on its way to be prepared automatically for printing. Radio and television news rooms are similar in appearance, except that the reporters pay far more attention to audio or videotape recordings.

Nevertheless, the excitement is still there—the thrill of being first to know what is happening, the satisfying feeling of writing for an audience. The same excitement, thrill, and satisfaction can resound through a school newspaper office. Within their communities, school newspapers can be every bit as vital to the distribution of information as are network broadcasts or metropolitan newspapers.

The general business of collecting, writing, and distributing news to the public is called **journalism.** A **journalist** may gather news, write it, or prepare it for publication or broadcasting. A **reporter** is a journalist who interviews news sources or attends news events in order to obtain information and then writes a news story for publication or broadcast. An **editor** supervises preparation of all or part of a newspaper, news magazine, or newscast. Various editorial positions may be described as managing editor, sports editor, entertainment editor, and so on. Contemporary journalism represents one of the most important kinds of communication today. How millions of people live their lives and what they think, feel, and believe are greatly influenced by what journalists communicate to them.

Communicating in Today's World

All parts of the contemporary world have been linked by communication. You have become an instant knower of global happenings. In fact, it is almost impossible to avoid being involved. You are surrounded by words and ideas—communicated by television, radio, magazines, newspapers, advertising, and so on. **Mass communication,** the name given to this concept, provides information, influences thinking, incites action, and entertains.

Your school newspaper is an important part of this broad process. Before you begin to work on developing and improving your skills in newswriting and editing, it is important that you understand something about the techniques of mass communication, the tradition of the American newspaper, and especially your responsibilities in connection with freedom of the press.

Transferring Ideas from Sender to Receiver

Any kind of communication, whether to a large audience or to a single individual, whether oral or written, must have both a **sender** and a **receiver.** If this communication is to succeed, there must be not only the words or actions used to convey the **message** but also an understanding by both sender and receiver that such a message will be sent.

The sender, or **communicator,** must recognize that it is possible to be influenced by his or her own feelings, attitudes toward the topic, and past experiences. The sender (speaker or writer) must therefore choose language that is clear and effective in transmitting the real meaning of the message to the receiver (listener or reader). Typically, this language will involve the use of words.

The sender must recognize that words are symbols that carry different shades of meaning. In the statement "The weather was cool," what is really meant? As to temperature, "cool" is a relative term. To one person it may mean cold, to another not quite as hot as usual. The sender must carefully choose words that truly communicate the thought in mind.

The ability of the receiver to understand the words chosen is also essential. The listener or reader, like the speaker or writer, is affected by personal attitudes and experiences and may, therefore, have a tendency to misunderstand or misinterpret the ideas received. A typical example might be a series of instructions given by an employer. The employee may regard them as merely standard procedure to be followed in a general way, while the employer expects each item to be followed exactly. Further, the receiver may not be conscious of misinterpreting a message or even of the reasons why he or she distorts its meaning. Therefore, communicators must recognize a special responsibility to write or speak exactly and clearly.

Recognizing Two Basic Kinds of Communication

Communication may be divided into two kinds: interpersonal communication and mass communication. A conversation, letter, or telephone call would be considered individual or **interpersonal communication.** Here, sender and receiver communicate back and forth on equal terms. However, when a communicator directs a message in a purposeful, organized manner to a large audience that is not expected to react with the sender on a face-

In interpersonal communication, senders and receivers communicate with one another on equal terms. The face-to-face conversation shown above enables the speaker to get immediate feedback from the listeners.

Photo by Owen Franken from Stock, Boston

to-face basis, it becomes mass communication. Examples include an announcement over a public-address system, an article in a magazine, or a radio news broadcast. In none of these three cases can the audience provide immediate, direct **feedback** to the sender.

Because of such lack of interaction and feedback between receiver and sender in mass communication, an audience can easily distort or even turn off the message being sent. Excellent results are possible, of course. You might say that the communicative process is working quite well when you are completely absorbed in a television mystery drama. But most of the time, a message is not conveyed under such ideal conditions. In fact, much mass communication depends on the knowledge that even if the receiver is paying little attention some part of a message will generally be received. Most television advertising, constantly repeating slogans, jingles, or persuasive ideas, is based on this understanding.

Whatever the kind of communication, the channel of communication between sender and receiver (a letter, a radio broadcast, a book) is called a **medium.** Collectively, the instruments of mass communication—television, radio, books, magazines, newspapers, recordings, movies, billboards, and others—are called **mass media,** or sometimes just **the media.**

This magazine reader is a receiver within the process called mass communication. In this kind of communication, the audience normally cannot provide immediate, direct feedback to the sender.

Understanding the Purposes and Value of Mass Communication

Mass communication has several purposes. The four principal ones are to provide information (including news), to present opinions, to persuade people to take a certain course of action, and to entertain.

Any one message may have more than one purpose, and the purpose may be understood differently by the sender and receiver. The sender's purpose, the receiver's purpose, and whether the two happen to coincide are all important in determining how successfully the message will be transmitted.

The value of mass communication is immeasurable. It offers great benefits in learning, information, and ease of living. You know far more about the world and its people than anyone did a few generations ago. You have become more aware of these people, how they live, and what they are doing. Consequently, you are likely to be more concerned about their problems.

However, so much information reaches you via the mass media that you cannot really absorb it all. Your knowledge of a topic may consist of scattered fragments rather than a well-rounded whole. Then, too, it is easier for you to be influenced, for you can't avoid the incessant messages sent to you by others. As a result, you may have less experience in thinking for yourself. Advertising tells you to "buy this"; spoken directions explain exactly how to do something. You may listen placidly and follow instructions blindly, instead of considering them critically and following the course of action that your common sense directs. Hence, the great value of mass communication goes hand in hand with the need to be intelligent and responsible when receiving all that it offers.

The checklist at the top of page 19 is intended to help you exercise intelligence and responsibility when exposed to the media.

✓ **Checklist for Recognizing Your Own Involvement with Mass Media**

☐ 1. For what proportion of my waking hours am I receiving some sort of mass communication?

☐ 2. Am I being informed, offered opinions, persuaded, or entertained?

☐ 3. If I am being informed, how well do I understand and use this information?

☐ 4. If I am receiving opinions, do I always make my own judgments about these viewpoints?

☐ 5. If I am being persuaded (for instance, by commercials) do I find myself wanting to take the requested action?

☐ 6. For what part of the time that I am exposed to the mass media each day am I making conscious choices about the communication I receive?

☐ 7. For what reasons do I make these choices?

☐ 8. How well am I making these choices?

☐ 9. What opportunities do I have to be a sender of mass communication rather than a receiver?

☐ 10. How well am I doing this?

Activity 1: Analyzing Your Own Involvement with Mass Media

1. For 24 hours of an average day, keep a record of the mass media with which you come in contact. List each radio or TV show, magazine, newspaper, book, phonograph record, movie, play, and so on that you watch, listen to, or read. Note the amount of time consumed by each. In addition to listing TV and radio programs, keep a record of commercials.

2. Make a summary of your record, showing (a) the total time spent on each of the various kinds of mass media and (b) the reasons for your participation—for general information, for entertainment, as a learning assignment, or for whatever other reason.

3. Be prepared to compare your list with those of the other members of your class and to discuss the lists in class. On the average, how many of your waking hours are consumed by mass media? What differences are there among the members of your class? How can these be explained or justified?

4. Referring again to your 24-hour record, mark the instances in which you participated without choice—as a class assignment, because your family or friends were involved, because you couldn't avoid it, and so on. What proportion of the total is this?

5. Consider the extent to which your 24-hour involvement with mass media offered you opportunities to make decisions for yourself. How much did you merely accept without taking the chance to do any careful thinking?

6. In what ways could you have improved your own selection of mass media offerings during the 24-hour period?

7. Prepare a list of 10 or 15 purchases you have made during the past few weeks. In how many of these were you influenced by mass media?

Discovering How the Mass Media Handle News

The mass media influence your life in many ways. One of the most important of these is their function as conveyors of news. You may be waiting in suspense to hear the outcome of some sports event. You may want to know who has won an election. Or you may be following any of a number of other current events with a keen desire to know what will happen next.

Imagine, for example, a spaceflight that has run into difficulties. Astronauts report that a vital control mechanism is jammed and that they may have problems landing their spacecraft at the end of its scheduled flight. Technicians on the ground, working feverishly, announce, "If we can't make it function properly, maybe we can prepare a substitute control that will do the job."

Within minutes, television and radio newscasters will be on the air. Newspapers will follow, providing the details in print. The story will spread across America, Europe, Asia, Africa, Australia . . . and all the world will wait breathlessly while the crippled craft skims on through space, anticipating the "moment of truth" when the landing must be undertaken. Hour after hour, millions of people will listen to newscasts, read their newspapers, think about the astronauts, until at last word comes through—"They made it!"

News has the power to affect people deeply. And today's mass media are designed to make the most of this news impact. They direct news at you with the speed and strength of a bullet. Because people want to know quickly and accurately what is happening, as well as why and how it is happening, newspapers and other news media exist.

News is one of the most important and desired commodities furnished by mass media. People want to know what is going on around them. It is more than a matter of curiosity. In the modern world, whole nations are dependent on other parts of the earth for food, clothing, raw materials, even their way of life. How people get along with one another in a remote part of the world may very well decide whether you will complete your education, work in industry, or wear a military uniform.

News is perishable. It must be delivered to its consumers while it is still fresh; otherwise, it is no longer news. The simplest way of spreading news is by word of mouth. One person tells another what he or she has seen or heard. The earliest way of distributing news, this method still conveys information about families, friends, or neighborhood activities. But something more is needed in the modern world. To meet these needs, better news-gathering methods have been developed. Modern inventions—the printing press, steamship, railroad, airplane, telegraph, telephone, radio, television, satellite, and computer—have improved the speed with which news can be distributed and have increased the distances over which it can travel. These and other instruments of mass communication have revolutionized the ways news is spread.

Modern inventions have also led to a number of different and often competing channels of communication. The four major **news media**—radio, television, news magazines, and newspapers—all have their own special ways of handling news.

Exploring Newscasts

Both radio and television feature frequent reports of current happenings all over the world. Some of these appear as live broadcasts of actual news events, which give listeners and viewers immediate information about sports contests, speeches, political conventions, and other newsworthy happenings. Generally, these broadcasts are of events that were planned in advance.

Radio and television also schedule regular news summaries, or **newscasts.** Although television has greater potential for news coverage than radio does, given its ability to use **videotapes** of actual news events, TV newscasts are ordinarily presented only at special times during the day. Meanwhile, radio stations (and certain cable TV stations), which are not so restricted by demands upon their time by other programs, may cover local and world news more frequently and in greater detail. Some stations, in fact, devote all their hours to news broadcasts and news analysis.

In early days, radio and television, collectively known as the **electronic media,** were more concerned with entertaining their audiences than with providing information. However, both radio and television have now become major forces in the spreading of news as well as entertainment.

Pittsburgh radio station KDKA created a sensation in 1920 when it broadcast the returns of the Harding–Cox presidential election. Today, over 4,000 AM stations and approximately 3,000 FM stations broadcast daily to some 400,000,000 radio receivers in the United States. There is, in fact, an average of two radios for each person in the United States.

Programs were being televised on a regular schedule by WGY of Schenectady as early as 1938, but it was not until the 1950s that television spread widely. Some 1,000 TV stations now broadcast to sets in 98 percent of the homes in the United States. Worldwide, there are some 350,000,000 TV sets, most of which can now be linked by satellite for special broadcasts.

The fact that the electronic media can show or discuss an event as it actually happens has added new dimensions to news reporting. According to a recent Roper survey, 47 percent of Americans consider TV the most believable medium, while only 23 percent prefer newspapers. More and more people are obtaining "headlines" from radio or television and then reading newspapers or news magazines for detailed accounts, explanations, background information, and local news items.

National or international items for a newscast are provided by network news staffs, as well as by the same **press associations** that supply this material to newspapers. Local news may be collected by the station's own reporters and camera operators or by the reporting staff of a local newspaper. A special editorial staff usually assembles the news reports for broadcasting.

It is important to distinguish between newscasts—the "news pages" of the air—and broadcast **commentaries**—the "editorial pages." A **commentator,** presumably an expert in a particular field, expresses personal opinions about the news. The commentator's remarks are designed to help listeners think for themselves.

Another form of broadcast news report is the **documentary,** an edited film or videotape report of a current event or issue prepared for television showing. Documentaries may present background information and in-depth coverage. They may be essentially factual, or they may present a single viewpoint about the chosen topic.

News broadcasts owe many of their standards to longstanding newspaper traditions. They are also subject to substantially the same privileges regarding freedom of expression and the same limitations of ethics and responsibility as printed news reports. However, certain legal requirements unique to broadcasting should be kept in mind when judging radio and TV presentations.

To begin with, broadcast media must be licensed by the federal government to avoid conflicts in the use of the airwaves. This is based on the

On-the-spot reporting is characteristic of both radio and television newscasts. Thanks to videotape, television has an even greater potential for such news coverage than radio does.

fact that only a limited number of channels are available in any one area. In contrast, any number of different newspapers, books, and magazines can be published in any area. Because of the limited number of channels, license renewal hearings are held to consider whether a radio or television station serves the public interest through its exclusive use of an assigned channel.

Broadcast stations are also bound by the **equal-time law** and the **Fairness Doctrine.** The first, a federal law, requires that stations providing time for a candidate for political office must also supply the same amount of time to any other "legitimate" candidate for the same office. The Fairness Doctrine, a **Federal Communications Commission** regulation, demands that comparable time be afforded to opposing viewpoints on any controversial or debatable topic or to any person specifically attacked in a broadcast. The equal-time law specifically exempts news broadcasts and news events such as debates, but the Fairness Doctrine encourages, indeed requires, news programs and other broadcasts to seek out controversial topics of current interest and give fair treatment to both sides.

Activity 2: Looking at Broadcast News

1. Using TV and radio schedules for a given day, chart the newscasts for each channel and station as to number, time of day for each, and total time involved. Which channels or stations present the most news? Which present it at prime viewing or listening hours? Summarize your conclusions from this survey.

2. Select a particular newscast, listen to it for several days, and prepare a brief report covering the following points:

   a. To what kind of audience does the newscast seem to be appealing?

   b. Are news items reported in some detail or just as "headlines"?

   c. Is a clear distinction made between facts and opinions?

   d. Is there any evidence of presentations favoring just one side of an issue?

   e. What evidence is there of a plan for the newscasts? To what extent do they relate one item to another, present a variety of news, and contrast serious news with human-interest items?

   f. How appropriate is the newscaster's voice? Is it clear? Can you understand the words? Does the newscaster become emotional at times or allow any hint of personal opinion to creep into his or her voice?

   g. What is your overall judgment as to whether the news is accurately and impartially presented?

3. Compare the results obtained by various class members in answer to Items 1 and 2. Then develop a chart that ranks the various channels and stations according to the emphasis they place on presenting accurate, useful news.

4. Television newscasts are sometimes criticized for emphasizing news events for which they were able to have camera crews present. Watch a regular evening newscast, listing its news items and the approximate amount of time spent on each. Then compare its coverage with the next morning's newspaper. Prepare a brief report to present to your class.

Inspecting the News Magazines

Most of the approximately 10,000 magazines published in the United States appeal to groups of people with special interests. Aside from a few widely circulated general audience magazines, most periodicals serve readers interested in a particular profession, kind of work, hobby, or recreational activity. There are also almost as many additional magazines published by industries or companies for their employees and friends.

Successful magazines are circulated widely. *TV Guide* has a paid circulation of approximately 18,000,000 copies a week. *Reader's Digest* sells almost the same number of copies each month in the United States alone and publishes several international editions as well. Over 60 other magazines distribute more than 1,000,000 copies of each issue.

While many periodicals include information and some specialized news, only a limited number of magazines are concerned with giving a rounded picture of current events. Henry Luce and Briton Hadden founded *Time* in 1923; its weekly paid circulation is now well over 4,000,000 copies. *Time*'s lively, organized presentation of news in condensed writing style has clearly influenced magazine journalism. Other major United States news magazines are *Newsweek* and *U.S. News & World Report. Sports Illustrated, Business Week,* and several other publications are essentially news magazines concentrating on specific fields of interest.

Life, a weekly magazine created by the publishers of *Time* in 1936, added a new dimension to the recording of news: **photojournalism.** During its first 36 years of publication, its often brilliant photographic essays—pictures plus vivid captions and brief explanatory paragraphs—described wars, the lives of personalities, and advances in science in a way that captured the public imagination. Eventually *Life* and similar magazines became victims of increased publishing costs and competition from television. After a gap of several years, *Life* has recently reappeared as a monthly.

News magazines offer an obvious advantage to the busy reader by collecting, in one place, a concise summary of the week's important current events. Certain special problems, however, do arise from summarized and condensed news. When many news items are available and space is limited, how will choices be made? When every story must be rewritten, not by the original reporters but by an editor who may be unfamiliar with all its details, how great will be the dangers of slanting? The intelligent reader must be constantly alert to these questions.

Activity 3: Comparing News Magazines

1. Collect three different weekly news magazines, all concentrating on general news. Study them and make comparisons covering the following points:

   a. What categories of news are covered in each magazine? What categories are emphasized? What differences do you find?

   b. Do the magazines use different formats or arrangements to present the news? If so, which do you prefer?

   c. Do you notice any differences in writing style? If so, which style seems to be the most effective?

   d. To what kind of audience do you think each magazine would appeal?

   e. Compare the treatment of the same news event in each magazine. What differences in emphasis do you find? Is there evidence of slant or bias in any of the magazines? Explain.

   f. Describe the editorial policy of each magazine, as you now understand it. Do you detect any evidence of general bias or partisanship? If so, identify it.

2. What might be some of the disadvantages of relying entirely on news magazines for your knowledge of current events?

Understanding Newspapers

Of all the various channels of news, newspapers are the only ones that concern themselves primarily with news. Most radio and television stations

For millions of people, newspapers are as much a part of their daily lives as their trips to and from work.

Photo by Barbara Alpe from Stock, Boston

offer much more than news. Only a few magazines focus primarily on general news.

Newspapers also have the distinction of being the first channel for the mass communication of news. Newspapers have a long history, dating back to the early seventeenth century. Newspaper procedures and traditions, developed over several centuries, have thus set worldwide standards for the presentation of news.

In fact, newspapers are still the preeminent conveyors of news for many. Whereas TV images and broadcast words are fleeting and impermanent, printed words last. Whereas news magazines offer a once-a-week summary of news for those with little time to keep up with events, newspapers are an important and satisfying part of the lives of all those who hunger for news every day. The importance and value of newspapers remain undiminished by the rise of the newer news media.

The next chapter will explore the American newspaper in much greater detail.

Activity 4:   Thinking About Newspapers

1. Drawing on your own experience with newspapers, explain in writing what value they have for you, as against the other news media. Include an explanation of why you sometimes will read newspaper reports of an event that you learned about earlier from a television newscast or a radio newscast.

2. Write a brief report in which you compare newspapers with television, radio, and news magazines with respect to the following: amount of news presented, range of coverage (local, national, international), degree of detail in coverage, accuracy and reliability, appeal and convenience to readers, and anything else that you regard as useful in such a comparison.

Investigating School Newspapers

Like other news media, school newspapers serve the needs of a number of people. Their particular audiences are their communities, centering on the schools in which they are published. School newspapers may be published monthly or every two or three weeks. A few appear weekly, or even daily. They include news about past and future school events, articles about students and their special interests, and presentations of teacher and student opinion. Advertisements may also be printed. A number of college newspapers are published daily and may print world news as well as school news. More than 25,000 school newspapers are now published in the United States, according to estimates.

Like commercial newspapers, school papers may appeal to different kinds of audiences. Some school papers resemble daily newspapers in size,

—Photo by Ellis Herwig from Stock, Boston

These students in their cafeteria represent the primary readership of their school paper. However, other members of the community in which this school is located may also be served by the paper, particularly if an effort is made to recognize the broader readership.

arrangement, and emphasis on current news. Others have the appearance of magazines. They are the same size, have illustrated covers, and contain pages that resemble typical magazine layouts, although the material is news-related. The majority of school newspapers, though, are **tabloids.** Their pages are about half the size of a standard newspaper, perhaps five columns wide. These pages include a combination of current news reports, photographs, articles of opinion, and expanded reports on topics of high student interest.

As later chapters will make clear, school newspapers resemble commercial newspapers in a number of ways. Moreover, the methods of writing, editing, and otherwise preparing news for a school paper are essentially the same as used by professional newspeople. The chief differences between school and commercial papers are three. First, school papers are generally published less often than commercial ones. Second, their readerships are limited to the school-centered community. And, third, they are an educational rather than a profit-making enterprise. These differences enter into the advice given in later chapters that deal with the writing and producing of a school newspaper. Nevertheless, the work of school journalists is true journalism, and at its best it stands comparison with the work done by professionals.

—Orange R, Roseburg Senior High School, Roseburg, Oregon; The Kirkwood Call, Kirkwood High School, Kirkwood, Missouri

FORESTRY STUDENTS IN THE WOODS SEE PAGE 7

DO STUDENTS CHEAT? SEE PAGE 8

INDIANS WIN RELAYS SEE PAGE 6

Orange R

VOLUME 55, NO. 9   ROSEBURG SENIOR HIGH SCHOOL   ROSEBURG, OREGON   APRIL 7, 1983

Forensics more than speechmaking

BY SUZANNE VERKOREN
Reporter

As you enter the room of Daphne Sturtz's Forensics class the scene is one of organized chaos. Some students are typing, while some are arguing with each other and others are making posters. These 17 students are all a part of the RHS Forensics Team.

Forensics is another word for competitive speech activities. The team runs a lot like

tial. "When they're juniors and seniors we should have a good team as their skills will have improved," the advisor says. Sturtz does have some experienced speakers on the team however. Seniors Randy Rubin and Tony Motschenbacher have each been involved in speech for three years. Both plan to become lawyers and find speech a very helpful.

"It helps me prepare for my career as a lawyer," Motschenbacher claims. Rubin is very active in debate. He

Class cuts to mee

Because of the state's newly imposed graduation requirements, there is a definite possibility that one or more electives may be cut from the curriculum offered at RHS next year.

Fairly recently the Oregon State School Board added classes such as economics, global studies, government, and more English to graduation requirements. This has stirred up some problems concerning staffing the classes.

"The real bind," according to assistant principal Steve Iverson, "is that we have to

teach more of the ular classes with number of teacher

The classes con cutting are Journ II, Photography Speed Reading, Writing, and Bibl

To help decide es would be cu completed and sub proposed schedule year. These were computer which possible students The results were for easy reference These results w

ON TO STATE!—From left, Sundancers Ruth Loveday, Kari Liesinger, Connie Chaffin, Melissa Phelps, Nicole Palmateer, Michelle Tunno, Teresa Puhl, Kari Kramer,

Dance team gets

"Alright girls, let's go! And 5, 6, 7, 8!"

These words of enthusiasm will be heard repeatedly this week from Coach Zuber by the dance team, preparing them for state competition to be

held at West Linn April 8-9.

The team will be to a routine to Juliet and the The Wizard of Oz. T through a preli

---

the Kirkwood CALL   jan. 29, 1982

Kirkwood High School
Kirkwood, Mo. 63122   Volume 73, Issue 9

World of athletics changes with time

Inflation, shortage of coaches, practice space and government regulations force athletic department to change policy (see related stories on pg. 6-7)

"All the teams should have record boards, because all of them work equally as hard."
—Tracy Fritzche, junior

GOING UP FOR a jumpshot, John Loudenslager, center, reaches above his Parkway North opponent as Lee Meyer, guard, and Bret Berthold, forward, await the rebound. The Pioneers wear the new uniforms which the athletic department budgeted into this year's expenditures (photo by Dave Mohler).

AS HE TURNS for the last lap of the 100-yard breaststroke against Parkway South, Jan. 20, Joe Witte, senior, takes a breath (photo by Dave Keiser).

AMY FRANK, FRESHMAN, dribbles past Angie Thorps, freshman, as Mrs. Leslie Goodwin, freshman girls' basketball coach, watches (photo by Dave Mohler).

"I think this new system (taking turns practicing at North) is fair."
—John Banjak, freshman

The Orange R *is a tabloid published every three weeks by the Journalism II class of Roseburg High School.* The Kirkwood Call *is a magazine-size paper published biweekly at Kirkwood High School.*

Activity 5: Examining School Newspapers

1. Answer the following questions from your current knowledge about your own school newspaper, without making any further investigation for the present:

   a. Who receives the paper (all students, students who subscribe, students holding activity cards)?

   b. Are there readers or subscribers in the community outside of teachers' and students' families? If so, approximately how many of them are there?

   c. Does the paper publish advertisements? If so, what kind of advertisements does it publish? Do the advertisements have any special placement in the paper? If so, where are the advertisements generally placed?

   d. What source or sources supply the money needed to publish your school paper?

   e. By what process is your school newspaper printed (professionally printed by letterpress or offset process, mimeographed, dittoed)? Where is it printed and by whom?

   f. Does the paper have a written statement of editorial policy? Who established it? What are its main points?

   g. Who is responsible for selecting articles for publication?

   h. Who is responsible for the truth and accuracy of articles published in the paper?

   i. Must material be submitted to anyone for review and approval before publication? If so, to whom and for what reasons?

   j. May any student in the school suggest or write material for the paper? How is student writing assigned or solicited?

2. Discuss and compare your answers with other class members. Work with other students to determine the answers to any questions not satisfactorily answered by the initial responses.

3. Examine your school paper's file of newspapers from other schools for the purpose of determining what types are represented. How many are news magazines as opposed to standard newspapers or tabloids? What kind of content does each paper emphasize?

4. As a class project, begin to assemble copies of a variety of different commercial newspapers. Examine these as they are brought in and decide what each one seems to emphasize.

5. Start a personal journalism notebook. Many assignments in this textbook will suggest that you find examples of various kinds of writing in daily or school newspapers. Paste each example on a separate page of your notebook, leaving room to add the date, the newspaper's name, and your comments about the example. Your collection of good and bad examples, together with the outlines and guides that you will add from time to time, will provide a practical and useful reference book to help solve your writing problems.

Summary

This chapter begins by discussing the communication process, particularly as it is carried out by the mass media. It goes on to consider how news is handled by radio, television, news magazines, and newspapers. It concludes with a brief examination of school newspapers.

COMMUNICATING IN TODAY'S WORLD. In the communication process, both sender and receiver must understand the purpose of each message. Mass communication results when a planned message is directed to a large audience. The mass media are the usual channels for such transmission. The major purposes of mass media are to inform, present opinions, persuade, and entertain.

DISCOVERING HOW THE MASS MEDIA HANDLE NEWS. The principal mass media involved in the distribution of news are radio, television, news magazines, and newspapers. Most Americans obtain their major news from the broadcast media but depend on the print media for details, explanations, and local news. Newscasts can present immediate news and catch watchers' or listeners' attention readily, but time limitations may prevent them from doing detailed reporting. They are also subject to licensing, equal-time, and fairness restrictions, which do not apply to print media. News magazines summarize important events in order to provide a concentrated review of one week's news. Newspapers, on the other hand, offer a detailed presentation of news on a day-to-day basis.

INVESTIGATING SCHOOL NEWSPAPERS. School newspapers serve their schools by publishing news, articles about students and their interests, student and teacher opinions, and advertisements. Most are printed in tabloid size. At their best, they can represent the finest in journalistic traditions.

Vocabulary

journalism	news media
journalist	newscast
reporter	videotape
editor	electronic media
mass communication	press association
sender	commentary
receiver	commentator
message	documentary
communicator	equal-time law
interpersonal communication	Fairness Doctrine
feedback	Federal Communications Commission
medium	photojournalism
mass media	tabloid
the media	

Review Questions

1. What is mass communication?

2. What are the four main purposes of mass communication?

3. What are the four main news media?

4. What are some of the differences between broadcast news, news magazine news, and newspaper news?

5. What are the similarities and differences between school newspapers and commercial newspapers?

Discussion Questions

1. Compare your daily activities with those of one of your grandparents when they were young or with those of a literary character of two or more generations ago. How much of the difference can you attribute to the influence of mass media? What are the advantages and disadvantages of this change?

2. In what ways might today's widespread exposure to mass media be both helpful and dangerous?

3. Why do many people depend on radio and television for their news? What are the limitations of these news programs? What solutions to these limitations are offered by other media?

4. Compare the radio or television presentation of a major news event with the printed account in a newspaper. Are the facts the same? Do you think they came from the same source? Do you detect any evidence of prejudice or slanting in any of the accounts? If so, state that evidence.

5. To what extent does your school paper approach the usefulness and interest of the commercial paper you most often read?

Chapter Project

Comparing the News Coverage of the Different Media

Choose a major national or world news event, one with some depth of information and one about which there might be conflicting opinions. Follow the event through the different news media. It would be desirable if you were to hear it first on the radio, since that medium is most likely to carry the earliest report. Follow the event for the next 24 hours, through broadcasts on an all-news or mostly news radio station, through at least one regular television newscast, and through the published reports in one or more daily newspapers. Then wait for a news magazine to appear with an account of the event's significance, and examine the account. Finally, prepare a brief written report in which you compare the way the various news media have dealt with the event. Pay special attention to how much information has been presented by each, as well as to how each has handled any conflicting reports or opinions.

THE AMERICAN NEWSPAPER: PAST AND PRESENT

When you have completed this chapter you should be able to

Identify major events in the development of the American newspaper.

Recognize the different kinds of newspapers and the ways in which newspapers serve their readers.

Classify the different kinds of material presented in newspapers.

Understand the basic elements of newspaper production.

Computers today can transfer reporters' news stories to editors for correction and approval, set them into type, space the lines properly, and arrange complete pages for printing. Newspapers have long been moving toward automated systems, a development that represents the greatest technological advance in newspaper publishing since inventors of the nineteenth century revolutionized news gathering and printing with the telegraph and power machinery. Nevertheless, reporters, writers, and editors still remain the key people at the heart of the newspaper business.

The history of newspapers has always been a combination of events and people. An early ancestor of the newspaper dates back to 60 B.C., when Julius Caesar posted the handwritten *Acta Diurna (Day's Events)* in the Forum and sent copies to military leaders. Real newspapers appeared in the Western world in the seventeenth century. They were made possible by Gutenberg's invention of movable type for the printing of books a century and a half earlier. In Germany, then in England in 1622 with the *Weekly News*, printed newspapers began to appear.

The history of American newspapers began soon after, when America was still an English colony. The real story of the American newspaper, of course, lies in the hopes and actions of the men and women of the press. A few of these individuals are named in the following account, but hundreds of others have contributed.

Surveying the History of the American Newspaper

A publication entitled *Publick Occurrences Both Forreign and Domestick* was created by Benjamin Harris in Boston in 1690. It was the first American newspaper and contained much that would be news by today's standards. In it, however, Harris criticized the King of France. As a result, the paper was promptly suppressed. It was followed by other hand-printed weeklies. One, the Boston *News-Letter,* appeared continuously from 1704 until the Revolutionary War. It was America's first regularly published newspaper. In 1735, John Peter Zenger's trial (details appear in Chapter 3) laid the foundation for American freedom of the press and established a newspaper's right to present editorial opinion.

Elizabeth Timothy became editor of the South Carolina *Gazette* in 1738. She was America's first woman editor, and she has been followed by many others.

Many small newspapers were published during the time of the Revolutionary War. Some spoke violently against British colonial rule—for example, James Franklin's *New-England Courant,* which included many articles by his more famous brother, Benjamin. After the Revolution, the new Constitution expressly guaranteed freedom of the press, but Congress soon passed the Alien and Sedition Acts, which prohibited criticism of government officials. When Thomas Jefferson became President, he opposed these acts, and they were allowed to expire.

Until about 1830, the new nation's newspapers appealed mostly to political and business interests and, as a result, were read by relatively few people. Then, led by Benjamin Day and James Gordon Bennett, newspapers began to print more sensational news in a more readable form. With prices reduced to as little as one penny, the general public became interested. Thus began what is known as the **penny press**—inexpensive, readable papers emphasizing stories with mass appeal. In their papers, Horace Greeley and Henry J. Raymond increased editorial influence and improved news coverage to further this general interest.

With these developments, the modern newspaper was born, and new inventions helped speed its growth. Telegraph lines and cables encouraged better and faster news gathering. The development of steam-driven printing presses to replace hand-operated machines made possible more rapid news publication. Finally, the invention of the **linotype** made newspaper preparation simpler and faster by eliminating the tedious work of selecting and placing each piece of type by hand. Newspapers gained wider circulation, especially during the 1870s and 1880s.

As papers competed for readers, the full truth was often disregarded. In the 1890s, Joseph Pulitzer, owner of the New York *World*, and William Randolph Hearst of the New York *Journal* waged a bitter war for readers, each trying to outdo the other in creating sensational news. The result, in their papers and in many others of the same period, was what is called **yellow journalism.** Derived from "The Yellow Kid," a comic section that appeared in both Pulitzer's and Hearst's newspapers, the term was used to point out the sometimes extreme lengths to which the papers went to attract readers.

The desire for greater circulation and profits also led to the formation by Hearst and Edward W. Scripps of two major **newspaper chains,** parts of which still exist. Then, after World War I, the number of newspapers decreased rapidly because of higher production costs. Those remaining began to be more objective in their news stories and more constructive in their editorial columns.

Large city newspapers, especially, came under pressure from all sides. Their older printing plants contained obsolete, expensive-to-operate equipment. Labor unions often resisted introduction of modern methods that would result in fewer workers. Television stations, most of them located in the same cities, became major news sources for numbers of people. And much advertising moved from newspapers to television. Today, fewer than 30 cities in the United States have competing newspapers. Even these papers may combine their mechanical operations, such as printing, circulation, and advertising, while retaining separate editorial policies.

The number of daily newspapers has remained fairly constant over the past 25 years. For almost every large city daily that has suspended publication, a new suburban daily newspaper has been established. Surveys have shown that Americans still rely heavily on newspapers for their local

The term yellow journalism was coined for reporting that offered sensationalism rather than authentic news. As this cartoon shows, yellow journalism was recognized by many as harmful to the American public.

news. At present, 1,730 daily and 755 Sunday newspapers are published in the United States. Some 9,000 weekly publications supplement these by printing news of small towns or suburban areas.

Writing for the nation's newspapers has changed radically since the time of Benjamin Harris. Emphasis has shifted from rambling personal opinion to objective and complete news reporting. The trend has been to more detailed accounts and to the background information that radio and television cannot present in their limited time slots. More and more newspapers are giving their readers information with which to answer the question *Why* did this happen?

The opportunities for women and representatives of minority groups to fill important positions in American journalism have also increased. Robert Maynard of the Oakland *Tribune* is regarded as the first black editor and publisher of a major metropolitan newspaper. Albert Fitzpatrick has been executive editor of the Akron *Beacon Journal* for a number of years.

From time to time, surveys are made to determine which newspapers most closely approach the ideas of good journalism. *The New York Times* is frequently named as the nation's best, with the following papers often appearing on the list: *The Wall Street Journal, The Washington Post,* the Los Angeles *Times,* the Chicago *Tribune,* the Louisville *Courier-Journal,* the St. Louis *Post-Dispatch,* and *The Christian Science Monitor,* among others.

The table of dates on page 36 is intended to give you some sense of American newspaper history over the past three centuries.

DATES IN THE HISTORY OF THE AMERICAN NEWSPAPER	
1690	*Publick Occurrences,* first American newspaper, is published and suppressed after one issue.
1704	Boston *News-Letter,* first regularly published American newspaper, is founded.
1728	Benjamin Franklin's Pennsylvania *Gazette* is founded.
1735	Trial of John Peter Zenger is held.
1738	Elizabeth Timothy of the South Carolina *Gazette* becomes America's first woman newspaper editor.
1765	More than 30 colonial newspapers are available to public.
1776	Declaration of Independence is published in a number of colonial newspapers.
1783	Pennsylvania *Evening Post and Daily Advertiser,* first American daily newspaper, begins publication.
1791	First Amendment of the United States Constitution is ratified, providing a guarantee of freedom of the press.
1811	Steam-driven press is invented.
1830	About 1,000 newspapers are available to public.
1833	New York *Sun,* first of the penny-press newspapers, begins publication.
1844	Samuel F. B. Morse sends message ("What hath God wrought") by telegraph from Washington, D.C., to Baltimore.
1851	*The New York Times* is founded.
1866	First permanent transatlantic cable is laid.
1872	Photoengraving is developed.
1884	Linotype machine is invented.
1897	Yellow-journalism war between Joseph Pulitzer and William Randolph Hearst is waged.
1900	2,226 daily newspapers and 12,000 weekly newspapers are available to public.
1919	New York *Daily News* is founded.
1933	American Newspaper Guild, first union for journalists, is founded.
1950	Rapid advances are made in offset-printing technology.
1958	United Press and International News Service merge to form United Press International (UPI).
1963	Computerized typesetting becomes widespread method for producing major newspapers.
1971	Pentagon Papers are published in *The New York Times* and other papers.
1973	*The Washington Post* covers the Watergate affair.
1983	1,730 daily newspapers and 9,000 weekly newspapers are available to public.

Activity 1: Exploring the History of the American Press

1. Write a brief report on one of the following aspects of American newspaper history: Benjamin Harris and *Publick Occurrences;* John Campbell and the Boston *News-Letter;* the role of newspapers in the American Revolution; two rivals—Hamilton's and Jefferson's *Gazettes;* the *Liberator* and abolition; the penny press; the founding and development of *The New York Times;* yellow journalism; newspaper chains; changing styles of news reporting; and the rise and fall of newspaper competition.

2. Research and prepare an oral report on the journalistic career of any one of the following: Dorothy Thompson, Heywood C. Broun, John Gunther, Ernest Hemingway, Dorothy Kilgallen, James Reston, Marguerite Higgins, Carl Rowan, Eric Sevareid, John Steinbeck, Gloria Steinem, Walter Cronkite, Ben Hecht, Ann Landers, Ring Lardner, Damon Runyon, Jacob Riis, Ernie Pyle, Horace Greeley, William Randolph Hearst, Adolph S. Ochs, Joseph Pulitzer, and Edward W. Scripps.

Recognizing the Different Kinds of Newspapers and the Ways in Which They Serve the Public

Although the majority of people in the United States now receive most of their news from radio or television, newspapers remain vitally important because they combine speed, detailed information, and permanency. They enable people who have gotten only the bare facts about a news event from TV or radio to read a complete report. They are available whenever the reader wishes to pick them up. And they allow the reader to decide which stories to read and how much time to devote to each. More than 61,000,000 copies of newspapers are sold daily in the United States. These papers reach 185,000,000 readers.

Looking at Different Kinds of Newspapers

While all newspapers, by definition, deal with current events and have the same general goals, several specific types can be distinguished. In addition to school newspapers, these include daily newspapers, weekly newspapers, ethnic newspapers, and special-interest newspapers.

DAILY NEWSPAPERS.   Most city dailies provide complete coverage of all kinds of news—news from the far corners of the earth as well as all the important happenings in their own communities. Daily newspapers feature fresh news about events that have taken place during the previous 24 hours or that are to take place in the near future.

Virtually every medium-sized or larger city in the United States has its own daily newspaper. Dailies from major cities are widely distributed, often throughout several states. They bring their readers reports of every major happening—the detailed account of a battle, a President's speech, or a major strike—as well as the story of a local automobile accident.

Of all the different types of newspapers, dailies have the widest **circulation,** or average total number of copies sold. Circulation figures may be found on the front page, the editorial page, or at the beginning of the advertising pages.

Among the daily newspapers in the United States are a number with very large circulations: the Boston *Globe,* the Chicago *Sun-Times,* the Chicago *Tribune,* the Detroit *Free Press,* the Detroit *News,* the Los Angeles *Times,* the New York *Daily News,* the New York *Post, The New York Times,* the San Francisco *Chronicle, The Wall Street Journal,* and *The Washington Post.*

WEEKLY NEWSPAPERS.   Covering local news is the main purpose of the weekly newspapers published in small towns, in suburbs, or in community areas within cities. Because they are not issued often enough to compete with the dailies in world news, they specialize in the one news element that daily newspapers do not cover as comprehensively: detailed personal news about local people and events.

National weekly publications that feature sensational news items in newspaper format are normally regarded as magazines, not newspapers. The same is true of such highly opinionated, distinctive papers as *The Village Voice* of New York or *The Real Paper* of Boston, since their pages tend to feature opinions rather than news.

ETHNIC NEWSPAPERS.   In the nation's larger cities and in some other areas, a number of newspapers devoted to the interests of ethnic or cultural groups are published, sometimes in a mixture of English and another language. Among these papers are *El Diário, The Irish Echo, The Jewish Advocate, Die Deutsche Zeitung, La Notizia, The Hellenic Courier, Kashu Mainichi, The Lithuanian Free Press, The Scandinavian Tribune,* and *Chinese World. The Amsterdam News* is one of more than 200 black-oriented newspapers in the United States.

—Photo by Freda Leinwand from Monkmeyer

A resident of New York City's Chinatown keeps up with the news with a Chinese-language newspaper. Ethnic newspapers often have large readerships in the major cities of the United States.

Weather

Today—Partly cloudy and milder, high 30-35, increasing cloudiness with a chance of freezing rain tonight, low 25-30. Tuesday—Cloudy with a 50 percent chance of rain, high 35-40. Yesterday—Temp. range: 26-3. Details on Page D2.

The Washington Post

Index — 138 Pages, 6 Sections

Classified	B11	Movies	B 9
Comics	B28	Obituaries	D 6
Crossword	B30	Sports	C 1
Editorials	A14	Style	B 1
Federal Diary	D 2	Style Plus	B 5
Metro	D 1	Television	B10

Inside: Washington Business

107th Year — No. 49 — © 1984, The Washington Post Company — MONDAY, JANUARY 23, 1984 — Higher in Areas Approximately 75 Miles From District of Columbia (See Box on A2) — P — 25¢

Beginning of the end for Redskins: Derrick Jensen (31) blocks Jeff Hayes' punt before recovering the ball in end zone for Raiders' first touchdown.

By Richard Darcey—The Washington Post

Raiders Dismantle Redskins, Records In Super Bowl, 38-9

By Gary Pomerantz
Washington Post Staff Writer

TAMPA, Fla., Jan. 22—After a season of bold conquest, the Washington Redskins were reduced to ashes today.

As plain as can be, the Los Angeles Raiders dominated the Redskins in a 38-9 victory in Super Bowl XVIII before 72,920 in Tampa Stadium, denying the Redskins' bid for a second consecutive National Football League championship.

This was the most one-sided game in Super Bowl history, even worse than Green Bay's 35-10 defeat of Kansas City in the first Super Bowl. This was the Redskins' worst defeat since Jack Pardee coached a 38-7 regular-season defeat to Pittsburgh in 1979.

The 38 points were the most ever scored in a Super Bowl.

In the grizzly end, Raiders running back Marcus Allen was voted unanimously the game's most valuable player. He gained a Super Bowl record 191 yards on 20 carries and scored two touchdowns.

Allen, who came on strong in the playoffs to help get the Raiders to the Super Bowl, broke John Riggins' record of 166 yards with his spectacular performance.

How strange it seemed to see the Redskins trailing, 21-3, at halftime. And it seemed even stranger that the Raiders' heroes to that point were named Derrick Jensen and Jack Squirek.

Jensen, a reserve tight end, blocked a first-quarter punt by Jeff Hayes and recovered it in the end zone for the game's first touchdown. And Squirek, a reserve linebacker, turned a most peculiar play call by the Redskins—quarterback Joe Theismann throwing a swing pass from his 12-yard line with 12 seconds left in the half, instead of running out the clock—into an interception and a five-yard return for a touchdown.

Then, the Raiders' heroes became more predictable. Cornerbacks Mike Haynes and Lester Hayes entirely shut down Redskins receivers Charlie Brown and Art Monk, beating them in one-on-one coverage. And Riggins, last year's Super Bowl MVP, was limited to 64 yards on 20 carries.

After the Redskins, who finish 16-3 with their 11-game winning streak severed, had

See SUPER BOWL, A23, Col. 1

Close Fight Expected For Control of Senate

No Major Change Predicted for House

By T.R. Reid
Washington Post Staff Writer

During the next 10 months, 900 men and women will expend tens of thousands of hours, tens of millions of dollars and perhaps a few billion words in their campaigns for the House of Representatives.

But when the high-priced hullabaloo is over, the House probably will look almost exactly as it looks today.

Barring cataclysmic developments, the 1984 elections should produce little change in the partisan or ideological balance of the House, according to political professionals in both major parties.

With many protective mechanisms in place for incumbents and relatively few members relinquishing seats, the House this year should be one of the country's most stable political institutions. Of the 434 current members (one seat is vacant), more than 400 likely will be back when the 99th Congress convenes next January.

"This election is going to be boring on the House side," said Martin D. Franks, executive director of the Democrats' House campaign committee. It is a kind of boredom that Franks would be pleased to put up with because his party's current 100-seat margin over the Republicans gives the Democratic leadership reasonably solid House control.

Republicans, too, foresee minimal fireworks in House races. The GOP's campaign committee won't make firm predictions, but at this point not even the most wildly optimistic Republicans foresee picking up the 30 or so seats that would be needed to replicate the coalition of Republicans and conservative Democrats that spurned the Democratic leadership and passed President Reagan's economic program in 1981.

In standard fashion, Republicans are expected to focus much of their attention and money on the 52 Dem-

See HOUSE, A10, Col. 1

Outcome May Hinge On Refusals to Run

By Helen Dewar
Washington Post Staff Writer

The call to arms is being sounded, but the battle for control of the U.S. Senate in this fall's elections may already have been decided by a handful of political draft-dodgers—prospective challengers who refused to run.

If the final count is as close as both parties predict, the outcome could hinge as much on states where vulnerable incumbents got a free ride as it does on states with tight contests.

Both Republican and Democratic strategists concede that Senate control next year could be decided by one or two votes, even though the GOP begins with a 55-to-45 margin and a strong head of steam because of a rebounding economy, hopes for a strong reelection bid by President Reagan and plenty of money.

What makes the race tight from the start is that the majority party is defending 19 of the 33 seats at stake this year—a sure-fire prescription for trouble that contributed to the Democrats' loss of the Senate four years ago.

Moreover, most of the Democrats' 14 seats are considered safe, and early polls give them an even or better chance of picking up at least four seats currently held by Republicans: in Tennessee, Texas, Iowa and North Carolina.

Democrats are at least narrowly favored to win seats being vacated by two of the Senate's most powerful Republicans, Majority Leader Howard H. Baker Jr. of Tennessee and Armed Services Committee Chairman John G. Tower of Texas. Both states are traditionally Democratic, and the Democratic contenders for the two seats, especially Rep. Albert Gore Jr. in Tennessee, are considered strong.

In the other two Senate races that Democrats like to think about, Sen. Jesse Helms (R-N.C.) is trailing Democratic Gov. James B. Hunt Jr.,

See SENATE, A10, Col. 1

WILLIAM FRENCH SMITH
. . . to return to private law practice

Shultz Reverts To Hard Line Against Syria

By John M. Goshko
Washington Post Staff Writer

The Reagan administration shifted back toward a harder line against Syria yesterday as Secretary of State George P. Shultz accused the Damascus government of acquiescing in terrorism in Lebanon.

For nearly three weeks after Syrian President Hafez Assad released captured U.S. Navy Lt. Robert O. Goodman Jr., the administration had softened its attacks on Syria in hopes of negotiating a resolution of the Lebanese civil war.

Shultz, who was interviewed on "This Week With David Brinkley" (ABC, WJLA), charged yesterday that rising terrorism in the Middle East is "increasingly originating in Iran . . . with the acquiescence of Syria." He warned that the United States is prepared to take preemptive action against possible suicide attacks on U.S. forces in Lebanon.

Shultz also implied strongly that Syria and the Soviet Union were behind the recent assertion by the Lebanese Druze leader, Walid Jumblatt, that the U.S.-backed president of Lebanon, Amin Gemayel, must be forced to resign.

The secretary also quoted Syrian Foreign Minister Abdel Halim Khaddam as telling U.S. negotiators,

See SHULTZ, A18, Col. 1

Smith Quits Top Justice Job; Reagan to Nominate Meese

By David Hoffman
Washington Post Staff Writer

Attorney General William French Smith submitted his resignation to President Reagan last week, and Reagan has decided to nominate White House counselor Edwin Meese III to replace him, administration sources said yesterday.

Smith told the president in a private Oval Office meeting last Wednesday that he wanted to leave the administration to return to his Los Angeles law firm, Gibson, Dunn & Crutcher, where Smith had become a millionaire practicing corporate labor law before joining the administration, the sources said.

Meese will not be replaced as White House counselor, a job that put him at Reagan's elbow during the first three years of the administration and often brought him into conflict with Reagan's other senior advisers, the sources said.

Meese's appointment will thus leave White House chief of staff James A. Baker III in undisputed control of the presidential staff for the first time since the 1980 election, when Reagan's top three advisers first divided their responsibilities, officials said.

Reagan accepted Smith's resignation on Thursday and decided the same day to give the job to Meese, 52, a former prosecutor and law professor who has worked for Reagan since he began his terms as California governor.

Smith, 66, will announce his resignation today, the officials said. They said Reagan told his top three advisers—Meese, Baker and deputy chief of staff Michael K. Deaver—last Thursday of his decision to give Meese the job.

They said that it was not certain if Meese's nomination as attorney general would be announced immediately, but that the president had decided to make the nomination, which requires Senate confirmation.

Neither Meese nor Smith could be reached for comment yesterday. Asked about the shift as he returned to the White House yesterday afternoon from Camp David,

See SMITH, A4, Col. 1

Meese Seen Taking An Activist Approach

By Mary Thornton
Washington Post Staff Writer

In naming Edwin Meese III to succeed William French Smith as attorney general, President Reagan will be replacing a trusted, longtime friend who never had a strong impact at the Justice Department with a much tougher law-and-order activist.

Smith, who served for many years in California as Reagan's personal lawyer, was conservative in philosophy but so remote in style that some federal attorneys complained that his picture appeared in newspapers because of his attendance at social events more often than because of his

NEWS ANALYSIS

legal activities. For similar reasons, conservatives complained that he was ineffectual in carrying out the Reagan social agenda.

In fact, it was Meese who took the initiative behind the scenes on a number of those issues and forced the Justice Department to follow.

Meese, once an Alameda County, Calif., prosecutor, has been interested primarily in law enforcement issues and has repeatedly made clear to Reagan that he would like to be attorney general.

He has played a key role on a number of issues affecting the Justice Department:

• Meese was the driving force on the White House staff in urging the president to replace

See JUSTICE, A4, Col. 3

U.S. Drug Crackdown Stalls in Bolivia

By Jackson Diehl
Washington Post Foreign Service

LA PAZ, Bolivia—A costly effort by the Reagan administration to help Bolivia control illegal cocaine production has failed to produce results after being frustrated by delays, inefficiency and corruption, according to government officials and diplomats here.

Since Bolivia's return to democratic government in October 1982, the United States has pledged up to $75 million in aid and has provided technical direction for a major crackdown on the drug trade here. However, the illegal growing and processing of coca leaves, the raw material of cocaine, has appeared to increase during the past 15 months, drug enforcement officials said.

Bolivia, a poor, landlocked nation of 5.8 million people in South America's center, is believed to supply about half of the illegal cocaine consumed in the world. Officials say that growing areas for coca leaves have expanded without challenge in regions largely unpatrolled by police and suspected traffickers arrested with U.S. assistance have slipped easily through Bolivia's porous justice system.

An ambitious series of enforcement and crop reduction programs funded by the United States, formally approved in August after laborious negotiations, has yet to be implemented in the field.

Enforcement authorities complain, meanwhile, that corruption

See COCAINE, A20, Col. 1

Chinese Scientist Ordered to Leave

A federal immigration judge has ruled that a scientist who wants to defect must return to China.

Details On Page A17

Six East Germans who sought asylum in the U.S. Embassy in East Berlin were safely escorted to the West.

Details on Page A17

Fairfax Home Buyers, Taxpayers Suffer as Builders Default

By Molly Moore
Washington Post Staff Writer

Almost 16 months after they signed the contract on their new split-level house in suburban Virginia, Jack and Michele Stash and their three children were living in a cramped hotel room, sleeping on rollaway beds and eating a tiresome menu of fast-food hamburgers.

"The waiting was almost unbearable," said Michele Stash, describing the final months of the long wait spent on the ninth floor of an Alexandria hotel. "We were under the constant tension of wondering whether we were ever going to get out of there."

She is just one of the hundreds of homeowners in Fairfax County who have felt the repercussions of buying a new house in a county that officials say has the highest construction bond default rate in the nation.

Even though the house had been finished for months and contracts had been signed on most of the houses in the new North Springfield Park subdivision, the developer had not carried out his promise to the county: that, along with building a subdivision, he would provide the new homeowners and the county with streets, sidewalks, gutters and other public improvements for the neighborhood.

The developer defaulted on that promise, saying that after he paid for the construction of the houses he had no money left to finish the streets and other facilities. And until those improvements were made, the county refused to allow the buyers to move into their houses. Although the developer offered to release the potential homeowners, who had obtained loans but had not yet paid for the houses, from their contracts, Stash said: "After we spent this much time, there was no way we were going to pull out. At that point, it's basically a survival thing."

At least 38 percent of construction projects under way in Fairfax County are in default. In the worst cases, this means that the developers have walked away from unfinished jobs, forcing the county to pick up the bills for thousands of dollars to complete streets, sidewalks and drainage facilities.

In even the most innocuous cases, default can mean no snow removal, no street signs, no repairs for gaping potholes and no relief from rains that turn yards into ponds because of improper drainage. In Virginia, most streets and public improvements are maintained by the state and, until those facilities have been finished and received state approval, the state will not provide maintenance for them. Although the county occasionally will provide some services, officials acknowledge that it is a

See DEFAULTS, A21, Col. 1

—*The Washington Post*, used by permission

The Washington Post *has not only a large circulation but also a reputation for excellence in news coverage.*

SPECIAL-INTEREST NEWSPAPERS.   These are typically published by organizations, labor unions, or large industries for their own members. Their content is usually limited to matters that concern only members of the special-interest group. Thus, their circulation tends to be relatively small.

Activity 2:   Comparing Your Community's Newspapers

1. Obtain copies for the same date of all the daily newspapers that are published or read in your own community and in nearby communities. Compare the newspapers carefully and answer the following questions:

    a. How is each of the day's major news stories handled by the various newspapers? What differences do you find?

    b. What types of news stories are featured by each newspaper? Would you say that any of the papers are sensational or conservative in their news approach? Why?

    c. Which newspaper prints the most local news? The least? (If you are comparing a newspaper from your own community with dailies from a nearby large city, which of the city's papers prints the most news about your own community?)

    d. How do the circulations of the newspapers compare? Can you explain why some of these papers sell more copies than others?

    e. Which newspaper seems most interesting to you? Why did you select this one?

2. Obtain a copy of a weekly newspaper published in your community or in a nearby community. (Be sure you have a real newspaper and not a neighborhood shopping newspaper, often called an advertiser. An advertiser will generally include as news only a few meeting announcements or publicity items and devote the rest of its space to paid advertisements.) Compare the weekly newspaper with the daily newspapers used in Item 1. Point out how the weekly and daily papers are similar and how they are different.

3. Compare the weekly newspaper with your school newspaper. You will find differences, of course, but there are likely to be many similarities in the way these newspapers handle the news of their own communities. Describe the ways in which the two papers are alike.

Understanding the Ways in Which Newspapers Serve the Public

A free press may publish much that would not be printed if newspapers were controlled by the government. Most American editors and writers recognize a duty to their community and their readers. They hold in mind a number of ways in which they may serve these readers.

KEEPING READERS INFORMED ON CURRENT EVENTS.   Each newspaper tries to keep its readers well informed about local, national, and international affairs so that they may form opinions based on knowledge. The newspaper publishes news reports that are as complete as possible in view of the limited time available for their preparation. It also presents the opinions of commentators and columnists on current events. Finally, the newspaper states its own opinion in editorials. The influence of a widely read newspaper's editorials may be very great. Such editorials often become the basis of opinion for readers who do not have all the facts on which to form their own views.

HELPING READERS LIVE MORE COMFORTABLY. A newspaper furnishes up-to-the-minute information about products, services, and activities that can make life better, more interesting, or more worthwhile for its readers. Many newspaper items serve this function. They include news of club projects, meetings, plays, radio and television programs, and concerts; articles describing how to repair or build something; travel articles; reports on the latest developments in science or medicine; and information and advertisements concerning material things.

ENTERTAINING READERS. Some items are printed solely for the purpose of entertaining readers. News of unusual or humorous events, comics and cartoons, stories, puzzles, games and contests, and similar items are both entertaining and relaxing.

INFORMING AUTHORITIES OF THE NEEDS OF THE PUBLIC. In a democratic society, daily and weekly newspapers serve as a link between the public and its leaders. They must act as a sounding board for both sides, and they have a definite responsibility to each group.

Governments, from the smallest local unit up to national government agencies, are doing things that affect people and the most minute details of their lives. The public has a definite stake in these activities, develops clear feelings about them, and possesses certain needs that must be met. The

The freedom enjoyed by the American press enables it to gather and publish information of use not only to the public but also to leaders and officials.

—Photo by Ken Karp

American newspaper stands squarely in the middle. If it is to act constructively, it must serve as a means of communication between leaders and individuals, between governments or organizations and the public they serve. A newspaper tells its readers what local and national leaders are doing, what they are thinking, how they are acting. At the same time, it tells these leaders what the people want, how they feel, what they need. And it is in this sense, which is a step above the level of mere news reporting, that the American newspaper makes one of its greatest contributions.

The following checklist can be used to evaluate how well a newspaper serves the American public.

✔ Checklist for Evaluating How Well a Newspaper Serves the Public

☐ 1. Does the paper cover local news adequately?

☐ 2. Does the paper cover national news adequately?

☐ 3. Does the paper cover international news adequately?

☐ 4. Are the opinion articles (editorials, commentaries, and columns) informative, intelligent, and concerned with things that matter?

☐ 5. Does the paper notify me of local activities and current entertainment offerings that I might be interested in?

☐ 6. Are the how-to articles practical and clear?

☐ 7. Does the paper keep up with developments in science and medicine?

☐ 8. Are the items intended to entertain me amusing, suitable, and in good taste?

☐ 9. Would public servants and officeholders be able to learn of the public's needs, concerns, and problems from the paper?

☐ 10. Does reading this paper better prepare me for life in my society?

Activity 3:   Examining the Ways in Which Newspapers Serve the Public

Write a brief report on how well a newspaper you frequently read serves its readers. You should consider the following: how informative the paper is in its news reports and opinion articles, the kinds of articles it publishes to help readers live more comfortably, the ways in which it entertains its readers, and the kinds of information it publishes that responsible public officials should have.

Looking into a Newspaper's Pages

Within the pages of today's newspapers are many kinds of information, opinions, non-news items, and advertising. Most of these items can be classified according to their sources. The chart on pages 43 and 44 is an example of how the contents of a typical daily paper might be classified.

DAILY NEWSPAPER CONTENTS		
Group	*Kind of Item*	*Explanation*
Wire or telegraph news	World news	News coming from outside the United States; news of other countries, wars, or disasters.
	National news	News coming from anywhere in the United States outside your own state; news of the President, Congress, and the federal government; disasters and strikes; important speeches and statements; news of famous people or unusual activities by any person.
	State news	News coming from your own state, outside the city or metropolitan area in which the newspaper is published.
Local news	Local or city news	Events happening in your home town or within the circulation area of the newspaper. Unlike wire news, local or city news is collected by the staff of each newspaper.
Special-page news	Family or "people" news	News of people and their lives—weddings, social events, organization activities, fashions, and foods. This kind of news and the four kinds listed below are generally printed on special pages, not mixed with the wire and local news.
	Business news	News of finance and industry—the stock markets, corporations, money and tax matters, and the price of minerals and farm products.
	Entertainment news	News of programs and people—movies, television, radio, theater, art, music, and books. Entertainment news usually includes daily listings of radio and television programs.
	Sports news	News of all kinds of sports events and sports personalities.
	Miscellaneous news	Other subjects, which as a rule are allowed less space in a daily newspaper, sometimes appearing only once a week—weather reports, vital statistics (births and deaths), legal actions, shipping news, farming news, building and real estate news, automobile news, travel news, and religious activities.

Group	Kind of Item	Explanation
Opinion articles and non-news items	Editorials	Expressions of the opinion of the news-paper, usually concerning current news and rarely signed. They appear on the editorial page or on special occasions on the front page.
	Columns	Expressions of a writer's opinion about news events, movies, television, sports, or some other subject. They are generally written by the same person issue after issue.
	Commentaries	Signed interpretations of or expressions of opinion about current problems.
	Letters to the editor	Opinions of readers on current events.
	Non-news items	Comics, cartoons, crossword puzzles, contests, and other items that cannot be considered news but that are printed because they interest or entertain the newspaper's readers.
Advertisements	Display ads	Advertisements for foods, clothing, and thousands of other products or services, appearing in various sizes and shapes throughout the paper. Display advertisements may be divided into two groups: *national,* which advertise a nationally known product without reference to local stores selling this product; and *local,* which advertise the services or wares of local merchants.
	Classified or want ads	Inexpensive, brief advertisements placed by individuals or local businesses, classified by subject, and collected in one place in the newspaper.

Activity 4:   Analyzing the Contents of a Daily Newspaper

1. From a daily newspaper, clip one good example of each of the 16 items listed in the kind-of-item column of the preceding chart. Label them appropriately.

2. How well organized were the contents of the daily newspaper that you used? How easy was it to locate the 16 items?

3. Which types of item were the easiest to find? The most difficult?

4. About what proportion of the paper consisted of advertisements? Of special non-news items (cartoons, puzzles, and so on)?

Producing the News

For a brief explanation of how a news event actually reaches the page of a newspaper, study the various steps shown in the following flow chart.

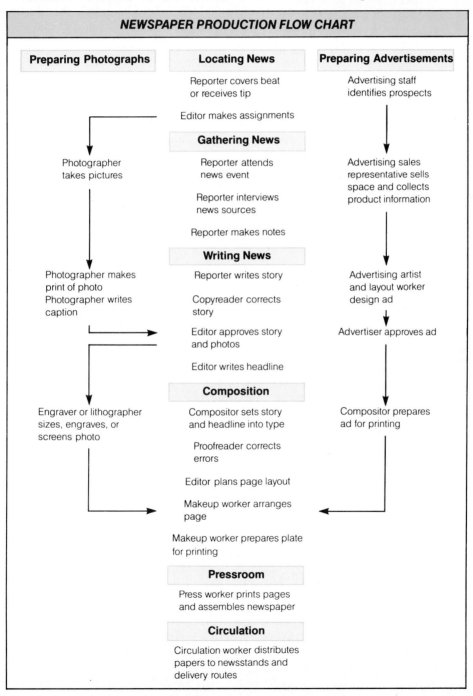

NEWSPAPER PRODUCTION FLOW CHART

Preparing Photographs	Locating News	Preparing Advertisements
	Reporter covers beat or receives tip	Advertising staff identifies prospects
	Editor makes assignments	
	Gathering News	
Photographer takes pictures	Reporter attends news event	Advertising sales representative sells space and collects product information
	Reporter interviews news sources	
	Reporter makes notes	
	Writing News	
Photographer makes print of photo	Reporter writes story	Advertising artist and layout worker design ad
Photographer writes caption	Copyreader corrects story	
	Editor approves story and photos	Advertiser approves ad
	Editor writes headline	
	Composition	
Engraver or lithographer sizes, engraves, or screens photo	Compositor sets story and headline into type	Compositor prepares ad for printing
	Proofreader corrects errors	
	Editor plans page layout	
	Makeup worker arranges page	
	Makeup worker prepares plate for printing	
	Pressroom	
	Press worker prints pages and assembles newspaper	
	Circulation	
	Circulation worker distributes papers to newsstands and delivery routes	

The chart on page 45 includes photographs and advertisements along with the steps for preparing news articles to help you gain a general idea of the process of newspaper production. The procedure shown is somewhat simplified. The process may also differ among various newspapers depending on local needs and the types of mechanical or computer-controlled equipment used by a particular staff.

Most of these procedures will become the topics of later chapters in the book. At this time, though, you may wish to look up unfamiliar terms in the Glossary that begins on page 502 and refer to the Index to locate an explanation of some of the processes.

Activity 5:   Studying Newspaper Production

1. Choose one step in the flow chart and use the Table of Contents or Index to locate a more detailed explanation of the step. Read about it in the appropriate chapter or in other books so that you fully understand it. Write a brief report on what is involved in the step.

2. Use the *Readers' Guide to Periodical Literature* in your library to find a magazine article explaining one of the computer-based techniques that are now used in newspaper production. Prepare a brief report, relating the technique to the steps presented in the flow chart.

Summary

This chapter begins with a brief historical survey of the newspaper in America. It then describes the basic kinds of newspapers and the ways in which they serve their readers. It goes on to show the different groupings of material in a typical daily paper. Finally, it charts the basic steps in newspaper production.

SURVEYING THE HISTORY OF THE AMERICAN NEWSPAPER. A table of Dates in the History of the American Newspaper is given on page 36. It provides a brief overview of the American newspaper from its beginnings in 1690 to 1983.

RECOGNIZING THE DIFFERENT KINDS OF NEWSPAPERS AND THE WAYS IN WHICH THEY SERVE THE PUBLIC. The basic kinds of newspapers are daily newspapers, weekly newspapers, ethnic newspapers, and special-interest newspapers. Newspapers serve the public in the following ways: by keeping readers informed on current events, by helping readers live more comfortably, by entertaining readers, and by informing authorities of the needs of the public.

LOOKING INTO A NEWSPAPER'S PAGES. The basic groups of material in a typical daily newspaper are the following: wire or telegraph news, local news, special-page news, opinion articles and non-news items, and advertisements.

PRODUCING THE NEWS. A flow chart on page 45 presents the basic steps of newspaper production from locating news to distributing papers.

Vocabulary

penny press
linotype

yellow journalism
newspaper chain

circulation

Review Questions

1. Explain the historical significance of each of the following: *Publick Occurrences,* the Boston *News-Letter,* John Peter Zenger's trial, Elizabeth Timothy, the penny press, Joseph Pulitzer and William Randolph Hearst, yellow journalism.

2. What are the basic kinds of newspapers?

3. What are some of the ways in which newspapers serve their readers?

4. What are the basic content groups of a typical daily newspaper?

5. What are some of the basic production steps between locating news events and distributing newspapers?

Discussion Questions

1. Is the future of the American newspaper bright or dim?

2. What effect do ethnic newspapers have on American society?

3. If newspapers ceased to exist in this country, could television and radio news and news magazines serve the public well enough that readers would not miss the papers?

4. What is the most valuable kind of information to be found in a newspaper?

5. What do you consider the most important step in the production of a newspaper?

Chapter Project

Surveying Newspaper Readers

Conduct a survey among people you know—both young people like yourself and older people—to find out the kind of importance newspapers have for people of today. Use the data from your survey to write a report entitled "Newspapers—What Readers Have To Say," or use a title that more closely links up with your main point. The following are some of the questions you might ask those you survey: What kinds of newspapers do you read (daily, weekly, ethnic, special-interest)? How much time do you devote to reading them? At what time of day? How much time do you devote to national and international news? To local news? To sports? To puzzles, cartoons, contests, and the like? To ads? To how-to articles? To TV, radio, film, and other entertainment listings? What do you value most in the papers you read? What do you dislike most in them? If you don't read any newspapers at all, or only once in a while, why? Have your newspaper reading habits changed over the years? In what way? Try to prepare other questions that will enable you to get a clear picture of what newspapers mean to each person you interview. And speak to as many people as possible. The more people you interview, the more substantial your report will be. Finally, think carefully about the data you accumulate, and see what general conclusions you can form about the role of newspapers in the lives of people around you.

3

THE POWER AND RESPONSIBILITY OF THE PRESS

When you have completed this chapter you should be able to

Understand the meaning of and the limitations on freedom of the press.

Understand a number of legal restrictions placed on the press in the United States.

Recognize the nonfactual material published in newspapers.

The governor of colonial New York stood before his council, angrily waving a newspaper.

"This *Journal* . . . it's making me the laughingstock of the whole colony!" he snorted.

A few members of the council smiled to themselves. Even though the verses criticized the governor for interfering with the courts, they had been funny.

"We must suppress the paper! Burn every copy! This man Zenger . . . he's broken the law by publishing scandalous libels about me, the King's personal representative in this miserable town!" The governor puffed out his chest importantly.

Council members nodded sagely. After all, John Peter Zenger's newspaper had been critical of the way the government was being run. People might object to other laws if this sort of thing were allowed to continue. Zenger and his New York *Weekly Journal* had to be silenced.

Zenger was thrown into prison in 1734 and brought to trial a year later. In spite of attempts by judges to force punishment, a jury made up of citizens set him free.

The famous trial helped to establish the right of American newspapers to publish the truth and to criticize public officials. Editorial opinion, previously forbidden, could now be regularly expressed. Fifty years later, a guarantee of freedom of the press was written into the United States Constitution.

Zenger's lawyer, Andrew Hamilton, defended his client on the ground that printing or publishing a paper does not amount to libel: "The words themselves must be libelous; that is, false, malicious, and seditious . . ."

Understanding the Right to Publish and Criticize

Student newspapers are similar to other newspapers in regard to the freedom of expression granted by the First Amendment of the United States Constitution. This famous amendment reads in part: "Congress shall make no law ... abridging the freedom of speech, or of the press ..."

The principle of freedom of expression includes both freedom of the press and freedom of speech. American publishers may distribute books, pamphlets, magazines, or newspapers without having to submit them in advance for government approval. The same rights apply to motion pictures, television, radio, and other media. Writers or speakers are, of course, subject to punishment if they broadcast or publish false, scandalous, or malicious material.

Freedom to print and the right to criticize are meaningless, however, unless journalists have access to all pertinent facts, especially those about what governments and organizations are doing. In practice, therefore, freedom of the press has been extended to embrace freedom of information—the right of the people to be fully informed about affairs of local or national interest.

Recent court decisions have established that student publications, including both school-sponsored and off-campus newspapers, come under this basic constitutional guarantee, which affects all print and broadcast media. Judges have pointed out two limitations, however. First, since high school students have had less experience in making decisions and judgments than college students and adults, their published material or activities may be subject to more careful supervision. Second, the publication or distribution of student newspapers must not interfere with the obligation of school administrators to maintain an orderly situation in which a young person may continue his or her education.

School newspapers also face a number of other limitations, both general and specific, that are placed on all newspapers in the United States.

Recognizing Valid Limitations on Freedom of Expression

Freedom of expression is probably greater for United States newspapers than for publications in any other country. Even so, a number of restrictions on absolute freedom do exist. In general, the effect of these limitations is to point out that every newspaper staff, professional or student, must act responsibly toward the public.

The limitations fall into two groups. Some of them are primarily a matter of common sense and standard ethics on the part of the press, government officials, advertisers, and the general public. The others result from certain legal restrictions that have been upheld by the United States Supreme Court as constitutional limitations on freedom of expression.

These Soviet citizens live in a society where freedom of the press and other forms of freedom of expression are severely limited. The paper they are reading is Pravda, *published by the Communist party.*

The first group includes the following: the need to act responsibly toward the general public, the need to protect national security, the need or desire to restrict certain kinds of information for one reason or another, and the need to consider the desires of advertisers and readers, whose interests are not always the same as those of news staffs.

The second group, made up of specific legal restrictions, is concerned with such matters as malicious or libelous statements, invasion of personal privacy, obscenity and vulgarity, copyright laws, and statements inciting violence.

Reporting the News Responsibly and Ethically

The American constitutional right of freedom of expression rests upon responsible use of this right. Reporters and editors, whether professional or scholastic, have an obligation to deal fairly with people in the news, as well as with their readers. This means that newspaper staff members must, through guidance, training, and experience, learn how to use their freedom responsibly.

Professional newspapers are commercial enterprises, often owned by members of the community in which they are published. Like other Americans in business, these publishers want to serve their communities honestly, while at the same time making a fair profit. Generally, they have earned good reputations and want to keep them. Daily newspaper staffs are well aware of their limited time for reporting and writing news, as well as a shortage of space in which to print all available information. Considering these limitations, most editors and reporters try to do an impartial job of presenting the news fairly.

Most professional and school newspapers have written or unwritten standards covering what to print. For example, few local newspapers would print your name if you, a minor with no previous police record, were arrested for shoplifting. The editor of such a paper would not be trying to protect you from proper punishment. Rather, he or she would be likely to take the position that you should be given every chance to mend your ways. The editor would not feel that telling the whole community about this incident would help you become a responsible citizen.

News media may also practice voluntary self-censorship if they feel it is not in the public interest to print all they know. For instance, Chicago newspapers cooperated in withholding news about a kidnapped child for two days while police searched for the child without the kidnapper's being aware of their movements. The effort was sucessful. The child was returned unharmed. Then the papers lifted their own censorship and published the entire story.

While newspapers may practice voluntary self-censorship upon occasion, censorship from an outside agency is another matter.

Avoiding Censorship
While Protecting National Interests

Censorship means inspection and approval of newspaper or broadcast material by a government or public agency *before* the material is released to the public. Censorship is based on the idea that some specific authority knows best what the public should read, hear, and see.

On this basis, censorship is unconstitutional in the United States. The news media may publish almost any information. However, they can in certain instances be subject to legal action *after* publication.

Responsible editors understand that confidential material affecting such things as the nation's security should not be broadcast to the eyes and ears of the world. Especially during wartime, information about movements and activities of the armed forces may be controlled to keep military facts out of enemy hands.

News from some foreign countries, even when written by American correspondents, may sometimes be carefully censored by the foreign government before it is released. Your newspaper may print it, but it is well to remember that such stories may include distortions of fact or **half-truths**— statements that are true but misleading because they omit important facts.

In public schools and universities, the term *censorship* is often used when administrators direct that certain words or stories not be published. This raises a fine distinction: Where does reasonable editing stop and unconstitutional censorship start? Chapter 4 discusses this topic.

Handling Other Restrictions on Information

Closely related to censorship is concealment of information by national or local governments. Governing bodies may hold secret meetings—

often called executive sessions—which are closed to reporters. In other cases, government agencies may simply not release important information.

In 1971 the Pentagon Papers, containing historical facts about United States government policy relating to the Vietnam War—facts which had previously been regarded as secret material—were obtained and published by *The New York Times*. When the Supreme Court finally halted government intervention and allowed the *Times* to continue publication, a full evaluation of the matter of restricted news was under way.

Many officials believe it is their duty to protect the public by withholding certain information from publication. The attitude of American newspapers remains that citizens have the right to know what their government is doing if they are to make intelligent judgments and continue to be a free people.

Another question in this area is whether reporters must reveal the names of people who give them confidential information. Obviously, stories received from confidential sources must at first be printed as rumors. But further investigation often leads to factual proof, perhaps from official records or reports. Reporters feel that if they are required to reveal the names of confidential news sources, they may no longer be given essential information that the public has a right to know. A few states protect reporters in the same way as they do lawyers—by **shield laws** that treat conversations with a client as confidential. But this is not true of other states or of the federal government. In any case, these shield laws provide little protection when information about criminal activity is involved, especially when withholding this material might interfere with an accused person's constitutional right to a fair trial. Reporters in New York, New Jersey, California, and other states have gone to jail rather than reveal the names of people who had given them information in confidence.

Satisfying Both Advertisers and Readers

To what extent do newspaper staffs have a responsibility to represent the views of their advertisers? Since advertising pays for most publishing costs, an editor or publisher must consider the possibility that advertising might be withdrawn from the newspaper if the advertiser is not pleased with the paper's content. In practice, most editors publish what they feel is right, not what their advertisers want them to. And most advertisers are quite willing to allow newspapers to determine what news items to publish and how to present these items to develop the greatest circulation.

While actual income from a newspaper's sales and subscriptions is small compared with income from advertising, the newspaper must be read if that advertising is to be profitable. Consequently, most newspapers seek the largest circulation possible. The newspaper that prints what its readers want will sell papers. Unfortunately, readers may prefer an emphasis on sensational news, rather than the more intelligent balance of information that many editors would prefer to print. A responsible staff may have to make some compromises to please readers.

Recognizing Legal Restrictions on the Press

As former Chief Justice Oliver Wendell Holmes once pointed out, no one has the right to cry "Fire!" in a crowded theater. This suggests that there must be certain legal limitations on freedom of expression. Some of these exist in various state laws, while others have developed through court decisions.

Avoiding Libel

Libel occurs when a published or broadcast statement unjustly exposes someone to hatred, makes that person seem ridiculous, or damages that person's reputation or earning power. The offended person may sue the writer, speaker, editor, or publisher. School administrators and newspaper advisers could be involved in such a lawsuit. Libel suits are usually civil actions—suits between two people that involve monetary claims rather than imprisonment. The damages claimed may sometimes amount to millions of dollars.

Newspapers must handle potentially libelous material carefully. For example, you would not write, "John Doe murdered his wife yesterday." You would qualify the statement: "Police arrested John Doe and charged him with murdering his wife." If you were to print the first statement and John Doe were to be proven innocent, he could make you pay for the harm you did to his reputation.

Truth is the best defense in a libel suit, but you must be able to prove that the offending statement is true. A second defense is what is legally termed **privilege.** It means that accurately reported information obtained from the public record or from sessions of such public bodies as Congress, state legislatures, and courts may be published. A third defense is known as **fair comment and criticism.** It means that public performances and the activities of people in public life may be criticized so long as the intent is not malicious. Since, however, libel laws change over time and vary from state to state and since the verdicts of juries are often unpredictable, reporters and other writers must be extraordinarily careful when saying anything negative about individuals, organizations, or products.

School publications are not exempt from libel actions. A $1,000,000 libel suit was filed against a New York state school district by a student's parents because a caption in the high school yearbook allegedly ridiculed her. The families of a teen-age boy and girl sued a school newspaper when its gossip columnist reported incorrectly that they were together in a car on a lovers' lane at 2:30 a.m. Explaining away a football team's losing season by calling the coach incompetent or reporting in an April Fools' Day edition that the student-body president left for Mexico with the activity fund can easily be cause for libel action. Letters to the editor are another danger area. Even when the writer's name is printed, the newspaper that publishes a malicious or untruthful letter can be held responsible.

Robert Trager, an authority on school press law, comments, "Courts will not protect a newspaper that has been proven to defame someone, with knowledge that the information was false or with reckless disregard of whether it was false or not."

The following checklist is a guide for school journalists dealing with the publication of negative comments about people or events in school papers. It is not, however, an authoritative guide to libel law. Since only a qualified lawyer can offer sound legal advice to journalists dealing with possibly libelous material, school newspapers should exercise caution by not publishing statements that could raise the issue of libel. An answer of no to any of the relevant checklist questions indicates that the material in question might be libelous.

✓ Checklist for Guarding Against Libel

☐ 1. Is the statement in question true?

☐ 2. Can it be proven true in court?

☐ 3. Is it free of malice in the sense of disregard for the rights of another person?

☐ 4. If it is concerned with privileged material—information gotten from public records, Congress, state legislatures, or court sessions—is it reported accurately?

☐ 5. If it is concerned with fair-comment material—performances or works open to the public (athletic events, entertainment, books, art exhibitions, and the like) or the activities of people in public life—are the criticisms responsible?

☐ 6. If it deals with someone in public life, does it avoid exposing that person's private life to hatred, contempt, or ridicule?

☐ 7. Does the statement suggest that its author is seeking to be truthful and accurate?

☐ 8. Was the writer thorough in checking the source of the statement?

Respecting the Right of Privacy

Publication of any information about someone's private life might also be cause for court action against a newspaper. In general, laws protecting privacy are similar to those covering libel. But whereas truth is the best

Even well-known public figures (like the one shown here) have the right of privacy with respect to their personal lives.

defense in a libel suit, newsworthiness is the best defense in a suit for invasion of privacy. Newspapers cannot pry into a citizen's private affairs, but if that citizen does something newsworthy, he or she loses the right of privacy in regard to the newsworthy activity. Even an innocent pedestrian hit by a car may have lost the legal right of privacy, because information about the accident is a matter of public interest.

While deciding what is or is not suitable to print about an individual is largely a matter of ethics, there are guidelines. When a person becomes a public figure by doing something newsworthy, information about that action may be freely reported, but details of the individual's personal life are still private. In addition, you cannot use someone's name in a fictional situation or print a photograph of a person doing one thing to illustrate something totally different. Using someone's name or photograph in an advertisement without that person's consent is also an illegal invasion of privacy.

Avoiding Obscenity

Obscene, vulgar, or profane statements are not protected by the First Amendment, according to the United States Supreme Court. Moreover, most states specifically prohibit vulgarity and profane language in their schools, and judges have supported these prohibitions.

What legally qualifies as an obscenity is still not completely clear in spite of recent court decisions. The present practice is to make obscenity judgments on the basis of "commonly accepted community standards."

However, there is little agreement as to what these standards may be in any given area. For instance, normally offensive words might be acceptable in a literary work where they add to its realism, but these same words would rarely be suitable in news columns. Material that could be considered pornographic might be acceptable for adults to read or see but would usually not be considered suitable for the young.

To quote Mr. Trager again, "If student journalists want to be assured of having their freedom of expression protected, they must not use *any* words or phrases that can be construed as obscene."

Respecting Copyrights

The right of authors or artists to prevent others from copying or reprinting their original work without permission is called **copyright.** Although most news stories are not copyrighted, some are. Such copyrighted stories may be carried by one news medium but not by others. In addition, school and professional newspapers may not reprint selections from books or magazines without permission, regardless of how pertinent the material might be in helping readers gain an understanding of current events.

Avoiding Incitements to Violence

As a matter of common sense as well as law, newspapers cannot publish material intended to encourage violence or criminal activity. In schools, this prohibition also applies to the publication or distribution of material that would disrupt the orderly educational process. This topic will be discussed in Chapter 4.

Newspapers can, of course, report *about* violent or criminal actions, as long as the reporting is fair and accurate. This is far different from the illegal act of inciting violence directly through an editorial or other opinion article.

Activity 2:　Looking at Legal Restrictions

1. Locate a published account of a libel case and prepare a brief report on the facts. The *Readers' Guide to Periodical Literature* will refer you to recent news magazine reports.

2. Read Paul F. Ashley's *Say It Safely*, a compact and informative study. Write a brief report on some of its major points.

3. After consulting the *Readers' Guide*, prepare a brief report on privacy suits brought by celebrities or other famous people. Tell how their privacy was allegedly violated and what legal judgment resulted.

4. Interview four adults about what they consider to be obscene or acceptable in movies, TV programs, or magazines. You may find this an emotionally charged topic, so your questions should be as objective as possible. Report your results.

Recognizing the Nonfactual Content of Newspapers

A certain amount of nonfactual material appears in almost every newspaper, professional or scholastic. The most important and usually most obvious kind of nonfactual material is opinion. Editorials, commentaries, columns, reviews, and reports based on interviews typically include opinions. In all of these, it is clear whose views a reader is receiving. Editorials state the opinion of the publisher or the staff. Commentaries and columns express the opinions of their writers, whose names are given to indicate the source of the views put forth. A review, again with the writer's name included, is likewise an opinion article. In addition, opinions may be included in news stories based on an interview. The opinions, though, are not the reporter's but rather those of the person interviewed. They must be placed within quotation marks and properly attributed or follow a phrase such as "Mr. Jones says that . . ."

Most newspaper readers want and welcome opinion when its source is clearly identified, because it helps them weigh the news and form their own viewpoints. But their major difficulty—and yours as a reporter—is to keep the difference between fact and opinion clear.

Distinguishing Between Fact and Opinion

A fact represents an actual event or situation. It is a statement of what happened, what plans were made, or what someone said. Even when your school newspaper publishes an article about a future occurrence, the report concerns something that has already happened—what a news source has told a reporter or what has already been planned by a committee or individual.

In some cases, people may argue about the facts. The real truth of the matter remains unchanged, even though no one agrees on exactly what that truth is. When there is such a discussion, it involves what people believe took place. In other words, the discussion consists of opinions.

If someone makes a statement concerning an event, the only immediately certain fact is that this particular statement was made. The content of the statement must be considered personal opinion until it is clearly established that it describes what actually happened. The reporter should note what was said, being careful to name the source. If there is reason to believe the statement is incorrect, the reporter may qualify it in the news story, perhaps with words such as *assert* or *allege*. Contradictory statements made by other sources may also be reported.

An opinion, then, is what someone thinks, believes, or wishes. That person may be an official, a reporter's source of information, or some other individual. What this individual has said may include both opinions and facts. The following paragraph is a mixture of fact and opinion. The facts appear in ordinary type, the opinions in italics.

To read a newspaper competently, it is necessary to recognize statements of fact and statements of opinion. Careful reading may often be necessary to tell when fact is giving way to opinion, or vice versa.

"*A tremendous number* of students—more than 150—were enrolled, but only 30 reported for the first class," stated Mrs. Irene Allen, school registrar. "Some of the 150-plus students had schedule conflicts and chose another elective. Some told me that they were dropping the course because they didn't need the credit to graduate. *And some, I guess,*" Mrs. Allen continued, "*probably felt the course was too hard.* Mr. Browne always assigns a 30-page term paper and two shorter papers, in addition to daily homework. *Not all students can handle that much work.*"

This paragraph could, of course, be included in an objective, straight-fact news story because it is a fact that Mrs. Allen made a statement about the enrollment for a certain course.

What might this distinction between fact and opinion mean to you? Serious difficulties may face an individual who cannot tell the difference. As a newspaper reader, you must be able to distinguish facts and opinions from one another in order to understand a news report. You should analyze the statements in the story, trying to identify which may be facts and which may be opinions. Moreover, you should watch for any conclusions that a writer may offer, since these are also opinions. Each time you find an opinion, first identify the source. Then consider it, accepting or rejecting it. Finally, use it to help form your own judgment about the news event.

Of course, school newspaper staff members are also concerned with the practical matter of publishing acceptable news stories. As a reporter, you must develop techniques for dealing with both facts and opinions in everything you write. To do so, you must first have a clear grasp of the distinction between the two.

Activity 3: Identifying Facts and Opinions

1. Make two columns on your paper. Head one Facts and the other Opinions. Then, study the following items and decide which sentences or parts of sentences belong in each column. List each under the proper heading. You may assume that statements that seem to be facts have been reported correctly.

   a. New auditorium footlights are being installed. They will enable the audience to gain more enjoyment from school performances.

   b. Cast members number close to 200. All realize the importance of teamwork in making "Allegro" the best play ever presented at Central High. Tickets for the performances are $1, and sales are in full swing at the moment.

   c. "If there are enough requests, German will be offered as a regular subject next year," stated Mr. Black. "Otherwise, I would imagine that our chances of having a second-year class are very low."

   d. "The cost is not high, as it averages out to about $1 per student and faculty member. The United Fund Drive will be a major success with your full-hearted support," remarked Gail Weber, head of publicity for the drive.

   e. The junior-senior prom will be held May 24. This is the event to which juniors and seniors have been looking forward all year long. This annual event was staged successfully last year, also at the country club.

2. Find in a daily newspaper a long news story containing both fact and opinion. A particularly useful story would be one describing a disaster, such as a major accident, fire, flood, or windstorm, that was obviously viewed by the reporter. Such a story should also include comments by other eyewitnesses or participants.

   a. Underline the statements of fact and circle the statements of opinion, including the conclusions drawn from the facts.

   b. Are the opinions fairly presented? Give reasons for your judgment.

   c. Can you detect any statements presented as facts that may in reality be opinions? If so, which statements are they? How did you decide whether they were truly factual or not?

3. Find another news story about a controversial topic. You might select a description of a law proposed to Congress or to your state legislature or a story about some local problem that includes the ideas of various officials. Mark the story as in Item 2. Then answer the following questions:

   a. If there is apparent disagreement, how is the controversy handled?

   b. Are opposing opinions presented to give the reader a chance to make up his or her own mind? Explain.

   c. Can you tell from the news story itself which side the paper favors? If so, how? (Do not be influenced by knowledge gained previously from editorials, cartoons, or other opinion articles.)

Considering the Source of Information

Another distinction newspaper readers and reporters must make is between facts and rumors—general statements made by someone who lacks sufficient information or authority to present facts. Most newspapers identify news sources by name or make clear the reporter's personal presence at a news event. But readers and reporters must judge the authority of the person who is the source of a given news story. A basic question to ask is "Does this person have the knowledge and qualifications to make reliable statements of fact?"

For example, suppose the mayor of a town in your area announces that the mayor of a city 500 miles away is a crooked politician. Before you even consider whether this statement might be true or untrue, you should question the first mayor's authority to make the statement. Where might the mayor have obtained the information? How reliable might this source be? Why is this statement being made? What business is it of the mayor's anyway? Perhaps most important, is there anything the mayor has to gain by making such a statement?

Even more questionable than the named news source who lacks authority to make a statement is the unnamed source. Unnamed sources appear frequently in news of national or international politics. As an example, a government official who is making a decision may not, for some reason, wish to announce it yet, but an alert reporter might guess or be "tipped off" as to what will be said. The reporter might then report it as a rumor without naming the authority. There may be no reference to a source, or the reporter may state that the information comes from an "informed source" or a "usually reliable source." How reliable are such reports? It is difficult to say, but in general it is reasonable to regard almost any report based on an unnamed source as requiring future verification.

Watching for Slanted News

Sometimes, a newspaper may present news in a biased or slanted way, either accidentally or intentionally. As a result of such **slanted news,** newspaper readers are likely to misunderstand the reality behind the story. Some of the facts may not be there, or they may be presented in such a way that their relative importance is distorted.

How might a news story be unintentionally slanted? In the limited time before a deadline, a reporter may not have time to gather all the facts and so may miss important information. News sources may not know all the facts or may deliberately lie about some of them. If the reporter has a strong personal opinion about the subject, his or her viewpoint may unconsciously determine which facts are emphasized and which are downplayed. Slanting may also result from the favorable or unfavorable connotations of words. Compare these paragraphs about the same news event. Which one strikes you as slanted? Why?

The school board today revealed plans for a $9,000,000 bond issue to enlarge and improve school facilities throughout the city. Of the $9,000,000, some $2,500,000 would be used to acquire land, while the remainder would rebuild two schools and provide for additions to eleven others.

The school board revealed today that it plans to condemn private property and homes worth $2,500,000, including a square block in the downtown area, for expansion of school facilities. The condemnation would be part of a $9,000,000 school bond issue going before voters in the general municipal election.

News may also be slanted by the way stories are arranged on a newspaper page or by the way a story is emphasized. A news item of major importance may be hidden on a back page while sensational, but unimportant, stories fill the front page. Stories with high news value may sometimes be left out entirely.

Responsible school and professional newspaper staffs do their best to avoid slanted news. Still, slanted news is not always the fault of staff members. A reporter might have received information from a news source who believes in **managed news**—that newspaper readers should be told only what that source's organization, company, or government agency wants them to know. In other cases, a newspaper's publisher may have directed that a certain policy be promoted in the paper.

Activity 4:   Detecting Rumors or Slanting

1. Search daily newspapers for statements based on rumors or unsupported by a reliable authority. Bring them to class and discuss them. Show how such statements could cause harm.

2. Select an item of local or regional news and clip two stories about it from two daily newspapers (perhaps an afternoon newspaper of one day and a morning newspaper of the following day or a community paper and a metropolitan area paper). Compare the two stories for evidence of slanting.

   a. Has one paper emphasized a particular portion of the news?

   b. Do the ways the two articles are written tend to make you draw different conclusions about the facts of the situation?

   c. Is there a difference in headline size, or are the stories placed differently on the pages of the two newspapers?

   d. Is any other kind of slanting noticeable?

Looking Out for Propaganda

Propaganda is the name given to any organized, widespread attempt to influence people's thinking or behavior. It may be good or bad, according to the purpose or intentions of its originator, the way it is used, or the manner of its reception by an audience. Reporters meet propaganda most often in the efforts of advertising managers, lobbyists, political campaign workers, or publicity people for various organizations. Today, anyone with anything to do with modern communications should be able to recognize and understand propaganda.

Nearly all advertising may be considered a form of propaganda, for it is designed to induce people to buy a product or service. Generally, the propaganda will be relatively mild and open, combined with a reasonably honest and straightforward presentation of facts. Some ads, however, are deliberately misleading or untruthful. Federal and state agencies recognize this and have taken action to ensure that advertisements for certain products are factual and truthful.

Whether mild or deliberately misleading, propaganda is designed to appeal to you in many ways. Half-truths are common: "This deodorant proved best in extensive tests." Best for what? Who conducted the tests? What kind of tests? With what other brands of deodorant was it compared? Or promoters may present arguments on only one side of a question, making it impossible for you to reason intelligently unless you are willing to seek out opposing arguments from other sources. Another device is to base a conclusion on too few examples: "These two teen-agers were caught shoplifting, so every teen-ager who enters a store should be watched carefully."

Other propagandists want you to do something because "everybody's doing it." "Follow the crowd! Everyone's voting for this candidate!" Or you hear a testimonial: "Famous movie star Liz Jones chews this gum." This implies that you should chew this brand because Liz is famous and wealthy and in this way you will share something with her. At election time, candidates become "just plain folks"; they chat with voters, kiss babies, or share a meal in some ordinary citizen's home.

Use of "loaded" or misleading words, names, or phrases is another common means of spreading propaganda. Speakers or writers may use evil-sounding words to attack an idea or a person—words such as *Nazi, dictatorship, agitator, addict, fascism, conspiracy,* and *antisocial.* Or they may support their program with words that have a positive connotation—words such as *crusader, home, love, honorable, truth,* and *American.*

Most of these devices appeal to people's emotions rather than to common sense. It is easier to relax and accept uncritically what is spoken or written than it is to stay alert and consider it carefully. This is why propaganda often succeeds. Those who don't bother to think statements through don't recognize propaganda when they encounter it. Therein lies one of the great dangers of today's high-speed methods of communication. They discourage slow, careful analysis and judgment.

Activity 5:   Identifying Propaganda

1. Select from advertisements in newspapers, magazines, or mailings five striking examples of propaganda. Explain the persuasive devices used by each advertiser.

2. Describe several television or radio commercials that use propaganda techniques to achieve their purposes.

3. Try to locate similar examples of propaganda in the news stories of daily newspapers or on news broadcasts. Did you have more difficulty locating propaganda in news material than in advertisements? If you did, explain why this might be.

4. Study propaganda techniques used in editorial cartoons in several daily newspapers, if possible choosing cartoons that deal with the same news material. How do they portray or symbolize various people, organizations, or ideas? Is their approach positive or negative? What propaganda devices can you detect?

Summary

This chapter begins by explaining the right to publish and report the news enjoyed by newspapers in the United States. It then discusses the chief restrictions on the power of the press. Finally, it discusses how newspapers present more than just facts on their pages.

UNDERSTANDING THE RIGHT TO PUBLISH AND CRITICIZE. Newspaper publishers in America enjoy freedom of the press, which is closely linked to freedom of information—the right to be fully informed about affairs of local and national interest. Freedom of the press is not absolute, however. Ethical and legal restrictions exist. The ethical restrictions include the need to deal fairly with the general public, the need to protect national security, the need or desire to withhold certain information for one reason or another, and the need to consider the desires of advertisers and readers. Censorship, which presumes that some authority knows best what the public should read, hear, and see, is unconstitutional in the United States. The concealment of information by the government is generally opposed by American newspapers. Instead, they try to publish what they feel they ought to, while maintaining a large enough circulation to keep up advertising income.

RECOGNIZING LEGAL RESTRICTIONS ON THE PRESS. Libel laws prohibit a paper from publishing material that unjustly exposes someone to hatred, makes that person seem ridiculous, or damages that person's reputation or earning power. Other laws restrict the publication of information about a person's private life. Obscene, vulgar, or profane statements may also result in legal action. Copyright laws seek to protect the right of authors or artists to prevent others from copying or reprinting their work without permission. Laws also forbid the publication of material intended to encourage violence or criminal activity.

RECOGNIZING THE NONFACTUAL CONTENT OF NEWSPAPERS. An opinion is a belief that is not absolutely certain or positive. It expresses what seems true or probable to someone. Both newspaper readers and journalists ought to have a sure grasp of the distinction between fact and opinion. A statement by someone who lacks the information or authority to present facts is a rumor, or at least an unreliable statement. A distortion of the facts, whether intentional or not, results in slanted news. An organized, widespread attempt to influence thinking or behavior is propaganda. Readers and reporters should be alert to the presence of such nonfactual material in newspapers.

Vocabulary

censorship

half-truth

shield law

libel

privilege

fair comment and criticism

copyright

slanted news

managed news

propaganda

Review Questions

1. What is meant by freedom of the press, and how is it related to freedom of information?

2. What is the difference between censorship and concealment of information?

3. What are the chief legal restrictions on the press?

4. What is libel, and what are the three basic defenses against a libel suit?

5. What are some of the basic kinds of nonfactual material that appear in print?

Discussion Questions

1. In what instances do you think newspapers should use voluntary self-censorship? What, if any, are the dangers of too much self-censorship?

2. In what ways might the influence of the general public have a negative effect on the quality of what gets published in American newspapers? In what ways might it have a positive effect?

3. Does your community have "commonly accepted standards" that make clear what kinds of

published material should be considered obscene, vulgar, or profane? If so, what are they?

4. Would you say that the staff of your school paper has a sure grasp of the distinction between fact and opinion?

5. Does your school paper publish news that is either intentionally or accidentally slanted?

Chapter Project

Investigating the Power and Responsibility of the Press

Research and report on one of the following subjects: conditions leading to the adoption of the First Amendment; recent judicial interpretations of the First Amendment; freedom of the press in countries with governments that are similar to or different from that of the United States; declarations made by the United Nations about freedom of expression; the question of national security in conflict with the First Amendment in the Pentagon Papers case; and conflicts between the First and Sixth Amendments in the conduct of fair trials.

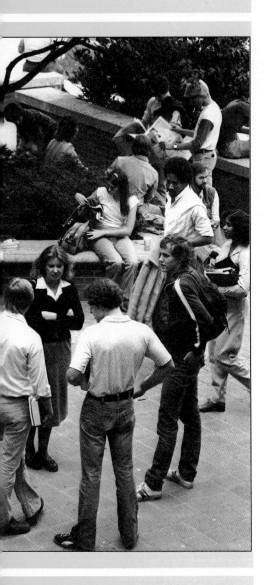

THE STUDENT PRESS

When you have completed this chapter you should be able to

Understand the meaning of freedom of expression as it applies to school journalism.

Enumerate the basic kinds of responsibility that a school newspaper has.

Form an accurate overall view of the school newspaper publishing process.

Last year's editorial staff had concentrated on current news items, covering everything that took place around school. But reader interest in the school paper had lagged. "We've heard it already" was the typical comment.

New staff members decided, "This year we'll print more relevant stories." They wrote detailed news reports and feature stories about students helping in hospitals and nurseries, school departments and their academic goals, and the problems faced by student dropouts.

As interest picked up, the staff plunged bravely into more controversial subjects—drug use in the community, the lack of interest in local elections, the ongoing effort to ease tensions between different local groups, and even the "do-nothing" student legislature. Readers applauded and urged reports on more sensitive topics. Some younger, less experienced staff members began to look into areas that had so far been taboo.

One story was prepared by a sophomore who had already made it clear in his conversations that he felt "the newspaper should be entirely a student forum, without faculty interference." He had investigated the cost of athletic equipment. One of his discoveries, which he featured in a sensationally worded story, was that the vice-principal had a major financial interest in the company supplying most of this equipment. The faculty adviser suggested that he modify the story to report only the facts of the case and, furthermore, that he carefully avoid any statements that might seem to be accusations of wrongdoing. The reporter, backed by some staff members, insisted that the story be used as prepared. Deadlines were rapidly approaching, and the editors finally decided to use the story as it stood.

The newspaper was barely in the hands of its readers before the trouble began. Some faculty members pointed out that an administrator's personal business was not a matter of student concern. The principal's and superintendent's phones were busy with calls from citizens who felt the charges must be false and malicious. The superintendent, reacting hastily, directed that the principal read all future newspaper copy before publication.

What went wrong? Staff members had not adequately recognized that freedom of the press must be accompanied by a full measure of responsibility. Editors and reporters must be aware of legal limitations on the freedom of the scholastic press. They must understand how their newspaper will affect the school and community. They must know where they stand with their school administration. And they must have developed clear, responsible goals.

Examining School Newspapers' Freedom of Expression

Court decisions have made it clear that students do not lose their basic constitutional rights to free expression merely because they attend school. On the other hand, since most high school students are not yet adults, they are not always expected to make mature judgments and decisions. Therefore, school administrators may exercise more guidance and control over their actions than would be necessary if they were adults. The Supreme Court, in the 1969 case of *Tinker v. Des Moines*, said: "A student may express his opinion on campus, even on controversial subjects . . . if he does so without materially and substantially interfering with the requirements of appropriate discipline and without colliding with the rights of others."

School newspapers are entitled to the constitutional protection of freedom of the press, and the courts have regarded them as worthy forms of student expression. This was best explained by a federal judge in the Connecticut case of *Eisner v. Stamford* in 1970: "Student newspapers are valuable educational tools, and also serve to aid school administrators by providing them with an insight into student thinking and student problems. They are valuable peaceful channels of student protest which should be encouraged, not suppressed."

School papers are subject to the general limitations upon freedom of expression outlined in Chapter 3, as well as to others that arise from the school situation itself. The courts have applied the same principles to both school-sponsored and to off-campus newspapers, often called **alternative newspapers.**

Comments in this section apply primarily to public schools, whose administrators are government officials and are therefore bound by the provisions of the First Amendment. While private school and parochial school students as individuals have basic constitutional rights, their administrators' relationship to the state is considerably different. In general, the school newspaper staffs at these schools occupy the same legal position as commercial newspaper staffs. Their publisher (in this case, the school or its administrators) has full authority to direct the work of staff members and to specify what may or may not be printed.

Understanding the Position of School Officials

Regulation by administrators in public schools is a matter of concern to many student staffs. Is it censorship when the faculty adviser or principal reads and criticizes student writing before publication? The answer would probably be yes if this criticism took the form of a flat prohibition of the publication of an article, with no effort made to discuss with the writer why the article violates certain reasonable limitations on the press and how these violations might be avoided or corrected. But when such an effort is made by an administrator or adviser, the situation no longer involves censorship but responsible **editing** and authority.

There is no publisher with absolute authority over a public school newspaper in the same sense that there is over a commercial paper or a private school paper. The primary responsibility for what is printed rests with student writers and editors. Nevertheless, the school board, the superintendent, the principal, and the faculty adviser have a clear right to supervise the newspaper's organization and management. The administrators

One of the keys to establishing a good working relationship with school officials is to remember that students are not your only audience. Adults also care about the contents and views in a school newspaper.

—Photo by Michael D. Sullivan

control a major part of a school paper's finances, pay the adviser's salary, provide office space, and often support the paper through the school's budget. Beyond that, they have an obligation as educators to see that the publication meets appropriate journalistic standards. To the extent that the adviser and school officials may read material proposed for publication, they probably also become responsible for its content. In fact, federal courts in most sections of the country have indicated that advisers are expected to prevent the publication of material that is libelous, obscene, or clearly disruptive of an orderly educational process.

Avoiding Disruption of School Operations

Administrators have the authority to make reasonable rules and regulations under which order and discipline may be maintained, so that the educational process may continue without disruption. The **distribution** of newspapers at the wrong time or place, resulting in excited students commenting about them in class, has been cause for court action. So also have printed articles that encouraged student strikes or defiance of school regulations.

Accordingly, freedom of expression may be limited if administrators determine that it will "materially and substantially" interfere with school operations. Just how much interference is "material and substantial interference" has not been well defined by any court; so the newspaper staff needs to tread cautiously in this area.

Some judges have pointed out that severe criticism of school administrators might make it difficult for them to control their schools. According to Robert Trager, a former high school newspaper adviser who has studied school press freedom, student writers "must be careful that criticism is constructive and based on demonstrable facts to avoid charges of disrupting the student body and causing 'material interference with good order.'"

Courts have consistently declared that distribution on school grounds of either school-sponsored or off-campus publications, as well as of posters, armbands, buttons, or other materials, cannot be regulated arbitrarily or on an individual basis. There must be a reasonable set of rules that apply to all situations and that allow for prompt appeals. In addition, freedom of the press does not extend to commercial activity, so school boards may properly refuse permission to sell any item, including publications, on the school grounds.

Activity 1: Looking at Freedom of the Press in Your School

1. Suppose an article published in your school newspaper contains libelous statements. What are the responsibilities of each of the following people in connection with its publication: the writer of the article, the editor of the paper, the faculty adviser, and the principal?

2. What are the regulations for distribution of publications or other materials at your school? How were they set up? What is the appeal process if a distribution request is denied?

3. Discuss in a brief report the relationship between the adviser and the student journalists as it has developed in your school. What are the responsibilities of each? How does the principal enter into school newspaper matters?

Recognizing the Responsibilities of the Student Press

What is your school newspaper's responsibility to its total community—to the students, faculty, and members of the general public who read the paper or support it financially? How does it fit into the life of this community? And what does the community expect of it?

A mature editorial staff recognizes its role as an interpreter of school life and student thought to the public and of community affairs to the student population. If staff members are to use their constitutional right of freedom of expression intelligently and responsibly by reflecting what students are doing and thinking, they need to understand something of the personality of the local community in which they publish a newspaper.

With this understanding in mind, the school paper can meet community expectations by publishing material that is in general accord with community standards. It can also act to improve relations between students and the community and to provide a forum for student opinions. Finally, the newspaper staff can develop, working with the school administration, broad guidelines that will ensure the continuation of this responsible relationship. Immediate goals can then be set up within this framework.

Meeting Community Expectations

Public schools are built and operated with taxpayers' money and run by school boards elected by community voters. The opinions of all these people are important in determining the kind of education you receive. Adult readers are likely to be looking for answers to such questions as the following as they read your paper: How much emphasis does the school place on formal education through classwork, as opposed to informal education through activities? Are students really interested in the academic goals of the school? In the activity program? In community projects? Are young people thinking only about trivial matters, or are they seriously concerned with problems facing them as they grow into maturity? Have they done constructive thinking about these problems? As a result, the pages of your paper need to show a certain sensitivity toward commonly accepted standards of public education—the professional standing of teachers, the responsibility of the students toward their school, and the dignity of learning.

The school board, acting through the superintendent and principal, authorizes the publication of your paper. Consequently, the board will usually expect your newspaper to be in harmony with the district's policies as well as to reflect the students' interests, although the two may not always coincide. Consider also that school newspapers almost never have direct competition. Even when there is an off-campus paper, it rarely appears with the same regularity, reaches the same students, or carries the same weight as the school-sponsored newspaper. This means that a school paper must be fair to all responsible points of view in its community, including that of the school board.

Improving Relations Between Students and the Community

Do people living near the school complain about student behavior? Do local police and young people have bad feelings toward each other? Do taxpayers grumble about the school's dramatic productions, athletic teams, or orchestra as "unnecessary frills"? Complaints like these may be products of poor community relations. The school newspaper staff can help influence and improve public feelings by being aware of potential problems and responsibly explaining school events and student opinions.

At the same time, staff members need to recognize that high school students are developing into participating and voting citizens. Young people who do not take an interest in the processes of community life miss out

A responsible school newspaper can affect for the better relations between the older and the younger members of a community by promoting worthwhile community activities or simply by providing a vehicle for the expression of ideas.

—Photo by Daniel S. Brody from Stock, Boston

on a vital part of their education. Your school paper can do much to make all students more aware of the world outside the school by publishing community-oriented stories and editorials.

Providing a Forum for Student Opinions

A major obligation of any worthwhile school newspaper is to reflect student thinking. Not only the staff's ideas but those of its student readership must be represented. While positive and constructive opinions are always desirable, negative ones can be effective as well. All reasonable ideas, especially those reflecting the thinking of large groups of students, need a chance for expression. It is only through the process of evaluation and discussion of new ideas that real change can take place.

Students, faculty members, and community readers all stand to gain much from the open-forum function of a school newspaper. The end result should be better understanding of what young people see as their real goals in education and life.

Activity 2:   Serving the Wider Community

1. Make a list of the various publications reaching homes in your school area. Include daily and weekly papers, neighborhood or community bulletins, company or union newspapers, other high school or college newspapers, and other local periodicals. Estimate as best you can the influence of these publications. Then make an estimate of the impor-

tance of your school newspaper in the area. Consider the approximate circulation of your school paper in comparison with that of other publications, the number of homes reached by your paper, and each publication's concern for local news.

2. Interview four or five adult members of the community concerning their impressions of your school and its students. Ask questions similar to the following:

   a. What is the main purpose for which this school exists?

   b. How well is progress being made toward this goal?

   c. Do the students seem really interested in learning and in preparing for the future?

   d. Is the student activity program of this school constructive and worthwhile?

   e. What do people in your neighborhood think about the general attitudes of students toward adults?

3. Discuss your interview results in class. Working with the other students, see whether you can assemble the comments into any sort of pattern. Then prepare a composite statement summarizing the feeling of the community toward your school.

4. List steps your newspaper can take to improve the community attitude or to maintain the present impression if you feel it is largely favorable.

5. From a recent issue of your school newspaper, select a story that might have been developed in greater detail. State what additional information could have been added to enrich or improve the story and to make it more valuable to students and the community.

—Photo by Richard Hutchings from Photo Researchers

Students have things to say, and a school paper can provide them with a forum above and beyond the forum of face-to-face conversation.

Developing Broad Guidelines

To clarify the relationship between student journalists and their adviser, school officials, and the community, a policy statement or set of permanent guidelines should be prepared. This statement will define what the people of the community, including residents, merchants, officials, administrators, and students, judge to be an appropriate school newspaper. With such a statement in hand, staff members will understand what they can and cannot do and will be able to exercise the privilege of publishing material that is interesting and useful to today's students. Administrators will also be guided by the statement whenever a specific problem or objection arises.

A statement of **editorial policy** is essential for any school paper that intends to handle sensitive or controversial matters and provide editorial leadership. The legal limits on student expression, the community's educational expectations, and the editorial staff's understanding of its purpose should all be considered. Such a policy should fix firmly in everyone's mind a general pattern for the operations and content of the school newspaper. It need not be in great detail but should outline broad areas. Such questions as the following need to be considered: What should be the main objectives of a student newspaper in this school? What kinds of content are or are not suitable for a school newspaper in this community? What should be the responsibilities of the adviser and the editorial staff? Is there to be an editorial board that will guide the handling of controversial matters and expressions of opinion? What will be its relationship to staff members? To the adviser? To the administration? How may students who are not members of the staff present their opinions in the paper?

Many different forms for a policy statement are possible. It might be a comprehensive statement of journalistic standards, including relevant court decisions on the First Amendment. It might emphasize procedural matters, listing the responsibilities of the principal, the adviser, and the staff members. It might be a contract between the administration and the staff, to be revised and then signed each year by the new staff. It might be a general expression of policy, leaving details to be filled in by the adviser and the staff.

Some school districts have dealt in a single statement with all media of expression. The board of education of Evanston Township, Illinois, set up a "Policy on Student Expression" that covers bulletin boards, printed materials, petitions, signs, and symbols and explains disciplinary and appeal procedures. The policy states that the board "desires to promote an orderly educational community which reflects traditional democratic values and constitutional principles, including freedom of expression by students."

Although there is general agreement among various sets of guidelines about purpose and content, the roles of the adviser and the school administration in relation to freedom of student expression may vary, as is shown in the two excerpts from school newspaper articles found at the top of the next page.

The Spyglass realizes that some amount of adult supervision is necessary to help guide the staff in publishing a newspaper. One such need for an adult is to guide the paper through the legal aspects of the printed word. We agree . . . that the adviser should act in this capacity, as well as inspire the staffers to develop and use good journalistic practices.

—*The Spyglass*, Memorial High School, Joplin, Missouri

Editorial views may not be changed or censored by the adviser without consultation and approval of the editorial board, which determines editorial views. The adviser may not change or censor articles without consultation and approval by the author. The adviser and editorial board shall be responsible for reading all articles prior to sending the materials to the printer.

—*Knight's Page*, Nicolet High School, Milwaukee, Wisconsin

If your newspaper does not presently operate within a framework of guidelines like these, your staff and adviser might consider developing a statement for submission to the administration and school board. Typical statements may be available from neighboring districts or from the schools with which you exchange newspapers. Many state departments of education (among them New York and California) have prepared samples. Model guidelines can be obtained from the Student Press Law Center, 800 18th Street NW, Suite 300, Washington, D.C. 20006.

Setting Immediate Goals

Within the framework of a broad policy statement, your staff or editorial board should also make specific decisions about your school newspaper's immediate purpose. The specific goals that your reporters and editors set out to accomplish will determine how successful your paper will be.

Only a few school newspapers have enough space to print all that it might be desirable to include on their pages. Most editorial staffs must focus their attention on selected areas, including other material on a space-available basis. In fact, many staffs prefer this alternative, for it gives them a chance to emphasize what they consider important.

Such questions as the following may be considered in deciding your newspaper's goals: Should we try to report all school happenings or focus in detail on a few? Should we emphasize stories that portray personalities? Should we report news events of local, national, or international importance or just school events? Should we focus on matters of serious concern to young people, whether on or off the campus? Should we provide a forum for all shades of student opinion? Should we try to lead and influence student opinion? To what extent should we include creative writing by students? How much should we entertain our readers with humor and other non-news items? How might we improve our school's image in the community? Are we responsible for building school spirit? Should we strive to make our newspaper a model of professional journalism in writing, makeup, and content, perhaps sacrificing other goals to do this?

As your staff discusses these questions, you are likely to decide that some of them matter greatly while others are of less importance. A pattern should emerge, establishing a set of goals for the current year. The following year, of course, may be different. Each new staff should have the right to its own interpretation of what a good newspaper should strive to accomplish.

A few staffs publish their goals from time to time. Others feel that the general tone of the newspaper shows their goals better than any written statement could. Would either of these statements of goals be appropriate for your school newspaper?

To publish news of events, ideas, and opinions of the school and community.

To broaden the range of thinking of staff members and readers.

To stimulate both reader and staff interest in high school publications.

To give opportunities for student expression.

To promote worthwhile projects of the school.

—*Trojan Tribune*, South High School, Grand Rapids, Michigan

In order to produce a quality newspaper, certain requirements must be met. The Virginian Times has chosen the following goals and editorial policies according to the principles of scholastic journalism:

1. To inform students of current affairs and activities at Virginia High, the community, and the world in general since we feel the student has an active role in all three.

2. To interpret complex events and issues that will bring constructive influence to bear on student and faculty opinion and hopefully stimulate thought and involvement.

3. To bring special achievements and improvements to the attention of the entire school community while at the same time point out problems and offer possible solutions.

—*Virginian Times*, Virginia High School, Bristol, Virginia

Activity 3:   Formulating Guidelines and Goals

1. Make up a set of broad guidelines that you feel would be suitable for your school paper by answering the questions in the section headed Developing Broad Guidelines. If your school paper already has a set of such guidelines, compare your own set with the one in use.

2. Make up a set of immediate goals suitable for your school paper by answering the questions in the section headed Setting Immediate Goals. If your paper already has immediate goals, compare your own set with the ones currently in use.

3. Analyze past issues of papers from other schools to determine and compare their broad guidelines and immediate goals. How do the guidelines and the goals differ from one paper to another? How do they differ from those of your school paper?

Publishing a School Newspaper

The activities involved in preparing your school newspaper for publication form the contents of the next 15 chapters of this book. In addition, information of special interest to your editorial staff and adviser are collected in the Editor's Handbook, which starts on page 449. A brief overview of the general process, however, will be valuable at this point to give you a broad framework within which you can fit each chapter's content as you come to it. You should first understand more about the kinds of material that you might find on the pages of school newspapers.

Establishing the Content of Your Pages

An interesting school newspaper contains many different kinds of material. The majority of items inform readers about school activities or policies, about students and their interests and accomplishments, and about local, national, or international events that may concern young adults. Other items present feature stories and opinions, whether those of the newspaper staff, of informed students and faculty members, or of readers. A few items may be published solely to entertain.

Advertisements also appear in most school newspapers. Occasionally, school administrations prohibit advertising in the school paper on the grounds that local merchants might not get a fair return for their money

A meeting of the newspaper staff and the adviser will often be part of the process of determining the contents of forthcoming issues of the school paper.

—Photo by Laimute E. Druskis from Taurus Photos

but may feel obliged to contribute to the school. Most school newspapers, however, gain a large part of their income from advertisers who welcome the opportunity to develop their business in the teen-age market.

The chart that begins below summarizes this variety of content.

SCHOOL NEWSPAPER CONTENT		
Group	*Kind of Item*	*Explanation*
Basic news	Academic news	Announcements by the school administration, changes in schedules or buildings, classroom news, or news relating to the instructional program.
	School activities news	News of programs, meetings, dances, and special events.
	Student government news	News of elections, student officers and their activities, and student legislative or planning groups.
	Faculty, student, or alumni news	News of accomplishments, plans, or personal events in the lives of people now connected with the school or formerly connected with it.
	Club news	Reports from various school clubs and organizations.
	Entertainment news	News about concerts, recordings, plays, movies, television, and other activities in the field of entertainment.
	Sports news	Reports on sports events, interscholastic and intramural, boys' and girls', and other athletic and physical education activities.
	Local, national, or international news	Happenings in the community, nation, or world having a bearing on the school, its students, or young people in general.
Feature stories	Topics of common interest	Articles on topics of particular interest to student readers.
	Personality sketches	Profiles of students, teachers, and other people in the school and community.
Opinion articles	Editorials	Expressions of the newspaper's opinion on events, policies, or plans.
	Commentaries	Views on school, local, or national problems, written and signed by students or faculty members.

Group	Kind of Item	Explanation
Opinion articles (continued)	Columns	Opinions or information appearing regularly and often written by the same person, about school events, entertainment, sports, or activities of students.
	Reviews	Evaluations of books, films, plays, and the like.
Non-news items	Miscellaneous	Puzzles, cartoons, jokes, poems, stories, exchange items from other school papers, and so on.
Advertisements	Display ads	Advertisements for various goods and services, usually placed by local merchants but occasionally by national advertisers.
	Classified or want ads	Inexpensive, brief advertisements, placed by individuals and collected in one location in a newspaper.

The following checklist will enable a school newspaper staff to determine the kinds of content its paper might include or whether a given issue covers the kinds of content that the paper customarily includes.

✓ Checklist on Newspaper Content

☐ 1. Does the paper cover basic news—academic news; school activities news; student government news; faculty, student, or alumni news; club news; entertainment news; sports news; local, national, or international news?

☐ 2. Does the paper include feature stories—articles covering interesting general topics or sketches of local personalities?

☐ 3. Does the paper include opinion articles—editorials, commentaries, columns, or reviews?

☐ 4. Does the paper include such non-news items as puzzles, cartoons, jokes, poems, stories, items from other school papers, and so on?

☐ 5. Does the paper include advertisements—display ads or classified ads?

Activity 4:   Analyzing the Content of a School Newspaper

1. Examine several issues of your school paper to determine which of the groups and kinds of items in the preceding chart are represented in it. Are any missing? If so, would the paper be improved if they were included?

2. Which of the groups and kinds of items are represented most often in your school paper? Which occupy the most space? Which are represented least often? Which occupy the least space? Would you change this arrangement? Why or why not?

Setting Up Your Staff

The organization of a student newspaper staff and its production procedures resemble those of professional newspapers. The staff, often divided into an editorial staff and a business staff, is headed by an editor, or editor in chief, who supervises all writing and production. Most of the editorial staff members are responsible for collecting and arranging material for certain pages. Meanwhile, reporters gather news and write stories. Business staff members handle advertising, circulation, and finances. The chart on page 81 shows one typical staff organization. The Editor's Handbook on pages 449–501 gives more details about staff organization and duties.

Planning Production Procedures

How does a news report make its way from the actual event to the pages of a newspaper? That, of course, is the subject of most of this book, but a brief sketch may be helpful here. The process starts when a reporter hears about an event or is assigned to find out about it. He or she will interview a number of people or observe what is happening and take notes. A photographer may also be present.

Next, the reporter assembles the information into a news story, following standard newswriting guidelines. Other staff members check, correct, and approve the story, which is then prepared for printing. An editor writes a headline and then places the story and photographs on an appropriate page, fitting them into place along with advertisements and other material. The staff may or may not be involved in the actual **typesetting** and printing processes, but they will manage the newspaper's distribution.

The chart on page 45 illustrates this general process. Your staff and adviser will plan the specific steps appropriate to your school paper. They should find the Editor's Handbook on pages 449–501 helpful.

Activity 5:   Understanding Your Staff Organization and Procedures

1. Using the staff organization chart on page 81 as a model, work out a chart showing the actual lines of responsibility for the staff of your school newspaper, as you understand them.

2. Trace the development of a news item for your school paper from idea to printed page. Compare your paper's procedures with those indicated in the central column of the chart on page 45. Point out any stages in the process where your paper's plan does not follow the chart.

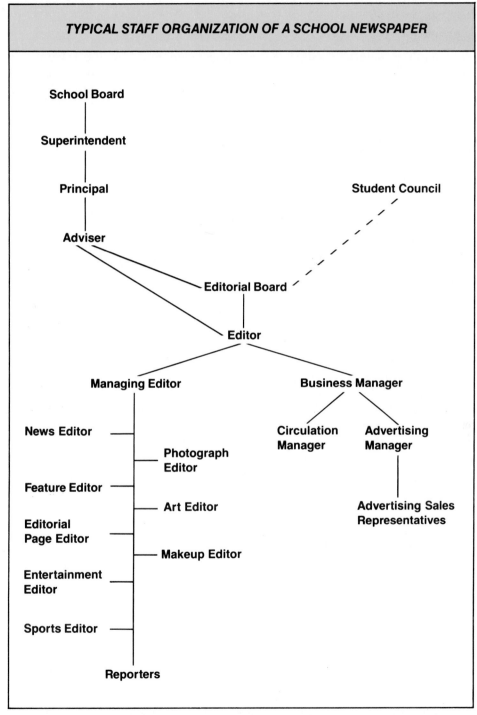

TYPICAL STAFF ORGANIZATION OF A SCHOOL NEWSPAPER

School Board

Superintendent

Principal

Student Council

Adviser

Editorial Board

Editor

Managing Editor

Business Manager

News Editor

Photograph Editor

Circulation Manager

Advertising Manager

Feature Editor

Art Editor

Editorial Page Editor

Makeup Editor

Advertising Sales Representatives

Entertainment Editor

Sports Editor

Reporters

The staff organization of a school newspaper usually takes into account the connection between the staff itself and those with a special interest in the paper, such as the adviser, the student council, and school officials.

Summary

This chapter begins by clarifying the scope and limits of the freedom of expression enjoyed by school newspapers. It then considers the kind of responsible relationship that should exist between a school paper and its community and goes on to suggest how broad guidelines and immediate goals may be formulated. Finally, it discusses the fundamentals of publishing a school newspaper.

EXAMINING SCHOOL NEWSPAPERS' FREEDOM OF EXPRESSION. School newspapers are entitled to the constitutional protection of freedom of the press. However, school officials and administrators have the right and responsibility to exercise reasonable authority over the management and content of student publications. They must see to it that neither the content of a paper nor its distribution interferes with school operations.

RECOGNIZING THE RESPONSIBILITIES OF THE STUDENT PRESS. A school paper must be sensitive to the feelings and educational standards of the community, whose taxpayers finance all school activities. It is expected to be in harmony with its district's policies as well as to reflect student interests. An effective school paper will improve relations between the school and community even as it provides a forum for students' views and ideas. To carry out its responsibilities, a paper may find it useful to have a set of permanent guidelines that define what it should be to its school and community, as well as a statement of immediate goals.

PUBLISHING A SCHOOL NEWSPAPER. An interesting school newspaper contains different kinds of materials, usually classifiable within five broad groups: basic news, feature stories, opinion articles, non-news items, and advertisements. The staff is often two-part, consisting of an editorial staff and a business staff. The chart on page 81 shows the organizational structure of a typical school newspaper. Most of the remaining chapters of this book are concerned with the writing and production of a school newspaper.

Vocabulary

alternative newspaper	distribution	typesetting
editing	editorial policy	

Review Questions

1. What are the basic limits and restrictions on freedom of expression in public schools?

2. How do public and private schools differ from each other in regard to the authority that administrators may exercise over publications?

3. Why should school newspaper staffs recognize a responsibility to their communities?

4. Why is it useful for a school paper to establish both broad guidelines and immediate goals?

5. What are the basic content groups found in typical school newspapers?

Discussion Questions

1. If the newspaper staff in your school were free of any authority or control exercised by an adviser or administrator, how would the paper put out compare with the paper currently published? Would it be better or worse according to the usual standards of journalism?

2. To what extent is your school paper a valuable educational tool? To what extent does it provide administrators with insights into student thinking and problems?

3. Does your school paper improve, worsen, or have no effect on relations between the school system and the community?

4. Does your school paper express primarily the thinking and interests of its staff, or does it also express the thinking and interests of the general student population?

5. Evaluate the organization of your paper's staff. Is there a person in a position of responsibility for every important function? Is the structure of authority adequate?

Chapter Project

Focusing on the Purpose of a School Newspaper

Examine the last two issues of your school newspaper. From these issues alone, make a list of what you as a reader would understand the paper's broad guidelines and immediate goals to be. Compare your findings with any broad guidelines and immediate goals already in effect in your school. If your school does not yet have such guidelines, compare your findings with the guidelines and goals you suggested in Activity 3. Summarize your findings in a brief report and add any suggestions you might have for future issues.

UNIT TWO

Reporting the News

5

GATHERING THE NEWS

When you have completed this chapter you should be able to

Recognize eight elements that make an event newsworthy.

Describe the qualities necessary for a person to be a good reporter.

Identify the four main techniques for locating news.

Describe the four steps involved in interviewing a news source.

Determine what reference materials a reporter might use to do research for a newspaper article.

It is 8:15 Monday morning. John Perry slams his front door and runs down the steps three at a time to meet his friend Fred Jones on the sidewalk.

A reporter for the Central High School *News,* John keeps his eyes and ears open for news while he and Fred walk to school. On the way, they discuss the Walk for Peace scheduled for Saturday. As they reach the school grounds, they whistle softly at the sight of Pete Terman riding his noisy motorbike into the parking lot. John knows that Pete has been working for two months rebuilding and repainting the bike.

John makes two entries in a small notebook:

Walk for Peace

Pete Terman's rebuilt bike

He walks through the *News* staff room and notices on the bulletin board that he has an assignment to cover the student council meeting Tuesday. He writes the time and place in his notebook and goes to class.

Carol Morton is called out of John's history class to see the principal, and when she returns she seems excited. Carol is an outstanding violinist in the school orchestra, and John wonders whether this has something to do with her excitement. Carol leaves so quickly at the end of the period that he has no chance to ask.

Near his locker, John meets Fred escorting a stranger. Fred introduces Werner Frisch, whose family has just come from Europe. Werner speaks little English but seems happy to be attending an American school.

In his French class, John takes a hard test and hopes he has passed it.

Passing Room 210, John notices an unfamiliar teacher standing by the desk. From a friend he learns that Miss Porter, who has taught math at Central High for 25 years, has suddenly retired because of ill health.

He meets Eloise Williams in the hall and chats with her about the school dance next Friday evening.

John completes a routine experiment in chemistry class. William Smith causes some excitement by burning his fingers in a near-explosion.

At lunch time, John finally sees Carol Morton and learns that she is to play as a soloist with the city symphony orchestra. He congratulates Carol on the honor.

John eats lunch with Donna Bennett, student council vice-president. Donna tells him that at its Tuesday meeting the student council will plan a fund-raising activity to help flood victims.

In the hall, one of his friends hands him a copy of *Between the Lines,* an off-campus newspaper, and points out an article accusing the *News* of failing to report on a student cafeteria boycott. He writes in his notebook, "Follow-up on *Between the Lines* story."

As John changes his clothes for physical education, the locker room buzzes with the rumor that Steve Henderson, Central High's star running back, won't play for a month because of a knee injury. John takes part in a quick game of basketball with his gym class. In the showers, he hears members of the school swim team boast that they now have the fastest relay group in the league.

After school, John studies in the school library. While there, he admires a clever display calling attention to science fiction books. Later, he walks slowly home, stopping to buy an afternoon newspaper. He notices a headline: "School Board Calls Bond Election to Replace High School Gym."

At dinner, John's father says, "I met Gus Cranston today. Twenty years ago he was all-state quarterback for Central High. Now he's back in town. He tells me he's going to coach one of the Recreation League Football teams at Cole Playground."

John finishes his homework, watches a television program, and looks at his news notebook before he goes to bed. He has jotted down notes on 15 different items for this week's *News*. John knows he will not write about all of these events himself. In fact, some may not develop into articles worth printing. Tomorrow morning, John will submit his list to the editor, who will decide which items merit coverage and which reporter will investigate each one.

John is sure of one fact. It is only because he and other reporters are alert to every news possibility that the *News* can advertise, "All the Central High News—About All the Central High Students."

In reviewing the possible news items John Perry discovered during his day at school, do you feel that there are more ideas, or fewer, than the 15 John counted? Which of these items do you consider most newsworthy? Why do you think these items are worth considering as news, and why might newspaper readers be interested in them?

If John Perry were to write a news story based on each of these ideas, he would meet two difficulties. First, he would not have enough time. Second, he would find other reporters covering the same news. How do you think a newspaper can organize its handling of news to avoid these difficulties but at the same time be certain that all important news ideas are developed?

Deciding What's Newsworthy

Jenny Andrews passed an English test today.

Jenny Andrews won a debating contest today.

One of the above items is news for the school newspaper. The other is not. Why? Successful reporters develop a "nose for news." They learn what appeals to their readers. If these reporters were to analyze why some happenings are news while others are not, they would tell you, "People are news. These people must be doing something. What they are doing must interest the newspaper reader."

This gives the following formula:

PEOPLE + ACTION + READER INTEREST = NEWS

This formula points out the difference between the two examples at the beginning of this section. There is a person in each, and there is action in each. But the debating contest is more unusual than the English test and is, therefore, more likely to interest readers.

Reader interest is the result of certain specific **news elements**—nearness, timeliness, importance, names, drama or conflict, variety, human interest, and humor. The more news elements, the more reader appeal the story has. Front page articles contain many of them. A description and an example of each of these news elements follow.

Nearness

A loud explosion severely damaged a building next to the school yesterday afternoon.

A loud explosion damaged a building in Shanghai, China, yesterday.

Which is the more interesting to readers in your community?

An event that takes place nearby is usually of more interest than a similar event occurring far away. Daily newspapers tell of many happenings in their own areas that would not appeal to readers in another city. The reader of a school newspaper wants to know about events that are happening in the school or on the campus.

Nearness is present in most news stories. If it is lacking, as in the case of foreign news in the daily newspaper, other elements, such as importance or drama, must be present.

Timeliness

The football team won most of its games in October and November.

The football team won its first league championship last Saturday.

The football team plays Chester High next Saturday for the state championship.

Which two of these contain more reader interest than the remaining one? A timely event is one that has occurred or will occur close to the time of a newspaper's appearance. Most school newspapers, because of the delay between writing and publication, cannot report what has happened during the two to five days preceding publication. Their most timely stories, therefore, are about events that will take place in the near future.

Timeliness alone does not make news. For example, consider this statement: "There will be the usual weekly mathematics test on Wednesday." The statement describes an occurrence that is timely, but it lacks other news elements and is, therefore, not a real news story.

Importance

My neighbor bought an expensive car.

The President of the United States bought a specially constructed bullet-proof car.

A change in high school graduation requirements affecting one student was announced today.

A change in high school graduation requirements affecting nearly 200 seniors was announced today.

One sentence in each pair has considerable news value. The other does not. Why?

The news element importance might also be called prominence, size, or consequence. The "bigness" of anything is one of the main factors in attracting readers. A daily newspaper can develop more interest with a report about a $1,000,000 fire than with one about a $100 fire.

Major announcements from school administrators, assemblies, holidays, or changes in school schedules are examples of this news element. In daily newspapers, important government activities, damage affecting many people, or major construction projects are important news items.

Names

Three police officers were honored by the mayor in a ceremony at City Hall this morning.

Officer Ralph K. Kendall, Officer Marie Williams, and Officer Robert Lopez were honored by the mayor in a ceremony at City Hall this morning.

You may not know these people. A number of people do, however. People will read a news story with names in it because they are interested in hearing about famous people or in seeing the names of friends or relatives. They enjoy finding their own names in print, of course. Inclusion of names makes many reports of past events, which otherwise have lost their timeliness, worth printing in a newspaper.

Drama or Conflict

Patsy Fuller is the only candidate running for election to the office of student council president.

Patsy Fuller, John Turner, and Joanne Cleveland have filed as candidates for election as student council president.

The element of drama or conflict makes the second statement more interesting. Elections, contests, discussions, and arguments appeal to readers because of opposing forces in verbal or physical conflict. Mystery and suspense may be present as well. In most sports stories, there are the conflict and suspense inherent in any game. Court trials create drama because of the clash between conflicting forces.

Variety

A boiler room explosion today caused minor injuries to Mr. Jake Johnson, head custodian.

Disasters and other extraordinary events, such as the one shown here, often contain several of the news elements that capture reader interest. The more news elements present in a subject, the more interesting the story can be.

A boiler room explosion today blew Mr. Jake Johnson, head custodian, through the basement door and left him standing, almost unharmed, on the school lawn.

The second statement is more appealing because it describes an unusual outcome of an explosion. Any event that is strange, original, has never happened before, or is not likely to happen again creates reader interest.

Human Interest

Students in home economics classes have just completed a three-week unit in child care.

Little children attending high school? Students were amazed to see a group of 3-year-olds going into Room 119. They came from nursery school to help dramatize a child care unit in the home economics classes.

Certainly, the second example is written in a more appealing way, but it also contains a hard-to-define news element called **human interest.** Either sadness or happiness may characterize human interest. The activities of the very young, of animals, of ordinary people with uncommon occupations—in short, any unusual items that have to do with daily living—are likely to have an element of human interest.

—Photo from UPI

Humor and human interest are often combined. Among the most interesting news elements in a story about a winter snowstorm might be the various ways, often humorous, that people have found to cope with the results.

Humor

"Property and sales taxes are used in this state to support education," stated Ms. Diane Hall, student teacher.

When student teacher Ms. Diane Hall asked Fred Simpson what kind of tax is used to support education, Fred replied, "Thumb tacks!"

Humor has a strong appeal to newspaper readers. Descriptions of comical incidents are always welcome. However, coarse or hurtful material, even though it may be funny, will repel more readers than it will attract.

Activity 1:   Identifying News Elements in the School Newspaper

1. Study the articles on the news pages of a recent issue of your school newspaper.

   a. For each news story, list the news elements represented. Remember that each article will probably contain several of the eight elements.

   b. Add the total number of elements listed and divide by the number of stories. What is the average number of news elements per story?

2. Compare the major news stories in this issue. Do certain news elements seem to be typical of the major stories? If so, which ones?

3. Circle all student names in the news articles. Count the names. Is a reasonable cross section of your student body represented? Could more (or different) names have been included successfully? If so, how?

4. Compare the news reports in your school paper with those in an exchange newspaper that has received favorable ratings from a press association. What suggestions can you make for the improvement of news stories in your paper?

Activity 2:　Analyzing News Elements in the Daily Newspaper

1. Study the front page of a local daily newspaper.
   a. List the news elements represented in each news article.
   b. Add the total number of elements listed and divide by the number of stories. What is the average number of news elements per story?
   c. Is this number greater or smaller than the average you computed for the school newspaper? What do you think is the reason for the difference?

2. Find examples from daily newspaper articles that illustrate the *intensity* of news elements. For example, the element of importance would be more intense in a report about a flood that left thousands homeless than in a story about a flood that damaged a dozen buildings. The element of drama or conflict would be more intense in a story about a battle on a war front than in a report of a fight between two people on a picket line.

3. The news stories that occupy the most prominent positions on the daily newspaper's front page are, of course, the most newsworthy. Is this because of the number of news elements they contain or because of the intensity of these elements? Give reasons for your answer.

Developing the Qualities of a Good Reporter

"There is no bigger word in newspapering than REPORTER," says the managing editor of an important western newspaper.

All news, whether intended for newspaper, magazine, radio, or television, must be collected by someone. The person who does this job is the reporter. As long as there is a free press that is privileged to distribute information, reporters will be needed to gather the facts.

Who are the men and women who perform the endless task of collecting bits of news and fitting them together into interesting reports? Why have they chosen this kind of work? How did they prepare for the job? Many of them are college graduates; many have had experience in other fields of work. Some have been trained in schools of journalism. Some have been writers, teachers, or salespeople. Some started without formal training by working for a small newspaper and learning journalism "the hard way."

Although their backgrounds may be different, all successful reporters have certain qualities in common. Some you may already see in yourself. The others can be developed by a student willing to work and learn. With these traits and skills, your work as a school newspaper reporter will be satisfying and successful. Moreover, journalistic training, with its emphasis on these qualities, builds a strong foundation for almost any occupation. Your efforts to improve your communication skills will repay you, regardless of your ambitions for the future. A description of each of these qualities follows.

Enthusiasm

Good reporters are interested in the job. The challenge of putting together a good news story is exciting to them. They accept assignments willingly, carry them out well, and develop each one into a good story. They go beyond what is required of them. For example, imagine that two reporters, both of them off duty, happen to be nearby when a big fire roars through a downtown office building. One has the attitude "I'm not supposed to be working tonight." This reporter just watches the fire. The other works through the night, getting eyewitness accounts and putting together the facts of the story. It's not hard to decide which of the two is the true reporter.

Initiative

Good reporters don't have to be told what to do. They think of potential stories and suggest them to their editors. They find new ways to ap-

"I went to the Chem Lab, but there's no news there!"

—Irwin Caplan in *Student and Publisher*

proach routine news items. They keep looking for facts until they have found them. They have learned to judge what is newsworthy and what the readers of their particular paper want to know about.

Curiosity

Good reporters are always curious. In other words, they have a "nose for news." They want to know what people are doing and why. At the same time, they respect other people's right to privacy, unless by words or actions these people have become public figures whose activities may ethically be reported as news. To satisfy their tremendous desire for facts, they read widely about people and events and, as a result, have gained some knowledge of many different fields of interest.

Responsibility

Good reporters know that they have a responsibility to print the truth. They check their information carefully because it is their job to report facts accurately. They report quotations exactly. They check dates and spell names correctly. On controversial issues, they realize there are at least two sides, and they try to present all viewpoints.

Outgoing Personality

Good reporters enjoy meeting and talking to people. They are careful not to offend or antagonize their news sources, but they search and question until they have their story. They are the kind of individuals in whom others confide. In this way, they get many unsought stories.

Writing Ability

Good reporters have learned to communicate an idea in correct and effective English. They write simple, direct prose. At the same time, their writing is lively and interesting. They have learned how to put bits of news together into an informative, well-organized story.

Activity 3: Becoming a Good Reporter

1. Select one or more news articles from daily newspapers and mark specific paragraphs whose content suggests to you that the reporter possesses one or more of the qualities just described. For example, to show responsibility, you might choose one or more paragraphs that indicate the reporter obtained several different opinions about the news event. Explain why you have chosen each example.

2. Interview a reporter for a newspaper, radio station, or television channel. Try to find out which of the qualities described in this section are most helpful, in this person's opinion, in his or her work.

Finding All the News

How does a newspaper staff go about securing news? The following are four main steps in locating news. The methods listed are used not only by newspaper journalists but by all journalists intent on presenting full coverage of the world around them.

Cover News Beats

Many reporters for school newspapers, like those for city newspapers, have definite **beats,** or **runs.** These beats are people, offices, or groups to whom reporters go regularly in search of news. A beat may include, for example, the school principal, the Honor Society, or the science department. A reporter covers a beat as the first step in finding news stories and is expected to check out each **news source** at least once for every issue of the school newspaper. Regardless of how unimportant the available news may seem, the reporter is expected to write it up or report it to the editor who will decide how the information is to be handled.

Use Special Assignments

The editor or another staff member makes **assignments** to reporters for every important news event. An assignment usually includes a **catch line** (the working title for the article), the name of the person to see, the time when the story is due, the number of words to be written, and a general idea of what the story should contain.

An important source of assignment ideas is the newspaper's **Future Book.** This is a loose-leaf folder with a page for each issue of the paper. As soon as anything is known about an upcoming school activity, an entry is made in the Future Book for each issue in which a story about this event might appear.

Certain guidelines are followed when determining which newspaper issues might contain news reports about a single major event. In weekly papers, stories might appear in two issues before the event and in one issue after the event. In newspapers that appear only twice a month or even less often, one preview story and one follow-up story would usually be sufficient.

In the Future Book example shown at the top of page 97, a school dance has been entered on the pages representing the two issues preceding the date of the dance and on the page representing the issue following the dance. As plans and preparations for the dance go forward, a reasonable amount of information should be available for each of the **advance stories.** Then there will probably be enough additional facts for a single **follow-up story.** Other news events would, of course, be listed on the same pages.

October 23 Issue

Halloween Dance Fri Oct 31 —
  date, place, theme,
  sponsor, cost

October 30 Issue

Halloween Dance Fri Oct 31 —
  How many attending?
  Final plans
  Important story

November 6 Issue

Halloween Dance Fri Oct 31 —
  Follow-up story
  What happened?

Follow Tips

A reporter will often hear of newsworthy events that would not ordinarily reach the newspaper through beats or assignments. Information about something that has just happened or is about to happen is called a **tip.** Typically, such information is unlooked for and unexpected. An anonymous caller lets a reporter know of a demonstration that is about to take place. A government official tells a few journalists in advance about a high-level decision to be announced the following day. Using the tip as a starting point, the reporter tries to find more information.

A tip differs from information gotten through a beat in that it represents news that may not be related to any of the newspaper's regular areas of coverage. It differs from an assignment in that it leads to a news story previously unknown to the editorial staff.

Create News Stories

It is sometimes possible to "invent" a news story. Of course, you can't make up a news story about an event that didn't happen, much as you might wish to! But there are certain kinds of stories waiting for an imaginative reporter to think of them. Incidents from the history of your school might provide interesting news stories. You might look into the files of your school paper or talk with a teacher who has been associated with the school for many years. Another possibility might be an article on the food service in the school cafeteria and the problems faced by the cafeteria manager. Many such news stories are developed through interpretive, in-depth reporting (described in Chapter 10).

Activity 4: Developing New Sources

1. Make a list of at least 25 persons, organizations, or other news sources around your school from which news could be obtained regularly enough for them to be considered beats.

2. Prepare a Future Book for your school newspaper by following the three steps listed below.

   a. Develop a list of 10 to 15 events that will take place at your school during the next three months. The following are some of the possible sources of information:

      Districtwide school calendar
      Activity calendar for your school
      Daily bulletins or bulletin boards
      Recent issues of the school newspaper
      Files of last year's paper (for events occurring every year)
      Faculty sponsors or student leaders of clubs or organizations

   b. Enter the events in a Future Book, which you make by using one sheet of paper for each issue of your school newspaper to be published during the three-month period. Place the date of publication at the top of each sheet. Then, enter each event on the sheet for each issue that should include a story about the event. Follow the sample on page 97.

   c. In class, compare your lists and discuss your entries. Make a composite Future Book that could be used as the basis for assignments to reporters.

3. Make a list of at least five topics that could be developed into news stories for the next issue of your school paper. Get them from the Future Book (prepared in Item 2) or from personal observation. Be ready to discuss the topics in class and to decide which ones contain enough reader interest to be worth developing.

4. Examine the stories treating local or suburban news on the pages of a daily newspaper. (These stories, called local or city news, are ordinarily those prepared by a newspaper's own reporters as distinguished from those prepared by large news-gathering organizations.) Try to decide which of the four devices named in this section might have been used to obtain each story.

5. After discussion, a committee might be delegated to interview the city editor of a daily newspaper regarding their means of finding local news, the extent to which beats and assignments are used by the paper, and the procedures their reporters are expected to follow when they get tips for stories. The committee can then report its results back to the class.

Interviewing for a News Story

Newspaper reporters get most of their news not by waiting for it but by going out, meeting people, and asking questions. The process of **interviewing** is the heart of reporting—the most fascinating and interesting part of newspaper work. Reporters for school newspapers seek out and talk with people who are "in the know" about school events, community activities, or student projects. When they have completed an interview, reporters have the satisfaction of being on the "inside." They know what is going to happen, often before many of the people who are directly affected do.

Which of the three different reporters in the following interviews will be most likely to have a story accepted for publication? After deciding, make a generalization about the best way in which to conduct an interview.

REPORTER: Uh . . . you don't have any news this week, do you?
STUDENT OFFICER OR FACULTY ADVISER: Well . . . no, I can't think of any.
REPORTER: Oh, I see. Well, thank you.

REPORTER: Good morning. I would like to talk to you about the semi-annual vocational conference.
NEWS SOURCE: Fine. What would you like to know?
REPORTER: Well, what it's all about. Who goes, and how many, and where it is, and what happens, and when it will be, and, oh . . . everything about it.
NEWS SOURCE: I guess I could tell you all that, but it would take much more time than I can spare right now. Why don't you go back and read about it in the files of your newspaper? There's a conference like this every semester, you know, and your paper had several long articles about the last conference that would answer most of your questions. Then come back to me, and I'll tell you the names of this semester's speakers and the schedule they're going to follow.

REPORTER (on the telephone): Hello, Mr. Casey. I'm a reporter from the Central High *News*. I'd like to ask you some questions about the Class of 1960 reunion this weekend.
MR. CASEY: Fine. Go ahead.
REPORTER: According to an article in the daily newspaper last week, you're all going to watch the football game Saturday and then have a banquet at the Hotel Smith. Who will be your speaker?
MR. CASEY: Joe Thompson. He was coach of our football team that won the state championship in 1960.
REPORTER: I see. And how many people do you expect?
MR. CASEY: We have reservations from about 125 so far.
REPORTER: That's a good representation, isn't it? The school records show 243 graduates in your class.
MR. CASEY: That's right. Say, you seem to be pretty well informed. Let's see what else I can tell you. . . .

When reporters are present at the events they are covering—a rally or a student council meeting, for example—they can write their stories from firsthand knowledge. But most reporting, and this includes reporting of future events, is done by getting the facts from one or more people who know them. This basic and essential process of interviewing news sources for information involves four steps: planning and preparing for the interview, setting up the interview, conducting the interview, and developing the information into a news story.

Prepare for the Interview

Most people are eager to tell a newspaper reporter about what they are doing. However, these people frequently need help in communicating what will be interesting to the reader. When interviewing to obtain information, you must plan ahead as carefully as possible. Only thorough preparation for an interview will result in a well-written, complete, and interesting story.

First of all, know whom you are to see. Then, think about possible topics to be covered in your interview. What will your readers want to learn? As the following chart shows, your approach and the kind of research you will do may vary depending on whether you are covering a beat or covering an assignment.

COVERING A BEAT	COVERING AN ASSIGNMENT
1. Check previous issues of your paper to see what type of story usually originates from this beat. 2. Check to see if previous stories give any hint of events that may have taken place since then or that may be coming up. 3. Get any additional information you can from the school bulletin or from conversations with teachers or students.	1. Make sure you know exactly what the editor has in mind. 2. If this event takes place on a regular basis, explore what happened last time. Familiarize yourself with the way it has been handled in your newspaper. 3. Remember that changes, which have the most news value, have more interest when they are compared with what happened previously. 4. If the subject is unfamiliar to you, read up on it in your library, using books, magazines, encyclopedias, dictionaries, or other sources of information.

After you have done your research, ask yourself, What will my readers want to learn? Then write out questions you will use as a guide to seeking information. Be prepared to ask further questions as the interview progresses. And remember: Good questions are the key to a good interview.

Activity 5:   Preparing for the Interview

1. Suppose you are assigned to see the drama teacher about a play that is to be presented in an assembly two weeks from today. The editor says, "This will be our main story in next week's paper. We must have all the facts." Your first step, of course, is to get as much information as you can. You uncover the following facts in the school newspaper office:

   The drama teacher is Ms. Marie Warkoff.
   The assembly will be first period, two weeks from today.
   The title of the play is "Geronimo in Gym."

   Write out the questions you plan to ask when you interview the drama teacher to get the rest of the information for your story.

2. Compare your questions with those prepared by other class members. Which of the questions do you think will get the best results?

Set Up the Interview

Once you have determined what it is your readers want to know, obtained as much information as possible about your topic, and written out a set of questions, you are ready to reach your news source, to ask your questions, and to collect notes from which you will write your story.

Contact the person you are planning to interview. If that person is a teacher, your school's master schedule will indicate whether you can do

Interviewing is the heart of reporting and often one of the most satisfying of a reporter's activities.

—Photo by Bob Daemmrich from Michael Sullivan

this best before or after school, during a lunch period, between classes, or at some other time. Let the person know that you are a reporter for your school newspaper, and make it clear what subject you are interested in. Ask when an interview would be convenient. Perhaps it will be at once. If so, go ahead. If not, make a definite appointment. Then be sure you keep the appointment!

Carry with you a pad of paper and several sharpened pencils so that you can take notes about facts, dates, and names of persons or places.

Will a tape recorder help? Some professional reporters think so. Others do not. Those who use tape recorders also take notes on major points and then turn to the tape for exact quotations, fact checking, and additional details. Your news source must agree to having the interview taped or else you should not use a recorder. And the recorder must work! Check the condition of the battery, and be sure the controls are set to "RECORD" and the volume is high enough.

The following checklist should help you conduct an informative, efficient interview.

✓ Checklist for Preparing and Setting Up an Interview

☐ 1. Do I have a clear idea of the purpose of the interview?

☐ 2. Have I consulted back issues of the newspaper or reference materials for information about the topic of the interview?

☐ 3. Have I written out good questions?

☐ 4. Am I familiar enough with the topic to be able to ask questions other than those I have prepared?

☐ 5. Have I scheduled my interview at the convenience of the person to be interviewed?

☐ 6. Have I prepared several sharpened pencils and a pad of paper to take with me?

☐ 7. If a tape recorder is to be used, do I have one that works?

Conduct the Interview

While interviewing your news source, be pleasant and courteous. Keep in mind that while the person may be busy with other matters, he or she is interested in accurate and complete coverage of this news event. During the course of the interview, you may have to deviate from your prepared questions. Do not hesitate to ask additional questions to be sure you fully understand the meaning of each statement and to draw your source out on points you consider important. Be sure to check the spelling of all names. Copy exactly any direct quotations that you think you will use. If you confine yourself to writing down important facts in abbreviated form, your news source will not mind waiting while you do it. The news source is personally interested in having these facts correct.

At the conclusion of the interview, go over whatever needs clarifying and read back any direct quotations you have copied. Then express your thanks. Politeness is good public relations for your newspaper and yourself.

Activity 6: Analyzing Interviewing Techniques

1. Observe two members of your class as they dramatize a scene in which a reporter interviews a news source. The news source may use information from an actual news story that the reporter has not read or may make up a set of facts. The reporter should have any information about the story that would ordinarily be available in the school newspaper office and should be prepared with a set of questions.

2. Write an evaluation of the work of the reporter in this interview. Include answers to these questions:

   a. How satisfactory was the reporter's approach to the news source?

   b. How well-prepared was the reporter?

   c. How many questions did the reporter ask?

   d. What other questions should have been asked?

   e. How did the reporter make sure of the facts?

Activity 7: Taking Notes During an Interview

1. To practice note taking, jot down the newsworthy facts that emerge from the following dialogue. Under the conditions of an actual interview, you would have little time to write, so use as few words as possible. Abbreviate wherever possible. Be sure to write down names, dates, and enough other facts so that you can reconstruct the story from your notes.

   REPORTER: Good morning, Miss Stevens. I'm a reporter for the *News,* and I'd like to get some information about the winners of the poster contest. Do you have time to talk to me now?

   MISS STEVENS: Yes, this will be fine. Won't you sit down?

   REPORTER: Thank you. I'm not sure I understand just what this contest was all about. Could you tell me something about it?

   MISS STEVENS: Well, the Chamber of Commerce wanted some posters to advertise our city's fiftieth anniversary celebration, so they set up a contest and offered prizes for the best posters.

   REPORTER: Was the contest just for students?

   MISS STEVENS: No, anyone could enter, but there were three categories—one for adults, one for high school students, and one for junior high students. We talked this over in our art classes, and many of our students decided to enter the contest.

   REPORTER: Did all the schools enter?

   MISS STEVENS: It was up to the teachers and their students. I think there were some posters entered from every school.

   REPORTER: How many entries were there from our school?

   MISS STEVENS: About 40. A few students entered more than one poster.

   REPORTER: And some of our students won prizes?

   MISS STEVENS: Yes, we did very well. John Friedman won first prize in the high school division.

   REPORTER: Let me get that down. JOHN . . . F-R-E-E-D-M-A-N—is that the correct spelling?

   MISS STEVENS: No. F-R-I-E-D-M-A-N.

   REPORTER: Thanks. What was John's prize?

MISS STEVENS: He won a $25 prize and a certificate. They were pre-
sented to him last Friday at the Chamber of Commerce luncheon.

REPORTER: Did we have any other prizewinners?

MISS STEVENS: Charlene Towner was in third place, and Kenny Hoffman got honorable mention.

REPORTER: C-H-A-R-L-E-N-E . . . how do you spell the last name?

MISS STEVENS: T-O-W-N-E-R. The other one is Kenny Hoffman—H-O-
F-F-M-A-N. Did you get those?

REPORTER: Yes, thank you. Charlene won third place, and Kenny an
honorable mention.

MISS STEVENS: That's right.

REPORTER: Were these posters used or displayed somewhere?

MISS STEVENS: They were all displayed at the art center last week. A
few of the best were printed and distributed all over the city.
John's was one of these. I saw copies yesterday in several different store windows in the downtown area.

REPORTER: Is there anything else I should know about the contest?

MISS STEVENS: I believe that's everything.

REPORTER: Thank you very much, Miss Stevens.

2. Evaluate your work on Item 1.

   a. Discuss with other members of your class the major facts needed to
   write the story properly. (One fact, for example, is "John Friedman
   first in H.S. division.")

   b. Go over your notes and compare them with the facts selected as
   most important by the class. Have you stated the facts briefly and
   clearly? How adequate are your notes for the purpose of writing this
   news story? Rate your work as excellent, good, fair, or poor.

3. Dramatize another interview between a reporter and a news source, similar to the one described in Activity 6. During the interview, take notes as
   though you were the reporter. Compare notes in class and rate your
   note taking as in Item 2.

Develop the Information into a Story

Write your news story immediately, while the interview is still fresh
in your mind and while your scribbled notes mean something to you. In
case a question of fact arises, get in touch with your news source and secure
additional information. Don't make a habit of this, however. Getting the
facts straight during, not after, the interview is good journalistic procedure.

After finishing a story, you might also take a moment to review your
questions. Which ones were most useful? Which were not? What changes
would be useful next time you conduct an interview?

Activity 8: Examining a Story Based on an Interview

The story at the top of page 105 was obviously based on an interview. Read
the story and then answer the questions that follow it.

Johnson to voice student opinion

Todd Johnson, senior, was recently elected student representative to the board of education.

"My goal is to earn the respect of the board so that the students' opinion is respected," said Todd.

Todd was chosen out of seven finalists to take a position with the board of trustees at district meetings.

As student representative, his main function will be to express the views of the 12,000 students in the district at board meetings.

"I'm really looking forward to an opportunity to work with the board," Todd stated.

Before being chosen as a finalist, he was required to write a 250-word essay and attend a 10-minute interview.

The final vote was taken by the ASB officers from all district schools. Todd was elected, with senior Laura Sue Cohen of Fremont High School coming in second.

—*The Epitaph*, Homestead High School, Cupertino, California

---

1. What questions do you think the interviewer asked?
2. Are there any further questions you would have asked?
3. What research do you think was done by the interviewer?
4. What further research would you have done?

Using the Newspaper Library to Find Information

When preparing to interview a news source and again while writing a news story, a reporter frequently needs information from previous newspaper reports or from other sources.

Major newspapers often maintain extensive libraries for the use of their reporters. The newspaper library is generally called the **morgue,** since one of its common uses is to supply information for **obituaries**—notices of deaths, which often include biographical accounts of the deceased. The librarian keeps files on prominent people, including clippings, photographs, family information, and business or professional data. As a result, a newspaper printed only a few hours after the death of a famous person may contain whole pages about this individual's life.

Large newspaper morgues also have **clipping files** on topics of current interest. Encyclopedias and other reference books are available, as well as news magazines and other newspapers.

There is, of course, a complete file of back issues of that particular newspaper. More and more libraries are using **microfilm** to store the contents of old newspapers. A reduced-size picture of a page is made and stored on film. Reporters may rapidly locate a particular page, use a special viewer to read it, and if necessary obtain a photocopy as well.

Small newspapers can rarely afford an extensive morgue. They are likely to have only a file of the paper's back issues. For other facts, they may rely on the public library or on the storehouse of information in the editor's mind.

In the staff room of your school newspaper, you should, ideally, find most of the aids listed in the following chart.

STAFF ROOM REFERENCE MATERIALS
Complete files of your newspaper for past years
Clipping files on selected important topics
Scrapbook of news about your school from city newspapers
Directory of teachers in your school or school district
Master schedule showing classes and free periods of each teacher
School activity calendar
Student directory or card file of pertinent information about students
Books on journalism, advertising, photography, printing
Dictionary—a standard, recent edition
Dictionary of synonyms (thesaurus)

Even though your school newspaper may not maintain its own complete library or morgue, you can find elsewhere a variety of additional aids to reporting and editing. Your school library will have such reference books as encyclopedias, almanacs, biographical dictionaries, and indexes to current magazines. These reference materials are also available in your public library.

There is one important thing to remember about the morgue and other sources of information: They are worthless to you unless you use them often!

Activity 9: Examining Your Newspaper Morgue

1. Make a chart showing the reference materials available for your use in connection with your work on your school newspaper. In the first column, copy the list of staff room reference materials from the preceding chart. In the second column, list the materials actually available to you.

2. List items that are lacking in your morgue. Describe in a few paragraphs a workable plan for improving the morgue of your newspaper, keeping in mind that a school newspaper morgue cannot be as extensive as that of a major newspaper.

Activity 10: Using the Morgue

1. Indicate which of the reference materials in your morgue you might consult and what information you might secure from each source if you were asked to write stories on the following:

   a. The construction of your school building

   b. The percentage of high school graduates in the United States who go on to college compared with the percentage in your school

   c. A highly regarded science teacher's announcement that he will be abandoning his teaching career for a job with a major chemical company

2. List sources in your school library or public library that could be used to supplement the information you would be able to find on each of the above subjects.

Summary

This chapter describes the elements that make a particular event newsworthy and lists the special qualities and skills characteristic of a good reporter. It discusses the techniques of finding news as well as the very important process of interviewing. Finally, the chapter details the sources of information available to the reporter.

DECIDING WHAT'S NEWSWORTHY. Editors and reporters must decide which news events will appeal to their readers. They are guided in these decisions by the formula

PEOPLE + ACTION + READER INTEREST = NEWS

Reader interest is the result of certain specific news elements. These include nearness, timeliness, importance, names, drama or conflict, variety, human interest, and humor.

DEVELOPING THE QUALITIES OF A GOOD REPORTER. Successful reporters develop a "nose for news." Although their training and experience may be quite different, all successful reporters have certain skills in dealing with people and in writing about news events. Special qualities possessed by reporters include enthusiasm, initiative, curiosity, responsibility, an outgoing personality, and writing ability.

FINDING ALL THE NEWS. Reporters and editors use four main techniques for locating news items—covering news beats, using special assignments, following tips, and creating news stories. The main source of ideas for assignments is the newspaper's Future Book, which contains entries for coming events.

INTERVIEWING FOR A NEWS STORY.   Newspaper reporters get most of their news by going out, meeting news sources, and asking questions. This process is called interviewing. An interview involves four steps. In carrying out the first step, a reporter prepares for the interview by collecting background information and formulating questions. In carrying out the second step, the reporter sets up the interview by making an appointment with the news source. In carrying out the third step, the reporter conducts the interview by asking questions and taking notes. In carrying out the fourth step, the reporter develops the information into a story by turning the notes into a readable, orderly piece of writing.

USING THE NEWSPAPER LIBRARY TO FIND INFORMATION.   Research is an important part of newspaper work. To provide information for their reporters, large newspapers maintain libraries that contain clipping files about people and various topics of interest, back issues of newspapers and news magazines, and other reference materials. School newspaper offices, however, vary in the amount and quality of their reference materials. Although a school newspaper library should be as complete as possible for the convenience of the students working on the paper, the school library and the public library can often provide many of the additional reference materials needed.

Vocabulary

news element	advance story
human interest	follow-up story
beat	tip
run	interviewing
news source	morgue
assignment	obituary
catch line	clipping file
Future Book	microfilm

Review Questions

1. List and define eight news elements that promote reader interest.

2. Describe the personal qualities and the skills that are needed in order to be a successful reporter.

3. Explain the four principal techniques for collecting news.

4. What are the four steps involved in interviewing?

5. How does the newspaper morgue assist a reporter?

Discussion Questions

1. Compare the news elements in the major stories on the front pages of several daily newspapers. Do certain news elements appear more regularly in some newspapers than in others? If so, which ones? Might a difference indicate that each newspaper tries to appeal to a different kind of reader? If so, what can you tell about the personality of the typical reader of each newspaper?

2. To what extent, in your opinion, is the reputation of a newspaper affected by the attitudes of its reporters when they interview news sources? How significantly might this apply to your school newspaper?

3. Which is more truly news: a "created" news story (see page 97) or what is called a "media event" a publicity happening staged for the purpose of attracting reporters and getting newspaper or television coverage? Give reasons for your opinion.

4. What problems are caused by the need to take notes at an interview? What problems can arise from the use of a tape recorder? What solutions can you propose to whatever problems might arise from note taking and tape recording?

5. Discuss ways of dealing with a situation in which a news source is reluctant to give information to a reporter.

Chapter Project

Carrying Out an Interview

After consulting with your journalism teacher or the faculty adviser of the school paper on a subject for a story and a person to interview, conduct an interview that can be the basis of a publishable story. Then, hand in the results of the interview (your notes), along with your questions, a list of sources you used to prepare for the interview, and a general evaluation both of the questions you used and the results you obtained.

6

WRITING THE NEWS LEAD

When you have completed this chapter you should be able to

Recognize why news stories are arranged in a special way.

Apply seven specific steps to the process of writing the lead paragraph for a news story.

Write several other special kinds of leads.

Four young people stood in the observation window of the airport waiting room. Outside, rain poured down in torrents.

"Dad's plane is due in 10 minutes," said Carolyn.

"Look!" exclaimed Harry. "The plane for New York is taking off."

Carolyn, Harry, and Ted were seniors at Central High School. Linda, who had been editor of the Central High *News* the year before, had gone to work after graduation. She was employed by the Midland *Times* as a cub reporter. Her work day of assembling obituary notices, writing club meeting reports, and running errands for staff members was over, and she had joined her friends at the airport to meet Carolyn's father when he arrived.

Outside in the driving rain, the plane bound for New York began to move down the runway, at first slowly, then more rapidly.

"It's off the ground," said Ted.

The plane began to ascend.

"Oh, no!" gasped Carolyn. "I think it's going to crash!"

Their faces pressed to the glass, the four watched as the plane veered downward, bounced crazily, and overturned at the far end of the runway.

Before the evening was over, all four of them had occasion to write about the accident. Both Ted and Harry used it as a topic for English compositions. Ted, planning to be an aeronautical engineer, wrote his composition with scientific exactness and attention to detail.

> The airplane, a DC-10, was bound for New York with 83 passengers and a crew of seven. Weather conditions were poor: Precipitation was rather heavy, visibility was about one-half mile, and ceiling was about 500 feet. The plane taxied to the runway and began its takeoff at exactly 4:47 p.m. When the plane was approximately 50 feet in the air . . .

Harry's composition was meant to be very elegant, with complicated sentences and poetic language. He wrote:

> The downpour was tempestuous. Out upon the rain-sodden field the shining silver airplane, resembling a grounded bird waiting for an opportunity to take flight through the upper-air currents toward the metropolis of New York, began to move slowly and ponderously along the runway. We watched as it gained speed, and then, not like a mechanical marvel with a heart of electronic and hydraulic gadgets, but like a great eagle with wings outstretched, it leaped forward into the damp air . . .

Carolyn wrote a letter to her sister, away at college:

> While we were waiting for Dad's plane to come in, an awful thing happened. We actually saw an airplane crash! It was terrible! The plane was taking off for New York when it lost altitude, crashed, and overturned at the end of the runway. We tried to go outside, but the guards wouldn't let us, so all we could do was watch the fire trucks and ambulances race out to the plane. We heard that 20 people were killed . . .

Linda was the first of the four to write about the crash. Almost immediately, she realized she had a job to do and began collecting facts for

The same event can be the subject of strikingly different stories. A newspaper reporter's account of any news event, however, will always focus on what makes the event newsworthy.

her newspaper. By the time another reporter arrived, Linda had a fairly complete story, which appeared in the late evening edition. Linda telephoned her story to the person at the Midland *Times* office whose job it was to rewrite phoned-in stories. She began this way:

> Twenty persons were killed and more than 60 were injured when a plane bound for New York crashed this afternoon at Midland City Airport. The plane had just left the ground in a heavy rainstorm when it was seen to lose altitude, bounce crazily, and overturn at the end of the runway . . .

Each of the four told essentially the same story, yet each report is different. Whenever you write, you write for a specific purpose. Ted's and Harry's compositions, although prepared from different viewpoints, both told about happenings in the order that they took place. To accomplish this, they included many details before describing the crash. Carolyn's informal letter, written much as she might have described the event to her father when he arrived, came closer to the way that news is reported. She first announced what took place and then filled in the details.

The special goal of Linda's news report was to answer instantly the question What happened? If you had seen the accident and were describing it to a friend, you would not have started out, "The rain was coming down hard," or "We were at the airport," or "The plane looked like a great silver bird." You would have begun with what was really important: "I saw an airplane crash!"

This is the way a **news story** begins. Its first paragraph tells *what* happened, *who* did it, *when* and *where*, and perhaps *why* or *how*. When the reader has finished the first paragraph, all essential facts should have emerged. The remainder of the story explains these facts, gives details, and adds less important information. There is no conclusion or moral at the end of a news story. Nor do news articles have surprise endings. If a story contains something unusual or surprising, it's right there in the first paragraph.

Summarizing a News Event

The first paragraph of a news story is called the **lead** (pronounced "leed"). Condensing the main facts or ideas about an entire news event into just a few lines of type is not easy. Learning to write good leads is one of the most important skills you will learn in your journalism studies.

In the following article from a high school newspaper, notice how the first paragraph, the lead, summarizes the important facts. Notice also the length of paragraphs in a news story. One or two sentences to a paragraph represent typical newswriting style.

School board considers curriculum changes

LEAD {

Almost 60 curriculum changes for the next school year have been proposed to the school board.

A special meeting of the board was held Monday night to discuss the curriculum proposals, which will affect physical education classes, art classes, and industrial arts classes, among others.

Changes were made to update the classes and their course descriptions and titles, according to Dr. Robert Brooks, principal. He said that changes were also made to accommodate students by putting emphasis on the areas where students were enrolling.

One of the proposed curriculum changes suggested that physical education classes be graded, and that the classes have two nine-week sessions instead of the three six-week sessions being used presently. This would cut down on paperwork for the department office and would fit in with the rest of the school's schedules.

—*Spotlight*, Valley High School, West Des Moines, Iowa

In a typical newspaper article, each news event is presented three times—in the **headline,** in the lead, and in the **body** of the story. Why does it make sense for a newspaper writer to summarize a news event in the lead?

First of all, the headline and lead answer at once the major questions a reader might have. When you think of news, you want to know immediately: What happened? Who did it? When and where? Why or how? You don't want to work through paragraph after paragraph to find the answers. A news story, putting important facts first, answers the questions in the order in which you would ask them.

The headline and lead also help you decide which stories to read. Most newspapers are put together on the assumption that few people will want to read everything. Therefore, the headline and the lead should enable readers to see at a glance whether a particular story will be of interest to them.

Another advantage of presenting a summary in the lead is the help it gives a busy reader. The individual who has only a few minutes for reading but wants to know what is going on in the world can get an overview of the day's news by reading only headlines and lead paragraphs.

This newswriting pattern is also helpful for the reporter. Writing a summary first and then detailing facts in the order of their importance is the natural way of thinking about a news event. It is easier for a reporter to write this way.

Finally, this arrangement meets the **cutoff test.** In the busy, rushed routine of the newspaper office, copyreaders or editors do not have time to rewrite a story if it is too long or if space is needed for another story or an advertisement. They simply cross out the last few paragraphs, which should contain the least important facts. A properly structured newspaper article can be cut at the end of any paragraph, and it will still tell essentially what happened.

Activity 1:   Analyzing the Way News Is Presented

1. From copies of your school newspaper, papers from other schools, or daily newspapers, select five leads, each of which summarizes the most important facts of its story. (Do not consider articles with fewer than four or five paragraphs.) Clip the complete stories, identify the leads, and be prepared to tell which key questions each lead answers.

2. Find six news articles of at least six paragraphs each. Three of them should be from school newspapers, and three of them should be from daily papers. Clip and mount the complete stories.

   a. Apply the cutoff test to each news story in this way: Read the entire article carefully to grasp its main idea and essential facts. Then, cover the last paragraph with a sheet of paper and see whether the main idea has been distorted or any of the essential facts have been hidden. Repeat this, moving your paper up one paragraph at a time. If you can cover all paragraphs except the lead without distorting the main idea or hiding any essential facts, the story passes the cutoff test with flying colors. If you cannot, mark the point where the article first fails to pass the test.

   b. Compare the school papers and the daily papers in the light of the cutoff test. Is there any difference between the results you got with the daily newspaper articles you selected and the results you got from the school newspaper articles? If so, what is the difference, and how do you account for it?

Building the Lead

The lead paragraph is the heart of the news story. A lively, well-constructed lead will attract readers to your story. A dull, uninformative one will not. Building a lead that appeals to readers and that summarizes the story in just a few lines of type takes practice. To do it right, follow the seven steps in this section.

Find the Five W's and One H

The first step in building a good lead is to answer the six one-word questions—known as the **five *W*'s and one *H***—in the following chart. These answers will serve as the foundation for your lead, although you might later decide not to emphasize every one of these facts.

THE FIVE *W*'S AND ONE *H*	
WHAT?	What happened? What is going to happen?
WHO?	Who did it? Who is involved in the event?
WHEN?	When did, or will, the event take place?
WHERE?	Where did, or will, the event take place?
WHY?	Why did, or will, the event take place? What is the reason behind it?
HOW?	How did, or will, the event take place? What is the method involved?

When you, as a reporter, interview a news source, you take notes that should include all the facts about an event. From these notes you must develop your lead. If you can answer the five *W*'s and one *H*, you will have the material for a satisfactory lead. If you cannot find answers to all six of these questions in your notes, it is likely that your interview was incomplete.

Check your notes carefully. Decide which major facts answer each question. Then, you may want to list the five *W* and one *H* questions down the left-hand side of a piece of paper and write the answers opposite each.

Next, look over your list, starting with WHAT? If you have more than one answer to WHAT? decide which answer is important for the heart of the story and which answers are of less importance. Cross out the less important details, leaving a single fact to answer the WHAT? question.

Then look at the answers to the remaining five questions, drawing a line through material not directly related to the statement that answers the WHAT? question. Probably you will now have only one answer to each question. In some cases, however, there may be more than one answer to the WHY? or HOW? question.

Activity 2: Identifying the Five *W*'s and One *H* in News Stories

Decide which words or groups of words in the following leads answer each of the six questions for leads. The example below shows how to write your answers. For each of the leads, you should be able to find answers to all six questions.

EXAMPLE: The new locker and shower rooms now being built on West Field will be ready for use in December, eliminating the present overcrowding, Principal Phyllis Marshall announced yesterday.

WHAT?	New locker and shower rooms will be ready for use
WHO?	Mrs. Marshall
WHEN?	In December
WHERE?	West Field
WHY?	To eliminate present overcrowding
HOW?	Being built now

1. To raise money for the new auditorium sound system, the drama class will present "Major Barbara," a comedy, Friday, October 15. Mr. Louis Kay, dramatics instructor, will direct this year's production in the Little Theater.

2. Pat Thomas and Paul Orlino were named last week to take leading parts in the school play, "The Bad Seed." Ms. Jane Hall, drama director, made the selections after a week of tryouts in the Little Theater.

3. A student's-eye view of school will be given parents of high school students November 12 at a Back-to-School Night sponsored by the PTA as part of National Education Week.

4. Taking part in the traditional initiation, 10 students will become members of Quill and Scroll November 26 in the high school cafeteria. They were chosen for outstanding work on the school newspaper.

5. "Being president of the State Student Council was the greatest experience I've ever had," stated Richard Wolfe, Central High's delegate to the Student Council Conference at State University October 15 and 16. Richard was elected president at the first conference session after a short but successful campaign.

Activity 3: Revising News Leads to Answer the Five *W*'s and One *H*

Each of the leads on page 117 answers only some of the five *W* and one *H* questions. For each lead, list the six questions in a column. Then (a) answer the questions for which the lead provides information; (b) circle the questions that cannot be answered from the information in the lead; and (c) answer the circled questions by making up information of the kind that would have been included if the question had been answered.

EXAMPLE: In honor of five retiring teachers, band and choir members will present the spring concert tomorrow. A musical number will be dedicated to each retiree.

    WHAT?   Spring concert
    WHO?   Band and choir members
    WHEN?   Tomorrow
    (WHERE?)   In the auditorium
    WHY?   To honor five retiring teachers
    HOW?   By dedicating numbers to them

1. The first meeting of the PTA will be Wednesday, October 6, at 7:30 p.m.
2. Intramural football teams will be organized in a few weeks.
3. Vocal tryouts for the state music contest were held yesterday afternoon and evening.
4. Fire damaged the vocational auto shop.
5. "Middle East in Crisis" will be the topic at the next World Affairs Club meeting.

Decide Which Facts Go into the Lead

As you worked with Activities 2 and 3, you may have realized that not all six questions need to be answered in every lead. Some of the answers are simply not essential to the story. Published leads rarely include the answers to all six questions. However, the only way to be sure that you are not overlooking an important fact is to search for the answers to all six questions. After you have discovered and listed all six, you can then take the second step in building a lead: Decide whether you should leave out some of these statements. If you take a short cut and use only those answers that you can find easily, you risk omitting material that is essential to a complete lead.

You will discover that you can safely omit some of the answers to these six questions from your lead *only* after you have found *all six* and considered the importance of each.

Certain of the answers to the five *W* and one *H* questions, though, are more likely than others to be essential to your story. The following are some points to consider as you write your lead.

WHAT?   You do not have a news story unless something has happened or is expected to take place. The answer to WHAT? will always be present.

WHO?   The name of a person who has done something noteworthy is essential. On the other hand, your WHO? may be the faculty sponsor or student chairperson. These names may not be important enough to be in the lead. They should be used later in your story. If you have many important names, you may wish to say in your lead "Eight students won . . ." and put the actual names in the second paragraph.

WHEN? The time or date is needed for events that occur at a specific time, whether past or future. It is unnecessary in stories about general announcements or about plans that are under way. The answer to WHEN? is rarely important enough to belong at the beginning of your lead. Except in special cases, it should be in the middle or toward the end of the paragraph.

WHERE? The location of a news event is often understood to be at school and can, therefore, be omitted from the lead. Your reader doesn't care whether the Key Club met in Room 12 or Room 318. The answer to WHERE? can also be omitted from articles about past events unless the place is directly involved in the story. On the other hand, WHERE? is important in future events, such as concerts or meetings that your reader may wish to attend. If used, the answer to WHERE? generally belongs at the end of the lead.

WHY? AND HOW? You will need to consider each of these carefully, for neither, either, or both may be essential. A story with an important WHY? statement may not have an important HOW? and vice versa. In the lead "Semester registration reached a state of total confusion last Friday because of hundreds of computer rejects," the WHY? (because of computer rejects) is essential to understanding the lead, but the HOW? (the kinds of confusion that took place) can easily be left to a later paragraph.

A lead that focuses on a game-winning score might answer the questions WHAT?, WHO?, and WHEN?, but perhaps not WHERE?, WHY?, or HOW? Published leads seldom answer all six of the five W and one H questions.

—Photo from *Westside's Lance*, Westside High School, Omaha, Nebraska

The following lead does not answer WHY? or HOW?, but it is a good lead for its purpose. In what ways are the other five *W* and one *H* questions answered?

> Ten Webster students will be attending a national journalism and write-off competition during the weekend of April 15–17 in San Francisco.
>
> —*Webster Warrior*, Daniel Webster
> Middle School, Stockton,
> California

Activity 4:   Determining the Important Facts

Study these reporters' notes on newsworthy events. For each event, list the five *W* and one *H* answers, as in Activities 2 and 3. Then circle the facts that are important enough to be used in the lead.

1. Mary Wilson won Voice of Democracy speech contest this year
   Contestants gave speeches in assembly last Thurs.
   Contest sponsored by local Junior Chamber of Commerce
   Mary is a senior
   Developed her speech around pledge to flag
   Dan Irvine won 2nd place and Jennie Malone 3rd
   Mary will compete against winners from other schools next week for city championship and $50 prize

2. Rehearsals start this wk. for this year's all-class play
   Date of play postponed from Nov. until Feb. 2; scripts late in arriving
   Name of play—"Court of Common Clay"
   Ms. Gene Turner is dramatics instructor
   Chris Botts will be student director
   First meeting of cast after school Wed.

3. Mr. H. I. Jones has had 30 years experience in education
   Has taught general shop, math, and phys. ed.
   Holds M.A. degree in ed. from Columbia U.
   Member of Phi Beta Kappa, honorary scholastic fraternity
   Was principal of Johnson H.S. for ten yrs.
   Then became superintendent of schools in Middletown in 1975
   Just hired as new superintendent of our school system; will take over new duties next semester

Select the Key Thought and Put It First

You have made an excellent beginning toward building a good news lead when you have selected the answers to the five *W* and one *H* questions and have picked the really essential facts from among these answers. The third step in building your lead is to consider the items you have chosen in order to determine which one fact will stand out as most important to your readers. This fact is your **key thought,** and you will begin your lead with it.

Your lead is the showcase for your story, and you must begin it with the most attention-getting material you have. Because newspaper columns are narrow, the first line of a news story may contain only five or six words. To assure that a reader will see the key thought, you should make sure it appears in the first line.

Examine, for example, the opening phrases of two sets of news stories. Would you read the stories that follow these opening lines?

> On November 26, three large . . .
>
> There will be a banquet in the . . .
>
> Preparations are under way for . . .

Or the stories that follow these?

> Vandals destroyed hundreds of . . .
>
> TV star Tom Selleck will . . .
>
> Monkeys, leopards, tigers, and . . .

In the examples in the second group, the key thought is in the lead's opening words. The resulting lively leads will make readers eager to find out more about the stories.

The key thought may be the answer to any of the five *W* and one *H* questions. It is more likely to be a WHAT?, WHO?, WHY?, or HOW? element than an answer to the question WHEN? or WHERE? Only in stories of future events, and then only in special cases, could either of these last two become the key thought.

The following examples show how any one of the five *W* and one *H* elements, even WHEN? and WHERE? in special situations, may be used to begin your lead.

WHAT? Black History Week will be celebrated February 13-20 with movies, a speaker, and special exhibits.

WHO? Kim Iurato was chosen president of the student council in an election September 18.

WHY? To explain senior high programs, Central's counselors will visit the junior high school next Wednesday to speak to ninth graders in an afternoon assembly.

HOW? Through its Christmas Care dance, the service council earned more than $500, which was spent to send food and warm clothing to needy youngsters. The December 11 dance was attended by 350 students.

WHEN? Monday, March 6, is the date now set for the opening of the new high school building. Over the preceding weekend, furniture and equipment will be moved.

WHERE? Sea World will be the destination of Mr. James Alden's biology classes when they embark on an all-day study trip December 13.

Activity 5:   Selecting the Key Thought

Each of the leads below is faulty because the reporter failed to find the key thought. Although necessary information is included, the most important or interesting fact is not at the beginning. Select the word or words that should be placed first in each of these leads and write them on your paper.

1. The Midvale school board met last week. Among the topics discussed was an announcement that local businesses would cooperate with the high school guidance office on a part-time jobs program.

2. At a special meeting of student officers next Tuesday, the juvenile justice system will be explained by Captain John Meyer of the city police force.

3. The clothing classes presented their annual fashion show and tea after school March 26 in the homemaking room. Parents, friends, and faculty members were invited.

4. Mr. Norman Coleman, president of the PTA, extends a cordial invitation to all parents to attend the next meeting, Tuesday, October 27, at 7:30 p.m., in the library. Mrs. Tracy Baker, assistant superintendent of schools, will describe the new report cards.

5. Students from Central High, East High, and West High will gather at the civic center Saturday morning to participate in a March on Hunger.

Activity 6:   Putting the Key Thought First

Rewrite each of the following weak leads to place the key thought first and to summarize the story in good form. You need not include all the facts or use the exact wording of these leads. If you feel there are any necessary facts missing, you may make them up and add them.

1. Recently 538 Central High students participated in a survey consisting of questions about radio stations and the music they play. The students' favorite stations are WXOA and WNUD.

2. "Do you want to see a good play? If you do, be sure to come Friday evening. That's when the drama department will be presenting the first play of the year," reports student director Eloise Hampton. "Our Town" is the name of the play to be presented in the gym.

3. Tuesday evening at 8 p.m. the PTA will hold a meeting. Dr. Gene Feldman, principal of the Federal Laboratory School, will give a talk on "Problems of Growing Up in a Troubled World." Also on the agenda will be the installation of officers. Mrs. Roberta Bell is the incoming president and Mr. Thomas Jones the incoming secretary.

4. The student council will again sponsor the annual Christmas dance Friday at 8 p.m. in the high school cafeteria. Free refreshments will be served. The cafeteria will be decorated to emphasize the theme "Winter Wonderland."

5. Mrs. Gail Rumsey, 4-H Club adviser, reports the enrollment of members has doubled since last year. The large enrollment of 126 members has caused the club to be divided into two groups.

Emphasize Your Key Thought

When department store managers advertise a big sale, they always include a few "specials" that are being sold at unusually low prices for the sole purpose of drawing customers into the store. In writing your lead, your first three or four words are your specials. They must attract readers to your story.

The fourth step in building a lead, then, is to state the key thought in striking, interesting, arresting words. Remember that because of the use of narrow columns, the first line of a news story may contain only five or six words. Among these words, you must include some with enough "spark" to catch a reader's interest. Notice how this has been done in the following leads.

"One lunch for us, four days for a refugee" was the theme of the Southeast Asian Relief Day held here January 11.

—*Trapeze*, Oak Park–River Forest High School, Oak Park, Illinois

Smoke, flashpots, and special sound effects will set the stage for tonight's opening performance of the spring musical, "The Wizard of Oz," being presented by Madison students.

—*The Scribe*, Madison Junior High School, Eugene, Oregon

To place the key thought at the beginning of the news lead and to state it in striking words, you have a wide choice of sentence constructions. Different parts of speech or different kinds of sentences are suited to emphasizing various elements in your lead. The chart that begins below illustrates some of the many possible ways to begin your lead.

WAYS TO BEGIN A LEAD	
With a noun	Computers will control student scheduling in all district schools next fall.
With a name	Jerry Vitez, new senior class president, plans to arrange an April tour to the state capital.
With a prepositional phrase	Without the proposed swimming pool, the new community college gymnasium complex will open for student use next Tuesday afternoon.
With a present participle	Headlining this evening's annual Christmas program will be the production of "The Magic Nutcracker," an operetta based on Tchaikovsky's "Nutcracker Suite."
With a past participle	Elected last week to the new post of student coordinator, Ramona Williams has already announced plans for a series of faculty-student conferences.

With an infinitive	To bring music to shut-ins, the advanced chorus will sing at seven different convalescent hospitals during the next two weeks.
With a striking statement	Hypnosis can be fun! Dr. Michael Herbert, one of the world's leading hypnotists, demonstrated this in the high school auditorium November 17.
With a quotation	"Our American ideals can be achieved only as they become a part of each American!" declared Lee Zayco in her prizewinning Voice of Democracy contest speech delivered in assembly March 12.
With a question	Could you win a color television set by writing an English composition? Senior James Butler did when he entered a nationwide essay contest.
With a noun clause	Russian and Japanese will be offered as new language courses next year, Principal Maria Cardoza revealed this week.
With an adverbial clause	If 250 more yearbook orders are received, this year's El Gaucho will include color photos of spring activities.

The best newswriters take pains with their leads. They will weigh and ponder their words until they are sure that they have chosen the most striking, interesting, and arresting ones to emphasize the key thought.

Selecting from among a variety of sentence constructions provides a major means of emphasizing your key thought. A word of caution is in order, though. Variations in lead beginnings can easily be overdone. The major goal is to bring the key thought to the front of the news story, not to display grammatical styles. Quotations and questions in particular are easy to overuse. Three fourths of your leads should start with a noun or a name as the subject of the sentence.

The important point to remember is to avoid using exactly the same approach again and again. If *all* your stories were presented in the same style, your readers would skip many of them. Suppose each story on your front page began the same way:

> A committee of the student council will meet today.
>
> A football game will be played Saturday.
>
> A dance attracted many students last night.

Not very interesting reading, is it? Without purposeful variety in word emphasis and sentence construction, leads can be dull.

As you build your leads, you should also be aware that nouns and verbs are the chief conveyors of meaning and sources of interest in writing. Articles *(a, an, the)*, prepositions *(of, in)*, and conjunctions *(and, or)* say little or nothing. While their use is frequently unavoidable, their lack of expressive power should be borne in mind.

Phrases such as *there is, there was,* or *there will be* also say nothing. Replace them with strong, lively words. Notice the difference between "There will be 10 prizes for lucky ticket holders at the concert" and "Ten prizes will go to lucky ticket holders at the concert."

In addition, avoid using the word *held* as the main verb in a sentence. Find a substitute whenever possible. Notice how much duller "A meeting of the student council will be held today" is than "Student council will meet today."

Activity 7:   Using Different Lead Openers

Rewrite each of the weak leads below, beginning with the words in parentheses. You may leave out any of the facts you do not need or make up additional facts if necessary.

1. Rewrite to begin with a name: (Marjorie Collier and . . .)

   The big news at the Central High Science Fair was the final result of the judging. Marjorie Collier and Bill Powers were the two grand-prize winners. The announcement was made after the formal opening of the fair.

2. Rewrite to begin with an infinitive: (To provide . . .)

   Central High is using an improved computer record-keeping system this year. The main reason is to provide quicker reports of grades, according to Mrs. Marian Villari, vice-principal.

3. Rewrite to begin with a quotation: ("City government . . .")

The school auditorium was the scene of a talk given by Mr. Alvin LaRue, city manager, January 9. Speaking to 300 eleventh-grade government students, he stated, "City government is the closest unit of government to the people."

4. Rewrite to begin with a prepositional phrase: (As a climax . . .)

    Members of Mrs. Dorothy Miller's geography class had a dinner at Canton Low last Wednesday night. This was a climax to their study of China.

5. Rewrite to begin with an adverbial clause: (Although it rained . . .)

    Central High defeated Ridgeway yesterday afternoon, 12-0. It was a miserable football game. It rained steadily all afternoon. By the end of the game, the field was nothing but mud. Spectators could not tell which team most of the players were on.

Activity 8: Rewriting Lead Openers for Variety

Rewrite the following leads placing the key thoughts at the beginning and using a variety of sentence constructions. You may leave out facts you do not need or make up additional facts if necessary. Try to avoid beginning with *a, an,* or *the.* Definitely avoid beginning with *there* or using the word *held.*

1. The marching band presented "Speedway," a series of unusual numbers, to entertain spectators before the West High football game last Saturday.

2. The Central High Glee Club is preparing songs for a program to be presented December 4 at the Kiwanis Club.

3. There was a good show of grades this term as every class but the juniors had a representative on the honor roll.

4. A total of eight instrumentalists were successful in the auditions for the all-state band, chorus, and orchestra. The auditions were held October 30 at Johnson High.

5. The National Merit Scholarship Test will be held October 24, according to Mr. Lewis McConnell, director of counseling. Approximately 30 students are to take the test.

Divide Your Lead into Two or More Sentences

Perhaps you noticed that some leads became complicated and burdensome as you tried to make them complete. You had to use too many words to say all that was needed to furnish a full summary. This may have been especially true when you tried to include all of the five *W* and one *H* facts. Even after you left out nonessential elements, your sentences may often have become long and involved.

Brief, direct, simple sentences are best for news stories. They are easier to read and more likely to be understood. For the fifth step in building a lead, put your facts into two, or perhaps three, shorter sentences, rather than one long, complicated sentence. The first should begin with the key thought and include other facts of primary importance. The second should contain the remaining important facts. You should still leave nonessential material for later paragraphs of your story.

Notice how the following one-sentence leads are improved by dividing the ideas between two sentences.

COMPLICATED: Four Central High math students, Martin Santoro, June Karas, Kim Hoffman, and Charles Hughes, members of the accelerated algebra class, presented their projects on the television show "Who Knows Best?" at 4 p.m. Wednesday, April 15.

SIMPLE: Four Central High math students appeared on the television show "Who Knows Best?" Wednesday, April 15. Martin Santoro, June Karas, Kim Hoffman, and Charles Hughes were chosen from the accelerated algebra class to present their math projects on the 4 p.m. program.

COMPLICATED: Nearly 230 business majors have each purchased $10 tickets permitting them to attend the luncheon and to participate in field trips connected with the sixth annual Business Education Day, April 2.

SIMPLE: Nearly 230 business majors will take part in the sixth annual Business Education Day, April 2. All have purchased $10 tickets permitting them to attend the luncheon and to participate in the field trips.

There will be times, of course, when a single short sentence summarizes your story better than two sentences. However, most lead paragraphs containing more than 20 words (three or four lines of type) can be improved by division into two, or even three, short sentences.

Activity 9: Dividing a Lead into Shorter Sentences

Rewrite the following leads, dividing each into two sentences. Put the key thought at the beginning. If you feel any of the given facts are unnecessary, leave them out. If you need additional facts, make them up. Your completed leads should be clear and concise.

1. Returning victorious with ratings of "1" or "Superior" from the district speech and drama contest, seven speech students and the five members of the cast of the play "Medea" are slated to attend the coming state finals at State Teachers' College.

2. Staging their first appearance of the year, participants in the one-act plays, under the direction of Mr. Robert Paulsen, will present "To Burn a Witch," "Trifles," and "Last Gasps" to the public next Friday.

3. That "Stairway to a Star" will be the theme of the junior-senior prom, to be held May 20, was announced by Loretta Gonzalez and Henry Walker, general co-directors.

4. Students of driving age or older who are interested in antique or modern cars are eligible to take out applications for membership in the newly formed Automobile Association, which will hold its first meeting in Room 211, Thursday at 3:15 p.m.

5. Four Central students, together with young people from other Midvale high schools, and Mr. Mark Glasser, tour adviser, are taking part in a workshop in Washington, D.C., this week, to gain insight into how the government works.

Capture Your Reader's Interest

Following the steps presented up to now will usually result in a good, lively lead. Sometimes, however, the lead, though properly put together, will be dull. In that case, a special method to capture the reader's interest can be employed. Notice the following leads from high school newspapers.

An underground river is the cause of shifting in the south gym and auditorium walls, said Mr. Floyd Converse, head custodian. Cracks caused by this movement have been apparent for some time, he added.

—*The Statesman*, Kennedy High School, Denver, Colorado

The kidnap and release of Chip Wittern, sophomore, attracted widespread attention and left his classmates and the community stunned.

—*Spotlight*, Valley High School, West Des Moines, Iowa

What do these leads have that others do not? It's the sixth *W*—WOW!

How can you write a lead that has the **WOW! element** in it? The trick is to find an item of unusual interest in the story and make this your key thought. The formula is simple. Stan Burroway, of the University of Arizona, showed in an article written for *Quill and Scroll* how to take a complete but uninteresting lead and put WOW! into it. This was the original lead:

The Stamp Club met at 3:30 p.m. last Wednesday in Miss Elsie Morgan's room to discuss the value and history of South American stamps.

It is short and direct. It answers all five *W* questions (the HOW? is not important in this case). But who besides Miss Morgan and the members of the Stamp Club would read past that lead?

You need something more than these facts if the story is to be worth publishing. Look at the rest of your notes: The guest speaker at the meeting was Mr. Phil Smith, a local businessman. He showed his collection of Venezuelan stamps. The collection is worth $800. The club members discussed their coming picnic. They are writing letters to West German pen pals and exchanging stamps. The club meeting broke up suddenly when Roger

—Photo by Harold M. Lambert from Frederic Lewis

A lead with a WOW! element in it captures attention much as something uncommon held up for viewing might. The WOW! element of a lead will often consist of something odd, extraordinary, or memorable.

Brace, the president, knocked over the speaker's water pitcher. Water soaked the cover of Mr. Smith's book, but the stamps were not damaged.

Take a sheet of copy paper and write the first word of your trial lead: "WOW!" Nothing else—just "WOW!" You now have on paper the hardest lead in the world to justify. You wouldn't dare turn in a story that said: "WOW! The Stamp Club met at 3:30 p.m. last Wednesday . . ."

You are right, it would look silly. Your job is to find the angle that justifies a "WOW!" You can eliminate the club picnic and the pen pals. Mr. Smith's stamps are worth $800. That comes closer, if you can't find anything better. Roger Brace knocked over a pitcher of water. That's not worth remembering—*except* that the stamps were almost damaged.

That's it. The Stamp Club almost had $800 worth of damage! After the "WOW!" on your paper write: "That's what Stamp Club members said Wednesday when Roger Brace knocked over the water pitcher and nearly ruined . . ." Of course, this lead is overdramatic, and you certainly cannot have every story in the paper starting with "WOW! . . ." So rewrite it, keeping the WOW! angle first:

A splash that almost damaged $800 worth of rare stamps ended the Stamp Club meeting Wednesday.

The accident came when Roger Brace, club president, overturned a water pitcher that doused Mr. Phil Smith's stamp book containing a collection of Venezuelan stamps. Mr. Smith was principal speaker at . . .

The sixth *W* is no longer missing. True, some of the first five are no longer in the lead. But the ones that are left out are not essential, and they appear further down in the story. And that's where an interested reader will get, too—further down in the story.

After a little practice, you can stop writing out the trial lead, the "WOW!" and the statement that justifies it. Do this part in your head and put on paper only the lead you're going to use. Soon you'll automatically be spotting any item of unusual interest in a story and featuring it in your lead.

Activity 10: Using the WOW! Formula to Write Better Leads

Rewrite the leads for the following stories, using the WOW! formula given in the preceding section. First, write "WOW!" Then, locate among the facts a statement that will justify this beginning and write it after your "WOW!" Now develop a good news lead to include this idea. You are given more than enough material for each lead. Choose only what is important, interesting, and striking. Remember to include necessary five *W* and one *H* elements and to leave out unnecessary ones. Divide your lead into short, snappy sentences.

1. The school driver-training car was completely destroyed by fire April 8 at 1:30 a.m. The apparent cause of the fire was either a short circuit under the dashboard or a smoldering cigarette. Mrs. Toni Federico, the driver education instructor, reported that all the final examination papers for her classes were on the car seat.

2. John Forte, an outstanding track athlete, is undefeated in the high jump in all track meets for the current season. He now holds the school record for the high jump, 6 feet 11½ inches. John established this amazing record in the meet against West High last Friday. John is considered a possible candidate for the next Olympics.

3. Music by The Shadows will entertain students at the dance October 18 from 9 p.m. to 1 a.m. in the girls' gym. The dance is sponsored by the student council, with Nicole DeJong in charge of publicity. The dance will be free to all students, and free refreshments will be served, according to Nicole. The student council decided to make the dance a dress-up occasion. Boys are to wear jackets and ties, and girls are to wear informal dresses.

Check Your Lead

Because leads are complex, carefully developed mechanisms of reporting, they should be checked to ensure that they "work"—that they perform the functions they are supposed to. The checklist on page 130 will help you to determine that the leads you write are in good working condition.

Checklist for Leads

☐ 1. Does the lead enable the reader to answer all relevant basic questions: WHAT? WHO? WHEN? WHERE? WHY? HOW?

☐ 2. Does the key thought—the most important or interesting fact—come first?

☐ 3. Does the wording or sentence structure help emphasize this key thought?

☐ 4. Does the lead consist of the most appropriate number of sentences? (Is the subject matter best handled in two sentences? Three? One?)

☐ 5. Does the lead read smoothly?

☐ 6. Would the meaning of the lead be clear even to a reader with no prior knowledge of the subject of the story?

☐ 7. Does the lead possess the sixth *W*—WOW!?

Activity 11:   Writing Good Leads

By this time you should be able to find the essential facts in a set of reporter's notes and to assemble them into the best possible lead paragraph. Using the notes that follow, go through each of the seven steps in building a lead. When you have finished writing each lead, be sure to apply the checklist questions to it.

1. Literary Society banquet
   Last Thurs.
   School cafeteria
   Parents and seniors were honored guests
   "Hawaii" theme carried out in decorations, food
   Program covers showed Hawaiian picture
   Mr. and Mrs. James Wood, who lived in Hawaii several years, were special guest speakers
   They showed movies of Hawaii
   Seniors given travel posters

2. Sachi Nakane
   Won $500 cash and scholarship to the Jeffers School of Business at Carter University
   For 4-year course
   She wrote essay "Why I Am Interested in Studying Economics"
   Plans to enroll in the school after graduation
   After finishes course wants to work for a large brokerage house as a securities analyst
   She scored 800 in the math achievement test

3. Special crafts class
   Producing puppet shows
   Students made puppets and stage
   "The Runaway Pancake" one of four plays produced
   Voices are taped beforehand
   Performances at Lincoln kindergarten and several nursery schools

Writing Special Kinds of Leads

Every lead paragraph must be developed according to the procedure outlined in the preceding seven steps. There will, however, be some occasions when story content calls for further development of these ideas.

Three such situations are outlined here—the complicated news story containing more than one thought, the story where a literary reference would be useful in attracting attention, and the story whose content suggests a novelty lead.

Information about other special kinds of leads will be discussed in later chapters. These include leads for speech stories, for interpretive, in-depth reports, and for feature stories.

Preparing a Lead When There Is More Than One Key Thought

What can be done with a complicated news report—one that contains several ideas of equal importance, all of which must be featured in the lead? The best way is to refer briefly to all of these main ideas in your lead. You can then deal separately with each topic in the body of your story.

A report on a science fair might treat a number of different ideas of equal importance, such as the three or four most interesting exhibits. A summary lead could be used to present all the separate ideas at the outset of the report.

—Photo by Jim Anderson from Woodfin Camp

Two basic styles can be used to handle stories with more than one key thought: **summary leads** or leads using **linking words.** Which to use depends on the particular facts to be reported.

SUMMARY LEADS.   Sometimes it is advisable to draw together into one story several sets of facts, each set representing a separate event but all related to the same general topic. This is done by referring to the separate events in a summary lead paragraph.

> Climaxing Homecoming Week will be a pep rally, a bonfire, and an open house tonight, a parade tomorrow morning, and the county championship football game tomorrow afternoon.

Here are three news reports combined into one—tonight's festivities, the parade, and the championship football game. All are related because they are Homecoming Week activities. In the body of the story each would be dealt with separately, following the sequence of the summary lead.

LEADS WITH LINKING WORDS.   By using conjunctions *(and, but, when, as, if . . .)* or other linking words, it is possible to tie two equally important facts together in a lead. Notice how in the following example the conjunction *when* serves to link (1) the opportunity of car owners to combat pollution and (2) the sponsoring of an ecology "tune-in."

> Car owners were provided with a unique opportunity to help combat pollution during the week of April 24 to May 1, when several Bergen County high schools sponsored an Ecology Tune-In at the Garden State Plaza Shopping Center. The purpose of the Tune-In was to offer a free service check on participating vehicles, particularly for pollution-causing vehicles.
>
> —*Crimson Crier*, Fair Lawn High
> School, Fair Lawn, New Jersey

The following chart shows some of the many different linking words and phrases that can be used to tie equally important ideas together in a lead.

COMMON LINKING WORDS AND PHRASES			
and	or	before	now that
but	so	even though	so that
for	because	if	while

Activity 12:   Writing Summary Leads

Write a summary lead for the three separate sets of facts presented in each of the following numbered items. Be sure that you first determine the one idea that ties each set together.

1. Leonard Robinson hired to teach chem & physics; taught 6 yrs. in Plainview H.S.; M.S. from State U.; plans to start science club; . . .

   New home economics teacher—Carol Browne; specialist in nutrition; worked for U.S. government 3 yrs.; says satisfaction of passing knowledge on to young people brought her here; . . .

   Assistant Principal John Stone announces new gym teacher will start next week; will coach hockey, soccer; named John Green; . . .

2. A fourth advanced placement course offered this year—a.p. biology; Mrs. Rosalie Grace will teach it; other a.p. courses are Eng., math, & American history; . . .

   Mr. Harvey Zallman says construction work in shop area completed; now can offer course in metal shop; will be taught 7th period, woodshop 8th period; . . .

   Board of ed approves new course—French 4; initiated by requests of 12 French 3 students; Mr. Pierre LeShay will teach it; . . .

3. Fire broke out in Nelson's Coffee Shop 3 a.m. Saturday; according to Mr. Al Nelson fire started in the wall (electrical wiring); $5,000 damage, he says; will reopen in week to 10 days; . . .

   Surface of Columbus Ave. has collapsed one block south of Nelson's; area of approx. 100 square feet; Mr. Ed Suarez, in charge of repairs, says collapse occurred last Fri. and was due to "some shifting of the base soil, plus wear and tear of constant use by vehicles"; . . .

   One block north of Nelson's, on Columbus, a fire hydrant was opened late on Friday, creating problems for cars returning from Movieland; police say incident will be investigated because this kind of prank is getting more common; . . .

Activity 13:   Using Linking Words in a Lead

Connect the two statements in each of the following pairs by using a linking word or phrase from the chart on page 132. Change capitalization and punctuation as necessary.

1. The Cardinals had the bases loaded in the eighth and ninth innings. They couldn't score a run, even with their best players at bat.

2. Principal David Smythe agreed to reopen the student lounge. The students pledged to set up a committee that would clean it daily.

3. More students are expected to be driving to school this year. Half of the south parking lot has been opened to them.

4. Dr. Edgar Ross will be giving an SAT prep course this year. SAT scores are likely to improve greatly over last year's scores.

5. The chief of police would not discuss the Henderson robbery case. The press turned to the arresting officers for the information that they needed.

Using Literary References to Interest Readers

Can you identify and explain the literary references or allusions in these leads?

To be or not to be soaked to the skin—that was the question faced by members of the choir last Saturday when a pouring rainstorm began just before their scheduled outdoor concert at the City Hall dedication.

Showing the strength of a Hercules, shot-put champ Harry Smith set a new state record last Friday.

Wheelchair-bound Marie Williams compares her problems in traveling through Central's halls to those of a hobbit making its way across Middle Earth.

The mental images suggested by the allusions in these leads are part of a common heritage, the world's great literature. You can add richness, color, and depth to your leads—in fact, to all your writing—by reference to the tremendous range of human experience portrayed in literature. To do so, however, you must acquire the necessary background from extensive reading, particularly among those books, poems, and plays that are considered everyone's heritage. These include some modern best sellers as well as the classics of the past. The literature that endures, whether it was created yesterday or 2,000 years ago, tells of timeless and universal experiences.

Successful reporters draw on the ideas and experiences encountered in their reading to help them express ideas in a meaningful and colorful way. They should, of course, be sure what allusions will be recognized and understood by their readers. They will not improve their writing merely by incorporating some obscure bit of knowledge, for allusions must be grasped if they are to enrich communication.

When should the writer of a lead resort to this device? There are no principles that make this question easy to answer. However, it may be said that allusions work best when (1) they seem to suggest themselves naturally to the writer, (2) they improve (rather than decorate) the lead, and (3) they are likely to enhance in some way the reader's response to the lead.

Activity 14:   Enriching Leads with Literary References

Go through issues of your school newspaper or of your favorite daily paper and find three stories whose leads could be altered so as to include literary references. Then either revise the leads to include references to the characters, events, or ideas in well-known works of literature or write new leads containing such references.

Designing Novelty Leads

When your story has an offbeat or unusual twist, you may wish to write a **novelty lead**—a lead that is "different" in that it relies on humorous or otherwise catchy writing. Novelty leads cannot substitute for intelligent reporting and good newswriting. They belong only in very special stories. More often than not, these special stories will be not news stories but feature stories (explained in Chapter 11). However, a news report with an intriguing WOW! element might benefit from an unusual approach in its lead.

A successful novelty lead must present the key thought in an especially engaging way. The following two stories open with novelty leads. Notice how these leads differ from conventional ones.

Who is the strange man circulating around the new Fine Arts Building bent over what looks like a Geiger counter? Is he seeking uranium?

That man is Mr. Al Brevnik, Pierce County television coordinator, who is making light meter tests for the TV showing of the departments in the Fine Arts Building.

The program will be shown at 10:30 a.m. Saturday on KTNT-TV.

—*Lincoln News*, Lincoln High School, Tacoma, Washington

Due to the lack of 6-foot invisible rabbits, the title role for "Harvey," the drama department's fall play, has not been cast. However, all other characters have been chosen.

The lead role of Elwood will be portrayed by senior Keith Bolton. Elwood insists upon the existence of a pukah, a type of kind spirit, which is in the form of a 6-foot rabbit named Harvey and is visible only to Elwood's eyes.

The John Muir drama department will present performances of "Harvey" November 17, 18, and 20.

—*Blazer*, John Muir High School, Pasadena, California

A true novelty lead tells you enough about the story to seize your attention and whet your appetite for more information. Imagination is the special ingredient in a successful novelty lead. But you still must have the main idea of the story clearly in mind. Regardless of how it is composed, your lead must reflect the key thought.

Novelty leads should be used sparingly. An occasional offbeat lead livens up a news page. More frequent use has the opposite effect. A page full of novelty leads will appear to lack true news value.

Activity 15: Preparing Novelty Leads

Select from issues of your school newspaper four or five articles with news leads written in standard form that you feel you can improve by using a novelty style. Write a novelty lead to replace each conventional lead.

Summary

This chapter focuses on the elements contained in a good news lead and offers steps to be followed to write good leads. It also deals with various other kinds of leads to be used in certain special situations.

SUMMARIZING A NEWS EVENT. News is presented in a special way. Each news article, in addition to having a headline, begins with a lead. The remainder of the story explains in detail what the headline and lead have summarized. This arrangement helps to answer readers' questions at once, enables them to decide which stories to read, and makes it easier for them to obtain an overview of the news. It also provides an organized way for reporters to write about news events.

BUILDING THE LEAD.   Reporters apply seven steps in preparing a lead. First, they uncover the answers to six questions: WHAT? WHO? WHEN? WHERE? WHY? and HOW? Second, they decide which of the important facts they have gotten from these questions are to be featured in the lead paragraph. Third, they decide what is the key thought—the single fact that possesses the most importance and interest. Fourth, they emphasize this key thought at the beginning of the lead through appropriate sentence construction. Fifth, they divide the lead paragraph into two or three short sentences if doing so will improve readability. Sixth, they make a special effort to capture the reader's interest with a WOW! element. Seventh, they check their lead and put the finishing touches on it, for they know that a well-written and interesting lead will attract readers to the entire news story.

WRITING SPECIAL KINDS OF LEADS. Certain stories require special leads. For a story with more than one key thought, a summary lead or a lead that uses linking words may work well. In other stories, a lead making use of a literary reference may prove effective. When a news story has an unusual twist, a novelty lead may be the best way to begin.

Vocabulary

news story	cutoff test	summary lead
lead	five *W*'s and one *H*	linking word
headline	key thought	novelty lead
body	WOW! element	

Review Questions

1. What is the purpose of the news lead?

2. What are the steps involved in building a lead?

3. What is the key thought, and why should it be placed first?

4. What are some of the methods that can be used to emphasize the key thought?

5. How should a lead be written when it must include more than one key thought?

Discussion Questions

1. Of the different reasons why news stories are put together in a special way, which one do you consider the most important? Explain your answer.

2. While a good lead can be read quickly and easily, writing one is usually not a quick and easy task. What are the chief difficulties encountered in writing good leads?

3. Analyze in terms of the questions WHAT? WHO? WHEN? WHERE? WHY? and HOW? the most newsworthy recent occurrence in your school. Which of the six questions is the hardest to answer? Which resists most strongly a short, simple answer? Which of the answers to the six questions is the most important? The second-most important? The least important?

4. Pick one or more recent events that are important but not immediately interesting. Discuss ways of using the lead to capture the reader's interest when reporting these events.

5. How might a reporter decide whether a newsworthy matter made up of separate sets of facts should be treated in a single story or in separate stories?

Chapter Project

Writing and Polishing a News Lead

From information you have collected by interviewing a news source, write a concise and appealing lead paragraph. Then, show how you have included answers to the five *W* and one *H* questions, or if some are not included, why they were not appropriate. Finally, show how you have applied the other steps from the section Building the Lead. Be able to justify your lead in terms of the Checklist for Leads on page 130.

7

PUTTING
THE NEWS
STORY
TOGETHER

When you have completed this chapter, you should be able to

Arrange news into the most important news story pattern—the inverted-pyramid story.

Recognize and use other basic news story patterns—the chronological story, the composite story, and the story that dictates its own arrangement.

Write a news story.

Tim Davidson, editor of the Central High *News,* faced his beginning reporters. He waved a piece of copy in his hand.

"Listen!" he said. "Tell me what's wrong with this story." He read from the copy:

> Janet Lanham received the first Gold *C* in the history of Central High at the recognition assembly last Friday. Awards were given to 37 athletes, and a fashion show was presented at the program.
>
> Students began preparing for the fashion show about six weeks ago under the direction of Mrs. Eileen Clay, homemaking instructor . . .

Tim continued, reading only the first few words of each paragraph:

> Fashions included clothes appropriate for spring wear . . .
> The following people took part in the fashion show: . . .
> Athletic awards in the form of pins and letters were given . . .
> First-year pins were received by . . .
> Letters for two years of participation were given to . . .
> Seven athletes were presented with three-year awards . . .
> The Gold *C* is given for four years of participation in . . .
> This is the first time it has ever been presented to . . .
> "Janet has been outstanding in sports," said Miss Lillian Grove, the physical education instructor. "She . . ."

"All right, what's good and what's bad about it?" asked Tim.

Comments came thick and fast from the reporters.

"The story has plenty of names. It's worth printing."

"The lead says what it should."

"The key thought is at the beginning."

"You're all correct so far," Tim conceded. "What else?"

"The story is all there," put in one of the reporters. "I helped plan the program. That's just the way it happened."

"Isn't that the trouble?" Tim demanded. "We've told the story in the order that things occurred. But is that the way our reader wants to hear about them?

"Janet's award is the biggest thing in this story," he went on. "Look— here's a diagram of the story the way it is now."

Tim drew this figure on the chalkboard:

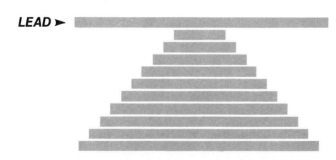

LEAD ►

"After the lead we have the weakest paragraph," Tim continued. "Then the paragraphs keep on growing in news value until we reach the last one, which tells us WHY Janet received the award. But that's the first question our readers will ask after they finish the lead. We should reverse the paragraphs, like this." Now Tim drew this figure:

LEAD ▶

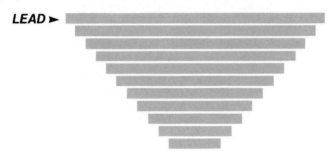

Arranging News into an Inverted Pyramid

Tim's second diagram shows the most common and effective way of arranging the body of a news story: the **inverted pyramid.** The top-heavy look is intentional. The arrangement puts the most important facts first and the least important details last. Read the following news story, noting the kinds of facts presented in each paragraph. You will see that each fact has more news value than the one following it.

Senior represents THS again in Voice of Democracy meet

For the second year, Con Poirier, Trojan senior, has been chosen in school competition to represent THS in the Voice of Democracy contest, sponsored by the Topeka Junior Chamber of Commerce.

Radio station KJAY sponsored the program for county competition. Mr. Joe Stavas of the station devoted a special program November 17 to broadcasting the speeches of the school winners. The final judging by various civic leaders in Topeka will be based on these scripts.

Other finalists in the Topeka area include Judy Paterson from Hayden, Nancy Schweitzer from Washburn Rural, and Virginia Epps from Highland Park. Each will be presented with a trophy, and the county winner will receive additional recognition.

Poirier, who placed second in county competition as a junior, is hoping to do even better this time. If he survives this elimination, he will go on to the state finals. The winner will represent Kansas in the national finals to be held in Washington, D.C., this February.

The top four finalists in the nation will each receive a $500 scholarship as well as a gold recording of their speech. Various activities will honor the national finalists at the Washington competition.

—*The World,* Topeka High School, Topeka, Kansas

Some of the reasons for writing a news story this way were discussed in Chapter 6. The reader finds desired information more readily and understands it better. The reporter thinks more logically while preparing the story. And the editor may adjust its length to fit space requirements because it meets the cutoff test. The first paragraphs after the lead contain essential details, and the last paragraphs of the story may be eliminated if there is no space for them, as in the following illustration. Many news stories could be improved and the appearance of news pages enlivened if the last paragraphs were eliminated.

LEAD►

} **Eliminated**

As you select material for each paragraph of an inverted-pyramid story, apply the same standards that you used when arranging your lead. Explain your key thought first. Then, tell other facts about the event in the order of their importance. Decide on their news value, according to the news elements they contain (nearness, timeliness, importance, names, drama or conflict, variety, human interest, and humor), to determine which ones are to be emphasized.

Activity 1: Examining Inverted Pyramids

1. Select a news story of six to eight paragraphs written in an inverted-pyramid form. Clip and mount the story.

   a. Label the lead. Then, summarize in a few words the main idea of each of the remaining paragraphs.

   b. Evaluate the arrangement of the paragraphs in this story by comparing their news value. Is the news value of each paragraph *less* (as it should be) than that of the paragraph before?

   c. Draw an inverted-pyramid diagram of the story in which the widths of the sections correspond to the news value of the paragraphs. Is the width of each section *less* (as it should be) than that of the section above?

2. Working in pairs, you and another student should each find in a daily newspaper a news story in inverted-pyramid form. Cut your own story into paragraphs after recording on paper the original paragraph order. Your partner is to do the same. Mix up the paragraphs and then exchange them for your partner's disarranged paragraphs. Each of you will try to restore the other's paragraphs to their original order. Compare your results with the original order as recorded on paper. If you succeed in restoring the paragraphs to their original order, what can you conclude about the story? If you do not, what then can you conclude?

Recognizing Other Basic News Story Patterns

Most news stories fit readily into the inverted-pyramid arrangement. However, other patterns may be more suited to particular sets of facts. Sometimes it will be most effective to narrate a news report in the order in which the events happened, preparing a **chronological story.** If you are combining several brief but related news reports into one, you will write a **composite story.** Finally, some news events are most effectively reported in a story that dictates its own arrangement.

The Chronological Story

When several related events take place over a period of time or when one occurrence causes another, you may wish to arrange the body of your story in chronological order. Notice how in the body of the following story each event connected with Homecoming is presented in the order in which it will take place. This sequence bears no relation to the importance of the event. It is used simply to present a convenient time schedule to readers.

'Decade of Progress' is theme of Homecoming festivities

"Activities on the theme 'A Decade of Progress' will honor the returning alumni of the Class of 1974," announced Tom Christy, chairman of Homecoming, which is scheduled for next weekend.

Two days of events, beginning with a pep rally Friday evening in the auditorium, are planned. Coaches and members of football and soccer teams of 1974 and 1984 will be introduced.

Mr. Kip Gunner, coach of the 1974 all-state football team and of Valley's interscholastic champions of that year, will be keynote speaker.

The Homecoming queen and her court will be announced. Jim Brough and Dick Cahill, co-captains of the football team, will crown the queen, who will reign over the weekend's festivities; and Ed Crosby and Carl Dailey, co-captains of the soccer team, will install the royal court.

Pat Downer, head cheerleader, will direct the squad in a presentation featuring new yells and songs.

The Homecoming parade Saturday morning will be led by Pete Ferrier and the marching band. The parade will feature our award-winning majorettes under Emily Gilbert and Carol Schwartz, co-leaders.

Saturday afternoon the alumni will join students in cheering the Panthers to victory as they battle Bordentown. Between halves of the varsity game, there will be demonstrations by the marching bands and majorettes of both schools.

Graduates will climax their Homecoming with a dinner-dance at the Embassy Club, while students will hold the Homecoming dance, "Harvest Moon," in the school gymnasium. Highlight of the alumni event will be the presentation of the Class of 1974 gift to the school.

The student dance, sponsored by the student council, features Ken Garcia's band and three skits by The Playcrafters.

Lee McEwen, head of the alumni committee, reports that more than 90 percent of the Class of 1974 has been reached and that "the response has been fantastic."

A chronological news story must have a good summary lead. Compare the successful story you have just read with another Homecoming story—one that reports all the events of a big weekend exactly in the order in which they happened, but that does not have such a lead.

Homecoming activities set stage for Central-North clash

Excitement and tension ran high Thursday night, October 17, at 7:45 p.m., when the band sounded the first notes of its opening song. Reason for this was the question of the evening: Who will be Homecoming king and queen?

Rita Jackson, student council president, welcomed all the guests and the student body. Jerry Burke played a trumpet solo. Rita then introduced a skit, "The Spirit of Homecoming."

After the skit ended, formal presentation of the king and queen candidates began. The five candidates for king were each introduced and took their places on the stage. To the music of a grand march, each of the candidates for Homecoming queen was presented by a member of the football team. Frank Dyer, who had played a swami in the skit, now announced that Kenny

Stuart had been elected king and gave him an envelope containing the queen's name. Kenny formally introduced Judith Pryor as queen. Delight shone on both of their faces as the band played the recessional.

The following afternoon the student body attended a 40-minute pep fest. Coach Don Douglas gave a talk on his idea of school spirit. Kenny then presented Judith with a corsage.

Friday, October 18, at 8 p.m., the Tigers met North High on the football field. At the opening kickoff, blue and gold balloons were released by cheerleaders and fans.

Following the game, there was a dance in the high school gym. The theme was "Fall Fantasy," and the gym was decorated in shades of yellow and gold.

What happens to such a story when the summary lead is eliminated? In what ways has the reporter failed to emphasize the key thought as well as other important facts?

A chronological story is not simply a chronicle of any and all events. To write one successfully you must choose the important ideas, applying the same principles that you learned in working with inverted-pyramid stories. Having selected the major facts according to their news value, you summarize them in the lead and then present them chronologically in the body of the story.

The Composite Story

A composite news story combines two or more news events because these events have a connecting theme. It is a story with more than one key thought. Chapter 6 pointed out that the lead may be written as a one-paragraph summary of all key thoughts or that the key thoughts may be expressed by connecting them with linking words.

The body of a composite news story may be arranged in several ways, all of them varieties of the inverted-pyramid or the chronological story. The simplest way is to treat each event as a separate story. Following a lead which refers to all events, tell the complete story of the first event, then the next, and so on. The events themselves may be arranged in an inverted pyramid order or in a chronological order.

The following diagram shows the use of the inverted-pyramid arrangement in a composite news story. Notice that not only the whole story follows this arrangement but each substory does, too.

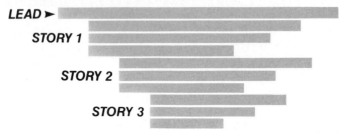

The following is a well-structured composite story. The lead summarizes in one paragraph the main idea—that the foreign students in an Arizona high school cherish the way Christmas is celebrated in their homelands. The body of the story treats each foreign student's description of Christmas at home as a separate item.

Glad Jul, Feliz Navidad, Fröhliche Weihnachten

By Sheri Marshall and Robert Cohen

While foreign Christmases are not a major thought or concern of the average student, some not-so-average students here, who come from other countries, hold their native Christmases close to heart.

Jackie Suazo, a senior from Mexico, remembers recent celebrations across the border.

Most Mexican families start the holiday season with elaborate posadas, or parties, she says. From December 18 to 23, neighborhood families gather at one house per night for several nights and sing and act out the scenes of Mary and Joseph trying to find room at an inn in Bethlehem. It's the now familiar La Posada, acted also each year in Tucson. After the skits, more fun comes with the breaking of piñatas.

Dagmar Reinike, a senior from West Germany, cherishes the Christmas season in her homeland.

Part of a Protestant family, Dagmar would start the holiday season with Advent, the preparation days before Christmas. Advent wreaths are used. Each holds four candles. One is lit every Sunday before Christmas.

In Sweden, Marie Falkman, a freshman, also begins the Christmas celebration with Advent, December 13. The boys and girls wear white and hold candles while singing songs and reading poems in school.

Agnes Mandal, a senior from the Philippines, says Santa arrives on Christmas Eve, as in America, stocking the tree with presents.

Agnes says, "We celebrate in the Philippines by singing carols, and then we go to Christmas Eve midnight Mass.''

Vinh Trann, a freshman from Vietnam, says his family tradition is to go to church on Christmas Day. "The streets are flooded with people. Cars can't even use the streets because they are so crowded."

—*Rincon Echo,* Rincon High School,
Tucson, Arizona

Another method of handling a composite article is to consider first one **angle** or one portion of each story, then another angle or portion, continuing in this way until you have covered all angles or portions. Take, for example, a typical school news story—one that announces that three one-act plays are to be presented. The lead might be a general statement about all of the plays. Then the reporter might compare or contrast the plots of the plays—angle 1. In the next section of the story, the names of all three directors might be introduced—angle 2. Then, the leading actors of each play might be named—angle 3. Finally, the chief people behind the scenes might be mentioned—angle 4.

Such an approach is practical when you wish to emphasize particular points common to all the stories. The lead should cover all angles but should feature the first angle you plan to consider.

The Story That Dictates Its Own Arrangement

Some purely factual news articles, as well as many interpretive and human-interest ones, may not fall easily into one of the standard news story formats. Such an article does not need to be forced into a rigid arrangement, especially if doing so might take away from its effectiveness. Instead, the reporter may arrange the material so that the ideas flow naturally, even though some of the advantages of the standard formats are lost. This type of story may be said to dictate its own arrangement. A good reporter may, however, still use the inverted-pyramid plan, the chronological plan, or both as a guide in organizing the information.

—Photo by Michal Heron from Woodfin Camp

A report on a student hot line might easily take the form of a composite story. If a summary lead identified the services offered by the hot line, the body of the story could then treat each service in turn.

Notice how much of the following story is in chronological form and how much is not. Where and how did the reporter use a nonchronological arrangement? Why?

Two counselors revive child by using artificial respiration

By Carol Raiffie

"I saw this little girl lying there helplessly on the line between life and death. I didn't hesitate for a moment thinking of what I should do. I knew instinctively to give her mouth-to-mouth resuscitation and I did just that," Allan Rosenbaum stated modestly. Allan, with the assistance of Jim Rand, helped save the life of an 8-year-old child at a recent session of the Saturday project sponsored by the junior class.

Both Allan and Jim are swimming instructors at the project for underprivileged youngsters. "The kids come and are involved in many activities around Ladue High School. Al and I help out in the pool area playing with them and teaching some how to swim," explained Jim.

It was during an afternoon period of swimming, and Jim was in the pool with some of the children. He was helping one of the girls, Diana, learn how to float on her back. "It was her first time in the water and she told me that she liked it very much," Jim recalls. When it was time for the children to get out of the pool, Diana asked him if she could be the last one out, so Jim helped the others out first.

"The next thing I noticed was Diana's body lying limply on the water. She must have passed out," stated Jim, speculating exhaustion as the possible cause. "The girl wasn't breathing," and according to Jim, "there wasn't any choice but to give her artificial respiration. After a few breaths she seemed to be revived."

However, Allan Rosenbaum noticed that she was not yet all right. "I slapped her on the back to clear her throat and give her mouth-to-mouth resuscitation for about a minute. She then began to breathe on her own, so I stopped, but after about 45 seconds I had to continue it again for about two minutes."

The two counselors commented that they had learned artificial respiration during sophomore health, but that they never had the opportunity to use the knowledge. Jim explained the procedure both had used. "After a slap on the back, I tilted her head back and pinched her nose shut. Then I opened her mouth and blew into it. Her stomach rose and I had to press it down to get the air out."

As Allan was trying to revive the girl, someone called the police. "They arrived shortly after Diana began breathing again," according to Allan.

An ambulance took the girl to County Hospital, and the parents were notified. A group of juniors then went down to the hospital and sat in the waiting room while the girl had lung X-rays. They talked with her and tried to cheer her up.

—*Panorama,* Horton Watkins (Ladue) High School, St. Louis, Missouri

Cutting Chronological, Composite, and Special-Arrangement Stories

A well-written story in inverted-pyramid arrangement presents no problems when it must be shortened. Its last paragraphs are designed to be expendable. With other arrangements, however, changing the length of the story becomes more difficult. The best way to avoid the problem of cutting a noninverted-pyramid story is to plan the story's length when it is first assigned and to write the story exactly that long. If cutting is still necessary, apply a rule similar to the one for cutting inverted-pyramid stories. Find the paragraphs having the least news value and eliminate them.

If it were your responsibility to cut the following story, which paragraph would you eliminate? Would you then have to rewrite any part of what comes before or after that paragraph?

Chess team checks for state

As the chess team prepares for the IHSA state team tournament in April and the Proviso West open March 19, the 6-2 team has hopes of winning several individual trophies.

Senior Shezad Bandukwala, the team captain, said that the team's goal is to finish second in the conference behind Hinsdale South.

"My goal is to get into the top 20 in the state," said senior co-captain Mark Stoermer.

The chess team receives support from the GE athletic boosters but very little student support. "I'm sick of people making jokes about the chess team," said Stoermer.

Although no tryouts are held for the team, only the top eight players are eligible to compete in meets. The top three players consist of Bandukwala, Stoermer, and junior Tom Beifuss, who are all nationally ranked in the U.S.

The best competitor plays on board one and receives 12 points for a win. The second best plays on board two and receives 11 points for a win. The pattern continues. Conference meets can take up to four hours, and tournaments like the Proviso open have lasted for 15 hours.

"The long hours of practice and tournament play are worth it, though, because it enables us as individuals to build up our mental stamina," Bandukwala said.

—*Echo*, Glenbard East High School,
Lombard, Illinois

Activity 2:   Examining Other Story Patterns

1. In a daily or school newspaper, find an example of a story written in chronological order. Explain why you think the reporter selected chronological order instead of an inverted-pyramid arrangement.

2. Find in a daily or school newspaper an example of a story that uses a special paragraph arrangement. Describe the apparent plan. Did the writer make any use of the standard arrangements? Evaluate the effectiveness of the plan used. Might the material have been better handled if the writer had used a standard news story form?

3. Find a chronological story, a composite story, and a story with a special arrangement, each about 12 paragraphs long. Cut each story by three paragraphs without, if possible, eliminating any important facts or otherwise distorting the story. Tell which story was the hardest to cut. Explain why.

Writing a News Story

You are now ready to assemble a complete news story, although additional skills must be mastered before you reach a professional level in reporting. Still, your work from now on will be with complete stories. The following series of eight steps will serve as guides.

Obtain All the Facts

The first step is to study your reporting notes carefully and get the event clearly in mind. Consider the news value of each fact and its potential reader interest. Decide which is the main idea of the entire story, what approach you will use, and what points you wish to emphasize.

Use reference sources to obtain additional information about your topic and to learn what has already been published about it. If you decide that you still lack essential information, check back with your original news source or interview other people.

Write Your Lead

The second step—writing your lead—is the most critical part of your writing. The quality of your lead determines whether your story will be accepted by your editors and your readers. (Review Chapter 6 for the specific steps to follow.)

Plan the Body of Your Story

For your third step, consider whether your story can best be presented in an inverted-pyramid arrangement or in another format. Usually you will have no alternative, since most news stories fall naturally into the inverted-pyramid plan. However, since chronological order or some other arrangement might be better for this particular story, you should consider all choices. Assuming that you will arrange your facts in an inverted pyramid, presenting them in the order of descending importance, you should do two things.

FIRST, EXPLAIN YOUR KEY THOUGHT.   In the paragraphs following the lead, give details about your key thought. This is the most newsworthy idea in your story, so it should be explained first.

THEN, EXPLAIN OTHER FACTS IN THE ORDER OF THEIR NEWS VALUE.   If your story is woven around a single, unified topic, all of the body will be devoted to amplifying and explaining your key thought. Within these paragraphs, you should arrange the details in the order of descending importance. If your news story must include other facts that are not that closely related to your key thought or to each other, you will need to determine the news value of each fact. Then present these after the main facts, placing the most important ones first.

Construct Good Newspaper Paragraphs

You have learned in English classes that a paragraph is a carefully organized group of sentences about one main idea and that a well-written paragraph usually includes a topic sentence giving the main thought of the paragraph. You will need to keep these principles in mind as you undertake the fourth step in preparing a news story—constructing good newspaper paragraphs. When you write newspaper paragraphs, though, you must also consider the special demands of a news page. The following three guidelines are especially important for the writing of newspaper paragraphs.

LIMIT A NEWSPAPER PARAGRAPH TO ONE TOPIC OR ONE ASPECT OF A TOPIC. This holds true for any paragraphing you may do, whether for formal composition or for newswriting. Consider only one topic as you write a paragraph.

KEEP A NEWSPAPER PARAGRAPH SHORT. Because of narrow newspaper columns, paragraphs must be brief to make a story visually attractive. Readers may skip over long paragraphs. A good length is 30 to 40 words—about two or three sentences. Paragraphs should seldom exceed 75 words. Even long lists of names may be broken into short paragraphs. One of the rules of newspaper makeup is that white space within and around a story makes it more appealing to the eye than unbroken walls of print.

START A NEWSPAPER PARAGRAPH WITH SIGNIFICANT WORDS. As you write each paragraph, consider its subject matter. Just as in your lead, put the paragraph's key thought at the beginning and describe it in forceful, striking words. Avoid vague, imprecise phrasing. Constructing a good lead paragraph will help you build successful paragraphs in the body of your story.

Notice how the paragraphs of the following news story begin with significant words, besides being short and limited to one topic or one aspect of a topic.

Ross likes new location

Ambition and talent are fundamentals needed by student journalists, according to Ken Ross, city editor for the Columbia Missourian.

"If you are interested, report for your high school or college paper," Ross said. "See if you like it."

Ross first became interested in journalism in junior high school when his class visited a local newspaper office. In his small-town high school, there weren't many other interested journalists. "I was the newspaper," he said candidly.

After graduating from the University of Michigan, Ross joined the staff of the Chicago Tribune. He held many positions, among them financial editor, feature editor, editorial writer, and assistant news editor.

Besides supervising the city desk, Ross teaches two classes of basic reporting at the university. "They're not classes in a class sense," said Ross. "They (students) report to the city desk just like any other reporter. It is practical experience for them."

Students cover news beats and do field work on or about the campus researching articles. They have few lectures.

"It's the only way to teach journalism," he stressed.

—*Workshop Missourian*, University of Missouri Summer Media Workshop, Columbia, Missouri

Activity 3: Paragraphing a Newspaper Story

1. The following story should appear as four or five paragraphs. On a piece of paper, write the first words of each new paragraph.

   Wood sculpture and silk screening will be featured at the spring art exhibit this year. The show, to be held in the cafeteria May 14, is open to the public. Two outstanding artists, Mona Larson, foreign exchange student, and Don Castillo, junior, will have individual exhibits displaying their best work. One of Mona's interesting pieces of work is a graceful but simple sculpture of a human body, done in redwood. Don's exhibit will feature some of his watercolors. Other art students whose outstanding work will be featured are Dave Clark, who has carved the form of a human head from a tree trunk; Esther Cooper, who has carved an abstract human form from driftwood; and George Foley, who also has constructed a head from wood. This year there will be more emphasis on print processes than ever before. The art classes' block printing and silk screening will be shown in the yearbook. At the exhibit, some of the students will demonstrate silk screening, scratchboard, and other processes. These processes are as close to commercial art as anything the art classes do.

2. Find one paragraph-opening sentence in Item 1 that fails to present the key thought at the beginning in forceful, striking words. Rewrite it so that it becomes a satisfactory paragraph opener.

Enliven Your Story with Direct Quotations

Study the following news story. Notice how the reporter employed brief direct quotations to tell part of the story and to add variety to it.

Futurism class offers alternatives

By Jeff Hindman

Alternatives for the future are the bases of material to be covered in history instructor Ed Cochrane's Futurism 210.

The course, "Alternatives for the Future," is described by Mr. Cochrane as "a study of the future and how we will do what we have to.

"The class will study what will happen in the future, based on current trends, and then concentrate on alternatives," he added.

"I also want people to be optimistic about their futures," he emphasized, "because if they have a good concept of the future, they will be looking forward to it."

Mr. Cochrane pointed out he intends the course to be "academic yet practical" and "applicable to life."

His plans for the class include covering topics such as "food for the future, energy consumption, nuclear energy, and waste problems."

Spring term may see the class on a field trip in the mountains.

"We will take a minimum amount of necessary items and try to live off the land for four or five days," Mr. Cochran elaborated.

—*Courier 4*, Chemetka Community College, Salem, Oregon

The fifth step, then, is to employ quotations where they may enhance a report. Doing so also enables you to include in a natural way the names of your news sources and other important people. Further, quotations allow you to print opinions without **editorializing**—without including your own opinions in the story. By quoting someone else's words, you are simply presenting the fact that the words were spoken, even though the words themselves express an opinion. And finally, quotations draw readers into your story, because the person quoted seems to be speaking directly to them.

A typical way of including quotations in news stories is to use them in alternate paragraphs. You may vary this plan, as in the example just given, to fit the particular story you are writing. And, of course, quotations must be significant ones that bring out important facts and not just examples of how a person speaks.

Some caution is necessary in employing direct quotations. When you enclose someone's words in quotation marks, you are responsible to him or her for the accuracy of the quotation. You and your newspaper could get into serious trouble if you **misquoted** someone, even by printing a single wrong word.

The only safe way to quote is to present exactly what a speaker has said. (You may, however, usually take the liberty of correcting grammatical errors and other slip-ups in language.) Accuracy in quoting requires extra attention while you are interviewing. Listen closely for short statements worth quoting and take careful notes.

Develop your own system of shorthand. Abbreviate words; leave out articles, conjunctions, and prepositions; invent symbols for words and

Quoting a news source adds variety to a story's arrangement and liveliness to its content. It also makes possible the inclusion of opinion within a factual report, for to state that someone said something is to state a fact.

names you use frequently. Your news source will usually be willing to wait while you copy short statements. You may find it advisable to read back what you have written so that both you and your news source can be sure it is accurate. Reporters often use a tape recorder, with the news source's permission, for the specific purpose of quoting correctly.

Be especially concerned about accuracy when quoting opinions, particularly on issues about which there may be differences. The viewpoints in the preceding story—for instance, "I want people to be optimistic about their futures"—are not controversial. But if, for example, a public official has made an unpopular decision and is giving you the reasons, be sure you quote exactly what you are told. Quotations do brighten your story, but they must be handled properly.

Identify Your Source

The following leads make statements typical of many that appear in school newspapers:

> Central High School has the most experienced first-string players of all the football teams in the league.
> The semester recess will be a day shorter this year.

If you write such leads, you can expect some of your readers to ask the question Who says so? Statements of this kind demand that you identify the people who provided the information that went into them and sometimes when, where, and why the information was released. After you add the authority of an identified source to each of these leads, they might sound like this:

> Central High School has the most experienced first-string players of all the football teams in the league, according to members of the Union High team interviewed at a practice session in preparation for Sunday's Central-Union game.
> The semester recess will be a day shorter this year, Principal Margaret Jones announced yesterday.

For your sixth step, then, you need to recognize that you must name a source in certain kinds of news reports—ones that include controversial statements, plans for special or unusual events, announcements of changes from established custom, and all personal opinions. You should also name your source for news you have not obtained from personal observation, for instance, news obtained from an interview. This protects you in case the information is incorrect. Then, too, by printing the name of your news source, you say "Thanks" and improve your chances of obtaining more news from that person for a future issue.

The source or authority for a story based on an opinion or a controversial statement should appear in your lead, ordinarily at the end of the last sentence. When you use the name of your news source in stories other than the special kinds just mentioned, the name belongs in a later paragraph.

Activity 4:   Identifying Sources

The following leads are incomplete because no authorities are given for statements of controversial facts and opinions. Rewrite the leads, (a) identifying a source for each statement and (b) specifying a suitable occasion (when, where, or why) for the statement.

1. Central High students are the most courteous in the entire state.

2. A student who accumulates five unexcused absences from any class will fail that course.

3. Names of more than 1,000 students will be printed in the Central High News this year.

4. Seventh graders are better spellers than ninth graders.

5. Because of the poor sportsmanship shown in last year's game, no boys' basketball game will be played this season between East High and West High.

Emphasize the Future, Explain the Past

"We've already heard all about it!" This is a frequent complaint against school newspapers. Reader interest cannot be maintained when the information in your stories is common knowledge around school before the paper comes out.

Since most news stories must be written four days to two weeks before the paper is published, a special effort must be made to make school news as fresh as possible. With this challenge in mind, the seventh step in school news story preparation is to anticipate the future while interpreting and explaining the past. Why did it happen? What will take place next? These become the questions your paper answers, instead of What happened last week?

Whether searching for news on your regular beat or covering a special assignment, be on the lookout for future happenings. News events taking place within the two weeks following your next publication date are what you want to know about. Ask questions and write your story with those future dates in mind.

Your newspaper has a place for past happenings, of course. Your readers are interested in your report of the dance they attended, the meeting in which they participated, the football game they saw. But in these stories they want explanations, reasons, and revelations of what is not common knowledge, rather than a rehash of the basic facts.

How can you successfully handle past news that is worth printing?

MAKE YOUR REPORT OF A PAST EVENT BRIEF.   If the event was covered by an advance story—a story about a forthcoming event—your only justification for a factual report is to introduce *new* facts. If you have very little to say that is new, make your report as brief as possible.

EMPHASIZE THE WHY? ANGLE.   Your story of a past event *can* be worthwhile if you interpret its meaning. Tell WHY a decision was made, what led up to it. Explain WHY the team was able to win, what this means to the next game. Interview news sources who can give you reasons for news events or suggest solutions to problems.

FEATURE THE FUTURE WHILE REPORTING THE PAST.   It requires knowhow and experience to talk about the future while treating the past. The following example of how this can be done comes from an article in the National Scholastic Press Association's publication *Helps*.

Suppose the Thespians elected new officers last week. It will be another week before the paper is out. Here are some important names, but the news will be two weeks old when it reaches your readers. How can you write this story to make it fresh and interesting a week hence?

Find out when the next meeting of the group will be held and what the program will be. Or perhaps the new president will comment that a committee is planning a spring picnic or that tryouts will be conducted soon for a class play. You now have something new to write about. Your story might read:

> Thespians will hear Miss Gloria Jones, director of Community Players, discuss new Broadway plays at their first meeting of the semester next Thursday. The meeting, scheduled for Room 101 in the activities period, will be open to any junior or senior, according to Tracy Abel, newly elected Thespian president.
>
> Officers chosen for the spring semester also include Susie Blank, vice-president; Jim Cole, secretary; and Janet Nelson, unanimously reelected treasurer.

Note that a stale date, two weeks old, has been eliminated. And, while the names of the new officers have been included, the real emphasis has been placed on what is going to happen.

Activity 5:   Evaluating News for Freshness

1. From the most recent issue of your school paper, select a story about a past event. Evaluate it by answering the following questions:

   a. How much of the information contained in the story had you known before the story was published?

   b. Did the story adequately emphasize why things had happened and what their consequences would be? Did the story reveal something not widely known about the past?

   c. Did the story feature the future adequately?

2. Read through the national or local news section of a daily paper and select another story about a past event.

   a. Compare the story with the school paper story by applying to it the three questions in Item 1. Which was the fresher story?

   b. Explain why a daily paper encounters less difficulty in publishing fresh news than a school paper.

When You Have Finished Reporting the Facts, Stop Writing

If you have followed the preceding seven steps, your written story is now complete. Next, check again for the five *W* and one *H* facts, as explained in Chapter 6. Whether or not these were included in your lead, all of them will usually appear somewhere in your story. Make sure you have answered all necessary questions.

When you have written the last fact of your story, write **—30—**, which stands for "The End," in the center of the next line on your paper:

—30—

Do not add a conclusion, a summary, or a moral. Do not add a plug ("Let's everyone come out to see this fine show"). Do not add any kind of editorializing ("We welcome Mr. Penn to the faculty"). To stop writing after stating the final fact may be a difficult matter for a beginning reporter. Yet doing so is necessary for a proper and effective ending.

If this reporter did his work properly, he wrote up all the facts summarized in the headline and the lead, made sure that the five W and one H questions were answered, and then stopped writing.

—Photo by Wil Blanche from DPI

Checklist for Constructing a News Story

☐ 1. Do I have a clear and complete grasp of my subject because I have assembled all the facts and information I need?

☐ 2. Have I followed all the steps in preparing a good lead?

☐ 3. Have I settled on the most suitable news story pattern for the material in my story?

☐ 4. If I am using an inverted-pyramid pattern, have I sorted out my facts so that each paragraph has less news value than the one before?

☐ 5. If I am using a chronological pattern, have I selected the important events and facts according to news value, summarized them in the lead, and presented them in correct sequence in the body?

☐ 6. If I am using a composite pattern, have I covered all key thoughts or all angles in the lead? Have I arranged the body so that each event is treated as a separate story, and have I chosen between an inverted-pyramid or a chronological pattern for these substories? Or, alternatively, have I arranged the body so that it treats first one angle, then another, and so on of my multiple subjects?

☐ 7. If I am departing from a standard overall story pattern, am I still making use where I can of a chronological or inverted-pyramid arrangement to keep my information well organized?

☐ 8. Are my paragraphs (a) limited to one topic each, (b) suitably brief, and (c) begun with the key thought expressed in forceful, striking words?

☐ 9. Have I made effective use of quotations?

☐ 10. Have I identified the sources of (a) all information I didn't get from personal observation, (b) all controversial statements and personal opinions, (c) all plans for upcoming events, and (d) all announcements of changes from custom?

☐ 11. Have I ensured that my news will be fresh by featuring the future or revealing something new about the past?

☐ 12. Have I concluded my story with a fact rather than with a nonfactual comment?

Activity 6:   Writing Good News Stories

1. Using the following set of reporter's notes, write a complete news story. Follow the steps explained in this chapter. Prepare your lead carefully. Then, arrange the facts of the story into approximately five paragraphs in inverted-pyramid order. Try to make the first words of each paragraph lively and interesting. You may make up details as necessary to develop the paragraphs.

   Best typists received awards
   In assembly last Friday
   Practiced speed typing daily in class for an entire week
   Each error counted against their speed
   From all typing classes of Miss Mary Bray
   17 students received certificates for typing 30–34 words a minute
   Bronze pins, 35–39 words a minute—Harriet Myers, Ronald Evans, Alice Johnson, Dorothy Flint
   Silver pins, 40–49 words—Maxine Peterson, Robert Wallace
   Gold pin, 50 words—Frank Egan

2. Complete the following steps.

   a. From the reporter's notes that follow, prepare a news story, the body of which is an chronological order. Write a good lead. You may make up details to develop the story.

   City Government Day
   One month from today (use an actual date)
   All three city high schools to take part
   Social studies classes studying city government in preparation
   Seniors in each school to nominate and elect 5 "council members" next week
   Those elected will meet to learn procedures of city council
   Other seniors to write application letters for positions as city department heads
   City council to select these on leadership and ability
   Day begins at 9 a.m.—council meets and dept. officials will work with respective city officials
   Luncheon served at 12:15 in civic center
   Mayor to speak
   Jobs to continue in afternoon; council members to visit various departments

   b. Which type of story, chronological or inverted-pyramid, seems better fitted to the news event described in *a*? Would it have been easier to write an inverted-pyramid story? Why or why not?

3. Prepare a composite news story from the following set of reporter's notes. Decide how to arrange your facts. Then, write a lead suitable for this particular arrangement. Keep the body of your story as interesting and factual as possible. Include the quotations found in the notes in appropriate places. Make up details as necessary.

   The following students from our school are going to Europe this summer:

   Kathy Murphy, senior, to Canada, England, and Scotland. She is one of four students from our city selected by British Embassy to represent the U.S. She will tour these countries with delegates from other English-speaking nations. "I hope to see the Queen," she says. She will stay with an English family.

   Jim Cole and Jerry Inman, juniors, will fly to Holland, then make their own way by land to Norway and Sweden. Jim says, "Looking for free rides is different over there. It's encouraged in those countries."

   Marjorie Barnard, freshman, and family, to Paris, Venice, the Alps. They plan to get their own car and drive.

   Becky MacDonald and Barbara Stillan, seniors, will visit Sue Miller, junior, whose father is stationed in Paris. "We plan to tour France, Germany, Switzerland, and Italy and return together," says Becky.

   Bill Neuhart, sophomore, will visit relatives in West Germany. He plans to live with a family all summer to "get the feel of living in a foreign country." Bill wants to go to college and then teach somewhere overseas.

Summary

This chapter explains the most important news story format—the inverted pyramid—and the three other basic ones: the chronological story, the composite story, and the story that dictates its own arrangement. It then presents eight steps that guide the writing of a news story.

    ARRANGING NEWS INTO AN INVERTED PYRAMID. In many news reports, the facts are arranged in the form of an inverted pyramid, with the most important ones first and the least significant last. As a result, the reader may find desired information more readily, a reporter is helped to think logically while writing the story, and the story's length may be easily adjusted to fit available space. The same standards apply to choosing facts for the paragraphs of an inverted-pyramid story as apply to choosing facts for a lead. Explain the key thought first and then present other facts according to their news value.

    RECOGNIZING OTHER BASIC NEWS STORY PATTERNS. Sometimes formats other than an inverted pyramid may be more suitable. A chronological arrangement may be used when occurrences should be narrated in the order in which they happened. Composite stories are suitable when you must handle a number of separate key thoughts linked by a common theme. And some stories dictate their own arrangement when their material resists one of the standard formats.

    WRITING A NEWS STORY. Reporters may apply eight steps to the process of writing a complete news story. The first is to obtain all the facts, getting a clear view of your subject, your main idea, your approach, and your emphases. The second is to write the lead, taking special care that the specific steps for writing a good one are followed. The third is to plan the body, having settled on a basic story pattern. The fourth is to construct good newspaper paragraphs by limiting each paragraph to one topic, keeping each paragraph short, and beginning each paragraph with a key thought, presented in forceful, striking words. The fifth step is to enliven your story with direct quotations, making sure that your quotations are accurate and significant. The sixth is to identify your sources, particularly when your information did not come from your own observation but also when your story involves controversy, opinion, plans for special or unusual events, or changes from what is customary or established. The seventh is to emphasize the future and explain the past—or (to put it another way) to see to it that you offer *fresh* news. The eighth is to stop writing when you've recorded your last fact, avoiding any conclusion, summary, moral, plug, or editorial.

Vocabulary

inverted pyramid	angle	misquote
chronological story	editorializing	—30—
composite story		

Review Questions

1. What are the most distinctive features of an inverted-pyramid news story?

2. Besides establishing the accurate time sequence of events, what else must be done to prepare a chronological news story?

3. How should a reporter go about preparing a composite news story?

4. What are the requirements for a good newspaper paragraph?

5. What principles should school news reporters follow to make sure that they report fresh news?

Discussion Questions

1. After reviewing the steps for writing a good lead, explain how these steps can help a reporter organize the rest of a story.

2. What can be said *against* writing a news story that dictates its own arrangement—against a story that makes no use of the standard news story patterns?

3. When does the use of quotations in a news story become excessive?

4. How easy would it be for a reporter to rely only on direct observation and disregard sources when covering news?

5. Why is it generally considered bad reporting to end a news story not with a fact but instead with an intelligent opinion, a conclusion, a well-intentioned request, or a suggestion? Are there times when ending a news story with something other than a fact is justified?

Chapter Project

Writing a Well-Constructed News Story

Working from a set of reporter's notes you have personally collected, write a complete news story. Include direct quotations. In a brief additional paragraph, point out examples from your story that demonstrate how you paid attention to as many of the steps in this chapter as possible.

WRITING IN NEWSPAPER STYLE

When you have completed this chapter you should be able to

Understand what "news English" is and follow eight key principles, or steps, in writing it effectively.

Present opinions without editorializing and state facts accurately and completely.

Handle correctly a few special aspects of newspaper style.

Develop and use a style sheet.

Doug Denison stared at the sheets of paper littering his study desk. How could he make this news story sound better? He had started to write it a dozen times! "How can I tell the news so that people will want to read it?" Beginning reporters struggle with this question, hoping to hit upon some magical solution to their problem.

Making Sentences Work for You

If your goal is to write in front page style, there is no substitute for day after day of practice: writing, listening to criticism, rewriting, striving to improve your work. But there are certain principles, or steps, that when followed put you on the right track for turning out news stories that have snap and sparkle.

The object of these steps—there are eight—is the writing of what may be called **news English.** City Editor Lee Merriman of the Pasadena *Star-News* called this "English with its sleeves rolled up" in his book *Between Deadlines*. News sentences are hard-working, direct, and full of life and vigor. Writing according to the following eight steps will "roll up the sleeves" of your sentences.

Start Sentences with Key Thoughts

The first step is to emphasize significant words. In most news sentences, this can be done by beginning with the subject—the word or words that tell what the sentence is about. Such an arrangement makes the sentence straightforward and easy to understand. Sometimes, of course, the key thought may best be emphasized by leading off a sentence with a prepositional phrase, participial phrase, dependent clause, or another construction. However, such sentences should not be used too frequently. They lend variety when introduced from time to time but make for difficult reading if overused. In any case, avoid unusual or awkward constructions.

Notice how the following weak sentences are improved by placing the subjects first:

WEAK:	Representing the club on the student council will be Joe Bradford and Susie Stoner.
BETTER:	Joe Bradford and Susie Stoner will represent the club on the student council.
WEAK:	There will be a talent show Friday night.
BETTER:	A talent show will be presented Friday night.
WEAK:	It is suggested that all student organizations have their pictures in the yearbook.
BETTER:	Every student organization should have its picture in the yearbook, according to committee members.

(In the first sentence of the last pair on page 161, "it" is technically the subject, but since it says nothing, it should be replaced by more significant words.)

Activity 1: Moving the Key Thought to the Front of a News Sentence

Rewrite each of the following sentences to place its key thought at the beginning. In most cases, you will accomplish this by putting the subject first. You may make other changes as necessary, but do not remove or distort any facts.

1. According to Miss Mary Nave, department head, "The majority of the students studying home economics are not planning to enter the field as a vocation."

2. Also to be represented at the senior assembly are Pacific University, Reed College, Seattle University, the University of Washington, and Washington State College.

3. Discussed also will be practical nursing and the state apprentice program.

4. It is planned to have the new shop building ready for the opening of school next fall.

5. Because teachers were attending the state convention, there was no school last Thursday or Friday.

Keep Sentences Short and Simple

The second step is to make most of your sentences simple sentences. In general, simple sentences are easier to read than compound sentences.

WEAK: The drama club will present "Death of a Salesman," and the music department will sponsor its annual musical.

BETTER: The drama club will present "Death of a Salesman." The music department will sponsor its annual musical.

The first of the two foregoing examples is a compound sentence because it is made up of two independent clauses joined by a comma and a coordinating conjunction *(and)*. The second of the two examples consists of two simple sentences (a simple sentence consists of a single independent clause).

Simple sentences also tend to work better than complex sentences.

WEAK: Key Club will sponsor a dance, for which The Raiders will provide music, in the gym after the awards ceremony.

BETTER: Key Club will sponsor a dance in the gym after the awards ceremony. The Raiders will provide the music.

The weaker of the two examples is a complex sentence because it consists of an independent clause ("Key Club will sponsor a dance . . . in the gym after the awards ceremony'') and a subordinate, or dependent, clause ("for which The Raiders will provide music").

Because short, simple sentences are easy to read, they make a news story seem brisk and quick-paced.

Activity 2:   Shortening and Simplifying a News Sentence

Rewrite the following sentences into good news English. Separate each into two or three shorter, simpler sentences. You may replace words if you wish but do not change any facts.

1. The art department, under the supervision of Mrs. Helene Selmer, made the decorations for the annual retirement dinner May 15 at Lincoln High, which is held to honor retired teachers and retiring teachers of the city schools.

2. When Mr. Franklin Davis was asked whether teen-age boys or teen-age girls committed the greater number of crimes, he said that 55 to 60 boys are placed in correctional institutions in our area each year and only about eight to ten girls.

3. Dr. Harmon A. Larson, superintendent of city schools, will open the program with a greeting, and the grade school choir and orchestra combined will present the first selection, directed by Ms. Janet Mathis, supervisor of music of the city schools.

4. Tickets for the all-school play, "The Music Man," are on sale at the activities office, which reports that almost all seats are sold for the Friday and Saturday performances and that not many are left for Wednesday or Thursday evenings.

5. Competition starts this afternoon for several stage bands at the Tri-State Music Festival in St. Louis, where the Central High stage band, having prepared a series of new numbers, will be shooting for its third consecutive win.

Use Familiar, Definite Words

The third step is to use familiar, definite words. Though you will want to develop a vocabulary of synonyms for common words, even these synonyms must be familiar to your reader. In the following pair of sentences, notice that the common word *named* communicates just as much as the less common word *designated* and does so in one-fourth the number of syllables.

WEAK: Pat Doherty has been designated editor of the News.

BETTER: Pat Doherty has been named editor of the News.

Moreover, each of your words should leave no doubt in the reader's mind what you mean. Be sure that your words communicate what you intend. For instance, does *very few* always mean the same thing to the reader as it does to the writer? Consider the sentences at the top of page 164.

WEAK: Very few students were present at the meeting.

BETTER: Eight students were present at the meeting.

How many students are "very few"? To the writer, eight. But to the reader, "very few" could mean any number from three on. Both "very" and "few" are too indefinite to give a clear idea. Changing "very few" to "eight" leaves no doubt what the writer meant.

Activity 3:   Choosing the Familiar, Definite Word

Use more familiar, more definite words to replace those in italics. Rewrite each sentence to include the new words of your choice.

1. *Several* plays will be *dramatized* this spring.
2. Teachers have been *perturbed* by *tumultuous* noise in the hall.
3. Seniors are *anticipating* the arrival of class rings *presently*.
4. The honor roll *customarily* is *promulgated* during the first week of the semester.
5. Parent-Teacher Night was scheduled for *shortly* after the *issuance* of report cards.

State Each Idea Briefly

The fourth step is to state each thought in a news sentence in the briefest way possible. Beginning reporters frequently use too many words to express an idea. The first of the two sentences that follow is made up of 15 words, the second of six. Both say the same thing.

WEAK: The newly accepted members will be formally admitted into the organization in an initiation ceremony.

BETTER: The organization will initiate new members.

You should think of excess words as fat. After you have written a sentence, look it over critically. Can you reduce several words to one word without loss of meaning? Can you simply throw out some words? Notice how much trimmer the second sentence is in the following pair:

WEAK: The day's agenda for those attending the picnic will include swimming, hiking, and riding.

BETTER: Picnic-goers will swim, hike, and ride.

Since a reader of your school newspaper assumes that its reports concern your school, omit the school name in most stories.

WEAK: Bob Walker, who is a Central High School senior . . .

BETTER: Senior Bob Walker . . .

That or *which* when used to introduce a subordinate clause may often be eliminated, as in the improved sentence shown on page 165. An even better solution in some cases may be to turn the clause into a phrase, thereby shortening the sentence.

News English at its simplest and briefest can be seen in the items that appear on public news boards like this one in Times Square, New York City. Trimming off excess words without loss of meaning is an important newswriting skill.

—Photo by Betty Schlossberg from Monkmeyer

WEAK: The Tigers lost the game that they played last Friday.
IMPROVED: The Tigers lost the game they played last Friday.
BETTER: The Tigers lost the game played last Friday.

Activity 4:   Rewriting a News Sentence for Brevity

The following sentences are wordy. Rewrite all or part of each to eliminate the wordiness without losing any of the ideas.

1. "The Silver Wedding" is the play that the junior college students are preparing for a one-act-play night.

2. In conclusion he again thanked everyone from the bottom of his heart for inviting him to take part.

3. At the end of each lecture there will be a discussion period of at least 45 minutes, during which the study group members will pose any questions and discuss what they have learned.

4. There is a deficiency of males in the Central High School drama class.

5. It seems there will be ample parking facilities at the new school for all of the students who drive automobiles to school.

6. Students are conscious that securing a complete education is of paramount importance to the success of their future lives.

7. Parent-Teacher Nights present an opportune time for the mothers and fathers to investigate the scholastic status of their children.

8. The Smith Sports Trophy is a sports award given every single year to a public secondary school that has attained the best overall sports records in athletics.

9. Readers would probably be interested in knowing that George Lee won first place, for which accomplishment he was awarded the first prize of $50.

10. The question that they discussed concerned dating on the part of teenagers.

Use Nouns as Modifiers

The fifth step—using nouns as modifiers—may appear, at first glance, to violate certain stylistic standards. However, this is not the case. Writers in general as well as writers of news English often employ nouns as modifying words both for brevity and for exactness. For example, the phrase *money problems* is somewhat briefer and often more appropriate than *monetary problems, financial problems,* or *fiscal problems.* Notice how in each of the following examples a single noun does the work of a phrase:

WEAK: An assembly for the students is planned.
BETTER: A student assembly is planned.

WEAK: The junior prom for this year . . .
BETTER: This year's junior prom . . .

WEAK: Lisa Stevens, a member of the sophomore class . . .
BETTER: Sophomore Lisa Stevens . . .

WEAK: Winners of the gold key are . . .
BETTER: Gold key winners are . . .

Activity 5:   Replacing Phrases with Nouns

Whenever possible, eliminate prepositional phrases in the following sentences by using nouns as modifiers. Remove other unnecessary words as well, when you can do so without changing the meaning.

1. Because of an error by the typist, the name of Don Compton was omitted from the list on page 3 of the last issue of the paper.

2. The play that won high praise at the drama festival at the city college will be presented in the auditorium.

3. Leaders of the student body from the junior high will be invited to attend a meeting of the student council at Central High, to make a tour of the campus of Central High, and to have lunch with members of the student council.

4. Members of the chapter of the National Honor Society at Central High will see a game of baseball as their activity for their half-holiday during this semester.

5. The Aquatic School of the Red Cross, at College Park from June 1 to June 10, will enroll students in water safety courses in preparation for summer jobs as lifeguards.

Write with Colorful Words

The sixth step is to visualize your subject matter as you write your sentences. Certain topics almost demand to be portrayed with colorful words. Descriptive or action stories in particular require words that convey sense impressions—impressions of something seen, heard, touched, smelled, or tasted—but all your stories will be improved if your sentences create word pictures. The following sentences show how various parts of speech may furnish interesting description:

VERBS: June's face *flushed* as the public-address system *trumpeted* her triumph.

NOUNS: The *murmurs* and *mutterings* increased in volume as the consequences of the new budget became ever more clear.

ADJECTIVES: At the yearbook photograph session, the *ruddy* cheeks and *bronze* arms of the golf and baseball teams seemed all the more *sun-baked* when viewed alongside the *lunar* paleness of the astronomy club.

ADVERBS: With 20 seconds left, Caldwell brought the ball up court so *casually*, so *thoughtlessly* (it seemed), that not even the hair-trigger responsiveness of Westlake's defense was up for the rapid pass he sent to Hagan.

Descriptive or action stories, such as those treating athletic events, require colorful words that convey sense impressions. If a reporter describes two players fighting for a rebound, the reader should be able to "see" the scene.

—Photo by Eric A. Roth from The Picture Cube

In writing news stories, you should give your reader a vivid impression by selecting bright, active, concrete words and phrases. Your descriptive terms need not be unusual. Choose widely used words, but look for ones that enable your readers to see with the eyes of the mind what you have seen with your physical eyes.

Whenever you read a newspaper story that draws you into the events reported, examine the kinds of words the writer used. You are likely to find that the words are specific, clear terms based on sense impressions. In your own writing, follow the practice of good reporters by searching for the right word to give the reader a vivid sense of what you have seen, heard, experienced, and learned.

The writer of the following humorous article chose his words with care. Notice how many of his words and phrases are based on sense impressions.

Frisbee throwers join in spring fling

By Scott Juengel

Sitting in class, my face pressed flat against the window pane, I watched the people play frisbee in the courtyard. As a class discussion droned on behind me, I realized for the first time that spring had sprung. At the sound of the bell, I bolted out the door, leaving papers hovering in my wake.

Reaching the grassy quadrangle, I fell to my knees, trembling. After two months of cabin fever and snow, the sight of something green had a unique effect on me. I pulled up handfuls of grass and threw them over my head, shrieking happily. Soon, however, a crowd began to gather, and I stopped before I made a complete fool of myself in front of my peers.

Eyeing one of the frisbee throwers across the yard, I hollered, "Fire it over here," and fire it he did. The saucer floated, dove, and bounced with the wind currents. Using my analytical mind and common sense, I bent over, figuring I would make the catch around my ankles. It struck me right on the chin.

I quickly came to, and finding the frisbee still spinning on my chest, I leapt to my feet to return the throw. My form was a little rusty though, and the saucer flew into a Spanish class in the opposite direction.

Suddenly an irate "hombre" came to the window. After a few choice Spanish phrases, he flung the plastic tortilla onto a neighboring rooftop.

I thought this was a dumb game anyway, so I proceeded to my next class. Once seated, I began to ponder the great questions of spring.

Should I wear shorts? Would my roll-on stay on, or would I have to move to the back of the room for the general welfare of the class? Would I stand out like a sore thumb because I did not look like I was cooked with the Thanksgiving turkey and did not go to Florida, getting only as far south as the Essex parking lot?

A bead of sweat rolled down my face and splattered my textbook, breaking my concentration and making me realize just how hot it really was. I then looked at my grimy pants and felt my jaw, still sore from where the flying saucer had utilized my face as a landing pad, and I remembered just how nice it was with snow on the ground.

—*The Kirkwood Call*, Kirkwood High School, Kirkwood, Missouri

Activity 6:   Drawing Word Pictures

Replace the words in italics with more colorful or vivid terms. Rewrite the sentences if necessary. Use your imagination! Try to see what the writer saw and then draw a word picture for the reader.

1. A basketball game *has plenty of fast action*.
2. Students and faculty have *worked hard to raise money* for a foreign exchange student.
3. Students *who are interested in* surfing may *get a chance to prove their skill* by entering the competition.
4. The band *performed an interesting demonstration of marching maneuvers*.
5. Central High *won all the awards* because of the *interesting drawings* entered in the art show.

Make Greater Use of Verbs and Verbals

The seventh step calls for using active and colorful verbs in place of duller adjectives and adverbs. Professional newswriters often use lively verbs to shorten their sentences and turn out vivid copy. One way to do this is to take the thought from a modifier and include it in the sentence's main verb, as shown in the following examples:

WEAK: He *walked slowly* down the hall.
BETTER: He *strolled* down the hall.

WEAK: Five new clubs *have made final* plans for the year.
BETTER: Five new clubs *have completed* plans for the year.

Another way is to use participles in place of adjectives or infinitives in place of weaker phrases or clauses. Such verbals—words derived from verbs but used as nouns, adjectives, or adverbs—carry a strong element of action.

WEAK: The association will award $50 for the *best* float.
BETTER: The association will award $50 for the *winning* float.

WEAK: Classes are learning *the operation of* office machines.
BETTER: Classes are learning *to operate* office machines.

Activity 7:   Improving Sentences with Verbs and Verbals

Improve these sentences by using strong verb forms to replace the phrases in italics. You may rewrite or rearrange the sentences if you wish.

1. His fist *struck hard against* the table to emphasize his words.
2. She *quickly wrote a nearly illegible* message and dropped it near him.
3. Everyone agreed that it was a *good* game.

4. Have you learned *the composition of* a business letter?

5. He promised *that more emphasis would be placed on* fundamentals.

Include Names

The eighth step is to include names in your sentences whenever possible. Since people make news, it makes sense to name the newsmakers. Not only do readers in general respond to names in news reports, but readers of school newspapers are especially interested when they come upon the names of people they know—other students, teachers, community figures, themselves.

A news story must be more than a list of names, of course. But after you answer the question What happened? the question Who did it? is the next one to answer. If a name is important enough, place it in the lead. If not, introduce it whenever it may be included in a natural way. A quotation is one handy way of adding names, since speakers must be identified.

WEAK: The decorations committee plans a color theme of white and silver.

BETTER: "The color theme will be white and silver," said Pam Scofield, head of the decorations committee.

WEAK: The advanced typing classes will also participate.

BETTER: Mr. Howard Kenyon's advanced typing classes will also participate.

Choir goes to national fest

By Anne Kenney

Due to the reputation and success of the South vocal jazz program, the Dorians have been invited to the National Association of Jazz Educators Convention in Kansas City, Mo., Jan. 12-16.

Audition tapes were sent in from all over the country, but the judges were not satisfied with the results, said Vocal Director James DeBusman. The South program was highly recomended by several people, so the judges invited the ensemble.

"This is the most prestigous jazz education event in the country," said DeBusman, "and this is the first time a school has been invited without auditioning."

At the convention, the Dorians will be the clinition group. They will do a 50-minute session with several different directors in front of an audience. The sessionwill be video-and cassette-taped and circulated nationally, said DeBusman.

Kansas City-bound Dorians are: (front row) George Helbling, Dave Gustafson, Chris Marko, Andrew Sherman, Dan Bray (second row) Jennifer Kemp, Heather James, Kristy Jacobsen, Pam Owens, Anna Lauris, Shannon Curran; (third row) Tracy Robertson, Chris Tarantola, Julie Keener,

Nigel Sellers, Jordan Schick, Holly Hill; (back row) Gary Graham, Chris Bolden, Brad Gray, Shawn Humes, Mike Vergamini, Dan Shively, Jeff Nielsen, director Jim DeBusman, Tim Clarke, Glen Bonney, Matt Elliott, Tim Farley.

The rest of the time students will go to other sessions, learning from some of the best jazz professionals in the world, including Count Basie, Joe Turner, Freddy Green and Jay McShane, said DeBusman.

For the trip the students need to raise $16,000, said Mary Inch, trip coordinator.

Parents of the Dorians have formed an organization to help raise the money. The parents are organizing such fund raisers as a garage sale and a bowl-a-thon.

A story such as this one of a school vocal group makes it natural to include not only a photograph of students but also a good number of names. School newspaper readers are pleased to see the names of friends and acquaintances in print.

—*The Axe*, South Eugene High School, Eugene, Oregon

The following checklist will help you to include all the names you reasonably can in a news story.

✓ Checklist for Names

Have I included the names of the following:

☐ 1. All major news sources?

☐ 2. Any other people who have offered useful comments or opinions?

☐ 3. The most important participants in an event?

☐ 4. Other participants who have played significant roles?

☐ 5. Present officers or leaders of an organization when relevant?

☐ 6. Past officers or leaders of an organization when relevant?

☐ 7. Members of classes, teams, clubs, and organizations who have played significant parts in an event?

☐ 8. Teachers, administrators, and other adults involved in a meeting, organization, or activity?

☐ 9. School board members or community residents involved in, affected by, or with something to say about an event?

☐ 10. People who may be significantly affected in the future by a present event?

Activity 8:   Getting Names into News Reports

Rewrite the following news sentences to add made-up names wherever you can. Do not, however, include so many names that they overload your new sentences.

1. The band and majorettes led the parade.

2. Final preparations for this year's annual science fair are being made this week.

3. Opening the talent show, to be staged before a dramatic background built by the stage crew, will be the jazz band.

4. Numerous students have earned service award pins, it was announced yesterday.

5. The club, expecting about 55 to attend, has reserved a special room at the restaurant.

6. Dr. Margaret Sanderson will be the new principal of Ralph Waldo Emerson High School.

7. Robert Kilmartin is school winner in this year's Voice of Democracy contest.

8. Andrea Roberts has been elected student-body president.

9. Mayor Paul Brown said that the village renovation program will temporarily inconvenience the owners of several business establishments in the general area.

10. The school board was divided over the value of the proposed Ecology Day.

Activity 9: Writing News English

1. Rewrite these sentences in news English. You should apply all eight of the steps for writing news English to each sentence. Make up additional facts or names as necessary.

   a. All academic activity ceased for about 40 minutes last Friday morning when the kitchen of the elementary school caught fire. Students in the east wing of the high school could see what was going on.

   b. This semester the advanced biology classes are going to start on some new projects. Some of the projects will be raising white rats and breeding them, trying to hatch eggs in an incubator, and raising guinea pigs and hamsters.

   c. The new building will house the gymnasium, which has been equipped with a folding stage so that it can be used as an auditorium until some future time when an auditorium proper can be constructed. The gym will seat 500.

2. Find a brief essay or other prose selection whose contents could be made into a news story. Rewrite it in lively news English. Add an explanation of what changes you made in the piece of writing with which you started.

Presenting Opinions and Facts Clearly

You have already read about the distinctions between fact and opinion, as well as about the responsibility of news people to be accurate and fair. Now you, as a reporter and writer, are concerned with the practical matter of preparing acceptable news stories. In everything you write, you must deal responsibly with factual statements and with people's opinions.

Avoid Editorializing in News Reports

When you are reporting news, state only facts. Keep your opinions out of your story. Do not let them affect your choice of facts or your way of reporting them. Be objective. Newspaper editors state their opinions in editorials. From this comes the term *editorializing*, which refers to a reporter's expressing his or her opinion in what should be a purely factual news story. Most newspaper readers do not want to know what a reporter may think about a news event. They wish to be told only what happened. If an opinion is desired, readers will turn to the editorial page.

Simple forms of editorializing are illustrated by the following statements:

> Come on, students, let's go to the game!
>
> It was a successful meeting.
>
> The News is happy to announce that . . .

Such editorializing is as easy for the reader to detect as it should have been for the reporter to avoid. Not so simple is the kind in which reporters permit personal feelings or opinions to color their factual writing. A careless choice of a single verb or adjective may change the reader's attitude toward the facts. News stories about political activities or controversial issues are most likely to include editorializing of this kind, for it is in these areas that reporters tend to have strong personal opinions. The following paragraph contains several examples of this kind of editorializing. Can you identify them?

> The governor, anticipating reelection even though his political fortunes have wavered recently, will address the state meeting Tuesday. Although known to be lukewarm toward the proposed tax reform, the governor is apparently satisfied to have the delegates come together and argue out an issue that seems likely to tear the party wide open at the July convention.

Notice particularly the phrases "political fortunes have wavered," "apparently satisfied," and "seems likely to tear the party wide open." While some of these may be factual, there is no evidence presented in this paragraph to support the statements or prove their truth. They must, for the moment, be considered expressive of the reporter's personal opinions and, therefore, editorializing. This brings up another point. What may in one sentence be editorializing may in another be factual reporting. The difference often depends on whether other statements make clear the factual nature of the statements in question.

Activity 10: Detecting and Eliminating Editorializing

1. List each instance of editorializing in the story below and in the story at the top of page 174. There are at least five in the first story, several of them stemming from single words. There are even more instances in the second story.

Town youth meeting draws 140 students

Despite the rain, 140 eager teenagers participated in the "Youth in Our Town" meeting held Saturday at Central High.

Mr. Edward G. Jones, administrative assistant to the city manager, narrated, with the help of slides, an interesting report entitled "Midtown: A Story of Growth and Change."

Mr. Jones described some of the social, political, and economic changes that have taken place during the last 50 years. He did not mention freeway development, which many people think has brought more change to Midtown than any other factor.

A panel discussion, full of exciting arguments, followed for an hour and a half.

After lunch, which was made enjoyable by the music of the talented Continentals, there were more talks about the role of youth in the community. The whole meeting was very worthwhile and educational.

New restaurant class draws attention

An interesting new class entitled "Restaurant Occupations" has recently been added to the curriculum, and students are encouraged to sign up for it.

The program will introduce students to the endless variety of high-paying jobs open to them in the food industry, where they will find a good future with considerable opportunities to advance.

Next week the students will begin working with the capable cooks in the cafeteria, where their duties will range from the drudgery of making sandwiches to the excitement of serving at the snack bar.

At the recent Back-to-School Night, class members served tasty doughnuts as well as peanut butter cookies that must have been made in class at least a month ago.

---

2. Rewrite the following story to eliminate all editorializing. Leave only the facts.

Cabinet reps to be elected Friday

First-year students will receive their first chance to gain valuable voices in student government next Friday, when they vote for fall semester cabinet representatives during lunch hour.

A primary election scheduled for last Tuesday unfortunately had to be canceled owing to the small number of candidates. Freshmen apparently do not yet understand the desirability of supporting their student government.

Voting will take place in the patio outside the office, and everyone who is eligible to vote should make an effort to be there. Each voter must have proof of identification in the form of a student-body card or library card. Some other kinds of proof are probably acceptable.

Jennifer Flint, the capable former student-body president of King Junior High, is the sole candidate for freshman president. Kelly Flynn, who had experience at King in secretarial work, and Dick Henderson are the candidates for corresponding secretary.

Use Direct or Indirect Quotations to Introduce Opinions

Opinion may be included in factual news stories only as the content of someone's reported statement. The actual reporting of such a statement—even one containing an opinion—is in itself a factual presentation. The statements should be reported either as **direct quotations** or as **indirect quotations.** A direct quotation presents the exact words of a speaker; it is enclosed in quotation marks. An indirect quotation presents what a speaker said but not the exact words; it is not enclosed in quotation marks. The difference can be seen in the sentences at the top of page 175.

DIRECT QUOTATION: "The conference was successful," said Jack Martin, student-body president.

INDIRECT QUOTATION: Student-body president Jack Martin said that the conference was successful.

When using direct or indirect quotations to report opinions, you should be doing so for the sake of factual accuracy. In other words, what somebody feels or believes should be as relevant a fact as what somebody has done. You should not be using quotations to slant the news in accordance with your own values, beliefs, or opinions. That would be bad reporting.

**Activity 11: Introducing Opinions
Through Direct and Indirect Quotations**

The following five sentences express opinions. Rewrite each first as a direct quotation and then as an indirect quotation. In each case, make up a suitable speaker and, if necessary, an occasion.

1. No doubt Dean of Studies Carol Stanton was proud of the superb results achieved by the advanced placement English students.

2. With eight seconds left in the fourth quarter, Heath lofted the 50-yard touchdown pass that will be remembered as long as there is a Central High football team.

3. The school budget for next year is not exactly one to make the teams and clubs leap for joy.

4. Because of the great interest in the production, those wishing to attend are advised to buy tickets early.

5. Going by his track record as Eastview's college admissions adviser, it seems that the addition this year of Mr. John Sarmiento to Central's guidance department can only raise the percentage of seniors getting into good four-year colleges.

State Facts Accurately and Completely

Assume that a well-known writer from *National Affairs* magazine, Mr. J. Q. Downing, had spent three days visiting Central High School. He collected information about the new building, school curriculum, student council, and community and visited many classes. When interviewed by a school newspaper reporter, he made the following comment: "I cannot positively say that the material I gathered will ever be used in *National Affairs* magazine. However, if it is accepted, it will probably be a part of a feature article explaining the makeup of a good high school."

The school reporter later wrote a story about Mr. Downing's visit to the school. The first three paragraphs of the story are shown at the top of page 176.

Central High is among several secondary schools to be featured in National Affairs magazine soon.

Mr. J. Q. Downing, a writer for the magazine, spent three days last week studying the new high school building and its educational program. He attended a student council meeting and visited many classes.

Mr. Downing stated that he would put his findings into a short article for his magazine, which would probably be a part of a feature concerning the makeup of a good high school.

A comparison of the school news paragraphs and the preceding information reveals a number of inaccuracies. For example, the information made no mention of "several secondary schools" nor did Mr. Downing say that Central High was "to be featured . . . soon." In fact, he did not promise that the school would be featured at all.

The inaccurate reporting was, no doubt, not deliberate. It was probably due to such things as defective note taking, lack of practice in using words to capture reality, and carelessness. One general lesson is plain. Extreme care is needed to report things accurately—care in finding out the facts, care in recording them as notes, and care in turning the notes into a news story.

A special kind of inaccuracy that you should watch out for is the half-truth. A half-truth is a statement that is misleading or puzzling not because facts have been presented inaccurately but because facts have been omitted. The following is an example.

Mrs. Dora Swenson has resigned from the Central High faculty. "A substitute will take over her classes until a new permanent teacher is hired," Principal A. F. Roberts announced.

This report is puzzling. Why did Mrs. Swenson resign? It may even be misleading. Not stating why Mrs. Swenson resigned may be a way of suggesting that her resignation was not voluntary—that she was asked to resign because her superiors were displeased with her in some way. A reporter should either tell the truth as completely as necessary or else not write the story.

Activity 12:   Reporting Accurately and Completely

1. Review the information given about the visit of Mr. Downing to Central High School. Then, write an evaluation of the accuracy of the following paragraphs.

   Because Central High is one of the best high schools in the United States, it will be featured in National Affairs magazine. Mr. J. Q. Downing, a writer for the magazine, spent three days last week visiting here and collecting material.

   Mr. Downing was particularly interested in the new building, which is said to be one of the country's finest. Central's student government was another object of his study.

   Many classes were visited by the writer in an attempt to understand the operation of a well-run high school class.

2. Explain why the following is an example of incomplete reporting:

   Chip Copeland, star Central running back, was carried from the field on a stretcher just before the end of the third quarter. The game continued without him, and Central scored twice in the final period to win, 13-6.

3. Select from a daily newspaper a story that you feel does not report the whole truth or all the essential facts. Indicate the unanswered questions.

Mastering the Details of Newspaper Style

Good newspaper style requires more than just the ability to write "English with its sleeves rolled up" and to handle opinions and facts properly. It requires mastery of a great many details of style and special features of reporting. A few that all good reporters must know about will now be considered. They have to do with using appropriate pronouns, keeping time references clear, and achieving reliability in the treatment of names, unfamiliar or hard-to-spell words, and facts and figures.

Use Pronouns Suitable for Newspaper Writing

News stories are supposed to be impersonal. Hence, they rely mainly on third-person pronouns (*he, she, it, they,* and their related forms). If a first-person pronoun (*I, we*) or a second-person pronoun (*you*) appears, it could mean that the reporter has lapsed into editorializing.

Once in a while, referring to yourself may be unavoidable. When this happens, say "I" or "me," rather than use a stilted expression like "this reporter." The need to refer to yourself is most likely to arise in an interview story, when you as a reporter are asking questions, or in an eyewitness account. Even then, you should avoid such references unless they are essential in making the story logical and clear.

In editorials, the first-person plural *(we* or *us)* may be used to suggest that the writer is expressing the views of the newspaper staff. This conventional use of *we* normally does not extend to any other kind of newspaper article.

You should also take care not to misuse third-person pronouns, particularly *they* and *them.* Make sure that the reader knows what noun your pronoun refers to. In the first of the following examples, the word *they* could represent either the Orioles or the Giants. In the second example, the first *they* stands for "yearbook sales," but the second *they* is totally unclear. Both examples need to be rewritten to make sure the reader will understand.

CONFUSING: In an intramural game yesterday between the Orioles and Giants, *they* scored seven runs in the first inning.

UNCLEAR: Yearbook sales are just about half of what *they* should be. *They* must sell 800 yearbooks and have at the present time sold 408.

Activity 13: Selecting the Right Pronoun

Rewrite each of the following news story passages so that all pronouns are appropriate to their news context as well as clear to the reader. You may have to change, add, or remove words.

1. Within minutes the fire engines arrived. The chief ordered me and the rest of the onlookers to cross the street and remain behind the police barriers. He repeated the order more forcibly when he saw that we were not moving off quickly enough.

2. As Harry Smith was being handcuffed and led away, he turned to this reporter and asked yours truly to phone his parents and tell them what had happened before they read about it in the papers.

3. Principal Carol LaRue's answer to the question was: "No, the schedule will be basically the same." When I asked if the schedule would still be unchanged next semester, she said to me that no final decision had been made.

4. Have you heard the moans and groans coming from the west gym? They are training for this year's first gymnast meet, reports Ms. Leslie Thornton, head of girls' phys ed.

5. Ninth and tenth graders are battling for first place in this year's annual fund-raising drive. They hope to be ahead after the carwash scheduled for this weekend.

Base Time References on Publication Dates

Imagine that a reporter sits down on a Monday, the first day of the month, to write a story that will be published on Monday, the fifteenth day of the month. The story is a report of an assembly that took place a few hours before the reporter sat down to write. It begins: "Five exchange students from Europe and Asia were introduced to Central's students at today's assembly." What is wrong with this lead? Nothing—except that when the story is read on the fifteenth of the month, "today" will refer not to the fifteenth but to the first day of the month. In other words, the reporter forgot to adjust time references to match the reader's time frame, which is based on the date of publication. The reader expects "today" to refer to the day the paper comes out, "next week" to refer to the week following that of publication, and so on. If these expectations are not met, confusion results.

The suggestion for reporters to follow is simply this: Make the **publication date** the basis of all time references. The date of publication should be referred to as "today," the day before publication as "yesterday," and the day after as "tomorrow." For events that will take place on other days during the week before and the week after publication, you should use the day of the week: "last Tuesday" or "next Tuesday." For any other time, use the date itself: "March 12." Do not include the year unless the date is more than a year away.

Activity 14: Clarifying Time References

Determine the publication date of the next issue of your school newspaper. Then, using a calendar, decide what would be the proper way to refer to each of the following dates.

1. Monday, the same week
2. Monday, the following week
3. Monday, the preceding week
4. Monday, the second week before
5. Monday, the second week after
6. Thursday, the same week
7. Wednesday, the same week
8. Friday, the following week
9. Friday, the preceding week
10. Wednesday, the following week

Check Names, Spelling, and Facts for Accuracy

Names make news. A reader is delighted when his or her name is printed. But that delight turns to disappointment and even to anger if the name is misspelled. Learn the correct spelling of a name when working on a story. Copy it accurately and legibly. If it is given orally, ask for the spelling. When necessary, look up the name. Your news office should have a di-

Careful newswriters will make the effort to check the spelling both of unfamiliar words and of familiar words whose spelling they are unsure of.

—Photo by David S. Strickler from The Picture Cube

rectory of teachers as well as a directory or card file of student names. If not, there's a file in the school office to which you can refer. A little extra time to check on the spelling of a name can save a lot of embarrassment. Also, type or print the correct name—don't write it—in your copy. Then there can be no excuse for typists' or printers' mistakes.

Next, be careful about the spelling of other words. A standard dictionary is your best authority on spelling and usage, but concise spelling dictionaries or lists of spelling demons are also helpful. When news sources use technical or unfamiliar words, be sure you understand them. One student reporter wrote "non-ten-year teachers" when the news source had been talking about "nontenured teachers." The reporter may have never before come across the word *tenure* and so was inclined to "hear" the more familiar words *ten* and *year*.

Finally, be critical of facts, figures, and statistics. Almost every such item in a story must be checked for accuracy. When covering school news, check them by requesting access to such official records and documents as are kept in the school office, the athletic director's office, and the attendance office. If you must check with a person, choose someone in a position to provide reliable factual information, such as an administrator. For facts, figures, and statistics concerning your community, check with government offices—city hall, village or town offices, for example—or your local public library (more and more public libraries are offering information services above and beyond the circulation of books). And, of course, learn how to use such standard reference sources as encyclopedias, almanacs, atlases, biographical dictionaries, books of quotations, standard handbooks for the sciences, the directories and statistical volumes published by the United States government, and so on. Checking facts, figures, and statistics for accuracy may not be fun. But mastery of the means to do so offers a satisfaction beyond fun.

Activity 15: Correcting Inaccuracies in Content

After examining the following passage from a feature story, list and correct the misspelled words and the factual errors.

After she arrived in the United States from her home in the port city of Bogotá, Columbia, Maria traveled throughout the United States. At the suggestion of her father, a former ambasador, she visited a number of state capitols and other prominent cities. "I really enjoyed Los Angeles," she said of California's capital. "I liked the accomodations in the big city hotels and did not find the people in your cities so agressive as I had been told they were. Mostly, they were nice."

Asked whether Americans were as nice as the people of her Central American homeland, Maria looked puzzled and did not reply. Her most memorable experience, she later said, was "getting my first view down into the Grand Canyon"—which in places cuts about 1 mile (1.6 kilometers) deep into Colorado and widens to about 18 miles (2.9 kilometers).

Using a Style Sheet

A newspaper should have a **style sheet** or **stylebook.** This is a collection of examples and rules of style for spelling, names, numbers, capitalization, abbreviations, punctuation, and so on. A style sheet makes it possible for all material in a particular newspaper to be consistent in the small details of writing and so smoother to read.

Consider the handling of an address. Any one of the following styles might be acceptable:

> 700 South Twenty-second Street
>
> 700 South 22nd Street
>
> 700 S. 22nd St.
>
> 700 S 22 St

But a mixture of styles would be unacceptable. Switching from one style of address to another and perhaps to yet another jars the reader and gives an impression of carelessness.

Readers can also be distracted by variations in other stylistic elements. A word may have two correct spellings, but if you use both of them you add needless confusion to your writing. Irregular capitalization or abbreviations can lead your reader to stop concentrating on your message and pause either to sort out the irregularities or to figure out what it is that is making the story hard to read. A consistent style keeps the focus on the message.

Many professional newspapers have adopted *The Associated Press Stylebook* or *The New York Times Manual of Style and Usage* for their reporters and editors. While such stylebooks should be readily available to school reporters, each school newspaper should assemble its own style sheet that will answer questions of style that arise from local names, places, and so on. Included in this style sheet will be spelling and capitalization rules for school courses and organizations, rules for abbreviations, and rules for referring to other matters that are peculiar to the school and its surroundings. Listings of examples will help reporters and editors to answer their stylistic questions quickly and with certainty.

Develop the habit of contributing and referring to your style sheet. The sample style sheet on pages 498–501 in the Editor's Handbook may be used until you assemble your own.

Activity 16: Developing a Style Sheet

Choose one of the numbered lists in the style sheet in the Editor's Handbook on pages 498–501 and adjust it to work better for your particular school and community. You can add useful local examples and any new items you think worthwhile. You can also change or take out items that you would like to see treated differently in your paper.

Summary

This chapter explains news English and presents eight principles, or steps, for writing in a vigorous newspaper style. Next, it considers how to treat fact and opinion properly. The chapter goes on to consider a few special aspects of reporting—using pronouns in keeping with newswriting conventions, keeping time references clear, and achieving reliability in details of content. Finally, the use and makeup of a style sheet are treated.

MAKING SENTENCES WORK FOR YOU.   Following certain useful steps can help you develop an effective newswriting style. Start a sentence with its key thought, usually by making this idea the subject of the sentence. Keep sentences short and simple. Use familiar, definite words. Express each idea briefly. Use nouns as modifiers. Write with colorful words. Make verbs and verbals do the work of weaker forms of expression. And include names.

PRESENTING OPINIONS AND FACTS CLEARLY.   Readers of news want a clear separation between what happened and what someone thinks about it. Always keep the reporter's personal viewpoint out of news reports, but do add the relevant, newsworthy opinions of news sources. These opinions may be presented in direct or indirect quotations. And they must always be properly attributed to their sources. Seek a clear grasp of the facts obtained from a news source and state them accurately, taking special care to avoid half-truths.

MASTERING THE DETAILS OF NEWSPAPER STYLE.   Because news stories are supposed to be impersonal, they are written in the third-person point of view. First- and second-person pronouns are usually improper. For clarity, time references should be based on the time of publication, not the time of writing. Reporters should check the spelling of names and other words and also check for accuracy of facts, figures, and statistics.

USING A STYLE SHEET.   Editors and newswriters make use of a style sheet to achieve consistency in the small details of writing and thus keep their stories readable.

Vocabulary

news English	indirect quotation	style sheet
direct quotation	publication date	stylebook

Review Questions

1. What is news English?

2. Why is editorializing inappropriate in a news story?

3. What are the basic kinds of inaccuracy that can damage a factual news story?

4. Which pronouns are the most appropriate for a factual story?

5. Why is a style sheet useful?

Discussion Questions

1. What qualities might the best news English share with literary English—the language of good novels, stories, and essays? What are a few of the most basic differences between the two kinds of English?

2. What limits, if any, should be placed on the number of names included in a news story?

3. Why might it be desirable to include fact and opinion in the same news story if it were made clear when facts are being reported and when opinions are being offered?

4. Why is impersonality—a reporter's not referring to himself or herself—a valued characteristic of reporting?

5. Is it really necessary for a school paper to have a style sheet? What problems might arise if there were no style sheet?

Chapter Project

Applying Newswriting Style

Write a factual news report on a recent event in your school or community. Make use of all the principles in this chapter that can possibly apply to your work. Include with your report a list of the principles that were especially important to your report and brief explanations of how you made use of them.

COVERING
SCHOOL
NEWS

When you have completed this chapter you should be able to

See the full range of school and community reporting possibilities for your school newspaper.

Plan and write a series of related stories about a major event or an ongoing activity in your school or community.

Write an eyewitness report on a meeting or speech at which you were present.

What happened? You worked hard on this issue of the school newspaper. It is attractive. The leads are interesting, and the stories are well written. You used names wherever you could. But your readers didn't like it. Now, staff members listen to the comments, trying to find out why.

"It's all stale news. We heard it last week."

"They only print their own and their friends' names. We want to read about other people."

"If the staff wants to promote something, it goes on the front page. If not, it doesn't get into the paper."

"Why don't they write about something interesting?"

Of course, you can't satisfy everyone. Some people always criticize, no matter how well your paper is written and edited. But when there is a great deal of criticism, it should be investigated. Start by asking some pointed questions:

Are we emphasizing the past or the future?

Do we explain and interpret the news or just report what our readers already know?

Are we covering all major student interests?

Are we making an effort to use different names in each issue?

Are we reporting about our school as a place of education or merely as a social center?

Do we include important news from outside the school?

Do we publicize the same students, organizations, and activities again and again?

Do we cover a variety of news sources?

Ways of handling problems uncovered in answering the first two questions are dealt with in other chapters. The importance of stressing the future is discussed in Chapter 5 as well as Chapter 7. The value of interpretive writing is treated in Chapter 10. Ways of handling problems uncovered in answering the other six questions are the subject matter of the present chapter.

Serving Your School and Community

Every newspaper serves a particular group of people who live or work in the same geographical area or whose interests are similar. The newspaper's job is to cover the news of this group or community completely and impartially. Readers must be confident that worthwhile news about community happenings—past, present, and future—will be reported.

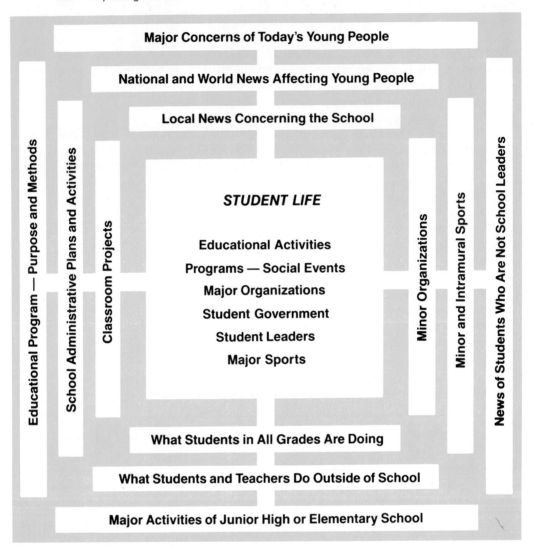

Major Concerns of Today's Young People

National and World News Affecting Young People

Local News Concerning the School

Educational Program — Purpose and Methods

School Administrative Plans and Activities

Classroom Projects

STUDENT LIFE

Educational Activities
Programs — Social Events
Major Organizations
Student Government
Student Leaders
Major Sports

Minor Organizations

Minor and Intramural Sports

News of Students Who Are Not School Leaders

What Students in All Grades Are Doing

What Students and Teachers Do Outside of School

Major Activities of Junior High or Elementary School

The community served by a school newspaper is a broad one. It includes a greater area and more people than most school reporters or their readers realize.

The area of influence of a school paper extends to students at all levels of the local school system as well as to teachers, administrators, office workers, and custodians. It also extends to parents, relatives, and family friends, to alumni of the school, to local advertisers and business people, and to citizens interested in education. While these readers are all interested in the reports on student activities that form the core of school newspapers, they will read your paper more avidly when it also includes news that is of particular concern to them.

To obtain this news, you must reach beyond school matters, even to national or international matters that may properly be treated in a school paper. The six steps that follow will help to improve your paper's coverage of your school and community, vitalize your news pages, and increase reader interest.

Consider Every Student a News Possibility

The most popular or active students often have their names in the paper. These are the busy people who hold major school offices, who star in athletics, or who are otherwise prominent. Their doings are important in news value and must be covered regularly. How can a school newspaper report what the other students, who make up a large percentage of the school, are doing? Although news about these individuals may not rate front page headlines, it may yet be well worth publishing. The first step in serving your school and community is to consider every student a news possibility.

Begin by making sure that every school organization is reached for news. Consider the activities or projects of each group, no matter what its size. Even bulletin board committees, intramural teams, or small clubs are engaged in newsworthy activities. By making every such source part of some reporter's beat, you can discover what the individuals in these groups are doing.

Each reporter should also be alert to classroom news—students doing unusual projects, humorous events, class trips, out-of-the-ordinary assignments. Special beats can be developed to reach classes with which staff members have no regular contact. You might consider selecting a **correspondent** in each homeroom. Like professional correspondents who provide special news from specific locations, these students can be assigned to pinpoint individuals doing newsworthy things.

Are you covering news of all grades? It is easy to overlook the lower grades in your school and in the other schools in your community. Some news about them may come through tips, but most of it must be discovered by reporters and correspondents. With guidance as to what to look for, reporters and correspondents in the lower grades can supply many stories, which an editor or more experienced reporter can help them prepare for publication. Some high school newspapers print news of lower grades in a separate section. Others distribute it throughout the pages. Whatever the arrangement, the quality of these articles must be as high as that of any of the others.

Frequently, a news item from a correspondent may deserve only a single paragraph. This is hardly adequate for a story. But don't throw it away. Combine it with other such paragraphs into a composite story or into a column of **news briefs.** The most widely read news in many newspapers appears in collections of short, lively paragraphs from a variety of sources.

What elements in the story at the top of page 188 made it desirable for publication in a high school newspaper?

Fetrow, Manwiller champions in junior high spelling bee

"The seventh graders outspell the eighth graders," states Mrs. Miriam Decker, English teacher in junior high grades. Mrs. Decker based her remarks on the results of the second annual spelling bee, January 29.

Janice Fetrow, school champion, and Dale Manwiller, runner-up, are both seventh graders. Janice and Dale will compete in the Tri-County contest.

Sixteen seventh and eighth graders participated in the contest. Two finalists were chosen from each of these sections.

Other seventh graders entered were Larry Pierce, 7A; Rosemary Diller, Carol Fortenbaugh, 7B; Betsy Kennedy, William Jones, 7C; Barbara Conley, Mary Bishop, 7D; Dean Anderson, Ron Zimmer, 7E.

Eighth graders in the contest were Donna Wilt, 8A; Barbara Davey, Jane Capito, 8B; Phyllis Estep, 8C; Pat Guistwhite, 8D; Carol Keefer, 8E; Rosalie Moore, Eva Hake, 8F; Darlene Harbold, 8G; Kenneth Ludeen, 8H.

—*Times*, New Cumberland High School, New Cumberland, Pennsylvania

Activity 1: Surveying Your Newspaper for Interest to All Grades

1. Using the last issue of your school newspaper, list the news items of specific interest to members of each grade in your school. For each item, write a brief explanation of why it is of interest to a particular grade.

2. Assume that it is your responsibility to plan the next issue of the school paper by listing the stories to be covered. Draw up your list, indicating alongside each entry the grade level or levels whose interest should be engaged. Try to include at least a dozen stories.

Print Many Different Names

A certain big-city daily, according to rumor, once hoped to print the name of every person living in the city it served at least one time a year. If a metropolitan paper entertained such a hope (however fanciful), how much more realistic would such a hope be for a school newspaper, and how much easier to fulfill. Names, of course, do not make news unless their owners are doing something. But most people are. Your second step for serving your school and community is to print many different names. Every time you expand your news coverage, you will accumulate more of them.

Reporters in one school discovered young people whose unusual outside interests were apparently unknown to other students. What possibilities do the items on page 189 suggest for stories about individuals in your own school?

Since most students, like most people in general, do things worth reading about, a school paper should be able to print many different names. A paper's appeal increases considerably when readers see their own names in print.

—Photo by Michael D. Sullivan

One 17-year-old girl had a steady income from trout flies that she tied herself and advertised in fishing and hunting publications. One of her original creations, Janet's Jest, had become a standard among fly-casters in her area.

A girl wove rugs of unusual designs. She had just completed one in the school colors, showing the emblem and mascot.

A boy whose habit of whittling had developed into a devotion to wood-carving erected in his backyard several 6-foot-high totem poles he had carved and painted himself.

Two girls got up at 3 a.m. each day to work as exercise girls at a local race track. One of the horses they exercised eventually won a number of major races.

A boy who had never played on his school basketball team developed into a star on a semiprofessional team.

For the purpose of checking to see whose names are appearing in the paper and whose are not, your school newspaper office might maintain a card file of all students. A staff member would then go through each issue of the newspaper and mark the cards, indicating how many times each name was printed. Some papers prohibit the printing of a name after it has appeared a certain number of times. This may be extreme, but it does point out the undesirability of featuring the student-body president or football captain in stories where a choice of names is possible. Personality sketches and "inquiring reporter" columns are among possibilities for printing less frequently used names.

When writing about groups of people, you may wish to present their names in an interesting format. If you treat a news story in an unusual way, though, you must be sure that your creative approach does not hide the story's news value.

Imaginative treatment raises the following honor roll story above the level of a mere list of names. Eleven additional paragraphs of names (not reprinted here) were enlivened by such phrases as "on the court for the Braves," "other stars," "will also play," and "complete the senior team." The special treatment was used effectively to make the names stand out.

Four juniors, five braves add straight A's to honor roll team

Tryouts for West's scholarship team reveal juniors Gerald Giolotto, Ted Hollander, Ramona Reed, and Sharon Strauss and sophomores Barbara Fleming, Lynn Gustafson, Marlene Jahss, Joseph Rokus, and Diane Swenson on the starting lineup with all A's for the second quarter.

Varsity team members include Mary Anderson, Sharon Anderson, Diane Andrews, Karen Braatz, William Brown, Dick Bulliet, Marilyn Cacciatore, Marilyn Carney, Gale Chandler, and Sari Culhane with all A's and B's.

—*West High Owl*, West High School, Rockford, Illinois

Activity 2:   Analyzing the Names in Your School Paper

1. Find out the total number of students enrolled in your own school and in other local schools in which your paper is read or distributed.

2. Count up the number of different names that appeared in the most recent issue of your paper.

3. Determine what percentage of the student body was represented in that issue (divide the number of names by the total number of students).

4. Decide whether or not the percentage you obtained in Item 3 is adequate. If not, how would you go about increasing the percentage?

5. Of the names that appeared in the most recent issue, what percentage belongs to especially prominent students, such as school officers, athletic stars, and student leaders? What percentage belongs to students who are not prominent or widely known?

6. Decide whether or not the percentages you obtained in Item 5 are justifiable. If you think they are, explain why. If you think they aren't, explain how and why you would change them.

Cover Educational Activities

One purpose of a good school newspaper is to reveal the school as an academic institution to its community. Stories reporting on teaching and learning play a big part in reaching this goal. The third step for serving your school and community is to cover educational activities.

Look into all kinds of educational affairs. Consider not only those activities going on during the regular school day but also those after school, including clubs, voluntary learning groups, and adult education programs.

Be sure that your regular beats include all academic departments and classes. Reporters covering these beats should be alert to happenings or announcements that may be developed into news stories.

You might arrange for class correspondents—students expected to send in information from their posts. They can work through regular reporters in turning in news about class trips, speakers, panel discussions, special reports, class honors, or humorous happenings connected with academic activities.

Cultivate the interest of classroom teachers in news. Many will give you tips about interesting happenings in other classes as well as detailed information concerning newsworthy events in their own.

From time to time, select one department or course and thoroughly investigate its activities. Your report might appear as a feature story, containing many names and illustrated with photographs if possible.

The following two stories are good examples of educational news coverage.

Chem II makes unique labs

By Alice Johnson and Kim Stopak

Following in the footsteps of Dr. Frankenstein, senior Chris Standaert tried to recreate the basis of life, and his fellow students taking Chemistry II designed sometimes bizarre, sometimes practical original projects.

Other experiments included developing inflammable substances, producing explosive gas from rotting fruit, developing nylon, and testing the resistance of dental fillings.

The purpose of these experiments is to have the students deal in total abstractions, according to chemistry teacher Mr. Robert George. It's a time when students go beyond regular classroom work and take off on their own.

STANDAERT ATTEMPTED to make amino acids, which are essential to life, by combining the gases ammonia, hydrogen, and methane with gaseous water in a simulation of the earth's original atmosphere. He tried to produce this atmosphere by vacuuming out all of the oxygen from a 2½-foot glass tube.

However, his vacuum wasn't strong enough, so when he added the gases and applied a spark to trigger reaction, the mixture exploded because of a presence of oxygen. No one was injured, according to Standaert.

Senior Richard Santucci developed chemical fire-retardants (inflammable substances) for his experiment. After testing known retardants, he developed his own using the chemicals he found most effective. He remarks that he was "able to improve upon old chemical fire-retardants."

A STRIP OF a bed sheet with his own retardant on it withstood being held over a Bunsen burner for an entire minute before blackening at all.

Senior Alisa Irvine made organic garbage using ripened fruit and placed it in a sealed trash can until it rotted. She then siphoned off the odorless, colorless gas and weighed it.

She found that it weighed less than air and assumed that it was methane because that is the only known gas that weighs less than air.

IN SPITE OF the projects' popularity with students, Mr. George is considering discontinuing mandatory original projects in the Chemistry II classes. Mr. George, the only Chemistry II teacher, feels that not enough students are gaining satisfactory end products; so he wants the projects to be optional.

—*Black and White*, Walt Whitman High School, Bethesda, Maryland

Teachers use 2,000-word list

Word games improve spelling, teacher says

"Playing scrabble, doing crossword puzzles, and playing other word games help students learn how to spell and how to use new words," says Miss Frieda Cook, English teacher. "These games help make the words more interesting to learn," she adds.

How well a student learns to spell depends largely upon his interest in learning how to spell. This interest in spelling is determined by how hard a student tries to learn new words and how he applies the words to everyday language, Miss Cook believes.

"I think the easiest way to learn to spell is by studying the word and breaking it into syllables," says Miss Cook.

Spelling is being stressed at Miami High this year because county statistics reveal that some high school students can't spell as well as they should.

"Spelling, however, has always been a part of the language arts program in our school," says Mrs. Helen Gwaltney, head of the English department, "but this year it will be particularly stressed. English teachers will use their own methods in their classes to help students with the 2,000-word spelling list, a copy of which every faculty member has received."

Parents are encouraged to help their children with spelling at home. The 2,000-word spelling list, which contains words which are most often used by people, is available to parents who want it.

—*Miami High Times*, Miami Senior High School, Miami, Florida

Activity 3:   Covering Your School's Academic Life

1. Survey three recent issues of your school paper and write an essay arguing that the paper does or does not adequately reveal the academic life of your school.

2. List six imaginative or unusual academic news subjects that your school paper might possibly cover in a future issue. For each listing, give a brief description of the kinds of details that the story should include.

Cover Outside News

A school newspaper staff needs to be aware of happenings beyond the school. Few students are involved only in school programs, whether academic or social. Most are concerned with local, national, and world issues that they perceive as affecting their present and future lives. Among these issues are career choices and the economy, family life and relationships, social change, poverty and hunger, and nuclear weapons and peace, to mention just a few. The fourth step for serving your school and community is to cover outside news that is of particular interest to students. A well-rounded school paper will include many articles, usually interpretive in nature, on nonschool issues that concern young people.

However, reporters should always be careful to treat the issues in a way that justifies their appearing in a school paper. This is done by making clear how these issues touch the lives and concerns of students. Even when writing about national or worldwide topics, reporters should try to include local examples or perhaps quote student opinions on these matters.

The four stories on pages 194 and 195 cover outside news. After reading each one, answer this question: Why might this story of a nonschool matter belong in a school newspaper?

A school paper's news coverage should go beyond the boundaries of the school. If, for instance, an organized carwash in the community involves or is of interest to students, it is a suitable subject for a story in the school paper.

—Photo by Joel Gordon

Voters to name officials, decide issues

By Karen Hickel

Incumbents and challengers for city council, mayor, and treasurer in the Salida city election Tuesday are in favor of passage of the proposed $280,000 swimming pool bond issue question with which they share the ballot.

Other candidate concerns dealing with young people are recreational sites, and many candidates said they feel renovation and remodeling of the pool will help solve much of that problem.

Also up for vote is an opinion poll concerning whether citizens here want to pursue the concept of home rule with an eye toward an eventual change.

Incumbent Ralph Coscarella is running for a two-year council seat in Ward 3. He said the youth of Salida have a lot of needs and they should "make some of their own recreation and really support it."

Salida lawyer Henry J. Florey is challenging Mr. Coscarella for the seat. He said, "I'd like to see the pool open year-round. I think the adults of Salida should not be adverse to some kind of recreational place for the youth of Salida to meet."

Mayor Edward Touber, a 20-year veteran in the office, is seeking to renew his two-year term for the eleventh consecutive time. He said he would like to see the swimming pool bond issue approved but added he feels youth of the city have "a lot" of recreational activities available.

He said, "I don't know of any special problems that youth have."

—Tenderfoot Times, Salida High School, Salida, Colorado

Registration dodgers to be denied collegiate loans from government

By Brian Hayashi

A document that makes any individual seeking financial aid ineligible if he has not registered for the draft was signed into law by President Reagan September 8, 1982.

This document, which is part of the Fiscal Year 1983 Defense Department Authorization Act, contains an amendment to the military Selective Service Act.

Since its inception, the Selective Service Act has been plagued with problems, the majority of which have involved low registration levels and the so-called "draft dodger."

The new program seeks to cut down these problems through financial incentives.

The enforcement of this program will be simple, as financial aid will be denied to all who don't receive a Registration Acknowledgement Letter Form 3A or 3A-S. This requirement is mandatory for students who reach their eighteenth birthday prior to April 1, 1983.

According to a school survey published by Bear Facts December 17, 53 percent stated that they would not serve. By the same token, that could render a large proportion of our student body ineligible for any form of financial assistance.

—Bear Facts, Bear Creek High School, Lakewood, Colorado

Queahpama boys rescue two men

Ray and Ken Queahpama, MSHS sophomore and junior, respectively, administered first aid to two Warm Springs men whose car was wrecked near the Queahpama home early Monday morning.

Ray and Ken had just gone to bed when the sound of a loud crash reached their ears. Upon reaching the accident scene, they discovered a late model Chevrolet lying on its side in the water.

Both occupants were unconscious, one completely submerged in the waist-deep water running through the car. Ken and Ray had considerable difficulty pulling the two men from the half-flooded automobile.

Nevertheless, they managed to carry the victims to the bank of the creek where they administered first aid. Because of their quick work, neither man is now in serious condition.

—*White Buffalo,* Madras Senior High
School, Madras, Oregon

SPCA needs owners, 10,000 pets need love

By Carol Whitten

If a small cuddly pet is on the shopping list, the Society for Prevention of Cruelty to Animals is an opportune place to shop. Located on Industrial Boulevard, it houses 120 to 150 animals. Customers are free to browse the aisles in search of satisfactory merchandise. If they choose to adopt a pet, they will be providing a home for an unwanted product of animal overpopulation.

The SPCA acquires animals through individuals. People give up their pets for reasons ranging from lack of funds to lack of interest. The animals usually range from 6 weeks to 7 or 8 years old. Sometimes older animals are received; however, they usually lack the adaptiveness of the younger ones. Some have been known to refuse nourishment and eventually die.

The SPCA also deals with animal abuse. As the field investigator, Mr. Darryl Chance handles this area. He received 84 calls last month. Thirty-six were severe enough to demand investigation.

According to Ms. Mary Rosen, the administrative assistant, most cases of abuse are simply the result of ignorance and negligence. One of the most common cases of unintentional abuse is leaving pets in the car. In just 10 minutes the temperature inside can reach 102 degrees or more. In 30 minutes the inside of a car may reach 120 degrees or more.

The SPCA features a volunteer program called TLC (Tender Loving Care). The program is constantly in need of volunteers. Anyone willing to help would perform such tasks as walking the dogs, combing the cats, working in exhibit booths, and simply loving the animals.

Ms. Rosen stresses that pets need love: "If you do choose to own a pet, the main thing is to continue to love your animal even after the first flush of excitement wears off."

—*Hillcrest Hurricane,* Hillcrest High
School, Dallas, Texas

Activity 4: Expanding News Coverage

1. Write the following six headings: In-School News (Students and Teachers), Out-of-School News (Students and Teachers), Alumni News, Community and Local News, National News, World News. Under the appropriate headings, list (by headline or subject) the stories that have appeared in the last three issues of your school paper.

2. Using each of the six headings, add story subjects of interest to young people that could have been covered in these issues. Underline your additions to distinguish them from the stories listed in the first part of this activity.

3. Of the story subjects you listed in the second part of this activity, take one from the heading Community and Local News, one from National News, and one from World News. For each of these subjects, write a brief explanation of why it would concern students at your school and should therefore be covered in your school paper.

Balance the Various Kinds of News

Heard in the halls: "The editor's best friend is the president of the drama club, so it's always on the front page. But our good debating team never gets any credit. They've won three tournaments this spring, and only one story has been printed about them."

—Gayle Goddard in *The Green Horn*, Springfield High School, Springfield, Vermont

Steps to The Future

The variety of academic subjects available in a typical curriculum is one example of the variety of kinds of news worth covering. A good school newspaper reflects this variety. It avoids the monotony of covering only a limited number of easily handled subjects.

It is easy to overemphasize a familiar activity from which news comes readily. It is also easy to underemphasize other, equally deserving events.

The fifth step for a staff eager to serve its school and community is to balance the various kinds of news covered. Some of this must be handled at the level of the editors, of course. But reporters are responsible, too. They must cover their beats and find news in spite of sources who think they have no information of interest to pass along. To do this, good reporters think up questions that will be answered with facts—facts that can be explored for further facts, until the material for a good story has been drawn out of a news source who, at first, had little to say.

Sometimes an alert imagination can help achieve balanced coverage by spotting news value in subjects often passed over. The following stories illustrate alertness to uncommon subjects.

Summer school value weighed by students, teachers

By Joe Feeney

Most students think of summer as a time for going to the beach, relaxing, and not thinking about homework. However, for some students, summer is a time for taking courses that they couldn't during the regular school year.

Don El-Etr '83 said that summer school is a good way to pick up extra credits. "Photography was really good because I got a half credit for only 15 days of work," he said.

However, there are also some disadvantages to taking classes during the summer. Craig Meyers '83, who took typing during summer school, said, "It didn't do me a whole lot of good. In summer school, I got by okay, but now I'm taking typing over to really learn how to type.

"In summer school, it's too short a time and the work is crammed in. Also, in summer, it's hard to do homework, especially when it gets really hot."

A one-credit summer school course takes six weeks, five days a week, 8 a.m. to 12:30 p.m. The session begins June 20.

As to how difficult the summer school courses really are, it usually depends upon the student.

Mr. Ken Lumb, who teaches U.S. History in the summer, said, "If students take the class seriously, the course is probably easier in the summer because the student doesn't have four or five other classes to worry about like he does during the regular school year. However, since everything is squeezed into six weeks, the summer school course doesn't expose the kids to everything the regular course does."

Mr. Aldo Mungai, who teaches English I and II during the summer, said, "The course I teach is easier because most of the kids in my class either failed or dropped the course the first time. So, to them, it's just makeup work."

Students' attitudes toward summer school are important. "First, people who take elective courses during the summer are here because they want to be," said Mr. Mungai.

Added Mr. Lumb, "We don't have many problems with students because most of them want to get the job done. Plus, these students pay good money to take summer school."

—*The Lion*, Lyons Township High School, LaGrange and Western Springs, Illinois

Debaters gain success through hard work

By Farida Moreau

Few students realize that Student Congress, Lincoln-Douglas, and two-man debaters spend up to $400 on supplies, hundreds of hours on research, endless afternoons practicing after school, and about two weekends per month at day-long tournaments.

Sophomore Sara Levine, president of Student Congress debate, was named "Outstanding Senator" last year in Maryland and attended the national tournament in San Francisco.

She explains, "This branch of debate is a mock congress where students present legislation on domestic, economic, and foreign areas of national concern. Speakers debate these bills and receive scores from judges indicating the strength of each speaker's performance."

Each week Levine goes "through the three major news magazines—U.S. News, Newsweek, and Time, the entire Sunday editions of The New York Times and The Washington Post and all of the local newspapers." She spends at least five hours per week organizing and researching her topics and preparing speeches.

Sophomore David Rudolph explains that two-man debate differs from Student Congress in that participants deal with one national topic for the entire year. This year's topic is national defense. Two people, working as partners, compete in rounds against other teams. One team presents a view on the topic, and the other team argues against it point by point.

Rudolph attended a debate program at Georgetown University last summer. For three weeks he researched, attended workshops, and presented speeches on many aspects of this year's topic.

Though the program cost about $300, Rudolph feels the investment was worthwhile because his participation prepared him for "the intense competition of two-man debate."

Lincoln-Douglas debate, named after the famous debates by Abraham Lincoln and Stephen Douglas, is similar to two-man debate except that the topic changes with each tournament and individuals rather than teams engage in debate.

Sophomore Mike LaBier spends around four hours per week on Lincoln-Douglas "to learn the most I can about topics."

—*Black and White*, Walt Whitman High School, Bethesda, Maryland

Balance also involves covering unhappy or unpleasant stories when the need arises. Even a school paper must sometimes publish an obituary. The obituary should be sympathetic and respectful but factual rather than emotional. It should tell when and how the person died and what his or her accomplishments and interests were. If editorial comment is necessary—in most cases it will not be—you should put it on the editorial page, not in the obituary.

Student suicides raise even more delicate questions. Some school staffs feel these reports may be too painful to the suicide's family, friends, and teachers for publication. If a story is printed, it must, even more than other obituaries, be simple and factual.

The following report of a death is in good taste. It was accompanied on the newspaper page by a photograph.

George Smith killed in car accident

George Smith was killed in an automobile accident Thanksgiving Day while returning home from the annual East-West game.

His car overturned when struck by a truck which had gone through a red light. Tom Ramsey, riding with him, was thrown clear and suffered only minor injuries.

George was a senior honor student and a member of Quill and Scroll, the tennis team, and the debating club. He had been chosen to be East's representative to Boys' State in January.

Officers of the school organizations of which George was a member acted as honorary pallbearers at his funeral Monday, November 27.

Set Up a System to Reach All News Sources

The intention of expanding your news coverage requires a means of fulfillment. The sixth step, then, is to set up a smooth-working system for collecting news from all desired sources. Some vital parts of this system include your Future Book, reporters' regular beats, staff meetings for developing story topics, and a catalog of general school news ideas.

A complete catalog of school news possibilities for all schools is impossible to assemble here. A detailed and specific listing of general news sources and ideas should, however, be developed for your own school, and you should refer to it regularly to keep your coverage extensive and thorough. The following checklist may be helpful in making sure you are reaching all appropriate news sources in your school and community.

✔ **Checklist of News Sources and Ideas**

☐ 1. Have we covered as many students as possible: student leaders as well as other students, students in the lower grades, students with special interests, and so on?

☐ 2. Have we covered enough other people who are directly or indirectly involved with the school: faculty, administrators, school board members, parents, staff members, alumni, and so on?

☐ 3. Have we covered as many educational activities as we might: classroom activities, trips, speakers, special awards, voluntary learning activities, adult education, other educational opportunities, educational policies, library resources, and so on?

☐ 4. Have we covered enough outside topics of interest to students: community affairs, social and economic issues, national and world events that affect students, and so on?

☐ 5. Have we covered enough aspects of school and life in general to present a balanced picture: changes in school policy or buildings, all school activities, any special events, deaths, and so on?

Activity 5: Locating Your School's News Possibilities

1. Work with other students to prepare a complete catalog of news possibilities to be used by the editors and reporters of your school paper. You might begin by having each student take a category such as Library or Adult Education. Then have each student fill in as many items as possible that might be covered under that category (specific people, specific policy matters, specific events, and so on).

2. Make a clipping scrapbook showing wide news coverage. Using newspapers from your school and others, find clippings on as many different topics as possible. Organize them into definite groups so that you can use them for news story ideas.

3. Study recent school newspaper issues to determine which school activities have received the most space, which have appeared least frequently, and which have not been covered at all. Make suggestions as to how news coverage may be balanced more evenly.

Writing a Series of Stories

One real reporting challenge comes when you are asked to develop a **series** of stories about a single topic. You may be assigned to write such a series about some ongoing activity, such as a fund-raising drive, about a group that is continually involved in newsworthy matters, such as the school band or the student government, or about a major all-school event, such as an annual talent show.

Sometimes a series may call for a story in each of a number of newspaper issues. "But," you say, "how can I write a story issue after issue about the same old news? There aren't that many ways of telling it." You are right. Your readers will lose interest in your reports rapidly if you merely repeat the basic facts of the first story. Intelligent reporting is the answer. You must develop fresh facts for each issue or a fresh angle—a new point of view on the subject and a different way of writing about it.

For example, assume you are the reporter assigned to the all-school talent show. The show is a major spring activity with enough news value to justify regular front page space in your newspaper, which is published twice a month.

The date of the show, March 1, is placed on the school calendar in November. You visit the faculty advisers. But so far they know only the date. A mere date will not make a story, so you start thinking. This is an annual event, isn't it? You turn to issues from past years to find facts for a story for the early December issue. The result is a story that begins in the following way:

March 1 is the date for this year's All-School Varieties, sponsored by the school service group.

Profits from the show have been used in past years to provide scholarships for Central High graduates. Winners of the talent competition enter the citywide Talent Search.

Last year's winners included . . .

Then, plans for the talent show are made, and these appear in the late December issue. The story might begin as follows:

Tryouts for the All-School Varieties will take place during the week of February 2-6, Bill Johnson, president of the school service group, announced.

All soloists and groups wishing to enter should . . .

Now your series is under way, and you need something new twice a month. Bill Johnson and the faculty advisers have no further plans to divulge. You could review the history of the show or see if any past talent winners became professional entertainers. These would make acceptable stories, but they are better feature story ideas. Again you go to past issues. Are some of last year's participants still enrolled in school? If so, you can write a timely story for early January:

"Fearless Four is going to win the All-School Varieties," brags Bobbi Freeland, leader of the instrumental group that placed high in last year's talent competition.

"We've added some new numbers and have been practicing hard all year," Bobbi added. Bobbi plays the piano. Other members of the group are . . .

Also returning to Varieties competition are . . .

Then, the judges for the talent show are chosen, and this is the springboard for the next story, in the late January issue:

Judges selecting All-School Varieties acts will be student-body president Melvin Stoneham, head cheerleader Kathy Kearney, and Mr. Wilson Farnsworth, drama instructor.

About 25 acts are to be chosen to enter the March 1 talent competition . . .

From now on, there should be developments enough to keep your typewriter clicking. For the early February issue, you try the stagecraft angle. It makes a good lead:

"Bandstand in the Park" will set the scene for the All-School Varieties, March 1 in the auditorium.

"A complete bandstand is being constructed on the stage by students in the stagecraft class," states Ms. Denise Jones, instructor.

Students working on the project are . . .

For the late February issue, you do a story on rehearsals. It includes personalities, interesting happenings, and names of some of the numbers:

Late for dinner every night.

This is an old story to some 75 All-School Varieties participants, who are rehearsing every afternoon to make next week's show the finest ever.

The auditorium curtain will rise on this year's talent competition next Friday evening at 7:30, announced Mr. Wilson Farnsworth, drama instructor. Curious sights at rehearsals include . . .

This event is entitled to one major follow-up story if you have something new to report. But don't repeat well-known facts unless you can add a new angle such as the following:

Having won the All-School Varieties competition last Friday, the Fearless Four instrumental group is already practicing for the citywide Talent Search. . . .

If you write for a monthly paper, your job is easier. You have only half as many stories to prepare. But you'll make a mistake if you decide that because your paper appears less frequently you can get by with rewording the same material you published weeks ago. Your readers will recognize it instantly.

Activity 6: Planning a Series of Related Stories

1. Outline a series of at least four stories about a forthcoming campaign or major activity in your school. Include all possible angles that the articles might take. Using actual publication dates of your school newspaper, suggest the best date for each story.

2. Plan a similar series of stories about a group that carries on newsworthy projects regularly (the band, the foreign student exchange program, or a major club, for instance). Indicate especially what different angle you would use in each article.

Writing Eyewitness Reports

Professional reporters are often present when a news event occurs. Therefore, they can write about what they have seen and heard, adding comments from news sources to amplify their information. This is called **eyewitness reporting,** as distinguished from reporting primarily by interviewing news sources and gathering already available information. Eyewitness reporting is common in daily newspapers, which deal with news of the recent past. At fires, court trials, or conventions, for instance, most of the action is seen by reporters.

Eyewitness Reporting for a School Newspaper

School papers are not so concerned with yesterday's happenings nor so likely to report unexpected events—the **spot news** that makes daily newspaper front pages. Certain school news items must be handled by eyewitness reporting, however. These may include speeches, sports events, and meetings—of the board of education, of community councils, of organizations, and so on.

When you cover one of these events, how can you sort and condense the vast array of facts, details, figures, and just plain words? Information obtained by interviewing a news source is already summarized, and its key thoughts are emphasized. Each story is relatively easy to organize. But not so with eyewitness stories. You start with everything that happened, including much trivial detail that doesn't deserve to be printed. First, you must find the key thought and other important facts, discarding ideas containing little news value. Then, you must condense your information into a brief, direct statement whose length reflects the overall news value of your subject.

Activity 7: Studying Eyewitness Reporting

1. Find in a daily newspaper a story that is clearly an instance of eyewitness reporting. Try to imagine the event as the reporter witnessed it. What kind of facts and details were probably omitted from the published account of the event? What difficulties in gathering information might the reporter have faced? Can you detect any evidences of editorializing in the story? If so, what are they? Do you feel that any of them are justified?

2. Find three or more eyewitness stories that include information or comments that come from sources other than the eyewitness reporter. Study the kinds of information and comments included in the stories. Then write a short report that answers this question: How should an eyewitness reporter best make use of the information and comments obtained from others?

Covering a Meeting

A story that tests your skill in deciding what is important and what is not is the eyewitness report of a business meeting, such as a session of the board of education or of the student council. Many things may be discussed at the meeting. You must decide which of these matters have news value to your newspaper's audience and which of these matters are mere details.

The mechanics of writing an interesting eyewitness meeting story are simple. First, attend the meeting and make your own notes. These should include the names of those conducting the meeting, of other chief participants, and of those in the audience who raise questions or offer opinions. Your notes should also include a few quotations, copied exactly, of statements you feel are significant. Second, select the event or decision that affects the largest number of people or that seems most significant for other reasons. This is the basis of your key thought. It should be featured in your lead and summarized in succeeding paragraphs. Finally, explain other happenings in the remaining paragraphs of the story, presenting them in the order of importance. If the meeting seemed dull or routine to you, you must

Photo by Ken Karp

Writing a good news report on a meeting requires the ability to distinguish significant from insignificant remarks—and, sometimes, the ability to write interestingly about uninteresting discussions.

use all your writing skills to interest your reader. Look for the WOW! element (see Chapter 6) and describe each happening in the most colorful way possible.

Activity 8: Writing an Eyewitness Meeting Story

From the following record of a student council meeting, write a news story. Find the key thought and emphasize it in the lead, along with other necessary five *W* and one *H* facts. The second paragraph should complete your treatment of the key thought as expressed in the lead. In the remaining paragraphs, report other actions in order of importance. Leave out details that have no news value. And be sure to use what you learned about writing news English (see Chapter 8) to turn the information into a story that is worth reading.

The regular weekly meeting of the student council was called to order by Carla Wells, president, in Room 103, Wednesday, January 12, at 2:15 p.m. The salute to the flag was led by Ray Staton. The minutes of the preceding meeting were read and approved.

Carla announced that a meeting would be held after school Monday, January 17, in Room 202, to plan calendar dates for spring semester activities. Representatives of all student activities and clubs should be present.

The proposal for raising the student activity fee next semester had been held over from the last meeting to give representatives a chance to discuss it with their own classes. In discussion, it was brought out that the extra money would be used to buy uniforms for the baseball team and sweaters for the cheerleaders, to provide transportation and materials for the school tutoring program at Neighborhood House, and to support student organizations. Ron Carson moved that the activity fee be raised from $3 to $5 for one semester only. The motion was seconded and passed. Carla directed Beverly Myers, in charge of finance, to take any action necessary to put the change into effect.

Sally Wilson asked that the council take action to find out if the water from the drinking fountain in the cafeteria could be cooled on hot days. Carla appointed Sally to see Mr. Joseph Hunter of the maintenance staff about this and to report back to the council next week.

Kenny Hewitt moved that the council sponsor a Valentine's Day dance. Because of lack of time for discussion, the motion was tabled until next week.

The meeting was adjourned at 3 p.m.

Covering a Speech

You may on occasion be assigned to write a story about a gathering that features a speaker. Reporting a speech accurately is difficult. You must sift through the many words spoken, find the essential facts, and present them in an interesting way. You also need to convey the personality of the speaker and the tone of the speech in your report. The guidelines in the following paragraphs should help you.

GET BACKGROUND INFORMATION. Start by interviewing the faculty sponsor or student leader in charge to get the speaker's name and topic. Ask the purpose of the speech. Obtain biographical data about the speaker from your news source, the library, or daily newspapers. If time permits, read up on the topic. This is especially desirable if you are faced with a technical or unfamiliar subject. On rare occasions, you may be able to obtain a copy of the speech in advance. Review this in preparation for listening. But attend the meeting in any case, for the speaker may not present the speech exactly as written.

LISTEN FOR THE MAIN IDEA. While listening to the speech, try to see what the speaker's aim or purpose is—what the speaker wants you to understand or believe. What principal information or arguments are presented? Make notes.

COPY OR RECORD A FEW KEY QUOTATIONS. Copy, in the exact words used, any statements that seem to express the speaker's main idea or arguments. Use abbreviations and your own shorthand in doing this or else tape-record the speech. If you plan to tape-record the speech, make sure you receive advance permission from the speaker or the person running the meeting.

INTERVIEW THE SPEAKER IF POSSIBLE. You can learn more about the speaker's personality and views if you interview him or her briefly before or after the meeting. Ask questions about the principal ideas in the speech or about related personal experiences. Any understanding you gain will help you write a clearer story.

BEGIN MOST LEADS WITH A QUOTATION. A speech story closely follows standard newswriting patterns. The lead should usually start with a direct or indirect quotation of a key statement from the speech. If the statement is long, place it by itself in the first paragraph. Then present other essential facts in the second paragraph.

The three examples that follow show different ways of writing a good speech story lead:

> "Opportunities in industry are always waiting for young people who have made the most of their education and are willing to work hard at their jobs."
>
> This statement was made by Mr. Clifton Jones, personnel manager of the California Steel Corporation, in an address to vocational students last week.

> "Speed isn't everything—if it were, jackrabbits would be running the world" were the words of advice given by Mr. Joseph Higgins of the Department of Motor Vehicles at an automobile safety conference attended by driver education students May 18.

> Emphasizing that a sound education is essential to success in today's competitive business world, Dr. Helen Keyes, dean of students at State University, spoke at the South High assembly last Friday.

BRIEFLY IDENTIFY THE SPEAKER AND OCCASION. A phrase or sentence in the lead or second paragraph is adequate for this purpose. As was done in the examples just given, tell who the speaker is, when the speech was made, and to whom. Then go on with your report of what was said. Other biographical information can be reflected in your summary of the talk or left for the final paragraphs.

VARY YOUR MANNER OF PRESENTATION. In writing the rest of the story, mix paragraphs of direct quotation, indirect quotation, and summary. One problem is to avoid repetition of *he said* or *she said*. This can be accomplished by using synonyms (*added, continued, remarked,* and so on) or suggesting this meaning in other ways.

The story on page 207 represents one writer's manner of covering a speech. The lead in this case is not a quotation because the writer wished instead to focus on two important points—the fact that the speaker had won a Pulitzer Prize and the fact that the speaker was an alumnus of the reporter's school. Several quotations are used, however, adding to the general variety of presentation.

Kennerly talks, gives slide show

By Dennis Fernandes

Mr. David Hume Kennerly, Pulitzer Prize winner in photojournalism and a former photographer for Roseburg Senior High School's Orange R, spoke at the annual Oregon Scholastic Press Conference, October 9, at the University of Oregon in Eugene.

Mr. Kennerly held two photo critique sessions in which he answered any questions that delegates from various Oregon high schools had about their photographs.

Mr. Kennerly then showed a slide show of his best photos, explaining how and why he took each one.

"I try to show what is going on when taking my photos," said Mr. Kennerly. "If it is positive, it's positive, and if it's negative, it's negative."

He then had an open mike session where delegates asked advice and more questions. One delegate asked Mr. Kennerly what he thought was the main problem with young photographers. Mr. Kennerly replied, "The main problem is their misuse of chemicals and care for their negatives."

Mr. Kennerly was a staff member of the Orange R during his earlier years in high school until he and his family moved to West Linn, Oregon.

He worked for both the Oregon Journal and the Oregonian before joining United Press International. While with UPI, he shot everything from the New York Mets' miracle year in 1969 to the war in Vietnam.

Mr. Kennerly did get some recognition for his pictures from Vietnam when he won the ultimate award—the Pulitzer Prize.

When he was asked if he ever felt fear while in dangerous situations, he said, "Fear? Oh, yes, Herrman Fear . . ." Then, he replied seriously, "Even if you are scared, you have to do your job."

—Orange R, Roseburg Senior High
School, Roseburg, Oregon

Activity 9: Reporting a Speech

1. In a daily or weekly newspaper, find a report of an important speech such as a politician, a business leader, or a representative of some organized group might give. Then answer these questions:

   a. What was the speech about? How clearly does the reporter present the speaker's main idea?

   b. How much of the story consists of direct quotations?

   c. Describe the personality of the speaker as reflected in the story. What details convey an impression of his or her personality?

   d. What expressions does the reporter use in place of *he said* or *she said*?

   e. What facts or details in the story indicate that the reporter got background information by interviews or research?

2. Following the guidelines in this section, write a story covering a speech or some comparable public address. You should look for a speech or address being given in your school or community, in a nearby college, or on radio or television.

Summary

This chapter begins by presenting guidelines for establishing a proper relationship between a school newspaper and its readership in the school and community. It then considers two common responsibilities of school reporters—writing a series of stories and reporting as an eyewitness.

SERVING YOUR SCHOOL AND COMMUNITY. A school newspaper's community includes a number of groups of readers—students and nonstudents, young people and adults, people in the school, and people in the community. Six steps can help reporters appeal to and serve their readers. First, consider every student, at every grade level, a possible subject for a news story. Second, print a variety of names, avoiding unnecessary repetition of the same prominent ones. Third, cover all the kinds of educational activities. Fourth, cover outside news—the local, national, and world events that affect students. Fifth, strike a balance among the various kinds of news subjects open to your paper. And sixth, develop a system and follow it to ensure that reporters remain aware of and in touch with every possible news source.

WRITING A SERIES OF STORIES. A difficult reporting challenge arises when a series of stories on one subject must be prepared. Fresh facts or a fresh angle must be developed for each issue if reader interest is to be sustained.

WRITING EYEWITNESS REPORTS. School reporters do less eyewitness reporting than professionals but face the same problems when they do. Reports about meetings, sports events, and speeches are the most likely topics. An eyewitness reporter must sift through the details and seize the key thought and other important facts, writing them up in a story whose length reflects the overall news value of the subject.

Vocabulary

correspondent	series	spot news
news brief	eyewitness reporting	

Review Questions

1. What readership groups of the school and community should a school paper reach and serve?

2. What steps can be taken to publish a variety of names in a school newspaper?

3. What considerations should govern the reporting of educational news? Of nonschool news?

4. What attitude of some news sources can make it difficult for a school paper to achieve a balance of the various kinds of news?

5. What skills are required to write a series of stories on a single subject? To write an eyewitness story?

Discussion Questions

1. For many school newspapers, expanded news coverage aggravates an already troublesome situation—lack of space in which to print all the worthwhile news stories. Discuss this problem, suggesting possible solutions that would be practical for your school paper.

2. What kind of treatment or angle would be needed to make the following national and international matters appropriate subjects for your school paper: the automobile industry, unemployment, political unrest in another country, and a development in medical treatment?

3. Assume that the editor of your school paper has decided to publish a series of six stories un-der the general title "Getting the Most Out of Our School." The purpose of the series is to report on educational activities of proven value and the ways that students can better themselves by taking advantage of the school's offerings. What subjects, angles, and news sources would you recommend for the six stories?

4. What are the advantages and disadvantages of writing a series of articles about a single major event?

5. What activities in your school and community would be especially interesting subjects for eyewitness stories?

Chapter Project

Breaking New Ground in Reporting

Choose a news source not ordinarily reached by your school paper—a class, organization, administrative body, or other group whose activities might interest your readers if reported skillfully. Attend a meeting of the group, conduct interviews, do some research, and prepare a news story suitable for publication in your school paper. Follow your story with an account of how you employed relevant guidelines from this chapter.

UNIT THREE

Specialized Writing

10

INTERPRETING
THE NEWS

When you have completed this chapter you should be able to

Understand what interpretive, in-depth news articles are and how they differ from ordinary news articles.

Prepare such articles by following five steps.

Write articles on broad or complex subjects.

On Monday morning the school buzzed with news that several well-known students had been arrested over the weekend, charged with drug possession. Rumors and questions, most of them based on misinformation, began to fly. "I heard they found pills in some kid's locker." "I heard it was cocaine." "They were selling drugs all around school last week." "The charge was only possession. It's not the same as selling the stuff!"

When the incident received sensational coverage in a local paper, suggesting a serious drug-abuse problem in the school, parents became alarmed. School administrators acted to reassure them, but questions and comments continued to circulate.

Drug problems had certainly not been solved when the school newspaper's next issue appeared. But several carefully prepared articles provided some answers to the questions. Among other topics, these articles explained the administration's position, reported on a proposed drug education curriculum, and analyzed the state's drug laws and their implications for young people.

The articles prepared can be summarized under one general term: **interpretive, in-depth news articles.** Unlike basic news stories, such articles require not just the facts but an explanation of the facts. They are also likely to include a number of opinions from various authoritative news sources. Naturally, they require fuller and more detailed research than ordinary news stories do. Award-winning school newspapers print interpretive, in-depth reports extensively. In fact, the trend today in most news publications is toward more explanation of events. The WHY? question must be answered quite thoroughly to satisfy today's news readers.

Interpretive, in-depth reports may often be identified by three basic characteristics. They are longer than most other news stories. They include a **byline**—a line printed above an article to identify the writer. And they give evidence that several news sources were reached and much research done.

An interpretive, in-depth report can serve various journalistic purposes. It might aim to correct misinformation about a group of people or a new movement. It might be used to help people deal with some unexpected or troubling event. It might also be used to reveal the humanity behind the statistics found in a survey or poll.

Investigative reporting is similar to the reporting that goes into interpretive, in-depth reports, but it is primarily concerned with uncovering hidden or suppressed facts behind a news event. Published results of investigative reporting often appear in a series of lengthy reports. Reporters may have searched out the truth behind rumors or charges, perhaps of corrupt acts in government or business. One famous example is *The Washington Post*'s revelation of the Watergate coverup, which was later detailed in the book *All the President's Men*. Most metropolitan newspapers engage in similar reporting, though usually on a lesser scale. Another kind of investigative reporting involves a reporter's going "under cover," perhaps posing as a member of a special group in order to unearth information about it.

—Photo from Wide World

Perhaps the best-known example in recent years of investigative reporting is The Washington Post's *coverage of the Watergate scandal. The* Post's *revelations were primarily the work of Carl Bernstein (left) and Bob Woodward (right).*

Unlike daily newspapers, school publications usually cannot publish sensational investigative reports. However, the subjects that school papers do cover can often be enhanced by intelligent interpretation and diligent investigation. School news reporters should see it as a challenge to take some unsensational subject—an upcoming event, an item of community news, a particular group or organization—and turn it into an interesting article by virtue of careful investigation and thoughtful interpretation.

Recognizing the Characteristics of Interpretive, In-Depth Reporting

The story on page 215 illustrates the distinguishing characteristics of interpretive, in-depth reporting. It includes facts—the basic one being that classes in self-defense are being taught in a particular high school. But it includes much more: background information, a good deal of explanation, the opinions and advice of expert sources, statistics, and even a brief quotation from a book.

Self-defense classes teach awareness, self-confidence

By Jackie Roth

Walking along a dark, misty street, each step being echoed by a similar step, glancing backward slyly, a teen-age girl sees two glowing eyes staring back. What should she do?

The answer to this question comes under the topic of self-defense. The need for individuals to know about self-defense is growing in West Des Moines and all over the country. At Valley, physical education classes in self-defense are being taught by Ms. Marjorie Wharff and Ms. Carolyn Caruthers.

Lieutenant Ray Fidler of the West Des Moines Police Department said that the number of assaults in West Des Moines has increased 14 percent. Personal thefts, Lieutenant Fidler added, are actually very uncommon, recalling only one purse-snatching case during the year.

Ms. Wharff feels that self-defense includes basically common-sense things. She added, "I feel that it's very important for people to be prepared in emergency situations so that they can react in a manner that will do them the least harm."

Original goals changed

According to Ms. Wharff, self-defense classes at Valley were first taught six years ago. They were started, she said, because there was a need for young girls to have a knowledge of how to protect themselves and how not to get into the situation in the first place.

The goals of the class have evolved to include both boys and girls, according to Ms. Wharff. She said that few boys still take self-defense, noting that only four boys are presently enrolled. Statistically, Ms. Wharff said, more women are attacked than men.

The six-week course started with discussions on safety precautions to prevent situations from occurring. Later in the course, a speaker from the Rape Crisis Center and one from Bell Telephone, speaking on annoying phone calls that may precede an attack, will be featured. Toward the end of the course, the students will be learning some basic release skills. These will include hitting, striking, kicking, and other methods of getting away if attacked.

Confidence is the key to self-defense, according to Ms. Wharff. This concept is explained in the book *Self-Defense and Assault Prevention for Girls and Women*, written by Bruce Tegner and Alice McGrath. The authors wrote, "Self-defense does not begin with the act of striking back; it starts with concepts of self-respect, self-reliance and autonomy."

Answers presented

As to the question "What should she do?" in the situation presented in the first paragraph, Detective Lyle McKinney of the West Des Moines Police Department would say that she shouldn't be there in the first place. He said that people should not be out walking at night but, if necessary, should take well-lighted streets. If attacked, he added, a person should, within reason, comply with the attacker's request. Detective McKinney said, however, that all self-defense depends upon the individual and that there is never any practical application until it's actually needed.

Ms. Carole Meade, director of the Rape Crisis Center, would say, in this situation, that she should walk into a nearby house or business. People sometimes won't do this, she said, because they are embarrassed.

Ms. Meade said, "Most people don't think of themselves as being vulnerable. The first step is to realize that they can be a victim."

—Spotlight, Valley High School, West Des Moines, Iowa

Carrying out an analysis and interpretation of all aspects of a situation is not easy. Instead of interviewing only one news source, you will talk with several. You may need to search out experts and people with special knowledge. You will wish to research your topic, locating and reading background material. You may need to attend meetings. And, since your readers will expect many and varied opinions and conclusions, you must explain the facts on which these opinions and conclusions are based. If the issue is a controversial one, you must make certain that all sides are fairly represented.

Interpretive, in-depth news articles may appear on your paper's news, feature, or editorial pages. They may cover classes and departments, activities, problems in your community, or special teen-age concerns, such as career opportunities and college loans. In some cases, your editorial staff may decide to devote a double-page **spread** or a special section to a topic, presenting more than one interpretive, in-depth report.

Activity 1:   Examining Interpretive, In-Depth Reports

1. Describe how the interpretive, in-depth news story on page 215 differs from a straight news report. List the similarities and differences. Which paragraphs or ideas have been added through interpretive, in-depth reporting? What additional sources did the reporter consult? Which paragraphs or sentences are factual statements? Which are the opinions of news sources? Which offer explanations?

2. Examine your school paper or exchange newspapers for other such articles. Clip three of the best. Explain what characteristics led you to identify each one as a good example of interpretive, in-depth reporting.

Preparing the Interpretive, In-Depth News Report

Real investigation of a newsworthy topic requires careful planning, much reporting time and skill, and great care in writing. The following five steps are suggested as the normal procedure for interpretive, in-depth reporting. Since interpretive, in-depth stories vary so greatly in their topics, purposes, and presentations, however, procedures may also vary from story to story.

Select Your Subject

Your first step is to decide on a suitable subject for your report. What are students discussing in and out of school? The answer to this question can offer a number of ideas for interpretive, in-depth reports. You can also look at the possibility of expanding a simple news story. For example, if an alumnus has become a candidate for a city office, this could become the **news peg** for reporting on an upcoming election as well as on its possible effects on the school community.

Finding a subject for an interpretive, in-depth report can be made easier by noting what students are talking about. Student conversations and discussions are likely to suggest subjects of special interest to your chief readers.

Notice the possibilities suggested in the following school newspaper leads. How many of these subjects might be suitable for interpretive, in-depth articles in your own school paper?

Darkness. It can be transformed into light by a simple flick of a switch. Unless you're blind.

—*The Tiger,* Central High School, Cape Girardeau, Missouri

The United States' record industry sales have dropped approximately 50 percent from last year. After 1978, the industry's last big year, business slid from a gross of more than $4,000,000 to $3,600,000 in 1981.

—*Hillcrest Hurricane,* Hillcrest High School, Dallas, Texas

Giant footprints, spray-painted bathrooms, bombs, and the disappearance of over 40 garbage cans have marked a continuing trend of vandalism on campus.

—*The Epitaph,* Homestead High School, Cupertino, California

In San Diego's Gompers Secondary School, a computer magnet school, ordinary students, not child geniuses, learn in unordinary situations.

—*Rincon Echo,* Rincon High School, Tucson, Arizona

The consensus among Whitman students and faculty members who have lived in other countries is that Christmas celebrations in other nations are more family-oriented and less commercialized than in the U.S.

—*Black and White,* Walt Whitman High School, Bethesda, Maryland

Activity 2: Finding Subjects for Interpretive, In-Depth Reporting

1. For each of the following groups, list three specific subjects that could be developed into interpretive, in-depth reports: (a) school activities, organizations, classes, or customs not recently covered in your school paper; (b) public matters currently being discussed by young people; (c) specific news events covered in short, factual stories in your school or local newspaper.

2. Choose a subject from this list that you could develop into an interpretive, in-depth story. (Activity 6 will require you to write this story. Each preceding activity will give you guidance as you proceed.)

Set Up a Guiding Question or Statement

Your second step is to decide on the general purpose of your story. Unlike a regular news story, where you may interview a single news source and then develop your article as you write it, interpretive, in-depth reporting requires that you begin by forming a relatively clear idea of your story. You may, of course, change direction as you encounter new ideas or new material. But you are not likely to make much progress unless you have in mind at the outset a clear conception of your objectives and your range of material.

After you decide on the general purpose of your story, you should put it in writing by preparing a short question or statement that indicates your story's scope and direction. The following examples show both a question and a statement:

How will student life differ if the 12-month school year is accepted?

Cross-country skiing is one of the fastest-growing sports in our area.

Although some writers find that a question or statement is enough, others find it useful to prepare an outline as well. The following is an outline for a story dealing with a crisis in school finances:

    I. Reasons
       A. Fewer school-age children
       B. Businesses are closing or relocating
       C. Voters don't want to increase school taxes
   II. Problems
       A. How to maintain current educational program
       B. How to meet new educational needs
  III. Proposals
       A. Close schools
       B. Shorten school day
       C. Lay off teachers

Be sure that your guiding question or statement, as well as any outline you prepare, is complete. If you are writing about a controversial or debatable topic, consider whether you are giving "equal time" to both sides.

Activity 3: Preparing Guiding Questions and Statements

1. The following question and statement are not complete enough to give a writer sufficient guidance. Rewrite each item.

   a. Why are people opposed to the new child care center?

   b. Many summer jobs are already filled.

2. Each of the following subjects could be treated in an in-depth, interpretive report. For each one, write a guiding question or statement that would give the reporter a sense of purpose and direction.

   a. A school board decision to add Latin to the curriculum

   b. A growing interest among local young people in part-time jobs

   c. The ever-expanding role of computers in daily life

   d. The increasing cost of entertainment and recreation

3. For the subject you chose in Activity 2, write a carefully thought out guiding question or statement. Bear in mind that your work here will largely determine the story you will write for Activity 6. If you think it will be useful, follow the question or statement with a brief outline that indicates the broad areas your story might, as presently conceived, cover.

Make a Plan of Action

For your third step, you will plan your course of action. You must decide what material and information you will need and where and how you will get it. You will wish to consult a variety of sources. Five or more different news sources—public records, published information, people, organizations, meetings, and other sources—might be the minimum you plan to consult.

If you were working with the topic of school finances, as outlined on page 218, you might make a tentative plan that looks something like the following one:

Plan for Story About Crisis in School Finances

1. Read articles in newspaper files at library about growth of school financial problems.
2. Interview budget officer on superintendent's staff. What has been done to date about problem?
3. Get information and statistics about industrial employment and community population from Chamber of Commerce.
4. Interview superintendent for additional facts.
5. Listen to discussion at school board meeting next week.
6. Interview officer of teachers' union about proposed layoffs.
7. Interview sample group of teachers and students. Which choice do they prefer? Why?

The checklist at the top of page 220 represents the kind of thinking that should enter into the forming of your plan of action.

✔ Checklist for Developing a Plan of Action

☐ 1. What specific information do I want to convey in my story?

☐ 2. What questions might my readers want answered?

☐ 3. Which items need to be given especially detailed treatment?

☐ 4. What background or explanatory information do I need in order to carry out my research?

☐ 5. How much research does this story deserve or need?

☐ 6. What kind of direct observation or first-hand experience do I need?

☐ 7. To whom should I turn for expert knowledge or informed opinion? For the testimony of experience? For the views and remarks of "ordinary people"?

☐ 8. What pictures, graphs, or charts should accompany the published story?

Activity 4:   Setting Up Your Plan

Prepare a plan of action for securing the information you will need to report on the subject you selected in Activity 2. Submit it, along with your guiding question or statement, to your teacher or adviser for evaluation.

Collect Your Information

Your fourth step is to gather your material and information. Especially if your topic is a debatable, controversial, or many-sided one, keep asking yourself: Am I getting a fair balance among all opposing opinions or differing perspectives? Are there additional viewpoints that should be expressed?

—Photo by Ann Hagen Griffiths from Omni

Subjects widely discussed and written about are the ones most likely to require research among published materials. Library skills and ease in using reference materials are invaluable to interpretive, in-depth reporters.

As you proceed, remain alert to the possibilities of researching other kinds of material or talking to additional people. Stories that at first seem simple assignments may develop into complex adventures as you carry out your research. For example, suppose you are preparing an article on the kinds and purposes of school field trips. While collecting this information, you might suddenly discover that your principal considers most such trips a waste of time and money. You might then shift your entire emphasis to an investigation of the values of field trips.

You should feel free to make such changes in your plan of action as may be needed to obtain all necessary information or viewpoints on your topic. Should you decide, however, that your original plan was inadequate, proceed more cautiously. Perhaps you will decide that your guiding question or statement was not well thought out, in which case it could be revised. If circumstances seem to dictate a radical change in your proposed story, your editor or adviser should be consulted.

Activity 5: Researching Your Subject

Following your plan of action, collect material on your subject.

Write Your Story

You have collected a great deal of material on your subject. Your next step is to write your story. All you have learned about writing leads and inverted-pyramid stories will be valuable to you. But with a more detailed topic, you will need to design a method of presenting your story in its most readable form, one that will carry out your purpose exactly. For interpretive, in-depth stories, the standard rules of news preparation are best regarded as guidelines, to be departed from as common sense dictates. Nevertheless, some suggestions can be given.

MAKE THE LEAD SET THE TONE. Leads for interpretive, in-depth reports do not always need to be complete. They must, however, tell enough to draw readers into the rest of the story, and they must set a tone that puts readers in the right frame of mind for all that follows.

Notice how the leads below and at the top of page 222 act, not simply to condense information, but rather to catch the readers' interest and launch them into the stories that follow.

Suppose you are walking down the hall on your way to class, and the man in front of you falls down, clutching his heart. Would you or anyone around you know what to do?

—*Catalyst*, Miami–Dade Community College South, Miami, Florida

Instead of dust, spiders, and cobwebs, the attic of Burton Gym is now the scene of a mechanical-drawing workshop for students interested in graphic arts.

—*The Pony Express*, David Lipscomb High School, Nashville, Tennessee

Civil Defense calls. An elk hunter is reported missing in the North River area. It is 4 a.m., and Mr. Jim Carossino picks up his 24-hour pack and heads for the door. Mr. Carossino, a 1970 graduate of Weatherwax, is the director of the local Explorer Search and Rescue unit.

—*Ocean Breeze*, J. M. Weatherwax High School, Aberdeen, Washington

Televisions, radios, billboards, and neon signs flaunt their incandescent propositions before the starry eyes of youth. For today's teen-ager, there are many more ways to spend money than to make it.

—*West Side Story*, West High School, Iowa City, Iowa

CUSTOM DESIGN THE BODY OF YOUR STORY. The inverted-pyramid arrangement will be useful when you are presenting a current news event and adding opinions and background material. A story narrating a series of events may fit naturally into the chronological approach. But in, for example, a report on the development of a grading system and proposed changes in it, neither of these formats may be suitable. You will probably have to design your story to harmonize with your material. You might adopt a logical arrangement suggested by a story outline; you might treat the main aspects of your subject one after another; or you might make use of comparison and contrast. The article on page 215 is a good example of a nonstandard story arrangement that fits its subject.

An interpretive, in-depth article is not expected to meet the cutoff test. However, it must be concisely written, and it must fit the allotted space. If it becomes necessary to shorten it, an editor will exercise judgment in eliminating or condensing paragraphs.

USE OPINIONS TO ENHANCE FACTS. A well-written interpretive, in-depth story presents a series of related facts. Opinions of people who are involved in, affected by, or knowledgeable in the matters covered should be quoted to amplify and explain these facts. Opinions can also be used to add interesting detail and to make a story more appealing.

Readers of interpretive, in-depth news stories may wonder what conclusions reporters have reached as a result of their investigations. A reporter's conclusions, if any, should be shown through the facts of the story. An editorial would be the proper place for outright conclusions. The facts, opinions, and observations in your article should make for accuracy and clarity of presentation and allow readers to make their own judgments. In any case, you should not attempt to promote your personal opinions, however strongly you may feel about the subject. It is in this area of interpretive, in-depth reporting that the main differences between responsible and irresponsible newspapers stand out.

The following story (presented here in somewhat shortened form) is an excellent example of a report in which opinions explain and enhance facts. What kind of preparation preceded the writing of it? How did the reporters structure the body of their story?

Shoplifting plagues holidays

**By Susan Larrabee
and Scott Mulcahy**

Shoplifters in Idaho will carry off over $7,000,000 worth of goods this Christmas season, according to a recent article in the Idaho Statesman.

Many department store managers in Boise believe a high percentage of these thefts are committed by teenagers, and undoubtedly if past years give any indication, some of these teens will be from Borah.

"We catch two to three shoplifters a week, and over 50 percent of them are teens," Mr. Phil Matlock, Loss Prevention Manager for Grand Central, reported.

K-MART ESTIMATES the rate of juvenile shoplifters to be even higher—anywhere from 60 to 70 percent, according to Mr. Mark Blackman, the store manager.

Shoplifting rates are highest during the Christmas season between Thanksgiving and Christmas.

Nationwide, over 3,000,000 people will be caught shoplifting between the beginning of the month of November and the end of the month of December. This comes to approximately 50,000 individuals a day.

"Shoplifting really skyrockets during Christmas," said Juvenile Probation Officer Dennis Holmes.

Teen-age males have a higher rate of arrests than teen females, the ratio being three boys to every two girls caught.

"The ratio is higher for boys because stores are more likely to turn in boys than they are girls," explained Officer Holmes. "The rates would probably be higher for both, but an overwhelming amount aren't getting caught," he noted.

MANY MERCHANTS place a copy of the Idaho Code dealing with shoplifting in their stores to try to discourage shoplifting, but even with this

warning Idaho stores lose a tremendous amount of money to shoplifters every year.

For instance, K-Mart estimates it loses 10 percent of each store's volume per year. Losses such as this force many stores to increase their prices as much as 2 to 3 percent.

While many adults steal out of anger or need, a majority of teen thieves steal for the challenge.

"KIDS SHOPLIFT for the fun of doing it," Officer Holmes explained. "They don't usually need the items they steal, and a lot of the time they don't really want them. They do it as a dare or for excitement."

Stores usually call the police when they catch a teen shoplifter. The police then call the resource officer at the juvenile's school. Then the resource officer takes the shoplifter to court.

"Although some of the shoplifters are repeat offenders and do go on to other, more serious crimes, many are only first time offenders and are so shaken up and embarrassed by being caught that they never do it again," observed Officer Holmes.

In court most teens plead "guilty." They are usually charged with petty theft if they have stolen items worth $150 or under or with grand theft when the items are valued over $150.

STORES ALSO may take civil action in which they sue the juvenile's parents for damages.

The courts have many options in dealing with the shoplifters. For instance, they may dismiss the case totally if it's a first offense and the teen has shown that he or she will not continue to steal.

Similarly, they may have the shoplifter sign an informal behavior agreement and judgment is withheld. If the person proves that he is responsible for his actions, after three months the case is dismissed.

For repeat offenders or even first-time offenders who have displayed attitude problems, the court may place the teen on a year's probation or sentence him or her to serve up to 30 days in jail.

"THIS SENTENCE is usually handed out because the court feels the kid isn't taking any of his crimes seriously," Officer Holmes said. "It would have a hard impact right away, and hopefully, it would stop him from doing it again," he added.

Myles (a fictitious name), a junior, tells how he was caught shoplifting.

"I went in the store and walked over to the record department. I found the album I wanted, and when I didn't think anyone was watching, I stuck it into my school folder. I turned around and started walking out of the store when a guy came up to me and asked me to open my folder," he said. "He took the album and made me go back to the security office with him. He called my dad, and when he got there, he was really mad."

"You can tell a shoplifter right away when he walks in the store," Mr. Matlock indicated. "He usually comes in with a friend who acts as a lookout. They head for the darker corners of the store with the items they want to steal, and the lookout watches for guards. When they're sure no one is looking, then the shoplifter sticks the item into his clothes."

—*The Senator*, Borah High School,
Boise, Idaho

Activity 6: Completing Your Story

1. Assemble all notes you have taken on your subject and mentally plan how you will use this material in your article.

2. Write a compelling lead that gives at least a partial summary of your findings and invites your reader to proceed into your story.

3. Complete the body of your story, using the most logical arrangement you can devise.

4. On a copy of your story, underline the factual material with a colored pencil. Using a second color, underline the opinions that you have quoted or summarized.

Extended Reporting of a Broad or Complex Subject

Some of the subjects that you listed when working on Activity 2 or that may have occurred to you since may be simply too broad or too complex to cover in a single article. In such a case, an editorial staff might consider publishing a variety of stories about this type of subject on a full page or more of its paper. It might even devote an entire issue to the subject. Another way would be to print a series of articles in several issues.

While a staff might also wish to include an editorial, it should keep in mind that its major purpose is to report the matter and responsible opinions on it to the readership. There is no harm in a paper's letting its readers

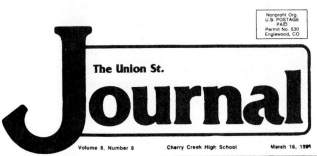

Nonprofit Org.
U.S. POSTAGE
PAID
Permit No. 530
Englewood, CO

The Union St.

Journal

Volume 8, Number 8   Cherry Creek High School   March 16, 1981

s   m   t   w   th   f   s

Graphic by Spencer Mains

SHORTENED WEEK

Four day school week could be wave of the future

BY RICK KORNFELD

It's four thirty in the afternoon on Thursday and, as the long awaited final bell sounds signifying the end of another school day, 3,400 Cherry Creek students leave school anticipating their three-day weekend. It's the end of another four day school week.

Although Cherry Creek School District is not officially considering a four day school week, this form of scheduling seems to be the wave of the future. Because many government and education officials believe that a four day school week would help conserve energy, school districts around the country — including fourteen in Colorado — have begun experimenting with this innovative new concept in schooling.

MANY STUDENTS would welcome the thought of a three day vacation each week. In addition, many teachers also favor such a program. There would be disadvantages, however, for the student as well as the teacher should Cherry Creek switch to a four day school week format. While the extra vacation day would give students and teachers extra leisure time, many students feel that, because two hours would be added to the school day, there would not be sufficient time to participate in extracurricular activities such as clubs and athletics.

Answering four day week proponent's claims that many classes are sufficiently taught in four days under the present system, Principal Henry Cotton said, "Any teacher can lower the quality of his or her class in order to teach it in three days if necessary. The good teachers don't have enough class time as it is."

Teachers foresee two major problems. First, they believe that their students could not tolerate an extra two periods per day because of restlessness or fatigue. More importantly, the instructors relate that they would not have enough time to properly teach the courses.

A staunch opponent of the four day week concept, Cotton, who has eliminated the "off day" in many classes, favors a longer school day or a six day school week like the ones utilized in many European countries, including Russia. "The quality of education in the United States has consistently gone down each year as is evident by the drop in S.A.T. scores." Cotton continued. "This country is mass producing students: we're more worried about how many we educate instead of how well we educate them." Because of his adherence to this philosophy, Cotton believes that school should not be compulsory because "then we'll get students who want to learn, and those who don't will be able to get into the job market early."

ALTHOUGH he emphasized that the United States needs to conserve energy — the main reason for the initiation of the four day school week program, — Cotton does not feel that reducing class time will actually help the country enough to outweigh the disadvantages of less learning time. "If we really value education in this country, we can't afford to cut down on it," he explained. "The country can't be as concerned with saving energy as it claims to be if we allow things like neon signs to waste our energy resources."

Like Cotton, Kurby Lyle, District Supervisor of Student Activities, also agrees

that education should not be reduced in order to save energy. In addition, Lyle doesn't believe that the district would save a great deal of energy by having a four day week. "Although we might be saving a little of the district's energy, I believe that we'd be wasting more of the country's energy with this program because the kids and teachers would probably waste more gasoline," he said. "Because they would have an extra day of leisure, there often would be more driving whether it be to go skiing or to go to a movie." On the subject of the extra leisure time which an extra vacation day provides, Lyle stated, "The last thing we need is more leisure time. This is a country of plenty, and we're more productive when we're busy."

Because the lengthened school day would shorten time for extra-curricular activities, Lyle also opposes the idea of a four day school week. "Although I believe that activities and athletics should not dictate the length or number of school days, these 'extras' are a vital part of the high school education," he interjected, "and it is important to continue to give the students the opportunity to participate in these activities."

WHILE there are many opponents of the four day school week concept, there are also many proponents of this new concept in education. One such proponent is Elbert County Public School District Superintendent Leroy Reams. Elbert County's public schools have had the four day school week for the entire 1980-1981 school year. Although cooks and bus drivers suffered a twenty percent salary cut, teachers and administrators have retained their original

salaries. Reams sights the fact that his district has saved a significant amount of energy as the main advantage to having a four day school week. In addition to saving fifteen percent on electricity, the district has also saved twenty percent on gasoline costs and twenty percent on food costs.

While most of the students and teachers in Elbert County favor the new system, only about sixty-five percent of the parents are pleased with it. Nevertheless, Reams still is in favor of it.

Elbert county has solved the extra-curricular activity problem by conducting these activities during the "off day" as well as the regular school days. Academically, Reams believes that the new format has had no adverse effect on the student's quality of education. "Under the new system, our classes are at the same point or ahead of what they were last year at this time," he said. Although the exact figures won't be known until the end of March, Reams also believes that the new format has made Elbert County's schools more efficient. "We're definitely more efficient this year because less time is wasted and the kids seem to work harder in anticipation of the three day weekend," he commented.

Eventually a four day school week might become a reality in the Cherry Creek School District because of federal budget cuts. If the final figures from the fourteen Colorado school districts participating in the four day school week program prove to be positive, it might not be long until Creekers are also enjoying a three day weekend.

The subject of this front page story is one of many that might call for extended treatment. In general, the broader or more complex a subject is the fuller its coverage must be.

know which side it is on so long as its opinion does not intrude on its objective reporting.

Many subjects lend themselves to extended treatment. The *Forum*, of South Houston High School, South Houston, Texas, published a group of articles defining prejudice and discussing its impact on blacks, women, Mexican Americans, and recent Oriental immigrants. Child labor law violations and their effects on teen-age workers were investigated by the *Echo*, of Glenbard East High School, Lombard, Illinois. Following the deaths of two popular students in an accident involving a drunk driver, the *Brighton Barb*, of Brighton High School, Salt Lake City, Utah, printed a group of stories on alcoholism and drunk driving. *The Nucleus*, of Albert Einstein High School, Kensington, Maryland, published an eight-page supplement entitled "High School: A Changing World."

Activity 7: Covering a Broad or Complex Subject

1. Choose a subject that you believe could be explored with a group of several articles. Prepare a plan showing what stories would be needed and what research would be done. Indicate the stories by brief descriptions of their contents. Your plan should include at least four stories.

2. In a daily newspaper, find an example of extended coverage—for example, reports on a major event in professional sports or an election. Write a report in which you explain what seems to have been the plan behind the related articles. Note the different purposes and approaches of the articles and describe the different kinds of news value in them. Also point out instances of unnecessary repetition.

Summary

This chapter describes interpretive, in-depth reports and explains how they are prepared. It concludes with suggestions for treating especially broad or complex subjects.

RECOGNIZING THE CHARACTERISTICS OF INTERPRETIVE, IN-DEPTH REPORTING. Interpretive, in-depth news articles explain news events by presenting opinions as well as facts. They are also fuller and more detailed than ordinary news stories. Investigative reporting, which calls for similar reporting skills, is primarily concerned with uncovering hidden or suppressed facts behind an event.

PREPARING THE INTERPRETIVE, IN-DEPTH NEWS REPORT. The process by which an interpretive, in-depth report is written may be divided into five steps. First, select a subject, perhaps by noting what students are talking about or by looking at a news event for possibilities of extended, detailed treatment. Second, set up a guiding question or statement that gives your work a purpose, perhaps followed by a rough outline of areas to cover. Third, make a plan of action for finding and gathering the material you will need. Fourth, collect your material and information, being sure to get enough for a thorough, balanced, and fair treatment of your subject. Fifth, write your story, taking care that the lead sets an attention-getting tone, that the body is structured to present your material in an orderly and appealing way, and that opinions are used to enhance the facts.

EXTENDED REPORTING OF A BROAD OR COMPLEX SUBJECT. When a subject is too broad or complex for treatment in a single interpretive, in-depth report, it can be handled in a number of related stories, either in a single issue of a paper or in a succession of issues.

Vocabulary

interpretive, in-depth news article
byline
investigative reporting

spread
news peg

Review Questions

1. How do interpretive, in-depth news articles differ from regular news stories?

2. How does investigative reporting differ from ordinary reporting?

3. What should a plan of action for an interpretive, in-depth story consist of?

4. What should the writer of an interpretive, in-depth story keep in mind regarding (a) the lead, (b) the body, and (c) opinions?

5. How might a school newspaper handle an especially broad or complex subject?

Discussion Questions

1. In daily papers, an interpretive, in-depth news article is often printed alongside a basic news story on the same topic. What are the benefits of this treatment? Might it be useful in your paper? Why or why not?

2. Many common news subjects can be expanded into longer interpretive reports. Which, if any, cannot be? Explain.

3. What changes might be made in a school newspaper's reference resources in order to en-

courage more thorough treatment of important news stories?

4. From the readers' viewpoint, what are the advantages and disadvantages of not being told the reporter's own opinion?

5. Schools sometimes devote entire issues to single topics. What problems might arise if this policy were followed too often? In your opinion, how often would such a policy be appropriate?

Chapter Project

Preparing an Interpretive, In-Depth Report on Manners and Behavior in Your School

Follow the steps in this chapter to prepare an interpretive, in-depth report on manners and behavior in your school. You may decide to narrow the subject and deal with some specific aspect of manners and behavior. Or you may decide to treat the entire subject.

11

WRITING COLORFUL FEATURE STORIES

When you have completed this chapter you should be able to

Understand the special characteristics of feature stories.

Conceive, develop, and write a feature story.

Interview a personality and write a vivid personality story.

A reporter stared vacantly at her typewriter. "There's hardly enough information here to make the story worth writing," she moaned. She read what she had typed:

> Dan Wagner was attacked and robbed of $520.92 while working at the Consolidated Station January 1.

"That's a good summary," she thought. "But that's all there is to the story—and everyone has heard about the robbery, anyway. How can I make it interesting enough to print?" She tried again:

> Attacked by two robbers while working at the Consolidated Station January 1, senior Dan Wagner is recovering from minor injuries.

The editor walked past. The reporter explained her problem.

"You're right," the editor agreed. "The facts of this story can be told in a single paragraph. We could put it in the news-briefs column."

"Then that's all I should write," said the reporter.

"There's more," the editor replied. "Dan had a really memorable experience that evening. Why can't we get some of that excitement into our story by the way we tell it? With a few more dramatic details and a bit of colorful narrative writing, this would make a fine feature story. Try to develop the human-interest angle and our readers will enjoy it."

If the reporter succeeded in writing the kind of story the editor had in mind, it might have been very much like the following.

Robbers attack ONHS senior

By Deb Krohn

"Can I help you, sir?" asked senior Dan Wagner.

"Yah, you can give me the money," chuckled the prospective customer, who began to strike Dan at the Consolidated Station where he was working January 1.

Dan had spotted a dark car parked alongside the road near the station while pumping gas but thought nothing of it. At about 7:30 p.m., the front door opened, so Dan went into the front room. He was then attacked by one of the two men. Dan said he had seen only one of the men, who made away with $520.92 from the cash register. One man tied Dan up and left him lying on the floor.

After about half an hour, Dan struggled to the light switch and continued to flash it on and off until an Appleton man found him.

—*North Star*, Oshkosh North High School, Oshkosh, Wisconsin

Developing Ideas for Feature Stories

Basic news is the heart of a newspaper. Interpretive, in-depth reports can help make such basic news more useful to the readers. But what about all the other things that may be of interest to readers yet do not qualify purely on the basis of their straight-news value? And what about situations such as the one in the introduction where the news itself takes only a few lines but the reporter feels there must be a story somewhere in the event? These are cases in which feature stories can be used to add interest to your paper while making it better able to meet the needs of your readers.

Feature stories, sometimes referred to simply as **features** or **news features,** are generally based at least indirectly on some news event. They may be used to expand in a brief and enlivening manner on an item of basic news, to provide information of general value or interest, to focus on some human-interest item, or to describe a personality.

The interest in a feature story should lie not only in the facts reported but also in the way the story is written. A lively narrative or descriptive style, often with a strong human-interest appeal, is typical of feature stories. Their leads are designed not to cover the facts but to draw readers' attention. The bodies of the stories are usually written in a style that is much less formal than that found in basic news coverage or in interpretive, in-depth reports.

Feature stories serve not only the readers but also the newspaper staff. They can generally be placed almost anywhere in a paper. They also allow reporters to write more creatively and informally on a broad range of news-related subjects.

"Features are the wide-screen, 3-D, technicolor side of the newspaper business. They provide scope, extra dimension, and, above all, color to the daily news diet," says Don Duncan, feature writer for the Tacoma *News Tribune.*

Finding Subjects for Feature Stories

What subjects are suitable for feature stories? This question is nearly impossible to answer since almost any subject is suitable for feature presentation. Feature stories include, for instance, profiles of organizations or

Personal experiences such as those that friends tell each other sometimes make excellent subjects for feature stories. A good feature writer will spot story possibilities in private matters appropriate for public consumption.

—Photo by Peter Vandermark from Stock, Boston

individuals, consumer surveys, promotional articles about worthwhile groups and activities, do-it-yourself items, and a variety of humorous pieces. Many feature stories even recount memorable personal experiences.

Finding a subject for a feature story may often come down to suddenly seeing some ordinary thing around you in a new light rather than discovering some extraordinary thing or occurrence. If you make an effort to maintain a lively, curious perspective on what lies around you, your everyday life will offer up subjects enough for feature writing. On the other hand, alertness to the extraordinary will enable you to catch those subjects that make for interesting feature stories no matter how plainly they are written.

In the following story, an extraordinary subject and a lively writing style come together to make up a good feature story. See if you can point out the characteristics that make this story different from an ordinary news report.

Model T cranks up

From out of the past, a 1926 Model T Ford rumbles up to the high school parking lot. Has Henry Ford emerged from a time warp? No, senior Dan Stanford has driven his antique car to school.

A PRESENT from his grandfather, Dan had the Model T shipped to him from Salem, Illinois.

As odd as the car looks from the outside, it looks even stranger on the inside. The accelerator is on the steering column, while the three foot pedals on the floor are the brakes and the forward and reverse gears. There are no turn signals, no speedometer, no fuel gauge, no windshield wipers, and no back seat.

DAN NOTED, "Without a speedometer, I just have to guess how fast I'm going. I only know the Model T has a top speed of 40 mph on a flat road."

Dan continued, "Driving around in the Model T really makes me feel like I'm back in the 1920s. I'm limited in speed and comfort, just as my grandfather was when he drove the car.

"I HAVE no real plans for the car. I might fix it up and enter it in car shows. But it's just fun to drive around on sunny, warm days," concluded Dan.

—*Jet Jotter*, Longmeadow High School,
Longmeadow, Massachusetts

Activity 1:   Analyzing Content and Style in Feature Stories

1. By going through issues of your school paper and a daily paper, find three feature stories based on unusual or extraordinary subjects. For each, write a brief description of the subject and an explanation of how the way of writing the story maximized its interest.

2. Do the same for three feature stories based on subjects that are not that unusual.

3. Explain in writing whether the foregoing Model T story could have been written effectively as a conventional straight-news story.

Developing Feature Stories from Observation

Reporters who write feature stories must be keen observers. Details that go unnoticed by the average person are yours to see and write about. Watch and listen for seemingly insignificant happenings whose potential news interest can be drawn out and made into a story that appeals to readers. What feature possibilities do you see in the following fragments of life?

A student says, "My great-grandfather was . . ."

Two students carry a telescope down the hall.

A teacher says, "When I was a student here . . ."

A student mentions, "My friend invented a new game . . ."

Extend your powers of observation as you collect information for any story. Train yourself to notice details. What was your news source wearing? What mannerisms did he or she have? What did your source do with his or her hands and feet while you talked? What was going on around you during the interview? What were the details of the setting? Teach yourself to absorb them and to recognize their feature story value. They may seem trivial, but some of the best literary and journalistic writing of the twentieth century consists of a vivid and exact representation of the details of ordinary life. What may be inconsequential in reality takes on meaning and vitality in the hands of a creative and imaginative writer.

Activity 2:   Sharpening Your Powers of Observation

1. Think back over your last few classes. In at least one of them, there was probably some kind of interruption. Someone was tardy for class; a messenger delivered a note or collected an absence slip; an administrator or teacher came in to ask a question. Who was it? What was he or she wearing? What happened? What was said? Was it a routine interruption, or did someone seem excited? What time did it happen? Write a paragraph describing the incident. Give as many significant details as you can.

2. Observe a teacher or student in your next class. Make no written notes during class. After you have left the room, write a paragraph describing this person's activities during the period.

Using Imagination to Create Feature Stories

The ability to observe with imagination can lead you to success in writing every kind of feature story, whether its main purpose may be to inform or to entertain. The examples presented so far in this chapter have been primarily of the human-interest variety. Since their subjects' news value is relatively limited, the success of these stories will be determined mainly by the way they are written. And the way stories are written is determined by how lively and resourceful the imagination is that penetrates a subject and either finds or injects interest into it.

A feature writer who had worked for the summer with a conservation corps might have material for a very interesting article. Many of the best feature stories are based on the simple recognition that something you are interested in may interest others as well.

Subjects for feature stories are everywhere around your school and community. You can often uncover them on your beat or while following a routine news assignment. Even the lost-and-found department and the attendance office can yield information or ideas for feature stories—not to mention the unusual happenings, peculiar situations, and funny remarks that punctuate every school day. Alertness, observation, and luck may help you come upon these subjects.

You should be especially watchful for occasions in which you can become personally and directly involved. When possible, take part in meetings, events, or experiences. Involvement can result in strong and effective stories. Many writers say that deep and true feelings can be expressed only by people who write about what they have experienced firsthand. In fact, a form of reporting, known as **new journalism,** is based on the idea that reporters should enter into and participate in what they are going to write about and then make use of the techniques of realistic fiction to convey the feel of authentic firsthand experience.

But however you arrive at a subject, it is your imagination that will determine whether it results in a good story. Often a subject will at first seem lifeless. Only when your imagination has had time to work on it will its kernel of vitality emerge. To aid in this process, it helps to keep a notebook of feature story ideas that you can develop when inspiration spurs your imagination.

The story on page 234 deals with a commonplace phenomenon of high school life: the apathy toward schoolwork that sets in among many seniors as graduation nears. Notice, however, that the writer saw in "senioritis" good material for a story. Notice also that the remarks and opinions she quotes indicate that she thought up questions designed to reveal what lies behind senioritis. Her creative grasp of her subject illustrates the feature story writer's imagination at work.

Sun, fun, tradition spur senioritis epidemic

By Kristin Johnsen

Sun. Sand. Sea.

Each year these forces beckon devoted students, urging them to hit the beach.

In the senior year, external factors strengthen these temptations, causing record absences and a marked drop in student dedication.

Senior Susan Ferris explained, "You cut classes. You're rude to teachers. Somehow everyone's attitude is different. Their attitude is, 'I don't care about grades. I want to do what I want to do.'"

One factor that changes seniors' views about school is college. Acceptances or rejections allow seniors to forget their college worries and cut study time.

"The reason you go to high school is to get into college. Once you've achieved that, high school is over," said senior Robert Pearson. He himself admitted cutting his study time 90 percent.

"Before, you might have wanted to go to the beach, but now it's not going to hurt your future," clarified senior Laura Onsted.

Freedom tantalizes seniors into foregoing studies and testing their limits.

"People are excited because they are jumping the last hurdle of childhood," said Chris Sodergren, senior. "They wish to get out into the adult world and fend for themselves."

Susan believes seniors try to thwart present controls and restrictions because they know that next year no one will control them.

"It's not that I'm tired of school," explained Robert. "It's just the fact that the end is near, and that's intensified the disease a bit."

Anticipating losing friends and their present social life, many students throw themselves into a frenzy of activity.

Senior Charlotte Garbers explained that seniors are working on other aspects of their life, such as their social life.

Laura agreed, saying that "in your last few months at high school, you want to have a good time to remember friends by."

Tradition plays a large role in seniors' habits. Many consider it their right to cut classes and work less.

"Senioritis is something you look forward to for four years," said Robert. "There's no way to break the tradition without totally destroying school morale."

—*The Epitaph*, Homestead High School, Cupertino, California

Activity 3:   Exercising Your Imagination

1. List five ordinary things or events in your school and community that you see as potentially interesting subjects for feature stories. For each, describe how you would approach it to bring out its interest for your readers.

2. Reread the story on senioritis and then explain another way of treating the subject of student apathy in a feature story.

3. Taking the first three paragraphs of the story on senioritis as the lead, which of the five *W* and one *H* questions are answered in the lead? Is

the lead's purpose primarily to inform or to lead the reader into the story? Does the story in its entirety conform to one of the standard news story formats (inverted-pyramid, chronological, or composite), or has a special arrangement been used? Can the cutoff test be applied to the closing paragraphs?

4. Briefly describe an event in which you were personally involved that would make a good subject for a feature story. Explain why you think it would be a good subject.

Writing Feature Stories

The writing of feature stories can, perhaps, best be approached by considering a representative type: the **human-interest story.** A human-interest story is one that appeals to people as human beings with capacities of joy, sorrow, amusement, and concern. More narrowly, it is a story that engages people's interest in other human beings, the most interesting of all feature story subjects.

Notice how much the quotes from the "victims" add to the human-interest angle of the following story. The story comes alive because of people's reactions to an unusual situation.

Owensboro students involved in 'major disaster'

By Judy Davenport

Six OHS students experienced a major disaster on the dreary night of Wednesday, October 24.

The six volunteer "victims" were senior Laurie Hicks, sophomores Kelly Lloyd, Janet Howard, Julie Head, Kathy Harris, and freshman Holly Hicks.

They all played different roles in a ficticious disaster at the Owensboro-Daviess County Airport. It was called the "Disaster Drill," and volunteers can agree to the name "disaster" even though it was all a put-on.

"Its purpose was to keep the medical team in practice," said sophomore Kathy Harris.

The "victims" are all from the volunteer workers at Mercy Hospital.

Kathy said, "I screamed and yelled, I got tied up, and I rode in the ambulance. I was supposed to be in hysteria!"

"I had blood rushing out of my face, and I was unconscious, too. It was really gross! I rode in the ambulance and was taken into intensive care. The doctors decided that I would die, so I did!" commented Kelly Lloyd.

Janet Howard encountered second- and third-degree burns all over her body and a bleeding artery and neck. She was put in the helicopter and then transferred to the ambulance. "While I was there, the paramedics were running out with me on the stretcher, and they dropped me!" said Janet with a slight smile.

—*The Scoop*, Owensboro High School, Owensboro, Kentucky

Follow a Logical Plan

When you set out to write a human-interest story (or any other kind of feature story), it is important to proceed in a logical way. While many of the same steps that work for basic newswriting must be followed here, other factors also come into play, particularly matters of approach and style. The following six steps should help.

COLLECT THE FACTS. Clever writing cannot hide a shortage of facts. Gather whatever you need by observation, interviews, and research. Remember that good note taking is as necessary for the feature story writer as for the straight-news reporter. So is accuracy.

DETERMINE AN APPROACH. Once you have enough facts, look over the material you've assembled and decide how to approach it. How, for example, would you handle a story about students who have overcome handicaps and gone on to become capable athletes or musicians? Would you tell their story largely through their words and from their point of view? Or would you arrange the facts about them into a narrative that you would simply report, maybe building up to a climax or surprise ending? The question of approach must be answered before you start writing.

WRITE A SUITABLE LEAD. In human-interest and other feature stories, the lead does not have to follow the strict one-paragraph format of a straight-news lead or include all essential facts. Rather, it must emphasize attention-getting statements, make clear what kind of story to expect, and set the tone. It should also establish the approach, or angle, from which your readers will view the story. How much of their stories do the following leads reveal? Do they make you want to read more? Why?

Colored lights blink on and off as paper printed with mathematical gibberish spews from a slot. Monitoring the machines are men in white coats who speak to each other in a language full of X's and Q's that only one of their group understands. The scene in a computer room, right? Wrong!

> —*The Owl*, Warren Central High School, Indianapolis, Indiana

What has two rubber hoses, one gallon jar partly filled with water, and one cigarette and creates a vacuum?

A smoking machine, of course.

To demonstrate the dangers of smoking, Ms. Pat Latimer, health teacher, created the machine.

> —*The Scribe*, Madison Junior High School, Eugene, Oregon

It's a thing that makes the blood run cold and the skin prickle on the neck. It's the old monster, ''The Research Paper,'' that comes every spring to trap the unwary in an endless mound of books, bibliography cards, and notes.

> —*The Redbird*, Loudonville High School, Loudonville, Ohio

In a cloud of dust, a pack of cyclists whizzed over the dirt trail. Scrawled on their leather jackets was the name of this ornery-looking bunch—''The Over-the-Hill Cycling Gang.''

A closer look at these characters might reveal some familiar faces since the gang is composed of pleasure seeking teachers out on a typical biking excursion.

> —*Black and White*, Walt Whitman High School, Bethesda, Maryland

ORGANIZE THE STORY IN THE BEST POSSIBLE WAY. Since a human-interest story is meant to be read from beginning to end, the standard inverted-pyramid arrangement is not necessary. A chronological or narrative pattern, on the other hand, may work quite well for some stories. For others, you may have to make up your own pattern. Concentrate on the primary impression you want to make on the reader and decide what arrangement of material will lead to that impression. Be prepared to experiment with different outlines until you hit upon one that works.

Keep in mind also that your last paragraph will complete the story and thus should in some way return the reader to the lead. This can be done by a clever summary statement, a final quotation, a reference to the future, or even a surprise ending.

FOCUS ON SIGNIFICANT DETAILS. The impression your story makes depends not only on the way it is organized but also on the details it includes. In view of this, some of the writing techniques often associated with new journalism can be recommended. One of these is to include the details of the setting, or the "scene." Another is to focus on aspects of a person's appearance, dress, mannerisms, and so on that suggest character, personality, or social status. A third is to include dialogue—a verbal interchange of thoughts and feelings that makes a human subject come alive for the reader.

WRITE WITH COLOR AND IMAGINATION. Imaginative, original writing is important to the success of any feature story. Here is your opportunity to unleash the descriptive words that will always need to be somewhat restrained in a basic news story simply because there you must stick to nothing but the facts.

Consider the description of a person such as a city editor. "In the straight-news story," says feature writer Don Duncan, "the person is simply a city editor, or at best, a veteran city editor. But in a feature story, the person might become a gimlet-eyed, bushy-haired, cigarette-puffing fugitive from Dante . . .

"The news story is a skeleton report of who's doing what and, possibly, why he's getting away with it. The feature story puts meat on the factual bones, gives the skeleton personality, and marches this 'blood and guts creature' through a series of neatly balanced paragraphs with a news twist.

"All feature writers have some basic tricks," continues Mr. Duncan. "They scorn passive verbs for those with action and sock. . . . They walk into a sentence headfirst, squeezing out excess words and confusing clauses. They try to make transitions from paragraph to paragraph so smooth the reader will be whisked along by the momentum of their prose. They know short sentences create a sense of urgency, long sentences a sense of leisure. And for the many-comma'd, preposition-ridden sentence, they have no use at all."

The meaning is clear. People in your feature stories must come alive as you tell what they are doing. Remember, however, that informal writing does not mean sloppy writing. You will still need to keep your writing within the bounds covered by your newspaper style sheet.

The following feature story "puts meat on the factual bones" of a tornado that struck parts of Missouri. Notice how much of the story consists of the words of the writer's schoolmates who were affected by the storm.

And it sounded like a train

By Karl Wunderlich

"We interrupt this broadcast . . . (static) . . . the National Weather Bureau has issued a tornado warning for the Missouri counties of St. Louis, St. Charles . . . (static) . . . thunderstorms, high winds, and heavy rain continuing . . . (static)"

As the radio broadcasts warned, Thursday, December 2, wasn't going to be a typical week night. Families dug out dusty flashlights and candles and huddled in basements, while thunder cracked outside and electric lights flickered and failed.

For many families, the storm was just an exciting diversion, but for Jenni Fly, senior, and her family, it was a taste of a tornado's fury.

"We lost two huge, old trees. One was a 100-foot pine that crashed onto our roof," she said. "The top 30 feet broke off and flipped into the back yard, and the rest fell against the house. The whole house shook and cracked plaster all over the walls. The tree broke a few rafters in the attic and leaned against the house all week until we could find someone to take it out."

Homes, however, were not the only targets of the storm.

"We had our car parked in front of our house on the street," said Robert Gregg, senior. "A big limb from a tree across the street broke off and smashed into it. Both doors got dented and the rear-view mirror smashed into the driver's window. We were lucky, though. Our neighbors had a limb smash through their front door, go through the wall into the kitchen, and knock the sliding glass door in the back of the house out of its frame."

The quickness of the storm took many people by surprise.

"I was upstairs in my room and I felt the pressure starting to build up," said Al Laudel, senior. "I made it to the stairs when I heard a noise like a train. When we looked outside later, most of our garage had been thrown into our back yard. The roof had been ripped off and turned upside down and the walls had been twisted around."

A few people remained oblivious to the danger.

"I was upstairs sleeping during the whole storm," said Adam Finch, junior. "I didn't even realize there was one until I got up and looked in the basement. We had about 10 gallons of water sloshing around in one corner."

—*The Kirkwood Call,* Kirkwood High School, Kirkwood, Missouri

---

Check Your Work

Since feature story writing is probably more of an art than other kinds of journalistic writing, it is especially necessary not to overlook the systematic parts of your work because of the attention you devote to the imaginative and creative parts. The following checklist will enable you to evaluate your work and make any needed revision.

> ✔ **Checklist for Feature Stories**
>
> ☐ 1. Have I chosen a subject appropriate for a feature story?
>
> ☐ 2. Have I gathered all the facts I need by observation, interviews, and research? If interviews have been involved, have I prepared and asked the right questions?
>
> ☐ 3. Have I settled on the best approach to my material?
>
> ☐ 4. Have I written a lead that contains attention-getting material, makes clear the
>
> kind of story the reader should expect, and sets the tone?
>
> ☐ 5. Have I organized my story in the best possible way in view of the primary impression I wish to make?
>
> ☐ 6. Have I focused on significant details?
>
> ☐ 7. Have I written my story in an imaginative, colorful way?
>
> ☐ 8. Is my story accurate as well as interesting?

Activity 4: Practicing Feature Story Skills

1. Carefully following the steps in the preceding section, write a brief feature story focusing on any new, unusual, or amusing thing that has happened at your school in the past month or so.

2. Choose a real-life experience or event in which you yourself were involved and write a brief feature story about it. Make use of the following new journalism methods:

   a. Recreate the setting of the experience or event concisely but vividly.

   b. Describe significant details of personal appearance.

   c. Include dialogue or other forms of speech to make the people of your story come alive for the readers.

Interviewing a Personality

A **personality story** is a special kind of feature story. It takes all of the skills covered in the previous section plus a number of specialized interviewing skills. As you will see, interviewing for the purpose of writing about a person's experiences and characteristics differs considerably from interviewing to obtain news. In a news report, you are primarily interested in collecting facts or opinions from your source. In a personality story, you must focus on the news source as a person.

Personality interviews may be approached in several ways, according to your purpose. Is your main goal to describe the person's characteristics? Will you be trying to develop a short biography? Are you mostly interested in this person's opinions on a current topic? Are you trying to place this individual in the context of a significant event or a special interest? Your answers to these and similar questions will determine how you conduct your interview and how you write your report.

Personality articles in school newspapers are generally of two kinds. One kind—the more common of the two—is about a student, teacher, or member of the community. The other, less common kind is about a famous person visiting the school or community.

Meeting the Famous Visitor

Did the writer of the following story make the most of this once-in-a-lifetime chance to interview a famous personality. Can you suggest ways in which the story might have been handled differently?

Actor Vincent Price says

'In all of us secretly there's a lot of ham'

"When I came out, everyone booed—it was the most wonderful thing," Mr. Vincent Price says of the "applause" he once received while playing a villain.

Mr. Price came to Saginaw for a Town Hall speaking engagement at the Temple Theater. He was also interviewed by student journalists from area high schools at the Bancroft Hotel. The interview is part of a program co-sponsored by Town Hall and the Saginaw News.

He explains his decision to go into acting as a career because "In all of us secretly there's a lot of ham."

Although he is best known for his horror films, only 20 of his 101 Hollywood films may be classed as such. He has played in more than 500 major television shows and 1,000 radio programs. Mr. Price usually does about three movies and 50 television shows a year. He also writes a regular arts column for the Chicago Sunday Tribune.

Mr. Price finds portraying villains more satisfying than good characters. "When I played several good characters, I found that there were no possibilities of making them anything but an extension of myself," he comments.

Mr. Price helped begin the Archives of American Art, which have since been taken over by the Smithsonian Institute. "Twenty years ago there was no center for American art. Unlike Europe, America has a great absence of national art pride," he says.

"If I have a mission in life, it is to tell the American people that art isn't just a painting on canvas. It's everything," he stresses.

—*The Arthur Hill News*, Arthur Hill High School, Saginaw, Michigan

---

One thing to avoid when writing a story such as the one above is the temptation to report your own experiences in reaching and speaking to the well-known person. Outstanding interview stories normally give no hint of the reporter's presence. They focus on the personality.

—Photo by Bettye Lane from Photo Researchers

This young reporter interviewing actress Candice Bergen is gathering information for one of the two basic kinds of personality stories: one based on an interview with a famous person.

Compare these two paragraphs:

I hesitatingly asked Governor Nelson about his opinion on federal aid to local school districts, for I knew from his recent speeches that he was against it. "I am sure," he replied, "that we can satisfactorily meet problems as they arise, without outside help."

Regarding federal aid to local school districts, Governor Nelson commented, "I am sure we can satisfactorily meet problems as they arise, without outside help."

In the first paragraph, the reader is aware of the reporter's presence. In the second, the reader is not. The second paragraph is the more professional.

Should you have the opportunity of interviewing a famous person, good preparation is especially important, because nervousness may impede your interviewing. To prepare properly, write out a number of well-thought-out questions. Some should deal with what your readers are most likely to want to know about the famous person. If the occasion of the interview is a visit to your school or community, some of your questions should touch on the occasion. Think twice about asking a question that the person may have answered countless times in the past. Such a question may not get a lively, interesting response. A fresh, unexpected question is more likely to stimulate an interesting reply and cause the person to reveal something of his or her true personality. And, needless to say, the more you read up in advance on the person you are interviewing, the better your interview will be.

Making the School Personality Come Alive

Personality sketches of students, teachers, or community figures are popular with readers. This is especially true when you consider an interesting student who is not constantly in the news. A student-personality story should give your readers a clear image and vivid sense of an individual. The story should reflect this personality so well that he or she becomes a living presence in the reader's mind. A flaw to avoid in preparing a student-personality story is the tendency to fall into a pattern. Week after week, the stories answer the same old questions in the same way. Asking about "favorites" (food, music, school subject, and so on) inevitably brings stock answers that produce colorless reporting.

What elements in the following story make it especially interesting?

Spirited Amy content

"Being blind is really not a handicap. There are actually advantages. I judge people on their personalities and reactions to me, not appearances like skin color or hair length."

AMY RUELL, a senior at Longmeadow High School, is often seen walking the halls to her next class. Many have marveled at how she manages to complete the same work they have trouble with. These people have not been exposed to anyone in these circumstances, so they do not know what to expect.

"I was once escorted across the street when I was perfectly capable of crossing it myself. I am more self-sufficient than most people think. A blind person's senses grow quite acute with the greater use one gives them," Amy explained.

"I HAVE to laugh," Amy admitted. "Many kids don't know how to act around me. I've heard all the Helen Keller jokes over and over. I suppose I am being related to a Helen Keller image, but it's not like that at all."

Amy does not feel that she is deprived. She says, "You can't miss anything if you've never had it." Amy leads a normal life. In her spare time, she cooks, takes and teaches guitar lessons, baby-sits, and leads a church choir. "I like to amuse myself by cooking, especially making popcorn," said Amy. She is also a member of the National Honor Society and the Spanish Club.

MOVIES DON'T bother her, because she can simply understand the movie's message by listening to the sound track. That is the same way she listens to television. But filmstrips do give her a problem. "I feel awkward when someone has to read them to me," she stated.

Amy has a cheerful outlook toward her situation and her future. She concluded, "Once a person accepts his or her problem, others will. You must make the best of it and, above all, have a sense of humor!"

—*Jet Jotter*, Longmeadow High School,
Longmeadow, Massachusetts

Activity 5: Analyzing Personality Stories

1. Write a paragraph that explains why personality stories are popular in school newspapers.

2. Find in your school newspaper or in exchange papers two student-personality stories, one that you consider good and one that you consider faulty. In a brief report, point out the good points of the first and the faults of the second. Explain in what ways the faulty story might have been improved.

Writing a Personality Story

Perhaps more than any other type of story, a personality story based on an interview requires planning. Most successful personality stories are the end result of considerable thought and preparation. In addition to previous suggestions, the following five steps should be followed.

CHOOSE A THEME. Find out as much as you can about the person you are to interview. Then, settle on a tentative theme (you might change it in the course of the interview). This theme, or **tie-in,** is one secret of successful

Writing an interesting personality story about someone with a special skill or unusual hobby requires planning. Not only must interview questions be thought out carefully, but some research on the person and the skill or hobby should be done.

—Photo by F. Siteman from Stock, Boston

personality interviewing. It pinpoints the reason the person is worth describing in print. The theme could be your subject's position, background, knowledge, expertise, ideas, skills, hobbies, or accomplishments—anything about the person that provides a focus.

PREPARE FOR THE INTERVIEW.   Write out questions that will lead your subject into the theme you have chosen. Try to word your questions in ways that will encourage people to give full and sincere answers. Such questions will generally arise from your own true interest in those you interview. People who believe that you are genuinely interested in them will warm up to you, feel at ease with you, and talk freely about themselves.

You should also make sure you have enough questions. Although you may not use them all, having the questions ready will guarantee that you will never be at a loss for something to say.

Finally, unless your subject is a student with whom you are friendly and can meet any time, you should make an appointment for the interview. Not only is it polite to do so but it decreases the likelihood of interruptions. If you wish to use a tape recorder, you might also use this opportunity to ask your subject's permission, since such permission must be obtained before you can do any taping.

START THE INTERVIEW INFORMALLY.   Begin the interview by getting acquainted. Be pleasant and courteous. Relax and enjoy the conversation. When the time seems right, use one of your prepared questions to lead your subject into talking easily.

Don't worry if the person you are interviewing decides to ramble on a bit in answer to one of your questions. In fact, the more your interview turns into a real-life conversation in which each speaker picks up and carries forward what the other has just said, the better. If the interview is going well and you and your subject are at ease with each other, you will no doubt find many opportunities to ask all the questions you prepared.

As the interview progresses, you should concentrate on what is being said. After the interview is under way, make brief notes on facts, figures, and main ideas. Copy the exact words of any statements you may wish to quote. Even if you use a tape recorder, take notes.

GO BEYOND THE WORDS BEING SPOKEN.   Notice how your subject looks. Study the person's face, smile, expression, clothes, and the movements of hands or eyes. Think about how you might describe your subject. Jot any ideas down.

Study the personality behind the voice. How does the subject make statements? What is his or her attitude toward the subject under discussion? How would you describe the voice and manner of speaking?

You may also find it useful to note the physical aspects of the interview. What is the setting? What objects are present? What is going on around you? Including a few well-chosen concrete details in your story can help give it a feeling of real life.

Before the close of the interview, remember to check facts, figures, the spelling of names, and the exact words of quotations. And be sure to express your thanks.

WRITE YOUR STORY. Put a first draft of the story on paper at once, while impressions are fresh in your mind. A personality story falls easily into the inverted-pyramid pattern, although some of the less formal techniques suggested for other feature stories may fit the kind of story you are preparing. If you have tape-recorded the interview, you could consider making use of a straightforward question-and-answer format—a simple transcription of the entire interview with only minor editing. Generally, however, you will find that the results are not as good as you might wish. While such a format does allow the views of the person being interviewed to be expressed in full, the story often loses focus and becomes much less readable.

Your lead should identify your subject, indicate or suggest the theme or tie-in, and catch the reader's interest. The following are good personality story leads.

Although they fit perfectly into size 3½ shoes, Cynthia Caiazza's tiny feet have the gigantic job of transporting her through a whirl of activities.

—*Echo*, Oneonta Senior High School, Oneonta, New York

Predicting the future comes easy for Mr. Kent Leutke-Stahlman. And he doesn't use astrology, a crystal ball, or mind reading. Mr. Leutke-Stahlman can see the future in computers.

—*Westside's Lance*, Westside High School, Omaha, Nebraska

Most girls, at one time or another, have had dreams of becoming ballerinas when they grew up. For freshman Elizabeth Le Vieux, this dream is not a passing one.

—*Hillcrest Hurricane*, Hillcrest High School, Dallas, Texas

Your main aim in the body of the story will be to make your subject come across to the reader as a vivid, interesting personality. Therefore, you should include a generous amount of quotations that convey your subject's thoughts, feelings, and manner of speech. Descriptive details should be used to make the reader see the personality as you did during the interview.

Arrange to have a photograph of your personality accompany the story, if at all possible.

Activity 6: Developing a Personality Story

Choose a school personality that you think could be the subject of an interesting personality story. Then follow the five steps you have just covered to develop the story. Be sure to approach the interview with a theme in mind. Watch for details whose inclusion in your story will help to convey a vivid sense of your subject. Make use of quotations that are long enough to give the reader a true idea of how your subject thinks and speaks.

Summary

This chapter begins with an explanation of what feature stories are and then goes on to explain how they are developed. Finally, it deals with the special considerations that go into writing personality stories.

DEVELOPING IDEAS FOR FEATURE STORIES. A feature story is a story whose interest derives not only from the facts reported but also from the way the story is written. Almost any subject may be suitable for feature story treatment, but memorable individuals, experiences, and happenings are most often the subjects. A keen sense of observation can help in the creation of ideas for future stories. It is the imagination, however, that determines whether a subject will really come alive in an interesting, readable story.

WRITING FEATURE STORIES. Whatever kind of feature story you are writing, you will benefit from following a logical plan. First, collect the facts through observation, interviews, and research. Second, determine the best approach to your material. Third, write a lead that attracts the reader's attention, indicates the kind of story to expect, and sets the tone. Fourth, organize your story according to the primary impression you want to make. Fifth, focus on significant details. Sixth, write with color and imagination.

INTERVIEWING A PERSONALITY. Personality stories consider people as interesting in themselves, rather than as sources of information. Whether you are interviewing a famous personality or a school personality, you should begin by deciding on a theme and preparing a number of good, nonpredictable questions. During the interview, you should try to create a friendly atmosphere, while noting details about the person as well as about what the person says. When writing the story, you should concentrate on making your subject come across to the reader as a vivid, interesting personality.

Vocabulary

feature story	human-interest story
feature	personality story
news feature	tie-in
new journalism	

Review Questions

1. How does a feature story differ from a conventional news story?

2. What is a human-interest story?

3. What are the special methods and approaches of feature story writing?

4. How should an interview for a personality story be conducted?

5. What are the most important steps and procedures for writing a personality story?

Discussion Questions

1. Would it be desirable for a school newspaper to publish nothing but feature stories? Why or why not?

2. If someone were to object to the publication of human-interest stories in a newspaper on the grounds that such stories do not offer news—timely or fresh information on matters of importance—how would you reply?

3. What are the advantages and disadvantages of making use of the techniques associated with new journalism?

4. How should students be chosen for personality stories?

5. Would it be easy or hard to give in a personality story an accurate, vivid representation of your best friend's personality? Of a close relative's personality? Of your own personality?

Chapter Project

Writing a Full-Length Feature Story

Using the methods and advice presented in this chapter, write a full-length feature story on a subject of your choice drawn from one of the following areas: your school's academic program, public affairs in your community, special concerns of young people, or unusual people or happenings.

12

PREPARING OPINION ARTICLES, COLUMNS, AND REVIEWS

When you have completed this chapter, you should be able to

Recognize the different kinds of opinion articles newspapers publish and know how to prepare them.

Write a column.

Write a review.

Assemble effective editorial and op-ed pages.

"Our editorial and opinion pages are the most popular part of our newspaper. We try to plan them that way," reports a staff member of a school newspaper.

Editorial and opinion pages can be exciting, different, and attractive. But success doesn't just happen. These pages must be organized in advance and planned to include a wide variety of student opinions. Among the different opinion articles that are likely to appear along with editorials are **commentaries** (interpretations of recent events), **letters to the editor,** formal **surveys** of student opinion, and less formal **inquiring-reporter articles.** Other opinions may be presented in special **columns** that appear regularly in each issue and in **reviews** of books, plays, films, concerts, and records, which may appear either on these pages or in a separate entertainment section.

In a four-page school newspaper, editorials, opinion articles, columns, and reviews typically appear on the second page, called the **editorial page.** This page will contain no advertising and can be identified by the newspaper's **masthead** (a statement giving details of publication), which is generally found at the bottom of the page. When the newspaper grows to six or eight pages, the facing page frequently contains additional articles devoted to opinions. Newspaper people often refer to this page as the **op-ed page** (the page opposite from the editorial page). Opinions may, of course, appear elsewhere in school newspapers, especially on sports and entertainment pages.

In daily papers, the editorial page's location may vary from one paper to another, but it will generally be found in the same place in any given newspaper.

This chapter will focus on all of the various types of opinion articles noted above, including columns and reviews. Chapter 13 will look at editorials and editorial cartoons.

Presenting Opinions on the News

Daily newspapers have long included many timely opinion articles about current news events. A recent trend in school newspapers is to increase the number of opinion articles, giving students a greater opportunity to present their viewpoints. These opinion articles may appear in the form of signed commentaries (as opposed to editorials, which present the opinions of a newspaper publisher, the entire staff, or an editorial board and which are traditionally unsigned). Opinions of students who are not members of the staff may be published in the form of letters to the editor, although many newspapers also provide space for full-length commentaries by nonstaff members. Sometimes the newspaper staff deliberately sets out to collect a wide cross section of student opinion by conducting a survey or poll. A more limited, more informal way of presenting a collection of student opinions is in the form of an inquiring-reporter survey.

Voicing Opinions Through Responsible Commentaries

In a school paper, commentaries, sometimes called **news analyses,** explain and interpret school and community news from a student viewpoint. School journalists have a way of looking at national and worldwide matters with a fresh perspective, unburdened by preconceived ideas. Commentaries may include background information, sidelights on news events, and explanations of relationships among various events.

Disagreeable as the thought may be, many of your readers may have little acquaintance with the world around them. Their knowledge may be limited to headlines that catch their eye as they open a newspaper to the television listings or sports pages. Your paper can perform a real service to such readers by broadening their information about those events in the community, nation, or world that could directly affect them.

Good reporters who read widely in books, magazines, and newspapers are the best candidates to handle the difficult assignment of introducing uninterested readers to the events of the world. Their preparatory work will be similar to the research and investigation carried out by a writer of interpretive, in-depth reports. A writer of commentaries is permitted, however, to present the results of research and investigation as personal conclusions. This writer is not bound by the obligation of the writer of interpretive, in-depth reports to present and explain all facets of an issue or by the editorial writer's responsibility of voicing an opinion established by a publisher or an editorial board.

Student writers, perceptive as they may be, must realize that they rarely have the broad knowledge of current events possessed by most professional commentators, who have gained their experience from years of observation and reporting. They must also remember that they and their newspaper are legally responsible for everything published in opinion articles. This responsibility typically extends to the editor, the adviser, and the school district. Therefore, the editorial staff must exercise exceptional care and caution in voicing opinions and seeing to it that nothing said violates libel, obscenity, or privacy laws (see Chapter 3).

The writer of any commentary—whether an opinion about the news, a viewpoint on a matter of concern to young people, or some statement about local issues—may also benefit from studying the material about the preparation of editorials found in Chapter 13.

The commentary on page 251 argues that a school newspaper has an obligation to publish negative articles as well as favorable articles about its sponsoring school. Judge for yourself how convincingly the writer states her case.

The journalist's creed: fearless truth

By Amy Gendler

Amid accusations of "negativism" aimed toward the Lance, I would like to clarify some of the fundamental concepts of journalism.

First of all, the three-fold purpose of any journalistic publication is to inform, interpret, and entertain. If, in adherence to these guidelines, it is necessary to discuss controversial topics, then so be it.

In view of the reader's right to know the truth, to refrain from printing any given article because of its content would be unjust.

The Lance has an obligation to its readership to print the news. That is, we have an obligation to print "the whole truth and nothing but the truth."

The Lance would violate the standards it has set for itself, were it not to expose a given aspect of the Westside community on account of anticipated reaction. Mr. Walter Williams states it well in "The Journalist's Creed": "The journalism which succeeds best, and best deserves success . . . is stoutly independent, . . . always respectful of its readers, but always unafraid."

We print certain articles in the hope that readers will gain something. If the readers gain knowledge of which they were previously ignorant, we have succeeded. If the readers are shown another side of an issue, we have succeeded. If a statement we make causes conversation among readers, we have succeeded. And if an article we print brings about change in an institution or practice, three cheers!

It is our aim to show all sides of every issue we cover—to inform readers accurately—to interpret issues sincerely. We refuse to turn a deaf ear to local school problems. They should be exposed and ultimately corrected. If, in doing so, we offend our readers, we will not quit.

"Better the rudest work that tells a story or records a fact," said critic John Ruskin, "than the richest without meaning."

The printing of "negative" articles by the Lance does not alter Westside's image whatsoever. The Lance should merely be indicative of what is going on, what some of the problems are, and how they can be solved.

The Lance is doing its job as a newspaper by portraying the many sides of Westside—good, bad, or indifferent.

I heard on the news of a grade school's "Positive Week." The theory behind this special event was, in effect, to accentuate the positive and eliminate the negative. I totally disagree. Society without both positive and negative aspects is no society at all.

A newspaper which does not expose both the positive and negative components of its community is no newspaper.

—Westside's Lance, Westside High School, Omaha, Nebraska

Activity 1: Examining Commentaries

1. In daily or weekly newspapers, find several examples of commentaries. For each, write a brief evaluation of the opinions offered by pointing out whether or not they seem to be thoughtful, intelligent, and based on knowledge or trained judgment. Notice also the ways in which profes-

sional writers seek to persuade their readers and note any particularly effective methods.

2. From a recent issue of your school paper, select a commentary that deals with some matter about which you have thought and have some knowledge. Whether you agree with the remarks in the commentary or not, point out examples of effective, persuasive writing and examples of weak, unconvincing writing.

Printing Letters to the Editor

Readers' letters to the editor, whether asking for information, suggesting improvements, commending, or criticizing, are always popular. To the staff of a school paper, they offer an opportunity to present opinions from students who are not members of the staff and who might not otherwise be heard. Moreover, publishing such letters enables a paper to be a forum for different points of view, which is squarely in the American tradition of journalism. One way to encourage readers to contribute letters is to present a

Letters to the editor enhance a school newspaper in a number of ways. They are popular with readers. They give students who might otherwise not be heard a chance to voice their opinions. And they provide a forum for differing views.

question on some issue of the day and invite answers, which would be published in the next issue.

Many school newspapers try to print all the letters they receive. However, if it is necessary to choose some and reject others, the responsible staff member should apply certain principles. Appropriate letters are those that are thorough, tactful, constructive, and reasonable. Letters presenting new or interesting factual information on a subject are especially desirable. And the letters published should be a fair sampling of all those that the paper received on a given subject.

Your readers should understand that all letters must be signed, although you may promise not to publish names if the writers ask that you do not. A controversial letter should be checked to see whether it was actually written by the person whose name is signed. If it becomes necessary to shorten a letter, edit it as fairly as you can.

Answers to or comments on letters are rarely needed. They should be included only when they would furnish readers with worthwhile information, such as corrections of factual errors. When a reply seems necessary, avoid criticizing the writer. Be factual, even though you may disagree with the writer's viewpoint. If an argument between letter writers develops, your staff should neither judge it nor take part. Your purpose is to provide a means for the participants to air their views.

You should avoid publishing letters that may damage someone's character or reputation. Should a libel action develop, the editors could be among those held responsible. If a school paper receives such a letter, a responsible staff member may wish to discuss it with the writer or suggest an appropriate authority to whom the writer's case may be presented.

Would letters such as the one below and the one at the top of page 254 be good choices for publication?

'Keep the library open'

To the Editor:

Each lunch block, one of the librarians steps into a room of busy students and calmly states, ''B-lunch—the library is closed.'' When I am bothered by being told to evacuate the library in the middle of my studying, I have an urge to state calmly, ''I flatly refuse.'' However, the custom calls for students to obey the rules of the library.

Of course, the library belongs to all members of Newton High, faculty, and administration. Therefore, it is the responsibility of the working librarians to meet the needs of all school members. Obviously, there are students who want to use the library for study during B-lunch.

For example, walk by the library almost any B-lunch and you will see students sitting in the corridor reading or impatiently mingling outside the library door. To solve this minor problem, each librarian could choose to eat during a different lunch period, thus allowing a supervisor to be present throughout the lunch block. Also, students would be responsible for not abusing the extra time by unnecessary conversation. In other words—keep the library open!

Marc Wine

—*Newtonite*, Newton High School, Newtonville, Massachusetts

A reader writes . . .

Dear Editor:

Recently there have been many attacks on the quality of education our schools are giving. Critics have said that today's students are incompetent, and they have blamed teachers and administrators for this.

I know that in the past it has been traditional to knock the teachers when we receive bad marks on a test. But just this once, let's support these professionals, whose mission in life is to enlighten us with the knowledge they have gained.

Today's educational system has been sharply criticized by three types of people. First, there are those who blame the educational system for the recent decline in the SAT scores. Then, there are those who believe that the old methods are the only effective methods to teach students. Finally, there are those who believe that just about every other country has surpassed the United States when it comes to education.

I have this to say to all these critics. In the past 80 years, the number of kids being educated has increased tremendously. Children between the ages of 6 and 10 are reading better than ever before. Although they had slipped a little in the late 1960s, they have made something of a comeback lately.

As for the SAT scores, statistics show that the environment in which the child is raised plays a major role in the score the child achieves on the test.

Looked at internationally, American students—the top 9 percent—come out better on some test scores than the top 9 percent of students in 15 other countries.

Yes, our educational system has its faults, and it deserves criticism, but to say that it is a failing system is just plain wrong. It happens to be one of the best systems in the world—and a lot of the credit must go to those courageous crusaders of the chalkboard, our teachers!

Deirdra Brown

—*The Viking Viewpoint*, Valhalla High School, Valhalla, New York

Conducting a Survey

School newspaper staffs often wish to take a survey, or poll, to determine the viewpoints of an entire class or the whole school on a certain topic. This is a difficult and time-consuming process if the results are to mean anything. A poorly conducted survey may be worse than none at all, for it might publicize opinions that do not really reflect the views of the group under consideration. If the topic is personal or controversial or if the

—Photo by Michal Heron from Woodfin Camp

A survey requires a good deal of time-consuming work. If reasonably well conducted, however, it will almost certainly be of great interest to your readers.

survey will require entry into classrooms in order to obtain answers, your purpose and plan must be shared with your adviser before you start.

The following chart presents basic procedures for conducting a survey.

HOW TO CONDUCT A SURVEY

1. Know precisely the primary question you hope to answer.

2. If you do not intend to survey the entire student population of your school, select a sample. The opinions of 10 percent of the students can be considered representative of the entire school population or of a large group within it, provided that these students are representative of the larger group with respect to age, sex, grade, and other group characteristics.

3. In addition to questions that deal directly with the issue you are considering, ask questions that enable you to judge the meaning and validity of a person's answers. If, for example, you were conducting a survey concerned with whether seniors think it truly beneficial to attend out-of-state rather than nearby colleges, you should include questions designed to find out what *beneficial* means in this context to those being surveyed. You might also include a question that separates out those who intend not to go to college.

4. Decide what combination of yes and no questions (which can be readily tabulated) and written-answer questions (which cannot be, but which provide fuller information) you should use.

5. Decide how you will survey—by personal interview, telephone interview, mailed questionnaire, or in-class questionnaire.

6. Carry out the survey.

7. Tabulate the results, using percentages for a large sample or numbers for a small one.

8. Publish your findings. Your report should include the major questions asked, the size of the group surveyed, your basic methods, and so on. Charts can be used to report your findings in a concise, vivid way. Keep in mind that no matter how careful you have been, your findings are probably less than 90 percent accurate.

Compiling an Inquiring-Reporter Article

The inquiring-reporter article, or **symposium,** in which a number of people provide answers to the same question, is less accurate than a formal survey in discovering and revealing the opinions of a group. It is, nevertheless, interesting, for it provides an appropriate cross section of viewpoints on a newsworthy topic. It also enables a paper to print a variety of names, often with accompanying photographs.

Choosing a good, lively question is the secret to a successful inquiring-reporter article. Any subject of interest to your readers is acceptable. The best subjects are related to current news events or to matters of student concern. A well-phrased question will furnish intelligent, even entertaining, replies. It is usually desirable to ask a large number of people and then select a group of representative, informative answers.

You might relate your question to a current school event: What is your opinion of the proposed homeroom schedule? What do you think of the new method of electing student council representatives? You might relate it to a school topic of continuous interest: What is the value of grades for schoolwork? What kinds of noon recreation should the school plan? Or you might focus on a topic that concerns teen-agers: How can we get 18-year-olds to be more concerned about their voting responsibilities?

The following inquiring-reporter article resembles a formal survey, in that a large number of opinions were gathered and tabulated. How satisfactory would you rate the question posed and the answers given?

In the HALLS of RHS

By Jay Buster

After we posed the question "Would you like to see more space in The Shield devoted to articles and editorials concerning national issues?" to 118 Richwoods students, we found these results:

Yes 41%
No 39%
No Opinion 20%

CHUCK ROCK—"The scope of a newspaper *must* encompass the interests of the students. Activities of the school are only the smallest part of events affecting the lives of students. Unless The Shield allows its editors and staff to write material that is relevant to the students and the world, The Shield ceases to be a newspaper except in name only."

JANICE PRICE—"The students of Richwoods will someday be running the government, and I feel that they should start now in getting involved in the national issues. The school isn't the only world a student lives in. There is a world outside this school that we are going to have to get involved in."

LARRY BISCHOFF—"The Shield is a school newspaper and, therefore, shouldn't take on national issues that the city newspaper already reports on.

We, the students of Richwoods, can, if we want to, read the Journal Star to find out about national issues. The school newspaper is supposed to be about the school!"

JULIE WATSON—"National issues are too important to be ignored. They may not always affect us as students of Richwoods directly, but national affairs are none the less important to our lives."

MIKE MERGENER—"The Shield is a school paper which contains topics which pertain to school and should not be changed. I want to know what happens in schools from my school paper and what is happening nationally from the Peoria paper. Besides, I do not believe anyone here is *qualified* to speak on national issues."

BETH SCHNUPP—"I feel that before we can look into deeper problems, or national issues, we must be able to understand all there is to know about our own school, what's happening, interests of students about subjects concerning the school, and so on. How are we able to understand the issues of the world if we are unaware of what is going on around us here?"

—*The Shield*, Richwoods High School, Peoria, Illinois

Activity 2:   Presenting the Views of the Public

1. Prepare a brief notice inviting readers to submit letters to the editor in answer to a particular question. Write the notice exactly as it might appear in your school paper. Think up a question likely to inspire intelligent, interesting answers.

2. Prepare a questionnaire for a survey on a subject of your choice by (a) stating the primary question you would hope to answer, (b) listing other questions that deal directly with the subject, and (c) adding questions that would enable you to judge the meaning or validity of answers to the important questions. Be sure to use both objective, easily tabulated questions and written-answer questions.

3. Prepare an inquiring-reporter article in the following manner. Think up a good brief question. Present it to about two dozen students from different grades and record their answers. Then, choose six to eight of the best and most representative answers and include them in your article.

Writing Columns

Columns are features that appear regularly in a newspaper. They often take the form of commentaries on current events, although they can be totally informative or entertaining. The basic distinction between columns that act as commentaries and other forms of commentary is that the column carries the same title from issue to issue, usually appears in the same place, and is typically the work of the same writer. Many columns in daily newspapers are **syndicated**—sold to newspapers across the nation.

Authors of daily newspaper columns are often authorities or specialists in a particular field, as well as competent writers. Some daily newspapers, knowing that a particular columnist's reputation will attract readers, print only that person's name as a column heading (for example, "Mike Royko" or "Ann Landers"). Or the column may have an arresting title, perhaps incorporating the columnist's name, such as "The Lyons Den," written by Leonard Lyons.

Deciding Whether to Publish a Column

While almost any general topic that would interest many readers may have sufficient merit, several questions should be considered before valuable space is reserved for a regular column, issue after issue.

DOES THE SUBJECT HAVE WIDE APPEAL?   The subject should interest a large number of readers. You might have difficulty justifying stamp collecting or archery as a column subject, worthwhile as either might be for an occasional feature story.

CAN THE COLUMN BE KEPT INTERESTING?   Fresh material must be available on this topic for each column.

CAN IT APPEAR REGULARLY? It should not be labeled a column unless the subject and style can be continued over time. For this reason, many school staffs prefer the greater flexibility offered by individual commentaries or special features stories.

DOES THE AUTHOR HAVE EXCEPTIONAL WRITING ABILITY? A columnist should be capable of preparing lively, interesting material consistently. A school newspaper column may have more chance for survival if two or three skillful writers cooperate as co-authors or if many staff members contribute, with one individual putting the column into its final form.

WILL THE TITLE BE EYE-CATCHING? A column needs a clever title to indicate content or purpose. Good column titles, like those of hit songs, are appealing and easy to remember. For example, "Clothesline" might be used for a fashion column. Many school papers print the title in small type at the top of the column and then feature an attention-getting key thought below it in larger headline type. (Notice this plan in the column on page 260.)

CAN THE COLUMN BE GIVEN AN UNUSUAL APPEARANCE? A column often benefits from special treatment, such as a border, unusual type, or extra white space surrounding the paragraphs. Such treatment can add to its attractiveness, while helping to set it apart from regular news articles.

Finding the Basis of a Column

The basis, or theme, of a school newspaper column can be news briefs, school life, entertainment, hobbies, special interests, humor, opinion, or exchange notes—to name some of the likely possibilities.

NEWS BRIEFS. Columns of short news items are frequently found in newspapers having limited space. One purpose of this kind of column is to condense news articles and thereby provide more room for interpretive, indepth reports and feature stories.

Even papers without a space problem may find such a column a convenient way to handle news items that can't be easily developed into stories with headlines, leads, and bodies. Remember, however, that any story is more likely to be widely read if it is displayed alone with its own headline. Thus, important stories should not be carelessly stuck in a news-briefs column.

SCHOOL LIFE. The accomplishments of students and teachers, bits of interesting news too short for separate stories, humorous happenings in school, human-interest items, personality highlights, or even announcements of future activities can be combined into an appealing school life column. Successful columns of this sort include names in almost every item, cover a wide variety of matters, and collect items from the entire school instead of just from the people and organizations that appear in the major news stories. The school life column differs from a collection of news briefs primarily in its variety of topics and its emphasis on people.

The entire staff may participate in assembling a school life column. Reader contributions may also be encouraged. Column items should not lean too far either toward routine news or toward gossip. Reporting rumors soon undermines the appeal of a school life column. On the other hand, if too much routine news is included, the column becomes dull.

Writers of school life columns should keep in mind that every item must be considerate in nature. If a joke about a student is printed, this person, too, should be able to laugh about it. Also, since readers normally cannot reply through the column, personal comments about them are never appropriate. And finally, any humor in such a column must be clean humor and in good taste.

Paragraphs such as the following can be very effective in a school life column.

Mr. William Booth, manager of the Providence National Bank, generously came to the aid of Sr. Mary Anne Curtin and her American family class. Sister decided that an assignment on family budgeting would be more realistic if the students could use actual checks. In answer to her appeal, Mr. Booth contacted his district manager, who printed up and donated 2,000 nonnegotiable checks specifically for the use of the class.

—''Chart's Chatter,'' *The Turret,* Notre Dame High School, Moylan, Pennsylvania

The Tip-of-the-Hat goes, and deservedly so, to George Ware of Homeroom 311. He has done more than his share toward aiding Mrs. Mabel Smith with the tax stamp project this semester.

—''Scrolling About School,'' *Shaker Scroll,* Woodbury Junior High School, Shaker Heights, Ohio

Metamorphosis . . . Mr. George Webb was slightly annoyed when office messenger Kathie Klein asked him where the teacher was. Upon learning his identity, the sophomore excused herself by saying, ''Oh, I thought you were a student.''

—''Paw Marks,'' *The Beacon,* Woodrow Wilson High School, Washington, D.C.

ENTERTAINMENT, HOBBIES, AND SPECIAL INTERESTS. Columns devoted to entertainment, hobbies, concerts, records, movies, fashions, cars, and so on, prepared by a well-informed writer, can appeal greatly to student interests.

Such columns may be written in various ways. They may be purely informative, or they may be commentaries that present conclusions based on personal investigation. Columns about recordings or entertainment might be written as reviews. When one particular hobby is spotlighted, the column might appear in the form of personality sketches about hobbyists. Because, however, students are interested in so many different things, hobby and special-interest material may be more appropriate for interpretive, in-depth articles or single reviews than for regularly appearing columns.

HUMOR. A column using original humorous material is excellent if cleverly done—and terrible if poorly done! It takes a special kind of writer to succeed. Unless you have such an individual on your staff, your paper is better off without an attempt at original humor. School papers can provide laughs, however. There is creative humor in the funny retelling of comical or unusual happenings around school. You will generally find that school life columns or human-interest feature stories answer your need for humor more successfully than a tired-looking collection of jokes.

OPINION. In most daily newspapers, the majority of columns offer opinions—by analyzing the day's news or by commenting on current events. Opinion columns are popular in many school newspapers, too. Such columns differ from ordinary commentaries only in that they carry the same titles and have regular space reserved for them.

Since it may be a problem to find fresh material for successive issues, two or three writers may alternate or pool their efforts in an opinion column. Or the newspaper may open the column to anyone, staff member or not, who prepares an intelligent commentary.

Is the following opinion column effective? Would it appeal to readers in your school?

▌Between the lines ▌

Dating: a game too serious?

By Mary Jo Burkholder

Dating has changed a lot compared to 10 years ago. The change is not so much in the date itself but rather in the attitude toward it. What is the difference? Consider these questions:

If you went out with someone this weekend, would you consider going out with someone different next weekend?

Even if you're not romantically involved with anyone, when was the last time you and a boy/girl *friend* went somewhere just for fun?

The old idea of a friendly date is disappearing. Now it seems that going out has a more serious meaning to it. Looking back, going steady was the major step when a guy gave his ring to his girlfriend symbolizing their promise to date only each other. But now that step has just about disappeared. Now if a couple goes out on a date, even for the first time, they are considered a steady couple.

No doubt, this has got to put pressure on the guy asking for the date as well as the girl being asked. It is difficult to make such a commitment when there hasn't been enough time to get to know the other person. It's like having to make a choice without being given a selection.

Dating has traditionally been considered to be an opportunity of meeting people, getting to know them better, and from those experiences possibly forming ideas as to what is wanted in a marriage partner. It is sad to think that some may back away from such an opportunity because they are not ready for a commitment. Should there even be a commitment, or is it too late for something to be so uncomplicated as a date used to be? The question is worth answering.

—*Anokahi*, Anoka Senior High School, Anoka, Minnesota

EXCHANGE NOTES. Unusual happenings at other schools make entertaining reading, especially if they can be related to life in your own school.

Exchange notes are generally taken from the newspapers of other schools and rewritten into short summary paragraphs.

OTHER TYPES OF COLUMNS. Personality sketches or inquiring-reporter questions are frequently the basis of regularly appearing columns. Still other successful columns might focus on events in the lower grades, community recreational activities, or alumni news. Columns might also revolve about world events, creative writing, or books. In addition to all of these, columns of comment frequently appear on sports pages.

What about gossip columns? There is no doubt that if your paper includes such a column, many will read it. Gossip column readers are looking for people's names and a chance to be entertained. Unfortunately, several difficulties are faced by a school newspaper that prints gossip. First, such columns show a general lack of effort and imagination. It is always easier for reporters to repeat rumors than to dig out interesting news items. Second, one small group is usually featured and the same few students keep popping up week after week. Third, there is a definite danger of libel. If a half-truth is printed, or even a full truth that damages someone's reputation, the reporter, newspaper, and school may find themselves in serious trouble. Fourth, it is hard to avoid bad taste. And fifth, it is hard to avoid hurting the feelings of at least some of the people featured.

A gossip column obscures the fact that students have a wide range of interests. Other types of articles not only include the names your readers desire but also raise the content level of the paper.

Activity 3: Writing a Column

1. Study the columns from a daily newspaper and answer the following questions: (a) What is the purpose of each column? (b) To which groups of readers would it appeal? (c) Are the titles clever? Do they accurately reflect the content of each column?

2. Tell what visual devices daily newspapers use to attract column readers.

3. Select a basis for a column, using one of those suggested in this section or one of your own invention. Collect and organize your material and write the column as though it were scheduled to appear in the next issue of your school paper. Use at least five short paragraphs. Write informally but clearly in a lively, appealing style. Make up a catchy title for your column and offer suggestions as to any visual devices you would like to see employed.

Writing Reviews

Most school newspapers allot space to both news and comments on entertainment and the arts. Typical coverage might include a calendar of school and community entertainment and recreational activities, news and feature stories about forthcoming events and performers, and reviews.

Reviews offer opinions about movies, books, records, museum exhibits, plays, television programs, concerts, and other art or entertainment forms. Emphasis on judgment and evaluation makes a review different from a news story, an in-depth, interpretive article, or even a commentary on the news. To have some basis for intelligent comment, a reviewer must have a wide enough range of experience to make comparisons of what is under review with other successful or unsuccessful productions of the same kind. The reviewer must know something about the skills required for success in the form of art being considered.

Major newspapers pay reviewers well because of their extensive knowledge of their fields. Student reviews may not represent such informed viewpoints, but they have a definite place in your paper. On any staff, there are individuals whose familiarity with popular music, books, movies, plays, or art is good enough for them to prepare intelligent reviews. The very fact that these reviews are by students gives them a special interest for your student readers.

A review should be brief but thorough. Only meaningful comments should be included. Unimportant ones should be omitted. Whatever form of art or entertainment you are reviewing, keep in mind that your main purpose should be to enable your readers to decide whether it is worth their time, attention, and money. You should provide an account of the contents, describing objectively what is there to be seen, read, or listened to, and you should offer an evaluation. While your evaluation will necessarily be an expression of what *you* liked, what *you* disliked, and why, you should always keep your readers in mind. Thinking of your readers' needs will make your review objective and useful. Ignoring them will make it just the expression of your personal taste.

When reviewing a school production, such as a play or concert, you should bear in mind that the performers (like the reviewer) are not professionals and that student productions are learning experiences. The following chart presents guidelines for reviewing them.

GUIDELINES FOR REVIEWING SCHOOL PRODUCTIONS

1. The reviewer's standards of judgment should be appropriate to an amateur performance.
2. The reviewer should indicate his or her reactions honestly. Criticism as well as praise may be expressed.
3. Reasons for liking or disliking something should be made clear, and opinions should be supported by specific examples.
4. School productions may reasonably be compared with past school productions, not with professional ones.
5. Part of the review should be devoted to indicating the content of the production.
6. The review should also include comments on main performers, less prominent ones, costumes, lighting, and sets.
7. In addition, the review might include mention of the general audience response to the performance the reviewer attended.

School newspaper reviews may cover school-sponsored cultural events as well as professional ones. No matter what kind of event is being covered, the review should display intelligence of judgment and fairness in evaluation.

As you read the following review, do you gain the impression that the writer has done some real thinking? Do her judgments seem fair?

'King Stag' complements spring festival's gaiety

By Jessica Kohn, Arts Editor

The drama department's delightful production of "The King Stag" provided a perfect centerpiece for the happy, open-air mood of the spring festival, Thursday to Saturday.

"King Stag," written in the 1700s by Carlo Gozzi (complementing the festival's sixteenth-century Italian setting), is a fast-moving fantasy centering on a king and his court and their misadventures with magic.

Drama teacher Liucija Ambrosini, the director, said she chose the play because it was suited to an outdoor production and because it involved a large cast (35 people). Because the script does not offer much guidance for characterization, she felt also that the play would challenge the actors.

The actors met the challenge. The characterizations, full of subtle nuances, reflected thought and discipline. Particularly outstanding performances were given by senior Lee Handler as the stuttering, evil prime minister Tartagha; junior Ellen Meltzer as the dizzy country bumpkin Smeraldina; and senior Robert Cohen as the old, bumbling second minister Pantaloon.

More than 100 people put hundreds of hours into the production. That was obvious in its technical excellence. But technicalities aside, they produced a wonderful evening of entertainment.

—*U-High Midway*, University High School, Chicago, Illinois

Activity 4: Writing a Review

Write a review of a work in a field of art or entertainment with which you are familiar. Assume that your readers—the students of your school—will be turning to your review for useful information about the work under consideration. Conduct any research you find necessary. In the review itself, give both an overview of the work and opinions based on elements of the work.

Assembling Effective Editorial and Opinion Pages

The main goal of editorial and opinion pages is to furnish readers with background information and thoughtful opinions about the news of the day. Editorials serve this purpose by interpreting or explaining current events. Editorial cartoons, commentaries, and other articles that present opinions to the readers can also contribute to a better understanding of current happenings.

Articles for these pages do not result from routine work by reporters. Most are written to fulfill definite needs. Each editorial, commentary, or other article will be published because an editor planned it carefully and then assigned it to a writer for preparation. In most cases, these assignments are made in advance, often before the preceding issue of the paper goes to the printer.

Almost any type of material except a straight-news report is appropriate. But since the best opinion-related material has a definite news peg, the number of articles unrelated to current events should be limited. One good plan is to spotlight three or four items related to the same major news event. These items might include an editorial, a cartoon, an inquiring-reporter article, and a letter to the editor. Each approaches the event in a different way, adding to an understanding of its background, meaning, and consequences.

Apply the ideas in the accompanying checklist as you assemble your editorial page and any additional opinion pages. Some are quite practical; others call for creative decisions.

✔ Checklist for Assembling an Editorial Page

☐ 1. Has the newspaper's masthead (the newspaper's name, sponsoring school, address, phone, names of staff members and adviser, and a statement of frequency of publication) been included in a lower corner of the page?

☐ 2. Has at least one significant editorial been included?

☐ 3. Have three of four of the following kinds of editorial page articles been included: commentaries, letters to the editor, surveys, inquiring-reporter articles, columns, reviews (if not appearing elsewhere), and editorial cartoons?

☐ 4. Is there a good mix of editorial page articles?

☐ 5. Is there a balance of humorous and serious articles, longer and shorter ones, formal and informal ones?

☐ 6. Have relevant photographs, cartoons, or drawings been incorporated?

☐ 7. Do most of the items on the page relate to current news?

☐ 8. Can, and should, puzzles, games, or other light material be included?

☐ 9. Have the principles of good page makeup (see Chapter 17) been followed to ensure that the editorial page is attractively laid out?

☐ 10. Has the page been checked for libel, especially in letters to the editor?

Honor rolls needed

The honor roll is nonexistent at Truman High School; however, the National Honor Society (NHS) is prevalent.

The requirement for NHS is a 3.0 grade average. This average must be accumulated over the quarters and semesters of the school year. Once a membership is acquired, it is sustained. Even if grades fall below an M average (2.0), the membership remains.

An honor roll is based on quarterly achievement. A member of the honor roll in the first semester may not be a member the second semester, because of lower grades. Since a grade-point average is accumulated for NHS, a student must make high grades starting in ninth grade. NHS is not to be criticized for these requirements, but an honor roll should be created.

Principal LeRoy Brown's excuse for not having an honor roll is that by the time one would be released, the school year would be close to an end. He also doesn't see any need for an honor roll. Chrisman and Palmer junior high schools have both "E" and "S" honor rolls. But neither Truman nor Bridger have them.

Truman has never had an honor roll, and probably never will if the principal doesn't see a need for one. But students, mainly those not in NHS, are being deprived of the recognition they deserve.

COMPU-GRADE		
History	3.8	E
Biology	3.5	E
Algebra	3.1	S
P.E	2.5	M
Foods	3.4	S
GPA	3.3	

Grades from computers

This is the computer age. People everywhere — at home, in the office and at school — use computers everyday.

The computers at school are currently being used for the computer science classes.

Yet, within the next five years the school hopes to be using computers for nearly everything which involves keeping records.

According to LeRoy Brown, computers may be used for inventory control, attendance, class rank and grades.

In fact, computers could completely change the grade cards we now know. The new grade card would probably resemble a college grade report.

The grades would all be on one sheet and from the freshman year on the class rank and grade point average would be included on the grade sheet. The St. Louis area is already using this method.

Actually the only thing holding the new system up here is money. New computers are expensive and the school district just does not have the facilities.

"We've already been working with Mr. Harris trying to utilize some of the computers we already have. Of course they couldn't do anything too elaborate, but they would help," Brown explained.

Keeping information on computers would be beneficial and the day it becomes a common practice is anxiously awaited.

—Column—

Holiday for the birds

by Stan Williams

Valentine's Day is for the birds.

Every year, after the Christmas rush, stores start to stock cards decorated with hearts and cutesy sayings. For some people, Valentine's Day is a big deal. Couples who have been together for ages might find the holiday interesting. I don't fall into the category of being involved in a relationship and I think I'm too young to be celebrating this occasion because it would be like making a committment according to ancient Roman beliefs.

Valentine's Day probably has branched off the Roman feast of Lupercalia. During these days of feasting and partying, boys and girls drew lots to see who they would be paired with. The couples would then have to court for one year. That would be wonderful if one would be paired with someone he liked and that someone liked him, but for the unfortunate ones who got stuck with someone they couldn't stand, I imagine the feast was a dreaded occasion.

Other traditions may have come from . . . well . . . the mating habits of birds.

Some countries believe Feb. 14 to be a day to honor lovers because birds supposedly begin to mate on this day. I'm sure, for the birds, this day really is a special day.

Since it is a bird's holiday, I'll let them have the day for their celebration. Now that I think about it, maybe I will help the birds celebrate by tossing out some bird seed and refilling my bird feeder. I'll just get out my binoculars and do some bird watching.

THE **SPIRIT** OF '83

—Review—

Arcades everywhere

by Zach Zuber

If you've had it with the normal scene every Friday and Saturday night, cruising, partying, or whatever form of merriment you indulge in, why don't you take some of those spare quarters just lying around collecting dust, and try something new and exciting like video games?

Wherever you live there is no doubt a video game just around the corner. Almost every establishment where young people might be attracted has at least one machine, and there is one major arcade in each of the area's shopping malls.

Aladdin's Castle arcade at the Independence Center has a wide selection of new video games: Joust, Tron (this one features four different games in one), Burger Time and Donkey Kong, Jr. As well as such old standards as Pac-Man, Battle Zone, Galactica and Donkey Kong. The only gripe I have with Aladdin's Castle is that you have to use tokens instead of quarters, which causes a hassle when you try to get back your unused tokens. Also, there are no pinball machines for all you die-hard pinball addicts. The hours at Aladdin's Castle are 10-9 and 12-5:30 on Sundays.

Space Port (notice the clever names for these places) is the arcade at the Blue Ridge Mall. It also features a lot of new games, but you don't have to use tokens in their machines. Although pinball machines are becoming obsolete compared to video games, Space Port has a few. Space Port is open 10-10 on week nights, and 10-12 on Friday and Saturday nights.

Although the new and improved home video games are reaching a peak of popularity, the video arcades still prosper. As long as new, improved games keep hitting the market, I'm sure there will always be kids to play them.

Member of Missouri
Interscholastic Press Assn.
Columbia Scholastic Press Assn.
International Quill and Scroll
Pacemaker, All-Missouri, All-American, Medalist, Gallup Awards

The Spirit is the official publication of Truman High School, 3301 South Noland Road, Independence, MO 64055. Subscription for the bi-weekly publication is $3 per year or 25 cents per issue. It is printed by Little Blue Press, Inc., Blue Springs, MO 64015.

Editor-in-chief .... Stan Williams

Managing Editor .... Donna Segroves   Features Columnist .... Jill Coldsnow
Copy Editors .... Carrie Carter   Sports Columnist ...... Gary McCulley
                                   Elayna Evans   Sports Writer .... Chris Keene
Editorial Editor .... Kevin Nickle   Reviews Columnists ..... Lisa Sandage
News Editor .... Linda Lowderman   Zach Zuber
Features Editor ...... Kathy Zimmermann   Business Manager .... Jeff Wilson
Depth Editor .... Sara Landers   Advertising Manager ..... Melody Burns
Sports Editor .... Brad Jones   Circulation Manager ..... Terry McCulley
Photography Editor ...... Christi Pennel   Photographers .... John Cook
Cartoonists .... Bob Farley   Joe Logsdon
                            Rick Farley   Adviser .... Ron Clemons

Board of Publications: Ron Clemons, Norman Cox, Georgia Dorsch, Tim Green, Anne Hills, Frank Holueck, Al Hunter, Chris Keene, Sheila Pool, Sue Ridings, Mark Scherer, Donna Segroves, Stan Williams.
Editorial Board: Brad Jones, Kevin Nickle, Sara Landers, Donna Segroves, Stan Williams.

Straight-news reports are unsuitable for an editorial page, but, as this page shows, articles pegged to current events are desirable.

Activity 5:   Analyzing Editorial and Opinion Pages

1. Examine the editorial page of a daily newspaper, as well as the op-ed page, if one exists. List the articles and classify them as to type (editorial, commentary, column, and so on).

2. Explain what you believe to be the purpose and organizing principles of the editorial page. How do the articles relate to one another? How do the editorial and op-ed pages relate to each other?

3. To what groups of readers will the editorial page appeal?

4. What relation do you find between the articles here and the news of the day? What are the advantages of relating the content of the editorial page to current events?

Summary

This chapter begins by discussing in general the publishing of opinions on the news and, in particular, several kinds of opinion articles. It then considers two special kinds of opinion articles—columns and reviews. Finally, the assembling of effective editorial and opinion pages is covered.

PRESENTING OPINIONS ON THE NEWS.   Opinion articles such as editorials, commentaries, letters to the editor, surveys, and inquiring-reporter articles play an important part in school newspapers. Commentaries present signed opinions on the news and other items of current interest. Letters to the editor give the readership the opportunity to voice its views. Surveys conducted carefully and systematically can publicize the views of a large number of people. Though less accurate than formal surveys, inquiring-reporter articles enable a paper to present a cross section of opinions and to add to the number of names it prints.

WRITING COLUMNS.   A column is a special kind of opinion article that carries the same title from issue to issue, usually appears in the same place in a paper, and is typically the work of the same writer. A column should be published only after it has been decided that the subject of the column has wide appeal, that the column can be kept interesting, that it can appear regularly, that the columnist is an especially appealing writer, and that the title and appearance of the column are eye-catching. Bases for a column include news briefs, school life, entertainment, hobbies, special interests, humor, opinion, and exchange notes. As for gossip columns, there is perhaps more to be said against than for them.

WRITING REVIEWS.   Reviews present opinions about movies, books, records, museum exhibits, plays, television programs, concerts, and other art or entertainment forms. They should help readers decide whether what is being reviewed is worth their time, attention, and money. They should, therefore, include both an account of the contents of a work and an evaluation of it. Reviews of school productions should be based on standards appropriate to an amateur performance.

ASSEMBLING EFFECTIVE EDITORIAL AND OPINION PAGES. Most articles on editorial and opinion pages should be related to news events. One plan for assembling such a page is to include three or four different kinds of opinion articles that approach the same news event in different ways. At least one editorial must also appear on the editorial page.

Vocabulary

commentary	column	op-ed page
letter to the editor	review	news analysis
survey	editorial page	symposium
inquiring-reporter article	masthead	syndicated

Review Questions

1. What are some of the ways in which the editorial and op-ed pages are different from the other news pages?

2. What is the value to a newspaper of letters to the editor, surveys, and inquiring-reporter articles?

3. In what three ways do columns differ from basic forms of commentary?

4. What general principles should a reviewer follow?

5. What guidelines should be followed when assembling editorial and opinion pages?

Discussion Questions

1. What subjects would be most likely to inspire interesting and intelligent opinion articles in your school newspaper?

2. How should students be selected to answer inquiring-reporter questions?

3. What new column might best succeed in your school paper? Support your opinion by answering the questions given under the heading Deciding Whether to Publish a Column on page 257.

4. If the editorial staff of your paper decided to publish book reviews in every issue, how should the books for review be selected? (If your paper publishes book reviews, answer the question with some other art or entertainment form substituting for books.)

5. In addition to one or more editorials, which other kinds of opinion articles do you feel should be published on the editorial page of every issue of your school paper?

Chapter Project

Developing an Editorial Page

Develop a plan showing the material you would use on an ideal editorial page, as well as on the op-ed or other opinion pages if your school paper typically includes them. Include each of the following three steps: (1) Indicate article subjects, designating the form of opinion article you would devote to each. Be specific. For example, do not write just "editorial," but rather "editorial on student elections." Be ready to justify each choice. (2) Sketch the page arrangement(s), showing how you would lay out the different articles. (3) Write one of the opinion articles that you have suggested.

WRITING EDITORIALS

When you have completed this chapter you should be able to

Distinguish editorials from other opinion articles and understand their importance.

Classify editorials by purpose.

Write an editorial.

Understand how to present opinions in editorial cartoons.

Understand the many ways in which newspapers influence public opinion.

A major highway, filled with speeding traffic, ran directly in front of a high school in southern California. The school administration and newspaper staff, concerned about occasional crashes, frequent injuries, and an adult pedestrian's death at a highway intersection near the school, had from time to time demanded better traffic control. A sympathetic city council had improved the lighting and provided some police supervision. But to install automatic traffic signals on a state highway required state approval. Repeated appeals were made to the state highway commission, but no positive action resulted. After the excitement of each accident, the issue faded into the background of day-to-day school life.

Then, in quick succession, a student and a teacher were struck while crossing the highway, and both were critically injured. Adults talked hopefully about signals. Students took action.

Editorials, articles, and photographs in the school newspaper aroused interest and stirred up activity. Staff members secured 1,000 signatures on petitions that demanded the installation of traffic signals. They listed accidents that had occurred at the intersection where lights were needed, pointing out that relatively few student drivers had been involved. Local newspapers became interested and published stories on the matter.

The school newspaper editor then asked the cooperation of state legislators in presenting the petition, clippings, and editorials to the state highway commission. The local senator, learning that the editor was to visit the state capital for a YWCA Model Legislature, made an unprecedented arrangement for her personal appearance before the commission. She also had a chance to present the request directly to the governor.

Soon a traffic survey was made, and the needed signals were installed—the outcome of the editorial campaign carried out by *Anoranco,* the school paper of Anaheim Union High School, in Anaheim, California, as reported in *Quill and Scroll.*

Recognizing Editorials and Their Importance

An editorial is an article that presents the newspaper's opinion on an issue. Since it may be considered the voice of the newspaper (rather than the voice of any one reporter), it is normally unsigned. Each editorial seeks to encourage critical thinking, to mold opinion, and sometimes to promote action. What a newspaper says, if said logically, powerfully, and often enough, can influence public opinion and make people take action.

The traffic signal crusade is one instance of an effective campaign by a school newspaper. Great success has been achieved by other school papers in securing building improvements, attacking sources of juvenile delinquency, and improving student legislative organization or activities. Less spectacular but equally far-reaching have been campaigns for achieving better understanding between students of different backgrounds, for encouraging students to complete high school, and for promoting more conscientious studying. Even when the results are not outstanding, editorials are valuable because they stimulate thought, discussion, planning, and action.

The power and influence of daily newspaper editorials are even greater than those of the school newspaper. Many people will vote for a certain candidate because an editorial has so urged them. By persuading readers to take action, an editorial can promote many improvements in its local area. On the other hand, irresponsible editorials can harm a community.

Editorials appear in two places in a newspaper. The traditional position is on the editorial page, often at the top of the left-hand column. When an editorial is considered to be of special importance, it may be placed on the newspaper's front page. In this case, it would be labeled as an editorial. Editorials are generally printed in larger type and in a wider column than other material on the page. Some papers publish only one editorial in each issue, while others may publish several.

Since editorials state a school newspaper's position on school, community, or other matters, important ones are planned by an **editorial board**, which consists of the top editors. An editorial writer will then do the actual research and preparation. Editorials by other staff members might also be discussed by the board. On smaller newspapers, the **editor in chief** will write most of the editorials.

Activity 1: Understanding How Editorials Serve Their Readers

1. Find two editorials in your school newspaper and two in a daily or weekly paper that deal with current matters or events of importance. Write a brief report on each editorial by doing the following:

   a. Describe the issue or event that is the subject of the editorial.

   b. State the position or opinion that the editorial offers.

   c. Explain why the editorial may be considered an attempt to serve the newspaper's readers.

2. Choose a topic of current student interest, preferably one about which there is some controversy. First, describe how you would handle this topic in a news story. Then, decide how you would handle it in an editorial. How would the two stories differ?

Understanding Editorial Purposes

Many editorials may be classified by purpose. The four most common purposes are to explain or interpret, to criticize, to persuade, and to praise. Often, however, an editorial that has one of these purposes as its primary goal will have one or more of the others as secondary purposes.

Editorials That Explain or Interpret

One basic kind of editorial has as its primary goal to explain or interpret an issue or event in a way that is not possible in news reports. These editorials may include further information about the issue or event. While opinions may be included, they do not form a major part of this kind of editorial. Daily papers often use editorials to explain the reasons behind today's front page news. School newspapers may explain or interpret regulations, decisions, customs, the feelings or actions of students, and so on.

What is explained in the following editorial? Does it seem to have a secondary purpose? If so, what is it—to criticize, to persuade, or to praise?

Foreign languages today

Today in the United States, fewer than 1 percent of elementary students, 18 percent of high-schoolers, and 9 percent of college students are studying foreign languages—far below the corresponding enrollment figures for other developed nations. France, Switzerland, the Netherlands, Germany, and Sweden all require the study of at least one foreign language for a minimum of five years for the equivalent of a high school diploma. Neglect of foreign language study in America is producing a generation whose inability to communicate is threatening the nation's political and economic interests, according to an article in Better Homes and Gardens.

"We're behind virtually every country on the face of the globe in what we demand in the area of foreign languages," Illinois Representative Paul Simon said in the February, 1983, Kansas City Times. "We're the only nation on the face of the earth where you can go through grade school, high school, college, graduate school, get a Ph.D., and never have a year of foreign language. And that obviously has an adverse impact on some of our security interests and on foreign trade."

The United States loses 100,000 jobs yearly because of the lack of people trained in foreign languages. Approximately 10,000 English-speaking Japanese business persons work in America handling some of the billions of dollars in U.S.-Japanese trade. Yet very few of the 1,000 American business personnel in Japan can even begin to communicate in Japanese, according to the article in Better Homes and Gardens.

A lot more can be done with knowledge of a foreign language than just teaching. Learning another language is a sound educational investment these days. According to figures from the National Council for Foreign Language and International Study, one of every seven management jobs relies on foreign trade. Government agencies need employees with language skills. American corporations are being forced to fill thousands of jobs abroad with citizens of other countries—jobs which could mean our future.

—*The Spirit*, Truman High School, Independence, Missouri

Editorials That Criticize

Some editorials are basically critical of actions, decisions, or situations. Ideally, criticism should be constructive. While it may pinpoint what is bad, it should emphasize good features and try to offer solutions to the problem identified.

The following is an example of an editorial that criticizes. How well do you think it achieves its purpose?

Lack of preparing, caring causes UCS drive to fail

Recently, students and staff made donations to the United Way (UCS) in various ways. Westside's goal for collection was $1,700, and the minimum to be collected was $200 less than that, or $1,500.

When the total collection was revealed, there was no place to hide. The kids from "Hollywood High" could only scrounge up approximately $1,400, far less than the "dollar per person" goal anticipated.

Whether through sweet nothings, doughnut sales, or whatever, a bigger push should have been given by student government to push donations up, and the supposed "Cadillac of Schools" should have been able to surpass the goal set for itself.

Amy Miller, Student Advisory Board (SAB) president, admitted that the collection program lacked "better publicity and earlier planning." Why not tell the students via announcements exactly where their money goes after it leaves their wallets. What part of it goes where, and to whom?

Maybe if students knew what type of people were receiving their donations and where these people were located, students would be more apt to give.

The inactivity of many homerooms was also a major problem in collecting for the needy. Only 23.5 percent of homerooms gave $1 per person or more. Sure, there were the typical excuses of "I'm broke today" or "I've only got enough for lunch." However, homeroom donation went on for several days. One of those days, most students were bound to have an extra buck.

Putting things into perspective, think about someone who is always broke and never has any money to waste on Burger King for lunch. Then ask yourself how important that $1 was to you.

—Westside's Lance, Westside High School, Omaha, Nebraska

Editorials That Persuade

Editorials that persuade have as their basic goal the initiation of specific, positive action. They differ from critical editorials in that action is the immediate, not the eventual, objective. (In critical editorials, the immediate objective is to get the reader to see a problem and, often, a solution to it. Action will come later.) Persuasive editorials that achieve their aims represent one of the most powerful forms of journalism.

Notice the emphasis on immediate action in the editorial on page 273. There is a call to action in the headline of the editorial as well as the final paragraph.

People turn to newspapers not only for facts about events but also for interpretations and opinions. The best editorials strongly engage the reader's attention and intelligence.

Accept pass-fail grading

Pass-fail grading is now being considered by several faculty groups, the administration, and the student council. Accompanying the issue are many complexities, but these facts are fundamental to the entire issue:

A pass-fail grading system would mostly benefit those students who would like to take a class for credit but because of other factors cannot or don't wish to spend the time required to get an A or a B. These would be the only students who might do what teachers fear—"try to do the minimum amount of work." Learning and classroom participation need not suffer, in this situation, as some students are able to do less work and learn as much. In any event, the class would not be a first priority for these students. The other students who have a greater interest in the class, which is taken on a voluntary basis, already would have sufficient motivation to work hard and learn a great deal; they would not be "dragged down."

If indeed this is not the case, it is a signal that too many students are working for a grade, and this is the wrong kind of motivation. Grades have become goals; students work to achieve a grade and not to learn the material. Often, these two—learning and a high grade—are compatible. Many times, however, students endeavor to get around the work, to achieve the grade "dishonestly." A pass-fail grading system would relieve the tremendous emphasis placed on a grade in the home and the classroom. Hopefully, this de-emphasis would encourage learning for the sake of learning, produce more self-disciplined students, and provide a more realistic experience.

We encourage any efforts being made to bring pass-fail to Nicolet and hope it can be accepted into the structure of student evaluations.

—*Knight's Page,* Nicolet High School, Milwaukee, Wisconsin

Editorials That Praise

Another worthwhile goal for an editorial is to praise, congratulate, or commend people and organizations that have done something well. A feeling of good will results from such an editorial.

The following is an excellent brief example of an editorial of praise.

Maintenance engineers clean, beautify campus

Although no additional maintenance engineers have been hired, the campus has taken on a cleaner, better-kept appearance.

Hallways are virtually trash-free, floors and walls are clean, and graffiti seldom lasts over 24 hours. Better maintenance has also beautified the grounds. Lawns are mowed, and hedges are clipped regularly. In addition, grass has been planted in formerly barren areas.

Through hard work and devotion, the maintenance engineers have made the campus's appearance once again pleasant and enjoyable.

—*Rincon Echo*, Rincon High School, Tucson, Arizona

Activity 2: Classifying Editorials by Purpose

1. In daily or weekly newspapers, find one example of each of the kinds of editorials just described. Clip and mount your examples on paper. Label each according to its main purpose. Indicate any other, secondary purposes it may have.

2. Briefly explain how each editorial you selected achieves its main purpose. To clarify your explanations, quote portions of the editorials.

Writing an Editorial

Preparation of an editorial combines the best ideas you have learned for organizing a standard English composition with many of the principles of newswriting. Editorials are usually arranged into the standard composition pattern of introduction–body–conclusion, with ideas presented logically and supported by examples. However, the skills you have learned in journalistic writing—for instance, emphasizing main ideas, keeping sentences simple and brief, and using familiar, definite words—are also critical to editorial success.

The following seven steps will help you in editorial writing. (They may also be useful in the preparation of commentaries.)

Subjects for editorials will often be discussed at meetings of the editorial board. But whether a subject is selected by a writer or determined by a board, it should be one of current concern to the readership.

Choose a Significant Subject

The first step is to choose a significant subject. In general, topics with a news angle are the ones that most deserve editorial space. The best editorial subjects are those of current interest to the readers of your school paper. Choosing such subjects will make writing an editorial easier, too. While it may be difficult to convince your readers that they should celebrate Thanksgiving as something more than a day off from school, that they should read a book during Book Week, or that they should study harder in order to succeed, it should be easy to arouse their interest when you suggest a new examination schedule or point out how the student council can best use its funds.

You *can*, of course, write editorials about school spirit, studying harder, being quiet in the halls, and so forth. But unless these are linked with current news issues, such editorials will not be widely read. These subjects are hard to present adequately without preaching. When so much *is* happening around school, it is not hard to find good newsworthy topics. From these, you can prepare editorials that will be read, thought about, and acted upon.

Activity 3: Selecting Suitable Subjects for Editorials

1. Prepare a list of 20 subjects for editorials that might be used in your school newspaper. Five of the subjects should be suitable for explanatory or interpretive editorials, five for critical ones, five for persuasive ones, and five for editorials that praise. All 20 should be news-related or at least connected with what students are discussing among themselves.

2. From your list of subjects, choose six about which you can form thoughtful, reasonable opinions. For each subject, present your opinion in a single, carefully expressed sentence.

Collect All Needed Facts

Daily newspaper editorial writers may do seven or eight hours of research for each hour spent in actual writing. They leave no stone unturned in their search for facts and arguments. If this is true of professional writ-

Though a well-written editorial may leave the impression that the writer simply sat down and typed out thoughts and opinions, the fact is that considerable research and investigation may have been needed to produce the editorial.

—Photo by Bernard Wolf from Omni

ers, then you, as an amateur, can hardly expect to produce a good editorial during the last 20 minutes before a deadline. Your readers will recognize your hasty writing, and you will feel little satisfaction with your work.

Perhaps you cannot follow a professional's schedule because of your scholastic obligations. But you owe it to yourself, to your paper, and to your readers to do the best job you can of researching your subject. Collect all needed facts—this is your second step in writing an editorial.

If you have chosen your subject wisely, your editorial will generally be based on a news event. Some reporter has covered the event and written stories for your newspaper. You should begin with the facts in these articles. Ask the reporter for additional facts that may have been omitted from the stories.

Next, plan your research program. What sources, written or personal, should you seek out to get a complete picture? An editorial writer must be a careful investigator who will dig deeper for and try harder to understand the reasons behind a news event than the reporter preparing a news story.

Suppose you are assigned an editorial about a school bond proposal to be submitted to your community's voters. First, decide the purpose of your editorial—possibly to persuade your readers that the bonds are needed for your local school system. Then, turn to the news stories assembled for your paper. Get the facts collected by reporters for stories in the forthcoming issue, in which your editorial is to appear. Talk to the reporters to find out their feelings about the election, to collect unpublished facts, and to learn their news sources.

Now that you have some facts, consider what additional information you need. Learn the background of the bond proposal. Your principal or school superintendent can supply this information. Then, since the matter concerns the community, your local newspaper has probably covered it in detail. The paper may even have taken a definite stand. If so, its editorials may explain why. Your school library may keep issues of the local paper on file. If not, read back issues at the local library.

Find out the arguments for and against the plan. Arguments favoring the bonds can be learned from your principal, the school superintendent, a school board member, or a citizens' committee member. Arguments against the proposal may come from a taxpayers' association, a special committee, school board members who oppose the plan, or possibly the local paper.

Talk to voters—your parents, your friends' parents, family friends, and business people. You know these individuals. It's not hard to ask them what they think.

Activity 4: Obtaining Background Information

Select one of the editorial subjects you listed in Activity 3. Make a plan showing what research work you would do before writing your editorial. Indicate the questions you would want answered, the kind of information you would need, and where you would go or whom you would see to obtain these data. You might list the questions and your information needs on the left-hand side of a page, the sources on the right-hand side. At least some of your questions and information needs should center on the facts and arguments that support the opposing opinion.

Decide How to Present Your Ideas

Since editorials may be written about any topic and since their purposes are varied, they may be organized in virtually any form. The third step is to decide how to present your ideas. This decision will be based on the need to make your editorial interesting and convincing.

Many editorials follow a pattern consisting of the following three parts: (1) a brief, single-paragraph statement of the subject; (2) one or more paragraphs that develop the newspaper's position on the subject; and (3) a conclusion that drives home the main point.

The short introductory statement of your subject should—like a news story lead—summarize the issue and seize the attention of your reader. The reader should want to continue reading to find out what you have to say about it and what recommendations you will offer. Your opening words should be provocative. If the subject is controversial or touches your readers' lives, this in itself will attract them. Pointing out a fire hazard on the third floor will interest every student who has a class on that floor. With a more commonplace subject or one in which students have a noticeable lack of interest, your opening statement must be clever or startling if you are to arouse any interest.

The paragraphs that develop your position will consist of arguments supported by details, information, facts, figures, and quotations. In these paragraphs—the body of the editorial—you develop your case, using the best results of your research. If an opposing opinion exists, you will refute it in the course of establishing your own view.

Your conclusion drives home your point. The last paragraph or paragraphs should leave no doubt as to where you stand. You should leave your reader with a clear understanding of the issue as well as a desire to think further about the issue and, when appropriate, to do something about it.

Because this three-part arrangement is formal and logical, either lively writing or an interesting subject is necessary to avoid dullness.

For a topic that is not immediately interesting, try a creative approach. There is literally no limit to the forms an editorial can take. You might compose an **open letter** to an individual or to someone in authority. You might make up a tale, parable, or short story using action instead of argument to convey ideas. You might construct a dramatic sketch, telling the facts in lively conversation. You might write a poem. You might rely on emphatic statements, short, direct, and apparently unrelated, adding up to a powerful argument. You might take a "personalized" approach, referring to the reader as *you* and leading him or her personally into the situation. Or you might use a humorous piece.

These variations demand creative writing skill. They add appeal and interest to your editorial column. If well done, they may be far more effective than formal, logical editorials. If poorly done, they will be trite, ineffective, and scorned by your readers.

Note the story form used in the following editorial. Would a moral or conclusion have weakened or strengthened this editorial?

Buy it for a song . . .

Two hot rods sat quivering at a stop light, their teen-age owners eager to be speeding down the highway. Over the roar of the motors, the kid in the hopped-up red Ford yelled, ''Hey, Tom, that's a pretty fine custom you have there.''

''Yeh, I bought it for a song, too. You remember the guy who was killed about a month ago in that big wreck uptown? Well, I picked up his hot rod at a used-car lot. I had to do a lot of work on the body; it was a mess, but the motor was in fine condition. I bet it will beat anything on the road.''

''Want to prove that?'' Jim called as the light turned green. He gunned out with a loud roar, just asking for a drag.

Tom took his dare and went after him. Faster and faster the two cars went, neck and neck down the two-lane road. 70–75–80. Beads of sweat broke out on Tom's forehead. He was scared, but he wouldn't chicken out. Then, suddenly, a truck loomed up right in front of him! No time to turn, to get out of the way! Tom felt a sudden agonizing pain, then nothing.

His hot rod sits on the used-car lot again. The body is really mangled, but the motor is good. It can be bought for a song, and the car dealer says that with a little work it will beat anything on the road.

—*Life*, Excelsior High School, Norwalk, California
(Quoted in *Student and Publisher*)

Activity 5:   Analyzing Editorial Forms

1. In a daily or school newspaper, find an editorial arranged according to the three-part pattern. Clip it and mark the dividing points of the three sections. Summarize the editorial's main point and describe how the middle section develops the writer's case.

2. In daily or school newspapers, find an editorial showing a creative variation of the standard arrangement. Write a short statement describing the plan or pattern and telling why you think it was used.

Make Every Word Count

Because an editorial is like an essay, editorial writers have more freedom in wording and style than reporters have. But this freedom goes hand in hand with the responsibility of using language ably and efficiently. The fourth step is to make every word count. Nothing repels readers faster than long unbroken columns of wordy writing. Even daily newspapers, which frequently used to print 500-word editorials, are approaching a 200-word limit.

For reader appeal, try to observe this limit. Ruthlessly strike out words, sentences, and even whole paragraphs that do not carry their weight. Consider and use the devices given in Chapter 8 for shortening and brightening news sentences.

Moreover, every statement must not only have a clear, definite meaning but also advance your argument. Taking the time to think through your ideas logically and systematically will make it easier to write concise, argument-advancing sentences and paragraphs.

You should also follow one other special point of style. Editorials are normally written in the third person, just as news stories are. When you must use the first person, do not say *I* or *me,* but rather *we* or *us.* In an editorial, *we* stands for the newspaper and its staff. This is called the **editorial *we.***

Stimulate Thought

The fifth step is to stimulate thought. Your editorial will achieve its goal only to the extent that you make your readers think their way to the opinion that you are presenting. Hours of deliberation by your editorial board will prove worthless unless, by the sheer power of your words on the editorial page, you "start the wheels rolling" in a reader's mind.

One way to do this is to involve your readers personally. Talk directly to and about them and their friends. Make your statements striking. Ask questions. Present your facts so that readers will ask, "Did I do this?" or "How does this affect me?" Then help them find the answer to the next question: "What can I do about it?"

It is also important to avoid preaching. No one likes to be told what to do. A good editorial writer avoids preaching by giving constructive suggestions, by using examples to make a point, or by showing why readers would benefit from an improvement. Sometimes it is enough just to state the facts about the problem, without comment.

Read the following excerpt from an editorial on gossip and notice how easy it is to fall into what is essentially a preaching tone.

> Gossip is nothing to play with, and those who do are headed for serious trouble. Gossips have a very short period in which they have many friends, but they also have much longer periods with no friends.
>
> Have Amy, Ken, and Donna been avoiding you for some unknown reason? Do Phyllis, Dave, and Sherry want to see you only when you have some gossip for them? Take a little time. Think. What have you said about them?

Now read an excerpt from another editorial on gossip. Notice how the use of a specific example helps the writer avoid preaching.

Tad did not have anything against Nick, but nevertheless he ''bumped him off'' one evening.

It all came about when Tad was with his crowd over at the soda fountain. When they ran out of something to talk about, Tad, who did not want to appear boring, burst out with—''Say, have you heard the latest dirt on Nick? Why, I hear . . .''

That is how it began, and before long poor Nick was slaughtered, although Tad's weapon was just his tongue.

—*Journal*, Parkersburg High School, Parkersburg, West Virginia

---

Write a Headline That Says, "Read This!"

An editorial does not have the same kind of headline as a news story. A news story's headline provides information in summary form. An editorial headline has only one purpose—to attract readers and get them to read the editorial. The sixth step, then, is to write a headline that says, "Read this!"

Depending on your school newspaper style, you may have more freedom in headlining an editorial than in headlining a news story. The single word, phrase, or sentence that makes up the headline will typically be printed in a single line across the wide editorial column. Frequently, the headline will be in a style of type different from that of other headlines.

The following are examples of good editorial headlines.

Where were the crowds?

Try math this year

A new girls' gym?

One more regulation

Solving the parking problem

Check Your Editorial for Basic Correctness

Because an editorial writer enjoys the freedom of an essayist and yet must produce a piece of writing as terse and condensed as a straight-news report, it is all the more necessary that an editorial be reviewed for fundamental soundness. The seventh step is to check your editorial for basic correctness. The checklist on page 282 should prove useful.

✔ Checklist for Preparing an Editorial

☐ 1. Have I chosen a subject of current importance and interest to my readers?

☐ 2. Have I decided on the specific purpose of my editorial—to explain or interpret, to criticize, to persuade, or to praise?

☐ 3. Have I limited the scope of my topic so that I can focus clearly on the points I wish to make?

☐ 4. Have I gotten all the facts and background information I need?

☐ 5. If I have decided to structure my editorial according to a three-part pattern, have I stated my subject in a single, brief opening paragraph; developed my position with arguments supported by details, information, facts, figures, or quotations; and concluded with a paragraph that drives home my main point and persuades my readers to think or act?

☐ 6. If my subject is not in itself lively, have I been sufficiently creative in my approach to the subject?

☐ 7. Have I written sentences that not only are vivid, definite, and concise but also advance my position?

☐ 8. Have I written my editorial in such a manner that my readers will be spurred to think their own way to my opinion?

☐ 9. Have I written a headline that will attract readers and get them to read my editorial?

Activity 6:   Preparing Editorials

1. Collect a number of headlines from editorials in school and daily newspapers. Note which ones you think are particularly effective and why.

2. Choose one of the four basic kinds of editorials and after reviewing its characteristics, write an editorial of no more than 200 words. Follow the seven steps just presented.

3. Choose another of the basic kinds of editorials and write an editorial according to the directions in Item 2.

Presenting Opinions in Editorial Cartoons

Editorial cartoons are powerful forms of expression. Since they enable readers to take in at a glance a concretely rendered idea, they evoke strong reactions and promote much public discussion. In the past, daily newspapers considered them so important that they occupied a regular position on the front page. But, for a long time, the custom has been to place them on the editorial page, where they are often related to the leading editorial.

Editorial cartoons in a school paper will catch the attention of almost every reader. Students will react constructively if cartoons are planned and presented in a positive manner.

Good editorial cartoons are not hard to produce. Even if you don't have a staff cartoonist, there is a way to get cartoons: Recruit students from an art class. Your editorial board or editorial page staff can plan cartoon ideas and assign them to one of the art students. This combination of artist-plus-journalist usually produces very good editorial cartoons.

—*The Axe*, South Eugene High School, Eugene, Oregon (top);
The Epitaph, Homestead High School, Cupertino, California (middle and bottom)

Not only are editorial cartoons powerful forms of expression, but they are sure to catch the attention of everyone who opens up a school paper. Getting a good cartoon idea is the first step in the process of cartoon production.

Activity 7:   Preparing Editorial Cartoons

Choose three editorials from recent issues of your school paper that could have been linked to editorial cartoons. Then, for each editorial, state the idea you would want a cartoonist to express and suggest the kind of drawing that might be suitable.

Influencing Public Opinion: Final Considerations

Student attitudes are likely to be influenced, constructively or destructively, by your school newspaper. Editorials play a distinct part in wielding this influence. But the apparent purpose of the entire paper, as indicated by the selection, treatment, and placement of copy, is also involved. Your editorial staff, therefore, has a fine opportunity to lead student thinking.

The first essential to leadership is a strong editorial board. With your adviser's guidance, this board decides editorial subjects, considers whether editorial campaigns will be conducted, plans story emphasis, and makes other major decisions. Your editorial board may include the editor and several other experienced staff members, preferably a group of people with diverse opinions. Some of next year's leading staff members should also be on the board so that they may prepare for their future responsibilities.

Your editorial board's first step will be to consider and determine your newspaper's purpose. What goals will the staff be trying to accomplish through publication of the paper? Editorial guidelines also need to be established in cooperation with the school administration and school board. This is especially necessary if newspaper content will touch upon controversial topics or if the staff proposes to engage seriously in the task of influencing student and community attitudes and actions.

Once your staff has determined its purposes and established a definite understanding of its privileges and responsibilities, your newspaper is in a position to become an important force in your school and community by reflecting student thinking and promoting worthwhile goals.

In addition to thoughtful and provocative editorials, school papers have a number of means of extending their influence. They may expand and enrich news reports so that they explain curriculum and activities. Interpretive, in-depth articles on a variety of subjects can show what students are thinking and doing. The staff may arrange broad coverage of problems that are high in student and community concern. These and other staff-initiated actions are explained further in the Editor's Handbook on pages 494–496.

An editorial campaign for traffic signals was featured at the beginning of this chapter. Editorial crusades are the outgrowth of a creative editorial policy that seeks to *do* something, not merely to act as a mirror of school life. What is involved in a successful editorial campaign? First, the confidence of readers: You must have gained your readers' trust by truthful news coverage and intelligent editorials. Next, hard work: To build up public opinion to the point where major results are accomplished requires untiring effort and imagination. Careful timing is necessary to keep the problem in everyone's mind until your goal is reached.

An editorial campaign is a combination of all possible efforts to influence public opinion. News stories and pictures may be combined with editorials, cartoons, and features over several issues. In addition, a full-scale campaign calls for posters, talks, meetings, petitions, and other similar devices.

Activity 8: Providing Editorial Leadership

1. Examine editorials and related stories, pictures, and cartoons in a major daily or weekly newspaper, analyzing the aims and methods of the editorial writers and other staff members. Summarize your findings.

2. Using several different daily newspapers in your public library, locate a number of editorials on the same subject. In a brief report, compare them in approach, factual content, and conclusions.

3. Select a major problem about which you feel student opinion could be constructively aroused. Then, draw up a plan for an editorial campaign, including stories, editorials, and cartoons in several issues of your paper. Augment this with outside activities that could be promoted in the newspaper.

Summary

This chapter begins by explaining what editorials are and why they are important. It describes the basic types of editorials, by purpose. It then presents seven steps for writing an editorial and discusses the preparation of editorial cartoons. Finally, it focuses on the importance of a strong editorial board and the many ways, in addition to editorials, in which a newspaper can influence public opinion.

RECOGNIZING EDITORIALS AND THEIR IMPORTANCE. An editorial is an article that presents the newspaper's opinion on an issue. It is normally unsigned, since it represents the voice of the paper rather than of any one person. If written forcefully and convincingly, an editorial can influence public opinion and even spur people to action.

UNDERSTANDING EDITORIAL PURPOSES. Many editorials can be classified by purpose, the four most common ones being to explain or interpret, to criticize, to persuade, and to praise. While one of these purposes will usually be the dominant one in a given editorial, one or more of the other purposes may be present secondarily.

WRITING AN EDITORIAL.   Like a standard composition, editorials usually consist of an introduction, a body, and a conclusion. But they also have many of the stylistic features of good news reports. Main ideas are emphasized; sentences are kept simple and brief; familiar, definite words are preferred to harder ones. Seven steps are helpful in preparing editorials. First, choose a significant subject, preferably one of current interest to your readers. Second, collect all needed facts. Third, decide how to present your ideas. You will probably use either the introduction–body–conclusion arrangement or, for less interesting subjects, a more creative and imaginative form. Fourth, make every word count. Fifth, stimulate thought, for you want your readers to think their way to your opinion. Sixth, write a headline that says, "Read This!" Seventh, check your editorial for basic correctness.

PRESENTING OPINIONS IN EDITORIAL CARTOONS.   Editorial cartoons express ideas visually and forcefully. They seize the attention of almost every reader and often stir up strong reactions and public discussion. After editorial departments have settled on cartoon ideas, either staff artists or art students can turn them into drawings.

INFLUENCING PUBLIC OPINION: FINAL CONSIDERATIONS.   Newspapers influence public opinion both through editorials and through the choice, treatment, and placement of stories. An editorial board's determination of a newspaper's purpose and of editorial guidelines is the essential step in preparing to lead public opinion. Then editorials and expanded, enriched news reports can be used to advance the paper's purpose. In conducting an editorial campaign in behalf of some public good, the editorial board may find it useful to draw on all of a paper's resources for activating public opinion.

Vocabulary

editorial board

editor in chief

open letter

editorial *we*

editorial cartoon

Review Questions

1. Why are editorials called the voice of the newspaper?

2. What are the four basic kinds of editorials?

3. What steps should an editorial writer follow?

4. Why are editorial cartoons powerful forms of expression?

5. Aside from editorials, what is involved in a newspaper's effort to affect attitudes and influence public opinion?

Discussion Questions

1. How would you reply to the following remark: "Newspapers should publish nothing but news. Editorials are not news. Therefore, newspapers should not publish them"?

2. To what extent should an editorial board try to vary the purposes of its editorials from one issue to another? Why?

3. What subjects, if any, would not be appropriate for editorials in school newspapers?

4. Because of their visual nature, editorial cartoons can sometimes be thoughtlessly cruel. What steps, if any, should be taken to guard against this?

5. How might a school newspaper abuse its privilege of leading public (that is, student) opinion?

Chapter Project

Writing an Editorial on Editorial Policy

Write a formal (introduction–body–conclusion) editorial that explains what you would regard as appropriate goals, policies, and responsibilities of your school paper if you were chosen editor in chief for the coming year.

PRESENTING SPORTS ACTION

When you have completed this chapter you should be able to

Understand how different kinds of stories can be used to cover sports events.

Understand how a feature story, an interpretive, in-depth report, a column, or a commentary can be used to add variety to sports coverage.

Write a sports story in proper form.

Plan an interesting sports page.

Sports have great appeal in American schools, as in American life. Students attend, participate in, and read about athletic events. The extensiveness of sports coverage today reflects this widespread interest in athletics.

Some school papers devote one fourth or more of their limited space to sports coverage. Moreover, the sports page often sparkles with the vigorous actions re-created there. When it does, it is usually because of the imagination the sportswriters brought to their work.

An anecdote told by a veteran sports editor and quoted in *Student and Publisher* gives an example of a sports reporter's imagination at work. The reporter is the legendary Damon Runyon. According to the editor:

> Yale won a crew victory from Harvard by a sensational last-minute spurt. All of us racked our brains to bat out a lead that wouldn't be the same old trite thing. Here's how Runyon, who typed out his whole piece in 15 minutes, began his story:
> "The Yale crew today arched their backs like eight angry cats and clawed their way to victory."

Covering Sports Events

School newspapers seldom need to worry about having enough sports news to report. The challenge is to publish high-quality sportswriting. To do so, reporters and other writers have to guard against preparing stories that consist largely of dead facts and statistics with a few observations thrown in. Daily newspapers have an advantage over school papers when covering completed events, because scores and results may still be fresh news after 24 hours. But when the results of a sports event are two or three weeks old—as they often are when they appear in a school paper—they are virtually dead. This unavoidable condition of reporting for a school paper only makes clearer the need for imagination and sound sports-reporting practices.

Much of what follows in this chapter is designed to help you acquire the skills needed for superior sportswriting.

Emphasizing Advance Stories

From what has just been said, it is clear that an important kind of article for sports reporting is the advance story. It tells about upcoming games, comparing teams and players, discussing team records, giving line-ups, and perhaps indirectly, stirring up enthusiasm.

Information for an advance story may be obtained from many sources. Attend practice sessions. Ask coaches and players for facts and opinions. Read daily newspapers, including local papers in your opponents' communities. Study papers from other schools in your league or talk to their sports editors by telephone. When sufficient facts have been gathered, assemble them into a dramatic fact-packed story.

When writing the story, you should feature the news element of conflict. Discuss the possible consequences of the game. Point out the strong and weak points of both teams. Use names and quote opinions. Your readers want to know about your opponent's strength as well as your own team's. Keep in mind, however, that predictions, speculations, or controversial comments should generally be published only as quotations from competent authorities.

Writing Follow-Up Stories

There is little reason for accounts of past sports events to be filled with lengthy details when a daily newspaper is also covering your school's major games. Only when there is no outside coverage are your readers likely to expect complete game reports, no matter how late they are published.

Brief follow-up stories, however, may be practical in school papers even when daily papers do cover school sports. Student reporters have many advantages over reporters from daily newspapers. They are closer to a team and its coaches. They also have more time to write and more opportunity to develop interpretive, in-depth aspects of sports reporting.

Writing at your leisure rather than under deadline pressure a few hours after the game, you can explain why and how things happened in a way that the daily paper could not—why the team played in an unusual way, why particular athletes didn't seem to be playing their best, and how the critical play that won the game was planned. Such reporting can be excellent when deadlines are not imminent, when time is available for reflec-

—Photo by Harold M. Lambert from Frederic Lewis

In a well-planned sports page, much of what is written about a game like this will have been published well before the game, in an advance story. A brief follow-up can then provide insights about the outcome.

tive thinking, and when interviews can be arranged with coaches and players after they have rested.

These game reports should be thought of as follow-up stories because most of your readers will have already learned the outcome and many of the details. Hence, you will try to offer insights and new information.

In addition to reports on major games, brief follow-ups on other games or on other less prominent sports events will be widely read, especially if players' names are included. They furnish variety and reach readers not attracted by accounts of major games.

Good follow-up stories on games generally require eyewitness reporting. In this respect, they are similar to reports on speeches or meetings. You observe carefully, taking notes on what is important or interesting. If the scorekeeper's records are available to you, you may depend on these for basic facts, while adding colorful highlights gained from firsthand observation. If these records are not available, you must keep necessary records yourself, at the same time watching for outstanding plays. Post-game interviews with players, coaches, and officials will add to your understanding of the event. From all these facts and impressions, you will select items to feature in your story. In most school papers, you will not be allowed much space, so you must make every word convey an important idea.

Preparing Summary Stories

Summary stories that give the results of all games or review an entire sport may serve a number of purposes. They can review and highlight a team's complete season. They can present the major events in a sport when space cannot be allocated for reports on individual games. Or they can publicize the results of intramural competition, as well as other less well-known sports activities.

Such summaries need not be routine recitations of scores and dull facts. Briefly but vividly describe the highlights of the season. List the names of outstanding players. Where many games must be mentioned in a limited space, emphasize the outstanding ones. Then, combine the highlights of other games into brief sentences or list their scores. If you try to be "fair" by writing one sentence about each game, you will end up with a dull pattern of statements that monotonously repeat the same idea.

Combining Advance, Follow-Up, and Summary Stories

Typical sports pages do not have space enough for all possible advance, follow-up, and summary stories. Why not combine all three into a single article? The result, sometimes referred to as a follow-up/advance combination, can help you avoid repetition while giving your readers a total picture of one sport.

The following story clearly explains all baseball activities at Oneonta High. The coming game is featured, and previous games are followed up and summarized. Notice the generous use of names.

Yellowjackets seek win over LFHS nine

Oneonta High's baseball Yellowjackets travel to Little Falls Saturday afternoon in search of another Iroquois League victory.

Last Saturday, behind the one-hit pitching of right-hander Bruce Bouton, the Jacket diamondmen blanked Herkimer, 5-0, with Bouton striking out 18 Herkimer batsmen.

Tomorrow's probable starting lineup will consist of infielders John Colyer, Bill Crowley, Dick Ingraham, and Dave Cooper and outfielders Harold Howland, Larry Hubler, and Bill Hadsell.

Either Larry Santos or Bruce Bouton will pitch, with Joe Russo behind the plate.

"Little Falls is expected to field a stronger team this year," commented Coach "Hal" Hunt. Last year, the Huntmen beat the Rock City nine twice in league play.

In two previous nonleague games, the squad defeated Vestal, 6-3, and topped Deposit Central, 11-4.

The Vestal game saw Bill Crowley bang out three hits, including a double and a home run. Dick Ingraham also clouted a four-bagger.

Hurlers Larry Santos and Bruce Bouton combined to allow Vestal only two hits, with Santos receiving credit for the win.

Clutch hitting by Larry Hubler, Dave Cooper, Bill Crowley, Dick Ingraham, and Bill Hadsell paved the way for the victory over Deposit.

—Echo, Oneonta Senior High School, Oneonta, New York

Activity 1: Analyzing Sports Coverage

1. Find a daily or a weekly paper that has covered at least one of your school's major sports events. How does this paper's coverage of the event differ from the coverage found in your own school paper? Why?

2. Using your school paper, write a brief report analyzing how much of the sports coverage consists of advance stories, how much of follow-up stories, how much of summary stories, and how much of the three in combination. Conclude your report with an opinion as to how these different kinds of stories should be proportioned in your school paper.

Adding Variety to Sports Coverage

Besides competitive events, there are a number of other subjects that school sportswriters can cover. Among these are physical education activities and developments, athletic facilities, schedules, awards, and standings and statistics. A school paper might also cover sports personalities, training and exercise, local sports history, noncompetitive games and recrea-

Coverage of athletic activities other than a school's major sports is characteristic of superior sports pages. Variety of content as well as of approach should be a goal of sportswriters and sports editors.

—Photo by Kent and Donna Dannen from Photo Researchers

tions, and the social significance of sports. No doubt you can think of still more subjects that are suitable for the sports page of your school paper.

Such subjects may be presented in news stories. Many of them can also be treated in appealing ways in feature stories, interpretive, in-depth reports, columns, or commentaries. All that you learned in previous chapters about these articles applies to their use in sports coverage.

Enriching a Sports Page with Feature Stories and Interpretive, In-Depth Reports

Feature stories focusing on fishing, hunting, skiing, jogging, skating, hiking, and other such activities can provide a nice contrast with stories covering major team sports. Some of these features might center on individuals who participate in these activities. One value of such stories is that they keep the sports page from concentrating too much on the major sports—football, baseball, and basketball—and thereby alienating readers who practice or follow other sports.

Nevertheless, feature stories spotlighting star athletes, coaches, and alumni doing well in college or professional sports are also desirable. When writing about the star of a major sport, you might briefly recount his or her accomplishments and try to reveal the kind of effort and determination that made them possible. You might also mention the star's ambitions and plans and highlight some of the less known aspects of his or her life and personality.

The following excerpts are from typical sports feature stories. What sports feature subjects can you think of for your own school paper?

The alarm clock rings early in the morning. Then off to school for a two-hour session of swimming practice and six classes.

This is a typical day for two of Gateway's top swimmers, freshman Betsy Weber and junior Jeanette Bartick.

—*The Gateway Medallion*, Gateway High School, Aurora, Colorado

Pumping weights is the name of the game for many Crescent Valley athletes.

Several hours are spent each day by athletes from all sports fields pushing up the iron in the CV weightroom.

—*Crescent Crier*, Crescent Valley High School, Corvallis, Oregon

"Coaching is a completely new experience," said Amy Subryan, who is one of several Kennedy students who coach for the Southwest Denver Soccer Association.

—*The Statesman*, Kennedy High School, Denver, Colorado

The ball soars up—past the upstretched arms of players, into the basket. The crowd roars!

Unrecognized at the sidelines is a figure who helped to get the ball into the basket—the team manager.

—*U-High Midway*, University High School, Chicago, Illinois

While feature stories can add interest to your sports pages, interpretive, in-depth reports can satisfy your readers' desire for a second, more penetrating look into a subject treated in an advance, follow-up, or summary story—for example, an important league victory, a one-sided score, or a team's overall season. They are also useful for subjects that cannot be handled in a story that reports on contests or standings—for example, the relationship between school athletics and academic matters or the connection between sports and the general life of a community. In general, people who enjoy reading about games, contests, and meets often like to read about the deeper issues involved in sports as well. Hence, interpretive, in-depth reports have a real and important place on the sports page.

Varying Sports Coverage Through Columns and Commentaries

Sports pages are brightened and enhanced by varied approaches to athletics. For this reason, columns and commentaries can be desirable additions to a page of reports and feature stories. Much of what you learned in Chapter 12 about publishing opinions and columns applies to their use as sports articles.

Sports columns may fall into three general types, each of which serves a different purpose. One type consists of paragraphs containing information about physical fitness activities, personality notes, interesting incidents, bits of comment, or facts about team progress. Another type consists of news briefs. This is a good way to keep readers informed about a variety of minor or intramural sports activities. Such paragraphs might be written by many reporters and assembled by the sports editor or an assistant.

The third type—an opinion column—usually evaluates a single pertinent sports topic. The writer, often the sports editor, needs to develop broad knowledge in a wide range of sports. This individual personally attends school athletic contests and practice sessions, earns the trust and confidence of coaches and players, and reads widely in daily newspapers and sports magazines.

Occasionally, a sports column may feature comments or predictions about college or professional teams. Interesting as these topics might be, however, most school papers have neither space for them nor qualified writers.

What does the following sports column add to a sports page that a conventional report would not?

Into sports

By Rich Payne

Football and basketball are considered the main sports here at Central. However, these are not the only sports offered by Central's well-rounded athletic program. These other sports should also share the recognition Central gets for its sports program.

Most of the other, less-known sports have earned honors equal to or even surpassing the two major sports. The boys' cross-country team won first in its conference and picked up four first places in 11 meets. In its first year, the girls' cross-country placed second in two meets and sent Wendy Hager to the state cross-country meet.

The girls' volleyball team established an 11-5 record and knocked off fourth-seeded Sikeston in the district tournament. The girls' tennis team had a disappointing 7-5 season this year. But with most of their top players returning next year, there should be a marked improvement.

For the second time in three years, the girls' golf team has advanced to state play. This year the girls won second place. That's a bigger accomplishment than any achieved in the major sports, yet these girls get very little recognition.

Girls' basketball and boys' wrestling are now starting. The girls' varsity basketball team wasn't outstanding last year, but with help from a 15-0 JV squad, they should be tough competition this year.

I am not trying to belittle the accomplishments of the major sports, but I think the smaller sports should be recognized for their many accomplishments. Not only does Central have a well-rounded sports program, but we also have one in which all the teams are winners!

—*The Tiger*, Central High School,
Cape Girardeau, Missouri

Sports commentaries are generally like opinion columns, except that they do not appear in the same format issue after issue. The qualifications for writing sports commentaries are the same as those for writing opinion columns. In both cases, it is necessary that the writer choose a subject that deserves analysis or interpretation, gather all information needed to support the views offered, and write thoughtfully and well.

Activity 2:   Analyzing Different Forms of Sportswriting

1. Find outstanding examples of sports feature stories and interpretive, in-depth reports in school or professional papers. Using these examples, write a report on the qualities that make these articles models of sports journalism.

2. Find outstanding examples of sports opinion columns and commentaries in the sports pages of daily or weekly newspapers. Explain how these columns and commentaries resemble those concerned with matters other than sports and how they differ from them.

3. Examine sports columns and commentaries in your own and in other school newspapers and comment on the subject matter or general approach used in each. Do you think each column appeals to a wide group of readers? Give reasons for your opinion. What are the indications that the author is qualified to offer opinions on sports?

Writing a Sports Story

Good sportswriting follows the general newswriting standards presented in previous chapters. There are, however, three special considerations that sportswriters should keep in mind. The first is to avoid jargon and clichés. The second is to follow the conventions of sportswriting. The third is to stick to the facts unless you know the sport very well.

Avoid Jargon and Clichés

A lively style is, of course, one of the first requirements for good sportswriting. An informal tone, a generous use of correct sports terms, a wealth of vivid details, and imaginative writing give readers the feeling of being present at an athletic event. Inexperienced writers, however, often tend to fall back on **jargon** and **clichés.** Jargon is highly specialized language used by those in the same work or profession. It usually consists of words and expressions that are unfamiliar or even unintelligible to a more general audience. A cliché is a trite word or expression—one that has lost its freshness and expressive power from repeated use.

The following passage shows what jargon and clichés can do to a sports story.

In their last outing against North High, Central's hickorymen drew first blood in the bottom of the second. The Bears' Joe Jones blasted a circuit to knot it up at a horse each in the third frame. Manuel Garcia hurled the first four stanzas, giving up a trio of safeties and whuffing two.

Possibly, a reader can puzzle out the meaning of the sentences, but why should a sportswriter make it hard for the reader to understand what is written? When such writing *can* be understood, it is immediately seen as worn-out and stale. It would have been better to use *game* for *outing*, *baseball team* for *hickorymen*, and so on.

If you follow the general principles of newswriting style (see Chapter 8) and if you bring a lively mind and lively perceptions to your subject, you will achieve a lively sportswriting style.

Follow the Conventions of Sportswriting

Sportswriting style usually involves certain details that may be slightly different from the details of other newswriting forms. One of these involves proper forms of address. When referring to an athlete for the first time, state the full name—*Ed Smith*, for example. For each other reference in the same story, use the last name only. Say *Smith*, not *Ed*, even though a first name may be preferred on other news pages.

School newspaper style sheets usually require the titles *Mr., Miss, Mrs.,* or *Ms.* when referring to an adult. *Coach* is an acceptable substitute for these titles on the sports page. Write *Coach Howard Taylor* the first time the name appears, then *Coach Taylor* or *Mr. Taylor*.

Our boys, our girls, or *the locals* are poor forms of reference. Say *Wildcats* or *Central* or occasionally *the track squad* or *Coach Billie Ross's team*.

Another convention is to present league standings, records, **box scores,** and other such statistical material properly. To determine the proper form, examine the sports pages of good daily papers or *The Associated Press Stylebook*. If local papers have published box scores for interscholastic contests, you will probably not want to publish your own, since limited space is usually a problem for sportswriters and sports editors. However, keep in mind that sports fans love statistics. Records and league standings not appearing in local papers are, therefore, welcome enhancements of a school paper's sports page.

Interpret the Facts Only If You Are Qualified

Opinions about the facts of a sports event are a natural part of many sports columns and commentaries. They may also appear occasionally in basic sports stories that include bylines. The heated nature of sports events lends itself readily to the statement of opinions.

However, any opinions you offer should be backed up in two ways—by your thorough knowledge of the sport itself and by the facts of the event you are writing about. If you do not know a sport well, you should stick to the facts. If you *do* know the sport, you should make sure the facts directly support your opinions.

Scoreboard

NHL

Wales Conference
Patrick Division

	W	L	T	Pts.	GF	GA
NY Isles	28	14	2	58	203	153
NY Rangers	24	14	5	53	175	163
Philadelphia	23	12	6	52	187	152
Washington	20	20	3	43	149	147
Pittsburgh	9	28	5	23	130	182
New Jersey	9	31	2	20	120	189

Adams Division

	W	L	T	Pts.	GF	GA
Boston	26	12	3	55	181	126
Buffalo	25	13	4	54	172	149
Quebec	24	16	3	51	207	158
Montreal	20	20	2	42	159	154
Hartford	15	23	3	33	145	175

Campbell Conference
Norris Division

	W	L	T	Pts.	GF	GA
Minnesota	20	18	4	44	189	193
St. Louis	18	22	4	42	166	176
Chicago	17	23	3	37	149	163
Toronto	15	22	5	35	167	202
Detroit	15	23	4	34	153	181

Smythe Division

	W	L	T	Pts.	GF	GA
Edmonton	32	7	4	68	259	171
Vancouver	16	23	5	37	168	179
Calgary	15	19	7	37	153	180
Winnipeg	15	21	5	35	179	200
Los Angeles	14	21	7	35	183	196

Monday's Result
Edmonton 7, Detroit 3

Tuesday's Results
Quebec 7, Pittsburgh 1
N.Y. Islanders 4, New Jersey 2
Hartford 6, Minnesota 3
St. Louis 2, Vancouver 0

Today's Games
Boston at Detroit, 6:35 p.m.
Philadelphia at Buffalo, 6:35 p.m.
Montreal at Toronto, 7:05 p.m.
Edmonton at Chicago, 7:35 p.m.
Winnipeg at Calgary, 8:35 p.m.
Washington at Los Angeles, 9:35 p.m.

NBA standings

Eastern Conference

Atlantic Division

	W	L	Pct.	GB
Boston	27	8	.771	—
Philadelphia	24	10	.706	2½
New York	20	15	.571	7
Washington	17	17	.500	9½
New Jersey	17	19	.472	10½

Central Division

	W	L	Pct.	GB
Detroit	19	15	.559	—
Milwaukee	19	16	.543	½
Atlanta	18	18	.500	2
Chicago	14	17	.452	3½
Indiana	10	22	.313	8
Cleveland	11	25	.306	9

Monday's Results
New Jersey 107, Washington 103
New York 111, Philadelphia 73

Tuesday's Results
Los Angeles at Houston, night.
Atlanta 103, Golden State 101
Cleveland 117, Milwaukee 104
Kansas City 112, Dallas 102
Indiana at Chicago, night.
Phoenix at Utah, night.
San Diego at Seattle, night.
San Antonio at Portland, night.

Western Conference

Midwest Division

	W	L	Pct.	GB
Utah	22	12	.647	—
Dallas	19	16	.543	3½
Kansas City	15	19	.441	7
Denver	15	20	.429	7½
San Antonio	14	21	.400	8½
Houston	13	22	.371	9½

Pacific Division

	W	L	Pct.	GB
Portland	23	14	.622	—
Los Angeles	20	13	.606	1
Seattle	16	17	.485	5
Golden State	17	19	.472	5½
Phoenix	15	20	.429	7
San Diego	12	22	.353	9½

Today's Games
Golden State at Boston, 6:30 p.m.
Chicago at New Jersey, 6:35 p.m.
Washington at Philadelphia, 6:35 p.m.
Detroit at Indiana, 6:35 p.m.
Utah at Dallas, 7:35 p.m.
San Diego at Phoenix, 8:35 p.m.
San Antonio at Denver, 8:40 p.m.
Thursday's Games
Portland at Houston, 7:40 p.m.
Atlanta at Washington, 6:35 p.m.
Los Angeles at Kansas City, 7:35 p.m.

These pro hockey and basketball standings from the Houston Chronicle *are among many that could serve as a model for a school paper's sports page.*

Activity 3: Preparing Sports Stories

1. Attend in person or watch on television a contest in a sport with which you are familiar. Write a follow-up story on the contest, making use of the principles of basic newswriting as well as the special considerations in this section.

2. Write a feature story, an interpretive, in-depth report, a column, or a commentary on any aspect of sports in your school. Besides following the special considerations presented in this section, review those presented in the chapter that covers the kind of article you intend to write.

Planning an Interesting Sports Page

Your editorial board will allot space for sports news in proportion to space for other news. In many cases, sports will be covered on the back page of a four-page newspaper. Advertisements often fill part of this page, posing a problem for the sports editor. If the ads are well positioned by the advertising staff, a reasonable amount of space will be left for sports news.

When the paper has six or more pages, sports can have a whole page to itself, free of advertising. An alternative plan, more pleasing to your advertisers, is to reserve two facing pages for sports, printing advertisements on both pages.

As you plan any sports page, keep in mind that student readers have a wide variety of athletic and recreational interests. While they want to know the progress of your school's major sports teams, they are probably also concerned about less publicized athletic groups. In addition, many students participate in recreational sports, such as skiing, bowling, or backpacking. Brief stories on minor topics take up little space, make the page attractive, add to reader interest by publicizing different names, and attract different groups of readers.

The challenge faced by sportswriters and editors is to cover a variety of subjects in a variety of ways in a limited allotment of space. Planning sports coverage, therefore, must involve the entire sports staff. The sports page in its entirety as well as each article and photograph that appears on it must be thought out carefully. A delicate and complex balance among all sports items must be established if the page is to be both comprehensive and lively.

The following checklist touches on the basic considerations that go into the preparation of a sports page. Some of the items will be more useful to the sports editor, some to the sportswriter.

✔ Checklist for Sports Coverage

☐ 1. Have all stories and photographs been planned well enough in advance to allow for appropriate coverage?

☐ 2. Is there a good balance between factual reports (advance, follow-up, and summary stories) and other kinds of articles (feature stories, interpretive, in-depth reports, columns, and commentaries)?

☐ 3. In reporting on competition, is there more emphasis on previewing what is upcoming than on reviewing what is past?

☐ 4. In a follow-up story, is there more emphasis on why and how things happened than on what happened?

☐ 5. In an account of a contest, is there an angle that will hold the interest even of those who have read a local paper's account of the contest?

☐ 6. Have names been included wherever possible?

☐ 7. Is there adequate coverage of minor sports, intramurals, nonschool athletics in which students participate, and developments in physical education classes?

☐ 8. Has a column of news briefs been used to report on items that don't require separate stories?

May 13, 1983, Union St. Journal, Page 13

Summer Sports

BY PATTI WOLTER

SPORTS ARE an activity that almost any person can take part in, and during the summer many people do. Of the students polled in a survey taken by the *USJ*, most said that during the summer they swam, played tennis, or ran. Many other sports were mentioned, but most Creekers commented that they didn't have the right accessories for many of the sports in which they would like to participate. They also said that many types of sports interest them, but they didn't know how to get involved. As a result, the *USJ* decided to reoort on some of the soorts

Two-wheels

Students rated bicycling third in the poll, but the students did not specify how much they cycled. There are two types of biking: recreational and touring. For an average bike that would be used for rides around a park or to a friend's house, most students spend about $150. A good bike that is lightweight yet durable costs approximately $250. Accessories to accommodate food, clothing, and emergency materials cost extra. Panniers are one type of saddlebag to carry these items. They cost from $50 to $100. Pumps, for $18 are highly recommended.

Golf

Many students polled expressed an interest in golf. A typical golf game takes up an afternoon and costs an average of $6 for eighteen holes at most public golf courses. Golfing equipment of average quality, however, costs about $400. Clubs usually can't be rented. For a less serious, cheaper, and shorter game, however, students can try miniature golf. Eighteen holes, requiring a course with various contraptions, a ball, and a putter, cost an average of two dollars and fifty cents per round. Miniature golf doesn't require good golfing skills, and the students polled said they take part in this activity when short of time or money.

All photos by Kevin Wood

THE STUDENT who feels these sports are inaccessible because of price, time, or lack of interest, can still swim, play tennis, or simply jog. According to B and H Sports, a swimsuit costs, depending on gender and brand, from $20 to $35. An average tennis racket costs approximately $75 to $100. Or, for about $50, students can purchase a good pair of running shoes. Swimming pools and tennis courts abound, and running does not require any specific facility. Most of these sports, in addition to being physically and mentally beneficial, provide recreation during the summer months.

Team sports

Three common sports involving teams that don't necessarily have to be organized are baseball or softball, football, and soccer. Creek students said they play these sports in the summer generally for recreation, using available backyards or parks for playing. The accessories aren't expensive. According to B and H Sports, a soccer ball or football costs $30, and a baseball or softball costs six dollars. A bat costs close to $30. Students said that one advantage to these team sports is that most people already understand the rules and objectives of these games.

Volleyball

A team sport that is popular along California beaches, volleyball, rated sixth in the poll. Volleyball equipment consists of a net and poles, which cost close to $50, and a ball for approximately $30. The game is easy to set up in a park or backyard, making it useful in many different environments. Also, volleyball's rules are simple, and it is easy to play. Students interviewed felt that volleyball is enjoyable, though it is a fairly common team sport, because it is a deviation from more popular field sports and most people can play it without worrying about their ability.

Photo courtesy of Yearbook

Poll results

When asked to list 12 sports in order of favorite to least favorite, Creek students said:

1. Swimming
2. Tennis
3. Bicycling
4. Running
5. Baseball/Softball
6. Volleyball
7. Water Skiing
8. Frisbee
9. Soccer
10. Golf
11. Football
12. Sailing

Boating

For many Cherry Creek Reservoir is a convenient place to go boating during the summer. Average costs for marine equipment run high, but to get into the reservoir costs only two dollars. Rocky Mountain Marina quoted prices for sailboats which range from $300 to $30,000. For an average Sunfish sailboat, the cost is $1,800. A catamaran, a more expensive and perhaps more challenging sail boat, runs an average of $5,000. For those who can't afford to buy a boat but would like to give sailing a try, renting a boat at the reservoir is a cheaper alternative.

Water skiing

To go water skiing, students who can't afford the price of a boat and skis will have to go along with a friend because there's nowhere in Colorado to rent motor boats. At Kenney's Marine, the cost of a motor boat runs anywhere from $13,000 to $16,000, excluding gas and safety features. Life preservers at $40 each are a requirement for every person skiing or swimming at the reservoir. Water skiing is expensive, but a group of eight can share a boat and one pair of skis to help bring the price down. Creek students placed water skiing as their seventh choice for favorite summertime sports.

Photo courtesy of *Sports Illustrated*

—*The Union St. Journal,* Cherry Creek High School, Englewood, Colorado

—*Black and White,*
Walt Whitman High School, Bethesda, Maryland

Girls playoff-bound with 6-2 AA record

by George Bennett

By virtue of a 6-2 AA league record and a 14-5 overall mark, the girls' basketball team enters the first round of the state playoffs Monday against an undetermined opponent under the dome.

The regular season ends at 5 p.m. today when the Vikes host Damascus.

Maryland's playoff system consists of five rounds. While the final two rounds will be played at Catonsville, home-court advantage is a factor in the first three regional rounds. Whitman will enjoy the familiar confines of the dome for the first round only, unless county rival Blair and Eleanor Roosevelt High in Prince George's county are upset before the third round.

Co-captain Donna Kay feels playing on home court can be a tremendous advantage for the Vikings. "If a lot of fans show up, like that crowd when we played at Blair (about 700), it will be a big help." She also feels the girls will need teamwork and balanced scoring to be successful.

Co-captain Stephanie Hardman agrees and adds, "It's more important now than ever for Donna and I to provide leadership in the playoffs. Leadership has been a problem for us at times during the season, but when we have it and everyone gets along, we play well."

Both captains believe their team performs best when running set plays off a patterned offense and think the team must adhere to this game plan in the playoffs.

Sports

C-1 **Black & White** Friday, February 27, 1981

On Tuesday, the Vikings notched their sixth league win and earned half of the county AA title with a 54-48 decision over visiting Peary. The girls got the balanced scoring they needed as Hardman, Kay, and Missy Palman finished with 15, 14, and 13 points, respectively.

After Hardman scored 8 of the Vikings first 11 points, Sam Arnelle gave Whitman a 13-5 edge when she grabbed an offensive rebound and banked in a shot just before the end of the first quarter. The Vikes coasted from there, allowing the Huskies within four points only twice.

The Vikings lost an important AA game last Thursday at Blair, 58-53. The defeat was an especially bitter one because the Vikings had led by as much as 17 points.

Whitman never trailed until Blair's Wendy Jackson gave her team a 48-46 lead on a three-point play three and one half minutes into the fourth quarter. Jackson's basket and free throw capped a methodical blazer comeback that began after Sara Southard made a similar three-point play for Whitman in the second quarter. Southard's layup and foul shot had given the Vikes a comfortable 27-10 advantage with five minutes left in the half.

But Blair reduced the margin to 11 by intermission, then outscored their visitors 17-8 in the third quarter, to trail 42-40 when the final period began.

In the fourth quarter, the Vikes promptly scored four points to lead 46-40. But Blair answered with eight of their own to take the lead, 48-46, with 4:27 left on the clock. Though their lead had evaporated, the Vikes seemed unshaken. Southard tied the game at 48 with a banker high off the glass. Blair's Jackson followed with another basket, but Kay came back with a driving layup, and the score was 50-50 with 3:10 remaining.

Then the Vikings fell apart, and Blair laid claim to its half of the AA title.

photo by Ed Dixon

CHAIRMAN OF THE BOARDS . . . Sophomore Kathy Evans arcs a shot over a Blair opponent after grabbing an offensive rebound in Whitman's 58-53 loss to the Blazers. Evans and the Vikes enter the state playoffs next week.

Girls' b-ball slate

Whitman		Opponent
31	Gaithersburg	43
53	Walter Johnson	40
58	Magruder	40
44	Kennedy	27
52	Wootton	48
44	B-CC	43
61	Churchill	59
48	Blair	39
50	Springbrook	46
43	Wheaton	48
62	Seneca Valley	47
53	Einstein	52
39	Peary	38
55	Northwood	28
48	Springbrook	55
54	Churchill	42
51	Richard Montgomery	53
53	Blair	58
54	Peary	48
Feb. 27	Damascus	home

Swimmers capture division crown

by Eric Whisenhunt

With 49 members of the team's roster eligible to participate, the swim team should be a strong contender as it vies tonight and tomorrow in the Metro meet, featuring entrants from the 40 best teams in the Washington area.

Competing for the Vikes will be swimmers who registered a qualifying time in at least one regular season meet and divers who are able to perform the 11 prescribed dives.

Scheduled for 8 p.m. tonight at the Gaithersburg Aquatic Center is boys' diving. Although girls' diving was held last night, the results of this event were too late for BLACK & WHITE deadline. Trials for the other nine events are slated for 8 a.m. tomorrow at the George Washington University Smith Center, with the top eight finishers in each event advancing to the finals at 7 p.m.

According to Coach Dave Greene, "The girls' team has a good chance of finishing in third place, and the boys have the ability to rank among the top five. The rule change allowing the top eight finishers to advance to the finals instead of only the top six should work in our favor."

The girls' team proved its capabilities as it won the divisional meet last Saturday, thus capturing the Western Division Championship. Upsetting both Churchill and Wootton, Whitman is the first team to keep the title from falling into the grasp of one of these two powerhouse adversaries. Though the boys' team was unable to overcome Churchill and Wootton, the squad still rendered a respectable performance, placing third.

Taking only one first place, the girls' team accumulated points by collecting a host of seconds and thirds. The single victory was contributed by Lezlie Kesterman who won the one meter diving competition. Co-captain Amy Dilweg finished second in the 50 and 100-meter freestyle, as did Jackie Barth in the 100-meter backstroke, Anne Whitney in the 100-meter butterfly, and the 400-meter freestyle relay team.

Thirds were taken by Debbie Falb in the 200 and 500-meter freestyle, Barth in the 200-meter individual medley, and the 200-meter medley relay team. In addition, co-captain Beth Gilfrich finished fourth in the 100-meter breaststroke.

Leading the boys' squad was Ben Dubin who finished second in the 50-meter freestyle and fourth in the 100-meter freestyle. The third place 200-meter relay team and the fourth place 400-meter relay team also scored vital points for the team.

"I couldn't have asked the teams to swim better," said Greene.

photo by Stephanie Chaufornier

OUT IN FRONT . . . Sophomore Ralph Miller heads for first place in the butterfly during a swim meet at the Rockville campus of Montgomery College, Feb. 14. By season's end, Miller and the boy's team had finished third in the county's west division while their female counterparts captured first place. The swimmers will enter the Metros tomorrow.

Students lack spirit

First in football, second in soccer, and last in school spirit. School spirit, or lack thereof, is embarrassing to me both as a student and a member of the varsity basketball team.

Excluding the cheerleaders, parents, and junior varsity basketball team members, less than 25 Whitmanites made guest appearances at the Feb. 17 game.

In basketball, the crowd is what is known as the sixth man. Al McGuire, a former college basketball coach turned expert television analyst, claims the home team is considered at least a five point favorite (depending on the caliber of the team) before the game even begins due to this alleged "sixth man."

One of the things that makes basketball exciting is fan involvement. Even if they are not actually down on the court filling the hoops with points, they can play an important role in the outcome of the game. If that all important, intangible momentum is shifting away from the home team, the fans can give its team a boost through rhythmic clapping or vocal support.

Sports Clipboard

by Howard Derkay

Speaking from experience, if you are losing to a home team whose fans have created utter bedlam, the chances of winning range from slim to none. The atmosphere is so deafening that players can't hear their coach trying to give instructions, or teammates shouting out plays.

Any athlete will tell you that the thrill of playing in front of peers in a rocking, packed house generates enough adrenalin to last for weeks.

Just recently, a milestone was set in a game between Rockville and Seneca Valley at Seneca Valley. So many fans showed up that the Seneca Valley officials set up a closed circuit viewing of the game in the adjoining girls gym.

You'll never see that happen at Whitman. How can the people at this school expect a successful basketball program if more people from the visiting school attend the game then from the home team? From the bench or from the stands, it's embarrassing to hear more enthusiasm for every visiting squad basket, than for a Viking bucket.

Of course, if the basketball team had a winning record, that might bring some fans out, but I'm beginning to doubt it.

These pages illustrate the variety of coverage possible on the sports page. Major sports, less publicized sports, and noncompetitive recreational activities should all be given due coverage.

Activity 4: Planning Sports Coverage

Plan the copy you would include on the sports page of the next issue of your school newspaper. Determine what games and events, past and future, will be covered in that particular issue. Also determine what other sports subjects should be covered. Indicate the types of stories that will be used for the various subjects. Suggest the photographs that might be included. Finally, taking into consideration how much space is available for sports coverage, indicate the approximate length each story should be.

Summary

This chapter begins by discussing four basic kinds of sports reports—advance stories, follow-up stories, summary stories, and stories in which advance, follow-up, and summary stories are combined. It then explains how variety may be added to sports coverage by publishing other types of articles, such as feature stories and interpretive, in-depth reports. Next, three special considerations in sports coverage are presented. Finally, the planning of a sports page is discussed.

COVERING SPORTS EVENTS. In school papers, the advance story, which covers upcoming events, is one of the most important forms for sports reporting. Imaginative writing, solid factual information, and an emphasis on conflict are three of the key elements in a successful advance story. Follow-up stories on past events should be eyewitness accounts emphasizing why and how a contest turned out as it did. The writer of such a story should take advantage of the opportunity of interviewing players and coaches and of working without immediate deadline pressure to produce a reflective, concise account. Summary stories can be used to review a team's entire season, the major events in a sport, the results of intramural competition, or the activities in less well known athletic endeavors. Summary stories should normally concentrate on highlights and outstanding moments. Since the space allotted to sports coverage is frequently limited, advance, follow-up, and summary stories may be combined to provide a total picture of a sport.

ADDING VARIETY TO SPORTS COVERAGE. Many athletic and recreational activities besides major-team contests deserve coverage on a sports page. These activities can often be treated in an appealing way in a feature story, an interpretive, in-depth report, a column, or a commentary. The use of such articles also adds variety to sports coverage. Feature stories on noncompetitive sports or on the individuals who engage in them can contrast nicely with reports on major sports. Feature stories can also be used to spotlight star athletes, outstanding coaches, and alumni doing well in college or professional sports. Interpretive, in-depth stories can probe more deeply into subjects treated in brief, fact-based reports. They are also useful for the deeper issues involved in sports. Sports columns can offer sidelights on matters that do not require full-story coverage or opinions and evaluations on a single subject. Commentaries are similar to columns, except that they are not restricted to the same format issue after issue. For both forms, the subject should merit analysis and interpretation, the views put forth should be grounded in fact, and the writing should be thoughtful and stylistically distinguished.

WRITING A SPORTS STORY. Sportswriters should avoid jargon and clichés when trying to achieve a lively style. They should also follow the conventions of sportswriting, such as those that apply to the forms of address and the forms of presenting statistical material. Finally, they should interpret the facts only if they are qualified.

PLANNING AN INTERESTING SPORTS PAGE. A sports page should be planned with a view to the wide variety of athletic and recreational interests that students have. Hence, subjects other than major-team sports should be covered, and different kinds of coverage should be employed.

Vocabulary

jargon
cliché
box score

Review Questions

1. Explain the difference between an advance, a follow-up, and a summary story.

2. What is the special value of a combination advance–follow-up–summary story?

3. How may each of the following add variety to a sports page: a feature story, an interpretive, in-depth report, a column, and a commentary?

4. What special considerations in sports coverage should sportswriters keep in mind?

5. What concerns should govern the planning of a sports page?

Discussion Questions

1. If you were preparing to cover football in an issue to be published midseason—several games played, several yet to be played—what arrangement of advance, follow-up, and summary stories would you use to make your coverage as interesting and informative as possible?

2. What sports subjects does your school offer that would be especially suitable for feature stories? For interpretive, in-depth reports? For columns? For commentaries?

3. Many sportswriters feel that because they are writing for a special audience they may over-

look some of the accepted rules of newswriting. To what extent do you agree or disagree? Why?

4. In many school papers, there is simply not enough space to cover all the different sports a staff might wish to present. How should deci-

sions be made about which sports to include in which issues?

5. In view of what you learned in this chapter, how might the sports page of your school paper be improved?

Competing with the Pros

Attend in person or watch on television an athletic event that will almost certainly be reported on in a daily newspaper in your area. Write a sports story on the event such as might appear in the daily paper. Then, after the report by the professional sportswriter appears, evaluate your article against it. Write up your evaluation in a brief report.

Producing
and Financing
a School Newspaper

15

COPYREADING

When you have completed this chapter you should be able to

Appreciate the importance of copyreading.

Understand what is necessary for good copyreading.

Copyread systematically.

Carry out the final tasks of editing newspaper copy.

In the final hour before the news deadline, the staff room is alive with activity. Typewriters clack steadily. The usual loud conversations are muffled as reporters work urgently to meet the deadline.

Suddenly, from the copy desk, comes a low, anguished moan. The typewriters stop. Everyone looks up. Sally, the copyreader, is staring sadly at a typewritten sheet.

Curious, you look over her shoulder. The neatly typed story, identified with the name of a cub reporter, reads in the following manner.

```
     Most people think that agriculture and travel don't

go together.  Farmers stay put for years at a time.  How-

ever, there is more to Agriculture than farming.  Millions

of jobs are open for Agricultural College graduates, who

don't intend to become farmers.

     Take a look at some of these headlines from various

papers, you can see how some Americans have enjoyed travel

and adventure and have helped make a better world, they

prepared themselves by majoring in Agriculture in agriculture.

AGGIE GRADUATE DISCOVERS ETHIOPIAN TOWN VERY MUCH

LIKE OURS

     POULTRY EXPERT RETURNS FROM THAILAND POST

     WEED MAN GOES TO LIBERIA

     ENTOMOLOGIST ON LEAVE FROM CENTRAL AMERICA, WHERE SHE

HELPED QUELL LOCUST PLAGUE

     FOOD SPECIALIST AIDS BIBLE LAND

     EXTENSION WORKER HELPS AFRICAN VILLAGERS

     You can prepare for a job like one of these two.  Enroll

in Agriculture at State College.  For more details, right

to the dean at state college today.
```

The story has some news value, you decide. Vocational information adds to the variety of a school newspaper. Changes, however, are obviously needed if this item is to appear in print.

Who is responsible for improving a news story? To begin with, reporters **copyread** their own stories, for they are expected to submit **copy** in correct form. Copy without errors is called **clean copy.** Any successful reporter's copy is always reasonably clean; it requires few changes. But not all reporters have the same experience, information, or skill. Therefore, a newspaper must have a specialist to see that written material is accurate and clear. On a small newspaper, this work may be done by the editor. For most newspapers, however, there are **copyreaders** whose only job is to correct and improve copy. When there are several copyreaders, a **copy editor** may supervise their work.

Improving Newspaper Quality Through Copyreading

The purposes of copyreading are many. Perhaps the most important of these is to ensure truth. Accuracy, while not easy to attain in the rush of newspaper deadlines, is a major objective of every newspaper. A second purpose of copyreading is to present news in a direct and readable style. This includes improving the lead and the organization of the story. A third is to condense lengthy stories to a size that matches their actual news value. A fourth is to remove any elements of bad taste, to avoid libel, and to eliminate editorializing. A fifth is to check for proper grammar and general clarity. And a sixth is to see that copy conforms to the newspaper's writing style.

The copyreader may also write headlines and mark **typographical specifications**—giving details about the size and style of type. On some papers, however, these tasks are done by other editors. A typical procedure on school newspapers is for **page editors** to do this work. As they review each story for their assigned pages, the page editors evaluate its importance and then determine its placement on the page and the style of headline it should carry.

Activity 1: Analyzing Copyreading Goals

Reread the story on page 307 while considering the six purposes of copyreading listed in this section. Taking one purpose at a time, list improvements you think a copyreader could make in the story. For example, do you find evidence of lack of truth or accuracy in the story? List and comment on any errors you find. After you have considered the story in relation to the first purpose, go on to the second—presenting news in a direct and readable style—and so on. Do *not* correct the errors. Just list and comment on them.

Looking at the Copyreader's Work

When a story leaves the copyreader's desk, commonly known as the **copy desk,** it is in final form for publication, and no further corrections should be necessary. Various editors may make other alterations, but responsibility for thorough checking of content, grammar, style, and other such matters is the copyreader's, not the editor's.

A good copyreader is more than a mechanical checker of words and sentences. To do the job adequately, a copyreader must know a good deal. For example, each copyreader must know the names of people around school and their positions—teachers, administrators, clerical workers, student leaders, and so on—in order to make sure that names are properly spelled and titles are correctly used. The copyreader must have general knowledge of school organizations, policies, programs, and history. Many times a reporter's innocent factual error is caught and corrected by an alert copyreader who remembers how the matter was handled the previous year.

In addition, a copyreader must have a sound knowledge of the English language. Improper spelling, sentence structure, punctuation, capitaliza-

The copyreader for a school newspaper must have a sure command of English and the ability to spot and correct errors in writing, as well as knowledge of the school and its people.

—Photo by Mimi Forsyth from Monkmeyer

tion, and other common writing errors that hide or distort the reporter's meaning must be corrected.

Tools of the copyreader include a supply of soft black pencils (blue pencils may be preferable on handwritten copy), scissors, paste, transparent tape, a good recent dictionary, a thesaurus or dictionary of synonyms, and a handbook on grammar and usage. A copyreader should also have a copy of the newspaper's style sheet, an up-to-date directory of students and teachers, and a local telephone directory. A copyreader is expected to make changes directly on the submitted copy. This is why reporters double-space or triple-space typed copy (or write handwritten copy on every other line) and leave extra room at the top of each page.

A universal system of editing by way of **copyreaders' marks** has been developed. They save hours of rewriting or retyping. When properly used, these marks are clear to editors, typists, and printers. Reporters should also learn the marks to save time when making their own corrections of their work. Copyreaders use the marks so that **typesetters** will understand exactly what they are expected to do.

Notice how copyreaders' marks from the chart on page 313 have been used in the following example to correct mistakes without rewriting.

```
|The (7th) period ⌐ournalism ⌐lass t⌐ok a field trip
to our local newspaper , the richmond independent (Nov.)
(fifth) to learnⱷ more about the pro⌐ess of print‿ing a
news⌐paper.
```

Most daily newspapers, as well as some school papers, are now equipped with **video display terminals (VDTs).** With these computer-assisted machines, reporters' stories appear on a video screen as they are typed. The reporter, copyreader, or editor may correct the copy or even move sentences and paragraphs around by using the terminal's typewriter-style keyboard. Copy may be transferred electronically from the reporter to the copy desk, stored in the computer's memory, or set into type for printing. While this system changes the mechanics of copyreading, it does not affect its purposes and importance or lessen the need for competence in the copyreader.

Activity 2:   Developing Copyreading Skills

1. Write out the sentences and phrases in the right-hand column exactly as they appear. Then, carry out the directions in the left-hand column, using proper copyreaders' marks.

   a. Start all words except the name with lower-case letters.   Mr. David Pierce is Chairman of the Board of Directors and Vice-President of the Company.

b. Use capital letters for all names.

mr. and mrs. john dearborn built the house, but paul harris lives in it now.

c. Correct misspelled words by inserting necessary letters.

The committee is planing an excellnt menu.

d. Insert *High* before *School.*

Central School

e. Correct misspelled words by deleting letters and connecting when necessary.

School annuales are beeing soled.

f. Change to read *Central High School.*

Central Junior High School

g. Transpose letters to spell words correctly.

Libarry books must be retruned.

h. Transpose words into proper order.

She has been a member four for years.

i. Write out the figures and the abbreviations.

3 boys and 4 girls arrived from L.A., Calif.

j. Use figures.

Betty is seventeen years old and five feet tall.

k. Remove and add spaces.

In the sum mer youcan always find her in the swim mingpool.

l. Add commas and a period.

You may take typing shorthand accounting and bookkeeping

m. Mark the names for boldface type.

Seen at the party were Mary Ann Clark and Rod Herbert.

n. Indicate that the subhead is to be centered in the column.

Honor Roll

2. Prepare a 50-item "copyreader's test" for your school newspaper, together with the correct answers. Include in your test errors involving the following:

a. The spelling of the names of administrators and teachers (including "Miss," "Mrs.," "Ms.," "Mr.," or "Dr.," and all first names)

b. The spelling of the names of student-body leaders, class officers, and heads of important student organizations

c. The exact titles of positions held by administrators and student leaders

d. Facts about your school (for example, the enrollment in each grade and the names of athletic leagues, debating conferences, musical organizations, clubs, academic departments, courses, and so on)

e. Your newspaper's rules of style

3. Test your knowledge by taking the test prepared by another member of the class. When you have completed it, find out how well you did. In which areas do you need to learn more about your school?

4. Copy the first story on page 312 exactly as it appears. Then, using the final story on the right as a guide, correct all errors in the first story, inserting the proper copyreaders' marks.

Thespians to perform 'The Crucible'	***Thespians to perform 'The Crucible'***
"The Crucible," a Drama by Arthur Miller has been chosen by Thespian troup 246 for it's annual production. the single perfromance is to be on Thursday Night, Dec. 12. The 9-character cast will start rehersals the 4th of November.	"The Crucible," a drama by Arthur Miller, has been chosen by Thespian Troupe 264 for its annual production. The single performance is to be Thursday night, December 12. The nine-character cast will start rehearsals November 4.
The Troup presents acycel of 4 different type of plays over a 4-year period, this enables all student to see a variety of productions during there high school years. According to Mr. Mary Jones, Sponser.	The troupe presents a cycle of four different types of plays over a four-year period. This enables all students to see a variety of productions during their high school years, according to Mrs. Mary Jones, sponsor.

Copyreading a Story

The copyreader has much to keep in mind when reading a story. Copyreading, therefore, is more effective if problems are considered one at a time. Only an experienced copyreader can recognize and deal with every type of mistake in a single reading of the story.

When you copyread, you should thus go over the story several times, looking for a different type of error each time. The following six steps can help.

Be Certain That Every Statement Is Accurate

Factual accuracy holds top priority on every copy desk. The copyreader's first step is to be certain that every statement is accurate. Copyreaders who take pride in their work do not release copy until they are satisfied that every statement in it is correct and accurate. Specific points include correct names and titles; accurate figures, amounts, and dates; and consistency between the facts and details given in one part of the story and those given elsewhere in the story or in previously published stories.

Make Sure the Story Is Well Organized

As you start the second step, read the story quickly to see what it is about. Is its main idea presented in the lead? Is the key thought emphasized so that it stands out clearly? Do the first two or three words of the lead say something vital and important? Are the remaining paragraphs in

COPYREADERS' MARKS

L or ¶	Paragraph
no ¶	No paragraph
Write, check hedlines	Insert letter or word
Ⓘa. ③	Spell out
⬭Iowa	Abbreviate
⬭twelve	Change to figure
worke	Take out letter
worke ing	Take out letter and join separated elements
write a ~~good~~ story	Take out word and join separated elements
be nzine	Close up space
stet	Leave as originally written
in the building. Twelve students	Set in one unbroken line or join separated material
go home	Insert space
John Johnson, director	Transpose elements
wroking	Transpose letters
Des moines	Change to capital letter
John Johnson, Director	Change to lower-case letter
Folo copy	Set copy as it is written
⏋ ⌈	Indent both sides of text; center material in column
⊗ or ⊙	Emphasizes period so that printer won't overlook it
in the house	Set boldface
college	Set italics
Des Moines	Set in small capital letters
(more)	Copy continued on next page
−30− or #	End of story

If you cannot find a mark that fits your need, use any simple mark that you feel sure will tell the printer what you want done.

inverted-pyramid order or in some other appropriate order? Make sure the story is well organized.

If the story fails to meet these tests, start rebuilding it. When the complete plan of organization is poor, you may have to rewrite the story or, if time permits, return it to the reporter for rewriting. If the problem is one of paragraph arrangement, use scissors and paste or transparent tape to place the parts of the story in an acceptable sequence. Frequently, writing a new lead in the space above the first paragraph can salvage the remaining paragraphs.

More often, the story will be weak but will not require such drastic measures. The lead may not include enough necessary facts, or it may be flat and uninteresting. Add to it, improve its structure and meaning, and make minor changes throughout the story.

Notice how a copyreader improved the following lead by rearranging material:

> [Ability to speak easily is of tremendous importance in today's business world, according to ⌐
> Dr. Cornelius Q. Gabworthy, professor of speech at the
> *who addressed the drama classes last Wednesday*⊙⌐
> state university, ∧~~gave an interesting and informative talk~~
> ~~to the drama classes last Wednesday.~~
> ⌐Dr. Gabworthy said that more emphasis should be placed
> on oral practice in high schools. ~~He feels that the ability~~
> ~~to speak easily is of tremendous importance in today's~~
> ~~business world.~~

Activity 3:   Reorganizing a Story

Copy the following story. Then, using copyreaders' marks, improve the lead and rearrange the facts according to their news value.

> This year our students will again take part in a conservation project. Our freshmen will plant approximately 1,000 trees in Prospect State Forest May 10. Our freshmen have been doing this for eight years.
>
> Highlights of past years have included talks by forest rangers and races between competing schools.
>
> Participating students have been chosen from all six of the freshmen science classes, with choices based on academic achievement.
>
> Students will plant trees in the morning and then have a tour of the area in the afternoon, according to Miss Robin Garrity, science instructor, who will lead the group.

Boil It Down

Most beginning reporters, as well as some experienced ones who should know better, are wordy. They use too many words to state simple ideas. They repeat the same thought over and over. They include details that have no news value. In effect, they are not applying their knowledge of news English, as described in Chapter 8. The third step, then, in copyreading is to "boil it down"—prune away unimportant details and surplus words, making the facts stand out clearly enough that readers cannot fail to grasp them.

An efficient copyreader may improve the average school news story by eliminating up to one third or even one half of its words. The process often begins when a story is reorganized. In the example on page 314, the copyreader shortened a 53-word lead to 46 words merely by rearranging it. In boiling down copy, watch for unnecessary prepositional phrases, strings of adjectives or adverbs, and long, complicated sentences. Eliminate details that add little or nothing to the main ideas.

Activity 4: Condensing a Story

Make an initial copy of the following story, leaving out enough words to reduce its length by about one third. Then, using copyreaders' marks, make any further changes necessary.

A pantomime quiz entertained the members at the first meeting of the Wranglers last Monday, September 16. The group met in the Greeley Room at 3:30. President Sarah Cross welcomed everyone present and expressed her happiness at seeing new and old faces alike. She then introduced the other officers who in turn briefly explained what their duties were. The other officers are Betty Taylor, vice-president; Beverly Simmons, secretary; Don Stanberry, treasurer; and Phil Chapman, point recorder.

Mr. Carl Coleman, the Wranglers' new sponsor, was then introduced by Sarah Cross. Mr. Coleman said that he would sincerely help in every way that he could with the Wranglers and encouraged all the students to take an active part in the year's program,

The business portion of the meeting complete, the group then turned to the pantomime quiz. Betty Taylor and Mildred Reynolds, juniors at Central High, presented a pantomime of their experiences in Denver this summer. These girls were selected to attend the High School Institute at Denver University for five weeks.

Jim Holman played master of ceremony in good Central High fashion. Panel members, who were selected from the audience at random, made up the two four-member teams. Captains were Larry Engleman and Lucy Randall. After much hilarity, the quiz came to an end, and it was announced that Larry's team had won by three seconds. All contestants will receive points for participating.

Eliminate Statements That Are Unsuitable or in Poor Taste

Copyreaders are guardians of their newspaper's reputation for objective and fair reporting. It is their job to examine a story carefully for opinions presented without proper authority, for distortion or omission of facts, or for other statements that might not be suitable for publication. The fourth step in copyreading, then, is to eliminate statements that are unsuitable or in poor taste.

First, eliminate any editorializing. If an opinion is not properly attributed, it should not be published. Second, watch for any obscene or vulgar statements, as well as for material that might incite readers to disrupt the school or to commit criminal acts. Such statements are often legally questionable in school newspapers, and certainly they are unsuitable for publication. Next, look out for libel and invasions of privacy.

You should also examine the copy, particularly statements of opinion, for poor taste. Understanding your newspaper's editorial policy will help you recognize undesirable material. For example, the public expects a school newspaper to support education. An article making the point that going to school is a waste of time (even though some students might really feel this way) is probably improper for your newspaper's pages—except, perhaps, among the letters to the editor.

In case of doubt, especially about questionable taste, vulgarity, obscenity, or suspected libelous material, talk with your editor or faculty adviser.

Activity 5:   Making Certain That a Story Is Fit to Print

Copy the following story. Then, using copyreaders' marks, eliminate editorializing, vulgar or libelous statements, items in poor taste, and other unsuitable material.

Pep Club and K Club have set aside their disputes and have joined forces to sponsor the basketball Homecoming on Friday, March 2. Students are wondering how long the truce will last.

The festivities will begin with a pep assembly on Friday, after school. Cheerleader Rita Talbot will be mistress of ceremonies, and the band will toot a few sour notes in its usual fine rhythm.

Friday evening at the game between Central and South, the king and queen will be presented to the audience. During half time, there will be some very special entertainment conducted by Bob Collins and Greg Murray. But, until half time, this entertainment is top secret!

The Central-South game should prove to be an exciting battle, for both teams are evenly matched. High scorer of the evening is expected to be South's "Brick" Bradford, if he can keep his temper and avoid being put out of the game for fighting.

Homecoming will conclude with an informal dance in the cafeteria following the game. Roy Early's group is scheduled to provide musical moods for the dimly lit dance floor.

Make Sure the Meaning Is Clear

The fifth step is to make sure the meaning is clear. Newspaper copy should always be checked carefully to ensure clear, forceful, correct English. Grammatical rules are designed to help convey specific ideas in such a way that readers will grasp them clearly and easily. They may be thought of as "traffic rules" that both writer and reader understand in the same way.

The most common errors to watch out for are listed in the following paragraphs.

ERRORS IN SENTENCE STRUCTURE. A basic principle in English is that each sentence should convey one complete thought. Incomplete sentences and run-on sentences make it difficult for a reader to identify the main idea. Notice what happens when a sentence is not complete.

INCORRECT: Jean Erwin, who has been chosen head majorette for next year, and who is now one of three assistants.

IMPROVED: Jean Erwin has been chosen head majorette for next year. She is now one of three assistants.

Because clarity in writing is essential, the copyreader may in some ways be thought of as the guardian of a newspaper's reputation with its readers. Ideally, no sentence should need rereading because the sense is unclear.

POOR REFERENCE BETWEEN PRONOUN AND ANTECEDENT. Poor writing is often marked by the use of pronouns whose antecedents are not clearly indicated. A pronoun may be so far away from its antecedent that the reference is not clear. In other cases, a pronoun may not agree with its antecedent in number or gender. Or, as in the following example, a pronoun may be missing its true antecedent entirely.

INCORRECT: Only 200 copies of the yearbook have been sold. They are working hard to sell more copies before the deadline.

IMPROVED: Only 200 copies of the yearbook have been sold. Staff members are working hard to sell more copies before the deadline.

LACK OF AGREEMENT BETWEEN SUBJECT AND VERB. This can be somewhat troublesome because there are many cases in which a writer is tempted to use a singular subject with a plural verb and vice versa. For example, when a subject is followed by modifiers, the verb must still agree with the basic noun subject, no matter how many modifiers there are.

INCORRECT: The skill of the cheerleaders were displayed at the final game.

IMPROVED: The skill of the cheerleaders was displayed at the final game.

A similar problem occurs when a verb is followed by a predicate noun that differs in number from the subject. Again, the verb must agree with the subject.

INCORRECT: The major problem in arranging debates are overcrowded schedules.

IMPROVED: The major problem in arranging debates is overcrowded schedules.

Compound subjects may also present problems. Subjects joined by *and* require plural verbs. Those joined by *or* or *nor* usually take singular verbs.

INCORRECT: The problem and its solution was discussed in class today.

IMPROVED: The problem and its solution were discussed in class today.

INCORRECT: Neither Jim nor Ed have a chance to be elected class president.

IMPROVED: Neither Jim nor Ed has a chance to be elected class president.

Mixed compounds occur when the parts of a compound subject do not have the same number—when one part is singular and the other plural. Mixed compounds joined by *and* are automatically followed by a plural verb. But mixed compounds joined by *or* or *nor* present problems. In this event, when one part of a compound subject is singular and the other is plural, the number of the verb is determined by the noun nearer the verb.

CORRECT: Neither the teacher nor her students were aware of the noise in the hall.

When the nearer noun is plural, the plural verb seems natural. However, when the nearer noun is singular, the sentence is often awkward.

AWKWARD: Neither the staff members nor the adviser was in favor of running the ad.

While this is "correct," the sentence does not sound logical. Thus it is best to avoid such compounds, even if it means reworking the idea completely, as in the following sentence.

IMPROVED: The staff members were opposed to running the ad, and so was the adviser.

Collective nouns refer to groups of people, animals, or things and are dealt with according to meaning. If the noun refers to the group acting as a unit, a singular verb is used. If, however, the members of the group are acting individually, a plural verb is required. Both of the following sentences are correct.

AS A UNIT: The student council has prepared a schedule of its events for the year.

INDIVIDUALLY: The student council have been arguing among themselves over the proposed schedule of events for the year.

Collective nouns include such words as *average, class, group, committee, public, crowd,* and many others.

You should also note that the expression *the number* is singular, while *a number* is plural.

SINGULAR: The number of students involved in school clubs is very large.

PLURAL: A number of students are involved in school clubs.

Another problem is caused by words that are plural in form but singular in meaning. In most cases, these words take singular verbs. This group includes names of academic subjects, such as *civics, physics, linguistics,* and *mathematics;* areas of public activity, such as *politics* and *aeronautics;* and common diseases, such as *measles, mumps,* and *rickets.* Also included are terms for weights, amounts, distances, and periods of time, such as *grams, dollars, miles,* and *weeks,* and titles containing plurals, such as the title *Twice-Told Tales.*

INCORRECT: Acrobatics require skill and agility.
IMPROVED: Acrobatics requires skill and agility.

INCORRECT: Politics are of great interest to him.
IMPROVED: Politics is of great interest to him.

INCORRECT: Ten miles were too far to walk for help.
IMPROVED: Ten miles was too far to walk for help.

INCORRECT: *Tales of the South Pacific* were converted into a successful musical and motion picture.

IMPROVED: *Tales of the South Pacific* was converted into a successful
musical and motion picture.

On the other hand, when referring to groups of people, writers often
use words that are singular in form but plural in meaning. Words in this
group, which includes *any, every, anyone, everyone, anybody,* and *everybody,*
require singular verbs.

INCORRECT: Everybody who want to go to college must get a good
score on the Scholastic Aptitude Test.

IMPROVED: Everybody who wants to go to college must get a good
score on the Scholastic Aptitude Test.

Other words and expressions that imply more than one person but require singular verbs are *each, many a, either, kind, sort, part, type,* and *series.*

INCORRECT: Many a school newspaper reporter have gone on to success in publishing.

IMPROVED: Many a school newspaper reporter has gone on to success in publishing.

MISPLACED OR DANGLING PARTICIPLES. School newspaper reporters
often begin sentences with participles because these are active and lively
verb forms. But a participle is like an adjective: It must modify a noun.
That noun is the subject of the sentence. When the noun that the participle
should modify is missing or in the wrong place, the meaning of the sentence
becomes obscure.

INCORRECT: Electing new class officers, the school year has started.

IMPROVED: Electing new class officers, students have started the
school year.

LACK OF PARALLELISM. Whenever a series of parallel ideas is presented, they should be expressed in the same grammatical form. This is
called parallel structure. Failure to maintain parallelism results in a difficult and confusing sentence.

INCORRECT: John has had experience as a member of the band, in
orchestral work, plays the saxophone well, and his desire is to be a member of a symphony orchestra.

IMPROVED: John has had experience as a member of the band, is familiar with orchestral work, plays the saxophone well,
and wants to be a member of a symphony orchestra.

AWKWARD STATEMENTS. Finally, copyreaders must watch for statements that are unclear because they are too long, include too many dependent clauses, or for some reason just don't make sense. You should not release any story that is not completely clear and readable. Unless you, the
copyreader, grasp the meaning of each sentence instantly, some readers
will not understand it at all.

INCORRECT: Mr. Lawrence Hull, who is the drama teacher, has great hopes for this play because he feels it is exceptionally good, and has the opportunity to work again with many students with whom he has worked before, and several other students are helping to make the play a success.

IMPROVED: Mr. Lawrence Hull, drama teacher, has great hopes for this play because he feels it is exceptionally good. He said he was happy to have the opportunity to work again with many students who have previously participated. He added that several other students were helping to make the play a success.

Activity 6:   Improving Unclear, Incorrect Writing

Copy each of the following passages. Then use copyreaders' marks to eliminate grammatical errors and increase the clarity of the writing.

1. Running across the street, a car nearly struck the dog.

2. The change was made for three reasons: to improve scholarship, because more time was needed for study, and more students are expected to benefit from it.

3. When 11 new automobiles arrived and 10 were immediately put into use.

4. The runner approached the finish line as they roared in applause.

5. The team have completed a busy season and proved itself to be one of the strongest teams in the state.

6. Neither Ann Williams nor Polly Jackson have placed first in the district tennis tournament.

7. Placing first in a National Merit French test given here, an award was received by Sharon Bailey.

8. One of the topics concerning youth of the nation are cars versus education.

9. Three dollars were paid by each participant.

10. Each of the men arrested were charged with disorderly conduct.

Make Copy Conform to Style-Sheet Rules

The sixth step for copyreaders is to make copy conform to the rules in their newspaper's own style sheet. These are rules that have to do with correct or preferred punctuation, capitalization, spelling, and so on. Like the grammatical standards in the preceding section, these rules are intended to improve communication between reporter and reader. Paragraphs are easier to read if the same words are always capitalized, if titles are presented in the same form, and if other matters of style are handled uniformly. If your newspaper does not have its own style sheet, you may use the one in this book on pages 498–501 or refer to the *The Associated Press Stylebook* or *UPI's Newswire Stylebook*.

Activity 7: Correcting Errors in Punctuation and Spelling

1. Using your paper's own style sheet or the style sheet that is found on pages 498–501, supply all of the necessary punctuation in the following story.

Centrals band will present a concert in the boys gymnasium March 30 according to Mr. Chester Q Warner band director

Robin Shaw Michael Leach and Rayna Hammett will form a trumpet trio to play Marinuzzis Trumpet Serenade

Each section of the band will be spotlighted in Pan the Piper a legend set to music

We will also perform Clifton Williams Symphonic Suite which was awarded the Ostwald Prize for Composition not too many years ago said Mr Warner

Slippery Gentlemen will be played by a trio whose members are Kim Hamilton trombone Sharon Winter saxaphone and George Stoner trumpet

The band has presented a concert each year since 1971 For the past six years its been first in the annual contest sponsored by the Elks All bands in the area are invited to compete

Central has consistently sent the largest number of band members to the All State Band

2. The following items contain a number of words commonly misspelled by student reporters. Find the words, correct their spelling, and list them on your paper.

a. The auditoriam is large enough to acomodate an audiance of 500 students for an asembley. The rehersal took place Wednsday. Gloria will give a pantomine, the corus will sing two numbers, and John will play a coronet solor. Mr. Richard Jones, principle, will make a short speach. Captians of the atheletic teams will recieve awards for intramural sports championships.

b. Mrs. Anne Smith, counseller, will be in the libary after school to council commerical students about there programs for the comming semester. She reccomends that everyone take typeing and bookeeping and suggests biollogy as an elective.

c. "It will be alright for eligable students to take algerbra, geomitry, and chemestry in preparation for a junior collage coarse," says Mr. Dennis Green, new director of giudance. Mr. Green was formally professer of mathametics at State Univercity.

d. Senors will attend bacalauriate servises the Sunday evening before comencement. They will be lead in singing the school hymn by Mrs. Janet Van Dyke, class sponser. This is the tenth aniversary of the school's first graduation.

e. The counsil elected Martha Garvin secretery-treasurer of the new sosiety. Untill Friday she will be busy writting a report about the problem of school bus transportation.

Completing the Editing Process

After following the six outlined copyreading steps, in each case looking for a different kind of error or possible improvement, you should have a story that reads well, says what is intended, and is grammatically correct. Several final editing tasks, however, may still be needed.

The first of these is to double-check your copyreading. Use the following checklist to make sure that you have gone over the story for all the errors and flaws that a copyreader is expected to spot and correct.

✔ Checklist for Copyreading

☐ 1. Have I checked every statement for accuracy? Are all names and titles correct? Are figures, amounts, and dates accurate? Are facts and details consistent between one part of the story and another and between this story and previous ones?

☐ 2. Is the story well organized? Is the main idea in the lead? Do the first words say something vital and important? Are the paragraphs arranged in inverted-pyramid or some other suitable order?

☐ 3. Have I boiled the story down by eliminating or altering unnecessary prepositional phrases, strings of adjectives or adverbs, long and complicated sentences, useless details, and so on?

☐ 4. Have I eliminated statements that are unsuitable or in poor taste—editorializing, obscene or vulgar statements, statements inciting disruption or criminal activity, libel, or invasions of privacy?

☐ 5. Have I made sure the meaning is clear by checking over the grammar and style of the story?

☐ 6. Have I seen to it that the copy conforms to style-sheet rules for correct or preferred punctuation, capitalization, and spelling?

The second task is to make sure that the final copy is legible. If you have made only a few corrections, all you need to do is make sure that the corrections stand out clearly enough that a printer or typist can follow them easily.

If, however, you have made so many corrections that it would be difficult for anyone to follow the copy without having to pause frequently and study it, you should retype the story before it leaves the copy desk. After retyping it, copyread it again carefully to make sure you have not introduced new errors.

A third task is to mark typographical specifications. Every newspaper has one regular style of body type and one standard column width. Your printer or typist will set all copy to these specifications unless different treatment is clearly indicated.

Kinds of copy requiring special typographical specifications may include the following: subheads, captions, paragraphs or other words to be set in special type, stories to start with double-column or triple-column leads, and stories to be set in different column widths.

Every departure from the standard body type and column width on each of these pages had to be marked. Generally, it is the copyreader who is responsible for such typographical marking on a school paper.

Copyreaders should be familiar with the many special **type styles** available to them since most print shops or composing machines can provide a wide range of type. One of the most common of these is boldface type. Words to be set boldface can be indicated through underlining, generally with a wavy line. (The typewriter underline is traditionally the mark for italics. However, many typesetting machines used for newspaper work do not have italic type available, and the operators will set underlined words in boldface type instead. If you wish to use a simple underline for boldface, you should check first with your printer.)

For stories to be set in other type styles, larger or smaller type, or unusual column widths, you can write directions at the top of the page and circle them. The following directions specify a column 4 inches wide with boldface type ⅛ inch high. (There are 6 **picas** in an inch and 12 **points** in a pica. More details about these measures are given in Chapter 17.) If the directions apply only to certain paragraphs, be sure to indicate by lines or brackets just which paragraphs are intended.

Use reverse brackets, shown among the copyreaders' marks on page 313, to indicate material to be centered or set on a general indentation. When you wish copy indented, show the width of the indentation next to the bracket as in the following example:

The important thing to remember about marking typographical specifications is this: Never leave anything to chance. Mark every deviation from normal body type and normal column width.

The last editorial task of the copyreader is to headline the story. This may mean checking and revising a reporter's headline or writing a new one based on the lead of the story. The writing of headlines is discussed in the next chapter.

Activity 8: Doing the Final Editing

The following is a story printed as it might have appeared in a school newspaper. Begin by making a copy of the story as it might have looked before being printed. Then, mark the copy so that a printer would know how to achieve the typographical results shown in the finished product. Assume that all type is a standard size. Note that the wide column is 24 picas and that the narrow column is 20 picas. You can ignore the extra *vertical* space above and below the indented heads and paragraphs, since the printer would generally follow a standard spacing here.

Central adds new courses

In addition to all courses previously available to students, three new courses have been added to next year's curriculum.

German

GERMAN I WILL BE OFFERED in the language department. German I is a study of the basic language patterns and vocabulary for daily living situations. German II will be offered the following year.

Horticulture

NEW TO THE SCIENCE DEPARTMENT is horticulture. Horticulture is a noncollege preparatory class involving a study of the influence of environment on the growth of plants and some of the underlying principles of horticultural practices. Horticulture classes will have access to the greenhouse as a laboratory.

Harmony

HARMONY WILL BE OFFERED next year as a minor subject. Harmony is open to all students interested in music, elementary education, or music education. It is the study of the science of music theory.

A vocational diploma will again be available. One of the requirements of the vocational diploma is satisfactory completion of vocational home arts.

According to Miss Margaret C. Bradford, vice-principal, ''Registration is completed, and the administration is now making arrangements for teachers and equipment for next year.''

Summary

This chapter begins by discussing the several purposes of copyreading. It then looks more closely at the copyreader's work, responsibility, tools, and methods and presents a series of steps for copyreading systematically. Finally, it presents four additional tasks that copyreaders often perform.

IMPROVING NEWSPAPER QUALITY THROUGH COPYREADING. The chief purposes of copyreading are the following: to ensure truth; to present news in direct and readable style; to condense stories as necessary; to eliminate bad taste, libelous statements, and editorializing; to check for proper grammar and general clarity; and to make copy follow a paper's own style.

LOOKING AT THE COPYREADER'S WORK. The copyreader for a school paper should have a good knowledge of the people, activities, and organizations of the school. A command of English usage, the mechanics of writing (punctuation, spelling, and so on), and copyreaders' marks is also needed.

COPYREADING A STORY. Copyreading should be done according to the following six steps. First, a copyreader should make certain that every statement is accurate. Second, a copyreader should make sure the story is well organized. Third, a copyreader must condense the story as necessary.

Fourth, a copyreader should eliminate any statements that are unsuitable or in poor taste. Fifth, a copyreader should make sure the meaning is clear. Sixth, a copyreader must make copy conform to style-sheet rules.

COMPLETING THE EDITING PROCESS. Copyreaders usually have several additional tasks to carry out: to double-check their work for thoroughness; to retype the story, if necessary; to mark typographical specifications; and to make up headlines.

Vocabulary

copyread	typographical specification	video display terminal (VDT)
copy	page editor	type style
clean copy	copy desk	pica
copyreader	copyreaders' mark	point
copy editor	typesetter	

Review Questions

1. What are the main purposes of copyreading?

2. What skills and kinds of knowledge should a school newspaper copyreader have?

3. Of what value are copyreaders' marks?

4. What are the six steps of copyreading?

5. What are the final editing tasks that copyreaders often perform?

Discussion Questions

1. Could exceptional care on the part of reporters in checking over and revising their work ever remove the need for copyreaders?

2. Which of the copyreader's main duties do you consider the most important?

3. Of the skills and kinds of knowledge that a school newspaper copyreader should have, which do you think is the hardest to acquire?

4. Which one of the six copyreading steps would generally be the most difficult to carry out properly?

5. What guidelines and procedures might reporters and other newswriters be asked to follow so that retyping by copyreaders can be minimized?

Chapter Project

Copyreading Professional News Stories

Examine one or more daily or weekly newspapers for stories containing errors that a copyreader might have detected and corrected. Clip and mount the stories, and make corrections alongside the paragraphs in which the errors are found. Go over enough stories to yield a variety of errors, and make a record of the kinds that appear most often. (Note that, since you are dealing with printed material, some of the errors may have been caused by the printer, not missed by the copyreader. Thus, you can omit any errors that are totally unlikely to have appeared in the original copy.)

16

HEADLINING

When you have completed this chapter you should be able to

Understand the characteristics of headline language.

Write a good headline by carrying out six steps.

Make a headline lively, interesting, and informative.

Use a headline schedule to select headline styles and sizes for your school paper.

Use your knowledge of headlines to read headlines intelligently.

What do you see first when you look at a newspaper? Undoubtedly, the answer is headlines. But not all headlines are likely to attract your attention equally. Which of the following two headlines would make you want to continue reading to find out more?

**Several buildings
burned in fire**

**Million-dollar fire
sweeps city block**

A headline's purpose is to summarize and advertise its story. Even if you never read another word of a newspaper, you will get much information from its headlines. What, then, can headlines do for you as a reader?

Headlines can help you decide which news stories you will read and which you will not by indicating the general subject and interest level of the story. Headlines also furnish you with a brief summary of each story. A busy reader, looking only at headlines, should get a fairly complete picture of the news of the day. The headline size tells you how important each story is. The largest headlines are on stories that the editors feel have the most news value. The size and style of a newspaper's headlines also give you a good idea as to whether the newspaper is conservative or sensational in its approach.

Each news story is told three times—in the headline, in the lead, and in the body of the story. Of these, the shortest and hardest to write is the headline, yet it is the most important.

Who writes headlines? On many daily newspapers, this is the copyreader's job. After checking a story for accuracy, organization, and style, the copyreader prepares its headline according to the city editor's directions. Major newspapers, on the other hand, often employ special headline writers.

School newspapers may assign various people to the task of headline preparation. Copyreaders or headline writers may have this responsibility. Sometimes, when assigned a story, a reporter is told what kind of headline it will require, and the reporter is expected to write it. In other cases, the job is done by a page editor, whose duty it is to plan, arrange, and follow up production of one page.

Understanding the Characteristics of Headline Language

The headline, like the lead, summarizes important facts of the story. Because of space limitations, though, you do not have the same freedom to choose the words you might wish to use when expressing your idea. So, newspapers have developed a special kind of headline language. It is not

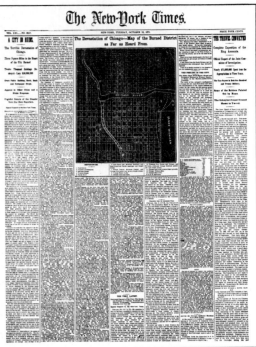

—New York *Tribune* from Culver; *The New York Times* from Bettmann

The increasing importance of headlines can be seen by comparing the New York Tribune *of April 10, 1841 (left) with* The New York Times *of October 10, 1871 (right). This development continued in the years that followed.*

hard to write, but it has several special characteristics. First, you use only key words that express the main idea of the story. Second, you use short words in place of long ones. Third, you leave out all unnecessary words. And, fourth, you use only two tenses of verbs, the present tense and the future tense.

In one essential way, the headline is like all other written work. Each headline expresses a complete thought. Nearly always, then, it is a sentence, containing a subject and a verb. Headlines are not titles or labels. They are live, informative, action-packed sentences.

Activity 1:   Identifying Headline Language

In daily newspapers find and list 10 headlines that make use of particularly expressive words. Look for words that serve a definite purpose in headlines because they are both brief and clear. (Examples might include such words as *flock*, meaning to attend in large crowds, *stage*, meaning to present a program, and *probe*, meaning to investigate.)

Writing a Headline

Writing a headline is like writing a telegram or a classified ad. You must make every word count. If you had to pay $1 per word, you wouldn't waste your money on words such as *there are* or on unnecessary adjectives. Headlines are limited in the same way. You must tell your story in one, two, or three lines, and each line can contain just so many letters and spaces.

You should not try to prepare your headline before you write your story. The reporter staring at a blank piece of paper, asking, "What can I say in the headline for a story I'm going to write?" is doing the job backward. Write your story first, taking special care with the lead. If your lead is well written, you can then use it as a basis for your headline.

There are six steps you can use to write effective headlines. First, select key words in the lead. Second, write a short telegraphic sentence using the key words. Third, if your headline is supposed to be more than one line, divide your sentence carefully into the desired number of lines. Fourth, use the correct verb form. Fifth, make your headline fit. Sixth, learn the standards for headline writing. The following pages will give you more information about each step.

Select Key Words in the Lead

You should begin by picking out words in the lead that tell the main idea of the story. Underline these words or list them on scratch paper.

Look, for example, at the following lead:

Competing with 17 other singing groups, the Boys' Choir will take part in the State Fair choral contest next Tuesday.

If you were writing a headline for this story, you might underline or list the following words: *Competing, Boys' Choir, State Fair,* and *contest.*

Activity 2: Choosing Words That Express the Main Idea

From each of the leads that follow, select and list about five words that give the main idea of the story.

1. Vocal and instrumental musicians will present their traditional spring Pops concert at 7:30 p.m., Thursday, in the auditorium.

2. Quill and Scroll will initiate 10 new members into its Central High chapter at a dinner tonight in the school cafeteria.

3. Joan White will hold the highest student office next fall when she takes office as student-body president, the second girl at Central High to attain this position.

4. Senior Thomas Foster recently achieved third place in the statewide American Legion oratorical competition.

5. Pottery, woodcarving, and oil painting will be exhibited at the annual arts festival, May 15 through 18.

Write a Short Telegraphic Sentence Using the Key Words

Your second step is to write a short telegraphic sentence using the key words. In this sentence, you should express the same idea as the lead does, but in shorter form. Rearrange the key words if necessary and add connecting words to make the sentence complete. Try to keep the sentence as short as possible.

The key words of the following lead are underlined:

Competing with 17 other singing groups, the Boys' Choir will take part in the State Fair choral contest next Tuesday.

Using these words, you might write the following brief telegraphic sentence:

Boys' Choir will compete in State Fair contest.

Activity 3:   Preparing a Brief Headline Sentence

From each of the following news leads, select the key words. Then, using these words and adding others as necessary, write a brief telegraphic sentence of not more than eight words. Leave out all unimportant words such as *the* or *a*. Be sure that each of your sentences states the main idea found in the lead.

1. "The theme for this year's junior dance is 'Winter Mist,' " announced Mary Elizabeth Warrington, class president. The dance will be held December 12.

2. The Central High band, under the baton of Mr. James Harrison, will play for the Founders' Day program at the civic center, October 24.

3. Senior Ron Miles, president of the school band, rescued a 5-year-old boy from drowning at Crystal Lake last Saturday.

4. Miss Anna Rosales, teacher of Spanish, attended a six-week summer session at the University of Mexico.

5. A multimedia presentation on the energy crisis will initiate Awareness Week activities this year.

Divide Your Sentence into Two or Three Lines

To complete this step, you must first know how many lines you are allowed to use and approximately how many words you can fit across a line. This information will depend on the general style chosen for your newspaper and on the width and number of columns in the story you are headlining.

If you find that the headline you have written can be fit on a single line, you may go on to the next step. Otherwise, you must now divide your headline sentence into the proper number of lines. To do this, you will need to shorten or lengthen the sentence so that you have approximately the right number of words in each line. As you break your headline sentence into lines, consider that the first line should show the key thought, just as a lead does. If you do not get this result, you will need to rewrite your sentence.

You should also keep in mind that groups of words that need to be read together should appear on the same line. These groups include verb phrases, prepositional phrases, proper names, or adjectives and nouns they closely modify. The headline sentence "Intramural season will begin on Monday" contains three such word groups: "Intramural season/will begin/ on Monday." None of these groups should be divided between one line and the next. "Intramural" and "season" must both be on the same line and so on throughout the headline.

Consider the headline sentence "Boys' Choir will compete in State Fair contest." If your headline is to appear as two long lines, you would need to divide it after the verb phrase: "Boys' Choir will compete/in State Fair contest." If your headline is to appear as three short lines, you might rewrite it in the following manner: "Boys' Choir/will compete/at State Fair."

Activity 4: Dividing a Headline Sentence into Lines

In each of the following leads, select the key words. Using these key words, write in telegraphic form a headline sentence of six to eight words. Adjust each of the first five sentences so that it fits in two lines of approximately equal length, with three for four words in each line. Adjust each of the last five sentences so that it fits in three lines of approximately equal length, with two or three words in each line. Remember not to divide word groups. Keep the key thought in the first line.

1. Mr. John Frederick spent Business Education Day in an airplane. He and 63 other teachers flew to Clear Lake, Point Arena, and down the coast to Monterey.

2. Construction work on the foundation of the girls' gym started this week. Contractor Lloyd Bennett expects to complete the building by next fall for use at the beginning of the new term.

3. Food and shelter are needed by flood victims. The Red Cross is sponsoring a drive to raise funds in all city schools, according to Laura Russell, club chairman.

4. Pioneer Service League has donated $700 to Guide Dogs for the Blind. The league started the fund about two years ago and has kept it up ever since through paper drives.

5. The school chorus, directed by Mrs. Alice Jordan, has been practicing every Monday for the annual holiday pageant in the civic auditorium, December 12 and 13.

6. Students will vote for new officers in a primary election February 17, with the final election February 18, Mr. Davis Chambers, student government sponsor, has announced.

7. A socialized medicine bill was debated and voted down by the Central High Model Senate at its annual session Friday.

8. Father's Day will be celebrated at the PTA meeting Thursday evening in the gym. A special program is planned.

9. Student government officers have planned, with the cooperation of the administration, to invite student government officers from other schools in the area to visit Central High.

10. Jean Odessa became badminton champion May 10, after a hard battle with Shirley Brinter. Ginger Franks earned third place, and Glenda Linsley fourth.

Use the Correct Verb Form

Your fourth step is to use the correct verb form. Headlines use two tenses only, present and future. Past-tense verbs are not appropriate.

USE THE PRESENT FOR PRESENT AND PAST EVENTS. Something that is now happening or has already happened is shown by the present tense of a verb. Regardless of when the event took place, the following headline is incorrect: "Stamp Club elected officers." Its correct form would be "Stamp Club elects officers."

The helping verbs *is* and *are* are usually left out of headlines. They can be used if you wish, but they are generally omitted to make a headline sentence shorter. When you omit them, it may at first appear that you are using the past tense: "Chess Club officers elected." The verb "elected" looks like a past-tense verb. Actually, however, your headline implies the verb *are* and the present tense. What you are really saying is "Chess Club officers are elected." The headline is correct with or without the helping verb. In practice, you are likely to leave *are* out, to save space.

When you find a word such as *elected* in a headline, there is a sure test to use to decide whether it is present or past. Try the helping verb *is* or *are* in front of it. If the headline makes sense, the verb is present. If it does not make sense, you have a past-tense verb that must be changed.

When you use *is* or *are* with a verb that appears to be past, you are employing the passive voice of the verb instead of the active voice. The active voice is more common. The subject is the doer, and the direct object receives the action of the verb. In the sentence "Student body chooses president," "Student body" is the subject, "chooses" is the verb, and "president" is the direct object.

The passive voice reverses this normal arrangement. The subject now receives the action of the verb, there is no direct object, and what was formerly the doer appears as the object of the preposition *by*, as in the following sentence: "President is chosen by student body." "President" is the subject, "is chosen" is the verb, and "by student body" is a prepositional phrase.

Notice that the sentences beginning with "Student body" and "President" say the same thing, but the first is more definite and more alive. Passive verbs should be used in headlines only when you need to emphasize certain words by placing them at the beginning of a headline. In the examples given, "President" has more news value than "Student body." Thus, there is some reason for the passive form. As a matter of good news practice, when you do use the passive, you should leave out the helping verb: "President chosen by student body."

In dealing with present and past events, the most important points to remember are the following. First, use the present, not the past. Second, avoid passive verbs whenever you can, for headlines must capture and hold a reader's interest, and active verbs are better suited to give this feeling of liveliness. Third, use passive verbs only when you wish to emphasize words that would be direct objects after active verbs. In such cases, you will generally find it advisable to omit the helping verb.

USE THE FUTURE OR AN INFINITIVE FOR FUTURE EVENTS. Future action in a headline may be shown by the future tense of a verb, with the helping verb *will*. However, most newspapers prefer the infinitive, beginning with the word *to*. When dealing with a future event, the present tense is definitely incorrect: "Aviation Club sees movie tomorrow." An acceptable alternative is the sentence "Aviation Club will see movie tomorrow." However, a better version would be the sentence "Aviation Club to see movie tomorrow."

CHECK YOUR HEADLINE CAREFULLY FOR THE CORRECT FORM. Returning to the headline about the Boys' Choir, you should first note that the event is to take place at a future time: "Boys' Choir will compete in State Fair contest." In a two-line headline format, an acceptable headline would be "Boys' Choir will compete/in State Fair contest." A better headline would be "Boys' Choir to compete/in State Fair contest." In a three-line headline format, an acceptable headline would be "Boys' Choir/will compete/at State Fair." A better headline would be "Boys' Choir/to compete/at State Fair."

Activity 5:   Using Correct Verb Forms in Headlines

The first five of the following leads describe past events. Write a two- or three-line headline for each one, using the present tense throughout, the active voice wherever possible, and the passive voice, where necessary, without a helping verb. The last five leads describe future events. Write a two- or three-line headline for each one, using an infinitive.

1. Two additional English teachers began instructing last Monday. Smaller classes have been formed, according to Principal A. J. Curtis.

2. The varsity basketball squad barely pushed its way past North High, 61-59, last Friday afternoon.

3. Mr. John Roberts, president of the First Federal Bank in Morgantown, spoke to Mr. Ralph Webster's business training classes recently on the history and functions of banks.

4. A sellout crowd of parents and students enjoyed their annual banquet last Wednesday in the school cafeteria.

5. Mary Castor, tenth grader, received a $100 bond as first prize in the Historical Society essay contest.

6. Foreign Students Union will welcome 25 new members at a party Friday. At present, there are 75 active members.

7. Student council will sponsor a ski trip to Bear Valley, Saturday, January 17. A special bus will be chartered.

8. "Fog Island," a one-act play, will highlight the next PTA meeting Tuesday at 7:30 p.m. It is to be presented by Mr. Joe Miller's drama class.

9. Student-body officers will head an anti-litterbug campaign next month. A rally will start the week-long crusade.

10. Walking across the floor of the gym for the last time, 397 high school seniors will receive their diplomas next Tuesday night.

Make Your Headline Fit

If you have had any contact with a print shop during your journalistic work, you have probably been told, "Type isn't made of rubber; it can't be squeezed!" This is especially true of headlines. Only a certain number of letters, punctuation marks, and spaces can be fit into a column width. What you can fit depends on the style and size of type.

Every newspaper, whether it be a small school paper or a big-city daily, has a **headline schedule**, which shows the various kinds of type that

—Photo by F. B. Grunzweig from Photo Researchers

The challenge of making a headline fit the space available for it is the same regardless of the language in which a newspaper is printed. The type for one language is as "unsqueezable" as the type for another.

can be used in that particular paper for headlines, as well as the number of letters, marks, and spaces that can be fit on a line. Reporters, copyreaders, and page editors must be familiar with this schedule, so they can prepare the headlines for which they are responsible.

Newspapers use either of two basic methods of measuring headlines to see whether they will fit. For all work in this chapter, you should count headlines according to the system employed by your school newspaper. It will be similar to one of the following plans: **flush-left headlines** (also called **no-count headlines**) and **strict-count headlines.**

Flush-left headlines are often used when newspaper columns are wide. Each line of a headline begins on the left above the column, but there is no need for any line to fill the entire space above the column. When following this pattern, you may count each **unit**—each letter, mark, and space—in the headline as one. Your headline schedule will give a minimum and maximum count for each line. For example, the count may be shown as 16–20. This means that you should have at least 16 units in each line, but not more than 20. If you have fewer, the headline will look weak and thin. If you have more, it won't fit.

The following headline has been counted correctly. Notice that the unit totals are written on the copy as a guide to editors and printers:

Council earns $102, ←⟨*19*⟩
purchases '83 pins ←⟨*18*⟩

Strict-count headlines are used with certain styles of type, as well as when you wish your headline to fill an exact amount of space. When following this pattern, you must do more than simply assign each unit a value of one. Looking at a printed page, you will notice that all letters are not the same width. The letters *M* and *W* are wider than all the other letters, and the letter *I* is narrower. Different unit values must be assigned to these letters to get an exact count. The following chart is used by many newspapers.

UNIT VALUES FOR STRICT-COUNT HEADLINES

For capitals, count *M* and *W* as 2 units; count *I* as 1 unit; count all other letters as 1½ units.

For lower-case letters, count *m* and *w* as 1½ units; count *f, i, l,* and *t* as ½ unit; count all other letters as 1 unit.

For numbers written as figures, count each figure as 1 unit.

For punctuation, count a period, comma, single quotation mark, colon, semicolon, and exclamation point as ½ unit; count all other marks as 1 unit.

For spaces, count each space as 1 unit.

The fifth step in writing a headline is to make your headline sentence fit the assigned pattern. If you had this pattern in mind as you divided your sentence into two or three lines, you probably have a headline that comes close to fitting the pattern. The next thing to do is to count the units in each line and write the number of units at the end of the line.

Then, if any line does not fit the unit count for the headline schedule you are using, revise it until it does. Do this by adding words, by taking out unnecessary words, by using longer or shorter synonyms, or by changing words. If none of these schemes works, start over again with a new telegraphic sentence.

Returning again to the headline about Boys' Choir, you would begin by counting units. The following examples show counts for two- and three-line headlines following the flush-left pattern:

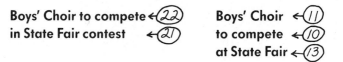

Assuming these are not within your allowable unit count, you can change the lines as necessary to make them fit:

Activity 6:   Finding Synonyms

Using *Roget's Thesaurus* or *Webster's Book of Synonyms*, find suitable synonyms that could be used in newspaper headlines to replace the words that follow: *choose, win, approve, see, hear, learn, plan, tell, entertain, participate, program, election, meeting, game,* and *student*. List as many synonyms as possible for each. You may be able to think of some words without using a reference book. However, you should become familiar with one or both of these specialized books. They are needed by every writer and particularly by every headline writer.

Learn the Standards for Headline Writing

As you have seen, headlines use language in special ways. The following checklist encompasses all of these uses. The first six items have been explained in detail earlier in the chapter. The last eight items represent other considerations that a headline writer must keep in mind.

✔ Checklist for Headline Language

☐ 1. Have I put the story's main idea in the headline, taking my facts from the lead?

☐ 2. Have I made the headline a complete sentence, with a subject and a verb?

☐ 3. Have I avoided using the articles *a, an,* or *the,* except when necessary to make my meaning clear?

☐ 4. Have I avoided dividing words, verb phrases, prepositional phrases, proper names, or closely related adjective-noun combinations from one line to the next?

☐ 5. Have I omitted *is* and *are* from headlines wherever possible?

☐ 6. Have I used the present tense to indicate current and past happenings, the infinitive to indicate future happenings, and the active voice of the verb, rather than the passive, wherever possible?

☐ 7. Have I avoided beginning a headline with a verb? (A headline such as "Choose new president" leaves the reader asking, "Who did it?")

☐ 8. Have I avoided using abbreviations that might cause confusion or look awkward? (Well-known abbreviations made up of capitals without periods—*PTA* and *TV,* for example—are fine. Unavoidable abbreviated titles such as *Mr.* and *Mrs.,* are also acceptable. Most other abbreviations, such as *Dept., Rep.,* or *Engl.* for "English," should be avoided at all costs.)

☐ 9. Have I used numbers only when they were important and never at the beginning of a headline? (When numbers *are* used, they should appear as figures, as in "Crash injures 2 children.")

☐ 10. Have I used single quotation marks instead of double quotation marks wherever quotation marks are needed?

☐ 11. Have I substituted a comma for the word *and* (as in "Teachers, students to complete survey")?

☐ 12. Have I used mostly short words (one or two syllables) and avoided long words wherever possible?

☐ 13. Have I avoided repeating an important word in a headline and used a synonym instead?

☐ 14. Have I followed the system of capitalization that my school paper has selected? (There are two systems commonly used by daily and school newspapers today. In **up style,** all words are capitalized except conjunctions, articles, and prepositions of fewer than four letters. Even these words are capitalized if they appear at the beginning of a line. In **down style,** words are capitalized as in ordinary sentences—capitals are used for the first word of the headline and for any proper nouns.)

Activity 7: Correcting Faulty Headlines

Each of the following headlines is faulty according to the standards in the checklist. Tell what is wrong with each, keeping in mind that several errors may appear in the same headline.

1. Latest student
   council minutes

2. New rule passed by
   student council

3. The Rams nipped Colts
   in very close game

4. Lockers will be in
   use by December

5. Vocational students
   attend vocational seminar

6. Eight students tried
   by student court

7. Mathematics department
   holds a survey

8. Appoint Johnson
   new principal

9. "The Tempest" Impresses
   Students And Teachers

10. Posts are assigned
    to Hall Comm.

Making Sure Your Headline Says Something

Consider two possible headlines for the same story:

Student council meeting

Student council has meeting

The first is not really a headline at all; it is merely a label. When a verb is added, as in the second example, a true headline emerges. But it still does not say anything; it is a "wooden" headline. You could set it in type, use it for every student council story, and it would always be correct. But would anyone read the story under this headline?

"Orchestra rehearses for concert" would be a wooden headline. A headline must capture the reader's attention by saying something of interest to the reader, something unknown or unexpected.

—Photo by Ann Hagen Griffiths from Omni

Improved versions are shown below. Notice how the focus on the meeting results makes the second headline even better than the first.

Student council discusses voter registration

'Register to vote,' urges student council

Sometimes wooden headlines result from wooden leads. If the lead merely reports that the student council met last week, one could hardly wonder why the headline says no more. But given an interesting lead, you can get life and interest into your headline. Use devices you have already learned for putting sparkle and color into your sentences. Above all, make your headline *say* something!

Activity 8: Removing the "Wood" from Wooden Headlines

Several dull headlines follow, together with the leads from which they were written. Improve each headline by making it more interesting. Following the six steps listed earlier in the chapter, write a two-line headline for each lead. Count the units in each line, so that the two lines are similar in length.

1. Principal speaks to county group

   "Science in the High School Curriculum" was the subject of Principal R. J. Smith's speech to the County Parent-Teachers' Association last Wednesday evening at the court house.

2. Class of '83 remembers

   An encyclopedia and other reference books have been purchased for the library with $890 left by the Class of 1983. Each year's graduating class donates something of value to the school.

3. Science Club sees pictures

   Fran Rohner showed slides of birds and exhibited her live barn owl at the Natural Science Club meeting last week. The owl, a rare bird in this section of the country, was of particular interest.

4. Newspaper places in national contest

   The highest award given by the Quill and Scroll Society, the George H. Gallup Award, was presented to the News. This recognition is bestowed on "distinctive high school papers" in the United States.

Working with a Headline Schedule

No newspaper can operate successfully without a headline schedule. This is a printed sample of available headline patterns, indicating type styles and sizes, as well as unit counts, and assigning a number to each pattern. With this number, the headline writers, editors, copyreaders, and printers all "speak the same language." Planning a headline schedule requires considerable study by the editor, adviser, and printer. Sample schedules are included in the Editor's Handbook on pages 462 and 480.

Your headline schedule will include various kinds of headlines, usually following the flush-left pattern. This pattern, combined with the use of capital and lower-case letters rather than all capital letters, produces modern-looking headlines that are particularly easy to read. Headlines may appear in various type sizes, numbers of lines, or column widths to suit a story's importance or its placement on the page. For proper appearance, each line should fill at least three quarters of its allowable width.

The two- and three-line "Boys' Choir" headlines on page 338 are typical examples of the once almost universal **single-column headline.**

With the modern preference for what is known as **horizontal makeup,** headlines extending across two, three, or four columns are becoming more and more popular. **Spreads,** as these headlines are called, can improve the appearance of a page by allowing for increased variety. They are generally limited to one or two lines. The vertical lines in the following examples show the columns covered by two spreads:

Centralites choose Homecoming queen

Ballet rehearsals to start for operetta 'Brigadoon'

Used to emphasize a story, a **banner** head, also called a **streamer,** may extend the full width of any page in your paper. Banners are generally at the top of a page but may be used elsewhere, especially near the bottom, for contrast. To reach across all the columns, they must be written to an exact unit count.

The short lines that sometimes appear above main headlines in order to highlight or introduce them are called **kickers.** Several points about kickers should be noted. A kicker is generally in smaller or lighter type than the main headline. It is often underlined. It may be followed by a dash or a series of dots, as in the following example. It is sometimes a complete sentence, with subject and verb, but this is not required. It never repeats words used in the main headline. It may begin a thought that continues into the main line (in which case it is called a **read-in**). It might, in special cases, contain more than one line.

'Brooksie's' proteges sing . . .

CHS musician leads Shrine program

—Pepper Bough, Colton High School,
Colton, California

A kicker is particularly useful in introducing a column. The kicker states the column's title. The main headline then emphasizes an appealing idea from the column itself, as in the following example:

Mark my words . . .

Blue chip stamp drive
merits student support

—The Mirror, Van Nuys High School,
Van Nuys, California

For feature stories, you may want to create unusual or specially designed headlines that will attract attention and brighten up your pages. While newspapers using magazine format rely heavily on such headlines, they can be employed effectively by any paper. You may have two or three good novelty headline patterns in your headline schedule from which you may choose, or you might wish to use your typographical resources to design a headline especially suitable for each feature story. Various kinds of kicker arrangements, borders around stories and headlines, unusual type styles, or even headlines in unusual positions say to your reader, "Here is something you'll want to read!" Notice how effective the following headline is for the story it introduces:

Computer turns on:
beep, buzz, bing

—The Lion, Lyons Township High School, LaGrange and Western Springs, Illinois

It is also possible to have a series of headlines for a single story. In newspaper terminology, each complete headline is called a **deck.** If another headline is added, the result is a **multiple-deck headline.** In horizontal makeup, multiple-deck headlines are seldom needed. Their place is generally taken by kickers or other short, special-format headlines based on the same principles as kickers but with their own distinctive patterns. You are probably most likely to use a two-deck headline when the top deck is a banner or spread and the story itself is only one or two columns wide. The use of a lower deck in this case can help the reader's eye locate the story.

A few special rules control the writing of two-deck headlines. First, each deck must have its own subject and verb and state a complete idea. Next, the second deck must not repeat the first. Instead, it must introduce a new idea, one that is important but not quite so important as the thought in the first deck.

Features Entertainment

THE AXE, FRIDAY, OCTOBER 16, 1981

Disaster: Are we prepared?

South may not be equipped to handle an unexpected disaster

By Kim Edwards and Adam Fendrich

Everyday, throughout the nation, disasters strike. Devastation seems highly unlikely to occur in the South Eugene area, but the p...

If a cr...
would w...
The inf...
such an...
challeng...
traits.

In Sep...
complied...
procedur...
which in...
occurs.

The f...
procedur...
Emergen...

Earth...
Oregon...
deal m...
generall...
occur at...

Acco...
happens...
they are...
under de...
should o...

In the...
would b...
Warning...
Broadca...
by emer...
the Lan...
would t...
who liv...
insuffici...

the fallout shelter or the most sheltered part of the building. The greatest building mass should be in between students and the ...

The bomb shelter under South would be home and protection for students faculty in the event of a nuclear disaster with insufficient warning to transport students home. School district regulations provide that food supplies and water in containers such as the one above be stored in the shelter.

Photos by Laura Brown

Ballard's shot sinks Tornado

BY MARK ADAMSKI
Orange R Reporter

It was a knock-down drag-out grind-your-teeth clench-your-fist kind of game. A real barnburner. It was the kind of game where people stood in line for an hour or two just to get a seat. Once inside, the 2000 fans found themselves standing in the tension-filled stadium for the whole second half of the game.

In a must-win situation to take the Southern Oregon Conference (SOC) title, Indian forward Troy Ballard hit a 10-foot jump shot with two seconds remaining the break the tie and win 81-79.

"That was the longest shot I've shot all season," grinned Ballard after the game.

Brad Seehawer led all scorers with a stunning 37-point effort, followed by Paul Robertson with 12, Doug Lafountaine and Ballard had 10 points apiece.

Jeff Noahr led Medford with 24 points in a balanced scoring attack. Robertson led the Tribe in rebounds with six, followed by Seehawer and Bill Michel with four.

With the win over the visiting Medford Black Tornado Monday night, the Tribe extends its season winning streak to 13 games, wins the SOC crown, and the trip to Portland next Wednesday for the AAA State Tournament.

There they face number one Benson High School, with All-State candidate A.C. Green, who recently announced his intentions to attend Oregon State in the fall.

If Ballard had known he was going to hit the jumper prior to his shot, he might have taken it a little easier the first half of the game.

Unfortunately, he found himself with four fouls.

"I wasn't really thinking about the fouls," he explains. "I thought this might be the last game here and I was just going for it."

From the first jump ball to the last shot, this was no ordinary game.

Medford grabbed the lead and rattled off to a 10-4 lead, but the Tribe came back and tied it up at 15. At the end of the first quarter, the Tribe led by three, 25-22.

Both teams played well.

Roseburg would catch up, tie the game, possibly go up by one or two, and then fade out while the Tornado would come back and grab the lead.

At half-time, the score was 46-41 Medford. Going in to the final quarter, the Tribe was tied with Medford 65-65. The two teams were never more than six points apart during the entire game.

"We couldn't quite capitalize," said Indian Seehawer. "Every time we got close there'd be a foul of something and we'd lose it."

As the Indians took the lead with a minute to go in the game, Medford quickly called two time outs to settle down and get organized.

Twenty seconds later the score was tied 79 - 79 on Noahr's short jumper.

Indian guard Seehawer brought the ball downcourt, but instead of calling time, the Tribe kept the ball in play, hoping for the last shot. It was a precarious proposition: hit and win the game, or miss and go into overtime.

With two seconds remaining, Ballard made the miracle shot, and the rest is history.

UP, UP, AND AWAY—Indian Brad Seehawer goes up for another of his 37 points in Monday's outstanding performance against Medford.

Photo by Mark Wood

Orange R Sports

Section B   March 5, 1981

Fans' mood 'electrifying' at game

The mood was electrifying. It was like hearing thunder while waiting to buy tickets for the Roseburg-Medford basketball game. Roseburg fans were ecstatic and the game had not yet begun.

Anyone could tell that the fans were going to play a large part in this playoff game and they lived up to their expectations. After the game got started, the Roseburg fans had absolutely no trouble getting themselves started. With every point that was made by

the Indians, the spectators were on their feet. The pulsating movements of the crowd was enough to keep the adrenaline going if nothing else.

The fans were always being encouraged on by the cheerleaders. These girls never gave up. Sitting on the bench, one said to herself, "Come on you guys. Lets go!" While she was saying this to herself, the fans were saying this to the players. These cheerleaders literally sweated the game out and for a good cause.

The bleacher bums were more than themselves at the game. One bum pointed out that the Medford fans were getting radical, but nothing could compare to the extremely high-spirited fans of RHS.

At the end, when Roseburg was declared victorious, practically every student ran out onto the court. All this could be called mass chaos, but it really sums up the true feelings of how the Roseburg fans feel about their school and their basketball team.

Swimmers do well at state

Roseburg swimmers went to state competition to do well and that's exactly what they did.

The girls' swim team placed twenty-first out of 58 teams. Roseburg's Jill Beecroft placed sixth in the diving competition, breaking school record. Lisa Zimmerman finished eighth in the diving competition. Female divers from RHS have never placed that high, according to coach Duffy Lederman. The girls' medley relay team took twelfth place. The team included Robin Ylitalo, Anne Heisleu, Lisa and Lynne Zimmerman.

Heislen also took sixteenth place in the 200 meter free style. "Coach Sanders gave Roseburg its best finish ever and enabled the girls' team to finish as well as they did," said Lederman.

The boys' swim team tied with 12 other teams in the meet with a total of 4 points. The Roseburg boys saw 19 All-Americans crown in the meet. As a fast meet to say the least. Mike Andrew placed tenth in the 100 meter breaststroke. Paul Cummings was twelfth in the 50 meter freestyle and was 1½ seconds off the All-American record. The race crowned four All-Americans. "The experience our boys got will be invaluable next year, and we will be back and better," said Coach Lederman.

Special Olympic team gets honor

BY MARK ADAMSKI
Orange R Reporter

They're not the Philadelphia 76'ers, but they're as interesting to watch as the pro club is. But you say to yourself: "Who can move like Dr. J and still have the soft touch of a Lionel Hollins?"

It's the Special Olympics basketball team.

Roseburg High School's Special Olympics basketball teams recently competed in an eight team—100 participant tournament at Joseph Lane Junior High School, finishing third and fourth in the "C" division, and fourth in the "B" division.

Of the 100 participants, 46 were from the Douglas County are, including 25 from Roseburg High.

Hidden Valley's Orange Team won the "B" tournament while Klamath Falls took the "C" title.

High scorers for Roseburg were Tim Bivens with 16 points for the tournament, followed by Larry Gregory's 14. Stan Johnson and Rod Rasmussen had two points a piece.

A more than special honor has been bestowed on Roseburg High's Ron Koch as he will be traveling to Vermont next year to compete in the International Olympic Games. Koch will enter the cross

country skiing competition, tentatively escorted by Trainable Mentally Handicapped teacher Irene Karsh.

Next in line for the Special Olympics athletes is preparation for the state basketball meet tomorrow and Saturday at Portland State University.

And though the winter sports season is drawing to a close for the Olympians, spring is in the air, with it the athletics involved in track and field. The season will kick off April 18 with an invitational track meet at RHS. Volunteers will be needed for practice and the actual meet, the highlight of the track season will be participation at the state meet to be held in Eugene soon after the Invitational.

—The Axe, South Eugene High School, Eugene, Oregon (top); Orange R, Roseburg Senior High School, Roseburg, Oregon (bottom)

The headline for the feature story on nuclear disaster is a two-deck headline. The top deck is a banner; the second deck is a spread. The headline announcing the winning shot is a more typical single-deck banner headline.

Another type of headline may prove useful in dealing with stories that are especially lengthy. Long stories give a gray appearance to a news page. This defect may be corrected by inserting subheads between paragraphs. **Subheads** are one-line boldface headlines, usually in the same size type as the body of the story. They may begin at the left of the column space or be centered on the column space. The minimum-length story for subheads has six paragraphs, since at least two subheads must appear if any are used and there should be at least two paragraphs between.

Each subhead is, in effect, a miniature headline for the paragraphs it precedes. It should summarize the key thought of what follows it, but like a kicker, it need not contain a subject and a verb.

Activity 9: Constructing a Headline with a Kicker

For each of the leads that follow, write a two-line headline introduced by a kicker. Follow in general the basic steps for headline writing. When you prepare your telegraphic sentence, however, you will also have to prepare an additional phrase or short sentence for the kicker. Your kicker and each line of your main headline should have three or four words.

1. Mr. Robert Johnson was recently named principal of Central High. Mr. Johnson, who is now administrative vice-principal at South High, attended a Central faculty meeting last Wednesday to be introduced to the teachers. He will assume his new duties next semester.

2. Cash prizes will be given to the three students who score highest in the United Nations contest, March 5. The national winner of the annual contest will receive a trip to Europe. The contest is in the form of an examination covering the United Nations and what it has done.

3. Elections for next year's student officers will take place at voting booths in the main lobby today. Since ballots will be tallied at intervals during the day by the math department computer, final results can be announced soon after the polls close at 3:30 p.m.

4. The new Student Board, with seven members appointed by the student council, will have authority to deal with all nonclassroom disciplinary cases this year. The board may withdraw privileges, place an offender on probation, or recommend a more severe penalty.

Activity 10: Using a Headline Schedule

For each lead that follows, write a different style of headline. Use your school paper's headline schedule if it is available. If not, use the headline schedule on page 462. Begin by finding the unit count for each of the headlines you will be writing. Study the schedule to determine the number of lines and whether kickers or other special arrangements are used in a particular pattern. Each of your finished headlines must follow the pattern given in the headline schedule. Be sure your headlines are correctly written in all other respects as well.

1. Barbara Hamilton, junior, left last Wednesday for five weeks in Africa. Barbara is accompanying her parents on a business trip and will return April 22.

2. The terrible experiences of life in a prisoner-of-war camp were related this week in two of Mrs. Rhoda Stewart's social studies classes by Mr. Harold Thornton, former Air Force pilot, whose plane was shot down in Southeast Asia.

3. As a tribute to the late Eubie Blake, the band will play a number of his compositions during its next half-time show.

4. "It's the answer to difficult assignments!" "All it leads to is gaps in your education." These were among various reactions expressed by students and faculty this week when it was learned that a company is selling term papers at some high schools and colleges.

Activity 11: Preparing Headlines for Feature Stories

Write a headline for each of the following excerpts from feature stories. Use an appropriate style from your school paper's headline schedule or design a special headline to fit each story.

1. During a recent session in first-aid class, Miss Joan Granger was explaining the process of anchoring a bandage on an accident victim. Addressing Peggy Anderson, she asked, "May I borrow your arm?" "Why, y-yes," Peggy stammered. "Well, bring it up here," Miss Granger instructed her.

2. At some schools, the problem is finding enough parking for all the cars. At Central High the problem is finding enough space for all the bikes. Each day more than 200 bicycles are chained to the racks and fences by the building.

3. Mr. James Young, physics instructor, asked his sixth-period class, "Does the sun really appear larger in the morning than it does later in the day?" Kelly Fleming, in a moment of inspiration, answered, "It must, because by afternoon some of it has been burned up!"

4. But she can't give you an aspirin. "Only a doctor may prescribe medicine," says Mrs. Carolyn Thomas. As school nurse, she serves students by giving health advice, watching for communicable disease, and supervising first aid.

Using Your Knowledge of Headlines

More than any other words in a newspaper, the headlines are intended to be read. What they say colors your impression of current news. Therefore, as you look at a newspaper's front page, you must be thinking as well as reading.

At best, a headline is a greatly abbreviated summary. It cannot cover the entire story and all its details, but it should be fairly representative. Some headlines, however, are not so trustworthy. The stories that follow them may contain details that will completely change the headline's impact on you.

In a poorly written headline, careless wording may add to the confusion caused by poor selection of information. Consider the rather gruesome implications of this headline: "Two eat, then rob proprietor."

Technical difficulties in the writing of a headline may also interfere with clear understanding of the story. For instance, to save space, a headline writer may use the word *choose* to mean "nominate." Good headline writers try to make each word express the precise meaning they wish to convey, but unit counting and the pressure of deadlines sometimes force them to do hasty work in spite of their good intentions.

Definite slant may creep into some headlines. Daily newspapers may feature crime, accidents, sordidness, or brutality in major headlines in an effort to sell more papers. When you buy one of these papers, you may sometimes have difficulty in finding the headlined detail, because it is of so little importance in the complete story. Even in the many papers that do not follow this practice, the headline writer's personal feelings may unconsciously influence the selection and treatment of facts.

The placement of a story and its headline on a page may also reflect a bias—an editor's or makeup artist's judgment. Your own standards of news values may not be the same as the editor's or the artist's, yet you are influenced by their ideas when you notice the size and placement of various headlines.

Activity 12: Examining Headlines

Make a collection of good and poor headlines from daily and school newspapers. Explain the reasons for your choices.

Summary

This chapter begins by presenting the special characteristics of headline language. It then explains the six steps for writing a headline. It goes on to consider the problem of writing lively, interesting headlines. Next, it discusses different headline patterns. Finally, it considers how to read a headline intelligently.

UNDERSTANDING THE CHARACTERISTICS OF HEADLINE LANGUAGE. Headline language is characterized by a reliance on short key words that convey the main idea of a story. All unnecessary words are left out, and only two verb tenses are used, the present and the future.

WRITING A HEADLINE. There are six steps for writing a headline. First, select the key words in the lead that convey the main idea of the story. Second, write a short telegraphic sentence using the key words; express the same idea as the lead does, but in shorter form. Third, divide your sentence into two or three lines (if the headline pattern you are using requires such division). Fourth, use the correct verb form, either present or future tense. Fifth, make your headline fit. And, sixth, learn and use the general standards of headline language.

MAKING SURE YOUR HEADLINE SAYS SOMETHING. Dull, lifeless leads give rise to dull, lifeless headlines. Using the methods for putting sparkle and color into newswriting in general will improve both leads and the headlines based on them. A headline such as "Student council has meeting" may be a true headline, but it is flat and wooden. The headline " 'Register to vote,' urges student council," on the other hand, says something that is concrete and particular.

WORKING WITH A HEADLINE SCHEDULE. A headline schedule is a sample of headline patterns indicating type styles, type sizes, and unit counts. A headline's type style, type size, number of lines, and column width will be determined by the story's importance and placement on the page. Standard headline patterns include single-column headlines, spreads across two or more columns, and banners or streamers across a full page. Kickers, multiple-deck headlines, and subheads are used to meet special needs.

USING YOUR KNOWLEDGE OF HEADLINES. Since every headline will not present a perfect summary of a story, readers should be careful not to jump to wrong conclusions about a news item. Moreover, some papers will deliberately inject sensationalism into headlines to sell more papers. The personal feelings of a writer, editor, or makeup artist may also help slant a headline. When reading headlines, people must think as well as read.

Vocabulary

headline schedule	down style	kicker
flush-left headline	single-column headline	read-in
no-count headline	horizontal makeup	deck
strict-count headline	spread	multiple-deck headline
unit	banner	subhead
up style	streamer	

Review Questions

1. What are the characteristics of headline language?

2. What are the six steps for writing a headline?

3. What is meant by a "wooden" headline?

4. What is a headline schedule, and why is it useful?

5. What should a reader keep in mind about headlines in order to read them intelligently?

Discussion Questions

1. To what extent do the headlines in the newspapers that you read help you to pick out the stories of greatest interest or importance to you?

2. Why are the tenses of headline verbs limited to the present and the future?

3. Which of the standard devices for writing news English are especially helpful when a headline writer is trying to write a lively, interesting headline?

4. Is there sufficient variety in the headline patterns used in your school paper?

5. Is the amount of sensationalism in today's headlines justified by the subjects being covered?

Chapter Project

Evaluating Current Headlines

Using daily or weekly papers widely read in your community, study and evaluate the headlines of major news stories. Ask such questions as the following: Do these headlines accurately indicate the contents of their stories? Do they help the reader to distinguish important from unimportant news? Are they interesting or dull? If they are interesting, is it because of the skill of the headline writer or because sensationalism is being resorted to for the sake of newspaper sales? What do these headlines indicate about the journalistic standards of the papers in which they appear? What do they indicate about the readers that the papers are trying to reach?

MAKEUP
AND DESIGN

When you have completed this chapter you should be able to

Prepare a basic design for your newspaper that will reflect an understanding of fundamental design principles.

Design individual pages of your newspaper according to modern standards of arrangement and emphasis.

Use typefaces, typographical devices, and graphic materials to enhance the appearance of your pages.

Lay out the pages of your school newspaper.

Coordinate the various aspects of makeup and design work.

"Our aim should be to sort out everything for the reader and present it in an orderly, detailed fashion." This is the way the Chicago *Tribune*'s handbook for its professional staff describes **makeup**—the process of designing a newspaper through careful selection and arrangement of headlines, stories, and pictures.

At this point, you are likely to have worked hard planning your newspaper's content, researching and collecting information, and writing your stories. You have a good mix of news, feature stories, and opinions. You have prepared headlines and arranged for photographs. Now you want your paper to be read and appreciated. To reach this goal, your pages must be attractive and interesting.

Makeup has several general purposes. It draws attention to the kind of material contained in a newspaper's pages. It shows the relative importance of each story. It suggests the relationship of stories to each other. It emphasizes stories that have substantial content or present especially good writing. It also helps a reader determine which stories will be read first or at all.

The *Tribune*'s statement about makeup continues: "Good design leads to better writing and a keener appreciation of story content." In today's newspapers, **design** is the key word in the planning of pages. This chapter will explore overall newspaper design, individual page design, the use of typographical resources, and the process of laying out a page.

Designing Your Newspaper

As recently as 25 years ago, makeup was regarded primarily as a means of displaying a paper's content. Stories would be arranged according to the way editors judged their importance. Makeup concerns were limited primarily to selecting good type styles, to creating a general balance of elements on a page, and to contrasting different items so each one would stand out.

The appearance of today's newspapers now emphasizes the idea of "packaging the news." Related material is placed together. Pages are almost always departmentalized with a general heading, such as State News, Entertainment, or Features. Boxes, lines, and other typographical devices tie together related items on each page. A major story may be positioned in such a way that all of its elements are pulled together. A significant article may stand alone on all or part of a page, surrounded by white space.

Attracting the reader's eye by "visualizing the news" is all-important. Content is no longer the only element that controls the arrangement. This is not to say that story content is less important. Rather, packages and visual devices call attention to story topics and writing. Weak reporting and poor newswriting will stand out more, not less, on modern pages.

The trend toward visual packaging has been brought about through three factors. First, newspapers have reacted to the impact of television

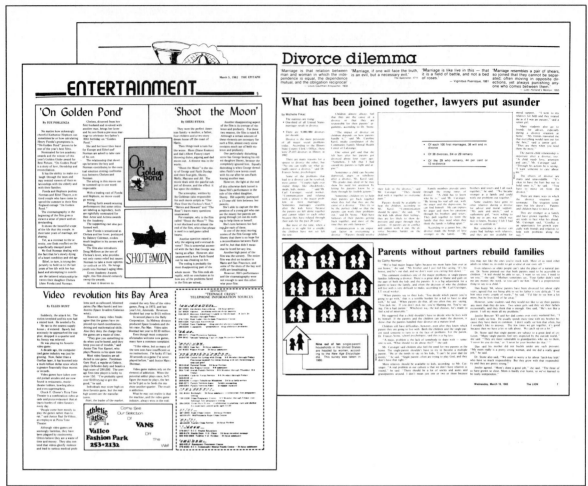

Both the entertainment page on the left and the spread of feature stories on the right illustrate packaged news. In particular, the two movie reviews are so arranged that their equality as prominent articles is immediately apparent.

upon consumers, who now receive much of their news and entertainment visually. Second, newspapers have had to keep up with the wide use of visual design in all kinds of printed materials. And, finally, newspapers have had to confront the tremendous growth in competition among the media for consumers' attention.

Good design not only packages and visualizes news but also reflects the personality of a newspaper. Casual observers may decide what kind of paper is before them and what sort of community it represents simply by taking in its appearance at a glance.

Appealing to Your Reader's Eye

"The modern reader wants to see as much as he or she reads," writes Jose Quevedo, adviser to the award-winning *Falcon Times* of Miami–Dade

Community College North. The key question in planning your newspaper's design is Will this arrangement attract the reader's eye to every item in the newspaper and encourage full reading of the paper?

Examine daily newspapers in almost any region of the United States or Canada. Compare them with copies of the same papers from a few years ago, perhaps in library files. Virtually every newspaper has changed its design at least once during recent years.

A few decades ago, forward-looking newspapers were trumpeting their change from traditional conservative layouts, with their hard-to-read patterned pages and headlines made up of nothing but capital letters, to streamlined layouts that featured free-flowing arrangements and flush-left headlines in capital and lower-case letters. By the time many newspapers had come to adopt this format, others were looking toward packaging the news and experimenting with a variety of visual appeals.

These two issues of The New York Times, *from 1930 (left) and from 1984 (right), illustrate the kind of design evolution American newspapers have undergone. Visual appeal is now of paramount importance with layout artists.*

What are the main elements of this newer visual presentation? One is the packaging of related stories and photos, often within a border. A second is the departmentalization of different kinds of stories and articles. A third is a trend away from crowded pages, with fewer stories on each page. A fourth is a corresponding increase in white space around stories. A fifth is the use of rectangular story packages, with horizontal rectangles more frequent than vertical. A sixth is the extensive use of informational graphics, such as charts and maps. And a seventh is a move toward wider columns and more variations in column widths.

Deciding on Your Basic Design

You are likely to have reached the decision to follow modern trends in design. What, then, will the basic look of your newspaper be? The answer to this question comes first of all from the purposes and goals of your newspaper. What sorts of material do you wish to emphasize? If, for example, current and future news is your central focus, you will probably choose a typical tabloid-size or even a full-size daily newspaper page, packaging news under regular headlines. If your emphasis is on feature stories or interpretive, in-depth reports, you may turn to news magazine size and format and even to a pictorial cover.

Many modern school newspapers have achieved successful combinations of these two extremes, using tabloid pages in a variety of ways that point up feature stories and feature-like material. Some of these possibilities will be examined as the chapter continues.

Another major consideration will be the personality you wish your newspaper to have. Which design elements would best reflect serious attention to young people's concerns? Which would display your school's variety of activities? Which would be lighthearted, as befits the laughter and high spirits of high school years? Which would harmonize with an emphasis on students' academic growth and career interests? Just as every school possesses a different personality, your newspaper will be correspondingly different from others in its character. Your design should reflect that character.

A decision about the size of your newspaper's pages may be your first concern. This decision begins to answer the questions in the preceding paragraph.

Standard, or full-size, pages are uncommon in school papers but are sometimes the most practical at a print shop. Such a page invariably says "news" to readers. Six columns rather than the traditional eight are now most widely used. You can study a variety of daily newspapers to see design elements appropriate to this size page.

Tabloid pages, usually 11 by 17 inches, can focus on straight-news stories, on feature stories, on single major stories, or on a variety of material. They offer the most flexibility to school newspapers. Four columns are more likely in modern design than five.

Smaller news pages, ranging from just below tabloid size, through 8½-by-11-inch pages, to as small as 7-by-8½-inch pages, are sometimes the only

These school newspapers illustrate a standard-size (full-size) paper, a tabloid, and a smaller paper with a news magazine format. The size of a paper is linked to the kind of content presented and the personality displayed.

choices offered to a staff by its print shop. Such pages contain four, three, or only two columns. These sizes offer real design challenges, but with creativity and effort they can attractively present the news and feature the elements of your choice.

News magazine format became popular in some high schools 20 years ago. It is especially effective as a display for feature stories, interpretive, in-depth reports, and art. A typical news magazine format would have a pictorial cover, display its articles in magazine style on full pages or pairs of facing pages, make extensive use of white space as a design element, and avoid clutter even when several brief stories are combined on the same page. It would also be likely to feature unusual headlines and interesting artistic design elements, while placing ads on a few back pages. By the 1980s, a strong trend was developing toward application of these news magazine elements to tabloid pages.

The **magtab** (magazine-tabloid) is a newspaper printed on tabloid-size pages but folded and turned so that the front and back covers are vertical half-size pages. The front cover then employs news magazine design. The back cover may be sold as advertising or might include departmentalized material such as news briefs. The magtab offers some obvious advantages of both the tabloid and news magazine formats. Its major problem lies in making sure every reader will automatically turn from the cover to the appropriate full-size inside page.

Using Modulars to Package Your News

As you begin to visualize news on your pages, you will want to define a news package and see how it appears on newspaper or news magazine pages. A typical package might consist of four elements: the story, its headline, a photograph, and a caption. There could, of course, be variations—no photo or a related secondary story, for instance.

In traditional newspapers, the design for stories has always been vertical. A long story might sometimes extend down a full column length. The

The illustration on the left shows vertical newspaper design, such as can be found most often in traditional newspapers. The illustration on the right shows horizontal design, usually emphasized in contemporary papers.

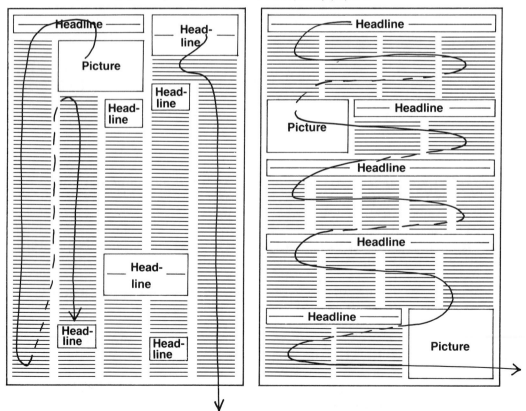

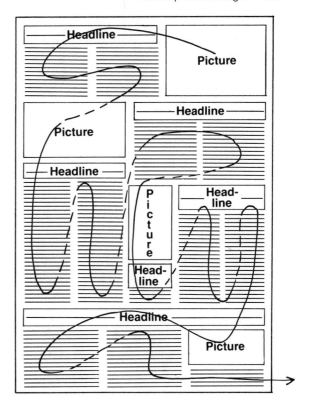

In modular design, news content is arranged in clean-looking rectangular packages, and these packages are, as far as possible, organized so that the reader's eye will move across and down the page.

total story package would look like an inverted L, starting at the top with two or three columns of headline, lead, and photo and then narrowing to a single column. The effect of this design is to lead a reader's eye down and off the page, often causing the reader to skip articles that are found in other columns.

The exact opposite, of course, would be a horizontal design. Each news package would appear under a banner-type headline that extends across the page, or the combination of story and photo would fill a section the width of the page. Here, the reader's eye might be carried off the right-hand side of the page. But since readers are accustomed to reading down as well as across, there would be a tendency for the eye to move to each lower article in turn.

This horizontal arrangement is one form of **modular design**—a design that places story packages in clean rectangular spaces, either horizontal or vertical. In a purely horizontal arrangement, each news package would fall within a rectangle extending across more than one column. The result would be totally unlike the inverted-L-shaped single column or the other irregular shapes found in the traditional vertical page structure. Modular rectangular shapes, whether horizontal or vertical, are the clear trend of newspaper design in the 1980s.

Obviously, pages containing all horizontal or all vertical rectangles would soon become monotonous to both the editorial staff and the readers. While the emphasis should remain on the horizontal modular, literally thousands of visually pleasing combinations may be designed.

In summary, modular design, sometimes called **structural design,** arranges page content into rectangular shapes, horizontal or vertical, that are placed into available space for the purpose of creating visual order. Each block or news package stands by itself and is visually attractive. The blocks do not wind around each other. Insofar as possible, the blocks or news packages should be arranged in such a way that a reader's eye will move across and down from the top to the bottom of the page, touching each story along its path.

Activity 1:   Developing a Sense of Newspaper Design

1. From a collection of school or daily newspapers, select two or three that you find especially attractive. Prepare a brief report explaining their visual appeal. Is it based on overall appearance, a clean look, use of photos or typographical devices, a balanced arrangement, artistic design, or some other factor? For each paper, list several of the elements that help make it attractive.

2. Redesign a page that you don't find visually attractive but that seems to you to have possibilities. Use a sketch to develop a visually appealing look. (You should be concerned here only with appearance, not with content.)

3. Do you feel that the design of your school paper fits the personality of your school? Explain your answer in a paragraph or two.

4. Redesign the front page of a recent issue of your school paper, making use of a modular arrangement. If the layout of this page was essentially vertical or seems to have no particular pattern, rearrange the stories, headlines, and photos into story packages that are either vertical or horizontal rectangles. If the page is already in modular form (horizontal, vertical, or a combination), choose another modular pattern for your new design. With a colored pencil, trace what you believe would be the path of the reader's eye on your revised page.

Designing the Pages

By this time you should have firm opinions as to the general design and size of your newspaper. You have considered how design and size relate to your paper's editorial goals and help establish its character in your school and community. You are beginning to understand why design is so important to the modern newspaper. Before working with actual page layouts, another aspect of design needs consideration. How will each page of your paper express its personality through appearance as well as content?

Because newspapers are meant primarily to be read rather than looked at, page design is less noticeable than design in the visual arts. Yet the visual impression of a newspaper page should be almost as carefully worked out as that of a work of sculpture.

—Photo by F. B. Grunzweig from Photo Researchers

Matching Your Front Page to Your Basic Design

It is your front page, of course, that most prominently displays the design principles you have chosen. This is the page that must tell your readers what kind of newspaper you are publishing. Here, also, you are likely to showcase your best writing. On this page, then, you have the best opportunity to create visual interest.

Typical front pages today present fewer stories than in earlier years. Three, four, or five major story packages, in addition to the paper's name, may appear here in contrast to the eight or 10 stories that could be crowded in if they were shorter or less significant.

Column widths may often be varied as you plan your front page story packages. One horizontal package could have four or five columns, while the next might have only three. The size and shape of an accompanying photo often dictates these choices. Similarly, side-by-side vertical packages could have different column widths for better visual display of their con-

THE CHRISTIAN SCIENCE MONITOR

COPYRIGHT © 1984 THE CHRISTIAN SCIENCE PUBLISHING SOCIETY
All rights reserved   VOL. 76, NO. 34   AN INTERNATIONAL DAILY NEWSPAPER   FRIDAY, JANUARY 13, 1984   R   A TWO SECTION PAPER   40¢ (50¢ Canadian)

SPRING TRAVEL
Small Paris
museums, the
wonders of Rome,
country inns **B1**

DUCK MOTIF
Crystal, brass,
pewter, and carved
ducks are the
latest rage **21**

One economist who wants tighter federal grip on US economy

By David R. Francis
Staff writer of The Christian Science Monitor

New York

Economist Wassily Leontief has a favorite image for talking about the economy. He likens it to a sailboat.

"The problem of guiding the economy is like sailing," he says. "You need the wind and a rudder. The wind is the private profit motive. The rudder is government influence."

The New York University professor continues: "The Russians have a big rudder, but have completely lost the wind." In contrast, President Reagan has put a big sail on the American economy and the wind is blowing hard. "But if he doesn't use the rudder he will end up on the rocks."

With that image, Dr. Leontief supports some modest degree of state planning.

"Planning," he says, "can never replace initiative, but initiative can never replace planning."

Many economists nowadays avoid the word "planning" — if they're in favor of it. It is a word with so many connotations and preconceptions that many Americans automatically turn off when an economist advocates it. They know that planning has failed to produce prosperity in communist countries and want nothing of it here. So economists talk of a "national industrial policy" or "reindustrialization," which involve some degree of government intervention in the economy.

Please see **LEONTIEF** back page

1985 budget dodges deficit action

By David T. Cook
Staff writer of The Christian Science Monitor

Washington

Huge federal budget deficits may scare economists and corporate executives. But Ronald Reagan apparently has decided the United States can tolerate them for at least one more year.

The President's proposed budget for fiscal year 1985 will not be officially unveiled until Feb. 1. But leaks from a variety of meetings the President has held make it clear that Mr. Reagan will propose only very modest spending cuts and no significant tax hikes for the coming budget year.

The bottom line on the administration's budget projections shows deficits hovering in the $200 billion range through fiscal 1987.

The President's well-advertised plans make chances for congressional action on the deficit even more remote than was already the case. For example, Senate Finance Committee chairman Robert Dole (R) of Kansas, a key advocate of congressional deficit-trimming action, is considering scaling back the scope of a Finance Committee package to clip the deficit by $150 billion over four years, aides say.

But Senator Dole warned this week that deficits "must be faced before they consume the country in an ocean of red ink and debt-service costs."

Although some conservative supporters of the President oppose tax hikes, bipartisan support for comprehensive deficit-trimming action appears to be growing. A call for quick action to control the deficits — using a package of spending cuts and tax hikes — was issued Thursday by the Committee to Fight Inflation, a bipartisan group of former government officials whose co-chairman is Herbert Stein, chairman of the Council of Economic Advis-

ers under President Nixon.

"In my opinion," Dr. Stein says, the deficit situation "is really frightening and deserves urgent consideration."

And a new Wall Street Journal poll found that six out of 10 executives at large- and medium-size companies think the deficit is the nation's biggest economic problem, and a majority think the President should do more to tackle the problem.

Please see **DEFICIT** page 6

TWO VIEWS OF THE FEDERAL BUDGET

In billions of dollars Numbers in parentheses represent dollar figure as a percent of gross national product.	Reagan Administration	Congressional Budget Office
1983 Receipts	$601 (18.6%)	$601 (18.6%)
Outlays	796 (24.6)	796 (24.6)
Deficit	195 (6.0)	195 (6.0)
1984* Receipts	669 (18.8)	665 (18.7)
Outlays	853 (24.5)	850 (23.9)
Deficit	184 (5.6)	185 (5.2)
1985* Receipts	738 (19.0)	733 (18.8)
Outlays	924 (24.1)	925 (23.8)
Deficit	186 (5.1)	192 (4.9)
1986* Receipts	805 (19.0)	796 (18.9)
Outlays	1,000 (23.9)	993 (23.5)
Deficit	195 (4.9)	197 (4.7)

FISCAL YEAR   * Projections
Sources: Congressional Budget Office, Lawrence Kurflow & Associates

Soviets harden stance before Stockholm

By Gary Thatcher
Staff writer of The Christian Science Monitor

Moscow

"We still have a leader who's firmly in control. We aren't softening our stance, and don't expect us to any time soon."

That seems to be the message coming from behind the walls of the Kremlin just days before two important events: the meeting of top United States and Soviet diplomats in Stockholm, and a major address on US-Soviet relations by President Ronald Reagan.

This rhetorical preemptive strike came in typically Soviet fashion — in a statement by Soviet leader Yuri Andropov issued by Tass, the official news agency, and in an article in Pravda, the official Soviet Communist

West unites on tactics at Stockholm, page 7

Party newspaper.

Taken together, they left no doubt that the Soviet Union is holding to its hard-line stance on negotiations over medium-range nuclear weapons in Europe. Further, they seemed to be aimed at quashing hopes for an early thaw in frigid relations between the two superpowers.

The Soviet Union walked out on negotiations over intermediate-range nuclear weapons last November. Shortly afterward, it threw two other sets of talks — on long-range intercontinental nuclear weapons and on conventional forces in Europe — into limbo by refusing to set dates for resumption.

Since then, the Soviet Union has blamed the US for the breakdown of the talks, arguing that the stationing of

Please see **STANCE** back page

Freestyle format promises lively Democratic debate, but Mondale is concerned

By John Dillin
Staff writer of The Christian Science Monitor

Washington

When Walter Mondale's staff members learned about the format for this Sunday's Democratic presidential debate, they were not pleased.

"We believe the voters want to hear a serious discussion of the issues. We don't think voters want to be entertained as if this were some kind of TV show," one top Mondale worker complains.

Such concern may be understandable. Mr. Mondale, who has steadily widened his lead over the seven other Democratic candidates, clearly has the most to lose in

Seven candidates at Harvard debate in October — plus, this Sunday, Jesse Jackson.

the debate to be broadcast nationwide (Sunday on PBS-TV, 3-6 p.m. EST). The program, sponsored by the House Democratic Caucus, features a "free form" style which could result in one of the

liveliest political performances in years. Even the audience may take part.

"It's a gamble, a leap of faith," to put on a show of this kind, says US Rep. Charles E. Schumer, the Brooklyn Demo-

crat who was the prime mover behind the debate. "We're trying to explore new ground" while avoiding the "very, very tedious" style of formal presidential debates, he says.

The first 90 minutes will be moderated by Ted Koppel, anchor man of ABC-TV's "Nightline" news program. Organizers are hoping that Mr. Koppel will keep the debate moving along at a brisk pace, while "not letting any of the candidates get away with anything."

The second 90 minutes will be turned over to TV personality Phil Donahue. His job will be to draw questions and com-

Please see **DEBATE** page 6

Variation in the number and width of columns in a news package partly accounts for the attractiveness of this front page of The Christian Science Monitor. *The front page of a newspaper can do much to reveal the paper's personality.*

tent. Study professional tabloid-size newspapers such as *The Christian Science Monitor* for interesting use of varied column widths.

Many tabloid newspapers that feature interpretive, in-depth reporting print one major story of this type as the lead article on the front page. This allows them to display prominently an interesting or timely topic. The story package may occupy one third or more of the page. The entire page can even be devoted to this article, with news items moved inside. Such an arrangement offers real possibilities for an exciting and creative display that carries a high level of visual appeal. You might consider a group of photos, a magazine-type headline, and extensive use of white space surrounding the copy.

Your **nameplate,** which gives the name of your newspaper in large type, is a significant part of your front page design. Since it is your trademark, its format may be fixed and unchanging, or it may be redesigned in accord with a new general plan. You may meet considerable resistance from your readers if you change it often, however. Readers tend to appreciate stability and to resist change in such things.

The nameplate usually extends across about three fifths of the width of a school newspaper page. A nameplate this size can be moved anywhere on the top half of the page (above the fold), allowing great flexibility in lay-

Each of these four attractive nameplates includes a folio line, which gives the name of the paper's sponsoring school, the city and state, the date of the issue, and the volume and issue number.

—*The Spirit,* Truman High School, Independence, Missouri; *The Lion,* Lyons Township High School, LaGrange and Western Springs, Illinois; *Sequoia Times,* Sequoia High School, Redwood City, California; *The Panther Press,* Griffith High School, Griffith, Indiana

out. If you do move it from issue to issue, your nameplate will be what is technically known as a **floating nameplate.** A nameplate may also occupy the full page width, either at the top of the page or below one horizontal story package. When space permits, you can place boxes known as **ears** on one or both sides of the newspaper's name. These little boxes might advertise features on inside pages, for instance.

Your nameplate is not complete without a **folio line**—one or more lines of small type that include the name of your school, the city and state, the full date of the issue, and perhaps the volume and issue number. (A similar but briefer folio line should appear on each of the other pages, as described on page 374.)

Creating Exciting Inside Page Designs

You may have spent hours working out an attractive, eye-catching front page design, picking your very best news and feature stories to showcase on that page. Everything else can be dropped somewhere on the inside pages—right?

Wrong! Each inside page should have a personality of its own, fitting within the personality of the total newspaper. Entertainment pages should be bold and eye-catching, to reflect their content. Sports pages should be active and exciting. Editorial pages should have a look that is serious but not dull. Feature story pages should attract readers to their unusual topics. Even an inside news page can look almost as exciting as the front page.

The back cover may be the first page to consider after the front page. If yours is a four-page paper, this is probably the place for sports stories. Should you have more than four pages, you will need to decide which important department fits easily on a single page.

As you plan inside pages, design each pair of **facing pages** (pages that appear across from each other) together. A pair of sports pages can be exciting and eye-catching. The editorial page may be effectively complemented by an op-ed page that extends the presentation of student opinions. Two news or two entertainment pages offer opportunities for balancing story packages. Even if space limits you to a single page per department, bright and similar facing-page designs can complement each other and build up reader interest.

Then there are the unlimited possibilities offered by the **centerfold,** the facing pages in the center of the paper, sometimes called a **doubletruck.** Here you can often print across the center, or **gutter,** so that the two pages can be designed as a single horizontal modular. This may be the place for a theme page or a special set of feature stories. With this amount of space, you can print several articles and a group of photos on the same general topic—perhaps basic facts plus a variety of opinions on a subject of high teen-age concern or controversy. Or you could showcase a long interpretive, in-depth report along with shorter, related articles. You might package all of the material into a single horizontal rectangle, using white space to em-

This is how one paper made use of the centerfold as a showcase. A set of feature stories, an interpretive, in-depth report, or a group of related articles and photos are just a few of the ways to make use of a centerfold's spaciousness.

phasize the elements. Your yearbook staff's source book of sample facing pages can help you design your centerfold, since many yearbook pages are planned in similar, though smaller, pairs.

Many of the inside pages—usually not the editorial page or the centerfold—must be designed to accommodate advertising. The typical arrangement of ads, as will be noted in Chapter 19, is a stairstep down the outside of the page. This makes modular packaging difficult. Often you must simply consider some of the ads as a visual part of a modular unit, arranging your copy around them to complete the rectangle.

Newspapers that emphasize full horizontal modulars often place all ads within a horizontal rectangle across the bottom of the page. This violates the general rule that every ad should touch copy, but it seems to improve the visual appeal of the page to such a point that all the ads will be read anyway.

Designing inside news pages may seem a difficult project, since the makeup worker will sometimes have only "leftover" stories. Some of these can be featured in major news packages similar to those on the front page. Other shorter news paragraphs can be combined into a package of news briefs. Such a package deserves a significant headline and at least one photo. Each paragraph should also have a short one- or two-line headline that makes a newsworthy statement. A mere label is not enough. Sometimes an effective head can be created by capitalizing the first few words of the paragraph or by placing them in boldface type. These words should reflect the key thought, though.

Making the Editorial Page Stand Out

After your front page, the most distinctive page in your newspaper should be your editorial page. This is the page that reveals your newspaper's spirit—light or serious, focused on hard news or on teen-age concerns, shallow or deep in reporting, narrow or broad in presentation of opinions. If your paper is large enough that an op-ed page faces the editorial page, the two should be designed together so that they will be similar in both content and appearance.

Your editorials should stand out. One or more editorials will normally appear in the upper-left corner of the page, typically in larger type than normal and generally in a wider column. If your pages have five columns, the editorial column may be double width. If four columns are your standard pattern, then the editorial column should still be wider than the others, perhaps one and one-half columns. With such a style, you will need to create a variety of column widths for the other modular packages on the page.

Headlines on editorial and op-ed pages are often printed in a lighter type than news headlines to add another distinctive element. They might also be in italics if your other headlines are not.

The publishing information that makes up the newspaper's masthead should be placed in a bottom corner of the editorial page, usually in a rectangular box. It should include the following: the newspaper's name, the school's full name, the complete school address, the newspaper's phone number, the editor's name and the names either of departmental editors or of the entire staff, the adviser's name, and a statement of frequency of publication.

Some newspapers also include a sentence or two summarizing the paper's editorial policy, especially when there is a desire to indicate the sources of published student opinions. Others cite their memberships and awards from press associations. Finally, the masthead is the place for any required legal statements, such as registration for second-class mail or other postage privileges.

April 15, 1983 THE EPITAPH

2 **OPINION**

Acts, not words

Acta non verba.

Translating as "Deeds, not words," this is Homestead's motto.

But evidently the school and the district need words to spur them to action.

The report published by the visiting accreditation committee fulfills this purpose. Administrators and teachers alike should carefully heed its recommendations if they hope for improvement in some of the school's wretched conditions.

Four issues dominate the report's life of major recommendations: poor relations between faculty and administration, curriculum development, guidance and scheduling.

A school cannot run effectively while a schism exists between its workers and its supervisors. Teachers and administrators should learn to cooperate with minimal friction.

Boundary changes resulting from the closure of Sunnyvale High have altered the nature of the student population, and the administration should adjust curriculum accordingly.

Guidance at all five schools has become a poor joke on the part of the district with a warped sense of humor. Counselors should return.

The administration has replaced the slow, clumsy mill system of scheduling, but the price of efficiency h
The present system often tramples upon stude
needs, and administrators should work to reme
tion. (Counselors would help immeasurably.)

Deeds, not words.

Unfortunately, this motto seems all too appr

Schwartz Illustrated/Jon Schwartz

Keep the memory alive

Relief for park

Finally, someone has taken action to alleviat
parking problem.

With the help of the Cupertino City Council,
mittee studying the issue devised a plan to c
parking spaces.

The initiative taken by the members of the
tee, juniors Stefan Kertesz, Doug Chang and
deserves applause, and the cooperation of the C
Council, especially Councilman John Plungy, ha
able.

The committee needs to see its plan thro
same determination that led to its formation. W
who launched the plan succeed in easing the
lem.

Analysis/Chimaine White

Presidenti

What do an ex-governor, an ex-vice-president and three senators have in common? They would all like to be President of the United States of America.

These five democrats are all hoping to become their party's candidate in 1984. To win that nomination, they must begin their campaign this early, almost a full year before the first caucus or primary and 20 months before the election.

The favorite is Walter Mondale, the widely-known vice-president to Jimmy Carter and middle-of-the-road democrat.

Next in line is Alan Cranston, the outspoken 68-year-old California senator who was also the first to announce his candidacy over two months ago.

The ex-governor is Reubin Askew of Florida, self-proclaimed dark horse in the race. Many see him trying to follow Carter's footsteps from obscurity.

National hero and Ohio senator John Glenn will not formally make

his bid until later t
he has expressed hi
ially and is already
ardently along with

The last is Gary
senator from Color
the youngest of th
the hardest to defi

A blend of cons
liberal stands, Hart
an exciting and har
tical innovator.

Elect '84

Hart is best kno
derboy technician
Govern's long-shot
presidency in 1972
feated in the electi
came to personify
alism, largely throu
work.

Hart is highly re
John F. Kennedy.
handsome and out
a book soon to be

PAGE 4 THE ORANGE R DECEMBER 16, 1982

editorials

Are video games harmful?

Are video games really harmful?

The reasons behind the great opposition to video games are totally ridiculous and unfounded.

Video games are simply a form of recreational activity just like any other. The fact that they are enjoyed by a staggering amount of people worldwide does not make them any more harmful than other recreational sports and activities.

Take basketball for instance. Few people, if any, complain about the harmful effects of basketball. It's simply a sport where players can let out their frustrations. Another reason is for pure enjoyment.

Those in opposition of video games claim that it is simply money going to waste. Like any form of entertainment it does require money. What about, then, the $3.50 spent for a two-hour movie?

Like sports, video games serve as an emotional outlet. They let out frustrations. They can also serve as a creative outlet, leading to an interest in learning to program games. In addition, video games serve to teach greater hand-eye coordination.

The level of violence in shooting down enemy ships and gobbling up dots does not make you want to go out and kill someone. The level of "violence" in video games could be compared to the level of "violence" in a football game. Certainly the level of violence by physical contact in a football game is much more exemplified, and yet there are few complaints about the aggressive nature of football.

Media in all forms is constantly exhibiting a level of violence much more realistic than that portrayed in video games. To claim that video games go against moral influences and to blame them for increasing levels of violence is yet unproven.

Orange R

The **Orange R** is published every three weeks, except during holidays and exam periods, by the Journalism II class of Roseburg Senior High School, 547 West Chapman Dr., Roseburg, Oregon 97470. Telephone 503/440-4173. Member of Oregon and National Scholastic Press Association and Quill & Scroll Society.
1979-82 NSPA All-American
1981-82 Regional Pacemaker Award

Editor	Diane Victoria
Opinion Editor	Carisa Cegavske
News Editor	John Politte
Sports Editor	Scott Burks
Advertising Manager	Melissa Baker
Business Manager	Brandi Black
Circulation Manager	Kevin Mooneyham
Photo Editor	Kelly Smothers
Production Team	Cindy Dunaway
	Kevin Mooneyham
	Mike Vaughn
Photographers	Lantz Shapiro
	Kelly Smothers
	Randy Thacker
	Scott Ylitalo
	CJ Brown
Reporters	Brad Collins
	Julie Durand
	Julie Graber
	Patty Kwon
	John Rehm
	Suzanne Verkoren
	Kela West
	Adam Rasmussen
Adviser	Rob Melton

Letters to be published in the next Orange R should be received no later than Jan. 7. Unsigned letters will not be published, but will be accepted as sources for further information

Is the Christmas spirit lost?

PATTY KWON

The very first Christmas on Earth was certainly not like the modern Christmases today. Its tale is told in the Bible as the birth of Jesus Christ. There was a very special meaning then that is rarely present today.

What is the true meaning of Christmas?

The true meaning of Christmas can be found in the purpose of why the original day of Christmas was celebrated.

Christmas marks the day when Jesus Christ was born and continues to be celebrated as a remembrance of this occasion. When the three wise men traveled afar to Bethelem, they bore as their gifts their greatest possessions—frankincense, gold and myrrh.

Christmas today has continued to stand for an occasion of remembrance yet it has a different meaning. People use Christmas as a time of year to remember others and it has gained a sentimental value. The tradition started by the three wise men continues on, as Christmas has become a time of presents under a lighted Christmas tree and of merriment.

Children remember Christmas the most as wishing for toys and other goodies. Santa Claus was invented for the very purpose of bringing presents to good little boys and girls. There are sentimental tales of hanging clean stockings over the fireplace to find them stuffed with surprises on Christmas morn.

Christmas brings a sense of family as well. It seems to draw others closer. Relatives from all over come to visit and bring good cheer.

It's a time for holly and kissing under the mistletoe. It's a time to go out and haul back a Christmas tree to decorate with ornaments and popcorn strings.

Certainly the first Christmas wasn't like this. As Christmas changed throughout the years, has the true meaning of Christmas been lost as well?

As people go Christmas shopping, gift giving often loses its value. People buy gifts simply to receive gifts in return. They stop thinking about how happy their gifts will make others and place more importance on the price tags. People forget to realize that it's the thought, not the gift, that counts.

In the midst of all this Christmas rush, people often forget the true meaning of Christmas. It's a time to gather with friends and relatives but it's also a time of remembrance. The purpose of the very first Christmas remains true today and it is to celebrate the birth of Christ.

Finding the impossible gift

DIANE VICTORIA

It's that time of year again. Everyone is running around asking for all sorts of gifts that they hope they will be opening on that very special magic day. But do they really know the torture the thoughtful gift giver goes through to get the gift?

I start out with the headache of spending long hours asking myself "What should I get them?"

After not getting any answer I decide to take my life into my own hands and go out into the mad world of —CHRISTMAS SHOPPERS. The Christmas shopper is one who runs through the mall in a hurry looking for bargains, singing Christmas carols and reminding themselves how many days they have left.

I stand just inside the doors of the mall watching these frantic people as they go a bout their business, wondering where I should start.

I go into stores looking up and down the aisle seeing people pushing to get the last home video game or cuddling up with an ET doll.

After hours of shopping that proved to be somewhat successful, only because I bought things that I wanted so that I could borrow them, my dreaded Christmas shopping is done.

Blood—an odd thing to give

KEVIN MOONEYHAM

Of all the nice things you can do for another person, giving blood is positively the oddest. I say odd because while donating blood is a great way to "give of yourself" it can also be downright scary. This is especially true if you've never given before. Usually a person can ask a friend what it's like but that's not always a good idea, as in the case of the following dialogue.

Bill— Whatcha been doin'?

Joe— I just gave blood.

Bill— Wow! What was it like?

Joe— Well, first this lady asked me all these questions like my name and address. Then I had to fill out a medical background paper. Then they tested me to see if it was ok for me to give.

Bill— How did you do?

Joe— Pretty good, the nurse said something about an A positive. You know that's the first A I've gotten this year. Anyway, then they had me drink some Tang.

Bill— Hey, didn't the astronauts drink Tang? Did they give blood in space?

Joe— Gee, I don't know. Well after that I had to wait around for awhile.

Bill— What for?

Joe— I'm not sure. I think it's so anyone who wants to chicken out has time to get away.

Bill— That makes sense.

Joe— Finally it was my turn. The nurse made me lie down on a fancy lawn chair and she took my blood pressure. Then she took this big long needle and after she found my vein she stuck me with it. All the blood started running through this little tube, kind of like a crazy straw...

Bill— I gotta go, Joe. I think I hear my mom calling me. Bye!

Joe— Hey, wait, I haven't got to the good part yet.

Actually giving blood is not at all like that so next time you get a chance why not give a pint. It'll make ya feel good and besides that, it's a great Christmas present.

—*The Epitaph*, Homestead High School, Cupertino, California (top); *Orange R*, Roseburg Senior High School, Roseburg, Oregon (bottom)

Italic and lighter type headlines are typical of editorial and op-ed pages. The use of wide columns is also common on editorial pages.

Activity 2: Working with Page Designs

1. Compare the design of your school paper's front page, as it now exists, with the front pages of a variety of school and daily newspapers. Make suggestions as to how you believe your own paper's front page could be improved.

2. If the front page of the last issue of your paper contains five or more stories, redesign it to showcase only three of these in modular packages. If there are two, three, or four stories, try a story package that displays just one major topic. If the page only contains one lead story, select two or three more from inside pages and present all of them in modular packages. If the front page is only a cover, design a page with at least three stories.

3. Choose one or more departmental pages (entertainment, sports, feature stories) and redesign the material to display modern packaging as well as to reflect a real personality for this department.

4. Take two facing pages from a recent issue of your school paper that do not seem to have been designed with each other in mind and redesign them so they complement each other visually.

5. Make suggestions for improving the appearance of your editorial or op-ed page. Redesign either one or both of these pages.

Understanding Typography and Graphic Art

The final major aspect of design is made up of the actual devices that appear on a printed page. These include such things as type, borders, boxes, charts, maps, graphs, and other artistic designs.

The words **typography** and **graphics** are generally interchangeable in a broad sense. Typographical devices enhance verbal content. They also communicate directly through their own visual content. Another of their purposes is to attract attention. Finally, they add to a newspaper's visual appeal. Typographical devices that do not serve one of these four purposes represent poor design. They may even turn a reader away from your pages. A common error is to include too many special devices, with the result that they either cancel each other out or result in a cluttered, disorganized appearance.

Understanding Type and Type Families

A **type family** includes a number of styles for the letters of the alphabet, all based on the same original design. A family might include, for example, **roman type** ("normal" letters), italics, boldface type, lightface type, condensed type, and expanded type.

Each of these styles, or **typefaces,** comes in several sizes. The following example shows a popular typeface called Times Roman printed in various sizes, which are measured in points (a measurement that is explained below).

8-point Times Roman

9-point Times Roman

10-point Times Roman

12-point Times Roman

14-point Times Roman

18-point Times Roman

24-point Times Roman

36-point Times Roman

When choosing a typeface for your newspaper, you will also need to understand the distinction between **serif** and **sans-serif** styles. Serifs are the little lines projecting from the ends of letters. The text you are reading right now is printed in a serif style. Sans-serif styles have no little lines added.

SERIF: T S R   SANS SERIF: T S R

Serif is often seen as more readable for text type, or **body type.** Sans serif is useful for headlines, captions, and such things as box scores.

While hundreds of typefaces are available, only a few are suitable for newspaper pages aside from advertisements and other special applications. Roy Paul Nelson, in his book *Publication Design*, lists a number of those that are particularly suitable for newspapers: Baskerville, Bodoni, Caslon, Clarendon, Garamond, Helvetica, and Times Roman.

When you are considering type sizes, measuring the length of a line of type, or deciding how much vertical space a story will occupy in a column, you will be dealing with printer's measurements. A pica is one sixth of an inch. This unit will be applied to all vertical and horizontal measurements on a printed page. One pica equals 12 points, making a total of 72 points per inch. Type sizes are measured in points.

For your basic body type, a simple serif face is most readable. Newspaper body type is typically 8 or 9 points high. The lines should be **leaded** (pronounced "led-ed"), or separated, by 1 or 2 extra points of space, called **leading.** Ten-point type can be used for editorials and special articles.

The following examples show 9-point type with no leading, with 1 point of leading, and with 2 points of leading.

This is a paragraph of 9-point Times Roman type set solid—without any leading between the lines.

This is a paragraph of 9-point Times Roman type set with 1 point of leading between the lines. This would be called 9-on-10-point.

This is a paragraph of 9-point Times Roman type set with 2 points of leading between the lines. This would be called 9-on-11-point.

As to the width of lines of body type, readability surveys have indicated that the traditional 12-pica newspaper column width is not ideal. According to the surveys, column widths from 14 to 19 picas are the ones preferred by readers. Though a paper should have a single standard column width, it may be varied to fit your modular packages and to increase the overall visual appeal.

The printing tradition of **justified lines**—lines that are even on the right-hand side as well as on the left—is also breaking down. According to surveys, readers are just as satisfied with unjustified lines as long as the column in which they appear is at least 14 picas wide. For narrower columns, though, such as columns of 10 or 12 picas, they find that justified lines are easier to read.

You should also choose a single type family for all basic headlines. Normally, this will be a clean sans-serif type, such as Helvetica. You might use boldface type on news pages and lightface type on the editorial page. A few headlines in italics will also provide contrast to the more prevalent use of roman type in headlines.

Most of the headlines on this page are sans serif. The occasional use of serif, in the folio line at the top of the page and at the top of the two boxes, adds interest without subtracting from the clean, basic look.

Emphasizing with Rules and Boxes

Straight lines can add much to your paper's visual appeal. Today, most lines, or **rules,** appear in the form of borders, or **boxes,** placed around individual stories, modular packages, or even entire pages. They serve to frame the material they surround and to focus attention on the complete package. They also help to emphasize the white space that is found inside the box.

The main purpose of a box is to call attention to the enclosed material. In this regard, it should have a functional relationship to the story. A heavy black rule was sometimes used in the past to enclose and designate an obituary; a decorative border was sometimes used to indicate a romantic tale. Today, though, this kind of emphasis would be indicated by the typography within the box.

Several guidelines are helpful in designing boxes. First, neatness is absolutely essential. The border should be plain and simple. A thin rule is adequate. A river of white space, 1½ to 3 picas wide, should separate the box from the headline, illustration, and text within the box. There should also be more white space between the headline and text and within the text itself than normal, perhaps in the form of larger type or more leading.

While the use of boxes must be disciplined, some creativity is permissible. Rounded corners are quite acceptable. A box may also be broken to accentuate a headline element. A rule at the top might be broken to fit in a kicker, or a left-hand rule might be broken for a side headline. In fact, there

A nicely restrained use of creativity can be seen in this box. Notice particularly the use of rounded corners and the break at the top to accentuate the headline. Here the kicker was placed outside the box.

—X-Ray, St. Charles High School, St. Charles, Illinois

TV studio

Cable set-up may come here

by Vicki Kaspar

CABLE TELEVISION may be coming to St. Charles and Geneva as the cities will be accepting proposals from cable t.v. companies Nov. 30. The franchise will be awarded to the company with the lowest bid that best meets the needs of the communities and their residents.

"There's a possibility a t.v. studio will be provided for St. Charles High School, as part of the cable company's agreement," said Tim Triplett, Editor of The Chronicle. If so, the company will provide all necessary equipment and assistance needed.

"Although this was put in as an extra, there's a good chance that they'll get the studio at the high school. This will be a good way to get students involved in broadcasting," stated Bill Birth, Administrative Services Manager of the City of St. Charles.

CABLE TELEVISION studios have been set up in high schools such as Downers Grove North and East Lansing, Michigan, a "model cable high school." A crew of 25 students at Downers Grove North programs up to five hours of air time six days a week, and the concept has been successful. "It's working pretty well and it's a good experience for everyone," stated one Downers Grove student.

"We judge companies by their responses to the Request For Proposals (terms and conditions set forth by Geneva and St. Charles)," said Mr. Birth.

A centralized facility will be located in St. Charles containing the cable company's head-end, necessary facilities and

EQUIPMENT for local production and presentation of programs will be available, at no extra cost to the public, and the cable operator shall permit its use for production and presentation of public access programs as well as educational, library, and hospital access programming.

A special cable is being proposed (institutional loop) which would link the schools, library, and hospitals together in an effort to promote interactive programming. "This way we can share programs. They can be broadcast here and received at other schools and libraries," said Mike Hill, head of the St. Charles H.S. media center.

An educational and library access channel will be made available for the use of schools and one channel will be provided for carrying each local television station in Kane, DuPage, and Cook counties. "The schools will receive full hook-ups (basic channels) and will be able to watch congressional hearings, etc. on more specialized stations," said Hill.

AS OF NOW, nothing's really been decided. Upon completion of the final evaluation process, which will include public hearings, the city councils will announce the successful applicant and award the franchises. The company will then file, within 60 days, the documents required to obtain all licenses and permits. Within 90 days, the company will provide the city with a construction schedule and every two months after the start of construction will report on the progress until the system is complete.

operating equipment, but will serve both Geneva and St. Charles. St. Charles is considering locating its public safety facilities in a shared-use building at this site, also.

will be times when a half box or three fourths of a box will be more effective than a full box. Finally, you may, if you wish, box an entire page instead of an individual package to pull all of the content together.

Single straight rules, once the standby on traditional pages, rarely appear in the modern newspaper. Vertical rules between columns have been replaced by 1 or 2 picas of white space or by an occasional rule that is part of a box. Horizontal lines used merely to indicate a story's conclusion are also rare. Sometimes, however, an **end rule** across several columns or even across your entire page may be a deliberate part of your design plan. Such rules may appear above and below your nameplate or below folio lines on any page. Horizontal rules instead of boxes may be your choice for visual separation of your modular packages as well.

Enhancing Design with Graphics

Strictly speaking, the term **graphic arts** covers the entire field of printing design, the general subject of this chapter. The following paragraphs will describe a rather limited area of graphic arts, that concerned with adding visual impact through special type, type materials, and art.

Sometimes unusually large letters, numbers, or even short words can create pictures of their own. For instance, in a question-and-answer feature story, huge Q. and A. letters could start paragraphs. A big YES and NO, or PRO and CON, could signal pairs of opinions. Large type could also be used for the first letter of the first word in each section of a long story to call attention to new sections. Such **initial letters** are usually more appropriate in magazines. If you do use them, each initial letter should be in the same typeface as the story's headline and must lead easily into the remainder of the first word.

The **standing heads,** or **logos,** that signal the titles of departmental pages or columns may also use type in creative ways, with or without added art work. This is one place where a non-newspaper type family may be suitable, since each logo, whether it signals the title of a department, a regularly appearing type of feature story, or a column, must be distinctive and have its own personality.

A **pulled quote**—one or two significant sentences from the story reprinted in larger type and set in a box or between rules to accompany the story—is a good graphic device when properly used. Pulled quotes do present makeup problems, however. For one thing, the reader may be attracted only to the quotes and not to the story. Then, if a pulled quote is positioned in the middle of a column of type, a reader's eye may hit it and bounce back to the top of the next column instead of continuing past the quote to the remainder of the story. For that reason, a pulled quote is best at the top or bottom of a story's columns.

Occasionally, an interesting effect can be obtained by printing over a lightly shaded **tint block** of gray. The gray must be very light, however, or it will interfere with legibility. Should you have a second color available, a light tint block of color can be even more attractive.

Reverse type—white letters on a black background—is creative and unusual but poses problems unless used prudently. Reverse type is hard to read unless the letters are large. It is best for headlines, pulled quotes, or other brief, special material. In addition, you should never use either type or reverse type over a photograph. A reader simply will not struggle through the variations in shading to discover what is said.

Type set in an unusual form, perhaps in the shape of a football or a crown or simply on a diagonal or curved line, can be visually interesting when well done. It may not, however, be easy to read. As Edmund Arnold points out in *Modern Newspaper Design*, "Anything that's hard to set or make up is hard to read!"

Graphs, such as a bar graph to illustrate the progress of a United Way campaign or a pie graph showing the numbers of summer jobs for teen-agers, are easy to draw and quite effective in any newspaper. Daily papers also employ maps frequently to show where something happened. Maps are usually small, perhaps one column wide, and extremely simple. You might sketch a map to show the location of the new parking lot or a proposed shopping center, for instance.

Small clever sketches are another graphic possibility that add visual appeal to dull areas of a page. Photographs are more appropriate to news pages, however.

Two principles should control your use of graphic devices. One is that you can be creative and experimental, using your imagination freely, as long as the graphics add to the appearance and impact of each story. The other is that too many graphic devices or overuse of any one device will limit or even destroy readability. As with all other typography, there is one rule to follow: Keep it simple.

Activity 3: Evaluating Typography

1. Identify the typeface, size, and leading of the body type now employed in your school paper. Compare its appearance with that of other newspapers, school or daily. What judgments can you make as to its looks and readability?

2. Make a 50-pica rule for your personal use by marking inches along the edge of a piece of cardboard and dividing each inch into six parts. Measure the column widths in your newspaper as well as in other papers that look attractive to you. Again, what judgments can you make about appearance and readability?

3. Identify the typeface and sizes of your newspaper's major headlines. Do you like their appearance? Give reasons for your answer.

4. Study the way boxes and rules are used in your school paper and in other newspapers. What suggestions for visual improvement can you make?

5. List other graphic devices employed in recent issues of your paper. Suggest ways in which type, typographical materials, graphs, or maps might have enhanced the visual appearance of specific articles or pages.

Laying Out Your Pages

Makeup is ultimately for the convenience of readers. Two preliminary steps will make the actual job of laying out pages for the current issue of your newspaper easier. First, your plan for designing the newspaper as a whole, as well as the individual pages, must be creatively and carefully completed. Second, long before major stories are written, their location in the paper should be determined by your editorial staff. If these steps are carried out, reporters can write their stories to specified lengths, the proper photographs can be taken, and headlines can be prepared to fit the anticipated spots on the pages.

A **page dummy**—a sketch showing where each story is to be placed—should be prepared for each page. Your advertising manager should start the dummy by arranging the advertisements. If it turns out that you have too much material for a page, you will need to cut stories, not paid advertisements, since ads involve contracts or business agreements.

Positioning the Stories

Like any other skill, good makeup takes know-how and practice. While it may seem complicated at first, it will become easier as you continue working at it and learn the tricks of the trade. Beyond the principles listed here, you will find more specific directions in the Editor's Handbook on pages 473–474. Other guidelines may come from your printer and editorial staff.

For a starter, you should carefully follow your general design, as well as the specific plan for a particular issue, arranging articles into story packages and fitting the packages on your dummy. Certain principles, in addition to the general guidelines already presented in this chapter, will govern your work.

First is the focal point, or **center of visual impact (CVI),** for a given page. When your editors planned the content of the page, they are likely to have decided on one lead story. Its package should appear somewhere in the upper third of the page (but never above the nameplate). If yours is a tabloid newspaper, the lead story's headline will probably be in 48-point type. Its package should form the page's center of visual impact.

Next, you need to establish a visual balance for the page. The page's appearance must be pleasing to the eye—neither top-heavy, bottom-heavy, nor swayed toward either side. Formal balance, achieved by placing matching stories opposite each other, is regarded as old-fashioned, although it is still acceptable. More likely, you will strive for an informal balance.

One approach to informal balance is to visualize your page in quarters and then make sure that each contains a piece of art (a photograph, a drawing, a box, or another graphic design, for example). Adviser Jose Quevedo suggests a triangular balance, in which you place three pieces of art at the points of an imaginary triangle. Your triangle could be of any shape as long as it extends into both the top and bottom thirds of the page.

Finally, you must create a smooth path for your reader's eye to follow across the page. A clear flow, or **transition,** must exist from one story to another. Your aim should be to guide the reader's eye from the CVI, or "target spot," where it will first rest, through all other material, to the least important item on the page. Some of the following hints should help.

Headlines should be placed above their stories. In certain instances, they may be acceptable at the left, but this kind of story package must be clearly defined by a box or other typographical device. Although the idea of putting a headline to the right of a story or even below a story may appear enticing to a creative designer, your reader's eye will not naturally return from such a headline placement to the proper story.

Stories with photographs or other illustrations should normally appear under the illustrations or within clearly defined story packages that

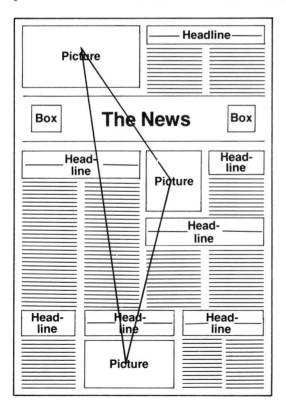

The triangular balance illustrated here is achieved by the placement of pictures. This arrangement represents one kind of the informal balance favored by makeup artists of contemporary newspapers.

include the illustrations. Keep in mind that readers tend to look at the art first and then at the text. Your arrangement must make this easy for them.

You should also try to avoid **tombstoning**—placing two headlines of equal size side by side so that your reader's eye runs from one into the other. A photo, a box, a column of type, or even two different headline styles can be used to separate them.

Your page corners should always be anchored with something strong— headlines or art at the top corners and boxes, art, or prominently displayed stories at the bottom corners.

Avoid **jump stories**—stories that are continued from one page to another. Readers rarely follow them, so you may be throwing away the latter part of a good story.

Deal carefully with an **overplay**, or **skyline streamer**—a story placed above a floating nameplate. This is not your lead story, yet it must be prominent enough that your reader's eye will return to the top of the page after focusing on your CVI. A headline in italic type may be useful here. A photograph or other art accompanying the overplay will help attract your reader's attention.

Finally, remember that each page needs a folio line. The information to be placed in the folio line that accompanies the front page nameplate is listed on page 362. On an inside page, the folio line should contain the page number, the name of the paper, and the date. The title of a department, such as Sports or Entertainment, can be placed in the folio line (perhaps in larger type) or elsewhere. Some newspapers print the folio line vertically in the margin or boxed in a single column near the top or even the bottom of the page.

Howard B. Taylor, in his pamphlet *Functional Makeup, Readable Makeup,* stresses simplicity as the greatest goal of makeup. Blocks of type should be squared off. There should be an element of punch in all four corners of the page. White space should be used to frame each package. Finally, he suggests, unnecessary ornamentation should definitely be avoided.

Positioning Photographs

Your photographs are target points on every page. They attract your reader's eye and set up transitions for you. Big pictures, as large as possible for your newspaper, are highly desirable, as long as the photographs are of good quality. The following guidelines for picture placement are intended to help these prominent items achieve their fullest potential on your pages.

A picture should never be placed between a story's headline and its lead. Since a headline and its story must always appear together, an accompanying photo and its **caption** (written description) must be placed somewhere else, either above the headline or in another position within a clearly defined story package.

Photo captions should generally be placed below their pictures. If a caption must be at one side, you will need to emphasize its relationship to the picture by surrounding it with white space.

Keep in mind that the reader's eye will tend to go to the picture first no matter where it may be placed, then to its caption, and finally to the nearest or most obvious headline. If you place the photo and caption above the headline, the transition will be particularly smooth.

Photos should not appear in the middle of a column of text. Just as with a pulled quote, the reader's eye may stop at the picture and jump to the top of the next column.

You can occasionally make good use of odd-shaped photos. The results can be quite attractive, as long as the use of such photos is not overdone.

Type of any sort—caption, headline, or story—should not be imposed across a picture. If either picture or text is good enough to print, it deserves undivided attention.

Be sure to align headline, story, photo, and caption into a block. This creates your modular package and helps your reader to see at once that all of its components belong together.

Note also that the people in photographs should be looking toward the page's center, rather than off its edges. This will help unify the look of your pages.

A one-column photograph of a person's face, commonly known as a **mug shot,** may be useful for emphasis. Such a picture does violate the general rule that news photos should portray action, but the photo can be appealing if the person is newsworthy. Today's daily newspapers make frequent use of mug shots. The formerly used half-column mug shot, however, is outdated and no longer appropriate.

The headline, story, picture, and caption presented here were laid out so as to form a block. As a result, a neat modular news package was created. A reader would immediately see that all the components of the package belong together.

—Black and White, Walt Whitman High School, Bethesda, Maryland

House displays past

by Mimi Kim

Walt Whitman history buffs or Revolutionary War fans might profit from a visit to one of the least known museums in Washington, DC, the Anderson House Museum, a historic mansion near Dupont Circle.

A private residence of Larz Anderson, a career diplomat and United States Ambassador to Japan from 1912 to 1913, relics from America's War of Independence fill the first floor of the museum. There are flags from regiments, paintings by early American artists, books, medals, swords, china, and some of George Washington's personal belongings such as his insignia ring, his seal stamps, a ring with locks of his hair inside, and an original prayer that he wrote for the new nation.

STILL FURNISHED as it was in the years occupied by the Andersons, the second floor rooms contain precious art objects. The French salon houses Ming vases from China and Flemish tapestries from the 16th century. The drawing room contains 18th century paintings, including the works of Reynolds, Hoppner, and Raeburn.

The house was given by his wife to the Society of the Cincinnati as its permanent headquarters. The 2,900 member Society of the Cincinnati is made up of male descendants of officers who served in the American Army or Navy during the Revolution.

THE SOCIETY'S main purposes are to support educational, cultural, and literary activities that aid the ideals of liberty and constitutional government, and to preserve the rights and liberties for which the founders fought in order to achieve independence.

Rules differ among the societies of the original 13 states, but generally membership passes to the eldest son. Honorary memberships are also given out.

photo by Jon Lerner

NOT JUST AN OLD HOUSE . . . the Anderson House at Dupont Circle offers a multitude of historical articles for Whitman students wanting to take a look at America's early history.

What if you have three photos for one story, all of them suitable? Consider placing the three together, either in a rectangle or in a visually pleasing arrangement surrounded by white space. One of the photos should be larger than the others so that it will be dominant. A single caption will do for all of the pictures.

**Activity 4: Using Design Principles
to Make Up a Page**

1. Obtain a blank page dummy or make one by drawing columns on a piece of paper the size of your newspaper's page. Practice the makeup process by preparing an exact sketch layout of one of the pages in the last issue of your paper. Show clearly each headline, photo, caption, story, box, and any other items.

2. Make another layout for the same page, arranging the material differently. See if you can improve on the original. Exchange with other students and evaluate each other's work.

3. Using a second color, trace the path you believe a reader's eye would follow across your new page.

4. Obtain as much information as you can about the stories and photographs assigned for a forthcoming page in your paper. Arrange this material into a visually attractive page layout, using your imagination to fill in any missing information. Keep the basic principles (CVI, informal balance, and transition) in mind.

5. Go through past issues of your school newspaper or exchange newspapers and make a collection of good and poor examples of photograph placement. Label and comment on each example according to the guidelines given in this section.

Coordinating the Different Aspects of Makeup

A great many different things are involved in newspaper makeup. They must, however, be coordinated if a unified and pleasing visual impression is to be created by the newspaper as a whole and by the individual pages. Hence, makeup artists must be able to keep in mind a host of considerations even while they are concentrating on a single one, such as story or photograph placement.

The checklist at the top of page 377 covers the basic areas of makeup and design that have been discussed in this chapter. Using it can help you to relate the many different kinds of work that must be done to achieve a professional-looking design. The last item in particular is one that should never be overlooked.

✓ Checklist for Makeup

☐ 1. Does our newspaper have a clear basic design plan to govern the work of makeup?

☐ 2. Are there design guidelines for each of the regular pages of the paper?

☐ 3. Do I understand why our particular style of body type (typeface, size, leading, and column width) was selected? Are there improvements that I could suggest?

☐ 4. Do I have a clear understanding of the sizes and styles of headlines that are available for use? Is there a headline schedule that will make my work easier?

☐ 5. Do I know what typographical devices are recommended and available for the pages of our newspaper?

☐ 6. As I start making up a page, have I placed the lead story so as to create a center of visual impact?

☐ 7. Have I placed three or four pieces of art work (photos, drawings, boxes, or other kinds of art) to develop informal balance on my page?

☐ 8. Have I created good transitions so that a reader's eye will smoothly cover all the items on the page?

☐ 9. Have I anchored the corners?

☐ 10. Am I placing photographs properly so that each one will enhance its story, not draw attention away from it?

☐ 11. Have I included a correct folio line?

☐ 12. Have I kept everything simple, even as I tried to be visually interesting and creative?

Activity 5: Examining a Design

Use the checklist to review the current design of your newspaper. What items are done particularly well in your paper? What items could be improved?

Summary

This chapter begins by discussing the most general design considerations for a newspaper and then takes up the designing of individual pages. It next explains fundamental aspects of typography and graphics and presents layout principles for positioning stories and photographs. The chapter concludes with a checklist for coordinating the various parts of makeup and design work.

DESIGNING YOUR NEWSPAPER.   Modern newspaper design must, first of all, be visually attractive. It is intended to compete for a reader's attention with visually appealing media, such as television. Good design also reflects the newspaper's personality and its editorial goals. Staffs may choose among full-size, tabloid, smaller news pages, and news magazine formats. Each story, together with related material such as photographs or art work, will generally be packaged into a modular rectangle, usually a horizontal one that sometimes extends the width of the page.

DESIGNING THE PAGES.   A newspaper's basic design is revealed most prominently in its front page layout. Fewer stories per page are presented in modern makeup, and more white space is used. Sometimes only one major story appears on a page. Each inside page, especially the editorial page, is designed so that it has a personality in harmony with its content. Attention should be paid to creating complementary designs for facing pages.

UNDERSTANDING TYPOGRAPHY AND GRAPHIC ART.   Typographical devices add to a newspaper's visual attractiveness and call attention to stories. While many styles of type are available, only a few are suitable for newspaper pages. Body type should not be sans serif, which is, however, suitable for headlines. Styles from the same type family are appropriate for all of a newspaper's basic headlines. Boxes and borders are widely used in modern makeup to frame story packages or even entire pages. Other graphic design elements include large letters, creative logos, pulled quotes, gray tint blocks, reverse type, unusual shapes, graphs, and maps.

LAYING OUT YOUR PAGES.   The actual process of makeup follows the design principles established for your newspaper. Stories are positioned according to their importance and in such a way that each story package stands out. Major layout principles include focusing on a center of visual impact, creating informal balance, and developing smooth transitions so that a reader's eye will move easily from one story to another. Simplicity is the key to good makeup. Photographs are special target points that add to a page's appearance and help make a newspaper easy to read.

COORDINATING THE DIFFERENT ASPECTS OF MAKEUP.   The various aspects of makeup and design must be coordinated if the desired look is to be achieved. A checklist is given on page 377 as an aid to such coordination.

Vocabulary

makeup	type family	logo
design	roman type	pulled quote
magtab	typeface	tint block
modular design	serif	reverse type
structural design	sans serif	page dummy
nameplate	body type	center of visual impact (CVI)
floating nameplate	leaded	transition
ears	leading	tombstoning
folio line	justified lines	jump story
facing pages	rule	overplay
centerfold	box	skyline streamer
doubletruck	end rule	caption
gutter	graphic arts	mug shot
typography	initial letter	
graphics	standing head	

Review Questions

1. Why is it so important that modern newspaper design be visually attractive?

2. What special considerations must be taken into account when designing an editorial page?

3. What are some of the special uses of type that can help create more attractive pages?

4. To guarantee a smooth transition, what is the best position for a photograph and caption that accompany a news story? Why?

5. How should the corners of a newspaper page be treated?

Discussion Questions

1. Virtually every American newspaper has changed its design at least once during the past 25 years. Discuss the reasons that have compelled newspapers, which are usually quite traditional and conservative in their outlook, to make such drastic changes. Have the changes been successful?

2. Should the personality or character of your school newspaper be the same as or different from the nature of your school as a whole? List arguments on both sides of this point.

3. Many school newspapers are limited by funds or staff size to four pages. These are typically news, editorial, feature story, and sports pages, in that order. Discuss ways of applying modern newspaper design to enhance this basic arrangement.

4. What limits should be placed on the number of photographs in a school paper?

5. Although a makeup artist will coordinate the different elements of a paper's design, the look achieved will be of interest to everyone on the staff. What methods should be used to assure that the right look has been achieved?

Chapter Project

Designing a Newspaper

Create a modern, original design plan for your school newspaper as an alternative to the one now in use. Draw on the suggestions in this chapter, as well as on those from any additional reading on makeup you have done. Change the paper's size, format, appearance, or any other design element if you feel it will improve visual attractiveness. Sketch some pages to show their personality through use of type, column widths, and other typographical devices.

NEWSPAPER
PHOTOGRAPHY

**When you have completed this chapter you should
be able to**

Decide how to use a photograph in a newspaper and
find a suitable subject.

Select appropriate photographic equipment and understand the basic aspects of its use.

Take a good news photograph.

Produce a print ready for publication.

From the day in 1936 when the pictorial news magazine *Life* first hit the newsstands, journalism was not quite the same. *Life* brought a new dimension—photojournalism—to the coverage of current events. Photojournalism is the telling of news through photographs and captions. The photographs present the main message, while the captions help identify the pictures and provide additional information. By 1972, when *Life* ceased weekly publication, photojournalism had long been firmly etched in the American news consumer's mind as one of the most effective ways to present news. While television is now America's prime source of news, newspapers continue to pictorialize current events. This is one reason for their continued success.

News publications had, of course, illustrated the day's events for many years before the coming of *Life*. Early newspapers printed crude drawings from hand-carved blocks. By the nineteenth century, American newspapers employed staffs of artists who could rapidly prepare drawings of current happenings. While these artists illustrated local events from personal observation, they relied heavily on their imaginations for distant news. Battle scenes were created by artists far from the front, and events on the advancing frontier were sketched by artists who had never been west of the Mississippi.

On the staff of a typical modern daily newspaper, a group of experienced photographers will provide most of the pictures needed. A newspaper may have, in addition, a photo editor or picture editor who schedules the work of these photographers. The actual picture assignments will usually come from a managing editor or city editor—the same person who assigns news stories to reporters. A competent photographer, in addition to having technical mastery of camera equipment and the artistic ability to compose a good picture, must be as well trained in news gathering as a reporter.

In like manner, news reporters must understand the way in which photographs may enhance their stories. Reporters are expected to see photo possibilities, envision actual pictures, and make suggestions to photographers. In fact, many reporters take their own pictures. They may carry and use a lightweight 35-millimeter camera with the same effectiveness as they do a cassette recorder.

Using Photos in the Newspaper

Perhaps 40 percent of a successful newspaper's pages will be filled with photographs. How will these photos be used? What kind of news will they represent?

Determining How a Picture Will Be Used

A photograph may appear in a newspaper in any manner that will enhance news presentation. Typically, though, a photo will be used in one of three different ways: as an illustration for a news story or a feature story, as a story complete in itself, or as one element in a story made up of a group of photos.

The largest proportion of newspaper photos appear as illustrations accompanying news stories or feature stories. These photos have several uses. They attract readers, perhaps more effectively than headlines. They picture the people, places, or situations about which the story is written. They help develop key thoughts. And they explain details that may be difficult to present in words.

When an editor makes a story assignment to a reporter, the editor also makes photo assignments. The editor may suggest what the photos should include. For instance, in addition to pictures of teachers being honored at a retirement dinner, an assignment might ask for such things as "student leaders talking with retiring teachers during the social hour." The photo editor may amplify these assignments, giving details about which camera, lens, and film to use or the particular angle from which each shot might best be taken.

A typical photo assignment sheet might look like the one below.

PHOTOGRAPH ASSIGNMENT SHEET

Photographer _____

Date photo is to be taken _____ Time _____ Place _____

Description of photo:

Names of persons to be in photograph:

Person to contact _____Phone number _____

Photo must fill shape checked below:

Date photo is needed _____Contacts _____Final print _____

Assigned by _____ Date _____

Ideas for illustrative photos may also come from the reporter who is covering the event. A reporter and photographer should ideally work as a team, each one supplementing the other's information. An alert reporter visualizes pictures of the news while it is being gathered. In fact, the reporter might also be taking some of the pictures.

In the case of major, scheduled school events, such as a Homecoming, or for interpretive, in-depth reports, the plans for both written material and photographs are likely to have come either from a meeting of the newspaper's editorial board or from a group session of the various editors concerned. The photo editor is an integral part of such boards or editorial groups. In these cases, photo coverage should be carefully planned in advance.

Sometimes a photo, with its accompanying caption, will serve as a very brief story all by itself. In essence, this is a two-paragraph news story. The key thought is emphasized in the photograph. The caption will redefine the key thought and add the major details that would ordinarily be written in the paragraph following the lead.

Finally, a group of photographs might be used to form what is known as a **photo story.** Each picture could have an accompanying caption. There would be no other text. A reader would obtain the full story by looking at

In this photo story, the phrase in large type functions as a headline, and the single paragraph of text includes caption-like matter.

Turning **Downtown** into a **Learning** and educational **Center**

Downtown Learning Center provides gifted students an opportunity to experience employment options in almost any professional field. Students work with mentors and learn from them what their job entails. Alteresa Owens is currently teaching a children's art class as part of her DLC contract with the Fine Arts Center. Loretta Tyree experienced the business end of an event such as last Sunday's Colonial Cup. DCL is expanding the walls of the classroom to cover the entire city.

Peggy Gentles/ Leaf photo

Bob Pullum/ Leaf photo

the pictures and reading the captions. Alternatively, a single headline and lead paragraph might introduce the entire story, and individual captions would simply identify the subjects of the photos.

A photo story differs substantially from a series of photos illustrating a written article. In the latter, the reporter's paragraphs present the story, while the pictures amplify and add interest to the written material. In a photo story, the pictures convey the story.

In your newspaper, you can often use either an illustrated story or a photo story quite successfully. For example, you could write an article about a child care program, perhaps as a feature story or an interpretive, in-depth report, and illustrate it with appealing photos of youngsters engaging in various activities. Or, by choosing your pictures carefully, perhaps intermixing photos of smiles and tears, eating and playing, and children with teachers and student helpers, you could establish the mood of the child care center and show what happens in a photo story that conveys the message in pictures rather than words.

Choosing Photo Topics

What topics are best for news pictures? You need only go back to Chapter 5 and its basic formula: PEOPLE + ACTION = NEWS. People doing

—Photo by J. Gerard Smith

Two to five people are the ideal number for a news photograph. Moreover, just as the key thought of a news story will generally concern the actions of an individual or group, so a good news photo will generally present people doing something.

something! Those words are the key to good news photography. When you write a news story or a feature story, your key thought does not describe someone who is just standing in one place. That is not news. Your key thought must describe someone doing something—speaking, giving or receiving, taking part in an activity. And that is exactly what every news photograph should show.

A news photo can portray a single individual, but it may be difficult to show what the person is doing unless there is someone else in the photo. Therefore, two to five people are regarded as ideal. You should envision a group of this size as you think about a picture.

Groups of more than five people are difficult to deal with on a newspaper page. For one thing, the printing processes used for newspapers make it hard to identify individual faces in a group photo. In addition, pictures of groups interfere with the portrayal of real action. Instead of a formal photo of, for example, an entire chorus, you might show two or three members studying the words of a new song. Instead of an entire football team, you might focus on the ball carrier, the blocker, and the tackler. Even though this may disappoint some group members who weren't portrayed, you have created far more reader interest in what the group as a whole is doing.

Occasionally, you may wish to create an effect with a larger number of people, even though individuals aren't identifiable. A shot of all the students in a section of the bleachers may tell more about what's really happening in a game than a shot of five students would. A picture of the crowd involved in a demonstration may reveal its real size and impact.

On rare occasions, a news photo might not include people. You might print an effective picture or even a photo story about the ice on the campus trees after a heavy storm, the new blossoms of spring, or the features of a new building. But even topics like these will draw more interest if people are included.

Activity 1: Looking at Subjects for News Photos

1. Select at least five news stories that are not illustrated by photographs, using the pages of your school newspaper, exchange papers, or the local news section of your community newspaper. For each story, describe a photograph that could have been added as a suitable illustration. Specify what the photo could have included.

2. Choose a news story that might have been presented in the form of a photograph with an accompanying caption. Briefly describe the photo that might have been used. Then, write a caption, using the material from the published story. Finally, tell why you feel no further written report would be needed.

3. Select a topic that you think would be suitable for a photo story—one with enough photos to fill an entire newspaper page, leaving just enough space for a headline and one paragraph of accompanying text. Briefly describe what material you would use in your photo story.

Selecting the Right Equipment

Your school newspaper may already possess cameras, flash units, and other equipment for use by staff photographers. If this is the case, you will need to become familiar with this equipment, learning how to use it effectively and understanding its limitations. As your photographic skills improve, you may recommend the purchase of other equipment by the school, or you may wish to buy and use your own camera and accessories. The following pages provide some helpful hints.

Picking the Best Camera for Your Purpose

Common camera choices today include the pocket camera, the instant-picture camera, the 35-millimeter camera, and the 2¼-by-2¼-inch reflex camera. Each has its advantages and disadvantages.

The inexpensive pocket camera is today's version of the old-fashioned box camera. When used on ordinary subjects in favorable photographic conditions, this kind of camera is virtually foolproof and requires little adjustment. You can make satisfactory indoor photographs with a built-in flash. There are disadvantages for news photography, though. Most of these cameras cannot be focused for sharp close-ups. Black-and-white film may not be readily available. And the quality of enlargements is not as good as with more expensive cameras.

Cameras that take pictures which develop in seconds are bulkier than the pocket styles but are limited in the same ways to undemanding picture taking. Because these cameras yield finished pictures quickly, you can retake a poor photo while the subjects are still available. Some school news staffs, especially those without darkrooms, find this type of camera quite valuable. The principal disadvantages for news photography are slow shutter speeds, which make action photos impossible, and a complicated process for making enlargements.

Serious photographers will soon find themselves limited by what pocket and instant-picture cameras can do. They are likely, therefore, to turn to one of the more versatile cameras.

The 35-millimeter camera is light in weight, easy to handle, and relatively inexpensive to use. It will produce either slides or prints. It can take excellent pictures under difficult light conditions. Thirty-five-millimeter cameras may have separate **viewfinders,** similar to those on pocket cameras, or through-the-lens viewing, generally called **reflex viewing,** with which you can see and compose the exact picture you are taking. On the latter type, you can interchange normal, **wide-angle, telephoto,** or **zoom lenses.**

Most 35-millimeter cameras have built-in **light meters** that measure the light which falls on the subject. On some cameras, you must match your settings to the light reading. On cameras with automatic controls, the **lens aperture,** the **shutter speed,** or both are set for you. Automatic focusing for distance is another optional feature.

The choice of many professional photographers continues to be the standard 2¼-by-2¼-inch reflex camera. It produces larger prints and slides than a 35-millimeter camera does and is thus often preferred for magazine work where large, clear prints are especially important. However, the pictures are more costly, and only the most expensive models will accept supplementary lenses.

If your camera offers a variety of settings but does not have a built-in light meter, you may want to purchase a separate **exposure meter.** These are versatile instruments employed by professionals as a guide to the best possible pictures.

Adding a Flash Unit

Flash equipment will be essential if you take pictures indoors or in poor light. Most modern cameras have either a built-in flash unit or a separate unit adapted specifically for the camera. Many automatic cameras will operate the flash only as needed. With older cameras, you may need flashcubes or individual flashbulbs that fit into separate attachments. A typical electronic flash unit will light subjects only within 15 feet of the camera. Large flashbulbs in reflectors can extend this distance.

Most 35-millimeter cameras, even with automatic exposure control, must be manually adjusted before making a flash picture. Flash settings are based on the film speed and the distance from subject to camera. Flash units generally require frequent battery replacement.

Determining the Proper Film

Your choice of film depends almost entirely on your purpose. Black-and-white film is typically used for newspaper, magazine, or book illustrations, since color printing on high-speed presses is difficult and expensive. Color film produces more-lifelike images and is essential for slides. When buying color film, you must decide in advance whether you will want prints or slides. Changing your plans after the film is developed will increase your costs.

Different films have different degrees of sensitivity, known as **film speeds.** These are commonly designated by **ASA ratings.** Black-and-white films used for news photography will generally have speeds of ASA 200 or 400. High-speed films (ASA 800 or 1200, for instance) are useful for taking pictures in poor light but may be too fast for sunlit subjects. Enlargements made from faster films also tend to be less sharp because of the films' texture. Slower films (ASA 25 or 64 in color, 100 or less in black-and-white) will produce sharper enlargements. If your camera has a built-in light meter, you must set the film speed when you load the film.

You will also discover that there are various other distinctions between types of film, each type produced for a specific kind of picture taking. Your photo dealer can usually suggest the best film for your particular needs.

Setting the Camera

Several camera adjustments are necessary for making sharp photographs. Even if your camera makes some of these settings automatically, you will need to know their purposes.

ADJUST YOUR LENS APERTURE. Your camera's lens opening can be adjusted, usually by means of **f-stops,** to allow more or less light to strike the film. The dimmer the light source, the more light must reach your film to make a picture. F-stop figures are actually ratios of the size of the lens opening to the size of the film. A large aperture is represented by a low number, such as f.2.8, and a small opening by a higher number, such as f.22. The proper aperture depends not only on available light but also on your film speed and shutter setting. The most often used lens aperture settings are f.8 and f.11.

CHOOSE THE RIGHT SHUTTER SPEED. In the same manner, the faster your shutter opens and closes, the less light hits your film. The effect on the picture is similar to opening or closing the lens aperture, and the two adjustments must, therefore, be considered in relation to each other. Shutter speeds are usually represented in fractions of one second, with the numerator not printed. For example, 125 means 1/125 of one second. If you were taking pictures of an auto race, you would use a high speed, such as 1/500, to freeze the motion. At speeds of 1/30 or 1/60, a camera must be held steady to avoid blurring the picture. For time exposures or for shutter speeds of less than 1/30, your camera must be attached to a **tripod.** Generally speaking, 1/100 or 1/125 are good speeds for ordinary picture taking.

FOCUS THE CAMERA FOR DISTANCE. Most cameras, even many of the automatic ones, require that you set the distance from your camera to your subject. Some cameras have **rangefinders,** or focusing devices, that help you determine this setting. On others, you must estimate the distance in meters or feet and then set a dial.

In bright sunlight, an approximate distance setting is accurate enough for all pictures except close-ups. In dimmer light, you must be more exact because of variations in what is called **depth of field.** The larger your lens opening, the less depth of field you have. With your focusing scale set at 10 feet, for example, at a lens opening of f.2.8, subjects in your photograph may be in exact focus only from 9 to 11 feet. At a setting of f.22, everything will be sharp from 5 feet to the distant background. Your camera probably has a printed scale defining these limits. Expert photographers frequently use their control over depth of field to blur out unwanted backgrounds.

PREPARE FOR USING FLASH. Unless your camera automatically sets itself for flash pictures, you must reduce the shutter speed to around 1/60 and adjust a dial on the flash unit to show both film speed and the distance from camera to subject. This dial then indicates the correct lens aperture, which you must set before taking the picture. Automatic flash units will do some or all of this for you. The most expensive ones will even adjust the intensity of the flash during the exposure. Keep in mind that most flash units have separate batteries that may last for only 20 or 30 flashes. (Your basic camera battery, on the other hand, will be good for a year or longer.)

The background of this photo is sufficiently blurred to allow the subject to stand out. Adjusting the f-stop enables a photographer to control depth of field and, thus, the clarity of background.

—Photo by Peter Vandermark from Stock, Boston

MAKE USE OF ADDITIONAL LENSES WHEN APPROPRIATE. A normal lens on a 35-millimeter camera will be rated as having a **focal length** of 50 millimeters or 55 millimeters. This lens is suitable for most picture taking. A wide-angle lens (usually 35 millimeters or 25 millimeters) will permit you to stand closer to your subject. This is useful in a small room or for action photos at a basketball game where you will be close to the players. A long lens, or telephoto lens (85 millimeters, 135 millimeters, or 200 millimeters, for instance), will create a larger picture of a subject that is some distance away—for example, on a football field. A zoom lens may also be helpful. It will commonly extend your normal range, perhaps from 35 millimeters to 85 millimeters. With a zoom lens, however, you do have to make an extra adjustment, in addition to adjusting lens aperture, setting shutter speed, and focusing for distance.

Establishing a Darkroom

Unless you are using an instant-picture camera, you will probably need a **darkroom** and related equipment. You might consider having your developing and printing done commercially if the service is convenient and rapid. Darkroom processes, though, are easy and enjoyable to learn. You must have a room with running water from which outside light can be excluded. Film developing is usually done in an inexpensive tank. Making a **contact print** requires an 8-by-10-inch or 11-by-14-inch printing frame, which can be handmade. Your most expensive piece of equipment will be

A telephoto lens, such as the one shown here, is necessary for photographs of subjects at great distances from the camera. Zoom lenses are also useful for long-distance photographs.

an **enlarger.** Safelights, trays, timer, thermometer, developing and fixing solutions, and photographic paper with light-tight storage are the major other items.

Activity 2: Learning How to Use Your Equipment

Learn about the camera elements affecting picture taking by practicing with a camera. Try to use the best camera you can by borrowing one if necessary. Take a roll or two of pictures, experimenting with the following variables: lens aperture; shutter speed; distance from the subject; wide-angle, telephoto, and zoom lenses; and various lighting conditions (indoor, bright sun, overcast, outdoor at night, and so on). Keep a careful record of the variables for each picture you shoot. Try to get as much variety as possible. After you go over your finished prints, write up your results, noting why each picture was satisfactory or not.

Taking a Picture

Once you have determined your photo topics and assembled your equipment, the most skill-demanding part of the photographic process begins— taking a picture for publication. Just as with reporting and newswriting, this will take practice, followed by evaluation and more practice, before you become really excellent in your work. You can, however, do creditable work from the beginning if you understand the basic principles. Additional reading of books about photography and photojournalism as well as courses on the subjects can help you improve your skills. For now, however, the focus is on taking creditable pictures for a school newspaper. The following five steps should help.

Prepare for the Assignment

Your first step is one of preparation. Too often a photographer grabs a camera and rushes off to the scene of the picture, only to realize upon arrival that he or she is not really ready. The results will, inevitably, be unsatisfactory.

Be sure you understand your assignment. Exactly what is it you are to do? If your assignment is to take a photo as an accompaniment to a news story, you will want to find out what the story's purpose and content are to be. Talk with the reporter who is to gather the news and write the story or ask questions of your editor.

From these sources, find out what your photograph's purpose is to be. Are you to emphasize a particular mood or portray the personality of a certain individual? Will your photo be expected to tell a story by itself, become one of a series of pictures, or be a part of a photo story? Such questions should be answered before you proceed further.

You should also collect background information just as though you were a reporter receiving a story assignment. You may obtain some facts from your editor or the reporter, but you will want to add some data for yourself. What is the topic about? Read about it in your morgue or library. Who are the people you are to photograph? Find out something about their experiences and personalities.

Arrange a time for the photo, making an appointment if necessary. Be sure that all of the people you are to photograph will be at the same place at the same time. Consider an appropriate location or background for the picture.

Assemble your equipment. In addition to one or more cameras and sufficient film, you may need a flash unit, light meter, supplemental lens, or tripod.

Since all equipment must be ready for use, you may find it useful to consult a checklist such as the one at the top of page 392 before proceeding with your picture taking.

✔ Checklist for Camera Preparation

☐ 1. Do you understand how to use all the controls on your camera?

☐ 2. Are the flash and camera batteries fresh?

☐ 3. Is the camera loaded with the proper film? Did you set the film speed on the camera dial?

☐ 4. Has the film been advanced from the previous picture?

☐ 5. Is the camera set for automatic or manual operation, whichever you plan to use?

☐ 6. Have you set the correct shutter speed?

☐ 7. Have you set the lens aperture (f-stop) to the setting indicated by the light meter?

☐ 8. If using a flash, have you set the dial on the flash unit to the proper film speed and to the proper distance?

☐ 9. Is the "ready" light of the flash unit on?

☐ 10. Did you take the lens cap off?

Pose Your Subject

As you begin your second step, consider what is likely to be the story's key thought according to your discussion with the reporter or your editor. What is the most important feature of the event? Try to show it in your picture. A contest judge may present an award to a winner. A speaker may display a certificate. A retiring club president may hand the gavel to an incoming officer. The yearbook editors may look over page layouts. The librarian may display a rare book. But always, someone is doing something! Your subjects should never be looking at your camera. They should be engrossed in their actions.

Posing your subject in an apparent position of action is much easier than trying to catch real action. Pose a high jumper just ready to start running, instead of trying to photograph one in midair. Pose a cheerleader on tiptoe instead of jumping. You cannot, of course, ask tennis players to stop their game while you pose a picture or freeze the movements of actors during a stage production. You can, however, get good shots on the sidelines or at points in the game or play just before the action starts. Real action photos, of course, are exciting when well done, but taking them demands a high level of photographic skill.

Move in close! Typical news photos are head-and-shoulders shots of up to five people. Place your subjects close together, even to the point where they complain that you are crowding them. Then, step closer with your camera so that their upper bodies are all you see in your viewfinder. Your goal is to have identifiable faces in the picture. There will, of course, be some occasions when you wish to include entire figures in a picture, and you will pose these pictures accordingly.

Most newspaper photos do not demand unusual lighting. As a newspaper photographer taking indoor pictures, you will generally be using nothing more than a simple flash. This will, of course, produce rather flat lighting. If you have a flash extension cord and if circumstances permit

—Photo by Bob Daemmrich from Michael Sullivan

A photographer will normally wish to pose a subject in a position of action that matches the key thought of a story. Sometimes, however, it will be desirable to take a candid action shot to catch people as they really are.

(you really need three hands!), hold the flash unit a few feet away from the camera and a little higher. This will create some shadows that will serve to enhance your subject. Outdoors, you will discover that bright sunlight creates harsh lines and dark shadows. Your best results when taking outdoor photos of people will come from the softer lighting you can find in open shade.

Try for a plain, neutral background behind most of your subjects or, alternatively, an especially appropriate background, such as bookshelves behind a teacher or librarian. A patterned background such as a brick wall can detract from your subject; move forward from the wall or look for a better background. Watch for trees and other objects that might on film seem to sprout from people's heads. By using a faster shutter speed and a correspondingly larger aperture, you can place the background out of focus, adding a pleasing professional touch.

Compose Your Picture

Composing the elements of a picture to ensure visual appeal takes much practice. As you begin your third step, you may want to study the composition section of a good photo handbook. This can help you understand the principles, also used by artists and designers, that are basic to taking a picture that tells its story effectively.

A few suggestions are possible here. Perhaps the most important thing to do is to consider your **center of interest.** This may be the certificate, the award, the handshake, the volleyball, or the face of the most important person to appear in your photograph. You will want this particular element near the center of your photo, but you should never place it at the exact center.

A rule of thirds is useful to photographers. Imagine the picture divided into three parts, both vertically and horizontally. If your picture is to be vertical, place the center of interest above or below the middle of the picture. If horizontal, place the center of interest to the right or left. Whether the picture is vertical or horizontal, make sure the center of interest falls toward or near one of the points where your imaginary dividing lines intersect. The circled areas in the diagram on page 395 stand for desirable centers of interest.

The helmets in this photo form two lines—one from the upper left corner, the other from the upper right—that converge on a center of interest slightly above and to the right of center.

—Photo by Ira Berger from Woodfin Camp

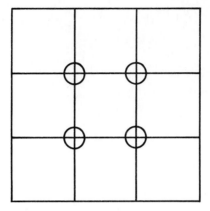

You should also be sure that there is only one center of interest—the one you have planned. Someone behind your subject staring at the camera would be a second, unwanted center of interest; so would a very light area at one side of the picture.

Diagonal lines, either formed by things in the picture or implied by your lighting, can add interest and strength. Lines, such as the edge of a tabletop, leading from the border of the picture toward your center of interest can also help the viewer focus on your subject.

Another way to add interest is to create a visual frame for your subject. The frame does not have to surround the center of interest. The curtain at one side of a stage can suggest a frame; so can a tree at one edge of an outdoor picture. A low shot of a play showing the edge of the stage along the bottom of the picture—just as an audience would see it—is another form of framing.

Take Pictures from Different Angles

Now you are ready, as your fourth step, to take a picture for publication. Be sure your camera is properly set. Take and hold a deep breath and then push the shutter button firmly but gently so as not to shake the camera. As you wind the film forward, look again to make sure that all of the faces are showing exactly as you want them. Then take another shot of the same pose. Move your position or change the pose slightly and take two more shots. You'll now have at least four shots from which your editor may choose.

Make Notes About Names and Occasions

As your fifth and final picture-taking step, make notes of your subjects' names and their positions within the picture before they move away. Check the spelling of each name and any titles carefully. Many photographers carry a small notebook in which they keep a running diary of each photo as they take it. This data should also be immediately entered on your photo assignment sheet, which you will return to the editor with your pictures.

"Boomer, Lhasa apso on boardwalk in Virginia Beach during tropical storm Dennis, on Thursday"—such is the information a photographer would record in a notebook to ensure that the meaning or significance of a photo was not lost.

—Photo from UPI

Signed releases are not needed for true news photographs. But every photographer must understand the legal implications of libel and invasion of privacy (outlined in Chapter 3).

Activity 3: Preparing for and Taking a News Photo

1. If you have not already done so, begin a collection of good news photographs, selecting them from school and daily newspapers or from magazines.

   a. Choose four of these photos that represent, in your estimation, well-posed shots. Mount them and write a paragraph about each, evaluating especially the arrangement of the people in connection with the purpose of the photo as you understand it.

   b. Choose four photos that you believe to be artistically well composed according to the principles suggested in this section. For each, point out the components of good composition.

   c. Find at least one photo that features a single individual (although other people might be incidentally included) and tell in writing how well you believe the photo reveals the personality of the subject.

2. From black-and-white photos in newspapers, magazines, or other sources, choose at least two that emphasize a particular mood or feeling. (Photos that make heavy use of black and dark gray tend to be gloomy, mysterious, and despondent. Photos that make heavy use of light gray and white tend to be happy, light, and springlike. Photos with a high black and white contrast may suggest action and excitement.) For each, point out how the details of the subject and the photographic techniques created the mood or feeling.

3. Make up a photo assignment for a story that might appear in the next issue of your school newspaper. Following the suggested steps, take several shots of the assigned situation. After the film has been developed and the contact prints made, mount your contact prints and prepare a written evaluation of your work. Indicate which photo you feel was your best and why.

Producing the Final Print

Once the photo has been taken, several steps remain before the finished picture, generally referred to as a **cut,** may be published. After the film has been developed, an appropriate picture will be selected and a print made. The center of interest will be emphasized by a trimming process called **cropping.** The actual size of the resulting picture on a printed page will then be determined and a caption will be written.

Preparing the Print in the Darkroom

Darkroom work is usually done by photographers. A number of excellent manuals covering developing and printing processes are available in photography stores. This work is not difficult, but your darkroom must be organized carefully and kept scrupulously clean. A few drops of the wrong solution or a few grains of dust may ruin a picture forever. The basic steps are film developing, contact printing, and enlarging.

To develop film, first load it into a tank. Two or three solutions are then used in order. It is possible in the developing process to "push" film that has been shot in poor light to a faster speed (ASA 400 to ASA 800, for instance). The film **negative** is then washed, dried, cut into convenient lengths, and placed in transparent envelopes.

A single contact print, or **contact,** of the entire roll of film is made on a sheet of photographic paper. Editors may then examine the pictures and determine which are to be considered for publication. Most film manufactured today has preprinted numbers for each picture, or **frame,** which makes identification easier.

Using the chosen frame from the film negative, the photographer then makes an **enlargement.** Photographic papers with a glossy or smooth finish will reproduce best. An experienced technician can improve the final print by bringing out details in light areas or holding back exceptionally dark areas.

The final print is usually made to a standard photographic size, generally 5 by 7 inches or 8 by 10 inches. Newspaper staffs that do all of their own printing preparation may wish at this time to make the enlargement to the exact width of one, two, or three columns. If this is the case, cropping marks, discussed below, should be made on the contact.

Cropping to Emphasize the Center of Interest

Photographers are told to move in close to their subjects. If this has been done, the print will probably contain only the heads and shoulders of the people pictured. Even so, there may be distracting elements along the picture's edges. You can remove these by the process of cropping. There may be too much empty space in the foreground or too much sky or wall above the subject. You might wish to remove an extra person from one side of the photo. Sometimes you may discover that you have two pictures in one and that you will need to block out half of your print in order to focus on the real center of interest.

Two pieces of cardboard cut into the shape of the letter L can be very helpful in cropping photos. Lay one across the top and one side of the print

Cropping enhances a photograph by making its center of interest more prominent. It removes clutter and all else that interferes with a clean, clear view of the subject.

and the other across the bottom and the other side. Now move the cardboard L's in until you see only the major elements of your picture. It is permissible to block out parts of a person's body, such as the outer edge of the arms, when doing this. But do not make cuts at the joints, because they would look like amputations. Remember also to keep the center of interest above, below, or to one side of the exact center.

When you have decided where to crop, indicate the places by marks with a felt-tip pen in the white margin of the print. The cutting point for the left- or right-hand side of the picture should be shown by vertical marks in the top and bottom margins, in line with each other. The cutting point for the top or bottom of the picture should be shown by horizontal marks at the left and right. Your printer will prepare a printing plate using only the portion of the picture you have indicated.

Activity 4: Cropping News Photos

In newspapers or magazines, find at least five photographs that you believe could be improved by cropping. You may use cropping to eliminate unnecessary background, to focus on the center of interest, or to improve the composition of the picture. Indicate by marginal markings how you would crop each photo. For the purposes of this assignment, you may ignore the size and shape of the finished photo. Exchange your work with another student and evaluate one another's results.

Scaling the Photo to Size

The picture size that results from cropping is probably not the size of the cut that will appear on your newspaper's printed page. The next step is that of **scaling** the picture to the desired publication size. Your editor will first decide the width in columns that the photo is to occupy. You will convert this width to a specific number of picas. One column might be 12 picas wide, two columns might be 25 picas, and so on.

You must then determine the height that the enlarged or reduced print will occupy on the printed page. Since you are dealing with a percentage increase or decrease, you can discover this measurement almost instantly with a pocket calculator. Figure the percentage that your desired width is of the present width. It will be less than 100 percent if it is a reduction and more than 100 percent if it is an enlargement. Apply this percentage to your present height, and you will have the new height. For example, if your present photo is 40 picas wide by 20 picas high and your desired column width is 30 picas, you will divide 30 by 40 and get 75 percent. Seventy-five percent of 20 picas is 15 picas—the new height. Inexpensive proportion wheels are also available to perform this calculation for you.

After determining the desired size, turn the photo over and put it face down on a hard surface. Write the new measurements as well as the percentage of reduction or enlargement on the back. Use only a felt-tip pen,

Photo by Brenda Brown

JOYOUS PAINTING ... Senior Wendy Peters helps to create "The Twelve Days of Christmas" on the windows of Mr. Steak. Wendy and other National Art Honor Society members compete with Chrisman students in a holiday contest sponsored by the restaurant.

Photo by Jeff Garrard

THE TOP FIVE STUDENTS of the senior class are (bottom) Kim Terrill, Jennifer Smith, Lewis Cohen, (top) Christi Clayton, and George Adams. All of these students have maintained a grade point average above 4.5 while at Hillcrest.

Photo by Dave Sanders

VROOM! Dave Newell hits a jump during recent motocross competition.

PAT DONAHUE, FIVE years old, searches for the great pumpkin at the A.P. History Booster Club's pumpkin sale. Proceeds will be used to buy video tapes and new books for the class.

—*The Spirit*, Truman High School, Independence, Missouri (top left); *Hillcrest Hurricane*, Hillcrest High School, Dallas, Texas (top right); *The Union St. Journal*, Cherry Creek High School, Englewood, Colorado (bottom left); *The Epitaph*, Homestead High School, Cupertino, California (bottom right)

The modern emphasis on visual appeal in newspaper design has increased the desirability of publishing good photographs. These photographs from four different student newspapers represent commendable work in newspaper photography.

never a pencil or ball point pen, which might create a ridge on the face of the print. Write out the necessary identification, the name of the photographer, and the date the picture was taken. Your editor will add a code—1A, 1B, and 1C for front page pictures, for example—telling the printer exactly where each cut is to appear in the newspaper.

Writing the Caption

The final but extremely important step is to write a caption, or **cutline**—the two or three lines that will appear under the cut and identify the people and the situation. The caption might be prepared by the photographer, the reporter covering the story, or an editor. In any case, the photographer's notes made at the time the picture was taken must be available.

Sometimes, a caption may begin with three or four words in capital letters. In other cases, it will simply be a sentence or two. You should follow the style used in your newspaper. Make sure that you identify the people in the picture and tell something about what they are doing. The caption should be written exactly as a news lead is, with the key thought in the first few words and the details following.

Avoid the phrase "from left to right" when identifying people. You can usually say, instead, something such as "Marcus Smith presents a certificate of excellence to Barbara Jordan while second-place winner Roberto Gonzales looks on." In most cases, it will be clear to your readers who each person is. If you feel there could be some confusion, you might say, "Marcus Smith, at left, presents . . ."

A good caption should tell its story in a lively way that would be interesting even if the photo were not present. Note the following examples.

This won't hurt a bit! You too may have heard this before, and certainly many GHS students will hear it January 26 when the Red Cross Blood Drive comes to Griffith.

—*The Panther Press*, Griffith High School, Griffith, Indiana

ON THE RUN. Senior Kathy Ludwig edges past an opponent in a recent win over Overland, 51-43.

—*The Union St. Journal*, Cherry Creek High School, Englewood, Colorado

---

The following suggestions can be helpful when writing captions. Keep the mood the same as in the story (light or serious). Don't repeat anything that is obvious in the cut, but do identify the people, place, and occasion to the extent necessary to help the reader fully appreciate the picture. Give the reader information that can't be derived from the picture. There should be just enough information, but not too much. Eliminate editorializing, such as "This is a good picture of . . ." Include a quotation if appropriate and accurate but don't make up quotations. Acknowledge the source of the photo, especially if it was obtained from an outside source. Identify your staff photographer if this is the custom of your newspaper. If the photo might be seen as a trick, give information as to how it was made.

Activity 5: Preparing Captions for Photos

1. Find five photographs without captions and prepare a suitable caption for each, following the style used in your newspaper. If you cannot determine the real names and positions of people in the photographs, make them up. Be sure each caption is written as a news lead would be, with an initial focus on the key thought.

2. Write an appropriate caption for the photograph that you prepared in Activity 3.

Summary

This chapter begins by explaining the uses of photographs in newspapers and presenting general principles for selecting subjects for photos. It then considers the different kinds of cameras and equipment and their correct use. Next, it presents the steps to be followed in taking a news photo. Finally, it discusses the last stages of producing a newspaper photo: developing, enlarging, cropping, scaling, and caption writing.

USING PHOTOS IN THE NEWSPAPER. A typical photograph might be used in one of three ways. Usually, it will accompany a news story to attract readers and enhance the story. It might occasionally appear by itself with a caption, presenting a very brief story. Or it might be part of a group of pictures arranged to tell a photo story. People and action are the keys to successful pictures. A typical photo might include from two to five people who are doing something.

SELECTING THE RIGHT EQUIPMENT. Of the available kinds of cameras, the 35-millimeter camera is probably the most versatile for news photography. An appropriate flash unit must be added and the proper film choice made. The photographer must also understand how to set the camera. Even if the camera is automatic, the photographer needs to know something about the function of the lens opening, shutter speed, and distance focusing. The operation of the flash unit and the use of supplementary lenses must also be understood. A darkroom is necessary if school newspaper photographers intend to make their own prints.

TAKING A PICTURE. Several steps are involved in the taking of a good news photograph. The photographer should understand the purpose of a photo assignment and do preliminary research. The subject should be posed carefully. The photograph should be composed properly. The subject should be photographed from different angles. And notes about names and occasion should be taken.

PRODUCING THE FINAL PRINT. Darkroom work involves film developing, making contact prints, and enlarging the selected picture. The photo must be cropped to feature the center of interest and then scaled to the appropriate size for printing in the newspaper. Finally, a caption must be written.

Vocabulary

photo story	film speed	center of interest
viewfinder	ASA rating	cut
reflex viewing	f-stop	cropping
wide-angle lens	tripod	negative
telephoto lens	rangefinder	contact
zoom lens	depth of field	frame
light meter	focal length	enlargement
lens aperture	darkroom	scaling
shutter speed	contact print	cutline
exposure meter	enlarger	

Review Questions

1. What are the basic uses of newspaper photographs?

2. What specific equipment should a news photographer have?

3. What camera settings and adjustments must be made before a picture is taken?

4. What are the steps involved in the taking of a good news photograph?

5. What considerations are involved in cropping, scaling, and caption writing?

Discussion Questions

1. What are the advantages and disadvantages of using a photograph with caption as a complete news story, in contrast to using a story accompanied by a photo?

2. How important do you think high-quality, expensive equipment is for taking outstanding photographs?

3. Discuss the following statement: "I am a competent photographer. I can size up a photo situation when I arrive at the scene. Doing research on my photo subject before I leave the newspaper office doesn't add anything to the quality of my finished photo."

4. What aspect of news photography do you believe requires the most skill?

5. Should a caption be omitted if the contents of a photo are made clear by the story that accompanies it?

Chapter Project

Making Photographs for a Newspaper

For either an assigned photo topic or one of your own choosing, take three good pictures suitable for publication in your school paper. Carefully attend to the technical details of camera work as well as to such artistic matters as posing and composition. Select your best frame, have it enlarged, crop it, and write an interesting caption.

ADVERTISING

When you have completed this chapter you should be able to

Recognize the role of advertising in the publication of a school newspaper.

Sell advertising space in your school's paper.

Prepare an advertisement.

Place ads on pages, create special kinds of advertising, and deal with ads that pose problems of taste or suitability.

Sixty-four billion dollars. Yes, billion!

That is the amount of money young people between the ages of 6 and 16 spend each year. Half of this comes from allowances, the other half from jobs held by teen-agers. Most of this income is spent on items young people may choose freely. Unlike adults, most do not have to budget regularly for housing, food, and medical care.

The purchasing power of young people is your newspaper's major appeal to local advertisers. Like commercial newspapers and magazines, your paper will depend on advertising to pay most of its publishing costs. **Subscriptions** simply can't bring in enough money to cover school newspaper expenses. Occasionally, school papers are fortunate enough to have a subsidy from their school district or the student activity fee. Or there may be a school print shop that produces the newspaper relatively cheaply. But at least three fourths of the school papers in the United States must turn to advertising for survival.

Like other aspects of journalism, advertising can be fascinating. Working in advertising will give you a chance to meet people you might not otherwise meet and to learn a good deal about public relations. Your experience in sales and in keeping business records will prove invaluable in your adult life. In short, advertising propels you into the world of business.

Managing the Advertising Program

How much advertising must you sell? This depends on the cost of publishing your newspaper. A newspaper staff might calculate the average cost for producing one issue, including operating expenses and printing, and then figure out how much advertising must be sold to meet this expense. Income from sales of subscriptions or from a student activity budget could then be applied to special expenses, such as camera equipment, photo and art supplies, books and magazines, and editing aids.

The staff may use various schemes to figure out how much advertising is needed. The equivalent of one full page of ads might pay for a four-page paper, one and one-half pages for a six-page issue, and so on. Another way is to deal in dollars—perhaps $100 per page. In this case, the total advertising income for each issue will determine the number of pages that can be printed.

With an intelligent sales plan, advertising can be sold almost anywhere. While it might appear easiest for students attending the only school near a major suburban shopping center, any number of school newspapers sell ads successfully in city neighborhoods with small, scattered stores. Ads can also be sold successfully when a school is so located that there is competition from other school papers. Generally speaking, teen-agers have money to spend regardless of where they live. The primary job of a seller of advertising, then, is to convince merchants that the ads in the school paper will reach these spenders.

Who on the newspaper staff is responsible for advertising? Your **business manager** will be in charge. This individual's role in making staff decisions will have much to do with the importance of advertising to your paper. If the business manager is looked upon merely as another member of the staff, advertising may rate low in everyone's eyes. On the other hand, if this person is second or third in staff ranking, the job of financing the paper can become much easier.

You may also have an **advertising manager** who is directly in charge of the sales program. Working with this staff member may be a number of sales representatives whose major job is to sell advertising space. Some individuals look upon this work as a challenge and enjoy it tremendously. It may, however, be the policy of your paper that everyone should have experience in advertising. This may prove a struggle for the shy staff member, but all will benefit from exposure to the business side of journalism.

Finally, your paper may assign a few **layout workers** to prepare most of the ads. Every staff member should have some experience, though, in planning an advertisement for publication. Artistic skill is not especially needed. What is more important is the ability, which you can develop, to visualize an ad's appearance and to have a sense of proportion and balance.

Activity 1:   Preparing for Advertising

1. What is the buying power of a typical student at your school? If a formal survey of the student body has not been made recently, your staff might consider conducting one, preferably an anonymous one since the subject can be somewhat touchy. In the absence of a complete survey, you might obtain informal, general figures by getting opinions from members of your journalism class and some of your friends. Estimate the average number of dollars each person has available for spending during a week and multiply that figure by the number of students at your school to reach a total.

2. How much influence do students have on family decisions about major purchases, such as TV sets, videotape equipment, cars, or furniture? You might be able to estimate a dollar figure for this purchasing influence as a supplement to the personal-spending figure.

3. How is your newspaper staff organized for the purpose of selling and preparing advertisements? Draw a chart showing this organization. How effective does this plan seem to you?

Selling Advertising Space

An efficient advertising sales representative does not start out by running down to the nearest store and asking breathlessly, "You wanna buy an ad in our paper?" Three major planning and preparatory steps must come before the sale itself. First, you should study your prospective buyers to learn more about their needs and how your advertising program might help them. Second, you should prepare a **sales kit** that includes not only printed material but also the general information each sales representative must have. And third, you should decide how each prospective buyer might advertise and prepare a sample ad to offer when you visit. Only after these three steps have been completed are you ready to approach your prospect.

As you proceed, you will want to keep in mind that you have a real service to offer. Your newspaper can serve local businesses by providing a means of increasing sales. You will at the same time serve your readers by supplying information useful to them as purchasers.

Studying Your Prospective Buyers

Every business within the area where the students of your school live is a prospective advertiser. The nearest downtown business district, even if some distance away from the school, may also have stores interested in attracting your school's students.

As your first step, list all these businesses. Some, of course, are more likely than others to want teen-agers' trade—record and stereo shops, fast-food restaurants, or clothing stores, for instance. Other stores may not be likely prospects. But there will not be many of these. Keep in mind that merchants whose trade is entirely with adults may be interested in reaching the parents who read your paper or in building good will with students in anticipation of future business. Even merchants who attract their customers in ways other than through school newspaper advertisements should be retained on your list. There is always the possibility that some sales representative will reach them with the right combination of service and selling appeal.

Many papers send each business prospect an advance letter in the fall. This letter might name the school and the newspaper, define the paper's purpose, give details about its circulation and its readers, suggest the degree of student buying power, and indicate the kinds of advertising space available. The letter might conclude by stating that a sales representative will call soon with more information and a sample ad.

Next, you need to assign a sales representative to each prospect. You may wish to divide your area into blocks or other units, giving each representative a "beat." Instead, you might divide your selling staff according to types of stores, or you may simply assign certain stores at random to each representative.

The sales representative will now begin to look into each business to learn what people the store appeals to, what products are sold or services provided, and what kinds of customers are actually coming to the store.

This should lead to answers to such questions as the following. What are the merchant's special problems? Are there slack times—certain hours, days, or seasons when the store might wish to improve business? Who does come into the store during these times? Are there parts of the store visited

Photo by Laimute E. Druskis from Taurus

Merchants place ads for many different reasons, but generally they will be looking for an increase in sales. A good sales representative should be able to offer a truly useful service to a merchant.

by few people? What items in the store don't seem to sell well? Your sales pitch will certainly be stronger if you are attacking one of the merchant's problem areas.

Preparing a Sales Kit

As your second step, collect all the material and information you might need when you approach the merchant. Most of this should be duplicated so that you may leave a copy at the place of business. It will include information about your paper, your school, and its students, all of which you must know thoroughly so you can answer questions.

Start your kit with sample copies of several issues of your newspaper. You will want to leave these with the merchant. Some newspapers have found that it also helps to give a free item, such as a school sports schedule or a pencil or calendar imprinted with the school paper's name and phone number.

You should also make sure the merchant understands the many reasons for advertising in a school newspaper. Because the newspaper is the only advertising medium at your school, it is a sure way to reach students and their families. In addition, a school paper is small enough in size that each ad is quite visible, unlike the multi-page daily where a small ad often appears in an obscure location. Then, too, the price of an ad in a school paper is quite low by comparison with the rates of daily or weekly newspapers. The unit cost per reader, figured by dividing the price of the ad by the number of readers, will be exceptionally low. Teen-age buying power is another good reason. Finally, a merchant can often hope to develop students who see a store's ads regularly into adult customers.

Be prepared to explain your paper's circulation. Tell who receives the paper—all students, all subscribers, all activity card holders, and so on—and how many there are in each group. Add faculty and administrators to whom it is delivered. You should also know how well it is read outside the school. Unless a formal survey has been made of outside readership, you will have to depend on a rough calculation made by asking a number of students whether they take it home and, if so, who reads it there.

Carry in your sales kit figures showing the buying power of your student population, as well as of your total readership. The ideal way to arrive at such figures would be through an anonymous survey in which you ask every student about allowances, work income, and spending habits. In the absence of such a survey, you can make rough estimates as suggested in Activity 1.

Your kit should also include an advertising **rate sheet.** Rates are usually quoted by the **column inch:** a certain price for a space one column wide and an inch high. Most advertisers are familiar with this measurement. Establish this rate by determining your normal operating and printing costs per issue and then dividing this figure by your projected total amount (in column inches) of advertising space. You will also want to find out the rate used by other school newspapers in your area, especially any with which you compete. Suppose you reach a figure of $5 per column inch. The smallest ad you might accept would be 2 column inches, or $10.

Another way of looking at rates is the **unitary method.** Here you would quote rates based on fractions of a page, although you would still use the column inch as a basis for your calculations. A typical five-column tabloid paper might have 16 inches in one column or 80 inches per page. A full-page rate would then be 80 times the column-inch rate, a half-page rate 40 times, and so on down to your minimum size. As a helpful visual aid, you might prepare a full-size sample page with the possible squares or shapes ruled off and the price shown in each square.

To encourage large sales, discounts might be arranged. Your full page, half page, or quarter page could be sold at a lower rate than one determined strictly by the number of column inches involved. You might, in addition, offer a lower rate to an advertiser who contracts for ads in more than one issue. As another incentive, if a merchant advertises in all of your issues for the year, the last ad might be free. You could also offer 10 percent off for prepayment when an ad is ordered or for immediate payment upon publication.

Your sales kit should definitely include a printed contract form. An advertising contract does not have to be full of legal language. All you need is a statement noting that a merchant agrees to purchase a certain amount of advertising in your newspaper. The contract should include most of the data in the following sample.

ADVERTISING CONTRACT

The News

Central High School

First and Main Streets

Phone 555-1111, Ext. 44

_____ (name and address of business)

agrees to purchase display advertising in the Central High <u>News</u> as follows:

Size and shape of ad _____

Date(s) of issue(s) _____

Cost per issue, according to rate sheet _____

Multiplied by total number of issues _____

Less discounts, if any, according to rate sheet _____

Additional charges for photography, reverse copy, or screened copy _____

Total cost for the 198__-198__ school year _____

Tear sheet will be provided and advertising charges will be billed on the date of publication. Interest of $1\frac{1}{2}$ percent per month will be added to bills not paid within 30 days after publication. Ten percent reduction will be granted when payment is made upon placement of order.

Copy to be furnished by advertiser _____ To be prepared by <u>News</u> _____
Copy deadline is two weeks before the date of publication; no changes may be made after that date.

Advertiser's signature _____ Date_____

Student sales rep's signature _____ Date_____

Designing a Sample Ad

The third step to take before you visit the merchant is to prepare a sketch of a sample ad, sometimes referred to as a **spec layout.**

What will you feature in your sample ad? Consider how an ad in your newspaper could serve the merchant's business. What goods or services offered by the merchant might your readers buy or use? What business problems have you identified that an ad might help solve? With these ideas in mind, choose an item or service to feature. How will it appeal to your readers? Why would they wish to buy it? What specific points about it will interest them? How will it help them?

Sketch an ad of the actual size you hope to sell. Include an attention-getting headline, a rough drawing of the visual content you propose, and the store's name with its address or location. At this point, it is not necessary to write out detailed copy. You may simply draw in a block to show how much space it might occupy.

Approaching a Client

Finally, with full information about your newspaper, its readers, and your school in mind and with a complete sales kit in hand, you are ready to attempt the sale.

Check your appearance. You want to give the impression that you are serious and businesslike. Most merchants will not be interested in talking with you if you are dressed too casually. You should wear clean, neat clothing that is informal but appropriate for business dealings. You will want to be relatively well groomed, and you should not be chewing gum. In addition, be sure to carry one or more pens.

Should you telephone first? Many business managers would advise against it. It is too easy for your prospect to say no over the phone. You want this person to see the material you have prepared, particularly your sample ad. An appointment may be desirable with an extremely busy store manager. Otherwise, simply plan to arrive at the store during a time you know will not be an especially busy one.

Before leaving for the store, you may find it useful to consult the following checklist to make sure you are ready.

✔ Checklist for Approaching a Client

☐ 1. Am I familiar with the kinds of customers the merchant seeks, the kinds who actually patronize the business, and the goods or services offered?

☐ 2. Do I know the merchant's special problems?

☐ 3. Have I assembled all needed information about the school paper, its circulation and readership, the buying power of its readers, and so on?

☐ 4. Can I give the merchant good reasons for advertising in our school paper?

☐ 5. In particular, can I convince the merchant that an ad in the school paper will reach sought-after customers?

☐ 6. Do I have an advertising-rate sheet? A contract form?

☐ 7. Can I arrange a discount for the merchant?

☐ 8. Have I brought along any free items for the merchant—pens, a calendar, or the like?

☐ 9. Have I brought along a sample ad specially prepared for the merchant?

☐ 10. Am I prepared to answer all questions?

☐ 11. Am I dressed appropriately for a business call?

☐ 12. Have I made an appointment if one was needed?

Once you have arrived, present your material and ideas, stressing the fact that you wish to serve the merchant. Talk briefly about your newspaper and how it can be of help. Explain your sample ad, telling why you chose that item and why you believe it will appeal to students at your school. Be ready to answer questions.

If the merchant appears interested in general but not in the item you chose for your sample ad, talk about what he or she wishes to sell. You can then promise to return the next day with a new layout. If there is a possibility of a series of ads, you might suggest an ongoing plan by preparing samples for each different issue.

Although a merchant may occasionally suggest a simple "Compliments of—" ad or some other donation to your school, the best policy is generally to make the ad a real ad. You want to help the merchant make sales or gain other definite results from the ad so that the business will continue to advertise. If the merchant insists, though, you might prepare an ad that simply states the type of business, its name, and location.

Don't be discouraged if you don't make a sale on the first visit. Go back later, perhaps with a new sample ad or a different approach. People successful in sales work say that 80 percent of their sales are made on the fifth call or even later.

Once the sale has been made, take care of details. Fill in the blanks on the contract. Have the merchant sign the contract and then sign it yourself. Be sure the cost is clear, especially if the merchant wants art work, photography, or other special treatment. Firm up the sample ad and promise to come back with the complete written text as well as a final layout if the merchant wishes. In some cases, the merchant may supply material for the ad. Larger stores often have their own ad designers; smaller ones may have printed material for your use. Keep the discussion businesslike but friendly. Thank the merchant and remind him or her that you'll be back on publication day with a **tear sheet** of the printed ad or a marked copy of the full paper. You might sell the next ad at that time!

Beginning sales representatives should not be discouraged if they fail to sell an ad the first time they approach a merchant. Several calls are often necessary before a sale is made.

—Photo by Laimute E. Druskis from Taurus

Activity 2: Developing a Sales Plan

1. Working with others in your class, prepare a list of the advertising prospects in your school community. Try not to overlook any prospect, including people maintaining offices and people operating businesses in their own homes. While you may not get in touch with all of these people immediately, you might later be happily surprised to find that some will buy advertising space to create good will between themselves and your readers and to make known their presence in the community. Go back through your newspaper files for several years and check off the businesses that have advertised. Determine which prospects also advertise in local daily newspapers or on local radio or television.

2. Make a specific list of all material that should be included in a sales kit at your school. Be sure to include items that were not suggested in the preceding section but that you consider necessary.

3. Assuming you have not done this already as a sales representative assigned to a specific prospect, choose a local business that has not advertised recently in your school paper and prepare a sample ad that could be presented to the store manager.

Preparing an Advertisement

Your advertising space is sold. The merchant has decided upon the size and shape of the forthcoming ad. If you have developed a sample ad that has met with the merchant's approval, your task now is to refine and complete this advertisement for publication. If you do not have an approved sample ad, you will need to start from the beginning and aim for the same general goal.

Ads must serve a basic purpose—to sell whatever is being advertised. They must also be visually striking even though they contain words. Unless an ad attracts the reader's eye, it will not be read. Factors that can help an ad catch the eye and attention of the reader are its general attractiveness on the page, an attention-getting headline or illustration, and even the white space setting it apart from the news columns.

Focusing on the Ad's Purpose

The basic purpose of an ad is to lead a prospective buyer through the four steps of the selling process. The first step, as noted above, is to attract the buyer's *attention*. The second and third steps are to arouse *interest* and create a *desire* for the product or service. The last step is to make a *sale*. The same steps apply to television commercials, to printed advertisements, and to person-to-person sales. Like other selling vehicles, a newspaper advertisement must lead its readers through these steps.

The white space in these ads is part of what will help them catch the reader's attention. Not only does it help set them apart from news text, it also makes their illustrations and messages stand out.

—*The Kirkwood Call*, Kirkwood High School, Kirkwood, Missouri (left); *Echo*, Glenbard East High School, Lombard, Illinois (right)

An ad must first attract the reader's eye and lead to an examination of the ad's content. If an ad does not gain a prospective buyer's *attention*, the selling process never starts.

Immediate *interest* in the content of the ad must now follow. This may be created through the topic, the headline, or the illustration. Interest in a school newspaper ad should generally be related to what teen-agers want or need. The ad might appeal to a general wish for good food, for better looks, for better school equipment, for leisure items, and so on.

The ad must then create a *desire* to find out more about the advertised item, to visit the store where it can be obtained, and, ultimately, to buy it. Now the reader is examining the ad's text. In the case of, say, ski equipment, the discovery that skis are presently on sale may develop an immediate desire.

Finally, if the ad is successful, at least some of the readers must be ready to take action leading to a *sale*.

Another aspect of an ad closely related to its purpose is its tone, or its style of appeal. Keeping in mind that you are providing services to both the advertiser and your reader, you will need to understand how the store approaches its customers. If the store is generally regarded as a friendly, pleasant place where a customer will feel welcome, then the ad should convey this feeling. If the atmosphere is a little more formal, as it would be perhaps at a department store, the ad should reflect this. In the case of a clothing store that features quality merchandise, the ad's content must reveal that quality. Other types of tone might reflect speed and efficiency, as at a fast-food restaurant, or an attitude of competent service, as at an auto-repair shop.

The tone of your reader's life is equally important. What kind of person is the typical high school student? Most students are, or wish to be, happy people enjoying a wide range of interests. Your ad's appeal should be appropriate to a young person with such a spirit. One award-winning school newspaper achieves this by using a "light touch"—a little humor, creativity, or fantasy in the ad's text—without neglecting solid information.

Making the Ad Attractive

Keep your ad layout simple. It must focus sharply on the particular merchant's service or product and point out why the reader should be interested in it. The described item might be available at half a dozen places around town, but you want your reader to purchase it at the store that has chosen to advertise in your paper.

An ad-layout person does not need to be an artist. What is far more important is a sense of spacing and the ability to focus on well-chosen material in a visually appealing manner. Artistic use of space is the key.

White space, or an absence of printed material, is likely to attract more attention than a mass of illustrations and text. It is the white space that sets the ad apart from the news columns next to it. Therefore, you don't have to fill all of the ad's space. Instead, you should be as stingy as possible with text.

A typical small ad contains a headline, an illustration or design, a few words of text or description, the store's name and address, and a border to keep these elements together.

The ad's headline should be limited to a few words that will attract the reader's eye and define the ad's topic. It does not need to be a headline in the journalistic sense of the word. It may or may not be a complete sentence, depending on the style and strategy of the ad.

Advertising headlines should generally be in capital and lower-case letters, as in ordinary writing, for better readability. The typeface should be chosen to match the tone of the ad, while remaining clear to the eye. It should normally be different from the typeface used in a paper's news headlines, to draw further attention to the ad.

The headline is usually placed at the top of the ad. It might also be appropriate to the left of the illustration or text. If you place it to the right or below, you are making the undesirable suggestion that it be read after the text.

An illustration is not always essential, but some contrast to printed words is desirable. It might be a drawing, a photograph, or the trademark name of the store or a product. It might also be an eye-catcher such as the words "½ OFF," the price in large type, or even a large area of white space.

The basic components of a typical small advertisement are displayed here: a headline ("IT MUST BE Homer Reed Ltd."), an illustration, some text, the name and address of the business, and an attractive border.

The text may be a few sentences or phrases describing the product or service offered. It can appear as a short printed paragraph under the headline, or it may consist of phrases appearing as subheads. Use as few words as possible. In some cases, you might want to leave unanswered questions, such as the exact price, for the purpose of drawing customers into the store.

The store's name and address should be simple but complete. Just the word *MAC'S* might be enough, if Mac's store is the teen-age meeting place across the street from school. Usually you will need to identify the store's location as well. The city name is rarely necessary unless your school serves several different areas. Printing the phone number may or may not be appropriate. You may wish to leave out a phone number when a merchant wants customers to come into the store. If phone inquiries are welcome, include the number. The proprietor's name or the store's slogan might also be added if these are familiar items that will increase appeal.

Enclose all of these elements in a simple border. Besides tying them together, a border will frame and emphasize the white space you have reserved. Like the other elements, the border should be simple. Just as in an art gallery, you don't want your viewer to murmur, "What a beautiful frame!" You want the eyes on what is inside.

Ads, like the photos described in Chapter 18, look best if the center of interest is not in the exact middle. Note the balancing of elements in the layouts on page 417.

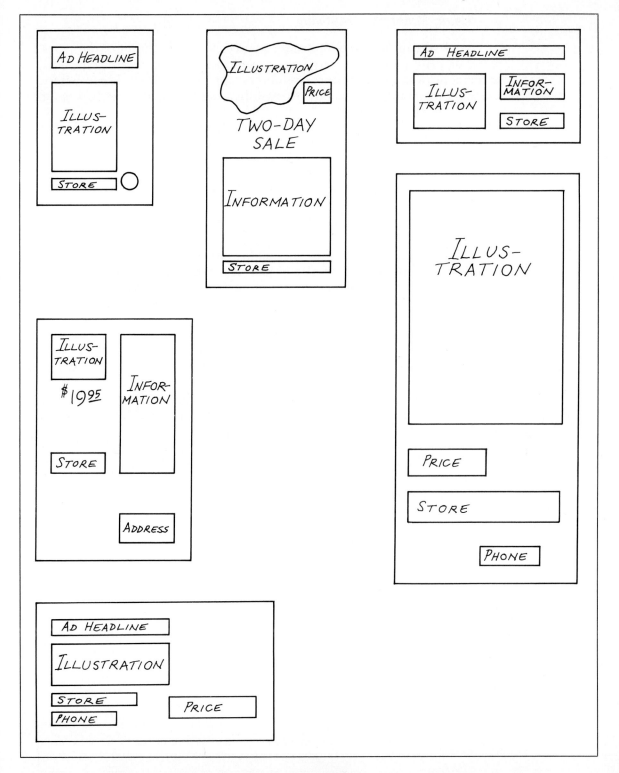

Using Materials Creatively

Look into all the typographical resources available through your newspaper or print shop. You may have access to a wide variety of typefaces, borders, or designs. From these resources, you will need to choose wisely, keeping everything in harmony. Readability and simplicity are the keys to an effective advertisement.

When you are preparing a layout for offset printing, you may be able to make extensive use of preprinted material. For instance, the store's business cards or letterhead may include attractive lettering, a design, or a trademark that will fit the ad. The merchant might also have catalogs with pictures of the products to be advertised. You can cut this material out and paste or tape it in place.

Drawings can be extremely effective in an ad. But what if you're not an artist and the merchant doesn't employ one? There is an easy solution, one used extensively by professional ad-layout workers. Several publishing services sell books or sheets of **clip art.** One page might contain football sketches, holiday designs, or pictures of hamburgers, for instance. Clip art is widely available and inexpensive. You simply cut out the design or picture you want and paste it in place.

Consider also adding appropriate photographs to your ad layouts. A photo of a popular student examining the advertised product in the store is a sure attention-getter. The advertiser will be expected to pay extra to cover photographic expenses, but this will not be a large amount. Photos should be clear and uncluttered. They should emphasize the student's face and show the product clearly. In your layout, the picture should be placed so the subject looks into, not out of, your ad.

You must have a signed release for commercial use of a person's photograph. The following sample can be used. If there has been a nominal payment to the person (often not necessary), the release should begin with the phrase "For value received."

PHOTO RELEASE

I hereby grant permission to _____(newspaper's name)

to publish photographs of me taken by _____(photographer's name)

in an advertisement for _____(store's name) to

be printed in the newspaper on or about _____ (date).

Signed _____

Date _____

Signature of witness _____

Signature of parent if student is a minor _____

In some cases, the commercial use of photos of student athletes may violate standards of a state athletic association. You will want to be sure where you and the athletes stand on this matter.

The accompanying ads show effective use of the various typographical resources likely to be available for use in school newspapers.

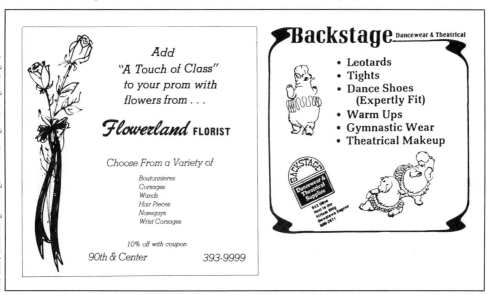

Activity 3: Evaluating and Designing Ads

1. Collect several effective, appealing ads. Identify the elements in each ad that you believe attract attention, spark interest, arouse desire, and lead to a sale.

2. Collect several ads that you believe match the tone of the store or business being advertised. Tell why you chose each.

3. Design an ad for a business that does not now advertise in your paper.

   a. Arrange all of the basic elements (headline, illustration, text, the name and address of the store or business, white space, and border) properly.

   b. Choose harmonious typefaces for the headline, text, and name in the ad and explain why they are appropriate to the tone you are trying to establish.

   c. Select a suitable illustration and explain how you would obtain it.

Supervising the Advertising Process

Advertising is not all selling and layout work. The business staff must make decisions about the general way in which ads will be placed in the newspaper. They must also make decisions about special kinds of ads that can be used to sell more advertising and even about matters of good taste in the ads that are submitted.

Placing Ads on a Page

The advertising manager usually positions the advertisements on the pages before any other makeup is done. Ad placement is marked on page dummies, which are then given to the page editors. They will fill in the remaining space with stories. Ads never appear on the front page and rarely on the editorial page.

The typical arrangement of advertising on a page is often referred to as a **half-pyramid**, or a **stairstep**, as illustrated in the following sketch.

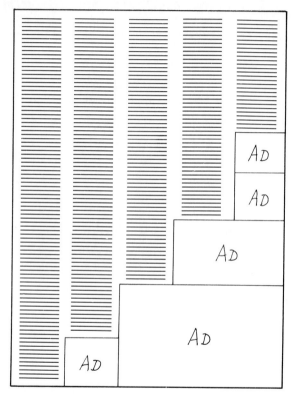

The principal advantage of this arrangement is that every advertisement will touch news copy. Your reader's eye, therefore, is more likely to be attracted to each ad. However, some newspapers have reported success in placing all the ads together. On a large page, the ads would generally form a rectangle across the bottom of the page. In a news magazine, an entire page might be filled with ads of assorted sizes.

Creating Special Kinds of Advertising

Sometimes related advertisements can be grouped to fill a complete page or even two facing pages, with or without accompanying stories. For

The basis for the grouping together of these ads is indicated in the upper left corner: All three businesses are located on Elm Street, in Bethesda, Maryland. Such an advertising arrangement requires early planning.

example, a number of different ads from clothing stores and department stores might be arranged to accompany a feature story on fall or spring fashions. Should a new shopping mall open, ads from the stores in the mall might appear in a rectangle around the edge of a page containing photos of the new mall in its center. Sometimes holiday, Homecoming, or graduation greetings from merchants or even from individuals are presented on a single page.

The advertising staff usually plans such pages far in advance. The idea is then presented to merchants to give them a chance to benefit from the impact of a complete page. In these cases, the stores may be charged enough to cover their share of the written or photographic publicity material on the page, since the material in effect becomes a part of their advertising message.

U-High Midway, the paper of University High School in Chicago, presented a clever spread about holiday shopping, telling a story that was continued from ad to ad. The story began, "Lucy needed ideas for holiday gift giving . . ." The individual ads were all the same size and design, each one featuring a photo of Lucy in the advertised store, examining a gift suggestion that was then described in the text under the photo.

Coupons are another idea that may develop interest and desire in prospective buyers. Each coupon, to be clipped from the paper, offers an incentive to patronize the store honoring the coupon. For example, a typical coupon offer from a popular eating place would be a free drink with the purchase of a sandwich. Obviously, coupon offers must be planned carefully with the store. A copy of the coupon as it will appear in your paper must be approved by the merchant before publication, for a misprinted coupon could be incredibly expensive or otherwise troublesome to the store.

A third type of special ad might be an **insert.** This usually consists of one or more pages the same size as your newspaper, printed separately and then inserted into the paper by hand. The principal advantage of an insert, besides attracting special attention, is that it may be printed in full color. A merchant may supply inserts or may order them through you and your printer. Your price will be based on the cost of color printing, the use of your paper as an advertising medium, and your labor in inserting the extra sheets.

Dealing with Controversial Ads

Advertisements are such an important source of publishing funds that refusing one seems almost beyond belief. Yet, the time may come when a prospective ad will raise a question as to whether it should be published. This might arise from poor taste in the ad's content. Another reason could be a product or service that your staff or the school administration considers unsuitable for a school publication.

A newspaper's editorial board has an established right to refuse advertising. Commercial newspapers and private and parochial school publications possess the absolute right to make such decisions. In the case of public school and public university newspapers, though, a number of court decisions have required that a decision to refuse an ad must be based on some good reason.

The most common cause for rejecting an ad is lack of available space. To be valid, such a decision would have to be based on a normal allotment of advertising space. Impartiality is also important. You could not refuse an ad from one beauty salon merely because a staff member had been dissatisfied with its work and print ads from other beauty salons. You could, however, refuse an ad that you felt was in poor taste and demand that it be revised. Courts have supported this right.

Most likely, though, the problems that arise with advertising will have to do with products or services that your school administration, the students, their parents, or the community may not feel are appropriate. What judgments would you make if ads containing the following were offered your paper: a political statement from a school board candidate, a suggestion that it's mature to drink a certain brand of beer, an invitation to join a recently established religious sect or cult, a computerized dating service's promise to improve subscribers' romantic lives, a statement by a student organization concerning the United States' policy in a foreign country?

In certain cases, the decision will have been made for you by a higher authority. Some states prohibit liquor advertising in public school and state university publications. One appeals court upheld the decision of a high school principal who, on the grounds of protecting student health, banned a publication containing a "headshop" ad. At least two court decisions have pointed out that a paid advertisement presenting a political opinion must be accepted by a public school newspaper that prints any other advertising.

Activity 4: Making Decisions About Ads

1. Evaluate the typical arrangement of ads on your school paper's pages by comparing it with the arrangements of other school newspapers. What improvements could you suggest?

2. Prepare concrete suggestions for increasing your paper's advertising through use of special page promotions or other creative ideas.

3. List a number of topics for ads that might be considered controversial. What do you think would be your paper's position about accepting each of them?

Summary

This chapter begins with an overview of the role of advertising in a school newspaper. It then discusses what must be done to sell advertising. Next, it explains the preparation of an advertisement. Finally, it considers ad placement, the creation of special kinds of ads, and problems concerning the acceptance of certain kinds of ads.

MANAGING THE ADVERTISING PROGRAM. Actual publishing costs determine the amount of advertising that must be sold. Most local businesses will buy advertising space if properly approached. The business manager supervises ad sales and preparation. There may also be an advertising manager, and there will certainly be advertising sales representatives and layout workers. Sometimes every staff member carries responsibility for selling and preparing ads.

SELLING ADVERTISING SPACE. Before approaching a merchant, three preparatory steps are essential. First, the staff must list and study its advertising prospects. Second, a complete sales kit including information about the school, its students, and the newspaper, as well as a statement of rates and a contract form, must be prepared. And third, an actual sample ad should be prepared to present to the prospect. Then, the merchant may be approached.

PREPARING AN ADVERTISEMENT. Ads must be visually oriented. They should draw the reader's attention, build up interest, create a desire for the product or service, and lead to a sale. They should also reflect the tone of the business. Ad layouts must be simple. Layouts consist of a headline, an illustration, a brief text, the store's name and address, white space, and a border that ties these elements together. The layout worker should make use of all available typographical elements, including preprinted materials, drawings, and photographs.

SUPERVISING THE ADVERTISING PROCESS. Appropriate placement of ads on a newspaper page, usually in a half-pyramid arrangement, helps make each ad effective. In addition, advertising managers should be alert to the possibility of grouping related ads around some special theme, to the use of coupons, and to advertising inserts. Sometimes decisions must also be made about matters of fairness, good taste, or controversial topics in advertisements.

Vocabulary

subscription	unitary method
business manager	spec layout
advertising manager	tear sheet
layout worker	clip art
sales kit	half-pyramid
rate sheet	stairstep
column inch	insert

Review Questions

1. How can a school paper's business manager determine how much advertising should be sold for a single issue of the paper?

2. What kinds of preparatory work should precede an advertising sales representative's approach to a prospective client?

3. What are the basic elements generally found in a typical small advertisement in a school paper?

4. How is attractiveness in an ad achieved?

5. What considerations should go into a decision to accept or reject a proposed ad that raises questions of taste or suitability?

Discussion Questions

1. Discuss the advantages and disadvantages of having each member of the staff responsible for selling and preparing advertising as opposed to relying on a special advertising staff.

2. To gain advertisers for your paper, how effective would a flyer or letter be that was sent out to local businesses at the start of a selling campaign? What should its contents be?

3. What businesses in your area could benefit substantially from advertisements in your school paper? What ones probably could not?

4. Which of the ads in the last issue of your school paper do you think was most effective? Why?

5. Why might an advertisement that is unobjectionable in a commercial newspaper be objectionable in a school newspaper?

Chapter Project

Advertising on a Large Scale

Plan and develop one of the following: a series of six ads for the different products or services of a single business or a page of advertising unified by a single theme that would attract advertising from a number of different merchants. Whichever you choose, prepare layouts and messages, including headlines and text, and indicate the illustrations you would use. You should have actual businesses in mind as you work on this project.

UNIT FIVE

Looking to
the Future

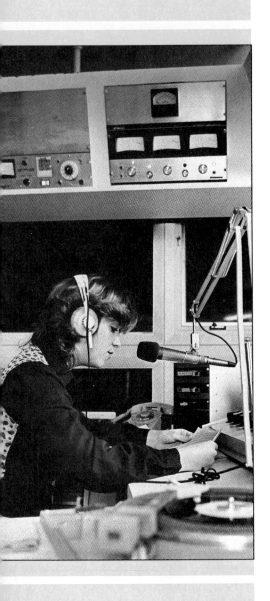

CAREERS
IN
JOURNALISM

When you have completed this chapter you should be able to

Recognize the wide range of jobs available to the person trained in journalism.

Identify the characteristics of those suited for work in journalism and related fields.

Plan your schooling and training if you decide to prepare yourself for a career in journalism or a related field.

Pursue the job of your choice in the right way.

"I awoke one day to the realization that careers are supposed to be fun," a young man told The Newspaper Fund recently. "Nothing is more important to me than choosing a life work I will always enjoy."

Journalism can be not only exciting but satisfying as well. The satisfaction can come from many different sources. It can come from meeting and talking to interesting and important people or from being "in the know" about local or distant events. It can come from anticipating the uncertainty of what news event might occur next or what today's work might bring. Satisfaction can also derive from helping people improve their lives through information you have discovered. And it can come from supporting American freedom by uncovering and explaining facts that citizens have a right to know.

The experiences of beginning reporter Camy Wilson offer an example. While carrying out routine assignments for the Minneapolis *Tribune,* she uncovered evidence of scandalous activities that were unfair to those victimized and expensive to taxpayers. One of her discoveries was that medical transportation services were charging $40 to $50 per trip to take elderly people to their doctors. Even though several would be carried in the same trip, they were being billed individually. Another discovery was that an administrator was selling an old man's home and possessions while the old man was in a nursing home recovering from a fall. The reporter's stories led to investigations and changes in the laws that had made these activities possible.

Typical questions asked about journalism as a career include what the educational requirements are, where and how people find jobs, what beginning salaries are, and what an employer looks for when hiring a new employee. Before examining these questions, a brief look at the entire picture of jobs in communications is desirable.

Recognizing the Wide Range of Jobs Available

As you are aware by this time, journalism includes every aspect of gathering, writing, editing, and publishing news, whether through the various print media or through radio or television. Writing is the key to much of this work. Because journalists are trained as writers, they can branch out into all forms of mass media work, including magazines, books, movies, and television. In addition, journalists are especially well suited to occupations in advertising and public relations.

Among the numerous jobs in the communications field are the following: (1) newspaper reporting, photography, and publishing; (2) magazine writing, illustrating, and publishing; (3) broadcast reporting, scriptwriting, directing, and camera or audio work; (4) book writing, illustrating, and publishing; (5) technical writing, illustrating, and publishing; (6) research

Superior writing ability and, more generally, a good command of English are characteristic of most of the successful people in the communications field, including radio and television reporters and announcers.

—*The Axe*, South Eugene High School, Eugene, Oregon

and data collection; (7) business communication, including writing and audiovisual work; (8) advertising copywriting, illustrating, and editing; (9) public relations, publicity, and promotional work; (10) commercial photography; (11) motion picture scriptwriting, film editing, directing, and camera or audio work; (12) translating and interpreting; and (13) teaching English and language arts.

Career possibilities are limitless for people who are trained in writing and communicating. It is impossible in one chapter of a book to do justice to the many jobs involving communication skills. Fortunately, much information is available from libraries, guidance offices, and professional organizations. In addition, the activities in this chapter will suggest a number of specialized sources.

Working in Print Journalism

Considering the field of newspaper work, with which you are most familiar as a result of your studies this year, what kinds of jobs are available?

Not surprisingly, the jobs available are similar to the ones you are likely to be doing now for your school newspaper. Of course, there are differences. On a larger newspaper, you would meet more people. Stories

Career Close-Up

Newspaper Feature Writer

Four years after earning a law degree, Peggy Mitchell Peterman was invited to write news articles for the St. Petersburg *Times*. She came to enjoy journalism so much that she stayed with the *Times* and has now been there for nearly two decades. Mrs. Peterman has been a feature writer since 1970.

"The world of the feature writer is quick-paced and varied. I write about all sorts of subjects, but I'm especially drawn to social is-sues—education, the family, the emotional stability of the home, the treatment of spouses and children, adoption, and other such sub-jects. I usually choose what I'll write about, though sometimes an editor will assign a sub-ject." Asked whether her feature stories ever grow out of direct observation of what is around her, Mrs. Peterman said that they fre-quently do. "There's always a story—maybe lots of stories—on every block. Going to work, I used to see every day an old, badly deteri-orated house set on stilts. One day I noticed that one side of it had been painted. When I investigated further, I discovered that the in-side was filled to overflowing with the most gorgeous flowers, like a botanical garden. I had to find out who had put so much love into the place, and I knew there must be a story here. There was: A very old man who used to own a farm had bought this place to be in-dependent of his children. He lived alone, and he ran the place as if it were his old farm, except that he grew nothing but flowers. I can't remember his words exactly, but one thing he said I can't forget: 'When I die, don't send any flowers, because I've had all the beauty of flowers while I lived.' There are a lot of stories like that all around us, but you've got to be observant if they're to catch your eye."

To start the process of turning her notes and observations on a subject into a story, Mrs. Peterman decides which observation or detail in her notes most forcibly seizes her at-tention and interest. That becomes the sub-ject of her lead, which she may rewrite as many as 10 times. When satisfied with the lead, she writes the rest of the story. She does not refer to her notes while she writes. "That would make my writing stiff and abrupt. It's only after I've written a draft that I'll turn to my notes to check for factual accuracy." Since she often rewrites her work at least once, it may take her two days to complete a 750-word story.

Does she still enjoy writing features after all these years? "Yes, but the nature of the enjoyment has changed. In 1970, I most en-joyed going out and doing research among people. Now, my chief satisfaction is in prac-ticing the craft of writing—in grooming, prun-ing, and polishing; in putting the right words in the right order; in making feature writing an art."

would often require more digging. Jobs would probably be more specialized. And, of course, you'd be paid. But, basically, working on a school newspaper is an excellent beginning for a journalism career.

There are a number of different kinds of entry-level jobs in the newspaper field. Among them are jobs as a stringer, reporter, desk (or rewrite) person, wire reporter, copyreader, headline writer, proofreader, specialized (or departmental) reporter, news photographer, editorial assistant, and circulation assistant. The following paragraphs will give more details about each of these starting-level positions.

The **stringer** represents a specific school, geographical area, or specialized subject, writing and submitting stories on a regular or occasional basis. Many high school and college students fill these jobs, gathering valuable experience to further their journalism careers.

A reporter, of course, carries out the basic work of the newspaper. The reporter's "nose for news" ensures a daily flow of information on which readers depend.

A **desk person,** or **rewrite person,** is also essential to any daily newspaper operation. He or she takes the reporter's basic story, often phoned in under pressure of deadline, rewrites it, and combines it with related stories to form a polished end product. This person must be able to think quickly and work economically with words.

A **wire reporter** has somewhat the same job as a reporter does, except that a wire service (or press association) may have hundreds of newspapers as its clients.

A copyreader, a headline writer, and a **proofreader** all have specific responsibilities similar to those carried out by people in corresponding positions on a school newspaper.

A **specialized reporter,** or **departmental reporter,** covers a specific field—sports, education, family life, medicine and health, entertainment, and so on. He or she must be well versed in that field and be able to present complicated technical matters in simple terms, if necessary. A specialized writer with a gift for humor or creativity may find a niche as a humor or feature story columnist.

A news photographer may accompany a reporter or work independently, recording events on film and preparing the prints for publication.

An **editorial assistant** performs tasks as an editor may direct. These can include typing, office tasks, reporting, research, and the like.

A **circulation assistant** carries out tasks related to all phases of distribution. The work may involve developing campaigns for increasing sales, updating mailing lists, keeping financial records, and collecting payments from subscribers and vendors.

Entering the Broadcast Media

Radio and television news rooms, either of individual stations or of networks, employ essentially the same kinds of workers as newspapers. Although the titles may differ from one news medium to another, the work is

Career Close-Up

TV News Editor

Joe Coscia is the executive editor of "News 4 New York," WNBC's news operation in New York. "I work a 10- to 12-hour day, supervising our assignment staff. But since there's no telling when a big story will break, I'm also on call nights and weekends. My staff is concerned with the practical problems of getting news events covered, as well as with the decisions as to what events will be covered, how they'll be presented, and the amount of time they'll take up. The assignment desk is the nucleus of the news-gathering operation. Each morning before dawn, the assignment editors go over the wire service reports, the daily papers, and other sources of news before they make any assignments. By midmorning, when many of our electronic-news crews have already hit the streets covering stories, show producers and managers meet to discuss the day's stories. The format for the evening broadcasts begins to take shape. As new developments occur, changes are made to keep coverage as timely as possible. A story that takes up two minutes on the air may have been preceded by four or five hours of logistical work."

Coscia got started in TV news as a freshman in college. To get information for a term paper on "happy-talk" news, he phoned WABC–TV's Channel 7 in New York repeatedly for over two weeks, pleaded for an interview, and finally got one. He was overwhelmed by the aura of the news room and expressed interest in taking any kind of summer job ABC might offer. A wish came true, and Coscia was offered a summer job in the news room. When a full-time position opened up in September, he took it. He kept up with his college studies, however, even while earning promotions and contributing substantially to award-winning broadcasts, and in 1974 he was graduated from Brooklyn College with a degree in broadcasting and journalism. In 1976, at the age of 23, he became chief city editor for Channel 7's "Eyewitness News" and also won an Emmy as producer of "White Line Fever: The Trucking Life," a special series on the trucking industry. "I broke into television," Coscia added, "without the benefit of a relative with pull: I'm the son of an Italian barber from Brooklyn."

For young people eager for a career in television, Coscia advocates internships combined with the kind of schooling that aims at both well-roundedness and specialization. "Good television journalists have to be well-rounded. History is one of the most important areas of study, since much of what is considered news is based on history and history repeats itself. But it's also a good idea to carve out a niche in a specialized area. Special features on the arts, health and science, and consumer and business news are of growing importance. There are wide-open opportunities in these areas and in the legal and technical aspects of broadcasting as well."

quite similar. Entry-level positions include reporter, news camera operator, news sound worker, broadcast scriptwriter, copyreader, videotape editor, and newscaster, or newsreader.

A reporter interviews news sources and develops stories. Television reporters must be more alert to the visual possibilities of news than print reporters, of course, and they often work with a **camera operator** and **sound worker** to produce a complete story. Some reporters may appear on camera for brief introductory or concluding remarks.

A **scriptwriter,** who works in the station news room, may perform the same tasks as a newspaper's rewrite person, assembling and completing a story when the reporter does not do so. A newscast script is more conversational in style than a newspaper story. A copyreader will check the script for conformity to the station's or network's guidelines.

A **videotape editor** and assistants will assemble the pictures and sound for a news report, according to an editor's directions.

A **newscaster** is the person who actually presents the story on the air. At a major television station or network, the newscaster may be a well-known anchorman or anchorwoman who is also highly skilled as a reporter. However, many radio stations employ less experienced newscasters, often called **newsreaders,** whose principal task is to read news items from wire service reports or prepared scripts.

Considering Related Jobs

Employment positions similar to those just discussed for newspapers, radio, and television exist in many other major fields of work. For instance, entry-level jobs in magazine or book publishing might include writer, copyreader, editorial assistant, **production assistant,** layout worker, proofreader, specialized (or departmental) writer, photographer, and illustrator.

Another major field that employs a large proportion of college journalism graduates each year is the field of technical writing. Skilled writers and editors with the appropriate technical backgrounds are needed to prepare industrial specifications and technical directions in nearly every manufacturing industry. Medical writers may work for hospitals, pharmaceutical distributors, or even busy doctors who must assemble reports about their patients. All levels of government employ writers and editors for reports and regulations. Researchers in scientific and other fields also need competent writers to prepare reports. Many large businesses employ writers and editors for their internal communications.

Writers, editors, and photographers may also work as **freelancers**—people who provide services but are not full-time members of a staff. While being your own boss can be a pleasant way to live, it produces little money until you have built up a reputation and established yourself with clients who can offer steady work at good rates of pay.

Advertising brings together selling, writing, and design skills. An advertising person must have communication skills plus good business sense.

Entry-level jobs, both on publications staffs and in advertising agencies, include advertising sales representative, classified ad writer, advertising designer, advertising copywriter, and market researcher.

In advertising, an advertising manager supervises advertising sales representatives, whose job it is to persuade business firms to buy advertising space or time. The advertising manager and the sales staff rarely prepare ads themselves, though they may suggest ideas or illustrations. A newspaper advertising department also promotes the sale of classified ads—simple, straight-text ads for such things as houses, jobs, or cars. These ads are often prepared for publication by a **classified ad writer.**

An **advertising designer** handles the visual and artistic aspects of ads created for publications, stores, corporations, or advertising agencies. An **advertising copywriter** prepares the actual text that appears in these advertisements.

The way a product is advertised may also be influenced by a **market researcher,** who through interviews, surveys, studies, and statistical analysis investigates the buying public's needs and wants.

Another major source of jobs requiring journalism skills is found in the **public relations** departments of many large companies and organizations. Public relations can be compared to advertising, except that in this case what is being advertised is the organization itself. Public relations people work to improve communication in at least two directions—between management and employees and between company and community. "PR" people must be able to establish good relationships with many different kinds of groups and have a wide understanding of the organization for which they work. Public relations work requires superior communication skills as well as social and organizational sense and sensitivity. Public relations work often involves writing, editing, and research.

A number of other communications jobs depend at least in part on journalistic training or ability. A list of these jobs would include the following, among others: commercial photographer, audiovisual worker, business manager for a publication, circulation manager, visual designer, graphic arts designer, printing technician, literary agent, literary-agency reader or editor, journalism or mass media teacher, information specialist or researcher, documentary producer, motion picture scriptwriter, and speech writer.

Activity 1:   Investigating Jobs in Communications

1. Choose a specific entry-level job from among those mentioned in the preceding pages. Collect information about this job from any available source and prepare a short report.

2. Send a self-addressed stamped envelope to the Council of Communication Societies, P.O. Box 1074, Silver Spring, Maryland 20910, asking for a copy of the pamphlet *Guide to Communication Careers*, which contains a summary of job functions, needed knowledge and skills, and

preparatory education for a wide variety of jobs, including most named in the preceding pages.

3. Interview a local person who works in the media (radio, TV, or print) at his or her place of work to find out exactly what the person does, how he or she does it, and how he or she feels about the job. Begin by preparing questions that will help draw out this information.

Identifying the Characteristics of a Journalist

Reg Murphy, former publisher of the San Francisco *Examiner*, told high school journalists a few years ago, "If you haven't read a newspaper in the last 24 hours, you aren't interested in working in journalism." Interest is the first requirement for journalism or any other profession.

Murphy and other authorities have also stressed the importance of being able to communicate easily and effectively in writing: to get ideas across, to paint word pictures—in a word, to communicate. Murphy has stated, "We are asking reporters today to be much better writers." And Ralph McGill of the Atlanta *Constitution* has said, "You can't really hope to be much of a writer, it seems to me, unless you like to read."

Curiosity is another trait often mentioned. Young people who can take a fresh look at the world around them, asking Why? and How?, may fit well into journalism.

Imagination counts as well. Peggy Mitchell Peterman of the St. Petersburg *Times* has commented, "As a writer you will have the opportunity to take a subject and soar to the outermost regions of your mind. You can paint pictures, titillate, excite, rectify, substantiate, clarify. It is an exciting occupation."

Journalists should be self-starters. Good ones have the ability to see news possibilities, decide what questions need to be asked and what should be investigated, and then go ahead and question and investigate. James Reston of *The New York Times* has emphasized "vitality, drive, aliveness" as essential qualities.

A journalist benefits from a probing, perceptive mind. Frequently, he or she must look beneath the surface—beyond the press release or the supposedly authoritative statement. Herbert Brucker of the Hartford *Courant* has mentioned the need for a person who will "ferret out the truth and tell it to people."

Journalists must be able to analyze and think rationally. They know that the reporting process has two parts and that these parts will be used over and over again. First is the gathering of the news, which means doing research and collecting information. Then, the facts are organized and written up. In the second part of this process, one first analyzes and thinks about the collected information and then organizes it logically.

Journalists should be knowledgeable. Their education should be broad, and they should continue it by reading widely. In their minds should be much pertinent information about the world in which they live. A ready memory for it is desirable.

One editor has said that a journalist must be "hungry"—hungry for information, hungry for reasons, never satisfied with less than the whole story, never satisfied until all sources have been pursued.

The following checklist should help you decide whether you are inclined toward a career in journalism. The more questions you can honestly answer yes to, the greater the likelihood that journalism might be a reasonable career choice for you.

✓ **Checklist for Considering a Career in Journalism**

☐ 1. Do I follow the news daily?

☐ 2. Do I like to read?

☐ 3. Do I have an interest in and talent for writing?

☐ 4. Am I curious about the *why* and *how* of the world around me?

☐ 5. Have I often come up with subjects that I wanted to investigate further?

☐ 6. Do I tend to look beneath the surface of things for greater understanding of them?

☐ 7. Am I good at analyzing data and information?

☐ 8. Do I make a constant effort to broaden my knowledge?

☐ 9. Am I "hungry" for information, reasons, and explanations?

Activity 2: Checking Your Skills

1. Write a short paragraph about your interest in journalism and the particular career possibilities you would be most interested in researching.

2. List the skills you believe are necessary for a reporter on your local newspaper and those you think would be needed by a reporter on your local TV or radio station.

3. Assess your own skills. Do you think you could qualify for a reporter's job? If not, what skills do you need to acquire or improve?

4. Assess your qualifications for at least two of the other jobs described in this chapter. On the basis of your evaluation, for which job do you feel you might be best qualified?

Planning Your Education and Training

Although there are some differences of opinion as to the best path to reach a career in journalism, everyone agrees on one basic idea. You must have training and practice in writing at every stage of your education.

High School Preparation for a Career in Journalism

At the high school level, the education of a future professional journalist should include a variety of courses that emphasize writing. Reporting, as you have seen, provides training in, among other things, finding main ideas, summarizing and being brief, and writing clear, sharp sentences. Courses that require creative writing, written analysis of literature, essay preparation, developing research techniques, and term paper writing are especially valuable. However, almost all courses—including vocational ones—can prove useful to a future journalist. The wider your knowledge, the better prepared you will be for whatever assignment may come your way.

Learning to type is absolutely essential. Whether you will in the future use a typewriter or a word processor, typing skill will be invaluable. A course in computers may also be helpful. While you may never need to program a computer in the same way as students who are studying business, math, or science may, you will be likely to use one for information retrieval and other purposes linked to journalism.

College Opportunities

Most editors today are looking only at college graduates when they hire new employees. Occasionally, of course, someone may get a position in journalism without a college degree. You will hear about famous journalists of the past who never attended college but simply went to work at an early age in a newspaper office and learned the trade there. Then, there might be the young person whose cousin owns a newspaper and offers him or her a job upon finishing high school. These examples, though, will be exceptions to the general rule.

Should you major in journalism at college or take a general liberal arts course with a major in some other subject? Professor M. L. Stein of New York University, who has written about journalism careers, points out: If you don't study journalism at college, who is going to teach you on the job? Press people are busy. They have little time to teach a cub reporter the fine points of newspaper style, interviewing skills, or the complexities of libel and privacy law. Few newspaper organizations are set up to provide formal on-the-job training. An untrained reporter will be left to sink or swim, and many will sink, according to Professor Stein.

You will not lack a traditional liberal arts education if you major in journalism. Accredited journalism schools, as well as many others, limit journalism courses to 25 percent of the total a student may take. This leaves three fourths of your college years to be devoted to a wide variety—the wider the better—of other courses. Then, too, some journalism courses, such as the history of mass media, are liberal arts studies in themselves.

Finally, being in a school of journalism may provide a better path to a job. Editors seeking new employees often come directly to these schools.

Generally speaking, a college degree is required of those seeking a career in journalism. The college students shown here could be preparing for jobs on a newspaper or magazine by getting experience in layout work.

—Photo by Martha Stewart from The Picture Cube

The journalism faculty is in touch with the job market and can provide advice and job leads.

What college should you select? You have a wide choice, ranging from small colleges with two or three instructors teaching in a friendly but often effective journalism department to huge universities with large communications faculties and a wide variety of courses. The biggest, the University of Texas, has over 2,000 journalism students. At the larger schools, you will have a choice of majors: print journalism, broadcast journalism, advertising, public relations, scriptwriting, business journalism, agricultural journalism, and so forth. Your choice of college will also depend to some extent on such things as location, costs, and scholarship aid. Still, you should make every effort to find out about the reputation of the schools you are considering, as well as to obtain personal impressions from journalism students actually attending these colleges.

You may also wish to consider a nearby community college for your first two college years. You may receive more personal attention and guidance there, as well as have a better chance for directed, practical experience on the college newspaper.

Practical Experience

Perhaps even more important than academic training in journalism is experience in writing for publication during your high school and college years. In addition to working on your school newspaper, you may be able to arrange part-time job experience at a local newspaper or broadcasting station. Though your lack of experience may work against you, you should be encouraged by the fact that even the most famous journalists once started out looking for work with no experience behind them. Walter Cronkite, one of the most famous television newscasters of all time, started out as a cub reporter on a local newspaper while he was still in high school. Myrna Oliver of the Los Angeles *Times* began her career at the age of 13 by writing feature, news, and sports stories for a weekly newspaper in her home community.

You may not even have to leave your campus to qualify as a school correspondent for your local paper. A campus stringer, as noted earlier, writes a regular column or submits occasional stories on school activities of interest to the wider reading public of a community newspaper. You might be paid little or nothing, but you will be building up a valuable collection of printed articles that will impress future employers.

At the high school level, another opportunity for extensive training exists. Summer institutes, usually on college campuses, are typically aimed at training next year's newspaper staff. They offer continuous practice and guided experience for periods ranging from one to five weeks. Scholastic journalism magazines list these institutes in their spring issues.

When you reach college, you should join the staff of the school newspaper. At smaller colleges and community colleges, the paper is likely to be a project of the journalism department, and so a journalism major will be automatically involved. At larger universities, the newspaper often is separate, frequently an independent off-campus publication, and you must make a special effort to join the staff as a reporter or editor.

Many other writing possibilities can be found on or near college campuses. A community newspaper or broadcasting station may have a job for you. There are also college radio stations, organizations that want publicity people, literary magazines or yearbooks, university offices where technical writing may be done, and university presses or other book publishers. The point is that you must find and use opportunities for writing or other work relevant to your career goals.

Internships

Internships are another valuable way of getting training. As a high school student, you may be able to take advantage of informal days in a local newspaper office, such as those arranged annually by the National Federation of Press Women. Some community newspapers offer high school students specific assignments to write school news for publication. Others, such as the Contra Costa *Times* in California, have planned formal internships through high school teachers.

Career Close-Up

Newspaper Editorial Writer

"People are surprised when they learn what editorial writers are really like," says Rena Pederson, who writes editorials for the Dallas *Morning News*. "It's often assumed that an editorial writer has been on staff for many years and occupies an ivory tower. Actually, many are young and more like reporters covering a beat than like aloof heavy thinkers. They may have to get to work by 7 a.m. or stay till 11 p.m. to meet a deadline. And besides writing editorials, they may be writing columns and doing proofreading and editing." Ms. Pederson, herself a young woman, writes a column and edits her paper's op-ed page, in addition to writing about three editorials a week. "Because of mistaken assumptions about the work, editorial writing is seldom depicted as the exciting, challenging, and attainable job it is, and even university journalism programs usually offer too few courses in it."

How did she reach her present position? "I had been a critic of television shows, and eventually I wanted to write on different subjects, especially telecommunications, the impact of computers, and social issues. After four years of bad television programs, I called the editorial director and proposed that I be considered for an editorial-writing position that had opened up. I got the job. Since then, I've taken on new subjects I'm interested in—local politics, the arts, women's concerns, the aged, social security, the environment, and most recently, the Far East."

Writing an editorial, according to Ms. Pederson, is much like writing a literary essay, "except that the general form is set—here's the issue; here's what we think; here's an opposing view; and here's the nut, or kernel, of the matter." Is she assigned a subject or told what to say? "We have daily staff meetings at which we discuss what's in the news. Usually, the editorial writers select subjects appropriate to them or within their areas of expertise. Since, of course, the editorial page is still the publisher's page, what we say is guided by our knowledge of the publisher's, and the community's, standards."

A tip for aspiring editorial writers: "Write opinion pieces for the op-ed pages of local and national papers. If they're published, not only will you be paid for them, but you can assemble them as work samples to show to prospective employers."

The Student Press Service offers year-long internships in Washington, D.C., to young people, usually just after high school graduation. Interns search out national news for the press service, which then distributes it to subscribing high school newspapers.

Internships enable many young men and women to get "hands-on" experience in a professional news room. They are often connected with college or university course work and can provide interns with a wide range of practical experience.

An internship may also be worked out in connection with a university course. The University of Missouri assigns journalism students to work regularly as reporters or copyreaders for the local community newspaper. A variety of summer internships are arranged locally or regionally for other college students. Internships typically provide you with experience rather than pay.

Activity 3: Deciding About Your Education

1. Send a stamped self-addressed envelope to the American Council on Education in Journalism and Mass Communication, School of Journalism, University of Missouri, Box 838, Columbia, Missouri 65205. Ask for a copy of the pamphlet *Accredited Journalism and Mass Communications Education.* This describes colleges currently having accredited programs.

2. Using the catalogs of several colleges or universities, prepare a brief report on the kind and extent of journalism and communications courses

at each school. What variety of choice is there? Do the courses lead to a degree in journalism? Does the school offer graduate courses? If so, how extensive are they and in what areas?

3. Write The Newspaper Fund, P.O. Box 300, Princeton, New Jersey 08540, for a copy of the *Journalism Scholarship Guide.* Examine this booklet, which describes more than $2,000,000 worth of scholarships and gives information about loan funds. List the offers at colleges of your choice for which you might be able to apply.

4. If possible, arrange to visit the editorial offices of the campus newspaper at a nearby university or college and report your impressions to the class.

Choosing and Finding a Job

With so many job options available to explore, how can you choose the right one? Journalism as a profession has become more and more popular in the last two decades. Schools of journalism have expanded their faculties and course offerings but still cannot take care of all the applicants. Reasons for this growth may be found in the rapid changes and improvements in the technology of news transmission and in a growing desire among young people for personally fulfilling or socially useful jobs rather than merely high-paying ones.

As a result, the job market in journalism and the media has become highly competitive in spite of the fact that the mass media are among the nation's largest sources of employment. Nevertheless, the market for skilled young people willing to work hard always remains open. Knowledge of specialized or technical subjects can be an asset in editors' eyes. Areas of journalism where the demand for new employees may increase include the following: photojournalism, to meet the continued interest in visual news brought about by television; graphic arts design, to make newspapers and magazines more inviting; sportswriting, to satisfy the growing interest in this field; and local news reporting, given the strength of newspaper circulation figures in small cities and suburban areas.

If you had a crystal ball, you could predict where you may find the greatest opportunities in journalism over the next 20 years. But even without one, an observer can note certain developments that will determine employment possibilities. For instance, television newscasts will almost certainly increase as cable reaches more American homes. A trend seems to be developing toward broader, perhaps national coverage of news about people, sports, and business, as demonstrated by Gannett Corporation's successful *USA Today.* Earlier predictions that newspapers would fade out or give way to computer-printed sheets reaching homes electronically do not seem to be coming true. However, computers will be used far more to store, call up, and distribute information, and journalism will be affected by this technology.

Surveying the Prospects

In spite of the competition, there are jobs for people who have worked hard in college and who are willing to search intensively. The Newspaper Fund reported that of each 100 new graduates surveyed in 1981, an average of 16 went to work for daily and weekly newspapers and 14 for radio and television stations. Public relations offices hired 11, as did advertising agencies. Seven went to work for magazines or took other media jobs. Twenty-four found nonmedia positions, eight went on to graduate school, and nine had not yet found work at the time of the survey.

The Newspaper Fund noted, "Students who find jobs in a particular field are the ones who prepared intensively in that field. Two thirds of the graduates who landed daily newspaper jobs were news-editorial majors in college. More than 90 percent of the students who found work at television stations were broadcasting majors, and more than 80 percent of those who started advertising-agency jobs were advertising or public relations majors."

Young journalists who have found work after college invariably report that the jobs are not on metropolitan newspapers. "You must have experience" is the common declaration of personnel directors at these publications. Openings do exist, though, on small city newspapers or even weekly papers; as a result, you may need to be willing to move in order to find employment.

Dorothy Butler Gilliam, a well-known black columnist, has said, "I would advise you to seek out small- and medium-sized newspapers for starters. The competition is usually less intense and there is room to develop your talent and to grow."

Experience on a small newspaper can be very valuable, for you will do almost everything needed to assemble and publish the paper. You may have to cover routine meetings, take telephone calls, prepare obituaries, copyread, and write headlines. It would not be unusual to be asked to take and process photographs, sell and prepare advertising, manage circulation, or even become involved in setting the type and printing the newspaper.

What about jobs in communications for women and minorities? Although a typical newspaper office 40 years ago was populated almost exclusively by white males, the picture has changed. Women, in particular, now make up nearly half of journalism school graduates and are finding jobs everywhere in reporting, editorial, and broadcasting positions. In addition, most news organizations have affirmative action policies, which encourage the hiring of minorities. Television, in part because it has expanded so rapidly over the last few decades, has drawn in large numbers of minority journalists.

At the management level of daily newspapers, women and minorities occupy fewer positions. A survey by the Associated Press Managing Editors suggested as a reason for this situation that most female and minority journalists are under 35 and have been in newspaper work for less than 10 years. If this is the case, management positions occupied by women and minorities are likely to increase as these groups gain more experience and seniority.

Career Close-Up

Magazine News Photographer

When David Hume Kennerly was a junior in high school, he started taking pictures for the school paper and yearbook. In 1972, at the age of 25, he won a Pulitzer Prize for his photographic coverage of the war in Vietnam. A couple of years later, he became President Gerald Ford's personal photographer. He is now on the staff of *Time* magazine, where he has worked for over a decade.

How did Kennerly get so far so fast, and what can he say to young people who hope to be professional photographers? "From an early age I knew that a professional photographer was what I wanted to be. I pursued my goal with a fierce desire. Besides taking pictures for the paper and yearbook, I took a photography course that the school offered—though mainly I learned by trial and error. I learned how to develop film, how to make prints, and the other things a pro should know. When it came to getting a job, I had to go it alone—nobody in my family was even remotely connected with the news business. I had to cling to the idea 'If you don't ask, you don't get.'

"To young people who want photography for their life's work, I'd say this: You have to want it more than anything else in your life. You must set your sights on the kind of job you want and head for it. There's a lot of competition out there, so you have to work longer and harder and be better than the rest. Also, you have to be informed and understand what you're covering. To be a news photographer, you have to be a newsperson first, a photographer second."

What special skills or kinds of knowledge are needed to photograph news events here and around the world for *Time*? "You must know how to get *to* a story, as well as how to photograph it—and how to get the film back to the magazine. So I have to know about the country I'm working in, the key politicians, and the airline schedules."

The satisfaction Kennerly gets from his work is that of photographing an event in a way that accurately portrays what happened and then seeing his photograph printed properly in the magazine. His work sometimes has its humorous aspects. When covering the India–Pakistan war of 1971, the Indian government was slow in issuing the pass he needed to get to the front lines. "So everyday I sneaked out to the battlefield in a taxi. Eventually my pass was ready—the day after the war ended."

Launching a Job Campaign

No matter what kind of job you are after, your search will probably entail three things: a letter, a résumé, and an interview. The letter should be concise (no more than a page), positive, and extremely neat. It should stress your qualifications, refer to the enclosed résumé, and request an interview. The résumé itself should present relevant personal data, work objectives, experience, and education. Standard reference books or your guidance counselor can give you further assistance in preparing your résumé. Before an interview, you should research the company where you are to be interviewed. Try to get an idea of what the newspaper or company considers as its basic purpose, what kinds of jobs it has open, and what kind of place it is to work. You should also have some idea of what salary you might reasonably expect.

If this sounds like a lot of work, it is! But, be assured that with persistence this work will eventually pay off, even if you are only looking for an internship or a part-time job. "If a position should open up in two or three years, those people who interviewed with us for intern spots may be in touch with us again," says Albert Dilthey, public relations and employee director of the Miami *Herald*. "Or, if we were impressed with them, we might keep their application on file and contact them."

Another suggestion when applying for a job is to have a neatly organized **stringbook,** a collection of your published stories. Clip each story and mount it on a single sheet of plain binder paper. Write the name of the publication and the date on each page. Then, assemble the pages in a ring binder with the most recent story on top. As your published work increases, add new stories and take out older ones that are not your best. A stringbook should aim at quality, not quantity. Also, your résumé should be in the front of the binder. Editors may wish to keep the stringbook for a while and later return it to you, so be sure your name, address, and phone number appear on its cover.

Noted journalist Lars-Erik Nelson reports, "I took Mark Twain's 'infallible advice' for getting a job. I went to the owner of a small-town weekly when I was 16 and offered to work for nothing. As a businessman he was delighted at the offer and found that he had made a good deal." Soon, Nelson was getting paid for his work.

Loren Ghiglione, now publisher and owner of a small daily, has recommended sending perhaps 50 enthusiastic letters to editors of small dailies or weeklies and then following up wherever possible with a visit to the editor's office. The editor will find it harder to turn you down in person, according to Ghiglione.

Activity 4: Preparing Job Search Materials

1. Prepare a standard job résumé for an after-school or summer job for which you might wish to apply. Ask your teacher or another student to read over the résumé and give reactions and suggestions for improvement.

2. Write a cover letter referring to your résumé and requesting an interview. Make your letter concise, positive, and very neat.

3. Collect your best writing in a stringbook, as suggested in the preceding section.

4. Make research notes about the newspaper or company to which you might send your résumé. Try to find out its organizational structure, the audience it serves, and the way it communicates information. How can this information help you in your job interview?

Summary

This chapter begins by surveying the jobs available in print and broadcast journalism and in related fields. It then describes the characteristics of people most suited for careers in journalism. It goes on to consider the kind of schooling and other preparation needed. Finally, it discusses employment prospects and the launching of a job campaign.

RECOGNIZING THE WIDE RANGE OF JOBS AVAILABLE. Communications and mass media cover a wide spectrum of jobs. Jobs in professional print journalism are similar to those you are likely to have had on a school newspaper. Work in broadcast news is also much the same, the main difference being television's emphasis on the visual. Large numbers of people with training in journalism also work in magazine or book publishing, advertising, public relations, and other jobs requiring skills related to journalism.

IDENTIFYING THE CHARACTERISTICS OF A JOURNALIST. A strong interest in reading and writing is characteristic of people most likely to succeed in careers in journalism. Other commonly mentioned traits are curiosity, imagination, initiative, clear and logical thinking, wide-ranging knowledge, and an insatiable appetite for the facts.

PLANNING YOUR EDUCATION AND TRAINING. For most careers in journalism, extensive practice in writing should begin at the high school level. Typing skill is necessary, and computer knowledge is desirable. Since most editors and managers prefer to employ college graduates, a college education is generally necessary. It should focus on journalism but extend over a wide area of the liberal arts. Practical experience in writing for publication should accompany a college education. Internships, in which you work without pay for a commercial publication, are one way of securing this experience.

CHOOSING AND FINDING A JOB. Since work in journalism is much sought after, the job market is highly competitive. Positions usually go to college graduates who are well prepared and have conducted an intensive search. Starting-level jobs are often in smaller communities where there is lower pay but much broader work experience. Getting a job usually involves requesting interviews by means of letters of application and résumés.

Vocabulary

stringer	circulation assistant	freelancer
desk person	camera operator	classified ad writer
rewrite person	sound worker	advertising designer
wire reporter	scriptwriter	advertising copywriter
proofreader	videotape editor	market researcher
specialized reporter	newscaster	public relations
departmental reporter	newsreader	internship
editorial assistant	production assistant	stringbook

Review Questions

1. What are some of the kinds of work inside and outside print and broadcast journalism available to someone with training in journalism?

2. What aspects of training in journalism are especially helpful to the person seeking employment outside the news media?

3. What are the characteristics of a person for whom journalism might be a suitable career?

4. What kinds of academic work and practical experience are desirable for the development of a future professional journalist?

5. What is the job market like for those seeking work in journalism?

Discussion Questions

1. In view of the expanding role of the visual media and computers, do you think the development of writing skills will continue to be an important part of getting a job in communications? Why or why not?

2. How might print journalism and broadcast journalism differ as to the kinds of satisfaction they offer? Which do you think would be more satisfying? Why?

3. In an age in which people are often encouraged to acquire specialized knowledge and skills, why should breadth of knowledge be useful in journalism and the other fields of work discussed in this chapter?

4. If you were planning on a career in journalism or a related field, which subjects would you take in college aside from those directly related to your career choice? Why?

5. What are the best methods of convincing a future employer that you are the one to hire?

Chapter Project

Preparing a Job Search Plan

Choose a job in journalism or a related field that you might wish to have when you are ready to start a career. Write up a detailed, step-by-step plan to secure this job. Your plan should make use of information and suggestions given in this chapter. It should also incorporate research and other kinds of work carried out to maximize your chances of getting an interview and demonstrating your fitness for the position.

Editor's Handbook

The Editor's Handbook contains practical plans and hints for publishing a school newspaper. Because no two newspapers face quite the same problems, you should not consider the material in the handbook as the only way to proceed. Rather, you may adapt the suggestions to meet your own journalistic requirements.

In general, the complete production program for a school newspaper is outlined here. Occasionally, reference is made to something explained more thoroughly in a chapter of this book. In these cases, you can use the Index that begins on page 513 to locate the desired material.

1 Organizing Your Staff

Although the staff organization will vary from one newspaper to another, the following general suggestions should prove useful.

Setting Qualifications for Staff Positions

To be eligible for the newspaper staff, students should have completed an apprenticeship of some kind. This might consist of a journalism course, during which students are given a chance to participate in the newspaper as they learn in class. Alternatively, students might simply work directly with reporters and other staff members, learning through a more traditional apprenticeship. Generally, candidates for top staff positions should have held lesser jobs during the preceding year. In addition, in most cases the editor of the entire paper should previously have been an assistant editor or a page editor.

Besides training in journalism, staff members should have good scholastic records, a willingness to work hard, and a cooperative attitude. Good scholastic records usually indicate students who are capable and are willing to spend necessary time on anything they undertake. Lack of good grades may indicate students who will treat both staff responsibilities and schoolwork indifferently.

Moreover, students must be able to devote time and energy to the paper and still keep up with their schoolwork.

Selecting Your Staff

There are several ways of choosing the editor of a paper: election by the staff; appointment by the retiring staff; appointment by the adviser; or appointment by the student council or principal from candidates presented by the staff or adviser. If election by the whole school is permitted, students may tend to use personality instead of journalistic ability as a criterion. Therefore, either election by the staff or appointment is generally a more dependable method.

Sometimes, the post of assistant editor and other special editorial positions are also filled by staff election or appointment. Together with the editor, these people constitute an editorial board that plans and directs the newspaper's policies. Either the editor or the editorial board can then make appointments to other staff positions, with the adviser's approval.

Using a Rotating Staff System

Some schools, particularly those with large newspaper staffs, rotate staff members in the various positions. An advantage of this plan is that it tends to give experience to more people. The major disadvantage is that a less effective newspaper may be produced because of lack of continuity and less experience on the part of staff members.

Several rotation methods have been developed. One way is to change all jobs every issue. Another is to create two staffs, publishing alternate issues. The resulting competition can be good for the paper. Some schools establish an experienced permanent staff, which acts in an advisory capacity to a rotating staff that actually carries the responsibility.

Assigning Duties of Staff Members

The jobs outlined below divide staff duties into basic functions. Assigning people to all or most of these positions provides staff responsibility for a large number of students. Better coordination of work, however, may result from combining some functions. Small staffs will combine jobs as a matter of necessity. Larger papers may divide up the jobs as they see fit.

Each of the jobs is described as applying to one individual. In some cases, several students might be assigned to a job. In other cases, several assistants may be required.

EDITOR (EDITOR IN CHIEF)

- Supervises the production of the paper.
- Determines how much space can be assigned to each department.
- Decides what important stories are to be used and where they are to be placed.
- Decides what artwork or photographs are to be used.
- Acts as head of the editorial board, which determines the editorial policy of the newspaper. Writes the editorials or sees that they are written.
- Checks important stories. Approves the page layouts and page proofs.

- With the approval of the faculty adviser, assigns and makes changes in staff positions. May also evaluate the performance of staff members.

ASSISTANT EDITOR (MANAGING EDITOR OR PRODUCTION MANAGER)

- Helps the editor in all duties. Serves as acting editor when the permanent editor is absent.
- Sets up the production schedule. Sees that all production steps are taken according to schedule.
- May receive stories from the copy desk to check for accuracy and form. May then distribute them to the proper page editors.
- Supervises the proofreaders.
- Supervises the assembling and folding (or stapling) of papers.

ASSIGNMENT EDITOR (NEWS EDITOR OR CITY EDITOR)

- Assigns the reporters' beats, checks to see that all beats are being covered regularly, and changes assignments as needed.
- Keeps the Future Book.
- Assigns all important stories to reporters, following up on plans made earlier by the editor and the page editors. (The editorial page editor and sports page editor may often be in charge of making their own assignments.)

PAGE EDITOR (ONE FOR EACH PAGE, EACH WITH ONE OR MORE ASSISTANTS)

- Plans the page by making a preliminary page dummy and then revising it to fit new assignments and completed stories.
- Determines what stories are to be used. Follows up to see that reporters are writing these stories.
- Checks the stories received from the copy desk for length, accuracy, and completeness.
- Writes or revises headlines.

- Prepares the final dummy after the advertising manager has placed the ads on the page. May paste up the finished page for reproduction.
- Checks the page proofs or finished stencils.

COPY EDITOR

- Supervises and assigns work to the copyreaders. Sets up the copyreaders' schedule.
- Works as a copyreader.

COPYREADER

- Reads and corrects the copy received from the reporters. Returns the copy for rewriting or other revision, if necessary. Checks for spelling, grammar, punctuation, accuracy, correct form, style, and completeness.
- May write headlines.
- Delivers corrected copy to the editor or page editors. (On some papers, copyreaders are assigned to specific pages and work with the page editors.)

PROOFREADER

- Working with a copyholder (who reads copy aloud to the proofreader), compares the proof, the column-width typing, or the typed stencil with the original copy and marks the corrections to be made. (Proofreading may sometimes be the responsibility of the page editors.)

COPYHOLDER

- Working with a proofreader, carefully reads copy aloud so that the original can be compared with the printed or final typed version.

EXCHANGE EDITOR

- Reads exchange papers and from them writes stories about happenings in other schools.
- Notes the outstanding story, department, or makeup ideas in other papers and passes them on to the appropriate members of the newspaper staff.

- Mails the paper to the schools on the exchange list.

CIRCULATION MANAGER

- Manages the sales campaign for subscriptions.
- Keeps a record of subscribers.
- Counts and distributes the papers.
- Prepares the papers for mailing to subscribers outside the school.

ART EDITOR

- Suggests and develops ideas for art.
- Does the artwork for the paper as directed by the editor or requested by other staff members.

HEADLINE WORKER

- On many offset papers, prepares headlines from type or printed alphabets.

LIBRARIAN

- Keeps a file containing past issues of the paper.
- Keeps a scrapbook of clippings about the school taken from daily and other newspapers.
- Keeps files of photographs, other illustrations, and advertisements.
- Clips from the paper and files in the morgue information about the school's history, students, teachers, or activities that may be useful to reporters for future issues.
- Maintains a collection of reference books.

TYPIST OR TYPESETTER

- May retype handwritten copy when necessary.
- For mimeographed papers and for some offset papers, types the copy in column widths so that margins may be justified.
- In a school with its own typesetting machine, operates the typesetting machine.
- May prepare mimeograph stencils.
- On stencils or offset copy, makes corrections as indicated by the proofreaders.

PHOTO EDITOR

- Suggests ideas for photographs. Works with the editor and page editors in deciding which stories should be illustrated with photographs.
- Schedules photographs, assigns them to photographers, and makes any special arrangements needed.
- Follows up on all photographs to be sure they are ready as needed.

PHOTOGRAPHER

- Takes photographs as assigned.
- May develop film and prepare prints for reproduction.
- Keeps the darkroom in order. Orders supplies through the business manager.

BUSINESS MANAGER

- Plans the budget with the editor and the adviser.
- Keeps records of income and expenses, checking them against budget allowances.
- Prepares regular business reports.
- Pays all bills by check.
- Receives all money and makes bank deposits.
- Orders or purchases supplies.

ADVERTISING MANAGER

- Plans the advertising sales campaign.
- Assigns and supervises the advertising sales representatives.
- Keeps records of all advertising sales.
- Arranges ads on page dummmies and submits them to the proper page editors.
- Checks completed ad layouts and submits them to the printer or, if no outside printer is involved, supervises and checks the work done in the school to prepare the ads for reproduction.

ADVERTISING SALES REPRESENTATIVE

- Sells advertising.
- Prepares ad layouts.
- Delivers the proofs or completed papers to the merchants.
- Collects money due from merchants.

ADVERTISING WORKER

- Prepares actual advertisements for offset reproduction, working from the layouts.

REPORTER

- Covers assigned beats.
- Writes stories discovered on a beat or assigned by editors.
- Takes each story back to the news source, as necessary, to check the accuracy of the facts.
- Turns stories in to the copy desk. Rewrites or corrects them, if necessary.

If you are producing a mimeographed paper, two additional staff positions will need to be filled.

MIMEOSCOPE WORKER

- Working on a special machine, transfers the nameplate, cartoons, lines, headline lettering, advertisements, and artwork to the stencil being used to prepare the paper.

MIMEOGRAPH WORKER

- Mimeographs pages according to the production schedule.
- Keeps the mimeograph machine clean and the supplies in order.

2 Setting Up Your News Room

Any organization functions more smoothly in the right surroundings. The school newspaper is no exception. Real news rooms are scarce in high schools, but you can do much to make an ordinary classroom serve as an efficient news room.

Sometimes, you can plan an ideal school news room in a new building or as part of a school remodeling program. It might be attached to a regular classroom but separated from it so that it can be used while the adviser is teaching other classes. An outside door and a connecting door to the classroom are necessary. The room should be large enough to permit 15 or 20 students to work comfortably at one time. It should contain desks for the editor and business manager, a copy desk, worktables, a telephone, typewriters, files, bulletin boards, a bookcase, and storage space. An adjoining darkroom can help assure quick results on news photography.

When the staff must use a classroom, working only when other classes are not being taught in it, an efficient working arrangement is still feasible. If possible, the room should be equipped with worktables rather than with typical small classroom-sized desks. A "half-and-half" arrangement is sometimes best from the standpoint of multiple use. This would consist of 20 or 24 classroom-sized desks in front and several worktables in back. The rear of the room can thus become the newspaper office. Cupboards may take the place of the editors' desk drawers and open shelves. They can be locked, if necessary, or opened wide for news room use. The inside of each cupboard door can provide space for the

schedules and the reference information that would otherwise be on bulletin boards. Ideally, each staff member should have a desk box or basket. These can be placed on the worktables when the staff members are working and stored in a cupboard at other times. The boxes also provide specific places where staff members may receive stories or mail, whether or not they are present.

Regardless of the type of room, you will definitely need as many typewriters as possible. You will also need extensive bulletin board or other posting space for assignments, production schedules, page dummies, editors' criticisms of the last paper, certificates, staff lists, and news photographs. A rack for displaying exchange newspapers is useful. In addition, you will need a labeled shelf or storage space for copy paper, scissors, paste, rulers, dummy sheets, printed forms, and other tools of the trade. Finally, you must have a recent edition of a good standard dictionary.

The staff of a mimeographed newspaper will need a few extra things: a table or stand for the duplicator; storage space for paper, stencils, and ink; a place to hang mimeograph workers' protective jackets or shop coats; and mimeoscope storage cabinets with door racks for styli and lettering guides.

3 | **Planning Your Newspaper**

You will need to make a number of decisions early in order to develop an efficient means of publishing your paper.

Deciding How to Produce the Paper

Most school newspapers today are produced by some form of offset printing. (The complete term is *offset lithography,* which describes the printing method.)

The cost of this kind of printing will vary according to the amount of production work the staff is willing and has the facilities to do. The first decision, then, is how much production work the staff will undertake.

Perhaps the ideal arrangement, leaving staff members free to concentrate on reporting and writing, is to have almost all of the production work done commercially. With this arrangement, the staff will prepare copy, headlines, and photographs. After the printer has set the copy into type, staff members will proofread the typeset copy and lay out the pages. The remainder of the work will be completed by the printer. Commercial production will probably cost more than $100 per page. Sometimes, a similar but far less expensive arrangement can be made with a school's vocational print shop.

Many school staffs choose instead to purchase typesetting equipment, setting copy into type and pasting up the pages themselves. In this case, only the final processing of photographs and the actual printing is generally done by a commercial shop. Obviously, this procedure saves money, but a great deal of time is required.

If a school chooses to buy photocopying equipment and an offset press, the staff can do nearly all the work. The equipment is expensive, though, even for a press that will print pages smaller than tabloid-size, and the equipment requires regular maintenance. The work may become a burden if it is the responsibility of a single small staff working under one adviser. Student production work must be done accurately and with close attention to detail. Otherwise, the results will appear amateurish, particularly to subscribers used to commercial-printing perfection. Consequently, fewer subscriptions and advertisements may be sold.

Three other printing processes may be considered. Related to offset lithography is the inexpensive "instant-printing" process, which reproduces prepared pages from a special paper "master." While typed material and simple unshaded drawings turn out as well as they do with more expensive processes, photographs do not reproduce very satisfactorily, and you are usually limited to a page size of 8½ by 11 or 8½ by 14 inches.

When very little money is available, a newspaper can be produced on a mimeograph machine or a similar duplicator. (See pages 476–485 for a more detailed description of this process.)

Finally, some print shops use the older "hot-type" process. With this method, copy is set into type on a linotype machine, and the printing is done from metal type. Preparation of material for this type of printing is the same as for commercial offset printing. Students are not likely to be involved in the typesetting or printing.

Deciding How Often the Paper Should Be Published

A few high schools publish daily newspapers, combining daily announcements with news. The facilities of a vocational print shop, however, are usually needed for this kind of publication.

Other schools publish weekly papers. This is very useful in terms of providing fresh news and maintaining reader interest. However, it also calls for rapid printing service and can be quite expensive.

Semimonthly publication is often chosen for financial reasons or because of the slower production process. Others choose this schedule because it places less pressure on the staff and the adviser and gives them a better chance to turn out a more finished product.

Finally, a number of schools publish their papers every three weeks or every month, making it possible to have more pages and giving students the opportunity to plan more carefully. Some schools with such a schedule have had noteworthy success with a news magazine format, in which the emphasis shifts to more use of interpretive, in-depth material. Others publish a monthly news magazine, plus weekly news sheets, which are frequently mimeographed to save money.

In determining frequency of publication, the following questions should be answered:

How much time do staff members have?

How much time does the adviser have?

What schedule do finances permit?

What are the advantages of publishing fresh news versus the advantages of taking more time for careful planning?

How much printing time is required?

How often will businesses advertise in the paper?

How often do students, faculty, and administrators want to see the paper published?

Planning a Production Schedule

The main steps in publishing a paper are illustrated in the chart on page 457. Following these general steps, you will need to work out your own more specific production schedule.

A well-planned, posted production schedule is a *must*. First, be sure to work out deadlines carefully, and clearly note the time allowed for each step. The schedule may be simple (day-by-day) or complicated (day-by-day and hour-by-hour). Then, post the schedule in a conspicuous place. Insist that everyone meet deadlines except in emergencies, and allow very few of the latter. You may find it helpful to use large manila envelopes—labeled clearly for contents and expected delivery times—to handle each batch of copy according to schedule.

A sample production schedule for a large high school semimonthly newspaper is shown on page 458. A production schedule for a mimeographed newspaper appears on page 477.

While you are planning your production schedule, you might also consider writing your own production handbook, covering all the processes of publishing your own paper. Set up a loose-leaf notebook with dividers listing the main steps in production. Insert instruction sheets as you develop them. Add pertinent ideas. When a question is asked, note the answer. By the end of a year, you will have the basic material from which a student group can write and duplicate a handbook. Keep copies handy in your staff room. Distribute copies to beginning staff members, perhaps asking them to study it and to pass a test on the contents.

Deciding on Page Size

The most common page size for a school newspaper is the tabloid—generally five columns wide. Its overall dimensions are approximately 11 by 17 inches. Some schools, of course, publish newspapers with standard full-size pages, approximately 15 by 24 inches. Both of these sizes can be produced efficiently on the type of press used by many weekly newspapers or available in large print shops. A smaller page size of approximately 9 by 12 inches may be more practical when your paper is printed in a school shop or by a neighborhood printer.

Typical newspaper columns are at least 12 picas (2 inches) wide. Narrower columns are uncommon. A growing trend is toward wider columns, perhaps six 14-pica columns on a standard page or four on a tabloid page. Column length will vary according to press capacity and paper dimensions.

In offset processing, the original layout may be reduced in size when the printing plate is made. This can increase the sharpness of line drawings and make typed material resemble commercial print in size. However, your body type should not become so small that there are fewer than eight lines in each inch of copy.

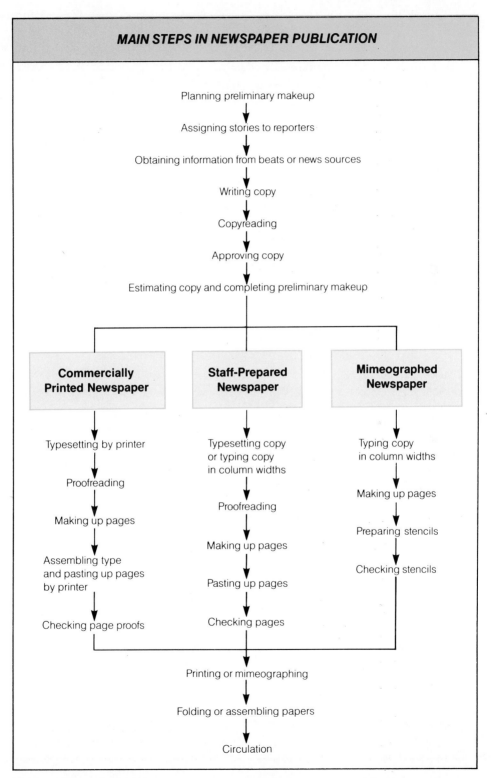

MAIN STEPS IN NEWSPAPER PUBLICATION

Planning preliminary makeup

↓

Assigning stories to reporters

↓

Obtaining information from beats or news sources

↓

Writing copy

↓

Copyreading

↓

Approving copy

↓

Estimating copy and completing preliminary makeup

Commercially Printed Newspaper	**Staff-Prepared Newspaper**	**Mimeographed Newspaper**
Typesetting by printer	Typesetting copy or typing copy in column widths	Typing copy in column widths
Proofreading	Proofreading	Making up pages
Making up pages	Making up pages	Preparing stencils
Assembling type and pasting up pages by printer	Pasting up pages	Checking stencils
Checking page proofs	Checking pages	

Printing or mimeographing

↓

Folding or assembling papers

↓

Circulation

SAMPLE PRODUCTION SCHEDULE

Semimonthly High School Newspaper
March 12 Issue

Wednesday, February 5	Preliminary page plans and story assignments due from page editors
Wednesday, February 12	Editorial-page assignments due to page editor Advertising copy due to business manager
Friday, February 14	Final advertising copy due Final editorial-page copy and page layout due First third of picture copy due First half of sports and feature story copy due
Wednesday, February 19	First third of news copy due
Friday, February 21	Second third of picture copy due Second third of news copy due
Wednesday, February 26	First third of copy to printer: advertising and editorial-page material
Thursday, February 27	Second third of copy to printer: feature stories, sports, and pictures
Friday, February 28	All news copy and all pictures to printer
Monday, March 3	Weekend news copy to printer Galley proofreading
Tuesday, March 4	Page makeup
Wednesday, March 5	Proofs and page makeups to printer
Thursday, March 6	Any changes
Friday, March 7	Page checking
Monday, March 10	Printing
Tuesday, March 11	Folding papers
Wednesday, March 12	Circulation Start of copy for next issue

—Adapted from schedules used by *The Arthur Hill News*, Arthur Hill High School, Saginaw, Michigan

If there is money and copy enough for more than four pages, you will have to decide whether to print more pages or to increase your page size. Keep in mind that a number of small pages may seem to contain more reading matter than just a few large pages.

Planning Your Pages

Practicality and appearance are important in developing a distinctive look for your school newspaper. Keep in mind that design devices requiring less handwork by printers will decrease the cost and reduce chances for error. Some of the specific decisions you will have to make relate to the following points.

LINES BETWEEN COLUMNS. Most newspapers now omit the vertical lines between columns known as column rules. You should, however, allow enough space between columns that the reader's eye won't jump from one column to the next.

LINES AT THE ENDS OF STORIES. Most modern newspapers also avoid dashes or horizontal lines between stories. Occasionally, they may insert lines for special emphasis—for instance, below an illustration and its caption.

BOXES AROUND STORIES OR HEADLINES. Various devices can be used to make a story stand out: a full box, heavy lines above and below a story, or three-quarter boxes around headlines only, for example.

SIZE AND POSITION OF NAMEPLATE. Should the name of your newspaper be in the traditional place across the top of the front page, or should it be smaller and "float" (appear in different locations on the page in different issues)? Typical nameplates for five-column papers spread across three or four columns and measure a little over an inch in height. You may vary your makeup by centering a nameplate of this size at the top of the page between "ears" (small boxes advertising stories or school events) or by moving it anywhere in the top half of the page (above the fold). Some schools include a slogan in the nameplate.

FOLIO LINES. On the front page just below the nameplate, you should list the school name, the city and state, the date of the issue, and possibly the volume and issue number between two lines extending the full width of the nameplate. On each of the other pages, you will need a simpler set of information—a line stating the name of the paper, the date, and the page number, the last always at the outside edge of your page. The folio line may extend the full width of the page, or it may be condensed to as little as one column. Some papers add a department head for the page, usually in larger type.

EDITORIAL PAGE LAYOUT. For the editorial page, you may want to have fewer, wider columns. Or you may decide to retain the standard column width but print the editorials double-column and in larger type, possibly with slightly more space between lines. You can open valuable display space for reading material at the top of the page by moving your masthead (the editorial page's general listing of detailed publishing information) to the bottom of the page.

SPECIAL COLUMN WIDTHS ON OTHER PAGES. You might occasionally vary your layout with two matching stories, each one and one-half columns wide. Or you might try one story in two columns of this width under a three-column headline. You can also use occasional illustrations of odd size, varying the column width accordingly.

ILLUSTRATIONS. In addition to photographs, line drawings and other kinds of illustrations lend interest, particularly on the editorial page.

STYLES AND SIZES OF TYPE. You should select the type that will present

the LION

Blasted!
Record lows limit local activities

'Everybody looks at gambling as the easy way to make big money. Unfortunately, it's not that easy.'

Betting against the odds
by Brad Severson

Medley
Black & White
Friday, December 19, 198-

Trolley returns to Georgetown
by Richard Weinstatzen

Retirees enjoy holiday spirit
by Andrea Vayda

...They feel this is really their home'

Holiday Events

---

the AXE

84TH YEAR, NUMBER 1 — SOUTH EUGENE HIGH SCHOOL, EUGENE, OREGON — WEDNESDAY, SEPTEMBER 30, 1981

9 students enter merit semifinals

Computer added

Store opens

Axe receives press award

Attendance policy changes
By Spencer Thal

College workshop planned for Oct. 7

Inside

X-RAY

Senior events

What's Inside

Planning for Prom... see pages 4 and 5

Girls' soccer season starts ... see page 7

Up to date

Board reviews options
by Trish Nagy

Cable TV negotiations held
by Vicki Kaspar

Seniors plan activities
by David Laird and Chris Russell

The appearance of each of these pages is a result of careful planning.

your message most effectively. The best criterion to use is what seems most readable. Avoid sans-serif and other modern faces for body type. They are decorative and appropriate for advertisements and special work, but tiring to read. Most newspaper body type is 8- or 9-point, although some daily papers now use larger type. Matching 10-point type is suitable for double-column stories, editorials, and other wide-column work.

BOLDFACE TYPE.   This type is available on most typesetting machines and can be mixed with your regular typeface at no extra charge. If you use 8-point body type, you can use 8-point bold for subheads, picture captions, boxed stories, paragraphs of emphasis within long stories, and special work. Larger bold type can also be used for some of these items. However, you should generally avoid mixing lines of different size type. Such mixtures must be made by hand and will increase printing cost.

ITALICS.   Newspaper typesetters seldom make use of italics in body copy. If this face is available, it will probably be in place of boldface, and you will use it accordingly. However, boldface is more suitable for newspapers.

TYPEFACES FOR ADVERTISEMENTS. Since each ad is a unit in itself, the use of different typefaces for different ads can help make their messages stand out. Typefaces within each ad should, however, harmonize. It is also a good idea not to use your headline type too extensively in advertisements.

Preparing a Headline Schedule

You should plan your headline schedule to attract readers and be typographically interesting, according to Professor Jack Z. Sissors of Northwestern University. To do this, you must first determine what typefaces and sizes the printer has for your use. You may be limited by this selection, or you may be offered a considerable array. Are they all set by hand, or are some prepared on typesetting machines? Machine setting saves time and money.

It helps to become familiar with type families. A family of type includes several different faces, each in a number of sizes. In any one size, you may find roman and italic styles; bold, medium, and light faces; and regular, expanded, and condensed letters. As a rule, you should select most of your headline types from the same family. A mixture of families may give your page a cluttered look. You can gain contrasts by mixing bold and medium faces in roman and italic styles. Avoid light faces on most pages. They might be suitable, however, if you wish a different kind of headline on your editorial page.

Several type families are especially suitable for headline type. Sans-serif types are quite appropriate here, as are Bodoni and some other serif faces. You should avoid ornate types that are hard to read. The use of capital and lower-case letters in all headlines will also improve readability.

In making up your schedule, you will need to include a number of headline patterns. First, select one or two banners (streamers) that will extend the full width of your page. Second, select two-, three-, and four-column-wide spreads. Pick two or three for each of these widths, and include both one- and two-line patterns. Third, select several one-column heads—perhaps two two-liners and two three-liners. Fourth, for minor stories select two subordinate one-column heads—one one-line head and one two-line head. Fifth, select about five headline patterns for feature stories. These should contrast with the patterns used for other kinds of stories. And, sixth, select as many patterns as are needed for the regularly appearing departments and columns.

Baron golf team plays Midtown Knights
No. 1   34–36 units

Student council will battle problems of jaywalking, reckless driving
No. 2   66–70 units

Senior Choir presents concert in National Cathedral Sunday
No. 3   22–27 units

Journalism student receives scholarship
No. 4   34–36 units

FINALISTS • 18 seniors pass second hurdle in Merit Scholarship competition

No. 5   Kicker 8–11 units/Main lines 25–30 units

Student government to present carnival
No. 6   15–18 units

20-member committee to inspect Central High
No. 7   17–22 units

'Ten Little Indians'
Public to see mystery play
No. 8   Kicker 15–25 units/Main line 22–26 units

Honor Society inducts 17 seniors, 19 juniors
No. 9   18–23 units

Students go on field trip
No. 10   22–27 units

Hi-Y, Tri-Hi-Y representatives plan Youth and Government Days
No. 11   25–30 units

Choral Club joins ——————
'Opera Sing'
—————— In All-School Chorus
No. 12   Kickers 12–20 units/Main line 10–18 units

Teens in government
Youths hold mock legislature
No. 13   Kicker 15–25 units/Main line 22–27 units

—Caesar comes to life—
English classes see Shakespearean film
No. 14   Kicker 15–20 units/Main line 30–35 units

Rebel cagers win, lose one in tourneys
No. 15   10–12 units

NHS to hold fall induction
No. 16   11–13 units

Debaters plan league tourney
No. 17   12–15 units

End of year
Tired students clean lockers
No. 18   Kicker 10–15 units/ Main lines 11–13 units

Bonfire climaxes 'Beat West Week'
No. 19   12–15 units

Musicians play before teachers
No. 20   13–16 units

Senior team wins in GAA basketball
No. 21   16–20 units

Etiquette Committee plans fall publication
No. 22   13–17 units

A few principles for determining headline size may be helpful. For example, minor one-column headlines should be 14 to 18 points high, or about twice the size of the body type. For more important stories and for each additional column, you can add about 6 points. Two-line spreads should generally be in smaller type than one-line spreads. When two-deck headlines are used, as with banners, the second deck should be half the size of the first. A kicker should be about half the size of the main headline; but on a special story, it could become the main element.

When setting up a new headline schedule, be prepared to experiment. As you use your schedule, you may decide that certain headlines are too large, too small, or otherwise unsuitable for your particular needs. Discard them. Develop additional headline patterns to meet needs you have encountered in your use of the schedule.

It is important to determine the maximum and minimum unit counts for each style of headline. For flush-left headlines, the maximum is the total units possible in the column width; the minimum, about three quarters of this number. Assign a number to each headline style. It is much simpler to write a single number rather than a complete description, such as "18-pt. Bodoni Bold Condensed, 1 column, 3 lines, flush left," every time you want a certain style of headline. Print (or paste) headline samples with numbers and unit counts on sheets of cardboard and distribute them to your staff members and printer. Note the sample headline schedule on page 462. While most spreads in this schedule have two lines, all of them could be written in single-line format as well.

4 Gathering and Preparing Copy

It is the content, appeal, and readability of your copy that will eventually determine whether your newspaper is a success. Your editorial board and page editors will start by making preliminary plans for the forthcoming issue of the paper. In most cases, these plans will include not only story content but also preliminary page layouts to suggest how the paper will look.

After reporters have secured information and prepared their stories, copyreaders will check them. Editors will make the final selection of material, including photographs, to be published. Headlines will be completed, and copy will be assembled for delivery to the printer (or to the typesetting-machine operator if staff members do this work).

Covering Beats and Assignments

News stories for your paper don't just happen. They are the result of real thinking and planning. Your reporters will turn in a few good stories without direction, but most major stories are brought to completion by following a system.

The first lines of defense against missing a story are your reporters' beats. List every possible news source in the school, even the teacher who has only one announcement a year for the paper. Assign each reporter one or more sources. Students new to journalism may handle the less important news sources. Expect every reporter to cover every assigned beat, every issue. Try awarding stars on

ASSIGNMENT LIST

Page ___1___ Date of issue ___May 17___ Story deadline ___9 a.m. May 13___

Reporter	Story	Estimated number of words	Headline to write	Initialed by reporter	Received at copy desk
J. Jones	Election: See Mr. Smith. Get names of candidates.	200	4A	*JJ*	5/11
B. Greene	Senior rings: See Miss Howe.	75	8C	*B.G.*	5/12

a posted list or bonus points toward a merit rating for those reporters who do cover their beats consistently. Take beats and related story opportunities away from those who do not.

Second, use the assignment system. Keep a Future Book and make assignments for all major stories. Whenever these assignments coincide with beats, be sure to assign the stories to the reporters whose beats are involved. Some of your page editors, such as the editorial page or sports page editor, may make their own assignments. Page editors of general news pages may plan their pages in conference with the editor and then work closely with the assignment or news editor, who divides the stories among the reporters.

Post assignment lists on your bulletin board or keep an assignment book. Require reporters to initial each assignment received. In addition, it sometimes helps to make out individual assignment sheets to give to reporters. The copy editor may check off each story on the assignment list as it is turned in. (A sample assignment list appears above.)

Estimating Copy

It is possible to estimate accurately the amount of space a typed story will oc-cupy on the printed page. Taking several printed lines in your paper, calculate the average number of characters (letters, spaces, and punctuation marks) in each line. Set the margin stops of your typewriter to allow twice this number of characters. For example, if your average number of characters per printed line is 35, you will require 70 characters per typed line. Reach this average by setting your margin stops to allow 75 characters, since most typed lines are not full width.

Next, count the number of printed lines per inch in your paper. You may now determine the number of column inches for any given story by this formula:

$$\frac{2 \times \text{number of typed lines}}{\text{number of printed lines per inch}}$$

For example, if you have seven printed lines per inch, you would multiply the number of typed lines by two, then divide by seven.

You may want to require all reporters to make this calculation when they type their stories and to write the number of column inches under the catch line (the word or two at the top of the story used to identify it). It is possible to prepare a relatively firm page layout from these measurements. However, you will probably find it more practical simply to add up the column inches in order to decide whether you have enough (or too much) material. Then, you can later prepare the page layouts from proofs.

Preparing Photographs

Working from the editorial board's or assignment editor's plans, the photo editor will schedule the taking of photographs and assign them to photographers. Some consideration must be given to the newspaper's printing process. While top-quality offset printing will produce excellent photo reproductions, some offset processes may be less than satisfactory. In the latter case, it will be the photo editor's job to see that suitable photos are taken—usually with high black-and-white contrast and large, clear faces.

The photo editor should follow up on the taking of photos and the preparation of finished prints. Generally, contact prints will be prepared from all negatives. Editors can make selections from these, and the photos can then be enlarged to fit properly on the page.

Since any printing process reduces photo quality, news photographs should be sharp prints on smooth white paper, with a full range of tones from deep blacks through grays to clear whites and with detail in the highlight areas. Crop your photos to avoid paying for sky or background areas that add nothing to the news value of your photos. Indicate where to crop by grease-pencil marks in the margins. When they are processed, the photos can be enlarged or reduced slightly to make printed pictures of the desired size.

Plan photo sizes as part of your page makeup, remembering that variety in size adds to the interest of the page. The sizes of faces, however, should be roughly equal. Limit a picture of one individual to one column or less. Extend group pictures across several columns.

Be sure to establish definite photo deadlines with your printer or processor. The preparation of photographic printing plates requires time and special care. Plan the proper screening size in advance with your printer. It will depend on the particular printing process to be used, as well as on the quality of paper.

Preparing Advertisements for Reproduction

Using layouts received from the advertising sales representatives, ad workers should prepare each ad on a separate sheet of white paper, using the newspaper's typographical resources to present the desired message. Line drawings, hand lettering, ad-headline type, other styles of type chosen especially for advertising, photographs, and available styles of typewriter type may be combined to make a tasteful and appealing ad. As a rule, commercial typesetting and photographs are not used unless the advertiser wishes to pay an extra charge to cover the additional expense.

You may wish to enlarge or reduce some of your ad copy to fit a particular space. This can be done by having a special offset negative of the material made at slight additional cost. When sending such an ad to the printer, do not include this copy in the ad but outline with blue pencil the space it is to occupy. Mark both the space and the copy with an identifying code (such as X1) and send both to the printer together.

Some merchants may furnish reproducible proofs of all or part of their ads. You merely trim these and rubber-cement them into place. Do not overlook the possibilities offered by other previously printed material, such as business cards, advertising circulars, or letterheads. Parts of any of these may be cut out and used to create very attractive advertisements.

Preparing Copy for the Printer

Prepare all copy following the general directions for preparing copy found in the chart below. When a story has more than one page, be sure that the same catch line appears at the top of each page and that the pages are numbered consecutively. Next, each story should be copyread carefully and marked with standard copyreaders' marks. If a story is hard to read because of changes, it should be retyped and copyread again.

Write headlines on separate sheets of paper. Put the same catch line on the headline sheet as on the original copy for quick reference by the printer and staff members. Some editors prefer to change the reporter's catch line when the headline is written so that it will correspond with the first few words of the headline. This facilitates the matching of the story and its headline by the makeup editor and printer.

Indicate both the type style and the form of the headline on the headline sheet. In the following example, the number tells the printer which type size and typeface to use (by referring to the headline schedule).

No. 3 | Students build
model stages

The vertical line indicates that the headline should be set flush left.

GENERAL DIRECTIONS FOR PREPARING COPY

1. Use 8½-by-11-inch paper on one side only.
2. Typewrite copy, double-spaced. Any copy that must be handwritten should be written clearly in ink or soft pencil. Print all proper names.
3. In the upper left-hand corner of each page, write the name, or catch line, of the story. Put the page number below it.
4. Write your name and the date in the upper right-hand corner of each page.
5. Begin the story one third of the way down the first page to allow space for editors' notes. Start about an inch from the top of succeeding pages.
6. Leave a 1-inch margin at the sides and bottom of all sheets.
7. Mark the beginning of each paragraph with the following symbol: ⌐‾‾‾‾ Skip an extra line between paragraphs.
8. Avoid dividing words between two lines. If it is necessary to break a word, divide it between syllables. Do not divide words between pages.
9. At the bottom of each page except the last, write the word *more* in parentheses.
10. At the bottom of the last paragraph, use the following end sign: —30—
11. If you use slang on purpose or misspell a word intentionally, write *Folo copy* (follow copy) in the margin.
12. Show, below your catch line on the first page, the number of words, the number of lines of typewritten copy, or the estimated number of inches, according to the policy of your paper. If you count words, also show the number of words in each paragraph in a circle at the end of the paragraph.

In addition to typing, copyreading, and headline writing, page editors or copyreaders may need to do several other things. They may need to write subheads for long stories. This requires placing them in their proper positions in the story and marking them to be set in boldface type and centered, as in the following example:

$$bf \underline{\hspace{1cm}}] \underset{\sim\sim\sim\sim\sim\sim\sim\sim\sim\sim\sim}{\text{Mark subheads this way.}} [$$

They may need to mark other things, too: lead paragraphs for 10-point or boldface type or for double-column width if special emphasis is desired; indentation or boldface type for other paragraphs; and any other special column widths that are needed. They may also indicate the proper type for bylines and prepare other things to complete the page, such as the folio line.

When the copy, headlines, and any other special material have been completed, all should be placed in a large manila envelope to be sent to the printer. Label the envelope with a production schedule for that page as a reminder to all concerned. (Note the sample envelope label below.)

Dealing with the Printer

Newspaper staffs that have established a pleasant working relationship with their printers find the results gratifying in terms of better-looking newspapers, cooperation in unusual situations, and finer training for their members.

Using a local print shop is often very advantageous. It is easier to keep in close touch with a local printer than with one located elsewhere, and staff members have more opportunity to see their paper in production. Local printers often take special interest in the school newspaper, not only because it directly or indirectly advertises their work but also because they are supporters of the local school system. Sometimes local print shops print a school newspaper at cost as a good-will gesture.

It is a good idea to have a written contract with your printer. Such an agreement is businesslike and offers ad-

---

CENTRAL HIGH <u>NEWS</u> Date of issue _____

This envelope contains all copy and headlines for page _____

Copy due at print shop (time) _____(date) _____

Three galley proofs of copy and headlines

      to be returned (time) _____(date) _____

Corrected galley proofs and completed page dummy

      due at print shop (time) _____(date) _____

Page proof to be returned (time) _____(date) _____

Corrected page proof due at print shop (time) _____(date) _____

vantages to both sides. The contract should cover such items as publication dates, deadlines, number of copies, page size, quality of paper, amount of allowable overset (type set but not used), cost rate for proof corrections (except typographical errors, which are corrected without charge), and other such matters.

Meeting deadlines punctually is the primary way of building a good relationship with your printer. Following your production schedule, the printer will assign people to your work at a specific time. If nothing is there for these people to do, the printer will lose money.

If you are lucky enough to be in the print shop while your paper is in production, remember that your status is that of guest. Discuss only those matters on which you are supposed to advise or assist. Depending on shop or union rules, you may or may not be permitted to help with actual work. Learn these rules and respect them.

The same principles apply to your dealings with a school print shop. Because the workers are students, the production schedule may be slower than an outside printer's would be. But it is just as important to follow that schedule precisely. You may need extra patience at times, since relatively inexperienced students will sometimes replace others who have completed their course work.

5 Dealing with Typesetting, Headlines, and Artwork

Your staff can save a considerable amount of money by doing its own typesetting, headline preparation, and artwork, as well as the final job of pasting up pages for reproduction. You can achieve professional results if staff members are willing to learn these processes and work carefully.

Setting the Stories into Type

You can choose from at least three different methods of typesetting: a typesetting machine, a word processor, or a typewriter. A typesetting machine is operated in the same way a typewriter is, but it will ordinarily have a video display screen to show the progress of your work. These machines usually prepare finished letters by a photographic process called phototypesetting. The copy appears in columns on white paper ready for you to paste into place on your page. Typesetting machines generally offer a choice of typefaces and type sizes, perhaps including some headline styles. Some even have dictionary applications for spelling or division of words at the end of a line.

Word processors are another possibility. These generally consist of a computer with keyboard and video display terminal, a word-processing program, and a printer. A simple desk-top computer may be adequate, or you may be able to arrange for a terminal attached to your school's computer. For good reproduction, the printer should be a "daisy-wheel" type, rather than the less expensive "dot-matrix" style. Daisy wheels also offer you a choice of type styles. If the equipment is sufficiently sophisticated to permit variable letter-spacing and lines with even margins on both sides, your pages can appear to be typeset, rather than prepared with a typewriter.

Even a typewriter can produce satisfactory copy for offset reproduction. An office-style electric machine will do the best work, of course, but you can prepare good-looking columns on a manual portable if you are willing to work carefully. If you desire even margins, you will in most cases have to type your copy twice. The first typing can be used to determine the amount of space needed on your page layout. The second typing will give you even margins. The process of justifying your margins is described in detail on page 481.

Careful typing and attention to detail produce perfection in this work. Brush your typewriter keys before starting. Use good-quality white bond paper of about 24-pound weight. Be sure your ribbon is relatively new and inks evenly. You may prefer a silk or carbon ribbon for sharper lettering. Type as evenly as possible. You can protect your finished typing from smearing by coating it with a plastic fixative. Spray the page lightly to avoid graying your black letters.

Work slowly to avoid mistakes. Untidy corrections show up in the final product. When a mistake is made, there are three ways to correct it. The first way is to use an opaque correction fluid designed for offset work. Brush the fluid over the error, allow it to dry, and retype. The second is to put in several x's to make the error stand out, space to the next line, and retype the line. The makeup worker will later cut out the incorrect line and move up the rest of the copy. The third is to retype a word or a line and paste it over the incorrect one. Consider this method only for errors found when rechecking finished work, since it is hard to align the correction perfectly.

Preparing Headlines

Several methods of headline preparation may be available to you. They vary considerably in the amount of effort required of staff members, as well as in

their cost. Regardless of the method you choose, you will want to establish and use a headline schedule, as suggested on pages 461–463.

The first method of preparing headlines involves a printer. When your copy is typeset commercially, your printer will also prepare headlines to your specifications. Even when you do your own typesetting or typing, you can ask your printer to typeset headlines. These will be returned to you as "repro proofs," ready to paste in place on your page layout.

The second method calls for the use of a typesetting machine. If you own your own typesetting machine, it may be able to set some headline sizes in addition to body copy.

The third method involves the purchase of special equipment. Headlining equipment consisting of type and a hand-operated proof press is readily available. The original cost is high, but the results are professional in appearance and the operating expenses are limited to ink and paper.

The fourth method involves the use of alphabets of type. Printed alphabets of headline type are in wide use. Their cost is relatively low, they produce good quality headlines, and they are fairly easy to use. Two general styles are manufactured. One consists of sheets containing printed alphabets, which are cut apart as needed. The letters have an adhesive backing and are mounted directly in place. The other style provides individually cut letters, which are assembled in a "composing stick" and fastened together with cellulose tape. Both varieties are available on white cardboard and on transparent film. The latter material may be necessary with certain offset processes that reproduce the edges of individual letter tabs as black lines. As the printed alphabets are used, replacements must be purchased.

The fifth method involves a process similar to the fourth. "Rub-on" sheets of headline type can be purchased at many stationery stores. They are suitable for newspaper work, but you may find it difficult to align the letters evenly and achieve a professional look.

The final method is the least expensive. Lettering guides similar to those used in mimeographing are also available for offset use. The letters are traced with a black ball point pen.

Using Artwork

Offset printing is unusually adaptable for reproducing line drawings. If drawings are the correct size and, therefore, do not require special handling in order to reduce or enlarge them, no extra expense is involved. Line drawings are suitable for advertisements, cartoons, illustrations, decorations, column titles, and department headings. The same drawing can be used issue after issue without appearing scratched, faded, or worn, if you handle it carefully and store it properly.

To reproduce well, a line drawing must be in solid blacks and whites, with no grays. (Any drawings containing various shades of gray, such as pencil sketches, must be processed in the same way as photographs.) Use India ink to make your drawing and to define all lines clearly. Correct your mistakes with opaquing fluid. Intermediate tones between black and white may be shown by shading with dots or lines. You can also purchase ready-made patterns printed on acetate with an adhesive backing. Apply these to the areas you wish to cover and trim away the excess with a razor blade.

6 Handling Proofreading and Page Makeup

Once your copy has been typeset, whether it has been done commercially or by staff members, the next steps will be to proofread the typeset material and to make up the pages. You will need two sets of galley proofs for these purposes. (The proofs may not appear on the old-fashioned long sheets of paper printed from a "galley" of type, but the name has not changed.) One set is for proofreading and returning to the printer. The second set is to be cut up for the page dummy that you will prepare. If the printer sends only one set or if you have done your own typesetting, it is a relatively simple matter to have photocopies made.

Proofreading

Proofreading is the process of comparing material set into type against the original copy to find any errors made in transcribing. Proofreading is quite different from copyreading. The copyreader is the last person who makes changes in a reporter's story. When you are proofreading, you watch only to see that the proof checks with the copy.

Correcting a reporter's mistakes at the time of proofreading can be difficult and wastes times that you cannot spare. If your paper is commercially printed, you pay extra for these corrections. Of course, if you do find an error that cannot be allowed to pass, you must correct it.

Proofreading is usually done by a team of two—a copyholder and a proofreader. The copyholder reads aloud from the copy, indicating paragraphs, commas, and other punctuation marks, while spelling out proper names. The proofreader follows on the proof, marking corrections.

PROOFREADERS' MARKS

Spelling and Missing Words

Mark	Description	Example
o/	Insert letter as indicated	He wn the medal. o/
o/	Change letter as indicated	He wan the medal. o/
the/	Insert word as indicated	He won/medal. the/

Typography

Mark	Description	Example
bf	Set in boldface type	He won the medal. bf
ital	Set in italics	ital He won the medal.
rom	Set in roman type	He won (the) medal. rom
cap	Set as capital letter	cap he won the medal.
lc	Set as lower-case letter	He won the Medal. lc
wf	Fix wrong font (type that varies in shape or size from others in the line)	wf He won the medal.
X	Fix worn or imperfect type	X He won the medal.
sc	Set small capital letters (capital letters the size of lower-case letters)	He won the medal. sc

Punctuation

Mark	Description	Example
,/	Insert comma	,/ Yes he won the medal.
;/	Insert semicolon	He won the medal the team won the trophy. ;/
:/	Insert colon	The members are as follows :/
V	Insert apostrophe	V He didn't win a medal.
V V	Insert quotation marks	He said, I am going. V V
⊙	Insert period	He won the medal ⊙
?/	Insert question mark	Did he win the medal ?/
!/	Insert exclamation point	He won the medal !/
|1em/	Insert one-em (short) dash	September 4, 1983 May 16, 1984 |1em/
|2em/	Insert two-em (long) dash	At last they left. |2em/
=/	Insert hyphen	It was very old fashioned. =/

Spacing

Mark	Description	Example
#	Insert space	# He won the medal yesterday.
◠	Close up space	He won the med al. ◠
#̄	Close up space, but not completely	He won the medal. #̄
lead	Add leading to space lines farther apart	He won the medal. He won the medal. lead
ℊ lead	Take out leading to close up space between lines	He won the medal. He won the medal. ℊ lead
eq. # √√	Equalize space between words	eq. # He won the medal.

PROOFREADERS' MARKS

Position

Mark	Meaning	Example
ꓘ (turn over symbol)	Turn letter over	He won the medal.
tr	Transpose position of letters or words	He won the medal. *tr*
stet	Disregard proofreaders' marks and let stand as originally set (You should also place dots under the material to be kept)	He won the gold medal. *stet*
⊏	Move material to the left	⊏—He won the medal.
⊐	Move material to the right	He won the medal.—⊐
]center[	Center material	]Sport Contest[— *center*
⌐	Raise type	He won the medal. ⌐
⊔	Lower type	He won the medal. ⊔
¶	Paragraph	¶ He won the medal.
No ¶	No paragraph (If the material should fall at the end of the preceding paragraph, you should also draw a line as shown)	He won the gold medal yesterday.) *No* ¶—The honor was a great surprise to him.
=	Straighten lines or words that are out of line horizontally	He won the medal. =
‖	Straighten lines or words that are out of line vertically	‖ He won the gold medal yesterday. The honor was a great surprise to him.
▫	Indent one em (short space)	▫—He won the medal.
▫▫	Indent two ems (long space)	▫▫—He won the medal.
ℓ (delete symbol)	Delete (take out) material indicated	He won the medal. ℓ

Miscellaneous

Mark	Meaning	Example
see copy	See attached copy since material to be corrected is too lengthy or confusing to mark in margin (Clip original copy to galley and clearly indicate copy to be corrected)	He great surprise to him. *see copy*
abbr.	Abbreviate spelled out words (If an abbreviation is not standard, write the abbreviation instead of the symbol *abbr.*)	He won the medal in Saint Louis. *abbr.* Missouri *Mo.*
spell out	Spell out figures or abbreviated words	He has won the medal 4 times. *spell out*
fig	Use figures instead of spelled out numbers	He has won the medal nineteen times. *fig*

Compare the first paragraph that follows with the second, which shows how a copyholder might read the first:

Beth Porter, senior, was recipient of the Herbert E. Harriss Scholarship at the second annual awards banquet February 21.

"Paragraph, capital B-E-T-H, capital P-O-R-T-E-R comma, senior comma, was recipient of the capital H-E-R-B-E-R-T, capital E period, capital H-A-R-R-I-S-S, capital Scholarship, at the second spelled out, annual awards banquet, capital February two one period."

Proofreading also differs from copyreading in the way the errors are marked. Proof corrections are never marked directly over the error. If they were, they would not be noticed. To indicate a correction on a printed proof, draw a line from the mistake out to the margin and show the correction there. Most errors are in spelling, and all you need to write is the proper letter.

To indicate other mistakes, use the standard proofreaders' marks shown on pages 471–472. Your printer will expect you to use them, for they are familiar to print shop workers wherever the English language is used.

There is another proofreading system, which is known as the book method because it is used by book publishers. The symbols are the same, but no lines are drawn to the margin. If your printer prefers this system, find out from the printer how errors are indicated.

If, instead of galley proofs, you are proofreading actual material that has been typeset or typed for reproduction, remember that you may make no marks over or near the typing. In the event that

it is inconvenient to make a photocopy for proofreading purposes, you can usually indicate corrections in the margins that will later be cut away. When there are no margins, you will need to make up a separate correction sheet, such as the one required for a mimeograph stencil and shown on page 485.

Making Up the Pages

Page makeup begins even before the stories are assigned. At that time, page editors will generally sketch preliminary layouts showing how the pages will look. As new assignments develop and as stories come in and their exact lengths become known, the layouts can be changed according to the lengths of the stories. If you follow this procedure, by the time you are ready for final page makeup you will know just where your stories are to be placed. You can use the limited time available to you for making the final layouts, or dummies, as nearly perfect as possible. (Makeup principles are discussed in Chapter 17. Only procedures are indicated here.)

For makeup work, you need a hand-drawn or printed dummy sheet, the same size as your finished page. If advertisements appear on the page, your advertising manager should start the dummy by marking where the ads are to be placed.

Cut your stories and headlines from the second set of galley proofs, trimming neatly at top and bottom. If the catch lines have been set into type, you may wish to cut them off at this time, or you may prefer to retain them for identification until the actual pasteup of the page is prepared. Using your preliminary layout as a guide, position the stories carefully. Allow sufficient white space above headlines and photographs. The minimum space is equal to one line of body type. Two lines of space are permissible, but more than this is undesirable.

Plan page bottoms so that they will be even. The printer can adjust minor shortages in column length by inserting a small amount of extra space between paragraphs. This will also be necessary in a two-column story with an odd number of lines. When cutting such a story apart for makeup, indicate which column will need spacing (or better, if practical, revise a paragraph on the galley proof to add or subtract a line).

You cannot squeeze extra lines into a column. Don't try! If you sacrifice your white space, the page will look cluttered. If you must cut a paragraph or sentence from a story, write "paragraph out" or "sentence out" at that point on the dummy as a guide to the printer. If you wish to cut a story in the middle of a paragraph, you must also mark the change on the galley proof, since several lines may have to be reset.

When you have finished organizing your page, paste the headlines and stories neatly in place on the dummy, exactly as you want them to appear when the true pasteup is done. The more even your dummy, the more likely it is that your printed page will look just as you want it to look. Write any special directions on a separate sheet of paper and clip the sheet to the dummy.

7 Pasting Up Pages and Carrying Out Final Checks

Even though the page editors may be planning to do the page pasteup themselves, it is generally desirable to begin by preparing a page dummy as described above. The more perfect the dummy, the easier and more accurate will be the pasteup itself, whether it is done by the staff or the printer. The extra work of planning a perfect dummy will ensure a professional appearance for your newspaper, instead of an amateur look.

Doing the Pasteup

Although content is important, your newspaper will often be judged by its appearance. The pasteup process determines to a great extent the appearance of each page. Careless or sloppy work in assembling the page will stand out in the finished newspaper, since, given the offset process, the printed page will be an exact duplicate of the pasteup.

To do this work yourself, you need a drawing board, a T-square and a triangle, opaquing fluid, a blue pencil, a ruler, scissors, a sheet of smooth white paper, masking tape to hold the paper to the board, and either rubber cement or a waxing machine.

Assemble all the material for the page: the repro proofs of your copy, headlines, advertisements, drawings, and photographs. Check each against the dummy and note any changes in spacing that you are expected to make. Trim your material about $1/16$ inch from the type. This allows room to retouch the page if the trimmed edge shows when it is photographed. With a blue pencil, draw light lines showing the page outline and the columns. Since light blue does not photograph, you may use this pencil for all such markings.

Start in one corner of the page, working down and across. Position a headline or story, using the T-square and triangle to be sure it is straight. If you are using a waxing machine that applies a thin coat of sticky wax to the back of your story, you may now press the story into place. The wax makes it easy to pick copy up and reposition it if necessary.

Otherwise, mark the corners of the story on the page with your blue pencil, turn it over, and spread the back lightly with rubber cement. Place it in position, cover it with a clean sheet of paper, and press down. The use of rubber cement prevents buckling or stretching and as with waxing makes it possible to lift copy and reposition it if necessary. Excess cement can be rubbed off when dry. Continue until the page is completed. Use your T-square and triangle throughout your work to assure straight columns, even lines of type, and square headlines. If borders or lines are necessary, draw them neatly with India ink.

Do not mount photographs or other material for which separate negatives are to be made. Cut a piece of black construction paper to the size of each finished photo and mount it in place of the photo. Mark both the space and the back of the photograph with an identifying number; a front page photo would be 1A or 1B, for example. Use a grease pencil to mark the back of the photos. A pen or pencil may produce a ridge on the front, which will show on the printed page. If special directions are necessary, type them on a small sheet of paper and cement it along one edge on the back of the photograph.

Finally, check your page carefully. Use opaquing solution to blot out unwanted black marks. Clean smears and pencil lines with an art gum eraser. Insert the page, the photographs, and other copy in a large envelope, between cardboard sheets. The material is now ready for reproduction.

Checking the Page Proof

If instead of doing your own pasteup, you have sent your page dummy directly to the printer, the printer will arrange the stories, headlines, and photographs on the page, pasting up the typeset material exactly as it is to appear in print.

(Printers who use "hot type" will perform the same process by assembling metal type into a form.) Depending on your printer's location, procedures, and the specifications in your contract, you may or may not have an opportunity to review each completed page before it is printed. Ideally, you will receive a photocopy of the pasteup or a printed page proof for checking. If you have pasted up your own pages, you can check them immediately upon completion.

This is no time for copyreading or even proofreading stories. But there are many things to check. Using the original galley proof, see if marked corrections have been made as indicated. Then, check the page proof against the page dummy to be certain that every story, headline, caption, and advertisement has been put in its proper place. Skim through each story to see that the lines are in correct order and to catch any typographical errors that may have been made in the lines corrected. Check the end of each story to make certain that no lines have been omitted in the transfer of material. You should also check the headlines to catch any errors and to see if they appear above the right stories. Be sure the photographs are in their proper positions, with the correct captions under them. Check the folio line for errors. Read each ad, watching particularly for errors in the names of businesses, addresses, phone numbers, or prices. Finally, check to see that the corners of the page are square, and make sure that there are no black spots or smudges between the words or lines on the page.

If you find any major errors in material from a printer, mark the errors as you would when proofreading and return the page proofs to the printer for correction. Errors found in a pasteup created by staff members should be marked on a separate correction sheet and attended to before the page is printed.

Finishing the Offset Newspaper

For many newspaper staffs, checking the pasteup is the final step. The printer then takes over and prepares the paper for circulation. A few staffs, however, perform some of the following steps to complete their newspaper production. If your staff does any of this work, remember that local sales representatives of your offset equipment company, who are familiar with your equipment and want it to function perfectly, will usually be happy to furnish you with information and instructions on the proper use of their products.

The first step in completing your own paper is to produce a photographic negative from the page pasteup, reducing it to finished size. This is done with a process camera and a lighted copying frame. A darkroom is needed to develop the film. Schools teaching vocational photography will have little difficulty in handling this work. Newspaper staffs can do it if equipment is available.

Next, the negative is retouched to black out all unnecessary marks. A lighted box similar to a mimeoscope is helpful.

With the right equipment, the staff can do this work, an expensive part of commercial preparation.

Special screened negatives must be made for individual photographs or shaded drawings. You will generally need to depend on the skill of an experienced lithographic photographer for this work to ensure sharply defined photographs.

The printing plate is then made from the negatives. A frame holds the negatives and plate together while a strong light makes the exposure. Screened negatives may be stripped into the main negative (a delicate process if margins are limited) or may be separately printed on the plate.

The newspaper can now be printed from the plate. Two pages (one side of a sheet) are usually printed at the same time. Then, the sheets are turned over, and the reverse pages printed. A small offset press is not much more difficult to operate than a duplicator, but the press itself is more expensive and requires regular maintenance for best results.

Finally, the printed sheets are folded and assembled.

8 Preparing a Mimeographed Newspaper

"We can't afford a printed newspaper. All we have is a mimeograph, and you can't turn out a *real* newspaper with that! Why try?"

This conclusion is far from the truth. With ingenuity, a mimeographed paper can be made a creditable, informative newspaper. The method of printing has no bearing on the quality of your news stories.

There are many good reasons for publishing a mimeographed paper. First, the low cost is an advantage. A few advertisements will pay your expenses. Because of the cost, you can distribute your newspaper frequently. In fact, some printed papers publish frequent mimeographed news sheets between their regular issues. Next, the size of your paper is limited only by the effort of your staff. And, in addition, the staff's pride in the finished product is likely to be especially great because they have done all the work themselves.

Start out by carefully organizing and evaluating your staff. In making assignments to reporters, for instance, insist that good newswriting practice be as faithfully followed as if you were publishing *The New York Times*. When you set up a production schedule, be sure to stay with it. For your guidance, a typical timetable for a semimonthly paper is shown below. Such a schedule completes one page per day. You may wish to work more quickly or slowly than this schedule indicates, depending on your typists, mimeoscope artists, and mimeograph workers.

You will find that creating and using special forms can make your work much easier. A progress chart for each page can make the production schedule

work. Effective assignment sheets, page dummies, and headline schedules can also be extremely helpful. The sample progress chart on page 478 shows how useful such forms can be. Dates at the left are entered from the posted production schedule. The page dummy can be placed on the back of the form. Corrections can be listed at the bottom of the form. Page copy and the stencil can be attached to the form with a paper clip.

As for preparation, you may have a choice of two ways of preparing your mimeograph or duplicator stencil: by electronic stencil preparation or by "cutting the stencil" with a typewriter. Electronic

SAMPLE PRODUCTION SCHEDULE

	Page 2 Editorial	Page 3 Activities (minor news)	Page 4 Sports	Page 1 News (major stories)
Start preliminary dummy; make assignments to reporters.	Mon. Mar. 2	Tues. Mar. 3	Wed. Mar. 4	Thurs. Mar. 5
Copy due.	Mon. Mar. 9	Tues. Mar. 10	Wed. Mar. 11	Thurs. Mar. 12
Copyread.	Tues. Mar. 10	Wed. Mar. 11	Thurs. Mar. 12	Fri. Mar. 13
Finish preliminary dummy; type copy in column widths.	Wed. Mar. 11	Thurs. Mar. 12	Fri. Mar. 13	Mon. Mar. 16
Make up final dummy.	Thurs. Mar. 12	Fri. Mar. 13	Mon. Mar. 16	Tues. Mar. 17
Type stencil.	Fri. Mar. 13	Mon. Mar. 16	Tues. Mar. 17	Wed. Mar. 18
Check stencil.	Mon. Mar. 16	Tues. Mar. 17	Wed. Mar. 18	Thurs. Mar. 19
Mimeograph.	Tues. Mar. 17	Wed. Mar. 18	Thurs. Mar. 19	Thurs. after school
Assemble papers, count, and distribute.	Fri. Mar. 20			

PAGE PROGRESS CHART

Page _____ Department _____ Date of issue _____

(Sign initials as work is completed)

Date _____ Preliminary dummy planned _____ (Page editor)
Approved by editor _____ (Editor)
Assignments made _____ (Assignment editor)
Art editor told of artwork needed _____ (Page editor)

Date _____ Copy deadline
Date _____ Copyreading completed _____ (Copy editor)

Date _____ Preliminary dummy completed _____ (Page editor)
Approved by editor _____ (Editor)
Approved by adviser _____ (Adviser)
Copy typed in column widths _____ (Typist)

Date _____ Stories placed on final dummy _____ (Page editor)
Artwork completed on stencil _____ (Art editor)

Date _____ Final dummy with headlines completed _____ (Page editor)
Approved by editor _____ (Editor)
Stencil typed _____ (Typist)
Headlines typed _____ (Typist)

Date _____ Lines and lettering completed _____ (Mimeoscope worker)
Stencil checked by page editor _____ (Page editor)
Stencil checked by editor _____ (Editor)
Corrections made _____ (Typist)

Date _____ Editor's final check _____ (Editor)
Adviser's final check _____ (Adviser)
Mimeographed _____ (Mimeograph workers)

(Turn in progress chart and copy to adviser; store the stencil.)

CORRECTION SHEET

Column	Line Number	Correction

processors prepare a stencil from a typed page or pasteup. Your school office may have such a machine, or you may be able to locate one through a store that sells or services duplicators. If you choose this process, you will paste up your page just as for an offset-printed page, except that you will cement the photographs in place rather than keep them separate. Some of the suggestions that follow about page planning and use of type will be helpful.

Planning Your Pages

Standard mimeograph pages are 8½ inches wide and 11 or 14 inches long. Paper measuring 14 by 17 inches can also be purchased, making it possible to mimeograph four pages on the same sheet by folding once, printing two inside pages, and then refolding. Pages 7 by 8½ inches are possible choices for news magazines. If you choose such pages, a wide-carriage typewriter will not be needed. You can cut the stencil in half for typing and then cement it together again. White or colored 24-pound paper can be mimeographed on both sides with a quick-drying ink. Lighter-weight tinted papers may also be suitable.

There are also a number of general hints that you can use to make your pages more attractive. Note, for example, that three columns look more like a newspaper than two. Changing your column width for feature stories or editorials can also improve the appearance and variety of your pages. Two or more spreads on each page can break the monotony of long columns of type. Three-column streamers can be used to attract readers to important stories. Long stories can help make the bottom of a page attractive if they are placed under three-column streamers. Boxes around brief stories or their headlines can also be used to add interest.

Using a Variety of Type

Most schools have typewriters with two sizes of type—pica (12-point) and elite (10-point). You may want to use elite for your body type and pica for editorials, special feature stories, subheads, and kickers.

Many modern typewriters are made with a number of different typefaces. You may be able to buy a machine with executive, gothic, or italic type, to contrast with your basic body type. If a special typewriter with interchangeable typefaces is available, plan to use it in an interesting way. Many schools also use a primary (18-point) typewriter for headlines and ads. However, you will probably not want to limit your headlines to this typeface.

Your nameplate should be especially neat and clear. An adequate size is 1 inch by three columns or 2 inches by two columns. A two-column nameplate can be moved to vary your front page makeup.

For headlines, you can use two or three sizes of lettering guides, both roman and italic, for contrast. For best results, you may want to plan a flush-left headline schedule, using capital letters and lower-case letters. Number each of the headlines, show the unit count and determine the number of lines each headline will occupy.

A sample headline schedule appears on page 480. The school from which the sample was taken uses a primary (18-point) typewriter for some of its minor headlines (marked with the letter *T* after the headline number). The first and fourth headlines shown on the schedule are used for nameplates and other special purposes. Many of the one- and two-column headlines have identical unit counts, giving additional options for flexible page makeup.

RAM'S TALE HEADLINE SCHEDULE

Ram's Tale Wins First
NO. 1 (5 SPACES)   18-21

Students Show Skills at Meeting
NO. 2 (5 SPACES)   (2-DECK: USE WITH NO. 19)   30-33

Student Association Members to See Movies
NO. 3 (3 SPACES)   (2-DECK: USE WITH NO. 18 OR 20)   38-42

Personalities
NO. 4 (5 SPACES)   12-14

Band Presents Concert
NO. 5 (5 SPACES)   18-22

Royals Have Picnic at Anza
NO. 6 (4 SPACES)   22-27

Student Association Members
To See 'Lost Horizon' Movie
NO. 7T (5 SPACES)   22-27 EACH LINE

Royals Have Picnic at Anza
NO. 8T (3 SPACES)   22-27

Personality of the Week
Eighth Grader Likes Sports
                                  Who Is She?
NO. 9 (6 SPACES)   KICKERS 10-25, MAIN LINE 22-27

Trampoline Artists --
Tumblers to Present Program
NO. 10 (4 SPACES)   KICKER 10-25, MAIN LINE 22-27
NO. 11 (3 SPACES) (MAIN LINE ONLY)   22-27

Student-Body
Officers Plan
New Calendar
NO. 19   10-13
(7 SPACES)   EACH LINE

Student-Body
Officers Plan
New Calendar
NO. 20T   10-13
(7 SPACES)   EACH LINE

Disc Data
NO. 12 (6 SPACES)   8-11

Rams Beat
Bears, 12-0
NO. 13 (6 SPACES)   8-11

Disc Data
NO. 14 (4 SPACES)   8-11

Teachers Say --
No Homework?
NO. 15   KICKER 10-15,
(5 SPACES) MAIN LINE 10-13

Officers Plan
New Calendar
NO. 16 (7 SPACES)   10-13
                         EACH LINE

Student Body
Has Meeting
NO. 17 (5 SPACES)   10-13
                         EACH LINE

Officers Plan
New Calendar
NO. 18T   10-13
(5 SPACES)   EACH LINE

—*Ram's Tale*, Roosevelt Junior High School, Richmond, California

Preparing Copy for Mimeographing

You should insist that your copy be written according to newspaper standards and that it be properly copyread. To estimate the space a story will occupy if copy is handwritten, have reporters count their words. About 25 words in elite type will fill a column inch. Estimate 20 words per inch for lists of names or for copy that has many short paragraphs. If reporters type their copy, use the method suggested on page 464.

Justifying Lines

To make mimeograph work look like a printed newspaper with even right-hand margins, you must type your copy twice. The first typing gets the words onto paper. It also serves another important purpose: With material typed to exact size, a page editor can accurately space stories on the dummy.

For the first typing, set the margin stops on your typewriter to print an exact number of characters, generally 26 characters for a standard three-column paper. Fill in unused spaces at the ends of lines with slashes to indicate extra spaces to be distributed through the line. Put check

marks where these extra spaces are to be inserted, trying to space between phrases and to avoid placing one wide space above or below another.

The two paragraphs on the left at the bottom of the page represent a first typing, with slashes and check marks. The two paragraphs on the right represent the second typing, with the extra spaces added to produce justified lines.

Making Up the Pages

Page editors should start the preliminary page dummies before assignments are made, in the same way as they would for a printed newspaper.

Makeup for a three-column page can follow, in general, all the standards suggested for wider pages in Chapter 17. Study these principles and plan how to apply them to the narrow page. One guiding principle is diagonal balance. If you have a "heavy" headline or story in one upper corner of the page, use another "heavy" item in the opposite lower corner to balance it.

You can readily mimeograph a dummy sheet by putting a stencil on the mimeoscope and tracing the general outline and columns of a page. Marks for

```
    You may type one extra
character/into the right-/
hand margin when there are
short words or punctuation
marks/in/the/same line.///
Circle this letter./ When/
typing the stencil, fit the
letter/in/by squeezing a//
short word together/or by/
leaving out/a space after/
a punctuation mark.
    Set up/definite rules/
as to the number of spaces
between sentences, the num-
ber of spaces to indent at
the beginning of each para-
graph, and other details.
```

```
    You may type one extra
character  into the right-
hand margin when there are
short words or punctuation
marks  in  the  same line.
Circle this letter.  When
typing the stencil,fit the
letter  in  by squeezing a
short word together  or by
leaving out  a space after
a punctuation mark.
    Set up  definite rules
as to the number of spaces
between sentences,the num-
ber of spaces to indent at
the beginningof each para-
graph, and other details.
```

each line of type are invaluable to the page editors and typists. They guarantee an even page bottom. Dotted lines may also be drawn across the dummy as guides for running heads and special nameplates.

After the dummy sheets are ready, paste the copy, typed in column widths, to the dummy. Make sure that lines across the page are exactly aligned. Make the bottom of the page even by interchanging headline styles, by cutting off paragraphs, by leaving out words or sentences at the end of a paragraph, or by allowing a little extra white space above a headline in a column.

Write headlines on the dummy, indicating the style number for each. Picture captions or fillers—material used to fill space in a column or on a page— should be typed (not handwritten) and pasted on the dummy to be sure the material fits properly. Indicate special styles of type by writing notes in the margins. Write any other special directions on another sheet of paper and fasten it to the dummy.

Laying Out Advertisements

In preparing an advertising message, use all the newspaper's resources. Make a list of the various sizes and styles of type, both those on typewriters used by the staff and those prepared with lettering guides. In addition to the headline styles, there may be other lettering guides for advertising use only.

Consider what can be done with artwork. Line drawings are not hard to trace on a stencil if someone on your staff can draw the original. Freehand lettering may be interesting in an ad. Completed artwork or printed designs for tracing can be purchased from duplicator manufacturers. Pictures, or perhaps entire ads, can be reproduced electronically from black-and-white copy and set into your stencil.

Typing the Stencil

Purchase top-quality stencils. In contrast to cheaper stencils, they produce finer mimeoscope work, print more clearly, and last through longer mimeograph runs. Special stencils with three-column newspaper markings can be ordered; these provide an added convenience. Film-covered stencils are also useful in that they make blacker letters and help keep the typewriter keys clean.

Brush your typewriter keys to clean them before typing each stencil. Disengage or remove the ribbon. (On older typewriters, you can generally disengage the ribbon by moving the ribbon lever halfway between black and red.) Use an even stroke, with lighter pressure on commas and periods and heavier pressure for *m*'s, *w*'s, and capital letters. If your typewriter cuts out *o*'s, use a film-covered stencil or have a repair person determine whether your roller is too hard.

If the dummy has been well made, you can type across all three columns; a ruler is used to guide your eye. Matching the lines from one column to another helps you space for headlines. Follow the directions on the stencil package for using cushion sheets or typing plates and for making corrections.

Doing Mimeoscope Work

The mimeoscope worker letters the headlines. A copy of your headline schedule marked up to show the proper lettering guide and stylus, or metal pencil, for each headline is a time-saver. Each lettering guide is designed for a particular stylus. The stylus number is often indicated on the guide.

Work with the stencil directly over a flexible writing plate. Remove the cushion sheet and slide the stencil backing through the slot at the top of the mimeoscope. Lock the metal ruler in place and slide the lettering guide along it. Pressing firmly with the stylus, go over each line until light shows evenly through it. When drawing lines that meet, work *toward* the junction to avoid tearing the stencil.

Notice the unit count of your headline and compare it with the headline schedule to see whether you should space letters out or crowd them together. Notice also the use of capitals and lowercase letters in the headline.

Drawings are mimeoscoped in a similar way. First, make a sketch on thin white paper. Then, put the flexible writing plate under your stencil, position the drawing under the plate, and trace it.

Learn the purposes of the various styli. A loop stylus is best for straight and curved lines. Ball point styli are used for detailed lines of varying thickness. Do not fill in solid areas, but use shading plates, which come in different patterns and degrees of blackness. Place the plate under the stencil and rub with a special round-pointed stylus. Wheel styli can be used for unusual lines or for shading.

Putting Insets into a Stencil

Photographs, nameplates, drawings, and other prepared designs can be glued into a stencil. Put the stencil on your mimeoscope with the flexible writing plate under it and the inset in position under the plate. With a razor blade, cut a hole in the stencil just a little larger than the actual design on the inset. Take the inset out and trim it, keeping it at least ⅛ inch larger on all sides than the hole. Place a slick cushion sheet or a piece of wax paper under the stencil. Brush a thin coat of stencil cement on the stencil around the edge of the hole. Move the backing sheet to a clean area and then put the inset in place on top of the stencil. Rub gently, being careful that the cement does not flow into your design. Allow the cement to dry completely.

You can make last-minute story changes in your completed stencils in the same manner. If you have ⅛ inch of space around a story, a worker with a steady hand can cut it out and glue in a new story prepared on an extra stencil.

Using Artwork and Photographs

A variety of artwork is possible with mimeograph duplication. Almost anything that can be drawn with simple lines and shading can be reproduced on a mimeoscope. Duplicator manufacturers sell portfolios of designs for tracing and also make die-impressed designs that can be cemented into your stencils. Your own nameplate or school emblem may be either die-impressed on a stencil or reproduced by a photochemical process.

Detailed black-and-white line drawings may also be placed on stencils with electronic stencil-making equipment. You may print directly from an electronically prepared stencil or cut it into insets to be cemented into your typed stencil.

Photographs may be reproduced on stencils by this process. They will not be comparable to photographs in printed papers, but clear photos, especially head-and-shoulders shots with good contrast, come out rather well. Mount the original photographs on a sheet of 8½-by-14-inch white paper, pasting lightly only at the top of each picture. After an electronic stencil has been made, inset the pictures wherever you wish on your pages.

The Redbird

JACS LOSERS: Kevin Rich, John Leland, and David Miller create their own Awards of Excellence for not winning.

Non-winners seek to enshrine feats

"Drum roll . . . and the losers are . . . third place, senior John Leland; second place, senior Dave Miller; and finally, first but not least, senior Kevin Rich."

Such a scene might become a trend in the '80s, if three REDBIRD editors have their way.

When REDBIRD and yearbook staffers came home from JACS competition with nine winners last fall, it gradually became evident (Continued on Page 2)

THE REDBIRD

Loudonville High School

Vol. 35, No. 6   Loudonville, Ohio 44842   Jan. 18, 1980

SUGGEST IMPROVEMENTS

North Central evaluators approve high school

Loudonville High School has "passed" the North Central Association evaluation conducted Nov. 12-14.

Schools in the North Central area are evaluated every seven years to determine whether they are maintaining the educational standards set by the association.

"I never had any doubts about the outcome, because we weren't in violation of any standards," Principal Alton Lance said.

One year before the evaluation, the faculty prepares a self-study which members of the evaluating team check.

"Their evaluation and our self-study outlined many of the same strengths and weaknesses," Mr. Lance said.

Now the school has 90 days to put the committee's recommendations and suggestions into priority.

"The most important phase of the whole evaluation is right now, though—how we're going to follow the suggestions for improvement," Mr. Lance concluded.

Musicians prep for contests

About 35 LHS students will participate the High School Sol Ensemble Contest F at Mansfield Senior

These students rated in three clas music: A—college le advanced; B—interme and C—easy.

LHS musicians in flute, clarinet, tr

Whirlwind

Library Book Suggestions Accepted

What books would you like to read?

Mrs. Ott welcomes suggestions from students and faculty members on new books for the library.

Juniors And Seniors To Tour Capitol

CHS's Juniors and Seniors will soon be leaving on their bi-annual trip to the capitol.

Leaving on March 16, and returning on the 19th, the students will be touring the legislature, watching the legislators work, and, if possible, attending some committee meetings.

Chaperones will be Mr. and Mrs. Thew and Mr. and Mrs. Thorne.

Mr. Thew commented, "It's a chance to see how government works.

"It shows most people you can affect how government works.

"It's not some people in Salem working magic."

Senior Betsy Defenbaugh said, "I can't wait!"

Caligraphy Classes To Be Given

"Handwriting when considered as an art... writing that is beautiful and individual" is the definition of caligraphy.

"What we're learning now is basic italic," said Mrs. Jean Goff, who is instructing a class on caligraphy from 4 to 5 o'clock Mondays and Wednesdays.

Because of the popularity of the class she is now teaching, Mrs. Goff plans to start another class soon, but because most of those interested are students, these classes will probably be held in the evenings so as not to interfere with track and tennis practices.

The class costs $15.00, which covers the cost of the special fountain pen and the other supplies necessary.

Anyone who is interested in taking the class should contact Mrs. Goff by March 11, so she can order the supplies needed.

WHIRLWIND

Crane Union High School   Crane, Oregon 97732

Vol. 25 No. 6   March 10, 1981

Soloists Compete At District

"Wow!" was Rise Thew's comment on the Instrumental and Vocal Solo and Ensemble District competition juniors Rise Thew and Harvey Gunkel, and freshman David Chamberlain competed in February 17.

Band director John Harding said, "I was very pleased with all three.

"Maybe now that we've broken the ice, next year we'll take more people."

David commented, "I enjoyed myself."

Competitors were judged on a scale from one to four, one being the best.

The judges scored the contestants on their tone, interpretation, musicality, and a number of other things, then averaged the scores for the final ratings.

Final scores were: Harvey Gunkel (Tuba solo) two-plus, David Chamberlain (Baritone horn solo) one minus, and Rise Thew (Flute solo) one.

Harvey and David came in second in their divisions, and Kise tied for first.

Heart Fund Drive A Success

The annual Heart Fund Drive, held at Crane on February 21, brought in about $1,800.

Mrs. Dorothy Oetter commented, "The Heart Fund Drive is a good community project.

"Members of our community work hard and work well together."

—*The Redbird*, Loudonville High School, Loudonville, Ohio; *Whirlwind*, Crane Union High School, Crane, Oregon

Photographs, drawings, appealing page designs, and even color printing are all possible in a mimeographed newspaper. With knowledge and ingenuity, a staff can make such a paper an admired school enterprise.

When mimeographing from electronic stencils, use the silk-screen inking process, if possible. With older machines, try two ink pads. Run your machine slowly. Note also that white paper generally gives much better results than tinted paper does.

Color printing enlivens your mimeographed pages and is not difficult. Directions are given in references available from your duplicator manufacturer. Color can be used for graphic designs, nameplates, headlines, cartoons, and special stories. Avoid two-color drawings, since most mimeographs do not feed paper accurately enough to align one color with the other. As a result, the colors will tend to look out of focus, and the general look will be one of carelessness, no matter how much work you have actually put into the drawing.

Checking and Correcting the Stencil

Check the stencil carefully when the typing is finished, comparing it with the original copy, not with the column-width typing. The two-person proofreading system described on page 470 will generally give the best results. Note, however, that errors should be marked not on the stencil but on a sheet of paper attached to the stencil. The Page Progress Chart on page 478 has a special place to indicate corrections. These are checked off as they are completed, and the typist then signs the chart in order to certify they have been made.

On your correction sheet, indicate the column number, line number (printed in white at the stencil margin), and the correction required. Show spelling errors by spelling the word properly. For other types of mistakes, you may use regular proofreaders' marks, clarifying if necessary the exact location of the correction. The example in the box at the bottom of the page shows how to mark errors.

When correcting a stencil, rub the errors gently with a rounded object. Then, cover that area with a thin coat of stencil correction fluid and retype, using a slightly lighter touch than usual.

Assembling Papers

Neat work in assembling pages improves your paper's appearance. Set up an assembly line. Be sure all pages are right side up, printed on both sides, not smeared or blotted. Stack the pages evenly, and staple them twice in the left-hand margin, keeping the staples out of the printed matter. Fastening the pages on the left instead of in an upper corner makes your product look more like a printed newspaper.

From the assemblers, the finished papers go to the checkers (who see that each paper is complete and neat) and then to the circulation staff for distribution.

```
(STENCIL)                              (CORRECTION SHEET)

41   The composing room  and the
42   ingraving room  were the last     Col. 1   42 engraving
43   we visited.  in the composing               43 cap I
44   room was the linotypemachine               44 #
45   which set the type.
```

9 Handling Circulation and Exchanges

You work hard preparing your school newspaper. You want every student in your school to read it. What problems do you face in building this kind of circulation?

Your circulation measures your reader interest. If you are publishing the kind of news your readers want, they will buy your newspaper. Technical perfection in journalism by itself does not guarantee attention from your readers. In fact, some prizewinning newspapers complain of poor circulation. They do not print the kind of material their readers desire.

To sell papers, you need wide school coverage, close attention to news of future events, notes about what people are doing, and information about the real interests of young adults. Contests and popular columns help. You need not stoop to the level of printing gossip to increase your circulation. But you do have to write, in an interesting way, the items your subscribers will read.

You will also have to consider school spirit. If students show little interest in student government and activities, they are not likely to pay much attention to your paper. Your staff cannot overcome this inertia by itself, but you can work steadily toward student participation in worthwhile extracurricular projects.

In general, your sales of advertising—the main revenue for your paper—will depend on good circulation. Advertisers buying space in your newspaper expect to reach most of your students. If your newspaper is distributed free of charge, you are relieved of the need for sales campaigns. But you are not relieved of the responsibility of putting out the best paper you can. Advertisers or taxpayers are paying your expenses. They are entitled to their money's worth.

Selling the Newspaper

Sales to 75 percent of a student body are considered good. First considerations toward reaching this goal are price and length of subscription. Some school papers successfully sell single issues at 25 cents each. This eliminates the need for keeping subscription records but requires constant promotion to make students want each issue. The low cost helps. Most students can spare a quarter on circulation day. Free copies of special issues may be given to homerooms that meet certain circulation quotas.

Most school newspapers sell subscriptions for one semester or one year. Rates may range from $1 a semester to $4 a year, depending on the financial needs of the paper and the number of issues printed during the subscription period. Lower semester rates make selling easier but also require a campaign twice a year instead of once.

Mail subscriptions may be sold at the student rate plus postage expense. If your paper qualifies for second-class or bulk-mailing privileges, postage costs can be quite low. The possibilities of selling your paper to alumni and friends who reside near the school are surprising. One midwestern high school paper aims for a circulation of 3,000, with about one half of the subscribers from outside the student population. If so many papers are sold, subscription rates can be low, which in turn makes the whole selling job easier.

A sales campaign is a promotional activity. It must be intelligently planned and enthusiastically carried out, building up to a climax. Base your method on the interests of your potential subscribers, using an approach that is familiar and acceptable to them. Choose a theme for each campaign, around which you can develop slogans, contests, and activities. Keep the campaign constantly before the students for about two weeks. Extending the period will not increase sales.

You may find it easiest to place the responsibility for conducting the campaign on the homerooms, with the student council representatives in charge. Run a contest among homerooms and award a prize to the homeroom with the highest number of sales. Point out that the winner must get alumni and outside subscriptions to achieve more than 100 percent sales. Push the idea of the public relations value to the school of the outside subscriptions.

A few other campaign ideas might also be mentioned. Start with an assembly, telling your story in an interesting or humorous way. Distribute the first issue of the paper to all students. Prepare posters and signs. Encourage competition between grades. Divide sales representatives into teams to compete against one another. Give cash prizes to top sales reps and other prizes to classrooms turning in 100 percent sales. Plan a variety show, dance, or party for all subscribers or for rooms that reach 100 percent in subscriptions. Get one room to challenge another and have the losing group give the winning group a party.

Be sure to keep careful sales records. A simple receipt book with a printed ticket to give each subscriber and a stub to fill out with name and homeroom (or street address) is sufficient. A single form requiring the same information will work, but sales representatives are less likely to omit names if they must hand a receipt to each subscriber. If you have stubs, you can also sort them by subscribers' locations for ease in delivery and then file them in alphabetical or numerical order for quick reference. Establish a regular time and place for sales representatives to turn in their completed books and

money. Follow up to see that they account for all ticket books issued them, sold or unsold.

You might consider deferred or installment payments. They require more bookkeeping, but it is estimated that they increase student sales 10 percent. Follow up as necessary until all students have paid up.

If the subscription is a part of an activity-card budget, you will not be solely responsible for the sales campaign. As one of the major beneficiaries of the activity fund, however, you must cooperate in the campaign. Many of the previously suggested devices will help sell activity cards.

Delivering the Paper

Delivery is usually done through homerooms. A typical method is for the circulation staff to count in advance the number of copies needed for each room. A room representative with a list of subscribers then picks up the papers for each class. The circulation manager notifies the room representative of any changes in the subscriptions. From this list, deliveries are made.

Another successful method is to organize subscription lists in the order of students' locker numbers. A circulation team moves through the halls, dropping a paper through the vent of each subscriber's locker.

If you sell individual issues of the paper, you will be most successful if you can send a circulation representative with papers and change to each homeroom. If the teacher allows a minute or two for the circulation person to explain the contents of the newspaper to a class, sales will be considerably improved.

If you distribute the paper to holders of activity cards, a circulation team may visit homerooms and give a copy to each person showing a card. Or you may distribute papers during lunch periods from a central point easily accessible to all students.

Even before the process of building circulation among students starts, a circulation staff member should prepare copies for mailing to outside subscribers and to exchange newspapers.

Making Good Use of Exchanges

Your exchange editor should work with the circulation staff to mail copies of your paper to all schools that send you their newspapers. The exchange editor has the additional responsibility of receiving these exchange newspapers and encouraging their use by reporters and staff members. The papers may be placed on racks or posted on bulletin boards. Finally, the exchange editor should constantly search for ideas about the handling of copy, page arrangement, story tips, promotion ideas, and production shortcuts and call these to the attention of appropriate staff members.

A good exchange list can be built around schools with common interests. One such group includes other schools in your city, town, or athletic conference. Another consists of schools of similar size all over the country that publish newspapers like yours. You can obtain the names of some of these papers by writing to scholastic press associations or by reading their magazines and other publications.

10 Managing Finances

Even the smallest school newspapers have expenses, purchase supplies, or receive money. Proper handling of funds and records is not only good business, but it also provides valuable training for staff members.

Business management of the school paper can be placed under the guidance of the journalism faculty or the commercial department. Each arrangement offers certain advantages. Appointing a business manager from a journalism class keeps the figures readily available to the staff, may make it easier to fix responsibility in case of error, and is less likely to cause confusion between the business and advertising staffs. Allowing the commercial department to handle this work provides the business students with a practical project, is likely to produce better records because of their training in accounting procedures, and relieves the overburdened newspaper adviser by providing a faculty business adviser.

Making a Budget

No school newspaper, whether it handles $100 or $10,000 a year, should be without a workable financial plan in the form of a budget to show where all monies are to come from and how they are to be spent. Your budget may be planned for a semester or a full year. It should be completed during the semester preceding the publication period it covers.

The first step in making your budget is to estimate realistically the sources of all income. List each source and the amount of income expected. Total these amounts.

Second, estimate carefully every expense anticipated. Check your past expenses, estimate possible price increases, and make adjustments allowing for these increases and for possible changes in your plans. If your paper is commercially printed, discuss your plans with your printer and ask for an estimate of the printing cost. If you have no records of previous expenses or if you are changing your printing method, you will have to estimate costs by gathering information from other schools, from printers, from sales representatives, and from other sources.

To the total sum of your expected costs, add 10 percent for a reserve fund. The main purpose of the reserve fund is to meet unexpected expenses, which will surely arise. Whatever remains at the end of the year is added to your permanent reserve, which helps pay bills arising before your income starts, keeps you solvent if you underestimate costs, or can be used to purchase special equipment.

Now compare your estimated total income and total expenses. To balance your budget, you must find some way to make the two figures equal. If expenses exceed income, you will need to find some way of increasing income or cutting expenses. If you have extra income, it should be relatively easy to decide how to spend it!

Your completed budget is usually approved by your student council, principal, or school superintendent. If your income comes from a student activity fund, the group that controls the fund should approve your budget.

When your budget is approved, make contracts if possible with printers, typesetters, and other firms involved with the publication of your newspaper. In return for your promise to give them your business and to meet certain deadlines, you gain the certainty of fixed costs for these expensive services.

Sample budgets for school newspapers are shown below.

Keeping Financial Records

Once approved, your budget becomes the basis of your financial records. It also controls the amount of money you

---

Sample Budget for a Semimonthly Printed Newspaper

Income		Expenses	
Student subscriptions	$3,600.00	Printing	$7,500.00
Subscriptions to alumni		Photography	600.00
and townspeople	1,500.00	Postage	300.00
Sales of advertising		Office supplies, tele-	
space	4,500.00	phone	300.00
		Reserve	900.00
	$9,600.00		$9,600.00

Sample Budget for a Semimonthly Mimeographed Newspaper

Income		Expenses	
Subscriptions, through		Paper	$400.00
activity fund	$300.00	Stencils, ink, mimeograph	
Mail subscriptions	50.00	service, and supplies . .	200.00
Sales of advertising space .	450.00	Office supplies, mimeo-	
		scope supplies, postage	120.00
		Reserve	80.00
	$800.00		$800.00

may spend on any one item. You should not exceed this allowance without a budget change, approved in the same way as your original budget.

Any business operating on a cash basis under a budget records all transactions twice. First, you will need a cash record, which shows the actual amount of money you have on hand. Enter each receipt or expenditure. Your checkbook can serve this purpose if sufficient detail as to source of income or purpose of expenditure is noted on each check stub. Your cash record should ensure that you will never spend more money than you actually have on hand.

Second, you will need budget accounts for all expenses. Head a separate page in your record book with the name of each budget item. For example, you will need a page headed Printing, another headed Office Supplies, and so on. Be sure to include all items in your budget. Enter at the top of the page the amount allowed for that item. Each time an expenditure is made, list it on the appropriate page and subtract it from the budgeted amount. The figure remaining shows

what still remains to be spent for this item.

You may also wish to set up a similar page for each source of income, to watch its progress during the year. If your income is from all fixed sources, this will not be necessary.

Your budget account records should be set up in a manner similar to the illustrations below.

A system in which all payments are made by check is suggested for school newspapers. It is a businesslike arrangement. It provides safeguards for handling money. And it simplifies recordkeeping. To make the system work, insist that every bit of money received, whatever the source, be deposited in the bank. Even though an advertising sales representative may have just turned in $6 and the business manager has to spend $6 for typewriter ribbons, the business manager may not use the same money. The cash goes to the bank, and the expenditure is paid by check. In the long run, you will save enough time in keeping accounts straight to justify the extra time spent writing the check. Checks should be made

Printing
(Expense Budget $7,500)

Date	To	Amount	Balance
Sept. 24	Miller Printing Co.	$532.12	$6,967.88
Oct. 8	Miller Printing Co.	544.50	6,423.38
Oct. 22	Miller Printing Co.	526.20	5,897.18

Advertising Space
(Income Budget $4,500)

Date	From	Amount	Total to date
Sept. 24	Cash collections	$212.00	$212.00
25	Cash collections	48.00	260.00
Oct. 8	Cash collections	140.00	400.00
9	Cash collections	124.00	524.00
12	Cash collections	50.00	574.00
12	General Mercantile Co.	48.00	622.00
13	Cash collections	128.00	750.00
15	North Star Clothing Co.	70.00	820.00

out by the business manager and should be countersigned by the business or newspaper adviser.

If incidental expenses are bothersome to handle by check, establish a petty cash system. A certain amount ($20, for example) is withdrawn from the bank. On budget account records, it is charged to the reserve under the heading Petty Cash. The business manager spends the money as necessary and obtains a receipt for each expenditure. When the fund diminishes, these receipts are submitted. Their amounts are posted against the proper budget accounts, and another check is written for the exact total of these expenses to replenish the fund.

Preparing Statements and Making Collections

While an issue of the paper is being printed, the business manager prepares for each advertiser a statement similar to the one below. (Refer to Chapter 19 for comments concerning the establishment of advertising rates.)

In cases where the sales representative is to present the statement to the merchant, the business manager should prepare each statement in triplicate. The sales rep takes two, and the business manager keeps the third. When the money has been collected, the sales rep marks the original statement "Paid" and gives it to the merchant. The sales rep then turns the money in to the business manager for deposit in the bank. At this time, the business manager marks both the file copy of the statement and the sales rep's copy "Paid." All parties then have a record of the transaction. The business manager prepares duplicate receipts for other cash and checks received. He or she keeps one copy and gives the other to the person from whom the money has been received.

When business firms prefer monthly billing, an account for each store must be maintained. You should post each charge and each payment promptly and accurately. At the first of each month, figure the amount due and mail a statement. Your accounts receivable ledger should have a page for each account, set up as shown in the example at the top of the next page.

CENTRAL HIGH NEWS

Statement

Date _____

To _____

_____

_____

For advertising in the Central High News: Date _____ $ _____

Please pay amount due to the sales representative who presents this statement or mail to the News, Central High School, Midtown.

Account No. 18
General Mercantile Co.
110 Main Street

Date	For	Charges	Credits	Balance due
Sept. 24	Ad 2 × 4	$24.00		$24.00
Oct. 8	Ad 2 × 4	24.00		48.00
Oct. 12	Payment		$24.00	24.00
Oct. 22	Ad 2 × 5	30.00		54.00

You may keep accounts of this kind for all advertisers. However, there is no real need to maintain them for merchants who pay for each ad separately if the statement and receipt system suggested previously is followed. Bring to the immediate attention of your business adviser all advertising accounts that are not paid promptly.

When you allow installment payments on subscriptions, the circulation manager sets up a collection system. Statements are not needed, since installment dates are fixed and can easily be announced to the school as a whole as they approach.

Circulation staff members who visit homerooms on this day make the collections. They then turn their money over to the business manager and receive receipts for it. Subscribers who do not complete their installments may be removed from the subscription list after delivery of the last of the papers for which they have actually paid.

To make bank deposits, the business manager prepares duplicate deposit slips. To the copy that is initialed by the bank and returned, the business manager attaches the copies of the original receipts, which indicate from whom this money was received and what these payments cover. At this point, the entries in the cash record and the income account can also be marked to show that the money has been deposited and acknowledged by the bank.

Issuing Reports

The business manager makes reports to the editor and adviser on a monthly basis or sometimes more frequently. The kind of report most useful to these people shows amounts budgeted, spent, and remaining, as well as the original estimate of expenses during the period, for comparison purposes. An example of such a monthly report is found on page 493. The report shows that the paper has cost only slightly more than its budget planners expected. But, as the report clearly shows, its income is falling below expectations. Adjustments are needed at once to avoid a deficit for the year.

This report was prepared on a cash basis. It records only money actually received or spent. Your bookkeeping instructor can help you set up records and reports that include unpaid accounts owing to the paper and those owed by it. However, if bills are paid when received and collections are kept up to date, the less complicated cash system provides sufficient operating information for most school newspapers. Of course, whatever system you use, the newspaper's business adviser should audit the records and reports regularly.

CENTRAL HIGH NEWS
Financial Report, November 1, 1984

Expenses	Budget	Expenses to date	Amount remaining	Estimated expenses to date
Printing	$7,500.00	$1,602.82	$5,897.18	$1,500.00
Photography	600.00	102.12	497.88	120.00
Postage	300.00	82.50	217.50	60.00
Office supplies, telephone . . .	300.00	24.19	275.81	60.00
Reserve	900.00	0.00	900.00	
Totals	$9,600.00	$1,811.63	$7,788.37	$1,740.00

Income	Budget	Income to date	Amount still due	Estimated income to date
Student subscriptions	$3,600.00	$2,912.50	$ 687.50	$3,600.00
Subscriptions to alumni and townspeople	1,500.00	721.30	778.70	1,500.00
Sales of advertising space . . .	4,500.00	544.00	3,956.00	900.00
Totals	$9,600.00	$4,177.80	$5,422.20	$6,000.00

Cash on hand, September 1	$ 216.90
Income to date	4,177.80
Total received	$4,394.70
Expenses to date	1,811.63
Cash on hand, November 1	$2,583.07

Making Purchases

The business manager makes whatever purchases are necessary for the paper. It is important to shop carefully, comparing prices and qualities from various dealers. The cheapest product is not always the most satisfactory. The costliest may be no better for a certain use than a less expensive product.

Quantity purchases can often save money. For example, in some areas there is a considerable discount on mimeograph paper when 50 reams are purchased at one time. Use of the school name may encourage other discounts. Frequently, wholesale distributors will deal directly with a newspaper, making further cost reduction possible. Consider, however, that local merchants support the school by taxes and perhaps by advertising and have a right to expect its business. You may not want to risk losing their good will. Sometimes you can arrange to buy through the school purchasing department, taking advantage of its regular procedure of buying in large quantities or its method of advertising for bids.

However you proceed, a purchase-order system is recommended. This ensures three things. Purchases will be approved in advance by the business manager. Merchants will honor the or-

```
                                          Purchase Order No. _____

                        CENTRAL HIGH NEWS

                                    Date _____

   To _____

      _____

      _____


   Deliver the following to the Central High News, Central High School, Midtown, or to the bearer. Please
   refer to the number of this Purchase Order when submitting your invoice.
```

Quantity	Item	Price	

```
                        Approved:


                        _____

                        Authorized Signature
```

der, since they know that approval has been given and that no complications will arise in receiving their money. And payments can be made by check when the merchant's invoice is received. A sample purchase-order form is shown above. The key point on the form is the authorized signature at the bottom.

11 Extending Your Newspaper's Influence

Your school newspaper is in a position to become an important force in your school and community by reflecting student thinking and promoting worthwhile goals. Several methods used by influential school newspapers follow.

Expanding Your News Stories

Articles discussing school curriculum or facilities, summarizing educational requirements, or explaining school board actions are examples of broad topics relating to both school and community. But more often than not, a school news story becomes richer and more meaningful by the way it is written, rather than by its content.

A personality sketch of a teacher may include information about educational background, personal philosophy of teaching, goals, and opinions on ways parents might help their children attain these goals.

A news story about an annual dance or a major school activity may cover some of the traditions behind the event or the reasons the school administration considers it a worthwhile part of the educational program.

A news report about a student project may be enriched by describing what has really been accomplished. Many special-interest groups (science or computer clubs, for example) reach points in learning far beyond what ordinary classroom instruction makes possible.

Guiding Opinion
with Thoughtful Editorials

Your editorial page offers unique opportunities for interpreting your school to the community. Thoughtful editorials on important topics indicate to many adult and student readers that the school is succeeding in training its students to think for themselves. Trite editorials on inconsequential topics suggest the opposite. Your editorial board, composed of several experienced staff members, can provide editorial leadership as well as visualize the impact of each editorial.

Making Extensive Use
of Interpretive, In-Depth Reports

Good reporting on significant topics relating to the school, community, or nation can result in powerful articles. These will be widely read and may suggest purposeful action to students or other readers. One of the functions of your editorial board might be to review such articles, particularly those on controversial subjects, to determine whether they support the paper's purpose, to decide whether they conform to its editorial standards, and to assess the reader impact.

Giving Full Coverage
to Major Issues

Influential school papers often assemble a variety of interpretive, in-depth reports, straight-news stories, and articles of opinion on some topic of critical interest to young people. These newspapers may devote a full page, a two-page spread, a special section, or even an entire issue to such material. Or they may publish a series of articles in several issues.

As an example, the *Redbird* (Loudonville High School, Loudonville, Ohio) explored a proposed multi-English curriculum with a series of articles, reporting on visits to other high schools where the program was already in use, interviewing students, teachers, and administrators, and commenting editorially. The paper reported, "After reading articles in the Redbird and visiting schools that have a multi-English program, LHS English teachers are enthusiastic about this innovation in teaching." Soon after, the school board approved the new program.

Recognizing the Way
in Which Advertising Links
the School and Community

Every advertisement in your newspaper develops closer relations between your school and community. Through advertisements, merchants hope they will be able to sell their goods or services to students. In addition, they hope that many people besides students will read their ads and respond to them. If your newspaper is being taken home by many students, it may very well be the most effective advertising medium merchants can use to reach buyers in the vicinity of the school.

Using a Multimedia Approach

Many school papers have expanded their sphere of influence by using a variety of media to get news and information to their readers. For instance, some staffs whose newspapers are published at three- or four-week intervals have concentrated on presenting interpretive, in-depth reports in these editions, often using magazine format. Then, between issues, perhaps weekly, they publish mimeographed news sheets. Other schools have obtained exciting results with a bulletin board newspaper, showing headlines, photographs, and typed stories but changing individual stories frequently as new material becomes available. Journalism classes in a few schools have prepared occasional newspapers especially for parents.

In schools with an intercom system, student journalists have experimented successfully with daily broadcasts, putting the morning announcements into news format and adding interesting news reports. The *Hoof Print* (Alamo Heights High School, San Antonio, Texas) produces a biweekly television broadcast to supplement the school paper. The show, including headlines, interviews, filmed items, features, and paid commercials, is seen in homerooms via closed-circuit television. Schools without closed-circuit equipment may use videotape, arranging several showings of the broadcast to reach their audience.

Supporting a Cause

The staff of the *Black and Gold* (Cleveland Heights High School, Cleveland Heights, Ohio) used editorials and news articles a few years ago to urge a change in an "antiquated" dress code. Prodded by the newspaper's editorial campaign, which was continued for most of a semester, the student council developed a new code that received administrative approval. When the new code went into effect amid some misunderstandings, the paper opened its columns to letters and student comments. By keeping the matter before the students and by maintaining steady pressure for continued progress, the newspaper may have helped avoid disruptions arising from sudden and unreasonable demands. And by providing an open forum, it helped to reduce the rumors that inevitably surround change.

Using News Releases to Local Newspapers

Most local newspapers consider school news well worth printing. Readers are interested not only in their children's educational progress but also in the tangible results achieved by their tax money. Alert reporters in your school news bureau, writing about the school for local daily and weekly newspapers, can interpret the school's purpose and program to the public. Local radio and television stations are also possible outlets for your news releases. Your news bureau might supply news scripts and make suggestions for interpretive, in-depth programs about school affairs. Suggestions for operating a school news bureau are given in the next section.

12 Setting Up a School News Bureau

A school news bureau prepares and delivers school news to local newspapers. It is composed of members of the school newspaper staff. On small staffs, the editor or assistant editor may be responsible for the operation of the news bureau. If the staff is large enough to permit it, assignment of separate staff members can provide more efficient news bureau operation. Important school news will inevitably arise when the editor is so busy with deadlines that he or she cannot give proper attention to the preparation of stories for other newspapers.

The news bureau is a spot for an outstanding reporter who can work independently and who will take an interest in the work of interpreting the school to the community. It gives the reporter a fine opportunity to get broader experience through contacts with professional journalists. One junior high school news bureau reporter so impressed the city editor of a local daily paper that he was offered summer work in the newspaper office. The following year, while still a sophomore, he edited a school news page for the daily.

At the beginning, select the newspapers to which you will send school news. Except in the largest cities, local daily newspapers are likely to welcome school news of all kinds. Metropolitan daily papers may be interested only in outstanding stories. They will outline their policy to you on request. Never overlook weekly newspapers, even if they serve only a portion of your school area. They thrive on the kind of news you can supply. News of future events and stories in which student and faculty names are presented in an interesting context offer outstanding reader interest in daily papers as well as in your school newspaper.

Write your stories in good news form. They should be typed, double-spaced on standard 8½-by-11-inch paper. At the top, the school name, the reporter's name, and the school paper's telephone number should appear. If the story is about an event in the near future, you may want to type "For Immediate Release" at the top of the first sheet. Leave space for the editor's notations above the story. Identify the school in the lead. Names or terms that are well known in the school but might be unfamiliar to the public, such as "CHS" or "Rally Committee," should be properly identified in the story.

Study the writing style of the daily papers in which the story will appear. This will sharpen your sense of news values and improve your means of expression. As for other writing details, the school paper's style sheet is probably similar enough to that of the daily newspaper. Copyreaders for the daily paper will make any minor changes that may be necessary.

Watch deadlines. Be sure the copy reaches the newspaper office in time. If your copy must be mailed, allow extra time for possible postal delays. Remember that school news does not merit fast handling in a daily newspaper office. Many of the pages on which such news would appear are made up 24 hours in advance of publication. Some papers print school news once a week on a special page. Learn the deadline for this page and meet it, planning so that advance stories will still be future news when they are printed.

Staffs of small daily papers and weeklies are notoriously overworked. If your copy is in acceptable form, they are likely to print it just as it was written. Otherwise, they may not bother with it at all. The copy can establish a reporter's reputation and that of the school. If clean, interesting, and readable copy is submitted, it will be used regularly. If it is known that a school reporter's copy always has to be rewritten or heavily edited, the copy will go to the bottom of the basket, for emergency use only.

While the school news bureau may report sports events for the daily newspaper, it is customary for the daily's sports editor to make arrangements personally for handling this news. Frequently, the sports editor of the school newspaper will be asked to cover certain school games for the daily, often meeting deadlines a few hours after the game is over.

13   Following a Style Sheet

The items in the following style sheet can be used as they are or adapted to fit your paper's own needs.

Names and Titles

1. Use *Mr., Mrs., Miss, Ms.,* or the proper title with names of teachers and other adults: Dr. Pearl Johnson, Coach Red Truman, Mr. Charles A. Anderson.
2. The first time a name appears in a story, use the full name plus a title for adults. Never use a single initial. Be sure names are spelled correctly: (adults) Miss Jeanette Jones, Mr. J. Paul Smith, Dr. N. W. Green; (students) George Swanson, Mary Lou McPherson.
3. The first time the name of someone with a special title appears in a story, use the title. Such titles usually follow the name but may precede it. They are not capitalized unless they replace *Mr., Mrs., Miss,* or *Ms.:* Mr. W. O. Nolen, assistant superintendent of schools; George Jones, secretary; student-body president Charles White; Principal J. C. Boone.
4. After the first time a name appears, use *Mr., Mrs., Miss,* or *Ms.* with the last name for adults; use only the first name for students, except in sports stories, where only the last name is preferred: Mr. Nolen, Jennifer, Williams.
5. Use *the* with *Rev.* and include *Mr.* when the first name does not appear: the Rev. Howard Stone, the Rev. Mr. Stone.

Capitalization

CAPITALIZE

1. All proper nouns, months, days of the week, holidays: New York, April, Tuesday, Fourth of July.
2. Names of sections of the country but not directions: He visited the Southwest. He walked west.
3. One-word titles when they precede names of adults: Coach Jerry Jones, Postmaster Gus Allen; but Dr. T. H. Gordon, superintendent.
4. Full names of schools, clubs, organizations, streets, geographical areas, or companies: Roosevelt Junior High School, Washington School, Stamp Club, Girls' Athletic Association, Ninth Street, San Francisco Bay, Carquinez Bridge, Standard Oil Company.
5. Proper names for races and nationalities: Caucasian, American, Indian, Negro, Oriental; but black, white.
6. Names of athletic teams: Giants, Gauchos.
7. Principal words in titles of books, plays, movies, or songs, including *a, an,* or *the* when it appears first in the title: *The House of the Seven Gables, A Christmas Carol.*

DO NOT CAPITALIZE

1. School subjects, except languages or specific course titles: social studies, algebra, journalism, history; but French, English, Algebra I.
2. Personal titles used without names: The dean came into the room.
3. *Street, company, club,* or similar words, unless they are a part of a specific name: The Science Club met yesterday. The club elected officers.
4. Abbreviations for the time of day: a.m., p.m.
5. Seasons of the year: summer, spring.
6. Academic departments, except for words derived from proper nouns: English department, mathematics department.
7. Names of classes: ninth grade, junior.
8. Boards and committees, unless given a distinctive name: student council,

dance committee, student body, student court; but Bar Association, Roman Senate.

9. School rooms and buildings, except for those with special names: auditorium, girls' gym; but Room 106, Harrison Gymnasium.

10. The subject of a debate or resolution, except the first word: Resolved, that capital punishment should be abolished.

Abbreviations

1. Abbreviate *Jr.* or *Sr.* following a name. Use no comma: Alfred Brent Jr. (This differs from general usage, which demands the comma.)

2. Abbreviate long names of organizations or other familiar names when there can be no confusion. Use no spaces or periods between letters: YMCA, PTA, FFA, UN, PE, TV.

3. Abbreviate the word *saint* in place names: St. Louis.

4. Do not abbreviate names of states, months, days of the week, or the words *street, avenue, Christmas, railroad, company, fort,* or *point* in place names: Iowa, January, Friday, Main Street, Union Pacific Railroad, Fort Hall.

5. Do not use symbols or abbreviations for distances, weights, or the words *percent* and *degrees*: 5 feet 8 inches, 2 pounds, 1 kilo, 25 percent, 27 degrees.

Dates and Times

1. Dates are written one way only: January 8; never January 8th, 8 January, or the 8th of January.

2. Never use the year for a date within the current year, nor the preceding or coming year unless there would be confusion: December 12, last April 5, next June.

3. Whenever possible, use terms such as *yesterday, today, tomorrow, next Tuesday,* or *last Friday* instead of the date.

4. Do not use the word *on* before days or dates: They met Wednesday. They will meet March 25.

5. Do not use the word *o'clock* in showing time. Omit the zeros for even hours: 3:10 p.m., 2 p.m., 11:45 a.m., 12 noon.

Figures

1. Always use figures for ages, dimensions, money, percents, days of the month, degrees, hours of the day, scores, room numbers, page or chapter numbers, and street numbers: 16 years old, 6 feet, 10 cents, 200 percent, Chapter 2.

2. Except for those numbers in the preceding rule, spell out numbers to and including nine and use figures for numbers 10 and over.

3. Use the abbreviations *st, nd, rd,* and *th* after numbered streets above Ninth but never with dates: First Street, South 21st Street, October 21.

4. For money under $1, use figures and the word *cents;* for $1 or over, use the dollar sign. Do not use zeros when they are not needed: 25 cents, $1.50, $10.

5. Do not begin a sentence with a figure. Spell it out or rewrite the sentence.

6. In a list containing numbers below and above 10, use figures for all.

Punctuation

COMMAS

1. Use to separate all words in a series: French, algebra, and social studies.

2. Use to set off parenthetical expressions or nonessential clauses: John Jones, whom I met yesterday, will be there. There is another way, namely, studying harder.

3. Use to set off appositives, nouns of address, or identifications: Mary White, sophomore, was chosen. Linda, will you be there?

4. Use to separate a quotation from the rest of the sentence: "I'll invite you," said John, "to my party."
5. Use in addresses: Mrs. Gordon Blake, 2431 South 17th Street, Richmond, California.
6. Use in numbers over 999, except for street numbers, telephone numbers, or item numbers: 1,436, No. 66-2431.
7. Use in sports scores: Roosevelt 21, East 7.
8. Use before *and, but,* and *or* connecting clauses in a compound sentence.
9. Use after an introductory clause: When the boy reached school, he went to his locker. If you go, I will not.
10. Do not use in place of a period to separate complete sentences.

SEMICOLONS

1. Use to separate independent clauses not connected by a conjunction: He was old; she was young.
2. Use between main divisions of a listing: Officers are Linda Clark, North, president; Tom Murray, Central, vice-president; and James Crain, West, secretary.
3. Use to divide enumerations when commas would not be clear: The three committees will handle theme and decoration planning; refreshment purchase, serving, and cleanup; and finances and sale of bids.

COLONS

1. Use to introduce a series after *the following* or a similar term but not after verbs such as *are* or *include:* The following officers were elected: Joe Smith, Jane Lutton, and Chris Fields. New officers are Joe Smith, Jane Lutton, and Chris Fields.
2. Use to introduce an example: He gave this example: If three boys were leading three cows, etc.

3. Use after characters' names in a dramatic sketch or joke: Jack: "Who told you that?"
4. Use in giving the time of day, but not in even hours: 3:15 p.m., 10 a.m.
5. Use along with a period to separate minutes and seconds in sports times: His time was 6:17.5 (six minutes 17.5 seconds).

APOSTROPHES

1. Use to form a possessive:
   To form the possessive of a singular word, add an apostrophe and *s:* Tim's shoes, Miss Burns's room.
   To form the possessive of a plural word not ending in *s,* add an apostrophe and *s:* children's toys, women's hats.
   To form the possessive of a plural word ending in *s,* add an apostrophe only: girls' sports, seniors' rings.
2. Use in contractions or to show omitted letters or figures: it's (meaning *it is*), don't, '74.
3. Use in plurals of letters and figures: S's, 7's.
4. Do not use in possessive pronouns: theirs, its, hers, yours, whose.
5. Do not use in such abbreviations as *phone, cello,* and *plane.*

QUOTATION MARKS

1. Use to show the exact words of a speaker. When not quoting exactly, use an indirect quotation without quotation marks: "That was a good game," said Mr. Stewart. He said it was one of the best he had ever seen.
2. If a quotation includes several paragraphs, use quotation marks at the beginning of each paragraph and at the end of the last one.
3. For a quotation within a quotation, use single quotation marks.
4. Periods and commas are always placed within quotation marks, ques-

tion marks and exclamation points only if they are part of the quotation: I heard a new record of "St. Louis Blues." Have you seen "Alexander the Great"? "Did you study your homework?" she asked.

5. Start a new paragraph each time there is a change of speaker.

HYPHENS

1. No general rule can be stated for the use of hyphens in compound words. You must learn the individual words or look them up. If you can write a compound word as a single word (*cheerleader*) or as two separate words (*police chief*), do not use a hyphen.

2. Use in certain common compound titles: vice-principal, vice-president, all-state team, sergeant-at-arms, and secretary-treasurer.

3. Do not use in such words as *weekend, bylaws, copyreader, makeup, textbook, cheerleader, homecoming, lineup,* or *basketball*.

4. Use with compound adjectives but not with the same words used as nouns: 50-yard line, six-day trip, cherry-red dress; but He ran 50 yards. The trip lasted six days.

5. Use in sports scores: North won 6-3.

6. Use, between syllables only, to divide words at the end of a line.

DASHES

1. Use after an introductory date in school calendars: February 27—Basketball Tournament.

2. Do not use to replace periods.

Titles

1. Enclose in quotation marks the titles of plays, poems, chapters, movies, songs, or radio and TV programs: "To a Skylark," "Smoke Gets in Your Eyes."

2. Underline book titles. (In printed newspapers, underlined words will be reproduced in italics. When italics are not available, the printer will set underlined words in boldface; in this case, you may prefer to put book titles in quotation marks.)

3. Capitalize newspaper and magazine names but do not underline or place them in quotation marks.

Spelling and Usage

1. *Webster's New World Dictionary* is a good standard source for spelling and division of words. When two spellings are given, the first is preferred.

2. Use the shorter spelling for *program, quartet,* and *catalog,* but do not use simplified forms such as *thru* or *nite*.

3. Use the *er* form for *theater*.

4. Do not add *s* to *forward, backward,* or *toward*.

5. Learn to spell the following common spelling "demons":

accommodate	led
airplane	library
all right	pantomime
badminton	principal (head
coming	of a school)
counselor	rehearsal
develop	sophomore
eligible	sponsor
embarrassment	until
intramural	writing

6. Distinguish between homonyms: their, there; it's, its; who's, whose; your, you're.

7. Use *alumnus* for masculine singular; use *alumni* for masculine plural and for a group of both sexes; use *alumna* for feminine singular; use *alumnae* for feminine plural.

Glossary

The following glossary contains all the words highlighted in the text as well as a number of others that may prove useful in your work in journalism.

advance story: news story about an event published before the event is scheduled to take place.

advertisement: space in a newspaper paid for by someone who has goods or services to sell.

advertising copywriter: person who writes advertisements.

advertising designer: person who plans the layout of an advertisement and the components that will be used.

advertising manager: person who supervises the selling and writing of advertisements for a publication.

advertising sales representative: person who contacts merchants or other business people and sells advertising space.

adviser: in school newspaper work, teacher responsible for helping students produce the school newspaper.

alternative (off-campus, underground) newspaper: publication published for the purpose of offering a different viewpoint from that of an official or regular newspaper.

anchor person: person in charge of a newscast, who reads and may comment on the news.

angle: one of several approaches to presenting or explaining a newsworthy topic.

ASA rating: number assigned to film to indicate its sensitivity to light.

assignment: instructions to a reporter about a specific news story.

assignment book (assignment sheet): listing of reporters' assignments, kept by the editor or news editor.

astonisher: see **kicker**.

balance: arrangement of items on a newspaper page so that stories and pictures on one part of the page balance as evenly as possible with similar material on the opposite part.

banner (streamer): headline that extends across the page.

beat (run): place or source which a reporter visits regularly in search of news.

blind interview: interview granted by a person in authority on condition that his or her name be withheld.

body: all of a news story after the lead paragraph.

body type: type in which all material other than ads or headlines is set.

boil down: shorten.

boldface: heavy black letters. **This is boldface type.**

border: lines drawn around an advertisement to separate it from other text; also, lines around a full page.

box: lines around a printed story or headline.

box score: statistical summary of a sports event, usually printed in small type at the end of a news story.

break: point in a column where a story is divided, to be continued on another page; also, to release a story for publication.

breaker: device, such as a quotation or subhead, that interrupts flow of print on a page. Used for contrast and to draw attention to key ideas in the body of an article.

broadcaster: person who presents radio or television programs.

broadcast media: channels of communication using some form of radio or television to relay messages, as opposed to **print media**.

bulletin: brief but important statement of last-minute news.

business manager: person who manages the finances of a newspaper or some other organization.

byline: small printed line below the headline, crediting the author of a story.

cable television: distribution of television signals from transmitter to receiver either partly or entirely by wire.

camera operator: photographer who takes pictures of news events for television broadcasts.

campus correspondent: see **stringer**.

caps (upper case): capital letters.

caption (cutline, legend): paragraph appearing below an illustration, describing the illustration.

catch line: one or two words that identify a piece of copy.

cathode ray tube (CRT): type of tube that displays the picture on a television set or monitor. See also **write-edit system**.

censorship: control by legally designated authority (usually governmental or religious) of what is said or written.

centerfold (doubletruck): pair of facing pages in the middle of the newspaper.

center of interest: most important item in a photograph, generally positioned near but not at the exact center of the photograph.

center of visual impact (CVI): item on a newspaper page, often the largest headline or photograph, that first attracts a reader.

channel: means by which messages are transmitted; a magazine or radio broadcast would be a channel of communication.

chase: metal frame for holding type on a press.

chronological story: story whose events are arranged in the order in which they took place or are scheduled to take place.

circulation: average total number of copies of a newspaper distributed per issue; also, the process of distributing a newspaper to its readers.

circulation assistant: person who carries out various tasks related to the distribution of a publication.

circulation manager: person who supervises the distribution of a publication to its readers.

city news: see **local news**.

classified ad: small advertisement in a newspaper or magazine, usually placed by individuals and grouped in categories.

classified ad writer: person who prepares classified ads for publication.

clean copy: written material containing relatively few errors and thus requiring little or no editing.

cliché: once-colorful phrase used so many times that it is no longer effective.

clip art: prepared sheets of drawings or lettering that can be cut up and used in advertisements or other printed matter.

clipping file: collection of printed material about the same subject. See also **morgue**.

cold type: type prepared by a typewriter, typesetting machine, word processor, or computer for reproduction through offset lithography, as opposed to **hot type** or **hot metal**.

column: article under a permanent title, written regularly by the same person and giving expression to his or her own opinion; also, vertical row of type on a printed page.

column inch: space measurement indicating a vertical inch, one column wide.

columnist: writer who regularly has a column appearing in a newspaper or distributed by a newspaper syndicate.

column rule: printed rule used to divide two columns.

commentary: interpretation of news by a qualified observer; frequently heard at the end of a news broadcast or found on the editorial pages of newspapers. See also **news analysis**.

commentator: qualified observer who offers comments on the news.

communicator (sender): person who initiates communication.

community: group of people who live in the same geographic area, share the same public and commercial services, and have similar interests.

composite story: news story with more than one key thought or dealing with more than a single event.

composition: photographer's arrangement of subjects to produce an eye-appealing picture; also, the process of preparing (composing) type for a printed page.

compositor: person who arranges type, either by hand or by machine.

condensed type: type narrower and spaced more closely than standard type, as opposed to **expanded** or **extended type**.

contact: see **contact print**.

contact print (contact): same-size print of a photographic negative for preliminary viewing.

continuous-tone work: printed material with shade gradations from black to white, such as photographs or wash drawings. See also **line work**.

contrast: use of varied styles and sizes of type to make each story stand out according to its relative importance.

copy: any written material intended to be put into type.

copy desk: table at which copyreaders work, often semicircular in shape; the city editor may sit in the **slot** at the center.

copy editor: person in charge of copyreaders and their work.

copyfitting: adjusting or rewriting copy to make it fit the space allotted.

copyholder: person who reads copy aloud so that a proofreader may check a proof for possible errors.

copy person: errand person and apprentice reporter in a newspaper office.

copyread: correct and improve copy submitted by reporters.

copyreader: person who corrects and improves copy submitted by reporters.

copyreaders' marks: universal system of symbols by which copyreaders indicate corrections to be made in copy.

copyright: author's or artist's right to control publication of his or her original work.

copywriter: see **advertising copywriter**.

correction fluid: liquid for covering unwanted marks on mimeograph stencils.

correspondent: reporter stationed away from the home newspaper office, perhaps in a foreign country; also, a **stringer**.

cover a story: secure all available facts about a news event.

credit line: line stating the source of a story or picture.

cropping: elimination of unwanted details in a picture by marking off those areas that are not to be included.

crossline: headline pattern made up of a single line of type extending the full column width.

cub reporter: inexperienced newspaper reporter.

cut: any illustration in a newspaper, such as a photograph or cartoon.

cutline: see **caption**.

cutoff rule: line extending completely across a column, above or below a story.

cutoff test: test applied to a newspaper story to determine whether the last paragraphs contain any essential facts.

darkroom: in photography, place where photographs can be processed without interference caused by normal light.

dateline: place of origin and sometimes the date printed at the beginning of a news story.

dead: term used to describe material set in type but not used or no longer suitable for use.

deadline: time at which all ad copy or stories are due.

deck (bank): one in a series of headlines above a single story.

delete: take out (a letter, word, sentence, or paragraph).

departmental reporter: see **specialized reporter**.

depth of field: in photography, measure of distance in front of and beyond the subject focused on, within which details will be acceptably clear and sharp.

depth reporting: full investigation of information and opinions related to a news event.

design: overall appearance of a newspaper, ad, or other printed material.

desk person: see **rewrite person**.

develop: process film by chemical means so that a negative image is produced.

direct quotation: exact words of a person, enclosed in quotation marks.

display: use of headlines and arrangement of pictures and copy on a page to make it easy to find and read a story.

display type: large or decorative type used in headlines and ads.

distribution: act of circulating a publication.

documentary: film or videotape that investigates a topic in depth.

doubletruck: see **centerfold**.

down style: newspaper style capitalizing as few words as possible. **Up style** is the opposite.

drop deck: see **lower deck**.

dropline (step head): headline pattern consisting of two or more lines of type, the first line touching the left margin only, the last line touching the right margin only.

dummy: sketch or mock-up of a page, created to show a printer where each ad, story, and picture is to be placed on the page. See also **makeup**.

ears: small boxes placed at the sides of the nameplate, containing brief messages or bits of information.

editing: process of improving copy and making it suitable for publication.

editor: person responsible for content of all or certain parts of a newspaper.

editorial: article explaining the newspaper's stand on an issue, written by the editor of the paper or prepared by the editorial board.

editorial assistant: person who performs various tasks related to editorial work.

editorial board: staff members who determine their newspaper's editorial position on debatable issues; they may also review material before publication.

editorial campaign: concerted effort by a newspaper staff to promote an idea by using all of the resources of a newspaper, as well as other media.

editorial cartoon: cartoon-type drawing that comments on a current event.

editorializing: expression of the reporter's own opinion in a news story.

editorial page: page containing editorials, columns, and other special material, usually of a serious nature.

editorial policy (platform): statement of a newspaper's purpose or goals; also, the paper's official attitude on debatable topics in the news.

editorial staff: reporters, photographers, editors, and other people concerned with collecting and preparing news for print or broadcast media, as opposed to the business staff, which manages financial matters such as advertising, circulation, purchasing, and financial records.

editorial *we*: first-person plural pronoun, referring to the newspaper's publisher or editor; used only in editorials.

editorial writer: staff member whose main duty is to write editorials.

editor in chief: person completely responsible for preparing a newspaper or some other publication.

electronic media: collective term, generally used to refer to radio and television.

electronic stencil: mimeograph stencil made mechanically from black-and-white copy.

elite: 10-point type, usually used in reference to the smaller of the two standard sizes of typewriter type. See also **pica**.

em: horizontal space in body type equal in width to the space occupied by the letter *M*; for example, in 8-point type, one em would be 8 points wide.

en: one-half em.

endmark: in newspaper work, mark that is written or typed at the end of a story to tell the printer that the story is complete. Symbols usually employed are —30— and #.

end rule: line placed at the bottom of a story, page, folio line, or nameplate as an element of the general design.

engraving (photoengraving): in printing process using hot metal, a metal or plastic plate created in order to print a photo or line drawing; also, the process of making such a plate.

enlargement: photograph that has been processed from a much smaller photographic negative. See also **contact print**.

enlarger: photographic equipment that produces photographs in the sizes desired.

equal-time law: federal law requiring that "legitimate" election opponents be allowed the same amount of time by a broadcasting station, except in broadcasts of events that are news-related.

ethnic newspaper: publication devoted to the interest of a particular ethnic or cultural group; often published in a mixture of English and some other language.

exchange: issue of another newspaper received in exchange for one's own publication.

expanded (extended) type: type somewhat wider and more spaced out than standard type. See also **condensed type**.

exposure meter: instrument that measures the intensity of light directed on or reflected from a subject being photographed.

eye movement: movement of a reader's eye from one item to another on a page.

eyewitness reporting: gathering material for a news story by actually being present at an event such as a meeting, speech, sports competition, or accident.

facing pages: opposite pages.

facsimile: picture or printed material transmitted electronically, as from one newspaper office to another, to a distant printing plant, or to various television screens; also, process for sending such material.

fair comment and criticism: principle that allows the publication of criticism of public actions by public figures as long as the intent of the criticism is not malicious.

Fairness Doctrine: Federal Communications Commission regulation requiring that broadcast media present all sides of an issue if any sides are to be presented.

feature: term used to describe a feature story or other similar material, as opposed to a straight-news story; also, the main idea of a story (see **key thought**).

feature story (feature, news feature): story generally about some topic in the news, written in an informal way, usually to add colorful details or to entertain and inform readers.

Federal Communications Commission: agency charged with regulating communication by wire and radio, including licensing television and radio stations.

feedback: responses from readers or listeners that reach the sender (communicator) of a message.

filler: story or brief informational matter that may be used at any time to fill space in a column or page.

film speed: a film's sensitivity to light.

five *W*'s and one *H*: questions (*What, Who, When, Where, Why,* and *How*) that a reporter should answer in a news story.

flag: see **masthead**.

flash unit: equipment for lighting a photographic subject with a brief flash of illumination.

flexible writing plate: translucent plastic plate used under a mimeograph stencil in order to provide a hard backing for hand lettering and drawing.

floating nameplate: nameplate that may appear in various positions on a page in successive issues.

flush-left (no-count, ragged-edge, streamlined) headline: headline pattern with lines beginning at the left and extending part way across the column.

focal length: see **lens**.

focus: vary the distance between lens and film so that the image of a subject will be optically sharp.

fold: imaginary horizontal line across the center of a newspaper page.

folio line (running head): line or two of type on each page of a newspaper giving information about the paper; on all but the front page, the information includes the paper's name, the date, and the page number; a departmental title may also be included.

follow-up story: story giving new information on news previously published.

folo copy: copyreaders' mark indicating that seemingly incorrect written material is to be set into type exactly as it appears.

font: complete set of type of one size and design, including complete alphabets in capital and lower-case letters plus numerals and special symbols.

form: page (or set of pages) of type prepared for printing.

format: physical size and makeup of a newspaper.

fotog: photographer.

frame: in photography, a single picture.

framer: instrument on a camera through which the photographer views the subject to see just what will show on film when the picture is taken.

freelancer: writer or other creative worker who offers his or her prepared material for sale, as opposed to working as a salaried employee.

f-stop: see **lens aperture**.

Future Book: list of stories planned for coming issues of a newspaper.

galley: long tray used to hold type; a galley is traditionally one column wide and a full column in length. See also **galley proof**.

galley proof (galley): printed impression made by hand from typeset material, used to check for errors.

glossy: photograph printed on shiny paper in order to produce a printed illustration that is sharp and clear.

graphic arts: communication by means of printing or similar processes.

graphics: visual devices used to enhance verbal content.

guideline: see **catch line**.

gutter: margin along the inside edge of a page.

half-pyramid: see **pyramid**.

halftone: cut made from a photograph.

half-truth: statement that is misleading because certain facts have been omitted.

handout: prepared material submitted to a newspaper for publication.

headline (head): title above a story.

headline schedule: printed examples of a newspaper's various headline patterns.

hold copy (holdover): material set in type and not included in one edition but held for possible future use.

horizontal makeup: makeup style that uses many headlines, illustrations, and stories extending across two or more columns.

horizontal packages (horizontal units): stories under multicolumn heads used partly to break up long, single, vertical columns.

hot type (hot metal): metal letters and engravings used in letterpress printing, as opposed to **cold type** used for offset printing.

human interest: news element that deals with people and their entertaining or unusual actions, particularly those actions that appeal to the emotions.

human-interest story: feature story designed to engage the reader's interest through the presentation of entertaining or unusual information about other people.

indent: set type a certain distance from the margin.

indirect quotation: general presentation of what a person has said, although not exact nor set in quotation marks.

initial letter: letter at the beginning of a word set in large type as a design device.

ink pad: cloth pad on a mimeograph machine used to create even ink distribution.

inquiring-reporter article (symposium): story presenting brief comments from a number of people about the same subject.

insert: place a word or sentence between those already in the story; also, a special advertising section added to a newspaper.

inset: cement a photograph or design into a mimeograph stencil.

intern: beginner in some professional field, working to obtain on-the-job training, with or without salary.

internship: beginning position in a professional field, offering on-the-job training, with or without salary.

interpersonal communication: direct communication between two or more people.

interpretive, in-depth news article: detailed explanation of a newsworthy topic, giving facts and quoted opinions.

interview: story based on facts obtained through conversation with the subject of the story.

interviewing: getting facts for a news story by talking with an appropriate individual.

inverted pyramid: normal arrangement for the body of a news story, in which the facts are placed in descending order of their news value.

inverted-pyramid head: headline pattern in which each succeeding line is shorter than the preceding line.

investigative reporting: probing into the background of a news story to determine facts that are not generally known or that have been concealed.

italics: slanted letters. *This is printed in italics.*

jargon: specialized language used by people sharing a particular interest or profession.

journalism: process of collecting, writing, editing, and publishing news.

journalist: person who collects, writes, or edits news.

jump head: headline used on a story continued from another page, repeating key words from the original headline.

jump story: story that begins on one page and continues elsewhere.

justified lines: spacing out type so that lines fit evenly along both left- and right-hand margins.

key thought: most important fact in a news story; the "feature" of the story.

kicker (astonisher, read-in, tag line, whiplash): short headline, usually in small type, placed above or to the side of a main head.

killed: deleted before publication.

layout: preliminary sketch of arrangement of various elements to appear in an ad or on a page. See also **makeup**.

layout worker: person who carries out preliminary and sometimes final work in preparing ads or pages.

lead (pronounced leed): first paragraph of a news story, giving a summary of the entire story.

leaded (pronounced led-ed): separated by thin lines of space.

leading: metal used to add space between lines of type.

lens: piece of glass or plastic used to change the direction of rays of light reflected from a subject in front of a camera. The **focal length** of a lens determines how much of the subject will be included in a picture. A **wide-angle lens** makes it possible for a photographer to stand close to a subject yet include all of it in the picture. A **telephoto (long) lens** brings a distant subject closer. A **zoom lens** permits changes in the focal length ranging from those achieved by the wide-angle lens to those achieved by the telephoto lens.

lens aperture: variable opening for a camera lens, changed according to available light; measured in **f-stops**.

lettering guide: plastic plate used for drawing letters.

letterpress: printing process that makes an inked impression directly from raised letters **(hot type)**.

letter to the editor: letter written to a newspaper or magazine, with the hope that it will be published.

libel: spoken, written, or pictorial material that unjustly damages someone's reputation or exposes him or her to ridicule.

light meter: instrument that measures the intensity of light directed on or reflected from a subject; used to indicate proper shutter speed and lens opening.

line work: printed material, such as line drawings, consisting of all black and white tones. See also **continuous-tone work**.

linking word: word used to connect related ideas in a single sentence; for example, *as, because, when*.

linotype: machine that casts a line of type in one piece.

lithography: see **offset**. True lithography is a finer and more detailed printing process than offset but is based on the same principle.

local news (city news): news of the community in which a newspaper is published; news covered directly by the staff of the newspaper.

logo (logotype): single piece of type or single plate bearing a name, such as a newspaper or column title or a trademark. See also **nameplate, sig cut, standing head**.

lower case: letters that are not capitals.

lower (drop) deck: any deck, except the first, of a multiple-deck headline.

magtab: tabloid-size newspaper folded so that the front page is half the normal size, making this page look like a magazine cover.

makeup: principles for arranging a newspaper page. A **layout** is the plan for arrangement of copy, headlines, illustrations, and advertisements as they appear on the finished page. A **dummy** is a sketch or mock-up of an actual page. To "make up" a page is to arrange all the material on the page.

managed news: news report, usually prepared by a public relations staff or press information office, that presents information in a manner favorable to the originating organization.

managing editor: person who supervises the work of several departmental editors.

market researcher: in advertising or sales, person who investigates what people will buy and suggests how best to present commercial information to them.

mass communication: distribution of printed or spoken words, pictures, or ideas in such a way as to reach and influence a large number of people.

mass media: instruments of mass communication—for example, books, newspapers, magazines, radio, or television.

masthead (flag): name, ownership, staff, and statement of policy of a newspaper, usually appearing in a box on the editorial page. Also, the name of the paper displayed at the top of the front page. See also **nameplate**.

mat (matrix): papier-mâché card on which has been made an impression from hot type.

medium: channel of communication.

message: information conveyed by a communicator.

microfilm: process of taking small pictures of a newspaper page or other printed material; also, the film containing these small pictures.

mimeograph: machine that prints by allowing ink to flow through a stencil.

mimeoscope: lighted box used for drawing on a stencil.

misquote: indicate in print that someone has said something he or she has not said.

modular (structural) design: style of makeup that deals with each news package (perhaps including story, headline, and photo) as a rectangular unit.

morgue: newspaper library.

mortise: material inset within a photograph or drawing.

mug shot: photo of a person's face.

multiple-deck headline: headline made up of one or more separate headlines, with the most important, generally also the largest and widest, placed at the top.

nameplate (title plate, title line, logo, flag): plate or line of type giving the newspaper's name; sometimes used to describe a departmental heading, such as Sports. See also **floating nameplate**.

negative: processed film that shows the reverse of the light and dark areas that will appear in the finished picture.

new journalism: reporting process that emphasizes personal involvement in the news event, as opposed to objective observation.

news: information about recent, current, or future events.

news analysis: explanation of a current event, usually by an expert. See also **commentary**.

news brief: single paragraph about a news event; usually a part of a column containing several such paragraphs.

news bureau: group of reporters who prepare stories about their own area or organization for release to newspapers or broadcasters.

newscast: radio or television broadcast of news.

newscaster: person who broadcasts news programs and may possibly also prepare them.

news element: one of several qualities, such as nearness, timeliness, or humor, that are likely to stimulate reader interest in a news event.

news English: direct, lively, and vigorous style of writing news.

news feature: story, based on a news event, that explains or entertains.

news impact: effect of news on people who read or hear it.

news magazine: periodical, generally appearing weekly, that summarizes major current events.

news media: broadcast or print media primarily concerned with reporting current events.

newspaper: regularly printed record of news; may also include items of entertainment, general information, and advertisements.

newspaper chain: group of newspapers owned by the same company.

news peg: specific current event on which an editorial or feature story is based.

newsreader: radio broadcaster who reads news reports prepared by reporters or received from wire services.

news source: person who may give information about a news event.

news story: article written about a news event.

no-count headline: see **flush-left headline**.

novelty (unorthodox) lead: lead paragraph that does not follow the usual pattern.

obituary (obit): news story about a death, generally including biographical information.

offset (photo-offset): printing process in which a specially processed photographic plate prints onto a rubber roller, which in turn transfers the ink to the page.

opaquing fluid: white liquid for covering unwanted marks or errors in typewritten material.

op-ed (opposite-editorial) page: page facing the editorial page in many newspapers, containing columns, opinions, letters, and similar material.

open letter: editorial or commentary addressed directly to a specific person, often someone in some position of authority.

opinion page: see **op-ed page**.

overline: headline appearing above an illustration.

overplay (skyline streamer): story above the nameplate on a page.

overset: stories set into type but not used in a newspaper.

page dummy: sketch or mock-up showing where each item is to be placed.

page editor: editor whose duty it is to plan, arrange, and follow up production of one page.

page layout: plan for arrangement of copy, headlines, illustrations, and advertisements as they are to appear on a finished page. See also **makeup**.

page proof: printed proof of an entire page used for final checking.

pasteup: completed page that will be photographed for reproduction through the offset process. See also **makeup**.

penny press: inexpensive newspapers introduced in the 1830s.

personality story: feature story concerning an individual.

photographer: in newspaper work, person who takes pictures to illustrate news stories.

photojournalism: reporting a news story by means of pictures. The text, if any, supplements the photos and their captions.

photojournalist: reporter-photographer who produces stories told mainly through photographs.

photo-offset lithography: see **offset**.

photo story: story told primarily through a series of photographs. See also **photojournalism**.

pica: printer's measure equal to 12 points or ⅙ inch; also, a corresponding size of typewriter type. See also **elite**.

plate: piece of metal on which a printing image appears.

platform: see **editorial policy**.

point: printer's measure of type size. There are 72 points to an inch. News stories are usually set in 8-, 9-, or 10-point type.

press: machine with which printing is done. A rotary press, used by daily newspapers, feeds paper in a continuous ribbon. A cylinder or flatbed press rolls single sheets of paper across the type. A platen press presses single sheets of paper against hot type. A proof press makes single copies for checking purposes.

press association (wire service): organization that collects news and sends it to newspapers or television and radio stations. Best known in the United States are the Associated Press (AP) and the United Press International (UPI).

press release: material given to a newspaper by an organization or individual seeking publicity.

printing technician (printer): general term for a person who reproduces words or artwork on paper.

print media: channels of communication that present information on paper, as opposed to **broadcast media**.

privacy: individual's legal right not to have personal information revealed.

privilege: principle under which certain information, such as material obtained from public records, can be published even though it might otherwise be libelous or invade a person's privacy.

production assistant: person who helps prepare copy to make it ready for printing.

proof: print made of a story as soon as it is set in type.

proofreader: person who compares proof with copy and makes necessary corrections.

proofreaders' marks: universal system of symbols by which proofreaders indicate corrections; they differ from **copyreaders' marks** particularly in that they are written in the margins of printed material.

propaganda: written, spoken, or pictorial material designed to influence thought or action.

prospect: business firm that may be interested in advertising in a newspaper.

publication date: date on which a newspaper or other publication will be ready for distribution.

public figure: person of prominence whose activities are newsworthy.

publicity: newsworthy information issued to gain public attention or support.

public official: person in a position of governmental authority; reporters have greater latitude in writing about public officials than about private individuals.

public record: official records in government offices or records of the meetings of public bodies such as legislatures.

public relations: activities of an organization to build and maintain productive relations with the public and to interpret itself to society as well as to its own members or employees.

public television: noncommercial television stations that present educational and informative programs.

publisher: owner or manager of a magazine, book, or newspaper business.

pulled quote: significant quotation printed in large type to attract attention to a story. See also **breaker**.

put the paper to bed: complete all checking so that the paper is ready for publication.

pyramid: arrangement of ads on a page, actually a **half-pyramid** or **stairstep** in shape.

ragged-edge headline: see **flush-left headline**.

rangefinder: mechanism on a camera that indicates whether a subject is in focus.

rate sheet (rate schedule): list of prices for ads in a newspaper.

read-in: line above a main headline that begins a thought continued in the main headline. See also **kicker**.

receiver: person who takes in a message.

reflex viewing: camera in which the subject is viewed through a lens instead of through a viewfinder.

release: news story prepared for publication in a newspaper, usually by an individual or organization not connected with the newspaper.

reporter: person who gathers news and usually writes the news story.

repro proof: good-quality proof on white paper, prepared for inclusion in a page that is to be reproduced by an offset printing process.

résumé: summary of a job applicant's qualifications.

reverse cut: printed area in which color values are reversed, as in **reverse type**.

reverse type: white letters on a black background.

review: critical discussion, usually about an event in the field of entertainment.

rewrite person: in a daily newspaper office, the person who takes stories over the telephone and then writes them up for the newspaper.

roman type: ordinary book or newspaper type with straight rather than slanted lines. This is roman type.

rule: any printed line, plain or ornamental.

run: see **beat**.

running head: see **folio line**.

sales kit: material giving details about benefits and costs of ads to potential advertisers.

sans serif: see **serif**.

scaling: enlarging or reducing a photograph so that it will fit a desired space on a page.

scoop: exclusive story or one published before other news media release it.

screening: photographing continuous-tone work through a screen to convert it to a series of dots so that it may be printed.

scriptwriter: person who writes dialogue and action for television programs or movies.

sender (communicator): person who initiates a message.

series: in newspaper work, several articles on the same topic, appearing in successive issues of the paper.

serif: small decorative line across the end of a stroke used in forming a letter. This letter has serifs: K. **Sans serif** is type without serifs: K.

set (compose): arrange letters of type into lines, either by hand or by machine.

shading plate: plastic plate used for making designs on a stencil.

shield law: state law that protects the right of reporters to keep information and names of news sources confidential.

shot: a single photograph.

shutter: on a camera, the device that opens and closes the lens; usually adjustable to various speeds.

shutter speed: speed with which the shutter on a camera works.

sidebar: secondary story presenting additional or related details about a major news story.

side head: headline placed to the left or right of an article instead of at the top.

sig cut (signature cut, logo): small piece of metal or plate containing the name of a business firm, usually in a special style of type; sometimes combined with an emblem or illustration.

single-column headline: headline that runs across just one column of a paper.

skyline streamer: see **overplay**.

slanted news: story intentionally or unintentionally written or placed in such a way that the reader misjudges its truth or importance.

slot: see **copy desk**.

slug: piece of metal used in printing from hot type.

sound worker: person who accompanies a camera operator and records sound to be broadcast with news films.

specialized (departmental) reporter: reporter who writes about a specific kind of news, such as science or entertainment, and usually possesses specialized knowledge in this field.

special newspaper: newspaper published by an organization, company, or group and devoted to its interests or to the specialized interests of its readers.

spec layout: sample advertisement offered to an advertising prospect in the hope of selling space.

sports advance: news story discussing a sports event scheduled to take place in the future.

sports report: news story about a sports event, generally by a reporter who has personally witnessed the event.

sports summary: news story or interpretive article covering a series of sports events or a complete sports season.

spot news: unexpected news, reported at once.

spread: headline across two, three, or four columns; also, two facing pages.

stairstep: see **pyramid**.

stale news: news so old that readers are not interested in it.

standard news lead: lead paragraph of a news story, which presents the facts in simple, direct language.

standing head: heading on a special feature or column, used repeatedly without change. See also **logo**.

stencil: wax-coated sheet that allows ink to flow through any marks made on it.

stereotyping: in newspaper work, process for casting a plate for letterpress printing from a mat.

stet: copyreaders' or proofreaders' designation meaning to restore crossed-out words or letters; usually written in the margin with dots under the words or letters to be kept.

stick: small metal holder for use by compositors setting heads by hand; also, the amount of type it contains (approximately 2 inches).

story: see **news story**.

streamer: see **banner**.

streamlined headline: see **flush-left headline**.

streamlined makeup: style of newspaper design that emphasizes easy readability and informality. Page arrangement does not follow a formal pattern.

strict-count headline: headline style that because of its size or placement must have letters counted in exact units to make certain they will fit.

stringbook: reporter's collection of his or her printed stories.

stringer (correspondent): part-time reporter, usually representing a specific geographical area or a specialized subject. Generally, a stringer is paid only for copy accepted for publication.

structural design: see **modular design**.

stylebook: see **style sheet**.

style sheet (stylebook): set of rules governing newspaper writing style.

stylus: metal pencil used for drawing on a stencil.

subhead: one-line headline, usually in boldface type, placed between paragraphs of a story.

subscription: money paid for regular receipt of a publication over a period of time.

summary lead: introductory paragraph containing most of the main points in a story.

survey: formal polling of a group's opinions.

symposium: see **inquiring-reporter article**.

syndicated: feature material bought from writers and sold to a number of newspapers.

tabloid: newspaper with pages approximately half the size of the standard full-size newspaper.

tag line: see **kicker**.

take: portion of copy given to a compositor.

tear sheet: page torn from a newspaper or magazine and given to an advertiser as proof that an ad has been published correctly.

telegraph news: see **wire news**.

telephoto lens: see **lens**.

teletype: machine similar to a typewriter, with which an operator in one city can transmit news reports to identical machines in many other cities.

the media: term often used to refer to all of the various channels of mass communication collectively.

—30—: symbol placed at the end of a story to show that it is complete.

thumbnail cut: one-half column illustration.

tie-in: topic used to set a theme for an interview of a personality.

tie-in ads: group of ads built around a central theme or event, such as a school dance, a Homecoming weekend, a school play, or a holiday.

tint block (tint): shaded block of color.

tip: suggestion for a possible news story.

title plate (title line): see **nameplate**.

tombstoning: use of similar headlines in adjoining columns.

top deck: first deck of a multiple-deck headline.

transition: in newspaper design, process by which a reader's eye is led from one part of the page to another.

tripod: three-legged stand used to support a camera.

type: letters used in printing.

typeface: all type of a single design, in all sizes.

type family: various sizes and styles of type, all from the same basic design.

typeset: prepared on a typesetting machine.

typesetter: person or machine that sets type to produce a printed image.

typesetting: process of arranging type for printing.

typesetting machine: any machine that arranges type for printing.

type style: any specific design for type.

typo: typographical error.

typographical specification: written instruction concerning kind and size of type, width of column, or other direction to the printer.

typography: design or appearance of printed material.

unit: in a headline, a horizontal measurement equivalent to the width of a normal lowercase letter; narrower letters such as *i*, wider letters such as *m*, punctuation marks, or capital letters are counted as more or less than one unit.

unitary method: method of quoting advertising rates according to a fraction of one page instead of by the column inch.

unorthodox lead: see **novelty lead**.

upper case: see **caps**.

up style: see **down style**.

video display terminal (VDT): television-type screen, accompanied by a keyboard, on which a story can be composed, corrected, called up from storage, or transmitted to another terminal. See also **cathode ray tube (CRT), write-edit system**.

videotape: process by which television programs can be recorded for later presentation.

videotape editor: person who arranges videotape pictures and sound into a final edition for broadcast.

viewfinder: camera device for viewing the subject of a photograph.

visual design: images created by artists or photographers to communicate ideas.

well: arrangement of ads on a page, reaching high points in both outside columns, but lower in center columns.

whiplash: see **kicker**.

wide-angle lens: see **lens**.

widow: final line in a paragraph, containing a single word or less than half a line of type; also, a line of type appearing alone at the top or bottom of a page or column.

wire news (telegraph news): news received by telephone, telegraph, or teletype, usually from a press association.

wire reporter: reporter who writes for a press association.

wire service: see **press association**.

wooden headline: headline that is little more than a label.

word processor: printing system used in connection with a computer.

WOW! element: part of a news lead that makes a reader want to continue reading the story.

write-edit system: computer-based writing system in which a reporter uses a keyboard to compose a story, with the typed material appearing on a television-type screen; the story can then be corrected by the reporter, transferred to an editor's screen for approval, and then sent to a typesetting machine. See also **cathode ray tube (CRT), video display terminal (VDT)**.

yellow journalism: news reports that emphasize sensational and perhaps one-sided information; historically, refers to newspapers of the 1890–1900 period.

zoom lens: see **lens**.

Acknowledgments

Without the help of many journalism instructors and school newspaper staffs, preparation of *Press Time* would have been impossible. The author wishes to thank all the busy school newspaper advisers and professional journalists who offered suggestions, replied to letters of inquiry, sent sample forms and copies of school newspapers, supplied photographs and cartoons, and gave permission for the use of excerpts from published newspapers.

Advisers and Schools

Sue Addicott, South Eugene High School, Eugene, Oregon
Marion Hahn Anderson, South High School, Sheboygan, Wisconsin
Robert E. Atwood, Walt Whitman High School, Bethesda, Maryland
Cynthia Baranowski, J. Sterling Morton East High School, Cicero, Illinois
John Bateman, Springfield High School, Springfield, Vermont
Christina D. Beeson, Colton High School, Colton, California
Emil Binotto, White Plains High School, White Plains, New York
Mary Blaskowitz, Camden High School, Camden, South Carolina
Regis L. Boyle, Walt Whitman High School, Bethesda, Maryland, and
    Woodrow Wilson High School, Washington, D.C.
Wayne Brasler, University High School, Chicago, Illinois
Gladys Brink and Patricia S. Moore, Oneonta Senior High School, Oneonta, New York
Marjorie G. Brittain, West High School, Rockford, Illinois
Janet Brovsky, Gateway High School, Aurora, Colorado
W. Michael Brown, William Chrisman High School, Independence, Missouri
Barbara Burns, John Muir High School, Pasadena, California
Ron Clemons, Truman High School, Independence, Missouri
Becky Peters Combs, Cherry Creek High School, Englewood, Colorado
Joe Contris, Lincoln High School, Tacoma, Washington
Madge Crumpler and Diane Stafford, South Houston High School,
    South Houston, Texas
Jeffrey S. Currie, Oak Park–River Forest High School, Oak Park, Illinois
Gary Daloyan, Lincoln High School, Stockton, California
Dick Dixon, Salida High School, Salida, Colorado
L. G. Docherty, Munich American High School, Munich, West Germany
Mary Ehling, Anoka Senior High School, Anoka, Minnesota
James Elkins, Owensboro High School, Owensboro, Kentucky
Nicholas Ferentinos, Homestead High School, Cupertino, California

Greg Franck, Valley High School, West Des Moines, Iowa

Patricia Gariepy, Griffith High School, Griffith, Indiana

Michael F. Gelinas, Longmeadow High School, Longmeadow, Massachusetts

Gary L. Gibson, J. M. Weatherwax High School, Aberdeen, Washington

Joe M. Gratton, Borah High School, Boise, Idaho

Lee Graves, Van Nuys High School, Van Nuys, California

Charles Haas, Randolph High School, Randolph, New Jersey

James A. Hagy, Albert Einstein High School, Kensington, Maryland

H. L. Hall, Kirkwood High School, Kirkwood, Missouri

Ron Harrell, Oshkosh North High School, Oshkosh, Wisconsin

Susan Hathaway, Wheeling High School, Wheeling, Illinois

Ron Hayes, Lewiston High School, Lewiston, Idaho

Mary Ellen Henderson, Madison Junior High School, Eugene, Oregon

Howard Hillis and Chris Luehring, Madras Senior High School, Madras, Oregon

Freeman B. Hover, Rincon High School, Tucson, Arizona

John Hudnall, Westside High School, Omaha, Nebraska

Jay Japka, Highland Park High School, Highland Park, New Jersey

Julia Jeffress, Hillcrest High School, Dallas, Texas

Marian Junker, Marshalltown High School, Marshalltown, Iowa

Mabel F. Kirk, Woodbury Junior High School, Shaker Heights, Ohio

Graham Knight, Sequoia High School, Redwood City, California

Raymond E. Kohtz, Lowell High School, San Francisco, California

Judi Krenek, Miami Senior High School, Miami, Florida

Marilyn Landers, Spring Hill High School, Spring Hill, Kansas

Elaine Levine, Fair Lawn High School, Fair Lawn, New Jersey

Richard P. Lloyd, Arroyo High School, San Lorenzo, California

Elizabeth Lockhart, Central High School, Cape Girardeau, Missouri

Sister Ann Lynch, Cathedral High School, Springfield, Massachusetts

James Macpherson, Crescent Valley High School, Corvallis, Oregon

Sister Marie Dolores, Notre Dame High School, Moylan, Pennsylvania

C. Marshall Matlock, Arthur Hill High School, Saginaw, Michigan

Carolyn McCune, Parkersburg High School, Parkersburg, West Virginia

Darin McDaniel and J. G. Carlton, Catalina High School, Tucson, Arizona

Rob Melton, Roseburg Senior High School, Roseburg, Oregon

Sister M. John Christian, Academia San Jose High School, Guaynabo, Puerto Rico

Jane Morehouse, Kimball County High School, Kimball, Nebraska

Sharlene E. Morris and Marjorie Robinson, Loudonville High School,
Loudonville, Ohio

Betty S. Morton, Virginia High School, Bristol, Virginia

Beverly J. Murphy, New Cumberland Junior High School, New Cumberland,
Pennsylvania

Michael T. Neubert, Nicolet High School, Milwaukee, Wisconsin

Elizabeth R. Nichols, Millard High School, Omaha, Nebraska

Charlotte L. Norton, Bear Creek High School, Lakewood, Colorado

Steve O'Donoghue, Fremont High School, Oakland, California

Candace M. Perkins, St. Charles High School, St. Charles, Illinois

Pege Rankin, Skyline High School, Oakland, California

Don Ridgway, Kennedy High School, Denver, Colorado

Nane Roberts and Charles R. Chumley, David Lipscomb High School,
Nashville, Tennessee

William Ross, Valhalla High School, Valhalla, New York
Antoinette R. Smith, Crane Union High School, Crane, Oregon
Marie E. Soricone, Rainier High School, Rainier, Washington
Howard Spanogle, Glenbard East High School, Lombard, Illinois
Carol Ann Stechow, South High School, Grand Rapids, Michigan
Wilma Taylor, Warren Central High School, Indianapolis, Indiana
Wayne L. Thallander, Tracy Joint Union High School, Tracy, California
Veronica E. Tucker, Newton High School, Newtonville, Massachusetts
E. T. Utley, Richwoods High School, Peoria, Illinois
Ben Van Zante, West High School, Iowa City, Iowa
Hilda Walker, Daniel Webster Middle School, Stockton, California
Brenda Wart, Topeka High School, Topeka, Kansas
Theresa Waterbury, Horace Greeley High School, Chappaqua, New York
Jerry Watson, Horton Watkins (Ladue) High School, St. Louis, Missouri
Jan Watt, Cleveland High School, Portland, Oregon
Bruce Watterson, Ole Main High School, North Little Rock, Arkansas
John Wheeler, Lyons Township High School, La Grange, Illinois
Mary C. Wieman, Memorial High School, Joplin, Missouri
Marjorie Wilson, Coronado High School, Lubbock, Texas

Others to Whom Special Thanks Are Due

Lester G. Benz and Richard Johns, Quill and Scroll Society, Iowa City, Iowa
Howard M. Brier, *Student and Publisher* magazine
Joseph Coscia, NBC, New York, New York
W. B. Daugherty, San Antonio College, San Antonio, Texas
Thomas E. Engleman, The Newspaper Fund, Princeton, New Jersey
Kristi Hedstrom, National Scholastic Press Association, Minneapolis, Minnesota
David Hume Kennerly, *Time*, New York, New York
Robert P. Knight, University of Missouri, Columbia, Missouri
Alan Koch, Chemetka Community College, Salem, Oregon
Sister Marie Louise, Colegio Espiritu Santo, Hato Rey, Puerto Rico
Rena Pederson, Dallas *Morning News*, Dallas, Texas
Peggy Mitchell Peterman, St. Petersburg *Times*, St. Petersburg, Florida
Tom Rolnicki, *Scholastic Editor*, Minneapolis, Minnesota
Robert M. Ruggles, The School of Journalism, Media, and Graphic Arts,
    Florida A & M University, Tallahassee, Florida
Jack Z. Sissors, Northwestern University, Evanston, Illinois
Mary Kahl Sparks, Angelo State University, San Angelo, Texas
Peter C. Townsend and J. Terence Kelly, Miami–Dade Community College South,
    Miami, Florida
Robert Trager, University of Minnesota, Minneapolis, Minnesota
Wendy Valentine, Valley High School, West Des Moines, Iowa

Photographs Used on Front Cover

Upper Left: Omni; *Upper Right:* J. Alex Langley from DPI; *Middle:* Ron Dorman from Shostal Associates; *Lower Right:* Mimi Forsyth from Monkmeyer

Photographs Used in Table of Contents

Page 5: Michal Heron from Woodfin Camp; *Page 6:* Bob Daemmrich from Michael Sullivan; *Page 7:* Mimi Forsyth from Monkmeyer; *Page 8:* Ann L. Reed from Taurus; *Page 9:* Mimi Forsyth from Monkmeyer

Photographs Used as Unit Openers

Unit One: Joel Gordon; *Unit Two:* Chuck Fishman from Contact; *Unit Three:* Paul Conklin from Monkmeyer; *Unit Four:* Laimute E. Druskis from Taurus; *Unit Five:* Michael Austin from Photo Researchers

Photographs Used as Chapter Openers

Chapter 1: Michal Heron from Woodfin Camp; *Chapter 2:* Culver Pictures, Inc.; *Chapter 3:* Bob Daemmrich from Michael Sullivan; *Chapter 4:* Paul Conklin; *Chapter 5:* Michal Heron from Woodfin Camp; *Chapter 6:* Bob Pullum, *Palmetto Leaf*, Camden High School, Camden, South Carolina; *Chapter 7:* Bob Daemmrich from Michael Sullivan; *Chapter 8:* Jim Anderson from Woodfin Camp; *Chapter 9:* Wil Blanche from DPI; *Chapter 10:* Donald Dietz from Stock, Boston; *Chapter 11:* Wil Blanche from DPI; *Chapter 12:* Mimi Forsyth from Monkmeyer; *Chapter 13:* Christopher Morrow from Stock, Boston; *Chapter 14:* David S. Strickler from Monkmeyer; *Chapter 15:* Wil Blanche from DPI; *Chapter 16:* Sybil Shelton from Monkmeyer; *Chapter 17:* Wil Blanche from DPI; *Chapter 18:* Ann L. Reed from Taurus; *Chapter 19:* Joseph Nettis from Photo Researchers; *Chapter 20:* Mimi Forsyth from Monkmeyer

Photographs Used in Career Close-Ups

Page 431: From "Newspaper Journalism . . . for Minorities," second edition, published by the Florida A&M University School of Journalism, Media, and Graphic Arts; *Page 433:* Supplied by Joseph Coscia; *Page 441:* Supplied by Rena Pederson; *Page 445:* Taken by Pete Souza, The White House

COPYREADERS' MARKS

L or ¶	Paragraph
no ¶	No paragraph
Write⟨check hedlines	Insert letter or word
(la.) (3)	Spell out
(Iowa)	Abbreviate
(twelve)	Change to figure
worke	Take out letter
workeing	Take out letter and join separated elements
write a good story	Take out word and join separated elements
benzine	Close up space
stet	Leave as originally written
in the building. Twelve students	Set in one unbroken line or join separated material
go home	Insert space
John Johnson, director	Transpose elements
wroking	Transpose letters
Des moines	Change to capital letter
John Johnson, Director	Change to lower-case letter
Folo copy	Set copy as it is written
] [	Indent both sides of text; center material in column
⊗ or ⊙	Emphasizes period so that printer won't overlook it
in the house	Set boldface
college	Set italics
Des Moines	Set in small capital letters
(more)	Copy continued on next page
—30— or #	End of story

If you cannot find a mark that fits your need, use any simple mark that you feel sure will tell the printer what you want done.

PROOFREADERS' MARKS

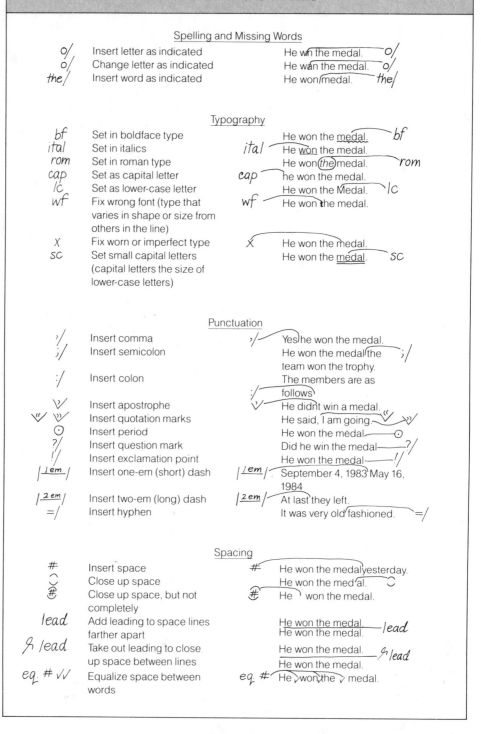

Spelling and Missing Words

Mark	Meaning	Example
○/	Insert letter as indicated	He wn the medal. ○/
○/	Change letter as indicated	He wan the medal. ○/
the/	Insert word as indicated	He won medal. the/

Typography

Mark	Meaning	Example
bf	Set in boldface type	He won the medal. bf
ital	Set in italics	ital He won the medal.
rom	Set in roman type	He won the medal. rom
cap	Set as capital letter	cap he won the medal.
lc	Set as lower-case letter	He won the Medal. lc
wf	Fix wrong font (type that varies in shape or size from others in the line)	wf He won the medal.
X	Fix worn or imperfect type	X He won the medal.
sc	Set small capital letters (capital letters the size of lower-case letters)	He won the medal. sc

Punctuation

Mark	Meaning	Example
,/	Insert comma	,/ Yes he won the medal.
;/	Insert semicolon	He won the medal the team won the trophy. ;/
:/	Insert colon	The members are as follows :/
V	Insert apostrophe	V He didnt win a medal.
\\" V	Insert quotation marks	He said, I am going. \\" V
⊙	Insert period	He won the medal ⊙
?/	Insert question mark	Did he win the medal ?/
!/	Insert exclamation point	He won the medal !/
|—1 em—|	Insert one-em (short) dash	|—1 em—| September 4, 1983 May 16, 1984
|—2 em—|	Insert two-em (long) dash	|—2 em—| At last they left.
=/	Insert hyphen	It was very old fashioned. =/

Spacing

Mark	Meaning	Example
#	Insert space	# He won the medal yesterday.
⌒	Close up space	He won the med al. ⌒
#̂	Close up space, but not completely	#̂ He won the medal.
lead	Add leading to space lines farther apart	He won the medal. He won the medal. lead
ꝗ lead	Take out leading to close up space between lines	He won the medal. He won the medal. ꝗ lead
eq. # √√	Equalize space between words	eq. # He won the medal.